THE FACTS ON FILE

Companion to Shakespeare

VOLUME V

THE FACTS ON FILE

Companion to Shakespeare

VOLUME V

WILLIAM BAKER AND KENNETH WOMACK

Facts On File
An Infobase Learning Company

The Facts On File Companion to Shakespeare

Copyright © 2012 William Baker and Kenneth Womack

Facts On File, Inc.
An imprint of Infobase Learning
132 West 31st Street
New York NY 10001

Library of Congress Cataloging-in-Publication Data
Baker, William, 1944–
    The facts on file companion to Shakespeare / William Baker and Kenneth Womack.
      p. cm.
    Includes bibliographical references and index.
    ISBN 978-0-8160-7820-2 (acid-free paper) 1. Shakespeare, William, 1564–1616—Encyclopedias.
I. Womack, Kenneth. II. Title.
    PR2892.B26 2011
    822.3'3—dc22   2010054012

Text design by Annie O'Donnell
Composition by Hermitage Publishing Services
Cover printed by Yurchak Printing, Landisville, Pa.
Book printed and bound by Yurchak Printing, Landisville, Pa.
Date printed: January 2012

Printed in the United States of America

10 9 8 7 6 5 4 3 2 1

This book is printed on acid-free paper.

Contents

Romeo and Juliet

INTRODUCTION

Romeo and Juliet is an immensely popular play, both on stage and in the classroom. Indeed, it enjoys such a strong cultural presence that even those who have not seen or read the play know its plot. Shakespeare's story of Romeo and Juliet is something of an archetype of tragic or forbidden romantic love, allowing for wide application and retellings in a variety of contexts or environments (as in, for example, the musical *West Side Story*). However, the tragic aspect is sometimes conveniently forgotten in these adaptations. Businesses catering to lovers frequently refer to *Romeo and Juliet*, evidently wishing to convey an air of romance and "true love" but conveniently forgetting the tragic end of the play.

The appeal of *Romeo and Juliet* possibly lies in its being the most romantic of Shakespeare's plays. (It is also probably the most sexually explicit.) It winningly depicts the young protagonists' sexual awakening and emotional coming of age. The more somber element is just as compelling. Comedy and tragedy come together in violence and an impossible dilemma, and the audience witnesses an entire younger generation destroyed through misplaced aggression, obstinacy, and conviction. *Romeo and Juliet* is a combination of widely appealing dramatic elements: love, romance, sex, violence, domestic tragedy, fighting, comedy, and pathos.

The conflation of the comic and tragic is a central aspect of the play. *Romeo and Juliet* was written about 1595, around the same time as *A Midsummer Night's Dream*. These plays are based upon similar stories; in both, we have a pair of lovers whose love is forbidden by parental rules. The lovers continue their courtship without consent, but then the genre of each play dictates the end result: Romeo and Juliet die, but the lovers in *A Midsummer Night's Dream* marry and live happily, as befits the genre of comedy. Interestingly, *A Midsummer Night's Dream* contains, albeit in recycled, parodied form, the tragic tale of Pyramus and Thisbe, whose forbidden love, catastrophic elopement, and separate, deluded suicides arguably both inform and are recalled by the narrative of *Romeo and Juliet*.

It is Shakespeare's linguistic skill in *Romeo and Juliet* that differentiates this play from contemporary plays with similar themes. The characterizations of, in particular, Juliet, Mercutio, and the Nurse are masterful, ensuring not only fascinating material for academic study but also the sympathy of ordinary playgoers. Audiences are not just amused by the Nurse and Mercutio, but they tend to care deeply about what happens to Romeo and Juliet. They cannot help but ask themselves: Are the lovers going to be married? How can Juliet get out of marrying Paris? Will their parents ever forgive them? Similarly, the death of Mercutio arrives seemingly out of the blue and in many performances is like a slap in the face for the audience. It is this crucial sympathy generated by the text that keeps *Romeo and Juliet* popular, relevant, and central to the Shakespearean canon.

Romeo (William Faversham) calls up to Juliet (Maude Adams) in Act II, Scene 2 of *Romeo and Juliet,* in this photograph (published by the Byron Company) of a 1899 production by Charles Frohman at the Empire Theatre.

BACKGROUND

Narratives of feuding families and forbidden relationships appeared in 16th-century Italian and French literature, some of which would have been available to contemporary English readers in translation. Shakespeare's story of *Romeo and Juliet* is based on a long line of sources. Most immediately, it comes from Arthur Brooke's *Tragicall Historye of Romeus and Juliet* (1562), an English poem that is itself a translation of a French prose work by Pierre Boiastuau (1559), which is an adaptation of Mattco Bandello's 1554 Italian version, "Romeo

e Giulietta," the narrative of which in turn had been appropriated from Luigi da Porto's *Giulietta e Romeo* (1525), which in fact is a version of a tale by Masuccio Salernitano (1476). The story also appears in English, again from Boiastuau, in William Painter's "Rhomeo and Julietta," in his collection of prose translations of French and Italian tales, *Palace of Pleasure* (1567). Though linguistic echoes of Brooke can be detected throughout the play, Shakespeare's retelling of this old story is an active one; he increases the pressure of events and the dramatic tension by condensing the action of Brooke's poem from nine months to a few days, develops the characters of Mercutio and the Nurse, and reduces Juliet's age from 16 (reduced from 18 in Bandello) to 13.

Juliet's age is an interesting point of discussion. Contrary to popular belief, the average age for marriage in 16th-century England was well into the 20s for both men and women. Marriage in one's teenage years was comparatively rare, and the only cases of marriage involving teenage girls as young as Juliet were in the extreme upper classes (though they were relatively common in this class). Shakespeare's alteration of Juliet's age would have various indications for a late-16th-century audience. It would imply her high social class, certainly, but also emphasize the essential Italianate nature of the story and perhaps convey a romantic historicity, as marriage in extreme youth was more common in England before the 16th century and the sources used do suggest a late medieval setting. Thematically, Juliet's youth adds pathos and provides an added dimension to the narrative in her and Romeo's coming of age and sexual awakening that lasts for a pathetically short time.

Romeo and Juliet is clearly informed by contemporary Elizabethan literature in the way Shakespeare presents a variety of both philosophies of love and ways of expressing love. Popular and conventional tropes of love poetry surface continually in the play. In particular, Romeo adopts the language of the Italian love poet Petrarch (1304–74), whose metaphors and images remained extremely popular in the love poetry of Shakespeare's day. Romeo uses popular Petrarchan metaphors to describe his love for Rosaline, and the conventional Petrarchan hyperbole, conceits, and wordplay fit his situation of unrequited love for a disdainful mistress. However, this use seems to deliberately contrast Romeo's codified "love" for Rosaline with his "real" feeling for Juliet. Romeo does continue his Petrarchan wooing when he and Juliet first meet at the Capulet feast, and Juliet joins him, but the language and imagery from courtly love poetry diminish as they explore their newfound feeling with a more extensive range of poetic language. The language of the play is often lyrical and stylized. After the sonnet-language of the ball, Juliet offers what closely resembles an epithalamium or nuptial poem alone on the night of her wedding, and a dawn song on the following morning. Furthermore, the Petrarchan convention can be widened to follow a Neoplatonic philosophy and a reading of the play as a parable of spiritual elevation. In this reading, the death of the lovers would be triumphant as they transcend their earthly bodies to enjoy an elevated, spiritual love. The elevated lyrical language is tempered and contrasted by bawdy language also used to reflect on love and sex. This language offers an

Romeo and Juliet meet at the Capulet feast in Act I, Scene 5 of *Romeo and Juliet.* This is a print from the Boydell Shakespeare Gallery project, which was first conceived in 1786 and lasted until 1805. *(Painting by William Miller; engraving by George Sigmund Facius)*

alternative to the Petrarchan rhetoric and figurative exaggeration, providing instead a more realistic, material view of love and sex in the society of the play. Eighteenth-century versions of *Romeo and Juliet* routinely cut the bawdy language, and some cut the parts of the bawdiest characters, the servants, Juliet's Nurse, and Mercutio, altogether. This demonstrates how the language and imagery thought appropriate in one period can be considered entirely inappropriate in another.

Furthermore, as Romeo and Juliet figure their love along popular models, the effect upon Romeo's friends also conveys contemporary ideas about relationships between the genders. Romeo's occupation with first Rosaline, then Juliet, removes him from his friends' company, either in antisocial preoccupation or in simply preferring to spend time with Juliet. This affects what critics refer to as the homosocial society of the play, that is, the all-male bonds of friends, brothers, business and political contacts. Romeo's absence irritates and confuses his friends, and his return to them is marked with mockery. In addition, Romeo himself suggests, after avoiding fights, that his relationship with Juliet has made him "effeminate," a standard view of the consequence of spending too much time with women in the period, and one that is echoed by Friar Lawrence, who calls Romeo's despair and suicidal thoughts "womanish" (3.3.110).

Date and Text of the Play

Romeo and Juliet is usually dated to around 1595. The reasoning behind this is multifaceted and varied, and different critics argue for a number of dates ranging from 1591 to 1596. The source material of *A Midsummer Night's Dream* and *Romeo and Juliet* shares similarities, but the play also shares sources with *The Two Gentlemen of Verona,* which is almost certainly earlier, perhaps 1592–93, but which draws upon Brooke's *Romeus and Juliet* for aspects of its featured forbidden love, suggesting a continuation in Shakespeare's reworking of material. As well as the relationship between *Romeo and Juliet* and other Shakespearean works, certain topical references assist in dating the play. The earthquake that the Nurse refers to in 1.3.24–36 in establishing Juliet's age (we are told she was three years old at the time, and the earthquake is said to be 11 years earlier) has been seized upon as a reference to historical English earth tremors, on the rather unfounded assumption that this reference both points to a real event, and that the writing of the play can thereby be dated as being set in the "present," that is, the time of writing. So, we learn of an earthquake on April 6, 1580, which would mean the "now" of the play's composition is 1591, and of an earthquake in early March 1584 or 1585. If this is the earthquake the Nurse refers to, then the play, it is argued, can be dated as 1595–96. Further earth movements in 1583 and 1585 mean that this method of enquiry gives a range of poten-tial dates between 1591 and 1596. A further topical reference is perhaps Mercutio's lines concerning the soldier's dream of "cutting foreign throats, / Of breaches, ambuscades, Spanish blades, / Of healths five fathom deep" (1.4.83–85). It has been suggested that this is a reference to the Cádiz expedition of June 1596.

Romeo and Juliet was first published in quarto format in 1597 (the text is known as Q1); this edition is generally agreed to be a "Bad" Quarto, compiled incompletely and inaccurately by actors. The next quarto, known as Q2, published in 1599, is a fuller text, probably derived from Shakespeare's own papers. The second quarto also seems to be the basis for Q3 (1609), Q4 (1623), and the First Folio (1623).

SYNOPSIS
Brief Synopsis

Romeo and Juliet is set in Verona, where an ancient feud between two powerful families, the Montagues and the Capulets, regularly disrupts daily life. The youngest members of these two families, Romeo Montague and Juliet Capulet, meet at a feast that Romeo and his friends have gate-crashed, much to the ire of Juliet's cousin Tybalt. Romeo and Juliet dance, kiss, and fall in love. This mutual love is declared hours later in a clandestine meeting in the famous "balcony scene," and they agree to marry. The following day, Juliet's nurse finds Romeo with instructions to meet Juliet at church, and they secretly wed. When Romeo returns to his friends, he finds trouble brewing as Tybalt, still furious about the Montagues' trespass, attempts to pick a fight with Romeo and is goaded by Romeo's friend Mercutio. In the ensuing fracas, Mercutio is mortally wounded by Tybalt when Romeo distractingly intervenes in their scuffle. Grief-stricken, guilty, and enraged, Romeo then pursues Tybalt and kills him. Romeo and Juliet spend one night together before he has to submit to his punishment for murdering Tybalt and is banished from the city. Meanwhile, Juliet's parents attempt to allay the family's grief by arranging to accelerate a proposed marriage between Juliet and Paris, a young

Title page of the second quarto of *Romeo and Juliet*, published in 1599.

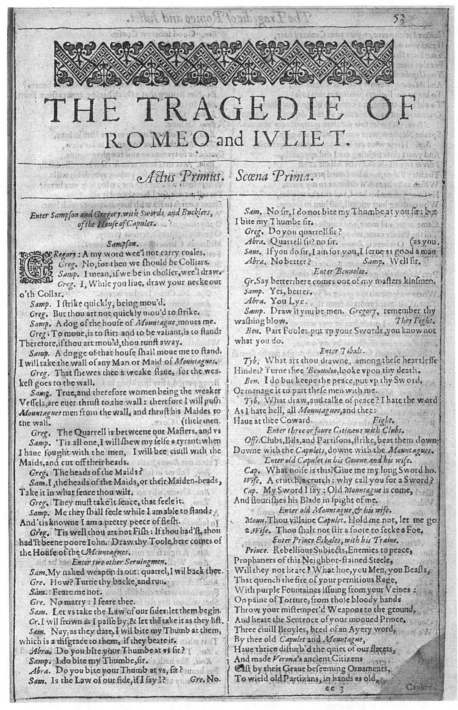

Title page of the First Folio edition of *Romeo and Juliet*, published in 1623.

nobleman. Juliet desperately seeks advice from Friar Lawrence who married the two young lovers thinking that their union, when revealed, would end the feud between their families. She threatens to kill herself, but Friar Lawrence proposes a plan. Under the friar's direction, Juliet takes a drug that renders her seemingly dead the following morning, and Friar Lawrence sends a letter to Romeo informing him of the plan. Tragically, the letter never reaches Romeo, but news of Juliet's "death" does. He hurries back to Verona, buys poison, and heads to Juliet's tomb. He is prevented from entering by Paris, they fight, and Paris is killed. Romeo then laments over Juliet's body, drinks the poison, and dies. When Juliet wakes up to find her dead love, she commits suicide with Romeo's dagger. Their bodies are found by their families and Friar Lawrence, who explains what has happened. The Capulets and the Montagues end their feud over the bodies of their dead children.

Act I, Scene 1

The play opens with two servants of the Capulets, Sampson and Gregory, involved in a pun-heavy discussion of their loyalties to their master in the feud with the Montagues. Their bravado is tested when they run into Montague servants, and a fight breaks out. This is interrupted by Benvolio, but Tybalt arrives and attacks him, leading to widespread fighting and the arrival of the elder Montague and Capulet. The fight is stopped by Officers of the watch, and Prince Escales, who is angry at the feud once again disrupting life in Verona. He proclaims that if any of the two houses fight again, then the crime is punishable by death. The street is cleared apart from Montague, Lady Montague, and Benvolio, who attempts to explain what happened. Their discussion turns to Romeo, who it seems has been melancholy and antisocial of late, walking alone in the early hours and staying in his darkened chamber during the day. Romeo's parents are concerned, and Benvolio says he will find out the cause of Romeo's misery. Romeo enters, his parents leave, and Benvolio engages him in discussing his mood. It seems Romeo is suffering from

unrequited love, and he describes his predicament to Benvolio in highly Petrarchan terms.

Act I, Scene 2

Capulet and Paris enter in the middle of a discussion of the Prince's judgment, but Paris changes the subject to ask about his proposal to marry Juliet. Capulet says that Juliet, at nearly 14, is too young and suggests Paris wait until she is 16, though he encourages Paris to woo her. Capulet then invites Paris to a feast that night and gives a servant a list of guests to invite. Capulet and Paris leave, and the servant reveals that he cannot read. He asks Romeo and Benvolio to read the list to him and, not knowing who they are, invites them too. On the list is the girl Romeo is pining for, Rosaline, so the cousins agree to go to the feast, Romeo to see Rosaline, and Benvolio to identify other women more worthy of Romeo's love.

Act I, Scene 3

Lady Capulet tells Juliet about Paris's proposal, interrupted by Juliet's bawdy nurse. Juliet is told she will see Paris that night at the feast, and she replies dutifully that she is open to considering the arrangement.

Act I, Scene 4

Romeo, Benvolio, Mercutio (who is actually invited), and their friends make their way to the feast, discussing and mocking Romeo's love-sickness. Romeo reveals he has an uneasy feeling about the evening.

Act I, Scene 5

Servants set up the feast, and the guests enter and start to dance. Romeo sees Juliet and is struck by her beauty. He is overheard by Tybalt, who recognizes his voice, is furious, and sends for his sword. He is, however, ordered by Capulet to ignore Romeo and do nothing. Romeo approaches Juliet, and they share a flirtatious interchange before Juliet is summoned by her mother. Romeo learns that Juliet is a Capulet, and Juliet that he is a Montague, and both are bitterly disappointed.

Romeo and Juliet meet in Act I, Scene 5 of *Romeo and Juliet*. This is a plate from *Retzsch's Outlines to Shakespeare: Romeo and Juliet,* published in 1836. *(Illustration by Moritz Retzsch)*

Act II, Scene 1

Romeo enters the Capulets' garden, avoiding his companions who are looking for him. Mercutio attempts to goad him into appearing, but they soon leave without him.

Act II, Scene 2

Romeo sees a light in a window of the house, which then reveals Juliet, and he listens to her monologue as Juliet articulates her desire for Romeo and the problem of his family. Romeo interrupts, and they declare their love for each other. Juliet is called inside by the Nurse but returns to instruct Romeo that if he intends to marry her, then to send her instruction via her Nurse the next day. She retires, but again returns to ascertain the time of the assignation, then finally retires.

Act II, Scene 3

Friar Lawrence enters, musing on herbs. Romeo enters, having not been to bed, and tells the friar of his love for Juliet and their intention of marriage. Friar Lawrence is initially unimpressed, pointing out Romeo's infidelity to Rosaline, but accepts Romeo's assurance that his love for Juliet is different. They leave to plan the wedding, Friar Lawrence hoping that the alliance will end the feud between the two families.

Act II, Scene 4

Benvolio and Mercutio discuss where Romeo can be, knowing that he did not return home all night and suspecting that he is pining for Rosaline somewhere. Benvolio reveals that Tybalt has written to Romeo, certainly challenging him to a duel. Mercutio starts to mock Tybalt's precision, skill, and adherence to rules of dueling, when Romeo enters. Romeo and Mercutio enter into dense comic banter, but Romeo reveals nothing. When the Nurse appears, Romeo defends her from his facetious friends and tells her to instruct Juliet to go to Friar Lawrence's cell that afternoon, where they will be married.

Act II, Scene 5

Juliet waits impatiently for her Nurse to return, and when she does, presses her for news of Romeo. The Nurse playfully keeps Juliet waiting, until she finally relents and joyfully tells her of the arrangements.

Act II, Scene 6

Friar Lawrence and Romeo are waiting for Juliet. She arrives, and they all go off to the wedding.

Romeo and Juliet in Friar Lawrence's cell in Act II, Scene 6 of *Romeo and Juliet*. This is a plate from *Retzsch's Outlines to Shakespeare: Romeo and Juliet,* published in 1836. *(Illustration by Moritz Retzsch)*

Act III, Scene 1

Mercutio and Benvolio are still relaxing and bantering when the Capulets turn up. Tybalt courteously asks to speak to them and asks where Romeo is, but Mercutio is relentlessly awkward and mocking. Romeo enters, and Tybalt challenges him. Romeo refuses to fight, claiming to love Tybalt and the house of Capulet. Mercutio sees this refusal as dishonorable, and he draws his sword instead, challenging Tybalt. Tybalt and Mercutio fight, while Romeo pleads with them to stop. When he steps between them, Tybalt stabs Mercutio underneath Romeo's arm. Mercutio knows he is mortally wounded yet continues to pun on the situation. He finally curses both the houses of Montague and Capulet and is assisted offstage by Benvolio. Benvolio returns moments later to announce that Mercutio is dead. Romeo is enraged, fights a willing Tybalt, and kills him. Benvolio urges Romeo to run as Officers enter, looking for Tybalt. The Prince, the Montagues, and the Capulets enter, and Benvolio is forced to explain exactly what happened. The Capulets grieve over Tybalt, and the Prince announces that Romeo is exiled for his crime.

Act III, Scene 2

Juliet is alone, longing for when her new husband will come and spend the night with her. When the Nurse enters, with a rope ladder for Romeo's access to Juliet's bedroom, she is distraught and tells Juliet, via a minor misunderstanding over whether it is Tybalt or Romeo who has been killed, of Tybalt's death. Juliet is horrified that Romeo's external attractive appearance could disguise any internal evil but chastises her Nurse for criticizing Romeo. Juliet is confused over how she should feel; she is distressed at the death of her cousin, but still loves Romeo, and is even more distressed at his banishment. She gives the Nurse a ring to deliver to Romeo.

Act III, Scene 3

Romeo is hiding at Friar Lawrence's cell and is horrified to learn that his punishment is exile, sep-arating him from Juliet. The friar tries to reason with him, but Romeo will not listen. The Nurse enters and tells Romeo of Juliet's confusion and distress. He offers to kill himself but is roundly chastised by Friar Lawrence, who counsels Romeo to see Juliet before he leaves for Mantua. The Nurse gives Romeo the ring, the friar tells him he will keep him informed while in Mantua, and Romeo leaves.

Act III, Scene 4

Capulet tells Paris that Juliet cannot see him that night as she is too upset about Tybalt. However, he then offers to bring the wedding forward to that very week. Paris is extremely satisfied with this, and Capulet instructs his wife to inform Juliet of this new plan.

Act III, Scene 5

It is the next morning, and Romeo is preparing to leave after spending the night with Juliet. Juliet pretends it is still the night so Romeo does not have to leave, but they are interrupted by the Nurse who warns them that Lady Capulet is on her way. Romeo leaves through the window, and Juliet goes to greet her mother, saying she is not well and still unsettled about Tybalt's death. Juliet joins her mother in wishing Romeo dead. Lady Capulet then tells Juliet she is to be married, and Juliet refuses. Capulet enters and is told of this development by the scornful Lady Capulet. Juliet's parents are extremely angry with her for refusing this match, and they leave, saying that if Juliet does not marry Paris, they will disown her. Juliet despairs, and her Nurse advises her to go ahead and marry Paris. Romeo is exiled, and Paris is noble and attractive. This counsel is disturbing to Juliet, and she decides to go and see Friar Lawrence.

Act IV, Scene 1

Paris is arranging his marriage with Friar Lawrence when Juliet enters. Paris is cordial and affectionate, and leaves her for her confession. Juliet tells Friar Lawrence that if he cannot help her, then she will kill herself. The friar gives Juliet a vial of a poison that has the effect of inducing a deathlike coma. He says he will write to Romeo, who will come from Mantua, release Juliet from the Capulets' vault, and take her back with him.

Act IV, Scene 2

The Capulets are busy making wedding preparations. Juliet enters and tells her parents she has been to confession, apologizes, and agrees to the wedding.

Act IV, Scene 3

Juliet asks the Nurse to leave her alone for the night and pretends to her mother to have everything ready for her marriage to Paris. Juliet prepares to take the drug, worrying briefly that it may be real poison, to cover up the friar's role in her and Romeo's relationship. She also fantasizes about the horror of the crypt but finally drinks the mysterious mixture and sleeps.

Act IV, Scene 4

It is the morning of the wedding, and the Capulet household is busily preparing. The Nurse is instructed to wake and dress Juliet as Paris has already arrived.

Act IV, Scene 5

The Nurse goes to wake Juliet and finds her, seemingly, dead. The Capulets enter at the commotion and lament their daughter, as does Paris when he also enters the bedchamber. Friar Lawrence quickly takes charge of organizing the funeral. Meanwhile, the hired musicians refuse to play for the servants and wonder if they are still going to get paid.

Act V, Scene 1

Romeo has been dreaming about Juliet reviving him from death with kisses, when Balthasar enters and tells him of Juliet's death. Romeo immediately sends for horses and intends to commit suicide. He finds an apothecary and buys poison.

Act V, Scene 2

Friar John, who apparently was sent by Friar Lawrence to Romeo, enters and reveals that he never made it to Mantua with Friar Lawrence's letter due to his being sealed in a plague-house. Friar Lawrence decides to go to Juliet's tomb to rescue her and bring her back to his cell while he writes again to Romeo.

Act V, Scene 3

Paris has brought flowers to Juliet's tomb. He is distributing them when Romeo enters and starts to break into the vault. Paris supposes that Romeo is going to violate the tomb in some way and confronts him. Romeo tells him to leave, but Paris will not, they fight, and Romeo kills him. All this is witnessed by Paris's servant who runs off to find the Watch. At his request, Romeo lays Paris within Juliet's tomb and laments over her body, noting how beautiful she looks in "death." He then drinks his poison and dies. Friar Lawrence enters and meets Balthasar, who informs him of Romeo's intentions. The friar finds Paris's body, and then Romeo. At this moment, Juliet stirs and awakes, asking for Romeo, and the Watch are heard outside. Friar Lawrence panics, points out Paris's and Romeo's bodies, and implores Juliet to come away with him

Juliet wakes up as Friar Lawrence enters to find Paris's and Romeo's bodies in Act V, Scene 3 of *Romeo and Juliet.* This is a print from the Boydell Shakespeare Gallery project, which was first conceived in 1786 and lasted until 1805. *(Painting by James Northcote; engraving by Jean Pierre Simon)*

so he can hide her in a nunnery. Juliet refuses, and the friar runs away. Off stage are heard the Watch still on their way, so Juliet quickly assesses the situation, kisses Romeo, and then stabs herself with his dagger and dies. The Captain of the Watch enters to discover the bodies, and members of the Watch apprehend Friar Lawrence and Balthasar. The Prince and the Capulets enter, then Montague, telling those present that his wife has died due to Romeo's exile. All are confused and distressed. Friar Lawrence tells everyone the full story, which is confirmed by Romeo's man Balthasar and Paris's servant. Capulet and Montague are reconciled in their grief, and the Prince somberly ends the play.

CHARACTER LIST

Juliet   Juliet is a young noblewoman, the daughter of Capulet. She is only 13 but demonstrates a depth of feeling and commitment that is surprisingly mature.

Romeo   Romeo is the son of Montague, the head of the Montague family locked in an ancient feud with the Capulets. He is a romantic, rash, and eloquent young man.

Mercutio   Mercutio is a close friend of Romeo's and the other young Montagues. He evidently belongs to a noble family respected by both the feuding families, as he and his brother are legitimately invited to the Capulets' feast. His name suggests "mercurial" (volatile and lively), and he proves to have a quick temper, a love of mockery, and a facetious outlook on the problems of his friends.

Benvolio   Benvolio is Romeo's cousin. He is loyal, amiable, and reluctant to take part in brawls and duels.

Tybalt   Tybalt is Juliet's cousin. He is proud and quick-tempered and revels in the opportunities for dueling offered by the feud. Tybalt is also referred to as the "Prince of Cats," which refers to medieval animal folktales and possibly to *catso*, Italian for "penis" and a slang term for a rogue.

Nurse   Juliet's nurse is an earthy, bawdy older woman who provides much of the sexual punning and jokes of the text. She is devoted to Juliet.

Friar Lawrence   The local friar and confessor of the other characters. He assists Romeo and Juliet in their covert relationship with good, though possibly misplaced, intentions.

Montague   Romeo's father. Committed to the feud with Capulet and concerned about his son.

Lady Montague   Romeo's mother. Less interested in the feud than her male relatives and also very concerned about Romeo.

Capulet   Juliet's father. He seems more reconciled to the feud developing into a "cold" stalemate and seems a genial man, until his daughter defies him.

Lady Capulet   Juliet's mother, who clearly wants the best for her daughter without being her confidant. Particularly fond of her nephew Tybalt.

Paris   A young nobleman in love with Juliet. A relative of the Prince, who would therefore be an advantageous match for Juliet.

Escales   The prince of Verona. His name possibly implies the scales of justice, and thereby his just nature.

Sampson   Servant to Capulet.

Gregory   Servant to Capulet.

Clown   Servant to Capulet.

Balthasar   Romeo's personal servant.

Peter   The Nurse's servant.

Friar John   An ally of Friar Lawrence. It is Friar John's failure to deliver the crucial letter that results in the tragedy.

Watchmen   These include the First Watch of Verona, who is a constable, supervising the Second and Third Watch.

Chorus   Though not technically a character in the usual sense, the Chorus introduces the play and appears between the first two acts. The function of the Chorus is to increase the dramatic sense of foreboding by revealing to the audience the tragic end to come and to make clear Romeo and Juliet's love.

CHARACTER STUDIES
Juliet

Juliet is the character who has attracted the most praise throughout the critical history of the play.

Juliet in Act II, Scene 2 of *Romeo and Juliet*. This is a print from Charles Heath's 1848 edition of *The Heroines of Shakspeare: Comprising the Principal Female Characters in the Plays of the Great Poet*. (Painting by J. Hayter; engraving by W. H. Egleton)

She appears at first relatively straightforward, but we see the extraordinary development and complexity of her character, revealed by her love, her conviction, and her imaginative language.

In 1.3, Juliet is introduced as demure and quiet, dutiful to her mother and dependent on her Nurse. She has only six lines in a scene of over 100. The main impression of her at this point is one of extreme youth and cloistered dependence. The Nurse infantilizes her with pet names like "lamb" and "ladybird" (1.3.3), and Juliet obediently bends her attraction to parental wishes, saying that she will not "endart" her eye deeper "Than your consent gives strength to make it fly." (1.3.99–100) Juliet is also, however, more than able to match Romeo's romantic tropes and overtures in their first meeting in 1.5. He introduces conventional imagery of pilgrims and worship, which she elaborates upon and develops flirtatiously, "Have not saints lips, and holy palmers too?" / "Ay, pilgrim, lips that they must use in prayer" (1.5.100–101). Juliet is evidently self-confident enough to indulge in such courtly banter and not so cloistered as to be fazed by Romeo's kisses, though it could be argued that they are received in a courtly manner. She does also, however, proactively seek out Romeo's name and makes evident her attraction: "If he be married, / My grave is like to be my wedding bed" (1.5.133–134). This suggests that her acceptance of the kissing, "You kiss by th'book" (109), while well-mannered, is based upon real, recognized attraction. Juliet is also astute enough to hide her feelings from her Nurse, explaining her couplets articulating her despair, "Prodigious birth of love it is to me, / That I must love a loathed enemy" (1.5.139–140), as "A rhyme I learnt even now / Of one I danced withal" (141–142). Juliet's complexity is here heard for the first time. This excuse is loaded with meaning; she has learned this "rhyme" of love from Romeo, as both a metaphor of her emotions and literally in their shared lyrical banter, and their meeting has inspired the feelings that in turn inspire her sorrow over their familial opposition.

Juliet's maturity is evident as events of the play develop and is demonstrated by her confidence in her decisions and in her language. She matures much quicker than Romeo; in the balcony scene, she is far more prudent and realistic, though no less smitten. Her initial focus, upon Romeo's revealing of his presence, is the danger and the practicalities; "The orchard walls are high and hard to climb, / And the place death, considering who thou art," "If they do see thee, they will murder thee," "By whose direction found'st thou out this place?" (2.2.63–66, 70, 79). However, her romantic nature is also evident in that Romeo's hyperbolic declarations of love and lack of concern for death unless it be caused by her rejection quickly override her possible embarrassment at being overheard and concerns for their safety. She also demonstrates an awareness of the conventions and pitfalls of love; she knows he will say "Ay" if she asks if he loves her (2.2.90), she worries about appearing "too quickly won" (2.2.95), and replies to his conventional poetic declarations with "O swear not by the moon / . . . / Do not swear at all" (2.2.109–111). In addition, her immediate thoughts, possibly as a result of her mother's and Nurse's previous insistence that this should be her concern at this stage in her life, are on legitimate marriage. This pragmatism is evidenced later in the play, where she makes Romeo leave in 3.5, after playfully persuading him to stay.

Even Juliet's dependence on her Nurse, whom she evidently loves, is outgrown in her rapid maturation. When she rejects the Nurse, "Thou and my bosom henceforth shall be twain" (3.5.240), following the Nurse's suggestion in 3.5 that she forget about her marriage to Romeo and marry Paris instead, she clearly demonstrates that the Nurse, though practical, has no concept of the depth of Romeo and Juliet's bond, and thus Juliet also rejects her childhood. This is also the final expulsion of the comic element of the play. At the end of 3.5, Juliet accepts responsibility for her actions. She is abandoned by her parents and her Nurse and, isolated, decides to go to Friar Lawrence to seek his help, proposing an alternative drastic plan if he cannot help her, "to know his remedy; / If all else fail, myself have power to die" (241–242). Her determination to commit suicide as a desperate last resort is reiterated to Friar Lawrence and finally tested in her last action.

Juliet's language of love is both more straightforward and more complex than Romeo's. It is more straightforward in that she does not use the rhetoric and Petrarchan metaphors and imagery to the extent that Romeo does, but it is more complex because her metaphors are more imaginative, more fantastic, and more original. Her musing on Romeo's name in 2.2 is followed to its conclusion, in that the erasing of his name would be in exchange for possession of herself, "for thy name, which is no part of thee, / Take all myself"

(2.2.48–49), and that his name does not define his "parts." In their following conversation, she objects to his conventional swearing by the moon, though she can herself sometimes only find conventional expression; she says her love is "as boundless as the sea, / My love as deep" (2.2.133–134). However, she then develops this with an expansive and more complex concept "the more I give to thee / The more I have, for both are infinite" (2.2.134–135) and introduces the creative imagery of Romeo as a hawk and herself as a falconer from line 158, "So loving-jealous of his liberty" (180). Her impassioned wait for Romeo to arrive on her wedding night in 3.2 also shows great linguistic imagination.

Juliet is also a focus for the linguistic links between love and death, particularly in her unusual personal epithalamium (nuptial poem) of 3.2. This interest in death could be seen as characteristically adolescent, but it also is possibly a product of the play's environment, as well as indicating a transcendent and again imaginative way of considering the liberating power of love. Juliet's latent focus on death is revealed earlier in the play. After meeting Romeo for the first time, she proffers the prophetic, "If he be married, / My grave is like to be my wedding bed" (1.5.133–134), unwittingly linking their marriage and death, and in conversation with Romeo in the balcony scene, as well as being excited and impressed by the risk of death, she also says, "I should kill thee with much cherishing" (2.2.183). The imagery in the epithalamium is extraordinary; Juliet's "and when I shall die, / Take him and cut him out in little stars" (3.2.21–22), an imaginative play on the Elizabethan meaning of *die* as orgasm and the transcendence of death in ascendance to the heavens. The epithalamium gives way to a further test of Juliet's linguistic skill in her resultant verbal negotiation of her conflicting feelings concerning Tybalt's murder, "But wherefore, villain, didst thou kill my cousin? / That villain cousin would have killed my husband. / Back, foolish tears, back to your native spring" (3.2.100–102). In addition, the dawn song of 3.5, where Juliet pretends it is not day but night, depicts her creating illusion through verbal trickery and willful false interpretation of evidence, "It was the nightingale, and not the lark" (3.5.2), and again evidences her love as constant, inventive, and imaginative.

Romeo

The Romeo of the opening act is almost a caricature of the despondent lover; he sighs, he stays inside in a darkened room like a moody teenager, and all he can think about is his love, Rosaline. Romeo's parents worry about him, "Away from light steals home my heavy son, / And private in his chamber pens himself, / Shuts up his windows, locks fair daylight out, / And makes himself an artificial night" (1.1.128–131), and he agrees to go to the Capulets' feast only because he will see Rosaline there. This existence is pinpointed by Shakespeare to be specifically Petrarchan; Romeo is "Out of her favour where I am in love" (1.1.159), and this rejection and unobtainable beloved is central to both his behavior and to the contemporary code of Petrarchanism. In falling in love with Juliet, Romeo's posturing disintegrates, and he learns, briefly, to live and love without this conventional set of symptoms as his character develops.

For some critics, Romeo's initial love-sickness and former love for Rosaline have raised troubling questions about his character and his love for Juliet. Is he merely fickle? Friar Lawrence asks, "Is Rosaline, that thou didst love so dear, / So soon forsaken?" (2.3.66–67) and calls him a "young waverer" (2.3.89). As such, can we as an audience accept him as a truly tragic figure? By the mid-18th century to the end of the 19th, any mention of Romeo's former love Rosaline was omitted as it was felt to lack propriety. However, what Romeo's former love does dramatically is allow the audience to witness his development from a false, superficial attraction presented in conventional terms to great love, great language, and great sacrifice. This, hopefully, is evidence enough that his love for Juliet is something different altogether, that it is "true."

When Romeo first meets Juliet, he remains cast in the Petrarchan model. In his first sighting

Publicity photo for the 1936 film version of *Romeo and Juliet,* with Leslie Howard as Romeo and Norma Shearer as Juliet.

of her, he compares her to a jewel and a "snowy dove" (1.5.45; 47) and their first exchanges employ Petrarchan imagery on his instigation of religious metaphors. The balcony scene of 2.2 also sees Romeo using conventional language to declare his love. Juliet is like the sun, her eyes are compared to "Two of the fairest stars in heaven" (2.2.20), her cheeks are bright, and she is an "angel." When Juliet protests at his swearing "by yonder blessed moon" (2.2.109), however, she inspires a simpler, perhaps more heartfelt tone from Romeo.

Romeo is demonstrably slower than Juliet to develop and retains an impulsive recklessness up to his banishment. That said, prior to the retaliatory murder of Tybalt, Romeo avoids the skirmishes of the feud, expressing disappointment with Benvolio over the squabble in 1.1: "O me! What fray was here? / Yet tell me not, for I have heard it all"

(1.1.164–165) and attempts to pacify the enraged Tybalt in 3.1, which ultimately leads to Mercutio's death. Romeo is clearly close to his male friends, evidenced most clearly in the banter with Mercutio of 1.4 and 2.4, but also accepts that his love will increasingly absent him from this group. Romeo evidences a new maturity in 5.1 when he believes Juliet to be dead, compared to his hysterical threats of suicide in 3.3. In 5.1, he is controlled, resolute, and committed. "Well, Juliet," he says, "I will lie with thee tonight" (5.1.34).

Mercutio

Mercutio is a relentless force. His speech, his humor, and his mockery drive the character on, and the scenes in which he appears are crammed with his banter (which he even manages when fatally wounded). As Romeo describes, he is "A gentleman . . . that loves to hear himself talk, and will speak more in a minute than he will stand to in a month" (2.4.123–124). Dryden reports a popular myth in the late 17th century that Shakespeare said he killed off Mercutio in the third act "to prevent being killed by him" (1672). This comment, though lacking in actual evidence, anecdotal or otherwise, was seized upon by earlier critics who took it both as proof of Mercutio's irrepressible nature and as an explanation, if they felt one was required, of why Shakespeare felt it necessary to kill the character off in the third act.

The name "Mercutio" suggests one who is "mercurial," volatile and lively, and the character is evidently both of these things. In the scene of his death, Mercutio proves to have a quick temper and a dangerous love of mockery. His opinion of Tybalt is already established in 2.4 where he describes him sarcastically as "the courageous captain of compliments" (2.4.18–19) and derides Tybalt's enthusiasm for the formalities, skills, and rules of dueling. Later, in 3.1, Mercutio mocks Benvolio's suggestion that they should "retire" because the Capulets "are abroad" (3.1.2), which suggests he is not above picking quarrels or deliberately antagonizing other characters, and this proves to be the case. Tybalt has no interest in fighting Mercutio, but initially Mer-

cutio purposefully finds offense: "Consort? What, dost thou make us minstrels?" (3.1.40), and then draws his sword on Tybalt as Romeo is attempting to avoid a confrontation. Mercutio's death divides the play in both structure and genre. With him dies comedy; with his death enters tragedy.

Mercutio contrasts with and comments upon Romeo's role as love-struck Petrarchan lover. This commentary is largely critical and does not take the misfortune of his friend in love as particularly serious or interesting. Mercutio describes Romeo as "poor Romeo, he is already dead, stabbed with a white wench's black eye" (2.4.13–14) and "Now he is for the numbers that Petrarch flowed in" (2.4.34–35). He advises, after some more sympathetic light wordplay, "If love be rough with you, be rough with love: / Prick love for pricking, and you beat love down" (1.4.27–28) and goes on to compare Romeo's lack of enthusiasm for the feast to an unsociable mouse (1.4.40) and to an old game of removing a log from mud, as Romeo is stuck "up to the ears" in love, making him, in this allusion, the proverbial stick-in-the-mud (1.4.41–43). Mercutio's irrepressible love of language, imagination, and exhibitionism is demonstrated in the famous "Queen Mab" speech, discussed in detail in the Difficult Passages section below. This speech proceeds rapidly through a description of the dream-bringing Mab that borders on nonsense and is by necessity cut off by Romeo's "Peace, peace, Mercutio, peace! / Thou talk'st of nothing" (1.4. 95–96). When Romeo gives his friends the slip after the feast, Mercutio tries to provoke him into appearing by again mocking his love-sick attitude, "Romeo! humours! madman! passion! lover! / Appear thou in the likeness of a sigh, / Speak but one rhyme and I am satisfied" (2.1.7–9) and goes on to "conjure" him by offering his own Petrarchan blazon of Rosaline, "I conjure thee by Rosaline's bright eyes, / By her high forehead and her scarlet lip, / By her fine foot, straight leg, and quivering thigh" (2.1.17–19). When Romeo does not appear, Mercutio's language becomes cruder and potentially reveals some misogyny in his character: "Now will he sit under a medlar tree,

/ And wish his mistress were that kind of fruit" (2.1.34–35), "O that she were / An open-arse, thou a pop'rin pear!" (37–38). *Medlar* is slang for female genitalia, as medlars are small apples with a large eye thought to resemble such, and hence "open-arse" was a slang term for medlar. "Pop'rin pear" refers to a Dutch pear used here, because of its shape, to refer to a penis, with further wordplay on "pop her in." Mercutio exhibits the same sexual bawdiness in reaction to Juliet's Nurse, who he intimates is both a bawd and a whore (2.4.109–116).

Mercutio continues his wordplay when Romeo does reappear in 2.4. His annoyance is clear, "Where the dev'l should this Romeo be? / Came he not home tonight?" (2.4.1–2), and directed toward Romeo, "Signior Romeo, bon jour! there's a French salutation to your French slop. You gave us the counterfeit fairly last night" (2.4.38–39). Mercutio thus also embodies the necessary divide between Romeo and his friends; his annoyance at Romeo's absence and general hostility toward heterosexual love (and, possibly, women) has led some modern critics to suggest the character is intended to be homosexual.

Friar Lawrence

Friar Lawrence is, at least in terms of plot, absolutely central to both Romeo and Juliet's love and tragedy, despite being on stage for only a short time. It is with his advice and approval that Romeo and Juliet are married, it is his plan Juliet follows in her pretended death, and it is arguably Friar Lawrence's mistakes (or unsuccessful action) that leads to the deaths of both protagonists. Nineteenth-century critics debated his role in moral terms: whether he could be seen as a choric voice (therefore expressing Shakespeare's opinion) or not. Concurrently, and throughout later criticism, some critics are overtly hostile to the character. Friar Lawrence fails to reveal the prior marriage of Juliet when her family are arranging the ceremony with Paris; his plot with the sleeping potion is extremely risky and open to error; and, in the final scene, he runs away rather than inform the awakening Juliet

Romeo and Juliet in Friar Lawrence's cell in Act II, Scene 6 of *Romeo and Juliet,* in this photogravure published by Gebbie & Husson Company in 1887.

of events. This summary would suggest a character who is dishonest, rash, shortsighted, and cowardly.

Friar Lawrence is first introduced in 2.3 as something of a choric voice explaining the potential for good and evil in all things in rhyming couplets. This in itself proves to be rather prophetic. The lines, "Virtue itself turns vice, being misapplied, / And vice sometime by action dignified" (2.3.21–22) could be applied to the results of his own actions, as described above. He is motivated to help Romeo and Juliet by a moral intention to end the feud between the families. This strong moral sense is evident in his previous counsel to Romeo regarding Rosaline ("Thou chid'st me oft for loving Rosaline" [2.3.81]) and his dry comments on Romeo's sudden change of heart. Overriding this, however, is his consideration of the greater moral good, "For this alliance may so happy prove / To turn your households' rancour to pure love" (2.3.91–92). It is also significant that it is Friar Lawrence that Romeo and Juliet continue to turn to for help throughout the play. Their faith in this figure suggests at least a presumption on their part that he can help, though as this faith is possibly misplaced, this aspect can add to the tragedy.

Friar Lawrence continues to advise well and with pragmatism in the face of Romeo's distress at his banishment in 3.3. He counters Romeo's hysterics with calm statements, advising "thy Juliet is alive, / . . . / There art thou happy. Tybalt would kill thee, / But thou slewest Tybalt: there art thou happy. / The law that threatened death becomes thy friend, / And turns it to exile: There art thou happy" (3.3.135–140). Events begin to unravel with the announcement of Juliet's marriage to Paris. Friar Lawrence really does not have much opportunity to do anything to stop this event, and his desperate solution (in the face of another distraught teenager) should, theoretically, work. The fact that it does not is beyond his control and part of the wider movement of the play in its inevitable descent toward a tragic end. The single failing on the friar's part is when he abandons Juliet in 5.3, "Come go, good Juliet, I dare no longer stay" (5.3.159), but given the pressure of events and the scene in the tomb, this is understandable, especially as the lines suggest the stage business of Juliet refusing to leave. Critics who debate whether the tragedy in the play is one of character or of fate are able to do so around the role of Friar Lawrence; if one of fate, then he is as much a victim of inevitable events as the main characters, if a tragedy of character, then Juliet and Romeo's actions are, too, out of his control. Despite this, the old friar accepts responsibility in requesting "the rigour of severest law" (5.3.269) for his part in the tragedy, arguably redeeming any momentary weakness.

DIFFICULTIES OF THE PLAY

Romeo and Juliet is not a particularly difficult play, which is why it is often assigned to younger students. However, like all Shakespeare's plays, it can give students some trouble. In particular, the tragic ending—a result, ultimately, of unfortunate coincidence and bad timing—can be difficult to accept. Many readers or audience members find Shakespeare's plotting of events after Romeo's banishment disappointingly "unrealistic," comprising a catalog of missed meetings, unread letters, and impulsive action; if only there had not been plague

on the road to Mantua, if only Balthasar had not been such an efficient and dedicated employee, if only Romeo had found Friar Lawrence earlier, or delayed his suicide, if only the Friar had not left Juliet, all could have been avoided. Such incidents, inconsequential failings, and coincidences can be hard to swallow, but it is precisely these that enhance the tragedy. Pathos is created precisely *because* the turns of fate are seemingly insignificant, *because* coincidence has devastating effect when part of a chain of events that culminate in tragedy. Furthermore, the vagaries of the action also have a thematic function. The question has been raised whether this play is a tragedy of fate or of character, or both, and both elements can be seen working in the final act. If the lovers are indeed "star-crossed" as the Chorus informs us, then their doom is set before they even meet, and every attempt to avoid their death, for example as in the friar's letter, must be thwarted by circumstances beyond human control.

The language of *Romeo and Juliet* is no more difficult than that of Shakespeare's other tragedies, but it, too, can be confusing. It is extremely lyrical, and stuffed full of puns and elaborate wordplay, a great deal of which is contextual. In particular, Mercutio's brilliant speeches can be hard to grasp. In addition, a modern audience has to reconcile the combination of sexual language with violence, both in the bawdily violent language of the lower-class characters (for example, Sampson and Gregory in 1.1), but also in Juliet's persistent romantic coupling of love and death. The bawdy language of 1.1 is also demonstrative of a young male-dominated social system where individuals need to assess and express their hierarchical roles.

Another important convention is that of the Petrarchan lover. Much of the play reflects Petrarchan techniques of expressing love and desire, evident in the Petrarchan language of both Romeo and Juliet in their initial meeting and in Romeo's self-fashioning as a rejected lover, as well as in Juliet's famous speeches in the forms of an epithalamium and dawn song. Such an abundance of stylized lyricism can seem both impenetrable and detrimental to the development and expression of individual character. However, an understanding of the tropes in use and the significance of where they appear in the play helps to clarify the text and opens up a variety of critical avenues. The different ways that Romeo uses or rejects convention can help us see the difference in the constructed love he feels for Rosaline and the real love he has for Juliet. The lovers also interrogate the received languages of love, Juliet replying to Romeo's hyperbolic promises with, "O swear not by the moon" (2.2.109), and embellish given tropes. As such, the romantic language of the play is in part a composite of a variety of contemporary philosophies and linguistic constructs of love relationships; Shakespeare's skill is in convincing the audience that Romeo and Juliet's love for each other goes beyond lyrical commonplace and conventional expression.

KEY PASSAGES
Act I, Scene 1, 1–40

SAMPSON. Gregory, on my word, we'll not carry coals.

GREGORY. No, for then we should be colliers.

SAMPSON. I mean, and we be in choler, we'll draw.

GREGORY. Ay, while you live, draw your neck out o' the collar.

SAMPSON. I strike quickly, being moved.

GREGORY. But thou art not quickly moved to strike.

SAMPSON. A dog of the house of Montague moves me.

GREGORY. To move is to stir, and to be valiant is to stand: therefore if thou art moved thou runn'st away.

SAMPSON. A dog of that house shall move me to stand: I will take the wall of any man or maid of Montague's.

GREGORY. That shows thee a weak slave, for the weakest goes to the wall.

SAMPSON. 'Tis true, and therefore women being the weaker vessels are ever thrust to the wall: therefore I will push Montague's men from the wall, and thrust his maids to the wall.

GREGORY. The quarrel is between our masters, and us their men.

SAMPSON. 'Tis all one, I will show myself a tyrant: when I have fought with the men, I will be cruel with the maids, and cut off their heads.

GREGORY. The heads of the maids?

SAMPSON. Ay, the heads of the maids, or their maidenheads, take it in what sense thou wilt.

GREGORY. They must take it in sense that feel it.

SAMPSON. Me they shall fall while I am able to stand, and 'tis known I am a pretty piece of flesh.

GREGORY. 'Tis well thou art not fish; if thou hadst, thou hadst been poor John. Draw thy tool! here comes two of the house of the Montagues.

SAMPSON. My naked weapon is out: quarrel, I will back thee.

This opening passage is valuable in the establishment of both narrative and thematic issues of the play. As servants of the Capulet household,

Sampson and Gregory are clearly as preoccupied with the feud with the Montagues as their employers. They enter the scene mid-conversation, discussing what they *would* do if challenged by any Montagues. This demonstrates the pervasive and all-encompassing aspect of the rift, as it divides factions through class lines, "The quarrel is between our masters, and us their men." As such, the feud has become a social problem rather than a political or professional rivalry of the upper classes. The passage also introduces the apparently routine expression of the feud in petty street brawls and disruptive skirmishes between opposing sides.

Moreover, Sampson and Gregory demonstrate a possible reading of the feud as intrinsically attached to their conception of their own, and others', masculinity. Their involvement is an opportunity for macho banter, for rabble-rousing, fighting, and disruption, and as such the feud as the audience witnesses it is very much the preoccupation of the young men of the households.

The link between the masculine "honor" achieved through fighting and masculine sexuality is also made clear here, as Sampson and Gregory express their bantering bravado largely through bawdy sexual puns, a linguistic fea-

ture underpinning the elevated language of love used by their social superiors throughout the play. Gregory's assertion that "to be valiant is to stand" explicitly links taking a firm opposing position in a fight with slang indicating an erection, and hence virility, and this idea is extended throughout the remaining interchange. This is echoed in the final lines of the extract with the pun on "My naked weapon is out." In addition, male Montagues will be pushed "from the wall," which Sampson persists in following through as the indicator of advantageous social position in the face of Gregory's suggestion that "the weakest goes to the wall," and counters this with threatening to "thrust" the Montague "maids to the wall" and wordplay concerning cutting off the women's (maiden) heads. In this swaggering fantasy of machismo, a male character proves he is a man by being adept both with his sword and sexually; he vanquishes other males and ravishes "their" females. As Sampson asserts, he is in his own construction, "a pretty piece of flesh," indicating his general perceived sexual attractiveness and emphasizing his penis. The following action, which is far more cautious than all this boasting suggests, offers no such opportunity for ravishing or seduction, as all participants are other young men. However, the conflation of violence, death, and sexual matters echoes throughout the play.

Members of the Montague and Capulet families fight in Act I, Scene 1 of *Romeo and Juliet*. This is a plate from *Retzsch's Outlines to Shakespeare: Romeo and Juliet*, published in 1836. (*Illustration by Moritz Retzsch*)

Act II, Scene 2, 33–69

JULIET. O Romeo, Romeo, wherefore art
   thou Romeo?
Deny thy father and refuse thy name;
Or if thou wilt not, be but sworn my love,
And I'll no longer be a Capulet.

ROMEO. Shall I hear more, or shall I speak
   at this?

JULIET. 'Tis but thy name that is my enemy;
Thou art thyself, though not a Montague.
What's Montague? It is not hand nor foot,
Nor arm nor face, nor any other part
Belonging to a man. O be some other name!

What's in a name? That which we call a rose
By any other name would smell as sweet;
So Romeo would, were he not Romeo called,
Retain that dear perfection which he owes
Without that title. Romeo, doff thy name,
And for thy name, which is no part of thee
Take all myself.

ROMEO. I take thee at thy word:
Call me but love, and I'll be new baptised;
Henceforth I never will be Romeo.

JULIET. What man art thou that thus
   bescreened in night
So stumblest on my counsel?

ROMEO. By a name
I know not how to tell thee who I am.
My name, dear saint, is hateful to myself,
Because it is an enemy to thee;
Had I it written, I would tear the word.

JULIET. My ears have yet not drunk a
   hundred words
Of that tongue's utterance, yet I know the
   sound.
Art thou not Romeo and a Montague?

ROMEO. Neither, fair maid, if either thee
   dislike.

JULIET. How cam'st thou hither, tell me, and
   wherefore?
The orchard walls are high and hard to climb,
And the place death, considering who thou art,
If any of my kinsmen find thee here.

ROMEO. With love's light wings did I
   o'erperch these walls,
For stony limits cannot hold love out,
And what love can do, that dares love attempt:
Therefore thy kinsmen are no let to me.

This passage establishes the instant attraction
and love between Romeo and Juliet and, signifi-

Romeo calls up to Juliet in Act II, Scene 2 of *Romeo and Juliet*. This is a print from Malcolm C. Salaman's 1916 edition of *Shakespeare in Pictorial Art. (Painting by R. Pyle; engraving by W. Elliott)*

cantly, that the desire is entirely mutual. Indeed, it is Juliet who first articulates her love as Romeo expresses his through action, his incentive to break into the Capulets' grounds, "With love's light wings did I o'erperch these walls." In addition, the way Juliet and Romeo verbally negotiate the issues and problems their union implies one of the themes of the play in the complexities of naming and names.

The barrier to Juliet and Romeo's relationship is, of course, the feud between their families, and family distinction is conveyed through family name. It is this name that either Romeo or Juliet would have to "refuse" ("Romeo, doff thy name" / . . . / "I'll no longer be a Capulet") in order to be able to be in love. As Romeo puts it, "Call me but love, and I'll be new baptised." This is also an implicit exchange; for losing his name Romeo gains Juliet, "for thy name, which is no part of thee, / Take all myself." Similarly, in being referred to only as "love," Romeo exchanges his name for his role as lover. His final speech in this extract, "what love can do, that dares love attempt," embodies himself as his love, his role as Montague exchanged for that of Juliet's lover. The desire for separation from constricting familial bonds is also a desire for new identity and thus is linked to the maturation of the young protagonists. The wish to break away from the family and form a new family is a sign of Juliet's burgeoning maturity. Characteristically, her expression of this is received by Romeo as a love-game, offering a reading of the characters that at this point sees Juliet as more mature than Romeo, who shows signs of still playing the role of Petrarchan lover.

In addition, Juliet's question, "What's in a name?" ponders the theoretical separation between the thing signified, that is, the object referred to, and the signifier, that is, the word. Juliet articulates this as she asserts that the thing called "rose" would be the same without the connotation supplied by the signifying word, hence Romeo is desirable separated from, or in spite of, his signifier of "Montague": "What's Montague? It is not hand nor foot, / Nor arm, nor face," "Romeo would, were he not Romeo called, / Retain that dear perfection which he owes / Without that title." This philosophical pondering, as well as articulating a structuralist approach to language, supports a reading of the play that interprets the deaths of Romeo and Juliet as ultimately triumphant in their successful dissolution of name and identity, driven by love.

Act II, Scene 4, 50–97

ROMEO. Good morrow to you both. What counterfeit did I give you?

MERCUTIO. The ship, sir, the slip, can you not conceive?

ROMEO. Pardon, good Mercutio, my business was great, and in such a case as mine a man may strain courtesy.

MERCUTIO. That's as much as to say, such a case as yours constrains a man to bow in the hams.

ROMEO. Meaning to court'sy.

MERCUTIO. Thou hast most kindly hit it.

ROMEO. A most courteous exposition.

MERCUTIO. Nay, I am the very pink of courtesy.

ROMEO. Pink for flower.

MERCUTIO. Right.

ROMEO. Why, then is my pump well flowered.

MERCUTIO. Well said: follow me this jest now till thou hast worn out thy pump, that when the single sole of it is worn, the jest may remain after the wearing solely singular.

ROMEO. O single-soled jest, solely singular for the singleness!

MERCUTIO. Come between us, good Benvolio, my wits faint.

ROMEO. Switch and spurs, switch and spurs, or I'll cry a match.

MERCUTIO. Nay, if thy wits run the wild-goose chase, I have done, for thou hast more of the wild-goose in one of thy wits than, I am sure, I have in my whole five. Was I with you there for the goose?

ROMEO. Thou wast never with me for any thing when thou wast not there for the goose.

MERCUTIO. I will bite thee by the ear for that jest.

ROMEO. Nay, good goose, bite not.

MERCUTIO. Thy wit is a very bitter sweeting, it is a most sharp sauce.

ROMEO. And is it not well served in to a sweet goose?

MERCUTIO. O here's a wit of cheveril, that stretches from an inch narrow to an ell broad!

ROMEO. I stretch it out for that word "broad," which, added to the goose, proves thee far and wide a broad goose.

MERCUTIO. Why, is not this better now than groaning for love? Now art thou sociable, now art thou Romeo; now art thou what thou art, by art as well as by nature, for this drivelling love is like a great natural, that runs lolling up and down to hide his bauble in a hole.

This is a significant scene as it depicts Romeo's close relationship with his friends, particularly Mercutio, through their banter and wordplay. It is the first time we have seen Romeo interact with his friends in good humor but also is an indication of the social group Romeo will neglect given the option of Juliet. Ironically, Mercutio, in his last speech here, attributes Romeo's change of mood to recovering from lovesickness rather than to the positive influence of requited love. Mercutio goes on to identify the lover, through implication, as antisocial, not his real self, and a "natural," that is, mentally challenged. In this way, this passage also perhaps punctures Romeo's previous posturing as an archetypal Petrarchan lover; Mercutio's criticism undermines such conventional preoccupations with love, thus supporting Romeo's development throughout the play.

Romeo's social circle of young men gives the audience a microcosm of a homosocial society, and it is this that is fractured by the invasion of heterosexual pairing off (though homosociality in a wider sense is retained in the relative mobility and socializing of men in contemporary patriarchal society). Mercutio expresses annoyance at Romeo's disappearance of the previous night, and the two fall into pun-heavy wordplay that figures Romeo's "business" to have been of sexual conquest. "Case" can be taken to refer to genitals (male or female), which are also gender specific in "pump" and "flower," to "bow in the hams" refers to the ruinous effects of venereal disease or sexual over-exertion, and to "hit it" conveys to sexually penetrate as well as to guess correctly. This laddish preoccupation can be seen to echo, in a more sophisticated battle of wits, the discussion of Sampson and Gregory in 1.1 (discussed above). In addition, the easy, rapid, and almost flirtatious bawdy banter has led some critics to suggest a deeper bond between Mercutio and Romeo than mere friendship. Why is Mercutio so annoyed about Romeo's disappearance and so obsessed with his supposed sexual occupation? In addition, Romeo figures Mercutio as a goose, punning on the common belief that geese are unintelligent, thereby also applied to foolish people, but "goose" also refers to a (female) prostitute. The banter culminating in Romeo's placatory "good goose, bite not" has led some readers to see the affection between the two friends as indicative of an additional sexual bond. Usually this is attributed to Mercutio alone, so Romeo is free to fulfill an uncomplicated role as a heterosexual lover (discussed further in Modern Criticism and Critical Controversies and The Play Today below).

Act III, Scene 5, 1–36

JULIET. Wilt thou be gone? It is not yet near day:
It was the nightingale, not the lark,
That pierced the fearful hollow of thine ear;
Nightly she sings on yon pomegranate tree.
Believe me, love, it was the nightingale.

ROMEO. It was the lark, the herald of the morn,

No nightingale. Look, love, what envious
  streaks
Do lace the severing clouds in yonder east:
Night's candles are burnt out, and jocund day
Stands tiptoe on the misty mountain tops.
I must be gone and live, or stay and die.

JULIET. Yon light is not daylight, I know it, I:
It is some meteor that the sun exhales
To be to thee this night a torch-bearer,
And light thee on thy way to Mantua:
Therefore stay yet, thou need'st not to be gone.

ROMEO. Let me be ta'en, let me be put to
  death;
I am content, so thou wilt have it so.
I'll say yon grey is not the morning's eye,
'Tis but the pale reflex of Cynthia's brow;
Nor that is not the lark, whose notes do beat
The vaulty heaven so high above our heads:
I have more care to stay than will to go:
Come death, and welcome! Juliet wills it so.
How is't, my soul? Let's talk, it is not day.

JULIET. It is, it is, hie hence, be gone, away!
It is the lark that sings so out of tune,
Straining harsh discords and unpleasing
  sharps.
Some say the lark makes sweet division;
This doth not so, for she divideth us:
Some say the lark and loathed toad change
  eyes;
O, now I would they had changed voices too,
Since arm from arm that voice doth us affray,
Hunting thee hence with hunt's-up to the day.
O, now be gone, more light and light it grows.

ROMEO. More light and light, more dark and
  dark our woes!

The opening of this scene can be taken in part
to constitute a dramatic version of the "aubade," or
dawn-song, sung by a lover at the start of the day.
Juliet also follows a fashionable poetic conceit in
attempting to persuade Romeo that it is not day-

break, it is still the night, and therefore he does
not have to leave. As Romeo says, it is not morning because "Juliet wills it so." Juliet says that the
dawn chorus of the lark was the nocturnal nightingale, and figures the breaking dawn as the light of
a meteor. Romeo relents with good humor, "Let
me be ta'en, let me be put to death," and ultimately
Juliet reveals her pragmatism; just as Romeo joins
in the game here, with "it is not day," she puts an
end to it, and makes him leave. Juliet continues
to assert her own interpretation of facts, however,
saying that the conventionally tuneful lark "sings
so out of tune, / Straining harsh discords and
unpleasing sharps" because the lark's song signifies
morning, and morning brings painful separation.

Romeo leaves as the Nurse enters in Act III, Scene 5
of *Romeo and Juliet*. This is a print from the Boydell
Shakespeare Gallery project, which was first conceived
in 1786 and lasted until 1805. *(Painting by John Francis;
engraving by James Stow)*

In terms of narrative, this scene informs the audience that Romeo and Juliet have indeed spent the night together and emphasizes their mutual love and compatibility in the easy, witty verbal game. Juliet cleverly interprets all signs of dawn as signs of night, as described, while Romeo introduces the tragic element of their love in his concentration on his promised execution if he does not leave, culminating in his contrast between the lightness of the day and the darkness of their seemingly doomed love. Interestingly, both refer to each other as "love," possibly referring back textually to the exchange of names for the opportunity of love discussed above in relation to 2.2, and Romeo also calls Juliet, "my soul," emphasizing their union in love and Neoplatonic union through sexual intercourse. Their union is also cemented in terms of style; their dialogue is ended and summarized before the entry of Juliet's Nurse with a shared couplet, "O now be gone, more light and light it grows." / "More light and light, more dark and dark our woes." Romeo's repetition of Juliet's words, "more light and light" also demonstrates their bond and union.

DIFFICULT PASSAGES
Act I, Scene 4, 54–95

MERCUTIO. O, then, I see Queen Mab hath
  been with you.
She is the fairies' midwife, and she comes
In shape no bigger than an agate-stone
On the finger of an alderman,
Drawn with a team of little atomies
Afhwart men's noses as they lie asleep;
. . .
And in this state she gallops night by night
Through lovers' brains, and then they dream
  of love;
O'er courtiers' knees, that dream on court'sies
  straight,
O'er lawyers' fingers, who straight dream on
  fees,
O'er ladies' lips, who straight on kisses dream,
Which oft the angry Mab with blisters plagues,
Because their breaths with sweetmeats tainted
  are:

Sometime she gallops o'er a courtier's nose,
And then dreams he of smelling out a suit;
And sometime comes she with a tithe-pig's tail
Tickling a parson's nose as a' lies asleep,
Then dreams he of another benefice:
Sometime she driveth o'er a soldier's neck,
And then dreams he of cutting foreign throats,
Of breaches, ambuscades, Spanish blades,
Of healths five fathom deep; and then anon
Drums in his ear, at which he starts and wakes,
And being thus frighted swears a prayer or two
And sleeps again. This is that very Mab
That plats the manes of horses in the night,
And bakes the elflocks in foul sluttish hairs,
Which once untangled, much misfortune
  bodes:
This is the hag, when maids lie on their backs,
That presses them and learns them first to
  bear,
Making them women of good carriage:
This is she—

ROMEO. Peace, peace, Mercutio, peace!
Thou talk'st of nothing.

Mercutio's speech on Queen Mab, the dream-bringing queen of the fairies, is one of the most obscure and fanciful in Shakespeare's plays. It arises out of Romeo's reluctance to go to the Capulets' feast, both because of his lovesickness and, more directly because, he says, he "dreamed a dream tonight" (1.4.50). Though Romeo does not elaborate on this dream, the implication is that he has had a bad premonition about the consequences of visiting the feast. Mercutio's response is to invent the mythology of the minute queen of the fairies who brings humans dreams. In part, the speech functions to illustrate Mercutio's characteristic verbosity and love of talking nonsense; as Romeo interrupts, "Peace" (meaning "be quiet") "Thou talk'st of nothing." The linguistic complexity and combination of invented and traditional fairy lore result in an interesting diversion from the action of the play. Mab is said to be tiny in size, no bigger than the carved agate stone of seal-rings, and, in the omitted lines, to travel in a chariot made from a hazelnut shell and insect-parts and driven by a gnat. Such diminutive fairies were unknown in contemporary fairy lore, as it was generally believed fairies were a similar size to humans or human children. Some critics have suggested that this speech offers another link to the contemporary *Midsummer Night's Dream*.

Mab is described as inspiring dreams in various social types and of mischief attributed to fairies. English domestic fairies were thought to despise lazy, "sluttish" housekeeping, and as punishment to mat and knot the hair of bad housewives or servants in order to create the pain and inconvenience of untangling it. Mercutio also links her with "the hag," probably the nightmare, who induced bad or sexual dreams by sitting on people's chests. This sexual link points towards the demonic incubus, who could impregnate women, hence the pun on "learns them first to bear." In addition, the origin of Mab's name is uncertain, and Shakespeare is the first in England to offer it as the name of the fairy queen. It is possible that Shakespeare is playing on the meaning of "quean" as a prostitute and "mab" as a sexually available woman, which complies with the implicit sexual direction of Mercutio's wit and the mysterious impregnation of unmarried women. Romeo's "nothing" also supports this reading in the contemporary slang usage of "nothing" to refer to female genitalia; Mercutio is indeed talking about "nothing" in the vulgar sense as well as the literal.

Act III, Scene 2, 1–31

JULIET. Gallop apace, you fiery-footed steeds,
Towards Phoebus' lodging; such a waggoner
As Phaeton would whip you to the west,
And bring in cloudy night immediately.
Spread thy close curtain, love-performing
  Night,
That runaways' eyes may wink, and Romeo
Leap to these arms, untalked of and unseen.
Lovers can see to do their amorous rites
By their own beauties; or if love be blind,
It best agrees with night. Come, civil night,

Thou sober-suited matron all in black,
And learn me how to lose a winning match,
Played for a pair of stainless maidenhoods:
Hood my unmann'd blood, bating in my
  cheeks,
With thy black mantle, till strange love, grown
  bold,
Think true love acted simple modesty.
Come, night; come, Romeo; come, thou day
  in night,
For thou wilt lie upon the wings of night,
Whiter than new snow upon a raven's back.
Come, gentle night, come, loving, black-
  brow'd night,
Give me my Romeo, and when I shall die,
Take him and cut him out in little stars,
And he will make the face of heaven so fine
That all the world will be in love with night,
And pay no worship to the garish sun.
O, I have bought the mansion of a love,
But not possess'd it, and though I am sold,
Not yet enjoyed: so tedious is this day
As is the night before some festival
To an impatient child that hath new robes
And may not wear them.

Juliet's personal epithalamium, a song traditionally sung by the bride just before her wedding night, sees her willing the onset of night as she waits for Romeo. This passage is potentially difficult in the surprising and complex language Juliet uses to express her impatience, desire, and love for Romeo, which are all combined within the same imaginative constructs. Particularly interesting is her employment of images of death, which may seem strange in a speech focusing on love, desire, and anticipation.

Juliet contrasts day and night in her longing for the safety of darkness by which Romeo can arrive. She acknowledges that it is the sun that is usually worshipped but focuses her language on how the night is superior. These claims are centered on the night being concealing, as Romeo can "Leap to these arms, untalked of and unseen" and on night being a time of lovers, "love-performing Night."

This is "proven" by Cupid's proverbial blindness and by how the darkness can also embolden virginal lovers, teaching them how to "lose a winning match" and their "maidenhoods." Romeo is thus "day in night," in his fairness, the joy or "light" he is bringing, and in the way he makes night preferable. Juliet also makes a pledge or bargain, that when she dies, Night, personified, can have Romeo, "cut . . . out in little stars, / And he will make the face of heaven so fine, / That all the world will be in love with night" and ignore the "garish" sun. This both confers immortality on Romeo and also darkly prophesies perhaps, in the violence of being cut into stars, their love's violent end. More implicitly, this violence is dependent upon Juliet's "dying"; in the 17th-century meaning of orgasm, Juliet's image couples desire and death as clearly linked.

CRITICAL INTRODUCTION TO THE PLAY

The narrative of *Romeo and Juliet* is not original to Shakespeare, and the general motif of doomed, separated, suicidal lovers as creators of pathos is a common one. Similarly, the linguistic images the author employs to depict the love between the protagonists is also not original, echoing courtly love poetry and conventional metaphor throughout the text. These elements are, however, grounded in a play that manages to present its subject matter sincerely as well as self-consciously. Shakespeare emphasizes the use of conventional romantic language by depicting his characters as they employ it self-consciously, as well as self-consciously and inventively depart from it. In addition, he creates a world in which the familial feud constitutes a highly fraught day-to-day life for the younger members of the families, and one in which the tragic end of Romeo and Juliet seems inevitable.

Tragedy, Fate, and Character

The tragic ending of *Romeo and Juliet* turns on a sequence of unfortunate, unrelated events but also on the decisions made by a number of characters. In addition, the text gives us a final scene of reconciliation between the feuding families.

Bereft of their children, Montague and Capulet settle their differences. That the Chorus's prologue informs the audience that Romeo and Juliet are "star-cross'd" and their love "death-mark'd" (6; 9) implies that the suicides of the protagonists are inescapable, set down by Fate, and the final reconciliation additionally suggests that this fate has some sort of purpose, if not meted out as a punishment. However, the events of the play are not visited upon characters that are represented as being passive victims in a sequence of events. Both Romeo and Juliet make decisions that influence or drive their circumstances, and in addition, Shakespeare's claustrophobic and feud-obsessed play world constitutes an environment that facilitates and encourages actions that later end in tragedy. The ambivalence of the nature of the tragedy of *Romeo and Juliet* has generated a great deal of criticism and is a key area of consideration in the play.

Fate seems to hasten Romeo's and Juliet's deaths, and work against their and the friar's plans most clearly in the disruption of the friar's letter to Romeo explaining the plot to drug Juliet and fake her death. The plague on the road to Mantua, which results in the messenger, Friar John, being sealed in a house to contain infection causes a crucial hiatus in Romeo's access to events in Verona, and the plague's biblical connotations and episodic appearance adds to the sense that the tragedy of the protagonists is fated. The fatal aspect of Romeo and Juliet's tragedy is also often alluded to through ironic premonition. Romeo's sense of foreboding on the way to the Capulets' feast is a result of a dream, which is never explained to the audience, but Romeo's hints that "I am done" (1.4.39) and his reply of "I dreamt a dream tonight" (1.4.49) to Mercutio's query concerning why Romeo thinks "'tis no wit to go" to the Capulets' suggests an ominous premonition of the deadly repercussions of the action. Similarly, at the feast, Juliet says "If he be married, / My grave is like to be my wedding bed" (1.5.133–134), superficially referring to her instant attraction to Romeo and hope that he is romantically available, but the statement also ironically describes her fate. When Romeo is married to

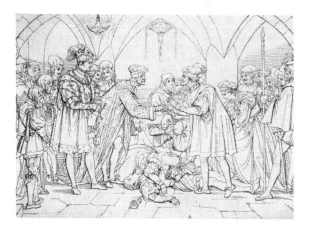

Over their children's bodies, the older Montagues and Capulets resolve their differences in Act V, Scene 3 of *Romeo and Juliet.* This is a plate from *Retzsch's Outlines to Shakespeare: Romeo and Juliet,* published in 1836. *(Illustration by Moritz Retzsch)*

Juliet, then she (like him) will die. The image of her wedding bed as a grave functions both metaphorically and literally; it is Juliet's own bed where she consummates her marriage with Romeo in which she first, falsely, "dies" due to the friar's potion on the morning of her second wedding, and her real death occurs within the arms of her lover. Juliet's linguistic links throughout the play perpetuate this concept, in her continual coupling of death and love.

However, the characters also induce the tragic end by acting according to their established characters. Both Romeo and Juliet are impulsive, impassioned, and reckless. This can be seen in their respective passionate natures and in the early risks Romeo takes physically in invading the Capulet grounds and Juliet takes emotionally in declaring her love for him. Romeo's return to Verona upon receiving the information of Juliet's death also demonstrates his impulsive nature, acknowledged as he claims, "I defy you, stars!" (5.1.24). A similar recklessness can be attributed to Mercutio and Tybalt, whose conflict, arguably sparked by Mercutio's aggressive mockery and finished by Tybalt's aggression and a shared chronic sense of "honor" ("O

calm, dishonourable, vile submission!" exclaims Mercutio, 3.1.66), sets in motion the events that lead to Romeo's banishment, Juliet's desperation, the flawed plan, and both their deaths. Evidently, such flaws in character, which lead the characters to act in this way, are a product of their environment, in this case a product of the obsession with the feud focused on the young male characters' bravado and violence. In addition, the character flaws of Friar Lawrence exacerbate the catastrophe. His reckless plan to drug Juliet and his cowardice in the tomb in 5.3 contribute to the tragedy.

Therefore, the nature of the tragedy in *Romeo and Juliet* seems to encompass both fate and character flaw; the audience is forewarned of their deaths by the Chorus at the beginning of the play, and the reconciliation of the families at the end seemingly encompasses a play about tragic fate. This presumption is undermined, however, by the inescapable succession of choices made by many of the characters (suggesting that the surrounding culture is also significant), which so influence the action and the tragic outcome of the play. The grand claims of fate-driven tragedy are also possibly undermined by the persistent presence of comedy within the play.

Comedy

The themes of love, sex, violence, and identity are manifested in the play in both comic and tragic form. The initial plot of lovers separated by familial pressure is familiar as a plot device of romantic comedy, evident in Shakespeare's contemporary *A Midsummer Night's Dream.* The nature of the play, be it comic or tragic, then depends on the effects and repercussions of this forbidden love. Until the play introduces death, with the murder of Mercutio, *Romeo and Juliet* could feasibly be read as a romantic comedy. Comic scenes and characters abound, in the lower-class characters of the male servants, in Juliet's Nurse, and the wit of the other characters such as Mercutio.

The feud and the resultant violence are expressed with an arguably comic dimension in the opening scene of the play, where Sampson and Gregory assert their own roles within this society and quibble over their martial and sexual prowess as fully analyzed in Key Passages above. Sampson and Gregory's conversation illustrates how the feud in Verona is so entrenched that it affects every level of society. They offer indicators of the ideological link between violence and sexual conquest and thereby the thematic links between love and death. In terms of comedy, Sampson and Gregory's witty contest offers an opportunity for a variety of puns based on "standing," as in holding one's ground and having an erection, on thrusting the Montague "maids to the wall" (i.e., sexually), and relieving them of their

Juliet and her nurse in Act II, Scene 5 of *Romeo and Juliet*. This is a print from the Boydell Shakespeare Gallery project, which was first conceived in 1786 and lasted until 1805. *(Painting by Robert Smirke; engraving by James Parker)*

"maidenheads" (1.1.8–25). Such focus on implied sexual violence can be exceedingly humorless, but Sampson and Gregory are arguably intended to seem ridiculous in their claims to sexual attractiveness and brawling capability. This assertion is supported by the succeeding ineffectual and cowardly hectoring of the Montagues, a contest that they only commit to and which only comes to blows when their superior and ally Benvolio appears.

Bawdy language is also used to underpin the romantic language of the text. Juliet's Nurse is a particular focus of this, and her earthy character is almost wholly comical. Juliet's mother attempts to talk to Juliet of love and marriage in 1.3, but the Nurse's presence undermines the discussion through allusion to physical matters. Even when the Nurse is asked to call Juliet in her first line, she does so first swearing "by my maidenhead at twelve years old" (1.3.2). Her recollection of Juliet's precise age leads to an extended reminiscence on breast-feeding and her "dugs" (1.3.16–49) and her deceased husband's joke about the childish Juliet learning to "fall backward when thou hast more wit," meaning the wit to be reciprocal to sexual intercourse (1.3.43), a joke she reiterates in her following speech. The Nurse's enthusiasm regarding Paris's proposal is also open to a highly comic enactment, and her immediate thought is that "women grow by men" (1.3.96) through pregnancy and a marriage's "happy nights" (1.3.106). The Nurse's teasing of Juliet by withholding the result of her clandestine meeting with Romeo as the facilitator of the couple's engagement (2.5), complaining about her head and back, and alluding to Romeo's attractiveness is also a comic scene.

Sexualized language also provides the comedy generated by Romeo and Mercutio in the scenes that establish the friendship of the group and the attitudes to love therein. Romeo and Mercutio's banter in 2.4 is highly witty and initially revolves around Mercutio's assertion that Romeo's absence the previous night was because he was busy with sexual "business," "bow in the hams [legs]," "Thou hast most kindly hit it" (achieved the sexual target), "Then is my pump well flowered" (2.4.42–55).

The opportunity for lewd gestures and actions on stage can result in this exchange provoking laughter from an audience, and the banter contrasts significantly with both Romeo's previous role as a Petrarchan lovelorn worshipper of woman and his intentionally more sincere wooing of, and declarations of love for, Juliet. The bond between Mercutio and Romeo especially is established throughout the previous scenes involving Mercutio's verbosity, and here in Romeo's comic figuring of him as a goose: "good goose, bite not" (2.4.65). Mercutio continues to generate comedy through disrespectful mockery of Juliet's Nurse in this scene and of Tybalt in 3.1, offering more opportunity for the actor to generate laughter.

Mercutio's death is the turning point of the play in terms of the comic element. This leads to some critical readings that see Mercutio himself as embodying the comic spirit, which dies with him. In addition, Juliet's rejection of her Nurse in 4.3 ("I pray thee leave me to myself tonight" [4.3.2]) constitutes a similar move away from the comic to the wholly tragic, and there are no scenes solely involving lower-class characters after Mercutio's demise. This ensures that the play can move toward its tragic conclusion with no inappropriate or anomalous comic element.

Gender Politics and Adolescence

Romeo and Juliet's youth, and their love presented as a coming-of-age experience, ensures that the play is in part a record of a particularly constrained adolescence. As this adolescence is strictly gendered, and Romeo and Juliet's lives and experiences so evidently differentiated, the gender politics of the play is another main consideration when endeavoring to understand the text.

Young masculinity is seemingly at the center of the feud and its method of perpetuation. It is the young male characters of all classes belonging to both houses who facilitate the continuation of the "ancient grudge" (Prologue, 3) by upholding the hostilities and manifesting them through violent conflict. As lower-class members of the Capulet household, Sampson and Gregory demonstrate the degree to which the feud affects Veronese society. Both are employees, not family members, but they enter enthusiastically into the conflict between the Montagues and their employers. It is reasonable to suggest that the feud allows an expression of masculine aggression and bravado and thereby functions as a release for these culturally encouraged indicators of mature masculinity. This can also be seen in the language of Sampson and Gregory, where they clearly associate violence released by the feud with sexual conquest and sexual prowess, further indicators of normative, heterosexual masculinity. Correspondingly, Benvolio, Romeo, Mercutio, Tybalt, and their friends and followers experience the feud as part of their social group and their status as young men of either household in Verona. The enthusiasm with which they view the feud varies according to character; even before he meets Juliet, Romeo seems exasperated and tired of the skirmishing ("O me! What fray was here? / Yet tell me not, for I have heard it all" [1.1.164–165]), and Benvolio similarly attempts to avoid conflict, reasoning with Tybalt, "I do but keep the peace. Put up thy sword, / Or manage it to part these men with me" (1.1.59–60). In contrast, Tybalt, in particular, has a sense of self and of proper masculine behavior focused on his honor and seems to enjoy the opportunity for dueling that the feud provides: ". . . peace? I hate the word, / As I hate hell, all Montagues, and thee" (1.1.61–62). This is further evidenced by his outrage at Romeo's presence at the feast, "'tis a shame" (1.5.84), noticeably a "shame" tolerated by the representative of the older members of the house, his uncle, and his resultant vow to settle the matter with Romeo and avenge his honor, leading to the death of Mercutio.

In contrast, Juliet seems isolated both in terms of being the only young female character in the play and in her apparent seclusion. We neither hear of nor see any of her contemporaries, and she seems cloistered in the domestic environment, depending on her childhood nurse for confidences and obedient to her mother. Juliet's participation in the feud is in duty to her family. She describes Romeo as "My only love sprung from my only hate"

(1.5.135), but offers no reasoning, understanding, or evident hostility toward her supposed enemies. Juliet's love for Romeo is a catalyst for her maturation and her move from dependence and obedience via a full awareness of her sexuality and emotional attachment to a casting off of her childhood self.

Romeo's circle of friends is an important part of the play's feud and of Romeo's social position. The scenes depicting Romeo's interactions with his friends, particularly Mercutio, establish both his position as already embedded within social loyalties and hierarchy and his choice to move away from this in his relationship with Juliet. Romeo's youthful society is a microcosm of the wider homosocial structure of political, cultural, and civic life, and this homosociality can again be seen in Romeo's comparative (to Juliet's) liberty to do as he pleases and exist in the public sphere. It is possible to read the events of the play as dramatizing an extreme version of what happens when the sexually mature members of a society move away from adolescent loyalties into heterosexual relationships. Here, Romeo's love for and marriage to Juliet takes him away from his group of friends, seen in Mercutio's indignant "You gave us the counterfeit fairly last night" (2.4.39), and ultimately destroys the group through Mercutio's murder, as it results from Romeo's refusing to fight. This psychosexual reading is at odds with a contextual reading, which would stress that though marriage removes women from social life, homosocial society is pervasive, and married men would be at liberty, in medieval Europe and early modern England, to continue to socialize with friends, colleagues, business associates, and family members in public places and away from the domestic sphere. The destruction of Romeo's friendship group, continued in his own banishment, as well as suggesting the comprehensive destructive nature of the feud and ensuing tragic events, perhaps also demonstrates clearly where Romeo's loyalties lie, and thereby the depth of his love for Juliet.

Sexuality and Death

Romeo's and Juliet's deaths can be read as either wholly tragic in that death triumphs, and they are victims of tragic circumstance and/or their tragic fate, or as their triumph *in* death as they are ultimately unified, transcending their earthly trauma to exist eternally and spiritually together in love. Certainly, the play provides ample support of both theories in the continual association of love and sexuality with violence and death.

The association of sexuality and death is introduced in the very first scene of the play where Sampson and Gregory figure their proposed vanquishing of the Montagues in a fight in sexualized language and go on to describe sexual matters in violent language, most particularly in cutting off the "maiden-heads." As Sampson concludes, "Me they shall feel while I am able to stand [see Comedy above], and 'tis known I am a pretty piece of flesh" (1.1.25–26), Juliet's epithalamium of 3.2 continues these links between sexual desire and death through more elevated language. As discussed previously in Difficult Passages, Juliet's desire for Romeo is expressed through imagining her own death and Romeo's destruction, "Give me my Romeo, and when I shall die, / Take him and cut him out in little stars" (3.2.21–22). This extraordinary image conveys the wish for the beloved (Romeo) to be made immortal and worshipped by everyone as he "will make the face of heaven so fine / That all the world will be in love with night" (3.2.23–24) and thereby functions as an expression of Juliet's love, but also conveys the literal elevation and transcendence Juliet attributes to Romeo, transformed into a constellation, following her own orgasm ("die"). Such a reading also implies a Neoplatonic philosophical basis, which sees the union of lovers in sexual intercourse as a union of souls and a transcendence of the material world to spiritual elevation. Romeo's similar premonition in 5.1, his dream that "my lady came and found me dead, / . . . / And breathed such life with kisses in my lips / That I revived and was an emperor" (5.1.6–9) is grounded in the concept that Juliet's love could bring him back from the dead and elevate him in status, again implying a transcendental interpretation of their love.

As described previously in Tragedy, Fate, and Character, Juliet's prophetic, "If he be married, /

My grave is like to be my wedding bed" (1.5.133–134) is the start of her continual association of love and death. Romeo and Juliet's love and marriage is indeed the cause of both their deaths, and the site of their death is reminiscent of a "wedding bed." Juliet's "death" on her second wedding day, the onstage depiction in 5.3 of the Capulet tomb, and Paris's arrival to "strew" Juliet's "bridal bed" with flowers though "thy canopy is dust and stones" (5.3.12–13) all lead up to the final scene of Romeo and Juliet together on her elevated, bedlike, open tomb in the Capulet crypt. Romeo's description of the supposedly dead Juliet, "Death, that hath sucked the honey of thy breath, / Hath had no power yet upon thy beauty: / Thou art not conquered, beauty's ensign yet / Is crimson in thy lips and in thy cheeks, / And Death's pale flag is not yet advanced there" (5.3.92–96) finds no barrier to her attractiveness in death, and Romeo marries love and death in suggesting that Death himself is in love with Juliet. Romeo's final kiss and salutation to Juliet with poison, "Here's to my love!" (5.3.119) is not unlike a wedding toast, and his promise to remain with Juliet forever (5.3.108–110), not unlike a wedding vow. Most productions maximize the implications of Romeo's words and

Juliet's family discovers her body in Act IV, Scene 5 of *Romeo and Juliet*. This is a plate from *Retzsch's Outlines to Shakespeare: Romeo and Juliet,* published in 1836. *(Illustration by Moritz Retzsch)*

have him lie embracing Juliet, as if in bed, as he dies. His final words again summarize the events of the play and the link between love and death, "Thus with a kiss I die" (5.3.120). When Juliet awakes, she reciprocates in kissing Romeo's dead body. Her suicide using Romeo's dagger can also be interpreted in sexualized terms, as she penetrates her body with a phallic instrument, "This is thy sheath" (5.3.170), in a violent enactment of sexual intercourse, and possibly ends with a final, grim pun, "let me die" (5.3.70).

The Language of Love

The language with which Romeo and Juliet articulate their feelings of desire and their love for one another (and, in Romeo's case, for Rosaline) employs a variety of methods and tropes of identifying and describing love. Romeo's initial appearance is intended to be that of a conventional Petrarchan lover; he is miserable, stays in his bedroom all day, and mopes around alone in secluded places, "With tears augmenting the fresh morning's dew" (1.1.123). Romeo complains that he is "Out of her favour where I am in love" (1.1.159), and this unrequited love is both the source of his misery and the classic Petrarchan situation. Romeo is mocked by his friends, particularly Mercutio, for his love sickness, and Mercutio offers a facetious version of Petrarchan language and imagery in an attempt to provoke Romeo, "Cry but 'Ay me!,' pronounce but 'love' and 'dove'" (2.1.10), "I conjure thee by Rosaline's bright eyes, / By her high forehead and her scarlet lip, / By her fine foot, straight leg, and quivering thigh" (2.1.17–19).

Romeo's situation changes once he has set eyes on Juliet. Initially, he remains within the Petrarchan conventions of describing Juliet's brightness, calling her a "rich jewel in an Ethiop's ear" and a "snowy dove" (1.5.43–47), and their first interaction revolves around religious metaphor. Crucially though, this interaction indicates mutual attraction, and Juliet is fully involved in the courtly game of wit. The balcony scene of 2.2 marks a move from the Petrarchan style. Romeo begins in a similar vein to his previous declarations,

"Two of the fairest stars in all the heaven, / Having some business, do entreat her eyes / To twinkle in their spheres till they return," "speak again, bright angel" (2.2.15–17; 26). However, in the following conversation with Juliet, Romeo is told not to swear his love, either by the moon or, ". . . at all; / Or if thou wilt, swear by thy gracious self" (2.2.112–113). Juliet's reluctance to participate in the codified exchange of conventional compliments and imagery results in a frank exchange of vows of love and honorable intentions. In addition, the characters, particularly Juliet, are somewhat self-conscious, aware of the roles they are playing and the conventions they possibly should be following. Juliet says, "if thou think I am too quickly won, / I'll frown and be perverse, and say thee nay" (2.2.95–96). The remainder of the play sees both characters mature and employ more imaginative and original language in order to express emotion. Juliet's epithalamium, with its praise of night (3.2), and Romeo's heartbroken accusations of Death, "Shall I believe / That unsubstantial Death is amorous, / And that the lean abhorred monster keeps / Thee here in the dark to be his paramour?" (5.3.102–105) illustrate this.

The language of love also raises questions regarding the relationship between language and the objects of love, as discussed above in Key Passages 2.2. This, in turn, questions identity. It is in the balcony scene during the mutual declaration of love that this is focused as Juliet laments the fact that Romeo is a Montague and muses on exactly what it means to be defined by that name. The distance between word and being is articulated here, as Juliet suggests that "Montague" does not convey the (implicitly attractive) "parts" of Romeo, "What's Montague? It is not hand nor foot, / Nor arm nor face, nor any other part / Belonging to a man" (2.2.40–42). The suggestion that Juliet makes that Romeo could "deny" his father (by not acknowledging him through his surname) and thereby "refuse thy name" or she could "no longer be a Capulet" (2.2.34–36) leads into the proposition of love as an exchange, as Juliet says that in return for "doffing" his

name, Romeo can "Take all myself" (2.2.48–49). Romeo's solution is that he shall have another name and figures himself as love, "what love can do, that dares love attempt" (2.2.68). In the play, Romeo and Juliet do choose to identify with love, rather than with their families, and exchange their "good" names for each other.

EXTRACTS OF CLASSIC CRITICISM

Samuel Johnson (1709–1784) [Excerpted from the notes section of *The Plays of William Shakespeare*, the great critic's landmark edition of 1765.]

This play is one of the most pleasing of our author's performances. The scenes are busy and various, the incidents numerous and important, the catastrophe irresistibly affecting, and the process of the action carried on with such probability, at least with such congruity to popular opinions, as tragedy requires.

Here is one of the few attempts of Shakespeare to exhibit the conversation of gentlemen, to represent the airy sprightliness of juvenile elegance. Mr Dryden mentions a tradition, which might easily reach his time, of a declaration made by Shakespeare, that *he was obliged to kill Mercutio in the third act, lest he should have been killed by him.* Yet he thinks him *no such formidable person but that he might have lived through the play and died in his bed,* without danger to a poet. Dryden well knew, had he been in quest of truth, that in a pointed sentence more regard is commonly had to the words than the thought, and that it is very seldom to be rigorously understood. Mercutio's wit, gaiety, and courage will always procure him friends that wish him longer life; but his death is not precipitated, he has lived out the time allotted him in the construction of the play; nor do I doubt the ability of Shakespeare to have continued his existence, though some of his sallies were perhaps out of the reach of Dryden, whose genius was not very fertile of merriment nor ductile to humour, but acute, argumentative, comprehensive, and sublime.

The nurse is one of the characters in which the author delighted; he has, with great subtilty of distinction, drawn her at once loquacious and secret, obsequious and insolent, trusty and dishonest.

His comic scenes are happily wrought, but his pathetic strains are always polluted with some unexpected depravations. His persons, however distressed, *have a conceit left them in their misery, a miserable conceit.*

A. W. Schlegel (1767–1845) [Excerpted from *Lectures on Dramatic Art and Literature* (1808). Schlegel translated the plays of Shakespeare into German and was an important influence on Samuel Coleridge and other romantics.]

Under his handling, it has become a glorious song of praise on that inexpressible feeling which ennobles the soul and gives to it its highest sublimity, and which elevates even the senses into soul, while at the same time it is a melancholy elegy on its inherent and imparted frailty; it is at once the apotheosis and the obsequies of love . . . their love survives them, and by their death they have obtained an endless triumph over every separating power.

[Excerpted from "A. W. Schlegel on Shakspeare's Romeo and Juliet," in *Olliers Literary Miscellany*, I, translated by J. C. Hare (1820).]

The poet has left out nothing of the stormy griefs of the lovers, it is on the other hand heavenly to behold how on the following morning their violence has been calmed amid the transports of love, how love speaks in them at their melancholy farewell at the same time full of confidence and boding evil. Henceforward Romeo, though in banishment, is no more cast down; hope, blooming, youthful hope has taken possession of him; he awaits tidings almost joyfully.

ↄↄ ↄↄ ↄↄ

The deliberation how he shall procure himself poison, and his bitterness against the world in his discourse with the apothecary have something of the tone of Hamlet.

ↄↄ ↄↄ ↄↄ

The well-meaning bridegroom [Paris], who believes he has loved Juliet right tenderly, resolves to do something extraordinary; his feeling ventures itself out of its every-day circle, though fearfully, even to the limits of the romantic. And yet how different is his funeral celebration from that of the beloved lover! How calmly he strews his flowers!

ↄↄ ↄↄ ↄↄ

As Juliet's whole being is love, so is truth her virtue. From the moment that she becomes Romeo's wife, her destiny is chained to his; she has the deepest horror for every thing that would seduce her from her husband, and dreads in an equal degree the

Juliet begs her parents not to force her to marry Paris in Act III, Scene 5 of *Romeo and Juliet.* This is a plate from *Retzsch's Outlines to Shakespeare: Romeo and Juliet,* published in 1836. *(Illustration by Moritz Retzsch)*

danger of being dishonoured and of being torn from him. The tyrannical violence of her father, the vulgarity in the behaviour of both parents is very offensive; but it saves Juliet from the struggle between love and daughterly feeling, which here would not have been at all in its place; for love is not here to be deduced from moral relations, nor to be represented as at war with duties, but in its original purity as the first command of nature. After such treatment Juliet could no longer very much esteem her parents; when she is compelled to dissemble, she does it therefore with firmness and without scruples of conscience.

℘ ℘ ℘

The part of the nurse was unquestionably executed by Shakspeare with pleasure and satisfaction; every thing about her has a speaking truth. As in her head the ideas cross one another according to arbitrary connections, so is there in her behaviour only the hanging together of inconsequence, and yet she thinks equally highly of her sly understanding and of her honesty. She belongs to the souls in whom nothing cleaves fast but prejudices, and whose morality always depends upon the change of the moment.

Samuel Taylor Coleridge (1772–1834) [Excerpted from *Lectures and Notes on Shakspere and Other English Poets* (1811–1818). Coleridge, best known for poems such as "The Rime of the Ancient Mariner," was also an inventive critic.]

The groundwork of the tale is altogether in family life, and the events of the play have their first origins in family feuds . . . in family quarrels, which have proved scarcely less injurious to states, wilfulness, and precipitancy, and passion from mere habit and custom, can alone be expected. With his accustomed judgement, Shakspere has begun by placing before us a lively picture of all the impulses of the play . . . he has, by way of a prelude, shown the laughable absurdity of the evil by the contagion of it reaching the servants, who have so little to do with it[.]

℘ ℘ ℘

Shakspere meant . . . Romeo and Juliet to approach to a poem, which, and indeed its early date, may be also inferred from the multitude of rhyming couplets throughout. And if we are right, from the internal evidence, in pronouncing this one of Shakspere's early dramas, it affords a strong instance of the fineness of his insight into the nature of the passions, that Romeo is introduced already love-bewildered. The necessity of loving creates an object for itself in man and woman; and yet there is a difference in this respect between the sexes, though only to be known by a perception of it. It would have displeased us if Juliet had been represented as already in love, or as fancying herself so;—but no one, I believe, ever experiences shock at Romeo's forgetting his Rosaline, who had been a mere name for the yearning of his youthful imagination, and rushing into his passion for Juliet. Rosaline was a mere creation of his fancy; and we should remark the boastful positiveness of Romeo in a love of his own making, which is never shown where love is really near the heart.

℘ ℘ ℘

The character of the Nurse is the nearest of anything in Shakspere to a direct borrowing from mere observation . . . Here you have the garrulity of age strengthened by the feelings of a long-trusted servant, whose sympathy with the mother's affections gives her privileges and rank in the household; and observe the mode of connection by accidents of time and place, and the childlike fondness for repetition in a second childhood, and also that happy, humble, ducking under, yet constant resurgence against, the check of her superiors!

❧ ❧ ❧

In the fourth scene we have Mercutio introduced to us. O! how shall I describe that exquisite ebullience and overflow of youthful life, wafted on over the laughing waves of pleasure and prosperity . . . Wit ever wakeful, fancy busy and procreative as an insect, courage, an easy mind that, without cares of its own, is at once disposed to laugh away those of others, and yet to be interested in them,—these and all congenial qualities, melting into the common *copula* of them all, the man of rank and the gentleman, with all its excellencies and all its weaknesses, constitute the character of Mercutio!

❧ ❧ ❧

All deep passions are a sort of atheists, that believe no future.

William   Hazlitt (1778–1830) [Excerpted from *Lectures on the Literature of the Age of Elizabeth, and Characters of Shakespear's Plays* (1817). Hazlitt was heavily influenced by Coleridge in his early years and went on to become one of the most important Shakespearean critics of the 19th century.]

'ROMEO AND JULIET' is the only tragedy which Shakespear has written entirely on a love-story . . . There is the buoyant spirit of youth in every line, in the rapturous intoxication of hope, and in the bitterness of despair . . . There is nothing of a sickly and sentimental cast. Romeo and Juliet are in love, but they are not love-sick. Everything speaks the very soul of pleasure, the high and healthy pulse of the passions . . . Their courtship is not an insipid interchange of sentiments lip-deep, learnt at second-hand from poems and plays . . . It

is Shakespear all over, and Shakespear when he was young.

We have heard it objected to "Romeo and Juliet," that it is founded on an idle passion between a boy and a girl, who have scarcely seen and can have but little sympathy or rational esteem for one another, who have had no experience of the good or ills of life, and whose raptures or despair must be therefore equally groundless and fantastical.

❧ ❧ ❧

But he has given a picture of human life, such as it is in the order of nature. He has founded the passion of the two lovers not on the pleasures they had experienced, but on all the pleasures they had *not* experienced. All that was to come of life was theirs . . . They were in full possession of their senses and their affections. Their hopes were of air, their desires of fire. Youth is the season of love, because the heart is then first melted in tenderness from the touch of novelty . . . Desire has no limit but itself. Passion, the love and expectation of pleasure, is infinite, extravagant, inexhaustible, till experience comes to check and kill it.

❧ ❧ ❧

Romeo is Hamlet in love. There is the same rich exuberance of passion and sentiment in the one, that there is of thought and sentiment in the other. Both are absent and self-involved, both live out of themselves in a world of imagination. Hamlet is abstracted from everything; Romeo is abstracted from everything but his love, and lost in it.

❧ ❧ ❧

The character of Mercutio in this play is one of the most mercurial and spirited of the productions of Shakespear's comic muse.

Anna Jameson (1794–1860) [Excerpted from *Shakespeare's Heroines: Characteristics of Women, Moral, Practical & Historical* (1833). An important early female critic of Shakespeare, Jameson saw

Shakespeare as the "Poet of Womankind," whose female characters exemplify all characteristics and complexities of women's natures.]

Such, in fact, is the simplicity, the truth, and the loveliness of Juliet's character, that we are not at first aware of its complexity, its depth, and its variety. There is in it an intensity of passion, a singleness of purpose, an entireness, a completeness of effect, which we feel as a whole;

ᑭ ᑭ ᑭ

All Shakespeare's women, being essentially women, either love or have loved, or are capable of loving; but Juliet is love itself. The passion is her state of being, and out of it she has no existence.

This incident [of Rosaline], which is found in the original story, has been retained by Shakespeare with equal feeling and judgment; and far from being a fault in taste and sentiment, far from prejudicing us against Romeo, by casting on him, at the outset of the piece, the stigma of inconstancy, it becomes, if properly considered, a beauty in the drama, and adds a fresh stroke of truth to the portrait of the lover[.]

ᑭ ᑭ ᑭ

With Juliet, imagination is, in the first instance, if not the source, the medium of passion; and passion again kindles her imagination. It is through the power of imagination that the eloquence of Juliet is so vividly poetical: that every feeling, every sentiment comes to her, clothed in the richest imagery . . . The poetry is not here the mere adornment, the outward garnishing of the character; but its result, or, rather, blended with its essence.

ᑭ ᑭ ᑭ

[*Romeo and Juliet*] is in truth a tale of love and sorrow, not of anguish and terror . . . Romeo and Juliet *must* die: their destiny is fulfilled: they have quaffed off the cup of life, with all its infinite of joys and ago-

Edward Hugh Sothern as Romeo and Julia Marlowe as Juliet in a 1904 production of *Romeo and Juliet*. *(Photographed by Hall's Studio)*

nies, in one intoxicating draught. What have they to do more upon this earth? . . . they descend together into the tomb: but Shakespeare has made that tomb a shrine of martyred and sainted affection consecrated for the worship of all hearts—not a dark charnel-vault, haunted by spectres of pain, rage, and desperation.

Georg Gottfried Gervinus (1805–1871) [Excerpted from *Shakespeare Commentaries* (1849–50), translated by F. E. Bunnet (1877). Gervinus was a renowned German literary historian who wrote a four-volume study of Shakespeare.]

For the outward form of the work bears in every way the marks of a youthful hand. The abundant rhymes, often used alternately, the sonnet-form, the thoughts and the expressions taken even from Shakespeare's sonnet-poetry and from that of his contemporaries, indicate distinctly the period of its origin. It is striking that in this admired piece there are more highly pathetic and pompously profound expressions and unnatural images than in any other of Shakespeare's works; the diction too in many passages, and in the most beautiful ones, is scarcely that of the dramatic style.

& *&* *&*

Every reader must feel that in Romeo and Juliet, in spite of the severe dramatic bearing of the whole, an essentially lyric character prevails in some parts. This lies in the nature of the subject. When the poet exhibits to us the love of Romeo and Juliet in collision with outward circumstances, he is throughout on dramatic ground; when he depicts the lovers in their happiness, in the idyllic peace of blissful union, he necessarily passes to lyric ground, where thoughts and feelings speak alone, and not actions, such as the drama demands. There are in our present play three such passages of an essentially lyric nature: Romeo's declaration of love at the ball, Juliet's soliloquy at the beginning of the bridal-night, and the parting of the two on the succeeding morning . . . In all three passages he has adhered to fixed lyric forms of poetry, each in harmony with the circumstances of the case and well filled with the usual images and ideas of the respective styles. The three species we allude to are: the sonnet, the epithalamium or nuptial poem, and the dawn song[.]

& *&* *&*

Thus this tragedy, which in its mode of treatment has always been considered as the representative of all love-poetry, has in these passages formally admitted three principal styles, which may represent the erotic lyric.

While it has profoundly made use of all that is most true and deep in the innermost nature of love, the poet has imbued himself also with those external forms which the human mind had long before created in this domain of poetry.

& *&* *&*

Here in the midst of the world agitated by love and hate he has placed Friar Laurence, whom experience, retirement, and age have deprived of inclination to either. He represents, as it were, the part of the chorus in this tragedy, and expresses the leading idea of the piece in all its fullness, namely, that excess in any enjoyment, however pure in itself, transforms its sweet into bitterness;

& *&* *&*

Shakespeare's wise morality . . . we may judge from those very sayings which he placed in the lips of Friar Lawrence in that first soliloquy[.]

& *&* *&*

We see two youthful beings of the highest nobility of character and position, endowed with tender hearts and with all the sensual fire of a southern race, standing isolated in two families, who are excited to hatred and murder against each other, and repeatedly fill the town of Verona with blood and uproar. Upon the dark ground of the family hatred the two figures come out the more clearly.

& *&* *&*

Tybalt appears as brawler by profession, distinguished by bitter animosity and outward elegance from the merry and cynical Mercutio, who calls him a "fashion-monger." Mercutio . . . affords a perfect contrast to Romeo. He is a man without culture; coarse, rude, and ugly; a scornful ridiculer of all sensibility and love, of all dreams and presentiments; a man who loves to hear himself talk . . . ; a man gifted with such a habit of wit, and such a humorous perception of all things, that even in the consciousness of his death-wound . . . he loses not the expression of his humour. According to the description of himself, which he draws in an ironical attack against the good Benvolio, he is a quarrel-seeking brawler, possessing a spirit of innate contradiction, and over-confident in his powers of strength, and as such he proves himself in his meeting with Tybalt. Our Romanticists, according to their fashion, [are] blindly in love with the merry fellow[.]

෮ ෮ ෮

How can she [Juliet]—with a mind so full of emotion, and a heart so tender, and with a

nature evidencing an originally cheerful disposition—how can she find pleasure in her paternal home, a home at once dull, joyless, and quarrelsome?

෮ ෮ ෮

The more tender being, in despair at the first moment, is soon comforted by her own reflection; she is soon even capable of comforting, and is bent upon means of remedy. The stronger man, on the contrary, is wholly crushed; he is quite incapable of self-command, quite inaccessible to consolation. The nature of the woman is not so much changed by this omnipotence of love, but the man's power and self-possession are destroyed by the excess of this one feeling.

Maud Granger as Juliet and Lawrence Atkins as Romeo in an 1866 production of *Romeo and Juliet*.

Edward Dowden (1843–1913) [Excerpted from *Shakspere: His Mind and Art* (1875). Dowden was an Irish critic, university lecturer, and poet.]

It is not Shakespere's practice to expound the moralities of his artistic creations; nor does he ever, by means of a chorus, stand above and outside the men and women of his plays . . . No! Friar Lawrence . . . is moving in the cloud, and misled by error as well as the rest. Shakspere has never made the moderate, self-possessed, sedate person a final or absolute judge of the impulsive and the passionate.

MODERN CRITICISM AND CRITICAL CONTROVERSIES

In the 20th century, criticism of the play moved away from the moral concerns of the preceding ages and largely concentrated on two areas: tragic form and responsibility, and the language of the play. However, the mixture of comedy with the tragedy and the love-death theme were also explored and, in the later part of the century, matters of gender, adolescence, and violence.

Discussions of the tragic element of *Romeo and Juliet* centered on whether the play is a tragedy of fate or of character, that is, of self-destructive human passion and individual fallibility. Franklin M. Dickey claimed in 1957 that "Critics are . . . embarrassed by Shakespeare's paradoxical treatment of the three great themes of the tragedy," and M. M. Mahood that "the question of whether the play is of character or of fate can be answered only by a neglect or distortion of the play as a dramatic experience." Critics like H. B. Charlton and Wolfgang Clemen who argued that the tragedy was one of fate follow an anti-psychological reading and instead emphasize the dramatic process and the conflict between love and destiny, focused on the feud itself. Those that assert the tragedy was a result of the characters of the lovers emphasized Shakespeare's choice of setting and the development of the characters. Further arguments suggested the play depicts a pattern of retribution with the lovers as instruments of a divine will that punishes, then reconciles, the feuding families, but more recent critics have opted for a conflation of concepts and see the tragedy of *Romeo and Juliet* to be a fatal combination of fate and character. As M. C. Bradbrook writes: "Both Romeo and Juliet are too impulsive to live safely in the electric atmosphere that surrounds them; put in terms of action, the speed of the plot carries everything along at such a pace that we feel the momentum cannot be checked; at this pace the smallest incident is fatal, the merest rub of circumstance will throw a life away." Such reliance of the plot on circumstance, accident, and caprice leads to frustrated criticism by some thinkers who find the chain of events and catastrophic coincidences generally unconvincing. This, too, however, is contested. Ruth Nevo writes in 1969, "Shakespeare, so far from mitigating the effect of unfortunate coincidence is evidently concerned to draw our attention to it. Bad luck, misfortune, sheer inexplicable contingency is a far from negligible source of the suffering and calamity in human life which is the subject of tragedy's mimesis; while of all the ancient and deep-seated responses of man to the world which he inhabits

the fear of some force beyond his control and indifferent, if not positively inimical, to his desires is one of the most persistent."

The tragic claims of *Romeo and Juliet* are also possibly undermined by the comic aspects of the text. These are both structural and overt in the action and language. Critics such as Nicholas Brooke in 1968 and Susan Snyder in 1970 highlight the generic clashes in the play and pinpoint Mercutio's death as the turning point in the action and tone of the text. This reading divides the play into the "comic" half before Mercutio's death, and the tragic part following it. Snyder comments, "In Mercutio's sudden, violent end, Shakespeare makes the birth of a tragedy coincide exactly with the symbolic death of comedy. The element of freedom and play dies with him, and where many courses were open before, now there seems only one." However, such commentators also stressed this generic shift does not constitute a lack of dramatic unity.

For critics not emphasizing the comic aspect of the play, the feud is entirely central to the action of *Romeo and Juliet* and constitutes a threatening background of underlying violence. As Coppélia Kahn observes in her "Coming of Age in Verona" (1983), "Structurally, the play's design reflects the prominence of the feud. It erupts in three scenes at the beginning, middle, and end (1.1, 3.1, 5.3) that deliberately echo each other, and the *peripeteia* [reversal of circumstances], at which Romeo's and Juliet's fortunes change decisively for the worse, occurs exactly in the middle when Romeo in killing Tybalt faces the two conflicting definitions of manhood between which he must make his tragic choice." It is in this environment that Romeo and Juliet have had to grow up and continue to mature in the play, and this maturation is of course strictly gendered. Participation in the feud is considered necessarily masculine, but it also threatens death. Kahn continues, "The feud in a realistic social sense is the primary tragic force in the play—not the feud as agent of fate, but the feud as an extreme and peculiar expression of patriarchal society, which Shakespeare shows to be tragically self-destructive. The feud is the deadly *rite de passage* that promotes masculinity at the price of life." In addition, the feud is demonstrably a focal point for language that ominously conflates violence and sexual matters in the play, as well as the preoccupation with "name."

Theories of structuralism from the 1960s and 1970s illuminate *Romeo and Juliet*'s interest in names and naming. The critic Jacques Derrida has considered the complexities of names and naming in the play, and Catherine Belsey writes that Juliet is unsuccessful in her attempt to isolate Romeo from his name. Julia Kristeva agrees, writing in 1992, "Juliet is mistaken and the name of her lover is not irrelevant to the triggering of their passion; quite the contrary, it determines it." Critical interest in the language of the play developed throughout the 20th century. The poetic quality of *Romeo and Juliet*'s courtship generated extensive critical commentary on both the poetic language they utilize and the philosophies of love the play illustrates. It is clear that their language is based on literary precedents. E. C. Pettet comments, that Romeo "habitually talks in oxymoron, hyperbole and extravagant conceit, and he is always close to the sonnet vein. On one occasion Shakespeare actually gives him a sonnet sestet to speak, while his first words to Juliet form a sonnet in the pseudo-religious style, in the recitation of which Juliet joins." Brooke, Mahood, Rosalie Colie, and many others focus at some point in their work on the effect of the stylized Petrarchan language of the play, and Colie in particular highlights the difference in the way Juliet uses poetic language, claiming that her "metaphoric daring is greater than Romeo's." Colie sees the poetic language of the play as elevating, whereas Bradbrook, Harley Granville-Barker, and Norman Rabkin feel the effect is, rather, distancing, Bradbrook stating, "Parts of the play are in a manner so rhetorical that they are emptied of all feeling." Also focused upon were the puns and bawdy language of the play. Some critics found the puns of some of the "higher" characters problematic. Juliet's punning in 3.2, upon thinking the Nurse's bad news is the death of Romeo, was considered by some to be inappropriate. However, Northrop Frye argued in that "she's not 'play-

Romeo drinks poison over Juliet's body in Act V, Scene 3 of *Romeo and Juliet.* This is a plate from *Retzsch's Outlines to Shakespeare: Romeo and Juliet,* published in 1836. (Illustration by Moritz Retzsch)

ing' with words: she's shredding them to bits in an agony of frustration and despair. The powerful explosion of words has nowhere to go, and simply disintegrates." Another key linguistic tendency of the text is continual opposition and paradox, exemplified in the pervasive imagery of light and dark.

Some critics developed the concept of the play by introducing a variety of philosophies of love, including Neoplatonism, to reconstruct the tragic deaths of Romeo and Juliet as ennobling and elevating. Nevo writes, "Their death is an act of freedom and of fidelity; hence an affirmation of the reality, vitality, and value of their experience." In this way, love is seen to overcome death, not be ended by it. The conflict between love and death is, according to Pettet, "the fundamental theme of *Romeo and Juliet,*" as well as another example of opposition, but the mass of critical thought, particularly in the latter part of the 20th century, reads these two opposing forces instead as inextricably linked. This is largely due to the sexual language used to figure violence, which pervades the text, as Frye identifies, the "macho jokes, 'draw thy tool' and the like, are the right way to introduce the theme that dominates this play: the theme of love bound up with, and part of, violent death. Weapons and fighting suggest sex as well as death." In addition, studies have also highlighted Juliet as particularly instrumental in aligning love with death in 3.2. Here, Brooke sees that "There is no gap here between the expression of love and the expression of death . . . This remarkable complex of associations is superb: this *is* desire, recognized and focused as it must be at that point where love and lust are identical, or love is not love but 'simple modesty' (a nonentity)." Kristeva's Freudian reading in "Love-Hatred in the Couple" also emphasizes the link between love and death in the text.

As indicated above in relation to the feud and Kahn's comments regarding it as being intrinsic to the patriarchal society in which Romeo and Juliet have to mature, 20th-century criticism also produced a combined interest in the contextual background of culture and history, which manifests in a wealth of considerations of the depiction of gender and adolescence in the text. The focus on adolescence is perhaps the reasoning behind many recent productions and films, which choose to aim their representation at a "youth" market—a decision that either irritates or infuriates many critics.

Gendered readings of *Romeo and Juliet* tend to focus on issues of masculinity, as in Robert Appelbaum (1997). As mentioned previously, the feud is the starting point for much of this criticism, as it condenses and stresses usual patriarchal social structures. The feud divides individuals into paternal households, and male members of the households "are constantly called upon to define themselves in terms of their families and to defend their families. Second, the feud provides a "psycho-sexual moratorium [postponement]" for the sons, an activity in which they prove themselves men by phallic violence on behalf of their fathers, instead of by the courtship and sexual experimentation that would lead toward marriage and separation from the paternal house" (Kahn, 1983). This homosocial environment, a society of men depending on men in contrast to the cloistered world of femininity, is disrupted by Romeo's love. As discussed in the Background and Character Studies sections, Romeo's attempts to spend time in the company of women are disruptive. Joseph A.

Porter claims that this central theme of the play is focused on the figure of Mercutio, a "priapic" and critical force who offers Romeo the stability of male friendship over the instability of heterosexual love. This view challenges the conventional view that sees the play as celebrating and privileging heterosexual love and romance.

Such concentration on the homosociality of the play is developed further by critics and more commonly in productions from the 1970s onward, which suggest Mercutio is more than aggressively homosocial and sociable, but actively hostile to heterosexual partnerships because of homosexual tendencies. This goes beyond the culturally influenced focus on the homosocial (the normal state of European societies from medieval Verona to 16th-century London) and is sometimes a point of contention between critics. Dympna Callaghan calls Mercutio "profoundly homoerotic" and claims that this homoeroticism would have been more evident in original productions able to exploit the potential homoerotics of all-male casts. In contrast, G. Blakemore Evans, in exasperation, calls this "character perversion" a desperate attempt to contemporize Shakespeare for modern audiences.

THE PLAY TODAY

Romeo and Juliet continues to be a popular play in performance and in study, engaging critics, audiences, students, and theater companies. The central narrative of doomed love is evidently as appealing now as at the time of the play's initial production. The most recent criticism of the play continues to reevaluate its depiction of distinctly gendered adolescence, homosociality, and tragic form, as well as the textual instability of the two quarto versions.

The majority of modern stage and film productions seem preoccupied with emphasizing the first two aspects, and it is a text open to a modernized setting (seen, for example, in Michael Bogdanov's 1986 Royal Shakespeare Company [RSC] production, complete with lethal injections and onstage sports car). However, a production of the play in 1985 in Paris instead chose to concentrate on the text's derivative, intertextual nature. Daniel Mesguich's production's set was that of an enormous library filled with books. When these are knocked off the shelves by Gregory and Abraham, they read out of them the interaction that opens the play. In death, Romeo and Juliet were led off into the stacks to begin a literary afterlife. Many more faithful productions echo this concept in, for example, using music from a variety of musical adaptations.

The text is also open to politicized productions to illustrate the feuding factions of the play. In place of antagonistic aristocratic Italian families, productions have offered racial divisions and, in Brisbane in 1993, the conflict between Christian and Muslim in contemporary Bosnia (directed by Aubrey Mellor). In contrast to productions that focus on a clear and overtly visual dichotomy are many productions that characterize their settings rather by focusing on the type of play-world in which such a feud could exist between families of similar race, religion, class, or creed. The majority of productions also choose to select an Italian setting (which, in the least, makes sense of the play's geographical references, "In fair Verona . . ."). A good example of these points is a recent RSC production directed by Neil Bartlett in 2008. This production was set in 1950s Italy, a world appropriately conservative, Catholic, and restrictive for its young female inhabitants. In addition, the hint of Mafia organization demonstrated how blood feuds and crime could affect whole communities. Indeed, Bartlett says that the music of the play was directly influenced by the Godfather films directed by Francis Ford Coppola.

The most influential production of the 20th century was that of Franco Zeffirelli at the Old Vic in 1960 and particularly the resulting film version of 1968, both of which emphasized the youth of the protagonists and the tensions within the families, described by Zeffirelli as the "breakdown of understanding between two generations." This emphasis continued throughout the rest of the century, with school-uniformed Juliets, teenage gangs, and so on. The dominance of youth, gangs, and violence over the concept of the play is illustrated by the concern of some British tabloid newspapers and organizations at the proposal of Shakespeare's Globe theater to give free performances of Bill Buckhurst's 2009 production to local teenage school pupils. The proposal raised fears concerning knife crime, a growing problem in parts of London, though it was uncertain how critics expected the play to influence the audience.

The youth-orientated trend reached its zenith with Baz Luhrman's highly successful film *William Shakespeare's Romeo + Juliet* (1996). In this version, the setting is modern, though fictional, guns are substituted for swords, and rival businesses are at the heart of the feud. The neo-Catholicism of massive churches, neon crosses, and elaborate religious tattoos (even on Friar Lawrence [Pete Postlethwaite]) suggest a religious cultural presence akin, at least in fervor, to that of medieval Italy. In addition, the action is high-octane, with still-frames, speeded-up scenes, and editorial tricks pervasive from the opening scenes. This, together with a highly contemporary sound track, led to the film being labeled as an "MTV" production.

Zeffirelli's film was also the first production to hint (but only hint) at the possibility of a reading of Mercutio as being homosexual. Following the critical interest in this aspect, the production in 1973 at Stratford, directed by Terry Hands, presented Mercutio as an overt and aggressive homosexual character. This was augmented by an emphasis on Mercutio's misogynist tendencies; in 2.1, during his blazon, or detailed description of the body parts, of Rosaline, the actor crudely dismembered a life-size female doll. Michael Boyd's 2000 production with the RSC also depicted Mercutio as a rival to Juliet for Romeo's affection. This theme continued after Mercutio's death, with the character haunting Romeo and Juliet's relationship; he is present when Juliet takes the sleeping potion and even puts the poison into Romeo's hands.

FIVE TOPICS FOR DISCUSSION AND WRITING

1. **Tragic form:** Is the play a tragedy of fate or of character? Does it depict self-destructive human

passion or individual fallibility? Do Romeo and Juliet's own actions and personalities lead to their deaths? How much is Friar Lawrence at fault? Can the play be read as following a pattern of retribution with the lovers as instruments of a divine will that punishes then reconciles the feuding families? Does the ending constitute frustration or fulfillment? Is the tragic ending inescapable?

2. **Comedy and tragedy:** How do the comic scenes and "low" bawdy language of some of the characters function within the tragic framework of the text? What elements of romantic comedy can be found within the play? Can you divide the characters into the comic and the tragic? Can you divide the structure of the play into comic and tragic? Is there a point in the structure of the play where the impetus changes? Why does Mercutio have to die? How do the themes of love, sex, violence, and identity manifest in both comic and tragic ways?

3. **Gender:** Consider the gendered roles of the individuals becoming adults in the Verona of the play. How are Romeo and Juliet "adolescent"? Is Juliet's young age an issue? What do Romeo's friends think of love? Why is the feud perpetuated by the young males of the play? Does Romeo change once he has fallen in love with Juliet? How are homosocial bonds depicted among Romeo's group of friends? In contrast, why does Juliet seemingly have no similar friendship group? Who are her female role models? Does it make sense to read Mercutio as potentially homosexual?

4. **Sex and death:** Is death presented as triumphing in this play? Or is there a triumph in death? How do ideas of transcendence link the areas of sex and death? Are the concepts of love/sex and death antithetical or linked? Consider the Renaissance meaning of "dying." How can this knowledge be related to some of the speeches of the play? Are Romeo and Juliet united in death? How else are sex and death related in the language of the play?

5. **The language of love:** How is Romeo and Juliet's love constructed by their language? What literary precedents can you find in their descriptions and pledges of their love? How aware do you think the characters are of these precedents? Would you describe their language as Petrarchan or anti-Petrarchan? Why does Shakespeare introduce the figure of Rosaline, who exists only in language? How does Romeo talk about Rosaline in comparison to Juliet once he and Juliet have met? Is it difficult to empathize with characters who speak in this way? How does Mercutio use language? What is the effect of the bawdy punning in contrast to the elevated language of love? How important are names and identity in this text? What are the implications of the suggestions about the names and nature of things and individuals in the balcony scene?

Bibliography

Andrews, John F., ed. *Romeo and Juliet: Critical Essays.* New York: Garland, 1993.

Appelbaum, Robert. "'Standing to the Wall': the Pressures of Masculinity in *Romeo and Juliet.*" *Shakespeare Quarterly* 48 (1997): 251–272.

Belsey, Catherine. "The Name of the Rose in *Romeo and Juliet.*" *Critical Essays on Shakespeare's Romeo and Juliet.* Edited by Joseph Porter. New York: G. K. Hall, 1997.

Brown, Carolyn E. "Juliet's Taming of Romeo." *Studies in English Literature 1500–1900* 36 (1996): 333–355.

Brown, John Russell. *Shakespeare's Dramatic Style* London: Heinemann, 1970.

Callaghan, Dympna, ed. *Romeo and Juliet: Texts and Contexts.* Basingstoke, England: Macmillan, 2003.

Cartwright, Kent. "Theater and Narrative in *Romeo and Juliet.*" In *Shakespearean Tragedy and Its Double: The Rhythms of Audience Response,* 43–88. University Park: Pennsylvania State University Press, 1991.

Colie, Rosalie L. *Shakespeare's Living Art.* Princeton, N.J.: Princeton University Press, 1974.

Davis, Lloyd. "'Death-Marked Love': desire and Presence in *Romeo and Juliet.*" *Shakespeare Survey* 49 (1996): 57–67.

Erne, Lukas, ed. *The First Quarto of Romeo and Juliet.* Cambridge: Cambridge University Press, 2007.

Fitter, Chris. "'The quarrel is between our masters and us their men': *Romeo and Juliet,* Dearth, and the London Riots." *English Literary Renaissance* 30 (2000): 154–183.

Franson, J. Karl. "'Too soon marr'd': Juliet's age as symbol in *Romeo and Juliet.*" *Papers on Language & Literature* 32 (1996): 244–262.

Frye, Northrop. *Northrop Frye on Shakespeare.* Edited by Robert Sandler. New Haven, Conn.: Yale University Press, 1986, 15–33.

Heyworth, G. G. "Missing and Mending: Romeo and Juliet at Play in the Romance Chronotope." *Yearbook of English Studies* 30 (2000): 5–20.

Hunter, Lynette. "Cankers in *Romeo and Juliet:* Sixteenth-Century Medicine at a Figural/Literal Cusp." In *Disease, Diagnosis, and Cure on the Early Modern Stage,* edited by Stephanie Moss and Kaara L. Peterson, 171–185. Aldershot, England: Ashgate, 2004.

Kahn, Coppélia. "Coming of Age in Verona." In *The Woman's Part: Feminist Criticism of Shakespeare,* edited by Carolyn Ruth Swift Lenz, Gayle Greene, and Carol Thomas Neely, 171–193. Chicago: University of Illinois Press, 1983.

Knowles, Ronald. "Carnival and Death in *Romeo and Juliet.*" In *Shakespeare and Carnival: After Bakhtin,* edited by Ronald Knowles, 36–60. Basingstoke, England: Macmillan, 1998.

Kristeva, Julia. "*Romeo and Juliet:* Love-Hatred in the Couple." In *Shakespearean Tragedy,* edited by John Drakakis, 296–315. Harlow, Essex, England: Longman, 1992.

Lehmann, Courtney. "Strictly Shakespeare? Dead Letters, Ghostly Fathers, and the Cultural Pathology of Authorship in Baz Luhrmann's *William Shakespeare's Romeo + Juliet.*" *Shakespeare Quarterly* 52 (2001): 189–220.

Levenson, Jill L. "Echoes Inhabit a Garden: The Narratives of *Romeo and Juliet.*" *Shakespeare Survey* 53 (2000): 39–48.

———. *Shakespeare in Performance: Romeo and Juliet.* Manchester, England: Manchester University Press, 1987.

Levin, Harry. "Form and Formality in *Romeo and Juliet.*" In *Shakespeare and the Revolution of the Times.* Oxford: Oxford University Press, 1976, 103–120.

Mason, H. A. *Shakespeare's Tragedies of Love.* London: Chatto & Windus, 1970.

Nevo, Ruth. "Tragic Form in *Romeo and Juliet.*" *Studies in English Literature* 9 (1969): 241–258.

Palmer, Daryl W. "Motion and Mercutio in *Romeo and Juliet.*" *Philosophy and Literature* 30 (2006): 540–554.

Porter, Joseph, ed. *Critical Essays on Shakespeare's Romeo and Juliet.* New York: G. K. Hall, 1997.

———. *Shakespeare's Mercutio: His History and Drama.* Chapel Hill: University of North Carolina Press, 1983.

Snow, Edward. "Language and Sexual Difference in *Romeo and Juliet.*" In *Shakespeare's "Rough Magic": Essays in Honor of C. L. Barber,* edited by Peter Erickson and Coppélia Kahn, 168–192. Newark, Del.: University of Delaware Press, 1985.

Snyder, Susan. "*Romeo and Juliet:* Comedy into Tragedy." *Essays in Criticism* 20 (1970): 391–402.

Sohmer, Steve. "Shakespeare's Time-Riddles in *Romeo and Juliet* Solved." *English Literary Renaissance* 35 (2005): 407–428.

Swann, Marjorie. "The Politics of Fairylore in Early Modern English Literature." *Renaissance Quarterly* 53 (2000): 449–473.

Taylor, Neil, and Bryan Loughrey, eds. *Shakespeare's Early Tragedies.* Basingstoke, England: Macmillan, 1990.

Wall, Wendy. "De-generation: Editions, Offspring, and *Romeo and Juliet.*" In *From performance to Print in Shakespeare's England,* edited by Peter Holland and Stephen Orgel. Basingstoke, England: Palgrave Macmillan, 2006.

Watts, Cedric Thomas. *Romeo and Juliet.* London: Harvester, 1991.

Wells, Robin Headlam. "Neo-Petrarchan Kitsch in *Romeo and Juliet.*" *Modern Language Review* 93 (1998): 913–933.

West, William N. "Mercutio's Bad Language." In *Rematerializing Shakespeare: Authority and Representation on the Early Modern English Stage.* Basingstoke, England: Palgrave Macmillan, 2005, 115–129.

White, R. S., ed. *Romeo and Juliet.* Basingstoke, England: Palgrave, 2001.

FILM AND VIDEO PRODUCTIONS

Kemp-Smith, Joan, dir. *Romeo and Juliet*. With Christopher Neame, Ann Hasson, Peter Jeffrey, Simon MacCorkindale. Fremantle, 1988.

Luhrmann, Baz, dir. *William Shakespeare's Romeo + Juliet*. With Leonardo DiCaprio, Clare Danes, John Leguizamo, Pete Postlethwaite. 20th Century Fox, 1996.

Zeffirelli, Franco, dir. *Romeo and Juliet*. With Leonard Whiting, Olivia Hussey, John McEnery, Milo O'Shea, Pat Heywood. Paramount, 1968.

—Sarah Carter

Sir Thomas More

INTRODUCTION

Shakespeare composed only a very small part of the play *Sir Thomas More*. The rest was probably written by his fellow dramatists Anthony Munday, Henry Chettle, Thomas Heywood, and Thomas Dekker. The collaborative writing of plays was not unusual, but this is one of only two known plays (the other is the play *Edward III*) where Shakespeare contributed little more than one scene to others' work. The date of composition of the play is uncertain; it was probably sometime between 1593 and 1603. It might not all have been written at one time but rather in two stints separated by several years.

The play is remarkable for one reason: Scholars believe that in the existing manuscript, Shakespeare's portion of the play is written in his own hand. The manuscript, classified as Harley 7368, is held in the British Library in London and comprises 22 leaves of paper—44 pages, not all written on and in different sizes. It became the subject of great excitement in the early 20th century when it was revealed to be, at least in part, one of Shakespeare's play manuscripts. Until then, it had been thought that all Shakespeare's play manuscripts were lost, presumed destroyed, leaving us only his signatures on certain nondramatic documents (including his will) to show what his handwriting looked like. Comparison of those signatures with the writing on three pages of Harley 7368 convinced experts that their handwriting, formerly known only as Hand D, was Shakespeare's (see Pollard et al., 1923). The rest of the manuscript (apart from these three pages) is in a variety of other hands. Other evidence corroborated the handwriting: Hand D uses uncommon spellings (including *straing* for modern *strange* and *scilens* for modern *silence*) that appear in early printed plays by Shakespeare, and the scene written in Hand D is stylistically similar to ones by Shakespeare.

The play tells of the rise of the historical figure More (1478–1535) from being one of the two undersheriffs of London to becoming a knight and a privy counsellor and finally gaining the Lord Chancellorship, one of the highest government offices in England, which brought him close to King Henry VIII. The second half of the play charts More's fall from power, arising from his refusal to sign a document accepting Henry VIII's assertion of himself as the head of the newly formed Church of England. The play does not name or depict the king and does not make specific the circumstances of More's moral dilemma—it comes down to whether to obey his king or his religious conscience—so presumably these details were thought to be well known to playgoers. More's book *Utopia*, written in Latin and first published in 1516, had been published in three English-language editions by the time the play was written, and his fame appears to have been widespread. In particular, More's role in the calming of a riot against foreigners in London (the so-called Ill May Day uprising of 1517), dramatized in Shakespeare's contribution to the play, seemed especially relevant to people in the 1590s as xenophobic tensions rose in the capital.

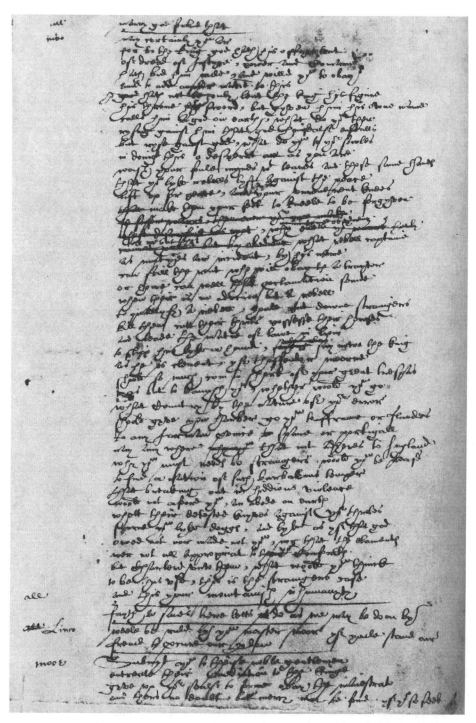

Facsimile of a page added to the manuscript of *Sir Thomas More*. The handwriting here is believed to be Shakespeare's.

The topic was clearly a sensitive one, since the manuscript contains extensive annotations by the state censor, the master of the revels, who checked every play script before it was performed. The master at this time was Edmund Tilney. Having made small changes to the ethnic identification of the foreigners (Lombards, Frenchmen, or generically "strangers"), he decided against any depiction of the riot. The Lombards came from what we now call Italy, so using this label projects the aliens' origin far into mainland Europe, while the rioters themselves refer to their enemies being French and Dutch, people from places on the western seaboard of Europe and hence much closer to England. The resulting manuscript contains multiple alterations and rewrites of scenes, making it an especially difficult task for editors to present the play to modern readers.

The account of the play given here is dependent on John Jowett's forthcoming Arden 3 edition, which he generously let the author see in advance of publication, although quotations are from Jowett's text of the play in the Oxford Complete Works of 2005. Jowett divides the play into scenes, numbered 1 to 17, but not into acts (as below). As this play contains relatively few lines actually by Shakespeare, it is here discussed in a somewhat abbreviated entry.

BACKGROUND

A play telling the life story of Thomas More was bound to be controversial in the 1590s. More was the most famous English public figure to suffer from the cataclysmic political and religious events known as the English Reformation, when a new Protestant Church of England was created and broke from the authority of the pope and the Roman Church to make the monarch (Henry VIII himself, and each successor) the supreme religious ruler. Before Henry fell out with Rome, More had long served him by hunting and executing heretical Protestants, which religious zeal was markedly at odds with the religious tolerance that More appeared to advocate in his fictional prose narrative *Utopia* published in 1516. The Utopians allow freedom of conscience to all faiths, condemning only outright atheism as a crime.

The historical More found himself unable to follow Henry's volte-face in 1534 and chose instead to be executed for the treason of denying the king's religious supremacy, for which martyrdom he was made a saint by the Catholic Church in 1935. Henry VIII's daughter Mary I returned England to Catholicism from 1553 to 1558, after which her half-sister Elizabeth I returned it to Protestantism, the official religion of the country to this day. The experience of three changes of official religion—each of which criminalized the religious beliefs of a sizable proportion of the population—was still raw in the 1590s. Curiously, however, the state censor seems not to have objected on principle to this Catholic martyr's life being dramatized but was gravely concerned about the representation of rioting in London. In the 1590s, there was considerable antipathy toward European exiles in London, in particular Protestants known as Huguenots fleeing persecution in Catholic France and Spanish-controlled Holland, and there were notable riots (partly xenophobic, partly economic) by apprentices (Pollard et al., 1923, 33–40). Inevitably, a dramatization of the Ill May Day riots of 1517 (which were essentially about economics, not religion) would in the 1590s take on fresh topical associations of religious strife, especially when tied to the story of More's martyrdom for refusing to abandon the Roman faith and take up Protestantism.

The main sources of the play are the 1587 edition of Raphael Holinshed's *Chronicles,* which is used particularly heavily for the first half of the play, and Nicholas Harpsfield's *Life of Thomas More,* which provided much of the second half. Harpsfield's biography was derived in part from material provided by More's son-in-law William Roper, who is present as a character in the play, and it circulated privately among secret Catholics in manuscript form in the second half of the 16th century. Anthony Munday, the main author of the play, could have had access to Harpsfield's biography via his employer, Richard Topcliffe, who certainly had a copy that he found while working for Elizabeth I's regime hunting down, torturing, and executing secret Catholics and extreme Protestants (Munday 1990, 6–11). One of the extraordinary facts of the play is Munday's involvement in it, since he had published in the early 1580s a series of vehemently anti-Catholic tracts, having previously stayed for a while in the English College in Rome. Munday may have stayed at this seminary for training Catholic priests because he was genuinely attracted to Catholicism, or else he may have been under cover so he could later detect the priests that Rome was sending to London.

SYNOPSIS

Foreigners from Europe residing in London early in 1517 are abusing the local population, abducting citizens' wives, and stealing their goods. Londoner John Lincoln makes out a bill of complaint to be read in public as an incitement to riot against the foreigners. Lincoln attracts a group of followers including Doll Williamson, who was nearly raped by one of the foreigners, and her husband. Thomas More is serving as one of the two sheriffs of London and gaining a reputation for decency and honesty, leavened with a mischievous sense of wit. At the sentencing of a pickpocket, More intervenes when one of the justices attempts to lay part of the blame on the victim of the crime for tempting the criminal by carrying around too much money and being too easy to rob. More adjourns the proceedings and persuades the pickpocket to pick the justice's own well-filled purse, thus exposing his hypocrisy. The jest successfully carried off earns the pickpocket a pardon. Meanwhile, the king's counsellors debate the growing unrest of the London population, which the king is unaware of even though it is in part due to his indulgence of the foreigners, which is encouraged by their ambassador. News arrives that the lord mayor is besieged by rioters, and as the privy counsellors leave to deal with this crisis, they agree to seek Sheriff More's help because he is popular with, and respected by, the citizens of London.

The rioters, some of them in armor, seek out the foreigners' houses and discuss how to deal with the forces they know are being mustered against them. The foreigners' houses are discovered to be empty—they earlier fled in fear—so the riot-

ers decide to set fire to them and make good their escape while the Lord Mayor is having his men put out the fires. More discovers that some of the rioters have broken open the prisons and swelled their insurrection with the criminals they have released, and he proposes a parley with the riot's ringleaders. Approaching the rioters, More rescues a sergeant-at-arms whom they are attacking, and he calls them to listen to him. For all their antipathy to the foreigners and the authorities that have let them down, the rioters respect Sheriff More and listen intently to a speech in which he persuasively argues that their rebellion is an offense against their king and hence against God who put the king in power over them. Moreover, if for their rebellion the rioters were banished from the kingdom, More points out, they would be foreigners in another country and would want to be tolerated by the natives. Promising them the king's mercy if they abandon their insurrection, More persuades the rioters to lay down their weapons, and the ringleaders agree to go to prison while he presents their case to the king. For this brave and peaceful suppression of rebellion, the king makes More a knight and one of his counsellors.

Despite More's promise, the ringleaders of the riot are sentenced to death, and the first of them, John Lincoln, is executed. Doll Williamson asks to be executed next (before her husband) and is on the ladder, reproving More for breaking his promise to them, when the king's pardon arrives. For his eloquent pleading on the rioters' behalf, More is made Lord Chancellor of England. More reflects on the moral dangers that come with such high office, but his gloom is lightened by further jests. When the Dutch humanist scholar Erasmus pays a visit to his house, More has his servant Randall dress as the master of the house while he, More, takes on Randall's role as servant to see if the wise man can spot the deception. Randall tries in vain to speak intelligently in English (having neatly avoided Erasmus's attempt to engage him in Latin) and is exposed. When More is presented with a long-haired ruffian who has been arrested for a public brawl, he finds that the man has taken a vow against haircuts. More's response is to offer to let the man keep his hair while languishing in jail, or to accept a haircut and a short sentence. The man first chooses to keep his hair but after a brief spell in jail decides to break his vow and is pardoned by More. At his home in Chelsea, More is visited by the Lord Mayor and aldermen of London and prepares an elaborate feast for them. A troupe of traveling players arrives and offers a performance; from their list of titles More picks *The Marriage of Wit and Wisdom.* More has the performance begin immediately even though one actor is away trying to procure a beard for the show. More offers to take this actor's part, that of Good Counsel (a role More plays in real life), and he extemporizes it. The evening is interrupted by More's being called to a meeting of the privy council.

In the council, matters of state policy are being debated when Palmer enters with papers (the Act of Supremacy) that the king has asked his counsellors to sign. One of the counsellors, Rochester, refuses and is arrested. More asks for time to consider the matter and is instructed to return to his house in Chelsea and remain there. The other counsellors immediately sign the papers. At his home, More's family seems to have presentiment of his fate in the form of dreams of his downfall and death. More arrives and behaves as if a great burden has been lifted from him. Although he is sure his family can survive without him—even his girls are educated and can make their way in the world—he is fearful of what will happen to his servants. Word arrives that More must sign the papers instantly or be conveyed to the Tower, and More chooses the latter. On his way there, crowds gather to see him pass. More's servants discover that he has left each of them 20 nobles, which is around two-and-a-half pounds, a great sum. In the Tower, More hears that he is to be executed the following morning, and despite the pleading of his wife and son-in-law Roper, he refuses to subscribe to the king's papers in order to avoid this fate. The next morning, More is taken to the place of beheading, and after a series of jokes about what is to happen and a speech that does not quite make the traditional admission of guilt, he is executed.

CHARACTERS
Thomas More

First seen as a sheriff of London, later knighted and made Lord Chancellor of England, More earns a reputation for sound judgment, first as a judge and advocate in lawsuits and later as an adviser to King Henry VIII. As much loved by the common citizens of London as the nobility, More combines humility and common sense with a love of jests, in particular puns and practical jokes. Hypocrisy he particularly detests, which is ironic, since he finds himself in a dispute with his monarch (about papal supremacy) that forces him to be hypocritical: either he must refuse to obey the king (which he had told the rioters was a sin of rebellion against God) or he must betray his lifelong religious conviction that the pope, not the king, is the highest spiritual leader. The reputation of More as a wise counsellor was established before composition of

Portrait of Sir Thomas More from 1527. *(Painting by Hans Holbein the Younger)*

the play began. It is present in the sources and is taken for granted in censor Tilney's instruction that the dramatists begin with "his good service done being Sheriff of London." At one level, the play presents More as a transparently virtuous man. When the player of the part of Good Counsel in the inset play in Scene 9 is unavailable, More steps in and extemporizes his part: This establishes that More personally embodies the principles of good counsel. The jesting that More displays throughout the play becomes somewhat tense in the last few scenes, and in performance it can be painfully awkward. On two occasions, in Scenes 13 and 16, More seems to tell his family that he will submit to the king's demands, and they express relief and excitement that he will be released, only for him to explain that they have misunderstood him and that he will stand firm and accept his execution. These moments of misunderstanding are related to More's fondness for verbal ambiguities: "I'll now satisfy the King's good pleasure" (13.171) means not that he will subscribe but that he will agree to go to the Tower, and "I have deceived myself, I must acknowledge" (16.91) turns out to be only a generalized admission of human weakness, not a specific admission of an error to be rectified. These moments of misunderstanding may be played comically, but the humor is grim in the cruelty it inflicts upon More's loved ones.

John Lincoln

A citizen of London (by occupation a broker, meaning a trader in commodities) who instigates the anti-foreigner riot of May 1517 by having a bill of complaint against them read aloud in the London streets. He leads the riot and is later executed for it, despite an assurance from More that the king will be merciful. Lincoln finds himself losing control of the rioters and becoming frustrated with them. He is paired with Doll Williamson in their last appearance (addressing the London crowds just before he is executed) and there is textual warrant for performers to suggest that Doll is more attracted to brave Lincoln than to her timid husband.

Doll Williamson

The strong-willed and feisty wife of a carpenter of London. The play's opening stage direction calls her "a lusty woman," which refers not to her sexual appetite but to her force of personality. Doll is the visible victim of the foreigners' crimes as she is dragged across the stage by Francis de Barde who means to rape her. She narrowly escapes execution for her part in the riot against the foreigners. Doll explicitly denies that she is physically attractive—"I have no beauty to like [please] a husband" (1.5–6)—but in performance she may be impressively assertive, putting to shame the husbands who, as she repeatedly points out, allow themselves to be abused and humiliated more thoroughly and publicly than any woman of London would tolerate. That is to say, from Doll's point of view, the men of London are being emasculated by the foreigners. When she appears with the rioters, she is in a shirt of chain mail and pieces of armor while holding a sword and shield, thus visibly usurping male power (rather like Joan of Arc of *Henry VI, Part 1,* Shakespeare's hit play of 1592). She also usurps official nomenclature in dubbing the ringleader "Captain Lincoln," as if they were an alternative army; More picks up this nomenclature and uses it ironically to ask how hierarchy can coexist with the anarchy of a riot. In the scene of the execution of the ringleaders, Doll might be played as more attracted to Lincoln than to her own husband (and he to her), although she kisses her husband and says that so long as any Englishman is available, she will never kiss a foreigner.

Williamson

Doll's husband, a carpenter of London who stands to lose not only his wife to the foreigners but also a pair of doves that are stolen from him. Williamson is not as belligerent as his wife but joins the rioting and is sentenced to death for it. He is noticeably less active than his wife in the rebellion. Like all the rioters, Williamson's role in the play ends with the execution in Scene 7.

Sherwin

A goldsmith of London. Before the start of the play, his wife was taken from him by the foreigner de Barde, who made Sherwin pay for her maintenance while keeping her; this scandal is widely known among Londoners of all classes. In the opening scene, Doll Williamson says that Sherwin's wife was "enticed" (1.10) from him, and Palmer uses the same word when recounting the story (3.19), which makes Sherwin seem rather more inadequate than Williamson, whose wife, Doll, forcefully resists de Barde.

George Betts

A broker (merchant) of London and, after Lincoln, the leading rioter, having been the first to advocate standing up to the foreigners. His catchphrase is a leader's "let us": "let's beat them down . . . Let us step in . . . let us along then" (1.30–31, 39, 148), "Let some of us enter the strangers' houses . . . Let's stand upon our swords" (4.47, 64), and "Let's mark him" (6.100).

Ralph Betts

George's brother (also a broker of London), a willing rioter, although seemingly more because he appreciates the opportunity for chaos and the sexual license it may bring than out of a strong sense of grievance.

Francis de Barde

One of the two foreigners seen in the play and much the worse behaved: The play begins with him dragging Doll Williamson across the stage in an attempt to abduct and rape her.

Cavaler

An associate of de Barde who steals Williamson's doves.

Lord Mayor of London

As the head of the London Corporation, the holder of the highest public office in the City. The rioters keep him confined in his house to prevent him marshalling his forces against them. Later, he and his wife are lavishly entertained by More.

Earl of Surrey

A poet and a counsellor, Surrey signs the Act of Supremacy "instantly" (10.98) upon seeing what happens to Rochester and More for refusing.

Earl of Shrewsbury

Seen almost always in the company of Surrey, and like him, Shrewsbury is almost indecently quick to sign the Act of Supremacy. Together with Surrey, Shrewsbury executes the warrant to arrest More and take him to the Tower.

John Fisher, Bishop of Rochester

The most implacable opponent of the king's Act of Supremacy, Rochester immediately refuses to sign the papers and patiently accepts his arrest, imprisonment, and execution with Christian fortitude. He undergoes the same fate as More but two days earlier. Scene 12, his entry to prison, shows him doing all the things that More will later do at greater length: comforting his friends, waxing philosophical about its being better to be locked up with one's private thoughts than out in the tempting world and saying how much he still loves his king.

Sir Thomas Palmer

A nobleman who was given the job of quelling the unrest in the city after the Sherwin scandal and who helps dampen of the embers of the riot after More has talked down the ringleaders. He later brings the king's paper containing the Act of Supremacy to the counsel.

Sir Roger Cholmley

Seen only in the company of Palmer, Cholmley blames the senior noblemen for allowing the foreigners' abuses and not informing the king.

Sir John Munday

A nobleman hurt while trying to disperse a gang of rioting apprentices.

Randall

More's servant who switches places with his master to play a trick on Erasmus.

William Roper

More's son-in-law, and somewhat like him in learning and fortitude.

Lady More

More's wife, who repeatedly tries to convince him to give up his principles and save himself by signing the Act of Supremacy.

More's Daughters

One of whom, Margaret, is married to William Roper.

Desiderius Erasmus of Rotterdam

A Catholic theologian and the leading humanist of Europe.

Justice Suresby

A hypocritical judge who blames Smart, the victim of pickpocketing, for his misfortune. More plays a practical joke on him to show that Suresby is as guilty as Smart of tempting pickpockets.

Lifter

A pickpocket who helps More play a joke on Suresby.

Smart

One of Lifter's victims.

Nicholas Downes

A sergeant-at-arms whom More rescues in the riot of May 1517 and who later arrests More for refusing to sign the Act of Supremacy.

Jack Falconer

A long-haired ruffian who reluctantly accepts a haircut instead of a jail sentence.

The Players, including Luggins

This is a small touring theatrical troupe (just four actors) of the kind common in the first half of the 16th century. This company is described as the Cardinal's Men, which might make early audiences think of the most famous cardinal of Henry VIII's reign, Cardinal Thomas Wolsey, who was More's predecessor as Lord Chancellor of England. In the middle of the 16th century, the state became increasingly involved in the regulation of acting, requiring that each troupe had an aristocratic patron. This forced out the smaller, less formally organized touring troupes and favored the formation of larger companies of between six and 12 permanent members plus additional hired men. These larger companies settled in the new purpose-built theaters that arose in London from 1567.

DIFFICULTIES OF THE PLAY

The chief difficulties of the play arise in relation to the contextual knowledge needed to make sense of the action. The play assumes that the reader or playgoer already knows the story of Thomas More's life and in particular the reason for his downfall and (since it was written for a London audience) understands the sometimes uneasy relationship between the monarchial power centered on Westminster and the City authority centered on the Guildhall. The name of the king is never spoken in the play—confusingly he is also a few times referred to as a prince—and just what is in the papers that he wants his privy counsellors to subscribe to is never mentioned. These difficulties can be overcome by reading the editor's introduction in a good critical edition. The language of the play is, by the standards of early-modern drama, relatively straightforward, and there is little complex poetry.

The motivations of the characters are straightforward, with perhaps the exception of the foreigners whose reason for being in London is never given and whose deeds are stereotypically evil. It is clear that the reader/playgoer is supposed to side with the abused Londoners, at least initially, but once in full flow, the rioting can appear to become simply driven by ugly xenophobia. This might be understood as a development necessary in order that More's suppression of the riot seems just, but there are considerable problems with the arguments about obedience that More offers. More's mix of moral flexibility in certain areas—such as his indulgence of a serial pickpocket in order to make fun of Justice Suresby—sits awkwardly with his rigid inflexibility in others, and it is difficult to know what we are supposed to make of this inconsistency. It may only be a consequence of the play's several dramatists failing to agree on just how to portray More (that is, it may be an accident), or else it may be interpreted as a fatal flaw in More's character.

KEY PASSAGES
Act I, Scene 2 (Scene 2)

MORE. Sirrah, you know that you are known
  to me,
And I have often saved ye from this place
Since first I came in office. Thou seest beside
That Justice Suresby is thy heavy friend,
For all the blame that he pretends to Smart
For tempting thee with such a sum of money.
I tell thee what: devise me but a means
To pick or cut his purse, and on my credit,
And as I am a Christian and a man,
I will procure thy pardon for that jest.

LIFTER. Good Master Sheriff seek not my
  overthrow.
You know, sir, I have many heavy friends,
And more indictments like to come upon me.
You are too deep for me to deal withal.
You are known to be one of the wisest men
That is in England. I pray ye, Master Sheriff,
Go not about to undermine my life.

MORE. Lifter, I am true subject to my king.
Thou much mistak'st me, and for thou shalt
  not think
I mean by this to hurt thy life at all,
I will maintain the act when thou hast done it.
Thou knowst there are such matters in my
  hands
As, if I pleased to give them to the jury,
I should not need this way to circumvent thee.
All that I aim at is a merry jest.
Perform it, Lifter, and expect my best.

(Scene numbers identified within parentheses are per Jowett.) This is the scene that the censor Edmund Tilney (whose instructions appear at the very beginning of the manuscript) wanted the play to begin with, rather than beginning with the crimes of the foreigners and the emerging resistance of the Londoners. Aside from other considerations, this preference suggests Tilney's imperfect grasp of how biographical dramas generally work: It is usual not to begin by showing the eponymous hero(es)—think of *Hamlet* or *Antony and Cleopatra*—but to come to them after developing the dramatic situation and the world in which they live. Here we see More for the first time, and he is setting up a practical joke. The pickpocket Lifter has been convicted and is about to be sentenced (death would be the usual punishment in such a case) when More intervenes and asks to be left alone with the prisoner. One of the justices, the appropriately named Suresby, had spoken in mitigation of the offense, describing the 10 pounds that the victim (Smart) was carrying in his purse as typical of the "fond baits that foolish people lay / To tempt the needy" (2.32). That is to say, the victim is partly guilty of the crime because he was at least negligent in carrying such a lot of money around and perhaps even tempted the pickpocket by bragging of his large purse, for which prize even an innocent man may be "provoked to that he never meant" (2.30). In modern legal language, this is known as entrapment and can form a defense.

More is not convinced by Suresby's line of reasoning and sets out to expose its falsity by having Lifter steal Suresby's purse in the courtroom. Here, for the first time, we see what will become a recurrent theme of the play, which is More's advocacy of the Christian golden rule of "whatsoever ye would that men should do to you, do ye even so to them" (Matthew 7:12). By reflecting Suresby's argument back upon Suresby, More hopes to expose his hypocrisy, for at the very least, Suresby will presumably not consider himself complicit in the theft of his own purse. As it turns out, the purse Lifter takes from Suresby contains seven pounds, so Suresby is also a hypocrite for having condemned Smart for carrying around a lot of money. This scene is easily overlooked as a simple piece of comedy that merely shows More's love of practical jokes, but it has a serious side too in More's exposure of Suresby's hypocrisy. Notice, too, Lifter's fear of what More intends, thinking perhaps that his purpose is to make matters worse for the criminal: "seek not my overthrow . . . Go not about to undermine my life" (2.61–67). To reassure Lifter, More has to promise that he will "maintain the act when thou hast done it" (2.71), which rather exposes More himself to a charge of hypocrisy: If stealing is an absolute wrong, then More is no better than Lifter. That More does not see this suggests that he is applying a relativistic notion of right and wrong in which the purpose of an act, not the act itself, determines how it is to be judged. If we really are to think that this is More's approach, it will become retrospectively ironic later in the play when we encounter a More who finds himself unable to follow others' pragmatic and context-sensitive approach to a request from the king.

Act II, Scene 4 (Scene 6)

MORE. Grant them removed, and grant that this your noise
Hath chid down all the majesty of England.
Imagine that you see the wretched strangers,
Their babies at their backs, with their poor luggage,
Plodding to th'ports and coasts for transportation,
And that you sit as kings in your desires,
Authority quite silenced by your brawl,
And you in ruff of your opinions clothed:
What had you got? I'll tell you: you had taught
How insolence and strong hand should prevail,
How order should be quelled. And by this pattern
Not one of you should live an agèd man;
For other ruffians, as their fancies wrought
With selfsame hand, self reasons, and self right,
Would shark on you, and men, like ravenous fishes,
Would feed on one another.

DOLL. Before God, that's as true as the gospel.

LINCOLN. Nay, this'a sound fellow, I tell you. Let's mark him.

MORE. Let me set up before your thoughts, good friends,
One supposition, which if you will mark
You shall perceive how horrible a shape
Your innovation bears. First, 'tis a sin
Which oft th'apostle did forewarn us of,
Urging obedience to authority;
And 'twere no error if I told you all
You were in arms 'gainst God.

This speech is the climax of Shakespeare's contribution to the play. Confronting an angry mob of rioting Londoners, More speaks calmly to them, first about their intended victims and then about the nature of their rebellion. Although the audience has seen only rapacious male foreigners (de Barde wanting to force himself upon Doll Williamson, Cavaler stealing Williamson's doves), More powerfully conjures up images of refugee families with children, forced from their homes to be repatriated. His next maneuver is even more subtle, as More applies the Christian golden rule ("Do unto others . . .") to the case of the rebels. Having established the wretchedness of the foreigners, More elevates the rebels, imagining them "kings" in their "desires," as "ruffians" absurdly decked out in the fancy starched-linen collars called ruffs. This topsy-turvydom achieved, the elevated rebels—having overturned the natural order that keeps them in obedience to their betters—would then be subject to the same overthrow by other rebels. If violence be allowed to disrupt hierarchy, then there can be no end of turmoil, for each new victor in the struggle would be overturned by the next in an endless succession of coups. Shakespeare dramatizes precisely such a sequence of overturnings in both his tetralogies of history plays: Once a group of rebels establishes that a monarch can be unseated, its own preferred holder of the throne finds himself attacked by yet another group seeking to repeat the process to establish their candidate. A ruff is also a small freshwater fish, and presumably having used the word to mean *collar,* Shakespeare was inspired to his image of "ravenous fishes" that would "feed on one another" (6.96–97).

Although More had not made explicit the religious application of the principle of reciprocity, the rebels pick up the latent suggestion: "that's as true as the gospel" (6.98). At this point, More brings in the connection between social upheaval and religious disobedience, arguing that since God put the king in a position of authority to act as his deputy on Earth, rebelling against the king entails rebelling against God. The rioters, of course, had not directed their violence toward the king but rather the foreigners, but it amounts to the same thing because they seek to take justice into their own hands rather than submit their grievances to the proper authorities the king has put in place. We learned earlier, in Scene 3, that the king has no knowledge of the Londoners' grievances or even of the abuses enacted by the foreigners, and the foreigners' ambassador has interceded to prevent their being held to account; as Cholmley says to the senior counsellors of the king, "Men of your place and greatness are to blame" (3.65) in this. Because the monarch and his appointed officers have the monopoly on redressing wrongdoing in society, the rebels are effectively not only in arms against the foreigners but also against their native social superiors and masters. More tells them that their political rebellion is tantamount to religious rebellion, and this is the argument that wins them over to peaceful submission.

Once again, this argument will in retrospect be ironized by More's response to the dilemma that his king asks him to subscribe to a religious principle, the Act of [Monarchial] Supremacy, that More is unable to accept. At this stage in the play, More rhetorically and oratorically wields to great effect the idea that monarchial and religious power form an alliance in that the king is God's deputy. Ironically, Henry's Act of Supremacy could plausibly be defended as a strengthening of this alliance since the king would then in one person represent the highest temporal and spiritual authority, while under the present arrangements, the ones More dies defending, the monarch is the highest temporal authority, but the pope in Rome is the highest spiritual authority. This division of authority adds a complexity that More does not present to the rioting Londoners, a rhetorical aporia that playgoers are doubtless meant to consider. Of course, More does not violently rise against his king, as the rioters do, but his is a kind of rebellion nonetheless; the nearest model parallel would be the nonviolent civil disobedience movement (as advocated by Mahondas Ghandi in India and Martin Luther King, Jr., in the United States) that encourages passive resistance to wrongdoing. Jesus Christ's teachings on passive resistance are one of the sources of this tradition.

Act III, Scene 1 (Scene 7)

LINCOLN. [*to Executioner*] Fellow, dispatch.
He goes up.
I was the foremost man in this rebellion,
And I the foremost that must die for it.

DOLL. Bravely, John Lincoln, let thy death
   express
That, as thou lived'st a man, thou died'st no less.

LINCOLN. Doll Williamson, thine eyes shall
   witness it.
Then to all you that come to view mine end
I must confess I had no ill intent
But against such as wronged us overmuch.
And now I can perceive it was not fit
That private men should carve out their redress
Which way they list. No, learn it now by me:
Obedience is the best in each degree.
And, asking mercy meekly of my king,
I patiently submit me to the law.
But God forgive them that were cause of it;
And, as a Christian, truly from my heart,
I likewise crave they would forgive me too,
. . .
That others by example of the same
Henceforth be warnèd to attempt the like
'Gainst any alien that repaireth hither,

Fare ye well all. The next time that we meet
I trust in heaven we shall each other greet.

He leaps off.

The construction of an onstage gibbet (gallows) for the execution of the ringleaders of the rioting necessarily generates tense anticipation in a playgoing audience that has seen More promise them the benefit of the king's mercy. Indeed, clemency had been a condition insisted upon by Lincoln when he led the rioters to surrender: "We'll be ruled by you, Master More, if you'll stand our friend to procure our pardon" (6.158–59). There is some uncertainty just why the execution proceeds, but the key culpability seems to lie with the Master Sheriff who tells his men "be speedy . . . make haste . . . and see no time be slacked" (7.10–14). Behind all this is the division of authority between the London Corporation (the City) and the monarch in Westminster. As an ordinary matter of civil unrest inside the city walls, the riot comes under the jurisdiction of the London authorities, but the Crown may be appealed to as the ultimate arbiter. More makes just such an appeal to Henry VIII while the City continues with the legal process. This sets up a tense race of the same kind as can be found in cinematic dramatizations of executions in 20th-century America: will word of the governor's stay of execution (in place of the king's pardon) arrive in time to save the condemned man? The division of authority between the monarch and the City also resonates with the division of authority between the king as temporal leader and the pope as spiritual leader. Or, to see it as the dramatists and their intended first audiences would have, the dramatization of the split authority in London—which is the dramatic motor of this scene—offered a way to glance at the fundamental split in authority that is central to the story of More's downfall.

John Lincoln's behavior conforms to the expected convention of a condemned man in making a speech admitting his crime. Typical examples in Shakespeare are Buckingham's "This, this All-Souls' day to my fearful soul / Is the determined

respite of my wrongs" (*Richard III* 5.1.18–19) and the reported end of the traitorous Thane of Cawdor (Macbeth's predecessor):

> MALCOLM. . . . very frankly he confessed his treasons,
> Implored your highness' pardon, and set forth
> A deep repentance. Nothing in his life
> Became him like the leaving it.
> (*Macbeth* 1.4.5–8)

Such behavior gave the condemned man a chance to redeem himself somewhat and to impress the spectators (on stage and in the theater audience) with his fortitude. To reject this opportunity was a sign of inveterate malice, as exampled by the close followers and flatterers of Richard II:

> BUSHY. More welcome is the stroke of death to me
> Than Bolingbroke to England.
>
> GREEN. My comfort is that heaven will take our souls,
> And plague injustice with the pains of hell.
> (*Richard II* 3.1.31–34)

A modern audience is likely to make its own judgments about the rights and wrongs of Bolingbroke's rebellion against Richard II, but we should take care to note that for the first audiences familiar with this convention Bushy's and Green's refusal to make a good end clearly tips the scales against Richard's party.

A limited amount of exculpation was permissible in such speeches, and John Lincoln takes this as far as possible without actually breaking with the conventional "good death." He refers to the foreigners who "wronged us overmuch" (7.54) but immediately acknowledges that the state has the monopoly on righting such wrongs: "it was not fit / That private men should carve out their redress / Which way they list" (7.55–57). To seek private redress is to undermine "Obedience," which he points out is a principle governing not only the ordinary people but "each degree" (7.58), that is, every social class. In performance, an actor might choose to make much of this "each degree" and although the Master Sheriff is the highest ranking official present, the lesson is applicable to the recently knighted former sheriff, More, who, this scene later reveals, has been elevated to lord chancellor for his pleading on behalf of the rioters. The principle of the golden rule recurs again in the play when Lincoln asks for reciprocal forgiveness: "God forgive them [the foreigners] that were cause of it; / . . . as . . . / I likewise crave they would forgive me too" (7.61–63).

After offering his death as an example to others—surely the most submissive of conservative acts—Lincoln throws himself off the ladder and is seen to hang. Because the character remains talking until the last moment, there is no opportunity to switch places with a dummy for the purpose of showing the dead body hanging from the gibbet, so we have to assume that somehow the actor himself was suspended for a realistic enactment of hanging. Other plays of the period staged hangings in full view of the audience, most notably Thomas Kyd's *The Spanish Tragedy,* which has two of them, and the trick seems to involve the actor wearing a concealed harness under his clothes to which the real suspension line was attached, while a rope, having just enough tension to stay taut without being uncomfortable, ran from the halter around the actor's neck to the gibbet (Astington 1983). Carried off professionally, this effect was doubtless spectacular and moving, and all the more so in the present scene because the audience would wonder if More had simply lied about attempting to secure the king's mercy for the ringleaders, or had tried and failed. In her execution speech that follows the lines quoted, Doll Williamson is explicitly disappointed in More: "Yet would I praise his honesty much more / If he had kept his word and saved our lives" (7.103–104). Pardon comes just in time to save Doll but too late for Lincoln, and to that extent, More has indeed broken his word given to Lincoln and somewhat loses the audience's sympathy.

The obvious scene to compare with this is the final one, Scene 17, which depicts More's own execution but stops short of this scene's realistic enactment. His love of wordplay stays with More until the end—"I shall forget my head," "good for the headache," "cutt'st not off my beard" (17.25, 87, 104–105)—but More also allows himself a little of the recriminatory and self-exculpatory tone of Lincoln. Indeed, Shrewsbury has to remind More of the conventional form of this ritual: "My lord, 'twere good you'd publish to the world / Your great offence unto his majesty" (17.70–71). In response, More will not name his offense but acknowledges favors done to him and offers his king in return "a reverent head . . . [and] because I think my body will then do me small pleasure, let him but bury it and take it" (17.78–82). Depending on the tone chosen by the actor, this may be a mild reproof or an extremely vehement one.

Act III, Scene 2 (Scene 8)

MORE. How long have you worn this hair?

FALCONER. I have worn this hair ever since
  I was born.

MORE. You know that's not my question: but
  how long
Hath this shag fleece hung dangling on thy
  head?

FALCONER. How long, my lord? Why,
  sometimes thus long,
Sometimes lower, as the Fates and humours
  please.
. . . .
My lord, Jack Falconer tells no Aesop's fables.
Troth, I was not at barber's this three years. I
  have not been cut, nor will not be cut, upon
  a foolish vow which, as the Destinies shall
  direct, I am sworn to keep.

MORE. When comes that vow out?

FALCONER. Why, when the humours are
  purged; not these three years.

MORE. Vows are recorded in the court of
  heaven,
For they are holy acts. Young man, I charge thee
And do advise thee start not from that vow.
And for I will be sure thou shalt not shear,
Besides because it is an odious sight
To see a man thus hairy, thou shalt lie
In Newgate till thy vow and thy three years
Be full expired.—Away with him.

FALCONER. My lord—

MORE. Cut off this fleece and lie there but a
  month.

FALCONER. I'll not lose a hair to be Lord
  Chancellor of Europe!

MORE. To Newgate then. Sirrah, great sins
  are bred
In all that body where there's a foul head.
Away with him.

Exeunt all but Randall

At first sight the interlude of Falconer's hair
seems an entirely pointless piece of comic business.
It comes at a point when the audience has been led
to expect, as More does, the arrival of Erasmus.
This gives the episode an urgent pointlessness to
complement its visual appeal. It may not be immediately apparent when reading the play that, in performance, a long head of hair offers a talented actor
considerable opportunities of amusing business, for
example by turning the head quickly so as almost
to leave the hair behind; actors playing Andrew
Aguecheek in *Twelfth Night* not infrequently make
such play with their long hair. Falconer's responses
to More's questioning have a mirroring quality to
them: Hitherto, we have seen only More play on
words in this fashion, and it comes as something
of a surprise to find another punster getting the
better of him. That Falconer is rather like More
in his person and his situation is signaled earlier
in the scene by his description of his occupation:

"I serve, next under God and my prince, Master
Morris" (8.81–83). Putting his masters in rank
order like this is just how More thinks about his
service, and it is a belief (that first comes God and
then the king) that More will die for. Falconer is
growing his hair because he took a vow not to visit
the barber for a haircut for three years, and More's
response is perhaps misleading: "Vows are recorded
in the court of heaven, / For they are holy acts"
(8.114–115). More presumably believes that such
a vow is not a holy act and need not be kept, but
he acts as though he takes the vow seriously and
would not have Falconer break it.

In offering Falconer the choice between a long
prison sentence until his vow be expired, or a short
one if he will break it, More treats the ruffian much
as the king will later treat More. The pressure
More comes under to sign the articles of the Act of
Supremacy has no effect because he is adamant to
the point of death, whereas Falconer quickly capitulates and soon reappears with his hair cut. (Doubtless in performance the actor merely removes a long
wig to effect the change.) At this stage in the drama,
it is merely comic that a spell of harsh punishment
can make a man forgo an avowed principle, but that
will become a central theme in the play's last few
scenes as More's friends and family plead with him
to sign the king's papers and save himself. On one
level, the audience is encouraged to admire More
for his defiance of his king on a point of principle,
but that admiration is leavened by the recollection
that in an analogous situation conducted in a comic
key, More behaved just like the king in attempting
to force a man to abandon his principles. That it is
done in a comic key does not diminish the hypocrisy, for More's own habitual jesting puts everything, including his own execution, into a comic
key; there is not so great a difference between him
and "ruffians," a term More earlier used for those
who defy their monarch (6.94).

CRITICAL INTRODUCTION
TO THE PLAY

The play is held together by the character of More,
whose rise and fall it depicts. Perhaps surprisingly,

the main activity for which More was known, his writing (in particular his book *Utopia*), is entirely omitted from the story in order to focus on various facets of his character by showing a sequence of events that illustrate them. This can tend to make the events portrayed seem rather episodic, rather like an unrelated series of disparate scenes. However, there are subtle connections between all the scenes, and the play has two central artistic aims: to show the rewarding of a popular man known for his integrity (a living embodiment of the marriage of wit and wisdom that forms the play-within-the-play) and to reveal the contradic-

tions that lie underneath that supposed integrity. The core problem that the play dramatizes is the division of authority, which is shown to be the condition of a series of interrelated institutions, each of which refracts the division in its own way. The first is the division between the authority of the City of London and the authority of the court at Westminster, which was a fact of life for Londoners in More's time (the early 16th century) and those alive when the play was written in the 1590s. The second division is between loyalty to the monarch as temporal ruler and loyalty to the pope as spiritual ruler, which division causes More's (and

Page from *The life and death of Sir Thomas Moore, Lord High Chancellour of England,* written by Cresacre More in 1630. This illustration shows members of the More family. *(Illustration by Cresacre More)*

Rochester's) downfall. These two main divisions are mirrored in a sequence of minor divisions that the play dramatizes.

In the opening scene, two groups of characters are established: the recently arrived foreigners and their victims, the native Londoners. The latter are rendered coherent as a group by their various citizen trades, for the occupations of all of them are named. Doll says that she is a carpenter's wife and introduces her husband, Sherwin says he is the goldsmith that they have heard about (because de Barde took his wife), and Lincoln says that he is a broker and that the Bettses are his "brethren" (also brokers). The honest, working Londoners are implicitly categorized in opposition to the strangers of no stated occupation, although later it will be complained that the foreigners are taking Londoners' work or otherwise harming their trade. The ethnic identity of the foreigners is not entirely clear. In Scene 4, Lincoln lists some of the aliens' names, and they sound Dutch; one of them is identified as a Picard and their Dutch/French origin is confirmed by Ralph Betts. This is somewhat at odds with his brother George Betts calling de Barde a "Lombard" in the opening scene (1.55). The power of the Londoners is their collective identification, one with another, while the power of the foreigners comes from their ambassador, who has the ear of the king. Implicitly, then, this opening scene establishes that the exercise of authority, and in particular the court's remoteness from events "on the ground" in London, creates tensions.

To understand the significance of the tension between the City and the court requires some knowledge of the geopolitics and economics of early-modern London. The river formed a natural southern boundary to the authority of the City, with the land on the south bank coming under the jurisdiction of the magistrates of Surrey and, in parts, the bishop of Winchester, although Southwark (where the open-air playhouses were located) was annexed as a suburb of the City in 1550 (Menzer 2006, 169–172). Although the monarch was the ultimate ruler and authority in early-modern England, London had considerable autonomy.

The significance of the city wall was that, within its bounds, the trades of London were regulated by the various guilds (also called livery companies) administered from the Guildhall. For each occupation, such as goldsmith (Sherwin's trade) or carpenter (Williamson's trade), there was a guild that regulated the business in that field. Members of the guild were said to be "free" of the company, meaning that they had met its conditions of membership, which could happen by patrimony (that is, by inheritance from a parent), or by redemption (paying a membership fee), or—and this was by far the most common route—by apprenticeship.

A freeman of a guild was allowed to engage a child worker as an apprentice for a fixed term of usually seven years, beginning somewhere between the age of 14 and 17 and ending with freedom of the company between the age of 21 and 24. An apprentice was not paid wages but was provided with food and lodging and taught the craft of his master. (In some trades, the apprenticeship would end with the production of a piece of work proving that all the skills of the trade had been acquired, known as a master-piece, whence our modern word for a great work of art.) Most apprentices were teenage boys or young men living away from the parental home and hence notoriously prone to antisocial behavior. In *Sir Thomas More,* Sir John Munday recounts being attacked by a "sort" (that is, a group) of apprentices wielding "cudgels" (5.3), meaning clubs. Apprentices were known to be keen to start or join in any kind of civil disturbance, and in the play, their presence helps turn the Londoners' uprising into a potentially uncontrollable riot. Thus, in preparation for the execution of the ringleaders, the master sheriff gives the order "Let proclamation once again be made / That every householder, on pain of death, / Keep in his prentices" (7.21–23).

The guild for each trade not only regulated the contracts of apprenticeship but also did the following: set the rates of pay for journeymen, those who had finished an apprenticeship but did not go on to be masters in their own right; controlled rates of production, for example by limiting the length of a book run to 1,500 copies so that typesetters would have enough work to do; settled trade disputes between members; and paid benefits to support the families of members who died. Trades that operated within the guild system were kept reasonably profitable, with members allowed neither to starve nor to become excessively wealthy. However, it was possible to work outside the guild system, especially in the suburbs such as Southwark. It was a recurrent complaint among guild members of late-16th-century London that skilled foreigners from Europe were moving into these areas and competing unfairly with members of the respective London company. There is a glance at such complaints in the rioters' references to the price of food and "the undoing of poor prentices" (6.11), although as the insurrection grows—and especially after the play was revised by the inclusion of the Additions (a process detailed in any good critical edition of the play)—this economic issue becomes hopelessly confused with sheer xenophobic fear of foreign foods.

As well as the guild system that had been developed over centuries, the late 16th century saw the growth of an entirely new way of organizing a business by forming what was called a joint-stock company. In such an arrangement, a group of sharers would pool their wealth to form a company to pursue a particular new venture (say, trading with an overseas colony or running a theater troupe), the money being spent on whatever capital was needed to carry out the endeavor (the purchase and rigging of a ship or the acquisition of costumes and manuscript playbooks). After paying whatever expenses were incurred (the wages of a crew or the rent on a theater), the profits made from the venture would be split equally among the sharers. In this system of business, there was no guild to limit the wealth that could be generated, but equally, there was no protection in the event of failure. Some members of successful joint-stock companies (such as Shakespeare, a sharer in the Chamberlain's Men, later the King's Men) became fabulously wealthy, while others who were less fortunate and/or skillful lost everything.

Whereas the guilds were controlled by the authorities of the City, joint-stock companies needed a license (typically one granting a monopoly) from the Crown or its officials. Because there was no guild for actors—the entire industry only really began when the Crown became involved in regulating playing in the mid-16th century (Egan 2003)—the theater companies were all necessarily joint-stock companies, each operating under a license from the senior aristocrat that gave it its name. One way to contrast the guilds and the joint-stock companies is to think of the former as an expression of how business was conducted at the end of the feudal epoch, and the latter as marking the beginning of the new capitalist organization of production in society. The tension between these two modes of production (as Marxists call them) is apparent across the history and art of late-16th- and early-17th-century England but does not feature directly in the play *Sir Thomas More*. It does, however, figure indirectly.

At the beginning of Scene 5, Shrewsbury, Surrey, Palmer, and Cholmley enter and report that the king has sent them to help the Lord Mayor, for the City is an authority over itself. At the end of Scene 6, the Lord Mayor comments that the king has honored the City by making one of its officials, a sheriff, into a knight and a privy counsellor. More assures "My lord and brethren" (that is, fellow servants of the City) that "this rising of my private blood"—meaning that he has earned it not as a sheriff but as a private man—will not make him forget and neglect the City's welfare (6.237, 242). In Scene 7, the execution of the riot's ringleaders, the division between the authority of the Crown and the authority of the City becomes explicit. The sheriff has a death warrant from the privy council and worries that if he does not see it rapidly carried out, "The city will be fined for this neglect" (7.29). The terrible mistake regarding the pardon for the ringleaders arises because there are two centers of power (court and City), or three if we factor in the privy council's capacity for independent action. The City (center I), fearful of the ill-favor of the privy council (center II), executes John Lincoln while More is pleading for clemency from the king (center III).

More himself comes from the City, not the court, and he rises through its hierarchy to become one of its two sheriffs before the play starts. In reward for quelling the riot, More is made a knight and a privy counselor, catapulting him out of the City hierarchy and into the heart of the court. This makes for much awkwardness of protocol when More meets his former "brethren," the lord mayor and aldermen of the City, as witnessed in the polite but pained disagreements about who should sit where when More is entertaining them at his house in Scene 9. At this point a contradiction emerges. At the start of the scene, More is told by a messenger that the lord mayor and aldermen are about to pay him an unexpected visit, but when More greets them—with an assurance of fraternal amity, "once I was your brother, / And so am still in heart" (9.94–95)—he speaks as if he invited them, saying he is grateful "That on so short a summons you would come / To visit" (9.110–111). This might only be a sign that the collaborating dramatists failed to make all the details of their collective labor cohere. Alternatively, if it is a deliberate contradiction, it might suggest that More feels the need to gloss over the inconsiderate and monarchlike behavior of turning up without an invitation and expecting extravagant hospitality. Elizabeth I, on the throne when the play was written, was said to do this to her senior courtiers.

There seems to be some connection between the rise of Protestantism and the rise of capitalism. In his early-20th-century book *The Protestant Ethic and the Spirit of Capitalism*, Max Weber argued that the widespread success of Protestantism in the 16th century—of which Henry VIII's conversion was a central part—made Christians behave in ways that promoted the growth of early capitalism. Many Catholic theologians called upon believers to display *contemptus mundi* (contempt for the world), meaning that since this earthly existence is only a short and transitory state before each soul comes to face God in heaven, it was pointless to concern oneself with one's position in the world. This idea underlies the disdain for the world shown by Rochester and More in the play: they simply do not love life enough to fear losing it. According to Weber, the Protestant doctrine of predestination, on the other hand, encouraged Christians to interpret successful pursuance of their trades as signs that they were "saved" (rather than "damned"), and since it also discouraged charity and forbade large donations to the church, Protestantism tended to promote the accumulation of hard-earned wealth that was needed for capitalism to get started.

These ideas form part of the intellectual background to *Sir Thomas More*, and we can trace their influence in the ways that the play stages the tensions between the City and the Crown. On the largest scale, the division of authority between the two is literalized in the staging at the beginning of the final scene, More's execution. The scene's opening stage direction is *"Enter the Sheriffs of London and their Officers at one door, the Warders with their halberds at another."* The Warders are the guards of the Tower of London (and halberds their weapons), and the Tower was one of the palaces owned by the monarch. It is situated at the southeastern corner of the fortified wall that marked the boundary of the City, where it meets the Thames, and as such is a liminal space where the authority of City and Crown interact. The Crown had independent access to the Tower because it could be reached by river, and More is said to be arriving that way at the start of Scene 14. The Tower was so strongly associated with its river access that in More's wife's nightmare, the couple are sucked into a whirlpool on the Thames right in front of the Tower (11.18–26). Although More is guilty of an offense against the Crown, in the final scene, it is the City that must execute him, and hence its opening stage direction prepares for his being handed back to the sheriffs after imprisonment by the Crown in the Tower. The stage of an open-air amphitheater playhouse of Shakespeare's time thrust out into the yard where the audience stood and was backed by a wall pierced with two stage doors, with possibly a larger central opening and/or discovery space between them. By having the sheriffs enter at one of these doors and the Tower's guards enter at the other to start the final scene, the play emblematizes this polarity of power. The theater stage stands as the space where the authority of the monarch meets that of the City.

Earlier in the play, as his fame and authority rose, More found himself the cause of divided authority. This is one of the points of the peculiar scene with Falconer, the man who has vowed not to cut his hair. Falconer has been arrested for fighting in the streets (perhaps depicted in a scene now lost from the manuscript) and insists on his case being heard by More: "I'll appear before no king christened but my good Lord Chancellor," and "I thought it stood not with my reputation and degree to come to my questions and answers before a city justice" (8.50–51, 88–90). Paradoxically, it seems that More's pure goodness can be corrosive of authority, undermining the power of the city's justices. Divided authority likewise underlies the seemingly pointless debate in the privy council about the loyalty of the emperor of Germany. More overcomes Surrey's fear that after a joint German-English military victory over the "perfidious French" (10.23) the German emperor would turn on the English and demand more than his share of the spoils. Imagining a world in which men fight for the honor of it rather than the rewards, More pictures one with "no court, no city" (10.64), a fantasy of unmediated temporal power. The play suggests that such fantasies are dangerous, because the simple moral principles that More imagines are powerful enough alone to govern behavior turn out to be self-contradictory.

The Christian golden rule is a clear example of the self-contradictory nature of simplistic ethical maxims. More tries to use it in Scene 2 to teach Justice Suresby the lesson of not condemning Smart, a victim of pickpocket Lifter, for a fault (the carrying of too much money) that he, Suresby, is also guilty of. Yet Suresby appears to be promoting what is now known as moral relativism, meaning that Lifter's crime cannot be judged absolutely but rather must be considered in the context of the motivation for it, including the temptation placed

in his way by Smart. In undermining Suresby, More stands for an absolutism of judgment and against the hypocrisy of judges, and yet More aims to promote leniency toward offenders like Lifter. Moreover, More's trick on Suresby invokes its own kind of moral relativism, since the picking of Suresby's purse cannot be judged in isolation, cannot be condemned by an absolute rule, since it was done at More's behest and in return for a pardon. Relativism sneaks back into the very procedure meant to undermine it. When Suresby is sent by More to hold a private talk with Lifter, he wants the pickpocket to confess to crimes that he has committed but not been charged with, and Suresby sounds rather like a Catholic priest: "Wilt thou discharge thy conscience . . . Confess but what thou knowst" (2.97, 110). Revealing further crimes cannot get Lifter into greater trouble since any one of his purse-lifting offenses is enough to hang him, so what is the point of recounting the rest? As Suresby's diction indicates, the good of such confession is a free conscience. Lifter complains to Suresby that he has been charged with more crimes than he has committed, and again from a practical point of view, this seems irrelevant since any one of them will do for a death sentence.

The point of the interview seems to be that establishing the number of the crimes nonetheless somehow matters, and this suggests the Catholic approach to sin and good deeds, which is that an account can be drawn up (each good deed canceling out a sin) to determine the overall state of the soul. It was precisely this kind of accountancy approach to sin, something like a modern profit-and-loss table, that was objected to by the Protestant reformers of the early 16th century such as Martin Luther and John Calvin. Suresby wants Lifter not only to further incriminate himself, for the purpose of clearing his soul, but also to incriminate others and to explain how the crime of pickpocketing is carried out. He exalts in the technical details and reveals a passionate zeal for information: "Ay, those are they I look for . . . 'Tis this I long to know . . . Excellent, excellent!" (2.118–134). Suresby sounds curiously like an interrogator extracting information about religious heterodoxy, which is precisely the work that the historical More undertook for Henry VIII in hunting Protestants and that the dramatist Munday, as Topcliffe's assistant, undertook for Elizabeth I in hunting Catholics. Munday's own writings on religion suggest a deeply ambivalent response to Catholicism—a mixture of attraction and repulsion—and perhaps this scene expresses a moral uncertainty underlying his virulently anti-Catholic tracts. The scene certainly displaces any hope of the kind of moral certainty that More was renowned for possessing; rather right and wrong become inextricably entwined in what should be the simple exercise of justice.

This problematizing of right and wrong can help to explain one of the central mysteries of the drama, which is why someone as apparently anti-Catholic as Munday would write a valorizing biography of the Catholic martyr More. Perhaps Munday felt about the man as he felt about the man's religion, being torn between liking and loathing. The principles that More stands for seem on the face of things to be admirable, but when looked into they contain horrors, and this is also how many readers respond to the historical More's most famous work, *Utopia*. In Stephen Greenblatt's influential reading, More's own personality and the ideas in his book are characterized as failed attempts to reconcile extremely opposed principles and opinions: "More brings together then a near-chaos of conflicting psychological, social, and religious pressures and fashions them into a vision that seems at once utterly clear and utterly elusive" (Greenblatt 1980, 57). The same could well be said of the play *Sir Thomas More*. One of the ways this is achieved is by unsettling the stable perspective that playgoers habitually take up when they begin to evaluate what characters say, and that can be done by forcing playgoers to see something from two points of view in rapid succession.

In the midst of the first scene's setting out the play's basic contrast between good native Londoners and bad immigrant foreigners, Doll Williamson utters what seems at first a simple lament: "I am ashamed that free-born Englishmen, having beaten strangers within their own bounds, should thus be braved and abused by them at home" (1.78–80). On reflection—which is something more readily available to a reader than a playgoer—this seems an ironic sentiment, since within the foreigners "own bounds" (that is, in their country) it was the English who were strangers and the foreigners who were "at home." Doll tries to contrast the triumphs of Englishmen fighting foreigners abroad with the humiliations they are now suffering in London, but because the terms are relative—"strangers," "own bounds," and "home" all depend on where you are—she seems to end up suggesting that the English have in the past been no better than those who now oppress them. This sounds like a pre-echo of More's golden rule speech to the rioters, but twisted into a vicious cycle rather than a virtuous one. If the English have already beaten the foreigners in their country then, according to the rule of reciprocity, what is happening in London is merely the Londoners' just deserts. This kind of reading makes the play particularly topical in times of terrorist attack against Western cities, as discussed below.

Linguistic details again express the slipperiness of ethical principles when Doll starts to use the word *captain*. First she says that she will be "a captain among" the rioters (1.144), which promise she seems to fulfill by entering in armor at the start of Scene 4. When Ralph Betts's song of rebellion threatens to drown out Lincoln's advice to the rebels, Doll calls for them to "Hear Captain Lincoln speak" (4.15). Betts picks up the word and calls Lincoln "Captain Courageous" (4.35). More, too, uses the expression when reporting the extent of the uprising ("The captains of this insurrection . . . came but now / To both the Counters," 5.9–11), but in his speech to the rioters, he explicitly denies the possibility that such an office can exist: "What rebel captain, / As mutinies are incident, by his name / Can still the rout? Who will obey a traitor?" (6.129–131). That is, since a core principle of an uprising is the refusal to recognize authority, how can anyone exercize authority over a rebellion? The notion of a rebel captain is, More insists,

A 1523 portrait of Erasmus *(Painting by Hans Holbein the Younger)*

a contradiction in terms. This is another version of the rhetorical maneuver by which he disarms the rioters, showing that their behavior is logically inconsistent just as the golden rule shows that it is ethically inconsistent. Yet by concentrating on this leading group of rioters, this "limb of riot" that More prevented from becoming "joined with other branches of the city" (6.197–198), the suppression of the riot depends upon the very notion of leadership-in-anarchy that it would deny.

A hypothetical switching of places with someone else lies behind the play's recurrent explorations of the ethics of reciprocity, but More's practical experiment in switching places with his servant Randall in Scene 8 shows its limitations. Erasmus is highly impressed with More-as-Randall who welcomed them into the house, reasoning that if even More's servants are educated enough to speak Latin, then

More himself must be all the more impressively learned: "What's the master, then, / When such good parts shine in his meanest men?" (8.152–153). But Randall-as-More cannot keep up his end of the exchange, lapsing into trivial questions such as "how long will the Holland cheese in your country keep without maggots?" (8.174–175). This would suggest that there are inherent differences between people—just as Erasmus is good despite being Dutch—and hence that wisdom and goodness are not merely a matter of public performances but of inner qualities. And yet, the play keeps at the forefront of the playgoers' attention the fact that it is a play, that More's wisdom and goodness are only a performance by its actors. The performativity of virtue is stressed by the recurrent metatheatrical comments: Lifter's name is "As his profession is" (2.10) because he (like the characters in the inset play) is a type rather than an individuated person, he shushes the audience with "Silence there, ho! Now doth the Justice enter" (2.95), and More takes a role in *The Marriage of Wit and Wisdom* that is no different from the role he plays in life. "Il n'y a pas de hors-drame": there is no outside to the play, to adapt a phrase popular with one school of modern critics (Derrida 1976, 158).

When the actors of *The Marriage of Wit and Wisdom* are revealed to be "My Lord Cardinal's players" (9.50), an early-modern audience would likely understand them to be in service to Cardinal Thomas Wolsey. He was More's predecessor as lord chamberlain and fell from grace by exactly the same cause that brings down More: Henry VIII's desire to overcome the considerable religious obstacles to his marrying Anne Boleyn. Yet logically these cannot be Cardinal Wolsey's men, since in historic fact, Wolsey's fall was the occasion of More's rise. By making the audience imagine More being entertained by Wolsey's servants, the play collapses the historical narrative in order to juxtapose their fates. The same temporal collapse is enacted in Roper's wife's nightmare presentiment of More's downfall: "I saw him here in Chelsea church, / Standing upon the rood-loft, now defaced" (11.37–38). The defacing of the ornate decoration in churches was part of the wave of iconoclasm within the English Reformation that followed Henry VIII's break from Rome, so Roper's wife's dream puts the More of the 1530s into a post-Reformation church of the 1590s. By closing the historical gap between the times depicted in the play and the occasion of its performance, the play makes More seem to adhere to an abandoned faith. This is not unintentional anachronism but rather part of the play's effort to make More, rather than Henry, seem to be someone out of step with his times.

CRITICISM, CONTROVERSIES, AND THE PLAY TODAY

Because the play was not widely recognized as Shakespeare's until the early 20th century, it was not included in Complete Works editions until Harold Jenkins provided a text for Charles Jasper Sisson's collection (Shakespeare 1954). Even the Oxford Complete Works of 1986, which brought a radical new treatment of the canon, included only the small section of the play believed to be written by Shakespeare, making it impossible to see the overall artistic design. (The second edition of 2005 remedied this defect by printing the whole play.) The neglect of the play by editors necessarily rendered it largely unread by critics of Shakespeare, and little has been written about it as a complete play. The focus of attention was first upon the manuscript in which the play is embodied and the theater practices from which it emerges (McMillin 1987; Howard-Hill 1989), and the connected claims that Shakespeare wrote part of the play and that part of the manuscript is in his handwriting. It is, of course, quite possible for someone to be the author of writing not in his hand—this would happen every time someone used a theater scribe to copy out his material for actors or printers to use— and for someone not to be the author of writing that is in his hand, as when he acted as a scribe for others. The claim that Hand D is Shakespeare's has not won universal assent, although most scholars find the paleographical arguments overwhelming (Pollard et al. 1923; Howard-Hill 1989). The case for Shakespeare being the author of the material

attributed to him was recently settled beyond dispute: The play contains unusual words and phrasings that are recurrent in Shakespeare's writing and no one else's (Jackson 2006).

Concerning the play's themes, Joan Fitzpatrick recently traced how the different kinds of food mentioned in it are readable as indices of early-modern attitudes towards alterity as well as class (Fitzpatrick 2004) and how the character of More himself is subtly undermined by the play's recurrent images of gluttony (Fitzpatrick 2008). More likes to play on his name, and Fitzpatrick suggests that the audience is encouraged to continue the process in respect to food (eating more) and the mouth (the maw). This suggests a further extension of the theme of hypocrisy that runs through the scenes of Justice Suresby's exposure, the quelling of the riot, and the cutting of Falconer's hair. One group of critics has been keen to connect the complex facts of the play's collaborative creation to its themes. Others have found parallels between the peculiar textual situation—the play's existence in a unique and messy manuscript—and the themes it handles. Jeffrey Masten sees a connection between the collaborative nature of the play's composition and the ways that it treats human individuation (Masten 2001). The play begins with a scene about distinguishing English property (women and food) and foreigners' property, and in quelling the riot More executes the opposite maneuver, making the Londoners see themselves as like the foreigners. For Masten, this implicates More in a kind of shape-shifting best exemplified in his extemporaneous performance in the play-within-the-play, *The Marriage of Wit and Wisdom*. Where in all this play is the real More? Stripped of his titles, he becomes "only 'More'" (11.70), a living oxymoron expressing both lack and excess. His verbal dexterity at turning words inside out is rebounded upon himself, and as Fitzpatrick points out, this is expressed in terms of his own body, "The fat is gone" (11.70), and much depends on the physique of the actor cast to play More.

Masten notices that running through the play's dramatic material in different hands is a recurrent concern for the rhetoric of selfhood, sameness, and strangeness. It seems that the censor Tilney disliked vagueness on this point, and where the dramatists had identified a wrongdoer as a "stranger," Tilney changed it to "Lombard" (3.49). Throughout this chapter, I have called them foreigners to avoid adjudicating between the dramatists and their censor, but Masten rightly points out that even the word *foreigner* could be ambiguous, meaning simply a person not from one's parish or recently arrived in town from the countryside. More wrote *Utopia*, a book about meeting a stranger (Hythloday) and hearing about the strange places he had been, and the play's writers seem to understand how slippery such definitions are. Nina Levine is also concerned with the collaborative nature of the play's composition, and she sees a parallel with the collaborative endeavor of rioting for which the Londoners come together (Levine 2007). The dramatists conjure up a mob for More to quell, but it is one that the audience has first seen as individuals (feisty Doll, leaderly Lincoln, bawdy Ralph Betts), so there is individuation within the collective. Censor Tilney, Levine reckons, probably changed the dialogue references to Frenchmen and strangers because there were lots of French Huguenots in London in the 1590s, and they might be offended, but there were not many Lombards. That is, the word *Lombard* was a convenient foreign label to use precisely because they were not around to object.

In Tilney's crossing out of speech prefixes, Levine sees a fussing over individuation: Did he perhaps object to the mob being identifiable characters, with individual motivations and personal grievances, that the audience had first seen suffering abuses earlier in the play? As she notes, Hand D (Shakespeare) gave the line "We'll be ruled by you, Master More, if you'll stand our friend to procure our pardon" (6.158–159) to "All" the rioters, but another writer, Hand C, reassigned it to Lincoln specifically, thereby generating a marked irony since Lincoln is the only rebel not pardoned. Hand C did a lot of such individuating of characters, giving speeches designated for "All" and "Others" to particular named speakers, and there is further

irony in the fact that we do not know whose hand it was, so his individuation as a person is lost to us. It might even be the same person as Hand D, that is Shakespeare, acting in a different mode of composition.

In Tracey Hill's reading of the play, the individuated personalities of the rebels are important because of the extraordinary audience sympathy evoked for them, which is why they attracted so much attention from the censor, and because they are clearly Londoners defending London (Hill 2005). Most plays of the period that show such uprisings present them as a threat to the City, with Jack Cade's rebellion in *The Contention of York and Lancaster/Henry VI, Part 2* a typical example. But *Sir Thomas More* daringly reverses this trend, and by recurrent references to precise locations in London, such as St. Martin's and Cheapside, it collapses the historical differences between 1517 when the Ill May Day uprising took place and the 1590s. In other words, playgoers were encouraged to see this as their contemporary London being defended. According to Hill, the most significant consequence of the revision of the manuscript by the dramatists who assisted Munday was the toning down of this sympathy for the uprising. By giving Ralph Betts more to say, and making the crowd more disorderly and xenophobic, Lincoln's and Doll's rational arguments for the uprising are undermined.

For many plays by Shakespeare, there is little or no evidence of performance in his own time, but we assume that performances occurred. With *Sir Thomas More*, it is distinctly possible that the problems arising from the sensitivity of the topics it handles made the players abandon the project, leaving it unperformed until recent times. The major recent productions were by the Stage One Theatre Company (directed by Michael Walling at the Shaw Theatre, London) in 1990 and by the Royal Shakespeare Company (directed by Robert Delamere at the Swan Theatre, Stratford-upon-Avon) in 2005, both coinciding with the publication of editions of the play (Munday 1990; Shakespeare 2005). *Sir Thomas More* reads today as extraordinarily prescient of three interrelated

21st-century concerns: the potentially fatal conflicts between religious doctrines, the economic consequences of migration, and the ways that xenophobic responses are engaged by these matters of religion and migration. However, the terms in which these concerns were formulated in the 16th century were very different from those of today, because of course the religions and the patterns of economic migration were entirely different. Nonetheless, suicide bombings by fundamentalist Islamists in London in July 2005 made the choices about race and religion in the Royal Shakespeare Company's production resonate particularly strongly. The misbehaving foreigners were played by black actors among a predominantly white cast, which strengthened the overtones of racism in the rioting of abused Londoners, which in Hill's terms means taking still further the adulteration by other dramatists of Munday's initial conception of a just rebellion.

In what is usually taken to be a slip of the pen in the manuscript, More expresses his revulsion at the rioters' "momtanish inhumanyty," which Jowett emends and modernizes to "mountainish [that is, mountainous] inhumanity" (6.155). Karl Wentersdorf argues, however, that *momtanish* is not a slip of the pen but a contraction of *mahometanish* and refers specifically to

"Thomas More Reflects," from William Hickman Smith's *The National and Domestic History of England,* published in 1878

Islamic barbarity (Wentersdorf 2006). As well as providing further topical interest, this reading strengthens the religious dimension of the play by making More accuse the rioters not only of rebellion against God (by rising against his anointed deputy, the monarch) but also of apostasy. This would further ironize More's downfall, caused by his adamant refusal to follow the change in the English state's religion, and give further shading to the play's theme of hypocrisy. In Wentersdorf's reading, More accuses the rioters of a barbarity so excessive that it can only be likened to the consequences of misguided religious fervor. Such fervor is readily apparent in the historical More himself, whose behavior as a persecutor and executioner of Christian heretics was so starkly contrasted with the ideals expressed in his *Utopia*. If the play is subtly drawing attention to this, the More who emerges is somewhat less attractive a figure than critics have generally assumed.

FIVE TOPICS FOR DISCUSSION AND WRITING

1. **More's tragic downfall:** To what extent are we encouraged to sympathize with More's adamant refusal to accommodate his king's wishes? Does More come across as an admirable man of principles or an obstinate fool? When considering this, do not forget the effect of More's refusal upon his wider family and household. How seriously do you take More's own assurances that his family can survive without him?

2. **Court versus city:** Do the authority figures of the court seem different from those of the City, and if they do, are we expected to feel differently about them as a consequence? As he rises, More makes the transition from one center of power to the other, but take a close look at what he says about the corrupting nature of power. Is there any evidence that he becomes corrupted, or that he changes (for good or ill) the behavior of others around him?

3. **Casting—what should these people look like?:** The casting of a stage play strongly conditions the meanings it generates, so the appearance of characters is no trivial matter. If the actor

playing More is thin, it can suggest a virtuous, even monklike, abstinence from the pleasures of food, while a plump and jovial More might be thought to be more in keeping with the fun-loving figure who is forever jesting. Should the foreigners look racially or ethnically different from the Londoners? Consider what difference it would make to the scenes of rioting, and the motivations underlying it, if the foreigners look like or unlike the Londoners.

4. **Oratory and rhetoric:** Why do some people's arguments fail to convince their hearers in the play and other people's succeed? Using a guide to rhetorical terms, see if those who manage to be persuasive are using language in fundamentally different ways from those who fail to persuade. Does the use of prose or verse have any bearing on this?

5. **Jests and puns:** Look for all the occasions when characters use puns in the play. Are the effects always supposed to be comic, or is there a place for tragic wordplay? What do you make of More's repeated feints at capitulation? Is he doing this deliberately to amuse those around him, or are the dramatists playing with the readers' and playgoers' expectations?

Bibliography

Astington, John H. "Gallows Scenes on the Elizabethan Stage." *Theatre Notebook* 37 (1983): 3–9.

Derrida, Jacques. *Of Grammatology.* Translated by Gayatri Chakrovorty Spivak. Baltimore: Johns Hopkins University Press, 1976.

Egan, Gabriel. "Theatre in London." In *Shakespeare: An Oxford Guide,* edited by Stanley Wells and Lena Cowen Orlin, 22–33. Oxford: Oxford University Press.

Fitzpatrick, Joan. "Food and Foreignness in *Sir Thomas More.*" *Early Theatre* 7, no. 2 (2004): 33–47.

———. "The 'Sweet-gorged Maw': Feeding and Physic in the Elizabethan Dramatic Life of Sir Thomas More." *Renaissance and Reformation/ Renaissance et Réforme* 31, no. 3 (2008): 51–67.

Greenblatt, Stephen. *Renaissance Self-fashioning: From More to Shakespeare.* Chicago: University of Chicago Press, 1980.

Hill, Tracey. "'The Cittie Is in an Uproare': Staging London in *The Booke of Sir Thomas More.*" *Early Modern Literary Studies* 11, no. 1 (2005). Available online. URL: http://purl.oclc.org/emls/11–1/ more.htm.

Howard-Hill, T. H., ed. *Shakespeare and* Sir Thomas More: *Essays on the Play and Its Shakespearian Interest.* New Cambridge Shakespeare Studies and Supplementary Texts. Cambridge: Cambridge University Press, 1989.

Jackson, MacDonald P. "The Date and Authorship of Hand D's Contribution to *Sir Thomas More:* Evidence from 'Literature Online.'" *Shakespeare Survey* 59 (2006): 69–78.

Levine, Nina. "Citizens' Games: Differentiating Collaboration and *Sir Thomas More.*" *Shakespeare Quarterly* 58 (2007): 31–64.

Masten, Jeffrey. "*More* or Less: Editing the Collaborative." *Shakespeare Studies* 29 (2001): 109–131.

McMillin, Scott. *The Elizabethan Theatre and* The Book of Sir Thomas More. Ithaca, N.Y.: Cornell University Press, 1987.

Menzer, Paul. "The Tragedians of the City? Q1 *Hamlet* and the Settlements of the 1590s." *Shakespeare Quarterly* 57 (2006): 162–182.

Munday, Anthony, et al. *Sir Thomas More.* In *The Revels Plays,* edited by Vittorio Gabrieli and Giorgio Melchiori, 49–192. Manchester, England: Manchester University Press, 1996.

Pollard, A. W., W. W. Greg, E. Maunde Thompson, J. Dover Wilson, and R. W. Chambers. *Shakespeare Problems.* Vol. 2. *Shakespeare's Hand in the Play of* Sir Thomas More. Cambridge: Cambridge University Press, 1923.

Shakespeare, William. *The Complete Works.* Edited by Charles Jasper Sisson. London: Odhams, 1954.

———. *William Shakespeare: The Complete Works.* 2nd ed. Edited by Stanley Wells, Gary Taylor, John Jowett, and William Montgomery. Oxford, England: Clarendon Press, 2005.

Wentersdorf, Karl P. "On 'Momtanish Inhumanyty' in *Sir Thomas More.*" *Studies in Philology* 103 (2006): 178–185.

—Gabriel Egan

The Taming of the Shrew

INTRODUCTION

The Taming of the Shrew, one of Shakespeare's ear-liest plays, remains one of his most popular com-edies. It demonstrates Shakespeare's knowledge of and desire to participate in existing and contem-porary literary tradition; "shrews" were popular characters, and stories involving shrews being domesticated were especially popular during the Renaissance. Compared to his tragedies, *The Tam-ing of the Shrew* naturally seems lighthearted and playful, but at the same time, it asks serious ques-tions about marriage, gender roles, and identity.

Though scholars do not classify *The Taming of the Shrew* as a "problem play," the play definitely presents weighty problems for its audience, espe-cially since the 1970s. What should readers and viewers make of Katherina's "taming"? She changes from independent (albeit angry and unfriendly) to obedient, in the end merely mimicking and agree-ing with her husband, even when he is blatantly wrong. Some critics find the play revolting, arguing that it represents Shakespeare as a sexist. Others, however, claim that Shakespeare merely depicted the dynamics and expectations of the culture in which he lived, and that *The Taming of the Shrew* neither endorses nor condemns Elizabethan ideol-ogy, since Katherina's actions can be read as either heartfelt or subversive. Regardless, the play focuses on the chronicle of a woman and man who marry more for money and love, but who also reach an understanding through which they live pleasantly, even happily, while others feel plagued with uneasi-ness about their new partners and marriages.

Some scholars have suggested that Shakespeare borrowed heavily from a very similarly named play, *The Taming of a Shrew.* Whether the plotline was Shakespeare's invention or not, the beauty and mastery of his writing style remains undeniable. Consider Samuel Johnson's claim: "Of this play the two plots are so well united, that they can hardly be called two without injury to the art with which they are interwoven. The attention is entertained with all the variety of a double plot, yet is not dis-tracted by unconnected incidents." *The Taming of the Shrew* provides readers with an engaging story, while simultaneously asking them to think care-fully about issues important not only in Shake-speare's era but in our own. Shakespeare entertains and entreats his readers with a tale of a battle of wills and a battle of the sexes.

BACKGROUND

Some readers have called Shakespeare a misogy-nist for having written *The Taming of the Shrew.* Shakespeare, however, did not invent the notion of taming a woman, of controlling and manipulating an independent woman into submission. Instead, he participates in a long-standing literary tradition, popular since the Middle Ages, in which a woman (like Shakespeare's Katherina) is put in her place. As Jan Harold Brunvand discusses in "The Folk-tale Origin of *The Taming of the Shrew,*" stories in this literary tradition often included husbands beating their wives or beating animals (a situation meant to allegorize taming one's wife or threat-ening a wife into behaving obediently). Though

Still photograph from the 1929 film version of *The Taming of the Shrew,* starring Douglas Fairbanks as Petruchio and Mary Pickford as Katherine

Shakespeare's participation in this tradition disappoints and unsettles some readers, others view the play as an example of Shakespeare simply catering to the needs and interest of his audience, who, in the patriarchal Elizabethan society, were highly entertained by these "shrew stories," in which an outspoken and tempestuous woman becomes silenced and broken.

In fact, scholars believe that certain shrew stories function as sources for Shakespeare's own composition, including *The Wicked Queen Reformed by a Cobbler* (as noted by Shakespearean scholar Stephen Miller) and *A Shrewde and Curste Wyfe* (suggested by Kenneth Muir, author of *The Sources of Shakespeare's Plays*), in which a woman is beaten into submission with birch rods. *The Taming of the Shrew* undeniably draws on this tradition, but tracing the sources for this early comedy is tricky,

particularly because of the existence of the other *Shrew* play, *The Taming of a Shrew*. For clarity, the plays will henceforth be referred to as *A Shrew* and *The Shrew*. Kenneth Muir writes that three primary theories exist about the source material for *The Shrew*. The first theory is that *A Shrew* is the primary source for *The Shrew;* the second theory is that *A Shrew* was "pirated" from *The Shrew;* and the third is that both *A Shrew* and *The Shrew* are based on what Muir calls "a lost play, the *Ur-Shrew*" (19), much like *Hamlet* and the *Ur-Hamlet*. Many scholars (like Richard Hosley) agree with the second theory, suggesting that a group of audience members or even actors attempted to write a version of *The Shrew,* and instead called it *A Shrew*. These scholars note that *A Shrew* is only one-third the length of *The Shrew,* which could suggest that those who pirated *The Shrew* had trouble remembering all the details.

Miller notes that *A Shrew* and *The Shrew* share very similar structures but also have significant differences (besides the length of the plays). *A Shrew* is set in Greece; almost all of its characters have different names; its Katherina has two sisters instead of one; and, significantly, its frame tale involving the tinker Christopher Sly has a conclusion. If *A Shrew* is simply a pirated version by audience members or actors, the authors definitely took some liberties with Shakespeare's material and even sought to finish what Shakespeare left undone, namely the plot strand involving Christopher Sly. Miller acknowledges the ongoing problems concerning the composition of *The Taming of the Shrew* most significantly when he asks, "Why, when *A Shrew* contains so much in common with *The Shrew,* does it have such a large amount of material that is different?" (3). The mysterious existence of these two plays remains ripe for critical exploration and debate.

Regardless of whether *The Shrew* or *A Shrew* appeared first, the two plays are based on the same sources. As noted earlier, the main plot of Petruchio's taming of Katherina builds on a healthy tradition of shrew stories. Muir notes specific examples that may have influenced Shakespeare's composition of the primary plot strand, including a scene with a tailor in *Access of Armoury* and a wager a group of men make on how obedient their wives are in *The Book of the Knight of La Tour-Landry* (20). Muir and Miller suggest that the source material for the secondary plotline, involving the story of Bianca and Lucentio, is Gascoigne's *Supposes,* from 1566; Gascoigne based his work on the Italian writer Ludovico Ariosto's *I Suppositi* from 1509. Muir and Miller also agree that the Christopher Sly story derives from a tale found in *The Arabian Nights,* "a variant of which," Muir claims, "Shakespeare could have read in *De rebus burgundicis* of Heuterus (1584)" (19).

Date and Text of the Play

The existence of *A Shrew* complicates matters for dating Shakespeare's composition of *The Shrew,* but most scholars believe Shakespeare wrote the play in the early 1590s, with some agreement on the year of 1592. If one agrees with the theory that *A Shrew* is merely a corrupt version of *The Shrew,* then the 1592 composition date for *The Shrew* makes sense, since *A Shrew* first appeared in the Stationer's Register in 1594. Shakespearean scholar Stephen Miller reports that on May 2, 1594, "the first quarto of *The Taming of a Shrew* was entered on the Stationer's Register by its printer: Peter Shorte Entred unto him for his copie under master warden Cawoodes hand a booke intituled *A pleasant Conceyted historie called 'the Tayminge of a Shrowe'*" (31). Another edition of *A Shrew* appeared in 1596. *The Shrew* was not published until 1623, with the release of the First Folio.

SYNOPSIS
Brief Synopsis

A lord and a group of hunters enter and find the drunken Christopher Sly, upon whom they decide to play a trick. The group puts Sly in fine clothes, and in an effort to test if Sly will forget his true identity, they try to convince Sly he is a nobleman with a wife. The lord convinces a group of players to stage a performance for Sly's benefit, and the play ensues.

Lucentio and his servant Tranio arrive in Padua and meet Baptista, a man with two daughters named Katherina and Bianca. Baptista wants to find a husband for Katherina, his elder daughter, known for her unpleasantness and "shrewish" behavior. If Katherina marries, he will allow his younger daughter Bianca (sweeter, more attractive, and more sought out than her sister) to marry as well. Lucentio immediately falls in love with Bianca and devises a plan to win her affections: Tranio, Lucentio's servant, poses as his master and begins wooing Bianca. He must contend with Hortensio and Gremio, two of Bianca's other suitors.

Petruchio, a man in search of wealth, arrives in Padua and decides he will woo and marry Katherina because, he knows, marrying her will provide him with a fortune. The first time Petruchio sees Katherina, he flatters her incessantly; the two engage in some heated verbal sparring and Katherina, unsettled by Petruchio's compliments, feels confused. The two soon become engaged, and Petruchio makes arrangements for the forthcoming nuptials. The wedding day arrives, and Petruchio is nowhere to be found. A tearful Katherina suffers only more embarrassment when Petruchio finally arrives, dressed like a beggar and riding an old horse. He and Katherina are wed, but the wedding is a fiasco. Petruchio's intent, readers know, is to break Katherina's feisty spirit and "tame" her. He continues this taming process by depriving her of food and sleep and insists he only does so out of love for her.

Tranio, on behalf of his master Lucentio, successfully woos Bianca. Baptista agrees to the marriage, especially now that Katherina has married Petruchio. Having lost in his suit for Bianca, her suitor Hortensio finds a (very wealthy) widow whom he decides to marry. After the joy and celebration at the three recent marriages (Katherina to Petruchio, Bianca to Lucentio, and the widow to Hortensio), the new husbands hold a friendly wager: Each bids his wife to come when he calls. Katherina, when summoned, appears immediately; the other wives do not come when asked. The triumphant Petruchio, all other characters, and Shakespeare's

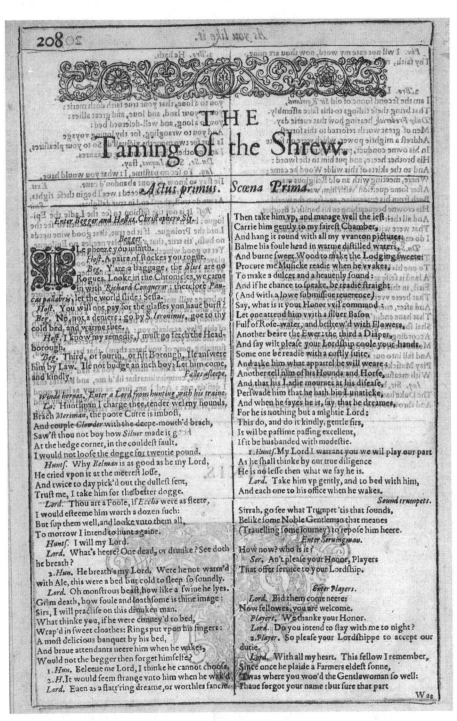

THE
Taming of the Shrew.

Actus primus. Scœna Prima.

Enter Begger and Hostes, Christophero Sly.

Begger.
Ile pheeze you infaith.

Host. A paire of stockes you rogue.

Beg. Y'are a baggage, the *Slies* are no
Rogues. Looke in the Chronicles, we came
in with *Richard Conqueror* : therefore *Pau-
cas pallabris*, let the world slide : Sessa.

Host. You will not pay for the glasses you haue burst?

Beg. No, not a deniere : go by S. *Ieronimie*, goe to thy
cold bed, and warme thee.

Host. I know my remedie, I must go fetch the Head-
borough.

Beg. Third, or fourth, or fift Borough, Ile answere
him by Law. Ile not budge an inch boy : Let him come,
and kindly.   *Falles asleepe.*

Winde hornes. Enter a Lord from hunting, with his traine.

Lo. Huntsman I charge thee, tender welmy hounds,
Brach *Meriman*, the poore Curre is imbost,
And couple *Clowder* with the deepe-mouth'd brach,
Saw'st thou not boy how *Siluer* made it good
At the hedge corner, in the couldest fault,
I would not loose the dogge for twentie pound.

Hunts. Why *Belman* is as good as he my Lord,
He cried vpon it at the meerest losse,
And twice to day pick'd out the dullest sent,
Trust me, I take him for the better dogge.

Lord. Thou art a Foole, if *Eccho* were as fleete,
I would esteeme him worth a dozen such :
But sup them well, and looke vnto them all,
To morrow I intend to hunt againe.

Hunts. I will my Lord.

Lord. What's heere? One dead, or drunke? See doth
he breath?

2.Hun. He breath's my Lord, Were he not warm'd
with Ale, this were a bed but cold to sleep so soundly.

Lord. Oh monstrous beast, how like a swine he lyes.
Grim death, how foule and loathsome is thine image :
Sirs, I will practise on this drunken man.
What thinke you, if he were conuey'd to bed,
Wrap'd in sweet cloathes : Rings put vpon his fingers :
A most delicious banquet by his bed,
And braue attendants neere him when he wakes,
Would not the begger then forget himselfe?

1.Hun. Beleeue me Lord, I thinke he cannot choose.

2.H. It would seem strange vnto him when he wak'd.

Lord. Euen as a flatt'ring dreame, or worthles fancie.

Then take him vp, and manage well the iest :
Carrie him gently to my fairest Chamber,
And hang it round with all my vvanton pictures :
Balme his foule head in warme distilled waters,
And burne sweet Wood to make the Lodging sweet :
Procure me Musicke readie when he vvakes,
To make a dulcet and a heauenly sound :
And if he chance to speake, be readie straight
(And with a lowe submissiue reuerence)
Say, what is it your Honor vvil command :
Let one attend him vvith a siluer Bason
Full of Rose-water, and bestrew'd with Flowers,
Another beare the Ewer : the third a Diaper,
And say wilt please your Lordship coole your hands.
Some one be readie with a costly suite,
And aske him what apparrel he will weare :
Another tell him of his Hounds and Horse,
And that his Ladie mournes at his disease,
Perswade him that he hath bin Lunaticke,
And when he sayes he is, say that he dreames,
For he is nothing but a mightie Lord :
This do, and do it kindly, gentle sirs,
It wil be pastime passing excellent,
If it be husbanded with modestie.

1.Hunt. My Lord I warrant you we wil play our part
As he shall thinke by our true diligence
He is no lesse then what we say he is.

Lord. Take him vp gently, and to bed with him,
And each one to his office when he wakes.

Sound trumpets.

Sirrah, go see what Trumpet 'tis that sounds,
Belike some Noble Gentleman that meanes
(Trauelling some iourney) to repose him heere.

Enter Seruingman.

How now? who is it?

Ser. An't please your Honor, Players
That offer seruice to your Lordship.

Enter Players.

Lord. Bid them come neere :
Now fellowes, you are welcome.

Players. We thanke your Honor.

Lord. Do you intend to stay with me to night?

2.Player. So please your Lordshippe to accept our
dutie.

Lord. With all my heart. This fellow I remember,
Since once he plaide a Farmers eldest sonne,
'Twas where you woo'd the Gentlewoman so well :
I haue forgot your name : but sure that part

W as

---

audience listen to Katherina explain that a wife must always obey and honor her husband.

Induction, Scene 1

A lord and a group of hunters find a drunken peasant, Christopher Sly, sleeping outside a pub. The lord decides to play a trick on Sly and enlists the help of his servants and a group of players to help him. He tells his servants to dress Sly in clothes fit for a noble and to treat him as though he were a nobleman who is sick and unable to recall his identity.

Induction, Scene 2

Sly wakes up, confused. The lord and his servants trick Sly into thinking that he even has a wife (played by the lord's page). The play, *The Taming of the Shrew,* performed by the group of players hired by the lord, begins.

Act I, Scene 1

Lucentio and his servant, Tranio, arrive in Padua where they soon meet one of its wealthy citizens, Baptista. Baptista's two daughters accompany him: the older daughter Katherina is known through the city as a shrew; younger daughter Bianca is sweeter and much more desired than her sister. Baptista explains that Bianca will be kept from marrying until Katherina is made a wife. Lucentio falls instantly in love with Bianca and enlists Tranio to helps him win her affection. The plan goes as follows: Tranio will pose as Lucentio and woo Bianca, while Lucentio will pose as one of Bianca's tutors so he can be close to her and get to know her better. In the meantime, two of Bianca's other suitors—Hortensio and Gremio—decide not to fight over Bianca any longer.

Act I, Scene 2

Petruchio and his servant Grumio also arrive in Padua. Petruchio has one mission on this trip: to find a wealthy wife. He seeks out his old friend, Hortensio, who mentions he knows of a wealthy woman in need of a husband, but that same woman, Hortensio explains, is a shrew. Undeterred by this information, Petruchio demands that Hor-

tensio reveal the woman's identity. Hortensio says her name is Katherina Minola. Petruchio declares that he will make Katherina his wife.

Meanwhile, Gremio and Hortensio (aware now of Bianca's new suitor, Lucentio) compete against each other again for the younger Minola daughter. Tranio poses as Lucentio while the real Lucentio, disguised as a tutor who will go by the name Cambio, arrives. Tranio/Lucentio asks where he can find the home of Baptista Minola, inciting suspicion in Gremio and Hortensio, who think Tranio/Lucentio may also be after Bianca's affection. To put the other suitors at ease, Tranio/Lucentio offers to buy the men drinks, and they depart.

Act II, Scene 1

Bianca and Katherina enter; Bianca's hands are tied behind her back, and she begs her sister to untie them. Katherina, clearly envious of the attention her sister receives, questions Bianca about her suitors and then strikes her. Baptista enters, tells Bianca to go inside, chides Kate for hitting her sister, and then sends her away also. Lucentio and Petruchio arrive and meet Baptista, who approves of Petruchio courting Katherina and Lucentio tutoring Bianca. Hortensio, acting as a music tutor, goes with Lucentio to give the daughters their first lesson. Hortensio returns shortly after Katherina breaks his lute on his head. Petruchio, hearing this, finds himself intrigued to meet Katherina for himself.

He finally meets her, and he and Katherina engage in a war of wits. Petruchio compliments Katherina while she insults him; resolved to marry her, Petruchio continues to flatter Katherina, only confusing her more. With Baptista's blessing, Petruchio sets the wedding date for the coming Sunday. Tranio/Lucentio and Gremio both vie for Bianca's attention and Tranio/Lucentio is victorious. Now one less of Bianca's suitors poses a threat to the real Lucentio.

Act III, Scene 1

The real Lucentio, disguised as the tutor Cambio, arrives; as does Hortensio, another of Bianca's suitors, dressed also as a tutor named Licio. Bianca says that she will have her lesson with Cambio first, filling the real Lucentio with hope, and Hortensio with despair. Lucentio/Cambio reveals his feeling for Bianca in Latin during the lesson, and she acknowledges his intentions but does nothing more. Hortensio/Licio also informs Bianca of his true feelings for her during his lesson with her; he does so less deftly than Lucentio/Cambio, and Hortensio realizes he may have to pursue a different woman as his future wife.

Act III, Scene 2

Sunday, the wedding day, arrives, and Baptista, Katherina, and all the guests wait for Petruchio to arrive. Katherina feels mortified by Petruchio's abandoning her and breaks down into tears. Biondello announces suddenly that Petruchio is coming. Feelings of relief are short-lived, however, when Baptista notices Petruchio's appearance: His future son-in-law is dressed in rags and riding on an old, decrepit horse. Baptista urges Petruchio to change his clothes, but Petruchio refuses, asking for Katherina. They are married, and Petruchio continues to embarrass Katherina with his behavior; the embarrassment Katherina suffers because of Petruchio's behavior, he decides, will be one way to start "taming" her into behaving like a good and obedient wife.

After the wedding, Petruchio and Katherina gather with their friends and family to celebrate. Petruchio commands that Katherina leave with him almost immediately, but she tells him she will leave when she feels ready. Petruchio claims thieves might steal his new bride—now his property—and whisks her away. Baptista, eager to marry off his other daughter, begins discussing wedding plans with Tranio/Lucentio.

Act IV, Scene 1

Grumio, one of Petruchio's servants, arrives at his master's house and explains to Curtis (another of Petruchio's servants) the trip that he, his master, and his master's new wife made from Padua, which was difficult. When Katherina and Petruchio arrive, they sit for dinner, which Petruchio throws from

Petruchio beats Grumio because Katherina's horse stumbled, as described in Act IV, Scene 1 of *The Taming of the Shrew*. This is a print from Malcolm C. Salaman's 1916 edition of *Shakespeare in Pictorial Art*. *(Painting by Sir Robert Ker Porter)*

the table, complaining the meat was burned (even though it was perfectly fine). Katherina says the food was fine for eating, but Petruchio disagrees, telling Katherina that he refuses to let her eat any of the food because she could fall ill. He then takes her to their bedroom. Shortly thereafter, Petruchio returns and explains, in detail, how he will "tame" his shrew of a wife: He will do anything he can to aggravate and torture his wife so he can break her tempestuous spirit and transform her into an obedient wife. He explains that when he returns to their bedroom, he will complain about the mattress so that she is unable to sleep, thus further depriving her of her needs and, in turn, wearing her down.

Act IV, Scene 2

The courting of Bianca continues. Lucentio/Cambio woos Bianca while Tranio/Lucentio and

Hortensio listen. Hortensio decides to withdraw from the battle for Bianca's affections and marry a widow. Tranio/Lucentio tells Bianca that Hortensio (disguised as Licio, the tutor) has left to attend "taming school," which Tranio/Lucentio explains is located at Petruchio's house. The real Lucentio and Bianca can now be together, but first they must find a man to pose as Lucentio's father so that Baptista can approve of the family into which his youngest daughter will marry. Tranio meets a Pedant, whom he convinces to pose as Lucentio's father.

Act IV, Scene 3

Katherina, still at Petruchio's house, talks with Grumio, expressing her misery. She wonders if Petruchio married her only to starve her and keep her from sleeping. A tailor and haberdasher arrive with new clothes for Katherina which she likes, but Petruchio causes a terrible scene and sends the tailor away, clothes in hand. Petruchio tells Kate they will leave to visit her father. Petruchio says it is seven o'clock; Katherina corrects him, explaining it is only two o'clock. Petruchio then cancels the trip to Baptista's, saying that they will not go to Padua until Katherina agrees with everything he says.

Act IV, Scene 4

Lucentio and the Pedant (who will pretend to be Lucentio's father) rehearse their story before meeting with Baptista. The Pedant must convince Baptista that his son Lucentio is a worthy match for his daughter Bianca. The sham convinces Baptista, who leaves with Lucentio and the Pedant to devise a marriage settlement. Biondello tells his master Lucentio/Cambio that Baptista has approved of the match, and encourages his master to find someone to perform the wedding for Lucentio/Cambio and Bianca.

Act IV, Scene 5

Petruchio decides that he and Katherina will visit Padua. On the trip there, and to further test Katherina, Petruchio compliments the moon for shining so brightly even though it is clearly daytime

and the sun is out. Katherina corrects her husband, who then scolds her again for questioning what he says. Petruchio threatens to turn back, but Katherina, noting that they have already come so far on the trip, concedes and says that whatever her husband says, she will agree with.

Continuing along their journey, the newlyweds encounter an older gentleman, whom Petruchio greets and treats like a young woman. Katherina, aware that the traveler is an elderly man, instead follows Petruchio's suit; she compliments his beauty, calls him a virgin, and says he will make a husband happy one day. Hearing this, Petruchio taxes Katherina even more by correcting her, telling his wife he hopes she has not gone mad because before them stands an old man, not a young woman. Without hesitation, Katherina addresses the traveler as an old man. She appears to finally have been "tamed" by Petruchio.

The old man's name is Vincentio, and he is searching for his son Lucentio. Petruchio informs the man that he and his wife are on their way to Padua where, in fact, Lucentio happens to reside. Vincentio joins them on their way to Padua.

Act V, Scene 1

The real Lucentio and Bianca go to visit a priest who will marry them. In the meantime, Petruchio, Katherina, and Vincentio (Lucentio's real father) arrive at Baptista's house. They attempt to enter the house, but the Pedant (claiming to already be Lucentio's father) will not let them in and calls out that Vincentio is a fake and should be arrested. Vincentio immediately recognizes Tranio (who is his son's servant), but Tranio pretends not to recognize his master's father.

Lucentio and Bianca, newly married, arrive, and Lucentio reveals the convoluted plan and disguises donned by numerous characters. He argues that he only instituted this plan of action because he was so deeply in love with Bianca. Before everyone enters Baptista's house, Petruchio demands that Katherina kiss him: The kiss will occur in front of everyone, in the middle of the street. Embarrassed, Katherina says she will not kiss him, but when

Petruchio threatens to leave Padua if she does not, she grants him a kiss.

Act V, Scene 2

A party ensues to celebrate the three recent marriages between Petruchio and Katherina, Lucentio and Bianca, and Hortensio and his wealthy widow. Amid the celebration, the three new husbands make a wager about whose wife is most obedient. When the husbands call for their wives, the results surprise them. Bianca refuses to come because she is busy; Hortensio's wife sends a similar response. But Katherina arrives promptly. Petruchio commands her to go get the other wives and to take off the hat she wears: she completes both tasks immediately. He then commands Kate to give a speech concerning wives' duties to their husbands, and how they should always obey them. She does so, unflinchingly. Others wonder about Katherina's transformation and how she has, indeed, been "tamed."

CHARACTER LIST

Petruchio   A gentleman from Verona; he desires wealth, and in turn searches for a rich wife. Knowing that marrying Katherina would award him a sizable dowry, he becomes her suitor, vowing to marry her, regardless of her shrewish nature. Petruchio devises a plan to tame Kate, which includes depriving of her food, sleep, and even seeing her family.

Katherina   Baptista's older daughter. She is "the shrew" in the play's title. The city of Padua knows Katherina for her biting wit, her hardened interactions, and her tempestuousness nature. A man must agree to marry her before her younger sister, Bianca, is allowed to marry. Characters in the play (and readers alike) feel amazement at Katherina's transformation, but whether this transformation is genuine or artificial remains debatable.

Lucentio   A young gentleman and Vincentio's son. He falls deeply in love with Bianca and devises a complicated scheme to win her affection, which he does with the help of his loyal servant Tranio.

Bianca   Baptista's younger daughter. She is beautiful and desired by many suitors. She is not allowed to marry, however, until someone marries Katherina. She appears more docile than her sister, but in reality, Bianca is as independent as her sister.

Baptista   A wealthy gentleman, father of Katherina and Bianca. He wants his daughters to be married, but he refuses to let his younger daughter Bianca marry until his older daughter, Katherina "the shrew," has a husband. He cares more about financial gain than the happiness of his daughters.

Hortensio   One of Bianca's suitors; his feelings for her are fickle, however, because by the end of the play he marries a wealthy widow instead.

Gremio   Another of Bianca's suitors.

Tranio   Lucentio's faithful servant who is instrumental in helping his master obtain Bianca's affection. Tranio poses as Lucentio and woos Bianca on his master's behalf, deftly manipulating each of Bianca's other suitors so that Lucentio can have Bianca to himself.

Grumio   One of Petruchio's servants; a clown.

Biondello   One of Lucentio's servants; he helps Lucentio win Bianca's affection.

Vincentio   A gentleman visiting Padua from Pisa. He is Lucentio's real father.

Widow   Woman Hortensio eventually marries.

A Lord   A genuine nobleman who tricks Christopher Sly into thinking he is a nobleman, watching a play performed for him.

Christopher Sly   Unassuming and drunken peasant who is duped into believing he is actually a nobleman, for whom a play is being performed.

Hostess, Players, Huntsmen, Page, and Servants   Those who assist the Lord in tricking Sly.

Curtis, Nathaniel, Philip, Joseph, Nicholas, and Peter   Servants to Petruchio.

Pedant   A man who agrees to impersonate Vincentio so Baptista will grant Lucentio permission to marry Bianca.

Tailor, Haberdasher, and Servants   Petruchio attacks them when they arrive at his home with new clothing for Katherina.

CHARACTER STUDIES
Katherina

The play's most important character by far, Katherina Minola (the shrew of the play's title) deserves extensive analysis. Shakespeare provides a host of descriptions for Katherina—known about Padua for her unpleasant nature—including shrew, "devil" (1.1), "an irksome brawling scold" (1.2), and "Katherina the curst" (1.2). This small catalog of insults for Katherina (many more exist) reinforces one of Shakespeare's major themes in *The Taming of the Shrew*: identity, and how one's identity can be transformed based on what others think of him or her. For instance, recall the character Christopher Sly, the drunken tinker who eventually believes

Katherina in Act II, Scene 1 of *The Taming of the Shrew*. This is a print from Charles Heath's 1848 edition of *The Heroines of Shakspeare: Comprising the Principal Female Characters in the Plays of the Great Poet*. (Painting by A. Egg; engraving by W. J. Edwards)

he is a lord, simply because numerous characters (including an actual lord) tell Sly that he *is* a lord. Most readers meet Katherina and believe her to be a hard-hearted, angry young woman; she definitely acts like one. However, if people constantly refer to her by names like those listed above, Katherina's identity is reinforced for her again and again, and she continues to be the shrew of Padua. Similarly, Petruchio's reinforcement that Katherina become an obedient wife serves as one reason for Kate's transformation by the end of the play (a point explored in depth below).

The catalysts for Katherina's shrewish nature warrant analysis. Shakespeare, a writer known for his moving and accurate depictions of the human condition, encourages readers to analyze the factors that influenced her to become the shrew she is when readers first meet her. Shakespeare suggests that Katherina's behavior stems primarily from her jealousy over Bianca. No passage captures Katherina's jealousy of her younger sister better than the following:

> KATHERINA. Of all thy suitors, here I charge thee, tell
> Whom thou lovest best: see thou dissemble not.

> BIANCA. Believe me, sister, of all the men alive
> I never yet beheld that special face
> Which I could fancy more than any other.

> KATHERINA. Minion, thou liest. Is't not Hortensio?

> BIANCA. If you affect him, sister, here I swear
> I'll plead for you myself, but you shall have him.

> KATHERINA. O then, belike, you fancy riches more:
> You will have Gremio to keep you fair.

> BIANCA. Is it for him you do envy me so?
> Nay then you jest, and now I well perceive

You have but jested with me all this while:
I prithee, sister Kate, untie my hands.

KATHERINA. If that be jest, then all the rest
   was so.

(2.1)

According to the stage directions, Katherina strikes her sister after the final line of this passage. Katherina, who also ties Bianca's hands together and drags her around, resorts to physical violence because of the fierce jealousy from which she suffers. This passage demonstrates that Katherina desires some attention and feels deeply hurt that suitors only arrive at the Minola home searching for her sister.

Katherina, sadly, also suffers from a lack of attention from her father, Baptista, who clearly favors Bianca. The following words Katherina utters to her father make her pain at being ignored exceptionally clear:

What, will you not suffer me? Nay, now I see
She is your treasure, she must have a husband;
I must dance barefoot on her wedding day
And for your love to her lead apes in hell.
Talk not to me: I will go sit and weep
Till I can find occasion of revenge.

(2.1)

The last line of this passage demonstrates Katherina's true anger, anger that stems from not only the attention suitors give her sister but the attention her father gives her sister as well. Baptista's insulting Katherina must compound her frustration. Consider Baptista's response after Petruchio asks to court Katherina: "But for my daughter Katherina, this I know, / She is not for your turn, the more my grief" (2.1). Though Katherina undoubtedly causes grief for Baptista, such a comment to a potential suitor could damn his daughter's chances at marriage and, likewise, his chances of seeing her provided for by a husband.

Women in Shakespeare's era were expected to be obedient, tamed, and submissive. So, when Petru-

chio tells Katherina "your father hath consented / That you shall be my wife; your dowry 'greed on; / And, will you, nill you, I will marry you" (2.1), she must obey. As further discussed in the analysis of Petruchio's character, women were viewed as property, and since Katherina's dowry had been "agreed on," she would cease to be her father's property and instead would become Petruchio's. Katherina resents her station and situation:

I must, forsooth, be forced
To give my hand opposed against my heart
Unto a mad-brain rudesby full of spleen;
Who woo'd in haste and means to wed at
   leisure. . . .
Now must the world point at poor Katherina,
And say, "Lo, there is mad Petruchio's wife,
If it would please him come and marry her!"

(3.2)

Baptista forces his daughter into the marriage; after the ceremony when the "taming" plot ensues, Petruchio also forces something from his new wife: a change in identity. Forced into her new wifely role, the expectations of which Petruchio consistently reinforces, Katherina in a very short time finds herself behaving obediently (much like Christopher Sly behaving like the lord he thinks he is). Granted, Petruchio forces Katherina to endure hardships—some may even say tortures—during this process of transforming her identity, but the play closes with a happy Kate, one so happy, in fact, that she calls her husband "love":

KATHERINA. Husband, let's follow, to see
   the end of this ado.

PETRUCHIO. First kiss me, Kate, and we
   will.

KATHERINA. What, in the midst of the
   street?

PETRUCHIO. What, art thou ashamed
   of me?

KATHERINA. No, sir, God forbid; but
ashamed to kiss.

PETRUCHIO. Why, then let's home again.
Come, sirrah, let's away.

KATHERINA. Nay, I will give thee a kiss:
now pray thee, love, stay.

PETRUCHIO. Is not this well? Come, my
sweet Kate:
Better once than never, for never too late

(5.1)

Katherina's significant change in identity, from the
shrew of Padua to a happy wife, only reinforces
Shakespeare's suggestion that identity is malleable,
fluctuating, and dependent on how others view a
person.

Petruchio

Petruchio, a bit of a madcap, has only one goal,
which readers learn immediately upon meeting
him: "I come to wive it wealthily in Padua; If
wealthily, then happily in Padua" (1.2). He explains
that he has "come abroad to see the world" and
has done so "haply to wive and thrive" (1.2). Marrying Katherina appeals to Petruchio because of
the large dowry she offers. As a typical example of
marriage during Shakespeare's era—a relationship
established more for security of wealth, property,
and safety of the people involved and less for love,
Petruchio feels extremely pleased with Baptista's
pronouncement that after he dies, Katherina would
receive "one half of my lands, and in possession
twenty thousand crowns" (2.1); this inheritance
would be Katherina's and hence, her husband's.
Though many of today's readers feel troubled by
viewing marriage as a business arrangement (rather
than something entered into out of love and partnership) and by Petruchio's eagerness to build
his fortune, readers must also acknowledge that,
as Katherina's future husband, Petruchio would
provide for his wife, if anything were to happen
to him:

And, for that dowry, I'll assure her of
Her widowhood, be it that she survive me,
In all my lands and leases whatsoever:
Let specialties be therefore drawn between us,
That covenants may be kept on either hand.

(2.1)

One cannot deny Petruchio's greediness, but
the marriage into which he and Katherina enter
provides them both with security, a concept
Katherina addresses in her final speech of the play
when she explains that a woman's husband is her
"lord," "life," and "keeper": in sum, her provider
and protector.

Petruchio reveals himself as a bit of a trickster
and sadist, however, since his pursuit and taming of Katherina are fun and exciting for him,
even though Katherina undergoes some torture
in the process. Petruchio definitely enjoys a challenge, demonstrated by his heightened interest in
Katherina after she smashes a lute on Hortensio's
head: "Now, by the world, it is a lusty wench; I
love her ten times more than e'er I did: O, how
I long to have some chat with her!" (2.1). Several
of Petruchio and Katherina's "chats," as he calls
them, receive detailed analysis in the Key Passages
section.

Though Baptista has already agreed to the
match, Petruchio makes a game of taming Kate.
The main technique Petruchio uses to tame her
involves torturing Katherina, which demonstrates
its effectiveness beginning at their marriage ceremony. Petruchio doubly embarrasses Kate, first
by arriving extremely late for the ceremony, and
second by the manner in which he finally appears.
Biondello explains Petruchio's appearance:

Why, Petruchio is coming in a new hat and an
old jerkin, a pair of old breeches thrice turned,
a pair of boots that have been candle-cases,
one buckled, another laced, an old rusty sword
ta'en out of the town-armory, with a broken
hilt, and chapeless; with two broken points:
his horse hipped with an old mothy saddle and
stirrups of no kindred. (3.2)

occurs, the woman is formally considered part of the man's property.

Petruchio does not shy away from using more ruthless methods to transform Katherina into an obedient woman and wife; as the play progresses, Petruchio's techniques become more sadistic, and some readers compare him to a torturer. For instance, embarrassing her at their wedding causes Katherina emotional distress, but depriving her of food and sleep cause her physical pain. Regardless, Petruchio explains that these methods allow him to begin his "reign," which he "hopes to end successfully" (4.1).

In Act 4, Scene 5, Petruchio appears to have obtained victory when Katherina relents and agrees with him that, even though they travel in broad daylight, the moon shines in the sky, just as Petruchio observes. A short time later, Katherina also obeys Petruchio's commands to kiss him in the street in front of onlookers, to remove a cap she wears because he does not like it, and to give her famous "obedience speech." Some readers believe that Katherina merely placates Petruchio and finally decides to play along with him (though, after not having eaten or slept well in days, it seems more likely that Katherina's will has finally broken). Whether Kate is genuine in her convictions does not matter to Petruchio though: He only cares about her obeying his wishes. In turn, Shakespeare reveals that Petruchio cares only about being obeyed, not loved.

Lucentio

Lucentio represents the obsessed lover who, without knowing much about Bianca, seeks to make her his wife. Lucentio provides a contrast to Petruchio who, fully aware of Katherina's tempestuous temper, still courts her. Lucentio and Petruchio also serve as opposites of one another because Lucentio desires Bianca because of her beauty, whereas Petruchio desires Katherina because of her dowry. Lucentio's pursuit of Bianca without knowing more about her character may shock some modern readers, but a common Renaissance ideology suggested that a person

John Drew as Petruchio in an 1888 production of *The Taming of the Shrew,* in this photograph published by the Gebbie & Husson Company

Petruchio knows that arriving at their marriage ceremony in such a manner will only demonstrate to Kate what he is capable of, what he is willing to do to tame and break her. Quickly following this episode, Petruchio drags Katherina away from their wedding celebration, and in another of his most famous speeches (analyzed in Key Passages), Petruchio claims Katherina as his property, comparing her to his field, barn, horse, and ox, among other things. He exemplifies the Elizabethan belief that women are goods, and when a marriage with an outwardly beautiful appearance must also be inwardly beautiful; in sum, in the Renaissance, if a person was beautiful, they were also assumed to be good and kind. Likewise, a person who was unattractive or who suffered from a physical deformity was often (and unfairly) assumed to have bad or even evil intentions. Many Shakespearean scholars agree that this philosophy contributed to Shakespeare's making the character of Richard III more physically grotesque than he was in real life, simply to signify his evil nature. Perhaps Lucentio believes the notion that one's outward appearance symbolizes his or her inherent nature, and that is why the stunningly beautiful Bianca appeals to him so greatly.

Lucentio makes both his interest in Bianca and his desperation to have her for himself obvious:

> Tranio, I burn, I pine, I perish, Tranio,
> If I achieve not this young modest girl.
> Counsel me, Tranio, for I know thou canst;
> Assist me, Tranio, for I know thou wilt.
>
> (1.1)

Lucentio must depend on the help of his servant to win Bianca for him; this plotline also suggests that not much substance exists in Lucentio and Bianca's relationship, since both know little about one another. Lucentio, for nearly the entire play, wears a disguise: few know the real Lucentio. Further, he tells Biondello that he must disguise himself because he killed a man. (This passage is further analyzed in the Difficult Passages section.) Lucentio's story is probably a lie, and as such, Shakespeare reinforces Lucentio as a fake, a man with a fondness for disguising who he truly is.

Though a lack of knowledge of one's partner would not have been unusual for people of Lucentio and Bianca's station, Shakespeare emphasizes the lack of connection between Bianca and Lucentio; Bianca's refusal to answer Lucentio's call at the end of the play—revealing a defiant side of her character—also suggests that these two, unacquainted with one another, will soon find themselves acquainted with problems.

Bianca

Bianca, the love object of many men in the play, provides a stark contrast to her sister, Katherina the shrew. Though she appears sweeter and humbler than her sister, Bianca proves to be a woman with a private independence that shocks her future husband, Lucentio, and readers as well.

As discussed in the in-depth analysis of Katherina's character, one possible catalyst for Katherina's shrewish nature may be the attention that men lavish on Bianca instead of her; even their father favors Bianca far above Katherina. The primary reason Bianca's suitors feel so taken with her is because of her beauty. Consider, for instance, Lucentio's description of Bianca: "Tranio, I saw her coral lips to move / And with her breath she did perfume the air: / Sacred and sweet was all I saw in her" (1.1). Her "coral lips" and breath that "did perfume the air" typify Shakespeare's ideal of beauty. His descriptions of Bianca are the opposite of details in Shakespeare's "Sonnet 130," a poem about a woman who is far from beautiful since "coral is far more red than her lips' red." The woman in Shakespeare's "Sonnet 130" also has horrible breath: "And in some perfumes is there more delight than in the breath that from my mistress reeks." The way Lucentio describes Bianca completely inverts the descriptions in Shakespeare's sonnet, thus depicting her as an example of ideal beauty.

Lucentio's claim that the "sacred and sweet was all I saw in [Bianca]" explains his surprise—as well as the surprise of readers—when, at the end of the play, the sweet new wife refuses to heed her husband's call, causing him to lose the bet he wagered with Petruchio and Hortensio. The following dialogue seems unnatural for the Bianca of earlier in the play:

> BIANCA. Fie! what a foolish duty call you this?
>
> LUCENTIO. I would your duty were as foolish too:
> The wisdom of your duty, fair Bianca,

Hath cost me an hundred crowns since
supper-time.

BIANCA. The more fool you, for laying on my
duty.

The character of Bianca, then, reminds readers of
the old cliché that one must never judge a book
by its cover. Most readers consider Bianca sweet
and kind, but she would naturally appear so in
comparison to the Katherina we meet early in
the play. Truthfully, Bianca is more deceptive and
disobedient than her sister (she does, after all, run
away with Lucentio to marry him, in contrast to
Katherina, who waits diligently by her father's side
on her wedding day).

Christopher Sly

Even though he qualifies as a minor character in
The Taming of the Shrew, Christopher Sly remains
significant. Shakespeare uses the Sly character to
introduce readers to major symbols and themes of
the play, including clothing, disguise, and identity.

When the lord and his servants dress Sly as a
lord, intent on making him believe he actually is
a lord, Shakespeare comments on clothing as a
symbol and how, in the Renaissance, clothes symbolized a person's status. Sly, confused that he no
longer wears the clothes he donned as a tinker, asks

What, would you make me mad? Am not I
  Christopher
Sly, old Sly's son of Burtonheath, by birth a
pedlar, by education a cardmaker, by
  transmutation a
bear-herd, and now by present profession a
  tinker?

(Induction.1)

His similar questions, "Am I a lord? and have I
such a lady? Or do I dream? or have I dream'd
till now?" emphasize the themes of disguise and
identity that Shakespeare highlights through the
performance of *The Taming of the Shrew* to follow,
staged for Sly's enjoyment.

Through the character of Sly, Shakespeare also
suggests that once a person is thrust into a role—
like Sly into that of a lord or Katherina into that of
a wife—they adapt to the demands and expectations of that role. Sly asks time and again for "the
smallest pot of ale," but when he—a lord—has a
wife, he suddenly demands the attention of his wife
as well: "Come, madam wife," he tells her, "sit by
my side and let the world slip: we shall ne'er be
younger" (Induction.2). Convinced by the lord
and his servants that he is also a lord, Sly has no
trouble suddenly acting like one.

DIFFICULTIES OF THE PLAY

The Taming of the Shrew, a play largely concerned
with the ideas of identity and disguise, poses difficulties in comprehension for readers because of
the many characters who pretend to be someone
else. Tranio pretends to be Lucentio for Bianca;
Lucentio presents himself as Cambio, the tutor, to
Bianca; while wooing Bianca, Hortensio disguises
himself as another of her tutors, Licio; and the
Pedant poses as Lucentio's father, Vincentio, to
address Baptista's concerns before he will allow
Lucentio to marry Bianca. Readers feel challenged
and confused by so many characters also doubling
as other characters.

Complicating this matter of disguise, all the
characters who disguise themselves as someone else
concern the secondary plot, the courtship of Bianca
and Lucentio. Readers, better acquainted with
such main characters as Katherina and Petruchio,
naturally struggle more with secondary characters
since Shakespeare presents them to his readers less
often. When these secondary characters also take
on personas other than their own, managing the
details can be quite difficult for readers.

Another difficulty in *The Taming of the Shrew* is
the prologue to the play, known as the Induction.
Here, Shakespeare introduces readers to the lov-
able Christopher Sly, a drunken commoner whom
a lord and his friends trick into thinking that he is
a nobleman with a wife. The lord hires a group of
players to perform *The Taming of the Shrew* for Sly,
but Shakespeare does not revisit Sly's story at the

end of the play (or after Act I, for that matter). The presence of this Induction suggests that the play that follows *(The Taming of the Shrew)* is a farce, a production used only to entertain. Critics grapple with the question yet today, wondering if the tale of the taming should be viewed as a mockery of Elizabethan values or a commendation of them.

Related to the concept that the play possibly is a farce, readers often have difficulty puzzling out the true intentions of each character. Petruchio, motivated by money, decides to marry Katherina based on her monetary situation; does he, however, also feel attracted to her? Perhaps Petruchio grows fond of Katherina and a real emotional bond develops between them during the course of the play, before they kiss each other happily at the end of Act 5. Similarly, Katherina's well-known and often quoted "obedience speech" at the close of the play, for instance, leaves some readers struggling with the true dynamics of Katherina and Petruchio's relationship: Does he tame her and break her spirit, or is the entire plot a ruse designed to make readers laugh? No definite answers to these questions exist.

The kneeling nobleman convinces Sly that he is a lord while the players prepare for a performance of *The Taming of the Shrew* in the Induction, Scene 2 of *The Taming of the Shrew*. This is a print from the Boydell Shakespeare Gallery project, which was first conceived in 1786 and lasted until 1805. *(Painting by Robert Smirke; engraving by Robert Thew)*

KEY PASSAGES
Induction, Scene 2, 63–77

LORD. Thou art a lord and nothing but a
   lord;
Thou hast a lady far more beautiful
Than any woman in this waning age.

SERVINGMAN. And till the tears that she
   hath shed for thee
Like envious floods o'errun her lovely face
She was the fairest creature in the world,
And yet she is inferior to none.

SLY. Am I a lord? and have I such a lady?
Or do I dream? or have I dream'd till now?
I do not sleep; I see, I hear, I speak;
I smell sweet savors and I feel soft things:
Upon my life, I am a lord indeed
And not a tinker nor Christopher Sly.
Well, bring our lady hither to our sight
And once again, a pot o' the smallest ale.

This passage remains key to a reader's understanding of *The Taming of the Shrew*. In this excerpt, the lord convinces Christopher Sly that he is a lord and not "a tinker nor Christopher Sly" as he has always considered himself to be. Shakespeare reminds readers that the play that ensues—the actual performance of *The Taming of the Shrew*—is a farce, simply because of the existence of the frame story involving Christopher Sly. More important, though, Shakespeare introduces a theme he will emphasize and explore in depth throughout the rest of the play: identity.

Convinced by the lord and his servingmen that he is a lord, Christopher Sly suddenly begins acting like a lord. He commands the servants to "bring our lady hither to our sight," and this forceful command to have his wife brought to him demonstrates his newfound confidence in the role as lord, a stark contrast to his power as a tinker. This situation with Christopher Sly foreshadows the fate of Kate. Formerly a spinster, Kate becomes a wife; indeed, with time, she begins acting like a wife as well. Much like Christopher Sly, Katherina's iden-

tity is transformed to meet the expectations placed upon her in her new role.

Similar to the theme of identity is the motif of disguise, a motif common throughout the entire play. Though Christopher Sly does not disguise himself voluntarily, the lord disguising him as a lord foreshadows the host of disguises that will soon occur in the play: Tranio as Lucentio, Lucentio as Cambio, Hortensio as Licio, the Pedant as Vincentio, and so forth.

Act I, Scene 2, 48–76

HORTENSIO. What happy gale
Blows you to Padua here from old Verona?

PETRUCHIO. Such wind as scatters young
  men through the world
To seek their fortunes farther than at home,
Where small experience grows. But in a few,
Signior Hortensio, thus it stands with me:
Antonio, my father, is deceas'd
And I have thrust myself into this maze,
Happily to wive and thrive as best I may.
Crowns in my purse I have and goods at home
And so am come abroad to see the world.

HORTENSIO. Petruchio, shall I then come
  roundly to thee
And wish thee to a shrewd ill-favor'd wife?
Thou'dst thank me but a little for my counsel
And yet I'll promise thee she shall be rich,
And very rich: but thou'rt too much my friend
And I'll not wish thee to her.

PETRUCHIO. Signior Hortensio, 'twixt such
  friends as we
Few words suffice; and therefore, if thou know
One rich enough to be Petruchio's wife,
As wealth is burthen of my wooing dance,
Be she as foul as was Florentius' love,
As old as Sibyl, and as curst and shrowd
As Socrates' Zentippe, or a worse,
She moves me not, or not removes, at least,
Affection's edge in me, were she as rough
As are the swelling Adriatic seas.

I come to wive it wealthily in Padua;
If wealthily, then happily in Padua.

This passage makes readers privy to Petruchio's goals: "I come to wive it wealthily in Padua; / If wealthily, then happily in Padua." When Hortensio reveals he knows of a woman who would meet Petruchio's financial needs, he tells him that she is "shrewd" and of "ill-favor" and that he would not wish such a woman upon his friend. Petruchio, on the other hand, explains he will weather a host of problems from a woman if she has a sizable dowry. He refers to the story of Florentius, a knight who was forced to marry an old and ugly woman, and says he would not mind suffering the same fate. He also says he would not mind marrying a woman like Socrates' wife, Xanthippe, who was known for her tempestuous nature, if he was assured the right fortune because of the marriage.

Petruchio's motives become clear when he tells Hortensio that he does not care about a woman's temperament but only about her financial background. He does not concern himself with marrying for love, which demonstrates itself repeatedly in his cruel behavior toward Katherina. He asserts that he will marry any woman, no matter her character, for the right price. His behavior in this scene also highlights another important theme of *The Taming of the Shrew*: greed. Petruchio is not the only man who places high value on money; Baptista, Katherina, and Bianca's father are also guilty of such behavior.

Act II, Scene 1, 197–220

KATHERINA. I knew you at the first,
You were a movable.

PETRUCHIO. Why, what's a movable?

KATHERINA. A joint stool.

PETRUCHIO. Thou hast hit it: come sit on me.

KATHERINA. Asses are made to bear and so
  are you.

PETRUCHIO. Women are made to bear and
so are you.

KATHERINA. No such jade as you, if me you
mean.

PETRUCHIO. Alas! good Kate, I will not
burthen thee;
For, knowing thee to be but young and light—

KATHERINA. Too light for such a swain as
you to catch
And yet as heavy as my weight should be.

PETRUCHIO. Should be! should—buzz!

KATHERINA. Well ta'en, and like a buzzard.

PETRUCHIO. O slow-wing'd turtle! shall a
buzzard take thee?

KATHERINA. Ay, for a turtle, as he takes a
buzzard.

PETRUCHIO. Come, come, you wasp: I' faith
you are too angry.

KATHERINA. If I be waspish best beware my
sting.

PETRUCHIO. My remedy is then to pluck it
out.

KATHERINA. Ay, if the fool could find it
where it lies.

PETRUCHIO. Who knows not where a wasp
does wear his sting?
In his tail.

KATHERINA. In his tongue.

PETRUCHIO. Whose tongue?

KATHERINA. Yours, if you talk of tales; and
so farewell.

PETRUCHIO. What! with my tongue in your
tail? nay, come again.
Good Kate, I am a gentleman.

KATHERINA. That I'll try.

She strikes him.

This brief passage is key to *The Taming of the
Shrew* because it truly captures the fiery dynamic
between Petruchio and Katherina. This selection
from the play demonstrates the first instance that
Katherina and Petruchio exchange words with one
another. The passage is laced with insults and sexually suggestive language, thus emphasizing and
foreshadowing the nature of Petruchio and Katherina's ensuing relationship.

Katherina calls Petruchio a "movable," meaning
a piece of furniture, and then expounds on this barb
by calling Petruchio a "joint stool," a stool made
by a joiner, and slang for an insult in Shakespeare's
era. The three lines following this insult highlight
Petruchio's confidence and his limited views on
women. Abounding with confidence, he first tells
Katherina to "come sit on me," a phrase with a literal meaning and a suggestive meaning. Literally,
he asks her to sit on his lap; suggestively, he implies
he would like her to have sex with him. Kate then
fires a pun, "Asses are made to bear and so are
you": literally, a donkey—an ass—bears goods or
its owner, and simultaneously, a person's "ass" or
bottom bears his weight when he sits. The double
meaning here, as well as Katherina insinuating that
Petruchio himself is an ass, demonstrates her wit-
tiness. Petruchio's response confirms his views on
women: that they live to bear children and, in turn,
serve their master's sexual needs. Katherina then
takes her turn in making a sexual allusion, when
she calls Petruchio "a jade," a word that refers to
a useless horse; it is also suggestive because Katherina's comparison implies that Petruchio, as a useless horse, has little energy, especially for breeding.

The following images relate to birds and wasps,
creatures that can fly. Shakespeare's imagery in this
passages functions to remind readers that these
two lovers flit and dart around and away from

one another; later in the play, Shakespeare builds on this imagery when Petruchio compares taming Katherina to taming a falcon.

Shakespeare also laces the end of this passage with sexual innuendos. The "talk of tales" Katherina mentions also has a double meaning, like so many other phrases in Shakespeare's canon. "Tales" can refer to gossip, much like "tall tales" or stories. On the other hand, "tales" is also slang for genitalia; in turn, Petruchio's comment about having his tongue in Katherina's "tale," followed by his declaration that he is a gentleman, serves as a great comedic scene and emphasizes the sexual tension and connection between the two future lovers.

This passage also provides an excellent example of *stichomythia*, a dramatic technique in which two characters engage in dialogue in which they invert each other's meaning. Petruchio and Katherina practice *stichomythia* when they exchange insults throughout this passage.

Act III, Scene 2, 217–241

PETRUCHIO. O Kate! content thee; prithee, be not angry.

KATHERINA. I will be angry; what hast thou to do?
Father, be quiet, he shall stay my leisure.

GREMIO. Ay, marry, sir, now it begins to work.

KATHERINA. Gentlemen, forward to the bridal dinner:
I see a woman may be made a fool
If she had not a spirit to resist.

PETRUCHIO. They shall go forward, Kate, at thy command.
Obey the bride, you that attend on her;
Go to the feast, revel and domineer,
Carouse full measure to her maidenhead,
Be mad and merry, or go hang yourselves;
But for my bonny Kate, she must with me.
Nay, look not big, nor stamp, nor stare, nor fret;
I will be master of what is mine own.

She is my goods, my chattels; she is my house,
My household stuff, my field, my barn,
My horse, my ox, my ass, my anything;
And here she stands, touch her whoever dare;
I'll bring mine action on the proudest he
That stops my way in Padua. Grumio,
Draw forth thy weapon, we are beset with thieves;
Rescue thy mistress, if thou be a man.
Fear not, sweet wench; they shall not touch thee, Kate:
I'll buckler thee against a million.

Exeunt Petruchio, Katherina [and Grumio].

This passage occurs directly after Petruchio and Katherina's marriage ceremony. Petruchio has thoroughly embarrassed Katherina by arriving late, dressed shabbily. This passage illustrates Kate's independent nature but also shows Petruchio's ideology about marriage and women.

Katherina says "a woman may be made a fool / If she had not a spirit to resist." Not wanting to look the fool again—since Petruchio just made an incredible fool of her at their wedding—Katherina

After their wedding, Petruchio commands Katherina to leave the celebrations in Act III, Scene 2 of *The Taming of the Shrew*. This is a print from the Boydell Shakespeare Gallery project, which was first conceived in 1786 and lasted until 1805. (*Painting by Francis Wheatley; engraving by Jean Pierre Simon*)

"resists" and orders that she and Petruchio stay at the wedding celebration, even though Petruchio wants to leave. Essentially, this passage functions as the last scene in which Katherina behaves truly independently and stubbornly, since henceforth Petruchio will enact his plan to break her, mentally and physically.

Petruchio's language here reveals his (and simultaneously the Elizabethan) ideology concerning marriage and wives. Katherina is now Petruchio's property and nothing more. He commands that "she must with me," adding that "I will be master of what is mine own." He compares her to other common property a man might own, including his home and livestock. The most significant indicator of Petruchio's ideology that woman are property is his threat, "touch her whoever dare; / I'll bring mine action on the proudest he / That stops my way in Padua." Essentially, Petruchio says that anyone who dares to touch what belongs to him will suffer the consequences. Though Petruchio says that thieves have arrived at the celebration and may steal his wife, truthfully no such event has occurred and Petruchio, with his now most valuable piece of property, simply seeks a fast escape.

Act IV, Scene 1, 171–214

KATHERINA. I pray you, husband, be not so disquiet:
The meat was well if you were so contented.

PETRUCHIO. I tell thee, Kate, 'twas burnt and dried away
And I expressly am forbid to touch it,
For it engenders choler, planteth anger,
And better 'twere that both of us did fast,
Since, of ourselves, ourselves are choleric,
Than feed it with such overroasted flesh.
Be patient; tomorrow 't shall be mended,
Come, I will bring thee to thy bridal chamber.

Exeunt.
Re-enter Servants severally.

NATHANIEL. Peter, didst ever see the like?

PETER. He kills her in her own humour.

Re-enter Curtis, a Servant.

GRUMIO. Where is he?

CURTIS. In her chamber, making a sermon of continency to her;
And rails, and swears, and rates, that she, poor soul,
Knows not which way to stand, to look, to speak,
And sits as one new-risen from a dream.
Away, away! for he is coming hither. [*Exeunt.*]

Re-enter Petruchio.

PETRUCHIO. Thus have I politicly begun my reign
And 'tis my hope to end successfully.
My falcon now is sharp and passing empty
And till she stoop she must not be full-gorged,
For then she never looks upon her lure.
Another way I have to man my haggard,
To make her come and know her keeper's call;
That is, to watch her, as we watch these kites
That bate and beat and will not be obedient.
She eat no meat today, nor none shall eat;
Last night she slept not, nor tonight she shall not;
As with the meat, some undeserved fault
I'll find about the making of the bed
And here I'll fling the pillow, there the bolster,
This way the coverlet, another way the sheets.
Ay, and amid this hurly I intend
That all is done in reverend care of her;
And in conclusion she shall watch all night;
And if she chance to nod I'll rail and brawl
And with the clamor keep her still awake.
This is a way to kill a wife with kindness,
And thus I'll curb her mad and headstrong humour.
He that knows better to tame a shrew,
Now let him speak: 'tis charity to show.

In this passage, Shakespeare reveals two significant plot elements: Katherina's strong and independent nature has begun to crumble, and Petruchio informs the audience of the plan he will use to continue to tame Katherina. This passage follows Petruchio's explosion at his servants that the meat served for dinner was burned. The meat was actually edible and prepared well, but under the guise of protecting his wife, Petruchio demands that she not eat the food in case it could sicken her.

After Petruchio escorts Katherina to bed, the servants—Nathaniel, Peter, Grumio, and Curtis—marvel over their master's techniques. Peter makes a keen observation when he states, "He kills her in her own humor," implying that Petruchio has adopted Katherina's strong-willed and angry nature to subdue her. When Grumio asks where Petruchio is, Curtis relays that their master "rails and swears and rates" while poor Katherina "knows not which way to stand, to look, to speak" and "sits as one new-risen from a dream." In other words, Petruchio's ranting and raging at Katherina has so unsettled and shocked her that she appears completely dumbfounded.

His servants leave and Petruchio arrives; he stands alone on stage. In one of the most famous passages of the play, Petruchio informs readers he has begun his "reign," a reign during which he essentially plans to torture Katherina into submission by depriving her of food and sleep. Ironically, Petruchio claims that in this manner he "will kill [his] wife with kindness." His goal to "curb her mad and headstrong humor" will only be met with such drastic means.

Shakespeare's choice to have Petruchio deliver this speech on stage alone deserves analysis, since Petruchio makes his plans privy to the audience and no one else. By sharing his plans with the audience, Petruchio makes those readers or viewers accomplices in his scheme to torture and tame Katherina. This disclosure of information also reinforces the play's farcical nature; surely this situation differs from an aside made by Richard III, who expects his viewers to watch in horror as he executes one person after another. Petruchio's plan to "kill his wife with kindness," coupled with his

revelation only to the audience, illustrates that he wants viewers and readers to know his plans and to chuckle along with him as they happen, rather than being shocked by the poor treatment to which he subjects Katherina.

Act IV, Scene 5, 1–23

PETRUCHIO. Come on, a God's name; once
  more toward our father's.
Good Lord, how bright and goodly shines the
  moon!

KATHERINA. The moon! the sun: it is not
  moonlight now.

PETRUCHIO. I say it is the moon that shines
  so bright.

KATHERINA. I know it is the sun that shines
  so bright.

PETRUCHIO. Now, by my mother's son, and
  that's myself,
It shall be moon or star or what I list,
Or ere I journey to your father's house.
Go on and fetch our horses back again.
Evermore cross'd and cross'd; nothing but
  cross'd!

HORTENSIO. Say as he says or we shall
  never go.

KATHERINA. Forward, I pray, since we have
  come so far,
And be it moon or sun or what you please.
And if you please to call it a rush-candle,
Henceforth I vow it shall be so for me.

PETRUCHIO. I say it is the moon.

KATHERINA. I know it is the moon.

PETRUCHIO. Nay, then you lie; it is the
  blessed sun.

KATHERINA. Then God be bless'd, it is the
   blessed sun!
But sun it is not when you say it is not,
And the moon changes even as your mind.
What you will have it nam'd, even that it is;
And so it shall be for Katherina.

HORTENSIO. Petruchio, go thy ways; the
   field is won.

This passage warrants analysis, because in it,
Katherina buckles and finally agrees with Petruchio's claims, no matter how outrageous they
might be. The passage also begs questions about
how genuine Katherina is and whether or not her
genuineness even matters to Petruchio. Katherina
tries to correct him at first by saying, "The moon!
the sun: it is not moonlight now," Petruchio rails
against her, claiming that things will always be
as he sees them, or as he says, "what I list." He
threatens to deprive Katherina of visiting her
family if she does not stop "crossing" (defying)
him. Though readers may question Katherina's
desire to see the family whom she seems to care
little about, one must also acknowledge that
with hardly any food or sleep, perhaps Katherina
remembers the comforts of the Minola home in
Padua, and for that reason alone she longs to go
there.

Hortensio tells Katherina flatly, "Say as he says
or we shall never go": In other words, Hortensio
informs Katherina that if she does not agree with
Petruchio, he will cancel the trip to Padua and they
will turn back for Petruchio's home. This advice
acts as a catalyst for Katherina to suddenly agree
with her husband and his observations from then
on. Her sudden obedience, however, prompts readers to consider whether Katherina's agreement is
genuine. Has she been broken, or has she decided
to simply humor Petruchio? More important,
Petruchio's further manipulation of Katherina in
this scene implies that her intentions mean nothing
to Petruchio, suggesting Katherina and her feelings
are meaningless to Petruchio; all he seems to desire
is her blind, unflinching obedience.

Act V, Scene 1, 147–155

KATHERINA. Husband, let's follow, to see
   the end of this ado.

PETRUCHIO. First kiss me, Kate, and we
   will.

KATHERINA. What, in the midst of the
   street?

PETRUCHIO. What, art thou ashamed of me?

KATHERINA. No, sir, God forbid; but
   ashamed to kiss.

PETRUCHIO. Why, then let's home again.
   Come, sirrah, let's away.

KATHERINA. Nay, I will give thee a kiss:
   now pray thee, love, stay.

PETRUCHIO. Is not this well? Come, my
   sweet Kate:
Better once than never, for never too late.
Exeunt

This passage remains key in depicting Katherina's transformation (whether genuine or feigned)
into Petruchio's obedient wife. Like the last passage discussed, when Katherina agrees with Petruchio's completely illogical observations, in this
passage she demonstrates further that she has been
tamed and will respect his wishes. She explains she
is "ashamed" only to kiss on a public street (even
though the rest of their company have relocated
inside Baptista's house), and not at all ashamed of
her husband, Katherina still kisses him, because he
demands it.

Petruchio's final lines in this passage also warrant attention. His question, "Is not this well?"
may be directed at Katherina but, simultaneously,
strikes a chord with Shakespeare's readers and
viewers, who must feel some contentment at seeing Petruchio and Katherina share (what seems to
be) a heartfelt kiss. Petruchio's comment, "Better

once than never, for never too late," acknowledges how he has anticipated this kiss, since sharing a kiss like this once is, as he says, "better . . . than never." It seems as if Petruchio, whose intentions about marrying Katherina seemed suspect, not only wanted to secure a fortune in marrying her, but also wanted to find a partner he could connect with emotionally and physically.

Act V, Scene 2, 100–131

KATHERINA. What is your will, sir, that you send for me?

PETRUCHIO. Where is your sister, and Hortensio's wife?

KATHERINA. They sit conferring by the parlor fire.

PETRUCHIO. Go fetch them hither: if they deny to come.
Swinge me them soundly forth unto their husbands:
Away, I say, and bring them hither straight.

Exit KATHERINA

LUCENTIO. Here is a wonder, if you talk of a wonder.

HORTENSIO. And so it is: I wonder what it bodes.

PETRUCHIO. Marry, peace it bodes, and love and quiet life,
And awful rule and right supremacy;
And, to be short, what not, that's sweet and happy?

BAPTISTA. Now, fair befal thee, good Petruchio!
The wager thou hast won; and I will add
Unto their losses twenty thousand crowns;
Another dowry to another daughter,
For she is changed, as she had never been.

PETRUCHIO. Nay, I will win my wager better yet
And show more sign of her obedience,
Her new-built virtue and obedience.
See where she comes and brings your froward wives
As prisoners to her womanly persuasion.
Re-enter KATHERINA, with BIANCA and WIDOW

Katherina, that cap of yours becomes you not:
Off with that bauble, throw it under-foot.

WIDOW. Lord, let me never have a cause to sigh,
Till I be brought to such a silly pass!

BIANCA. Fie! what a foolish duty call you this?

LUCENTIO. I would your duty were as foolish too:
The wisdom of your duty, fair Bianca,
Hath cost me an hundred crowns since supper-time.

BIANCA. The more fool you, for laying on my duty.

PETRUCHIO. Katherina, I charge thee, tell these headstrong women
What duty they do owe their lords and husbands.

This passage provides Shakespeare's readers with a comparison among the three brides: Katherina, Bianca, and Hortensio's widow. After making a wager to see whose wife would come when called by her husband, only Katherina arrived, whom Petruchio sent to fetch the other wives. The obedient Katherina provides a stark contrast to Bianca and the widow, who not only refuse to come when called at first but rebuke their husbands for participating in such a "silly pass," as the widow describes it. Bianca finds the wager "foolish" and calls her husband a "fool" for betting on her obedience.

This passage is also important because of the context in which Katherina behaves obediently. In the previous passage analyzed, Katherina agrees to kiss Petruchio in public, but not in the presence of her father. When she heeds Petruchio's call in Baptista's home, however, she demonstrates her unflinching obedience for not only her husband but her father as well. Shakespeare makes Baptista's shock at Katherina's transformation obvious:

> The wager thou hast won; and I will add
> Unto their losses twenty thousand crowns;
> Another dowry to another daughter,
> For she is changed, as she had never been.

The attention Petruchio pays Katherina provides a dynamic far different that the one she shared with her father, who often disregarded Katherina in favor for his younger, seemingly more pleasant daughter, Bianca. Having the attention and protection of a man causes Katherina's jealousy and anger to abide.

Act V, Scene 2, 130–180

PETRUCHIO. Katherina, I charge thee, tell these headstrong women
What duty they do owe their lords and husbands.

WIDOW. Come, come, you're mocking: we will have no telling.

PETRUCHIO. Come on, I say; and first begin with her.

WIDOW. She shall not.

PETRUCHIO. I say she shall: and first begin with her.

KATHERINA. Fie, fie! unknit that threatening unkind brow,
And dart not scornful glances from those eyes,
To wound thy lord, thy king, thy governor:
It blots thy beauty as frosts do bite the meads,
Confounds thy fame as whirlwinds shake fair buds,
And in no sense is meet or amiable.
A woman moved is like a fountain troubled,
Muddy, ill-seeming, thick, bereft of beauty;
And while it is so, none so dry or thirsty
Will deign to sip or touch one drop of it.
Thy husband is thy lord, thy life, thy keeper,
Thy head, thy sovereign; one that cares for thee,
And for thy maintenance commits his body
To painful labor both by sea and land,
To watch the night in storms, the day in cold,
Whilst thou lie'st warm at home, secure and safe;
And craves no other tribute at thy hands
But love, fair looks and true obedience;
Too little payment for so great a debt.
Such duty as the subject owes the prince
Even such a woman oweth to her husband;
And when she is froward, peevish, sullen, sour,
And not obedient to his honest will,
What is she but a foul contending rebel
And graceless traitor to her loving lord?
I am ashamed that women are so simple
To offer war where they should kneel for peace;
Or seek for rule, supremacy and sway,
When they are bound to serve, love and obey.
Why are our bodies soft and weak and smooth,
Unapt to toil and trouble in the world,
But that our soft conditions and our hearts
Should well agree with our external parts?
Come, come, you froward and unable worms!
My mind hath been as big as one of yours,
My heart as great, my reason haply more,
To bandy word for word and frown for frown;
But now I see our lances are but straws,
Our strength as weak, our weakness past compare,
That seeming to be most which we indeed least are.
Then vail your stomachs, for it is no boot,
And place your hands below your husband's foot:

In token of which duty, if he please,
My hand is ready; may it do him ease.

PETRUCHIO. Why, there's a wench! Come
   on, and kiss me, Kate.

This passage, found at the very close of the play, remains key to *The Taming of the Shrew*. Like the passage analyzed earlier, one must question Katherina's genuineness; does she truly believe what she says, or is her final speech an act that allows Petruchio to think that he has, indeed, tamed Katherina? Perhaps Katherina herself has transformed into the master manipulator and simply plays along with Petruchio to please him, so that she might also live a peaceful, comfortable life, even if she must appear as though she has lost some of her independence?

Consider the fate Katherina would face if she had not found a husband, either in Padua or England, at the end of the 16th century. Her claims that "Thy husband is thy lord, thy life, thy keeper / Thy head, thy sovereign" most likely resonated with Shakespeare's female audience members in particular and do not necessarily need to be read as sexist. She may be recognizing an important and difficult situation, true for women all over the world 400 years ago, which is that a woman needed what a man could provide for her, things she could not provide for herself, including a home and protection.

DIFFICULT PASSAGES
Act I, Scene 1, 226–242

LUCENTIO. Sirrah, where have you been?

BIONDELLO. Where have I been! Nay, how
   now! where are you?
Master, has my fellow Tranio stolen your
   clothes? Or
you stolen his? or both? pray, what's the news?

LUCENTIO. Sirrah, come hither: 'tis no time
   to jest,
And therefore frame your manners to the time.
Your fellow Tranio here, to save my life,

Puts my apparel and my countenance on,
And I for my escape have put on his;
For in a quarrel since I came ashore
I kill'd a man and fear I was descried:
Wait you on him, I charge you, as becomes,
While I make way from hence to save my life:
You understand me?

BIONDELLO. I, sir! Ne'er a whit.

LUCENTIO. And not a jot of Tranio in your
   mouth:
Tranio is changed into Lucentio.

This passage presents some difficulties for readers because of a detail Lucentio reveals about himself. When Biondello arrives and asks Lucentio why he and Tranio have exchanged clothing, Lucentio tells Biondello that "in a quarrel I came ashore / I kill'd a man and fear I was descried." Readers feel troubled by Lucentio's revelation that he is, in fact, a murderer. His desire to disguise himself and then woo Bianca takes on a troubling dynamic if readers take Lucentio at his word. However, scholars tend to agree that Lucentio's revelation to Biondello is fake, and that Lucentio fabricated the story of his murdering a man to scare Biondello into silence. Since Shakespeare does not reveal Lucentio's intentions to his audience, however, this passage continues to present readers with difficulty since Lucentio, if capable of committing murder, appears far more manipulative and ruthless in his pursuit of Bianca.

Act III, Scene 1, 26–46

BIANCA. Where left we last?

LUCENTIO. Here, madam:
'Hic ibat Simois; hic est Sigeia tellus;
Hic steterat Priami regia celsa senis.'

BIANCA. Construe them.

LUCENTIO. 'Hic ibat,' as I told you before,
   'Simois,' I am

Lucentio, 'hic est,' son unto Vincentio of Pisa, 'Sigeia tellus,' disguised thus to get your love; 'Hic steterat,' and that Lucentio that comes a-wooing, 'Priami,' is my man Tranio, 'regia,' bearing my port, 'celsa senis,' that we might beguile the old pantaloon.

HORTENSIO. Madam, my instrument's in tune.

BIANCA. Let's hear. O fie! the treble jars.

LUCENTIO. Spit in the hole, man, and tune again.

Lucentio and Hortensio disguise themselves as tutors in order to confess their feelings to Bianca in Act III, Scene I of *The Taming of the Shrew*. This drawing was designed for the Chiswick edition of Shakespeare, published in 1900. *(Illustration by John Byam Lister Shaw)*

BIANCA. Now let me see if I can construe it: 'Hic ibat Simois,' I know you not, 'hic est Sigeia tellus,' I trust you not; 'Hic steterat Priami,' take heed he hear us not, 'regia,' presume not, 'celsa senis,' despair not.

HORTENSIO. Madam, 'tis now in tune.

This passage presents difficulty for readers because of Shakespeare's use of Latin and the faulty "translations" both Lucentio and Bianca provide for the phrases. Lucentio begins by saying "Hic ibat Simois; hic est Sigeia tellus; Hic steterat Priami regia celsa senis," which translates from the Latin to "Here ran the river Simois; here is the Sigeian land; here stood old Priam's lofty palace," lines that appear in Ovid's *Heroides*. After Bianca asks Lucentio to translate them for her, he instead inserts phrases that, when compiled, reveal his true intentions to Bianca. After Hortensio interrupts, Bianca also "translates" the Latin by the same method as Lucentio: she inserts her message to her suitor. Since both characters "translate" the same passage but with different meanings (which obviously are completed unrelated to the original phrases), readers feel confused about the actual meaning.

CRITICAL INTRODUCTION TO THE PLAY
Gender Roles

The most prominent theme in *The Taming of the Shrew*, undoubtedly, concerns gender roles. In the play—and in Shakespeare's era—men are the masters and protectors, while the women are expected to remain silent, obedient, and chaste. Shakespeare does not reveal any information about Katherina's sexual experiences (we assume she is chaste), but she is definitely not silent or obedient. Shakespeare and his contemporaries held fast to the concept that a great "chain of being" existed, governed the world, and preserved order. This "chain of being" is a type of chart that defines the rank and place of every person, animal, plant, and even rock (see E. M. W. Tillyard's *The Elizabethan World Picture* for an extensive exploration of this notion). In respect to people and the "chain," nobles outranked the middle class, and the middle class obviously outranked the poor, but no matter the socioeconomic status, men always outranked women. When a woman, like Katherina, disregarded society's expectations for her and, in essence, acted like a man—she takes advantage of male privileges like speaking freely and doing as she wishes—Katherina disrupts the clearly defined order represented by the chain, and hence, others view her as a threat to order and stability.

In one of Petruchio's most important and studied speeches (analyzed in the Key Passages section), he affirms Elizabethan expectations for and views of men:

> PETRUCHIO. But for my bonny Kate, she
>   must with me.
> Nay, look not big, nor stamp, nor stare, nor
>   fret;
> I will be master of what is mine own:
> She is my goods, my chattels; she is my house,
> My household stuff, my field, my barn,
> My horse, my ox, my ass, my any thing;
> And here she stands, touch her whoever dare;
> I'll bring mine action on the proudest he
> That stops my way in Padua.

In this speech, Petruchio emphasizes his power dynamic with his wife: She is mere property, equivalent to a barnyard animal or household possession that belongs to him. Petruchio guards Katherina like any other property, threatening anyone who dares to even touch his new wife. Though Petruchio may appear controlling to modern readers, his behavior reflects Elizabethan expectations for men.

By the end of the play, when Katherina falls (seemingly) happily into her role as wife, she gives her famous "obedience speech" and reflects on the defined gender roles for both men and women in Elizabethan England. She says a woman's husband is her "lord," "king," "governor," "life," "keeper," "head," and "sovereign"; all of these terms emphasize the man's power and mastery

over his wife. Katherina continues, adding that a woman's husband

> cares for thee,
> And for thy maintenance commits his body
> To painful labor both by sea and land,
> To watch the night in storms, the day in cold,
> Whilst thou liest warm at home, secure and
>   safe;
> And craves no other tribute at thy hands
> But love, fair looks and true obedience;
> Too little payment for so great a debt.
> Such duty as the subject owes the prince
> Even such a woman oweth to her husband;
> And when she is froward, peevish, sullen, sour,
> And not obedient to his honest will,
> What is she but a foul contending rebel
> And graceless traitor to her loving lord?
> I am ashamed that women are so simple
> To offer war where they should kneel for peace;
> Or seek for rule, supremacy and sway,
> When they are bound to serve, love and obey.
> . . . Then vail your stomachs, for it is no boot,
> And place your hands below your husband's
>   foot:
> In token of which duty, if he please,
> My hand is ready; may it do him ease.
>
> (5.2)

Some readers question Katherina's sincerity in this passage: Is it possible for the shrew that broke a lute over Hortensio's head, physically assaulted her sister, and verbally sparred with Petruchio in the street to now preach obedience, mildness, and duty? Whether she only poses as content or speaks genuinely, Katherina (and inherently Shakespeare) represents the real, truthful expectations for men and women in Shakespeare's era.

Marriage as a Business Arrangement

A theme that consistently troubles modern readers is the way that Shakespeare emphasizes marriage as an economic institution, entered into for security instead of love. During the Renaissance, the husband was expected to provide his wife with a home and protection; the wife, on the other hand, was expected to provide her husband with children. Emotions like love and passion were unnecessary in these types of arrangements. Such notions unsettle contemporary readers, since marriage now represents the pinnacle of love and emotion and, unlike during the Renaissance, marriage is not commonly viewed as a business agreement.

Petruchio, who is very financially motivated and who has come to "wive it" in Padua, learns of Katherina's generous dowry and, even before meeting her, decides to marry her. Petruchio and Baptista establish the marriage/business arrangement within a few lines:

> PETRUCHIO. Signior Baptista, my business
>   asketh haste,
> And every day I cannot come to woo.
> You knew my father well, and in him me,
> Left solely heir to all his lands and goods,
> Which I have better'd rather than decreased:
> Then tell me, if I get your daughter's love,
> What dowry shall I have with her to wife?
>
> BAPTISTA. After my death the one half of my
>   lands,
> And in possession twenty thousand crowns.
>   (2.1)

As noted in the Character Studies section above, Katherina realizes she has no choice but to be traded like common goods since her father and Petruchio have entered into an agreement. Katherina, the goods, changes hands, and the business deal is complete. Similarly, Lucentio must prove his background and wealth to Baptista before the father agrees to the marriage between the young suitor and his daughter Bianca. Aware of the importance of the business aspects of a marriage, Tranio (as Lucentio) goes to great lengths to prove himself as a worthy man with whom Baptista may enter his daughter into an arrangement: He convinces a Pedant to pose as Lucentio's real father, Vincentio. Though contemporary readers sometimes attack Shakespeare for portraying mar-

riage as similar to a business merger, he accurately depicts the institution of marriage in Elizabethan England.

Disguise

Characters disguising themselves as others is a common occurrence in comedies, and *The Taming of the Shrew* is no exception. The theme of disguise, a popular motif in the comedic genre, makes the scene ripe for confusion, mistakes, and lighthearted trouble. A host of characters don disguises, including the following: Lucentio as Cambio, Tranio as Lucentio, Hortensio as Licio, and a Pedant as Vincentio. Much as Don Pedro does for Claudio in *Much Ado About Nothing*, Tranio woos Bianca for Lucentio so his master can be happy with the woman whose beauty has struck a chord with his very soul:

> LUCENTIO. We have not yet been seen in
>   any house,
> Nor can we lie distinguish'd by our faces
> For man or master; then it follows thus;
> Thou shalt be master, Tranio, in my stead,
> Keep house and port and servants as I should:
> I will some other be, some Florentine,
> Some Neapolitan, or meaner man of Pisa.
> 'Tis hatch'd and shall be so: Tranio, at once
> Uncase thee; take my colour'd hat and cloak:
> When Biondello comes, he waits on thee;
> But I will charm him first to keep his tongue.
>
> TRANIO. So had you need.
> In brief, sir, sith it your pleasure is,
> And I am tied to be obedient;
> For so your father charged me at our parting,
> 'Be serviceable to my son,' quoth he,
> Although I think 'twas in another sense;
> I am content to be Lucentio,
> Because so well I love Lucentio.
>
> LUCENTIO. Tranio, be so, because Lucentio
>   loves:
> And let me be a slave, to achieve that maid
> Whose sudden sight hath thrall'd my wounded
>   eye.

Tranio, posing as Lucentio, leaves his master open for the possibility of disguising himself and gaining further access to Bianca. In 3.1, Lucentio (and Hortensio) pose as tutors (Cambio and Licio, respectively) to gain access to Bianca, the woman each man hopes to marry. Similarly, in order to assuage Baptista's concerns about Bianca marrying Lucentio, Tranio convinces a Pedant to pose as Vincentio, Lucentio's father, to convince Baptista to consent to the marriage between Bianca and Lucentio.

Examining these disguises yields a telling pattern: All of these disguises concern the secondary plotline, focused on Bianca and Lucentio. Perhaps Shakespeare associates the theme of disguise so closely to the story thread concerning Bianca because Baptista's youngest daughter dons a disguise herself: Though she seems obedient and kind, she has a streak of independence—much like Katherina's—that, when revealed at the end of the play, surprises both readers and her husband. Few readers suspect Bianca will not come when her husband summons her, nor do readers expect her chastisement of Lucentio for placing a wager on her actions (5.2). Shakespeare supplies his readers with careful and masterful hints that a woman surrounded and courted by men in disguise must also be disguising something herself.

Structure

The structure of *The Taming of the Shrew* sets it apart from the rest of Shakespeare's works—it is the only play to open with an induction. An induction is a scene or series of scenes, apart from a play's main plotline, that comment on the play and its themes. The story of Sly and the lord who fools him focuses on the theme of disguise and identity, important topics throughout the play.

Marjorie Garber, in *Shakespeare: After All*, says that Inductions were common among Shakespeare and his contemporaries. Though inductions serve the useful purpose of furthering themes, motifs, or symbols significant to the main plotline, the induction in *The Taming of the Shrew* also functions as a confusing point for some readers and viewers since Sly does not appear again after his

final line in which he praises the plot concerning Katherina and Petruchio: "'Tis a very excellent piece of work, madam lady" (1.2). The frame story starring Sly has a conclusion in *The Taming of a Shrew,* but Shakespeare's readers must wonder about Sly's fate.

As discussed in the Background section, Shakespeare's use of an induction in this play presents readers with questions, especially since in *The Taming of a Shrew,* Sly's frame story is completed with Sly reappearing at the end of the play. In turn, readers wonder about Shakespeare's choice never to return to Sly's character after Act I. Did Shakespeare write this play so quickly that he forgot to provide a resolution for Sly? On the other hand, some readers believe Shakespeare disregards bringing closure to Sly's story because doing so is unnecessary: The Induction sets the tone for the play, and readers and viewers are responsible for remembering that the story involving Katherina, Petruchio, Lucentio, and Bianca is nothing more than a play itself, being performed for Sly.

Another aspect of the play's structure that interests readers remains the events of Act III. Shakespearean plays follow the same pattern: Rising action occurs in the first two acts, the crisis of the play happens in the third act, and then falling action with a resolution occurs in the last two acts. Some readers feel shocked by the brief "courtship" of Petruchio and Katherina and do not expect them to be married until later in the play. The fact that the marriage occurs in the middle of the play, however, reaffirms the main plot as that of Petruchio's attempt to tame Katherina, which he seems to have accomplished by the end of the fifth act.

Yet another important aspect of the play's structure concerns the primary plot and the secondary plot, which run almost independently of one another, until the final act. Petruchio's pursuit of Katherina (and likewise his plan to tame her) occurs almost completely in isolation from the scenes involving Lucentio and Bianca. Consider, for instance, the third and fourth acts of the play. Traditionally, the scenes in Act III appear as follows: The first scene concerns Lucentio and

Hortensio's attempts to woo Bianca by posing as her tutors; the second scene revolves around Petruchio and Katherina's marriage. Similarly, the scenes in Act IV also alternate between focusing on Katherina and on Bianca. The first, third, and fifth scenes all center on Katherina's struggles with Petruchio, while the action in the second and fourth scenes involves Lucentio's courting of Bianca. Though devoting scenes to one plotline in particular seems natural, what deserves further analysis is how the focus of each scene alternates between the two sisters. The alternating plotlines emphasize the two sisters and their very different corresponding stories. Katherina, already (and quickly) married, adjusts to the social construct of wife while Bianca delights in the attention several suitors pay her. In contrast, Shakespeare reminds readers that Bianca's courtship process is much longer than her sister's, a choice that insinuates that Bianca has not only more suitors from which she will help choose a husband, but also that she has more time than Katherina to make a choice about her future.

Clothing

Clothing functions as one of the most prominent symbols in *The Taming of the Shrew*. Clothing, closely related to the theme of identity, allows people to alter their appearances and become characters they are not. The symbol of clothing would have been especially powerful for Shakespeare's audience, who were forced to observe sumptuary laws: These laws governed the type and look of clothes a person was allowed to wear. Strict laws outlined who was allowed to wear certain fabrics, and even colors. For instance, only nobles were allowed to wear the color purple (because of its association with royalty) or the material velvet. Defying sumptuary laws led to serious punishment. Chaos remained a looming threat to those in the Elizabethan era, and rules like sumptuary laws helped create some sense of order. If someone threatened this sense of order, he or she would face dire consequences.

In turn, Sly's situation would have held special significance for and resounded deeply with Eliza-

Elsie Leslie as Katherine and Jefferson Winter as Petruchio in a 1903 production of *Katherine and Petruchio,* an adaptation of *The Taming of the Shrew.* This photograph was published by the Byron Company.

bethans. Unconvinced at first by the lord's prank, Sly feels uncomfortable when one of the lord's servants asks Sly what he plans to wear that day:

> THIRD SERVANT. What raiment will your honor wear to-day?

> SLY. I am Christophero Sly; call not me 'honor' nor 'lordship:' I ne'er drank sack in my life; and if you give me any conserves, give me conserves of beef: ne'er ask me what raiment I'll wear; for I have no more doublets than backs, no more stockings than legs, nor no more shoes than feet; nay, sometimes more feet than shoes, or such shoes as my toes look through the over-leather.

> (Induction)

Sly, a lowly, drunken tinker, suddenly finds himself thrust into a higher social rank because of the clothing he wears. Simultaneously, Sly feels anxious and uncomfortable—as demonstrated in the passage above—especially because of the new clothes he wears, clearly meant for those of much higher social class than his own.

Clothing also functions as an important symbol when Petruchio finally arrives for his wedding. Biondello explains Petruchio's startling appearance to Baptista:

> BIONDELLO. Why, Petruchio is coming
> in a new hat and an old jerkin, a pair of old
> breeches thrice turned, a pair of boots that
> have been candle-cases, one buckled, another
> laced, an old rusty sword ta'en out of the town-
> armory, with a broken hilt, and chapeless; with
> two broken points: his horse hipped with an
> old mothy saddle and stirrups of no kindred;
> besides, possessed with the glanders and like to
> mose in the chine; troubled with the lampass,
> infected with the fashions, full of wingdalls,
> sped with spavins, rayed with yellows, past cure
> of the fives, stark spoiled with the staggers,
> begnawn with the bots, swayed in the back
> and shoulder-shotten; near-legged before and
> with, a half-chequed bit and a head-stall of
> sheeps leather which, being restrained to keep
> him from stumbling, hath been often burst
> and now repaired with knots; one girth six
> time pieced and a woman's crupper of velure,
> which hath two letters for her name fairly set
> down in studs, and here and there pieced with
> packthread.
>
> (3.2)

Petruchio uses his mismatched clothing as a means to embarrass his future wife. On his wedding day, one would expect Petruchio to dress properly and not in an "old jerkin," "a pair of old breeches thrice turned," carrying a rusty, broken sword while riding on a haggard, old horse. Petruchio's clothing in this scene symbolizes his subversive nature. He loves a challenge and enjoys making sport out of serious events, including courting, marrying, and then taming Katherina. In contrast to Sly, Petruchio's clothes here reflect his character. In turn, Shakespeare reminds readers that clothing functions as a powerful tool, that can either reflect and amplify one's character (as with Petruchio), or that allow a man to change who he

is completely (like Sly). With Sly, however, Shakespeare also suggests that one's status changes when his clothes do.

Another important scene involving clothing occurs in Act IV, Scene 3, when a tailor and a haberdasher visit Petruchio's house; they bring some new clothes for Katherina with them. First, they present Katherina with a fashionable hat:

> HABERDASHER. Here is the cap your
> worship did bespeak.
>
> PETRUCHIO. Why, this was moulded on a
> porringer;
> A velvet dish: fie, fie! 'tis lewd and filthy:
> Why, 'tis a cockle or a walnut-shell,
> A knack, a toy, a trick, a baby's cap:
> Away with it! come, let me have a bigger.
>
> KATHERINA. I'll have no bigger: this doth
> fit the time,
> And gentlewomen wear such caps as these
>
> PETRUCHIO. When you are gentle, you shall
> have one too,
> And not till then.
>
> (4.3)

Petruchio realizes that Katherina finds the cap pleasing. Since, at this point in the play, his priority is to break his wife's resolve and, in doing so, tame her, he blatantly causes friction and reminds Katherina that she will not be allowed to wear things like the cap, fit for a gentlewoman, until she learns to behave like a gentlewoman herself. In turn, the cap in this scene is an expression of Petruchio's control over his wife. He dangles the fashionable item before her but refuses to let her have it because she has not yet bent to his will.

A similar situation occurs when the haberdasher and tailor show Katherina and Petruchio the dress they were commissioned to make for the new bride. When the tailor shows Petruchio the gown—which is expertly and beautifully made—he responds by saying,

O mercy, God! what masquing stuff is here?
What's this? a sleeve? 'tis like a demi-cannon:
What, up and down, carved like an apple-tart?
Here's snip and nip and cut and slish and slash,
Like to a censer in a barber's shop:
Why, what, i' devil's name, tailor, call'st thou
  this?

Shocked, the tailor tells Petruchio that he made the dress "orderly and well, according to the fashion and the time." In the following exchange, Petruchio once again frustrates Katherina by denying her the gown:

PETRUCHIO. Marry, and did; but if you be
  remember'd,

I did not bid you mar it to the time.
Go, hop me over every kennel home,
For you shall hop without my custom, sir:
I'll none of it: hence! make your best of it.

KATHERINA. I never saw a better-fashion'd
  gown,
More quaint, more pleasing, nor more
  commendable:
Belike you mean to make a puppet of me.

PETRUCHIO. Why, true; he means to make a
  puppet of thee.

TAILOR. She says your worship means to
  make a puppet of her.

Petruchio sends the tailor and haberdasher away in Act IV, Scene 3 of *The Taming of the Shrew*. This engraving is from an 1846 edition of the *Illustrated London News*. *(Illustration by Charles Robert Leslie; engraving by William Luson Thomas)*

ment one another nicely and reinforce the main plot thread of the story: Petruchio's taming of Katherina. *Come* and *now* emphasize and recall images of Petruchio commanding Kate to appear before him and obey him, especially during the final scene of the play when Kate gives her "obedience speech." The popularity of *say* highlights Katherina's voice and, implicitly, her independence, since women in Katherina's station in Shakespeare's world were expected to be quiet and obedient, far less opinionated. The appearance of *good,* then, reminds readers that Katherina must tame her tongue in order to fit the expectations of a "good" woman and wife.

EXTRACTS OF CLASSIC CRITICISM

Samuel Johnson (1709–1784) [Excerpted from *The Plays of William Shakespeare* (1765), Johnson's landmark edition of Shakespeare's plays. Revered as one of the greatest literary critics, Johnson's observations on Shakespeare's canon remain highly influential. Before offering some general comments on the play, Johnson provides an analysis of three passages in particular.]

Redime te captum quam queas minimo.

[In Act I]

Our author had this line from Lilly, which I mention, that it may not be brought as an argument of his learning.

GREMIO. Youngling! thou canst not
love so dear as I.

TRANIO. Grey-beard! thy love doth
freeze.

GREMIO. But thine doth fry.

[In Act II]

Old Gremio's notions are confirmed by Shadwell:

The fire of love in youthful blood,
Like what is kindled in brushwood,

But for a moment burns—
But when crept into aged veins,
It slowly burns, and long remains,
It glows, and with a sullen heat,
Like fire in logs, it burns, and warms us
long;
And though the flame be not so great
Yet is the heat as strange.

PETRUCHIO. A good swift simile.

[In Act V]

Swift, besides the original sense of speedy in motion, signified witty, quick-witted. So in *As You Like It,* the Duke says of the clown, "He is very swift and sententious." *Quick* is now used in almost the same sense, as *nimble* was in the age after that of our author. Heylin says of Hales, that he had known Laud for a nimble disputant.

. . .

Of this play the two plots are so well united, that they can hardly be called two without injury to the art with which they are interwoven. The attention is entertained with all the variety of a double plot, yet is not distracted by unconnected incidents.

The part between Catharine and Petruchio is eminently spritely and diverting. At the marriage of Bianca the arrival of the real father, perhaps, produces more perplexity than pleasure. The whole play is very popular and diverting.

William Hazlitt (1778–1830) [Excerpted from *Characters of Shakespear's Plays* (1817). Hazlitt's analysis of Shakespeare's work remains very influential.]

The Taming of the Shrew is almost the only one of Shakespeare's comedies that has a regular plot, and downright moral. It is full of bustle, animation, and rapidity of action. It shews admirably how self-will is only to be got the better of by stronger will, and how

At dinner with Katherina, Petruchio throws their food from the table in Act IV, Scene 1 of *The Taming of the Shrew*. This illustration was designed for a 1918 edition of Charles and Mary Lamb's *Tales from Shakespeare*. *(Illustration by Louis Rhead)*

which to admire most, the unaccountableness of his actions, or the unalterableness of his resolutions. It is a character which most husbands ought to study, unless perhaps the very audacity of Petruchio's attempt might alarm them more than his success would encourage them. What a sound must the following speech carry to some married ears!

> Think you a little din can daunt my ears?
> Have I not in my time heard lions roar?
> Have I not heard the sea, puff'd up with winds,
> Rage like an angry boar, chafed with sweat?
> Have I not heard great ordnance in the field?
> And heav'n's artillery thunder in the skies?
> Have I not in a pitched battle heard
> Loud larums, neighing steeds, and trumpets clang?
> And do you tell me of a woman's tongue,
> That gives not half so great a blow to hear,
> As will a chesnut in a farmer's fire?

Not all Petruchio's rhetoric would persuade more than "some dozen followers" to be of this heretical way of thinking. He unfolds his scheme for the *Taming of the Shrew,* on a principle contradiction, thus:

> I'll woo her with some spirit when she comes.
> Say that she rail, why then I'll tell her plain
> She sings sweetly as a nightingale;
> Say that she frown, I'll say she looks as clear
> As morning roses nearly wash'd with dew;
> Say she be mute, and will not speak a word,
> Then I'll commend her volubility,

one degree of ridiculous perversity is only to be driven out by another still greater. Petruchio is a madman in his sense; a very honest fellow, who hardly speaks a word of truth, and succeeds in all his tricks and impostures. He acts his assumed character to life, with the most fantastical extravagance, with complete presence of mind, with untired animal spirits, and without a particle of ill humour from beginning to end.—The situation of poor Katherine, worn out by his incessant persecutions, becomes at last almost as pitiable as it is ludicrous, and it is difficult to say

And say she uttereth piercing eloquence:
If she do bid me pack, I'll give her
  thanks,
As though she bid me stay by her a week;
If she deny to wed, I'll crave the day,
When I shall ask the banns, and when be
  married?

He accordingly gains her consent to the match, by telling her father than he has got it; disappoints her by not returning at the time he has promised to wed her, and when he returns, creates no small consternation by the oddity of his dress and equipage. This, however, is nothing to the astonishment excited by his mad-brained behaviour at the marriage . . .

The most striking and at the same time laughable feature in the character of Petruchio throughout, is the studied approximation to the intractable character of real madness, his apparent insensibility to all external considerations, and utter indifference to every thing but the wild and extravagant freaks of his own self-will. There is no contending with a person on whom nothing makes any impression but his own purposes, and who is bent on his own whims just in proportion as they seem to want common sense. With him a thing's being plain and reasonable is a reason against it. The airs he gives himself are infinite, and his caprices as sudden as they are groundless. The whole of his treatment of his wife at home is in the same spirit of ironical attention and inverted gallantry. Every thing flies before his will, like a conjuror's wand, and he only metamorphosing her sense and all the objects she sees, at a world's speaking. Such are his insisting that it is the moon and not the sun which they see, &c. This extravagance reaches its most pleasant and poetical height in the scene where, on their return to her father's, they meet old Vincentio, whom Petruchio immediately addresses as a young lady:

PETRUCHIO: Good morrow, gentle
  mistress, where away?
Tell me, sweet Kate, and tell me truly
  too,
Hast thou beheld a fresher
  gentlewoman?
Such war of white and red within her
  cheeks;
What stars do spangle heaven with such
  a beauty,
As those two eyes become that heav'nly
  face?
Fair lovely maid, once more good day to
  thee:
Sweet Kate, embrace her for beauty's
  sake.

HORTENSIO: He'll make the man mad
  to make a woman of him.

KATHERINE: Young budding virgin,
  fair and fresh and sweet,
Whither away, or where is thy abode?
Happy the parents of so fair a child;
Happier the man whom favourable stars
Allot thee for his lovely bed-fellow.

PETRUCHIO: Why, how now, Kate, I
  hope thou art not mad:
This is a man, old, wrinkled, faded,
  wither'd,
And not a maiden, as thou say'st he is.

KATHERINE: Pardon, old father, my
  mistaken eyes
That have been so bedazed with the sun
That every thing I look on seemeth
  green,
Now I perceive thou art a reverend
  father.

The whole is carried off with equal spirit, as if the poet's comic Muse had wings of fire. It is strange how one man could be so many things; but so it is. The concluding scene, in which trial is made of the obedience of the new-married wives (so triumphantly for Petruchio) is a very happy one.—In some parts of this play there is a little too much about music-masters and masters of philosophy. They were things of greater rarity in those days than they are now. Nothing however can be better than the advice which Tranio gives his master for the prosecution of his studies:

The mathematics, and the metaphysics,
Fall to them as you find your stomach
  serves you:
No profit grows, were is no pleasure
  ta'en:
In brief, sir, study what you most affect.

We have heard the *Honey-Moon* called "an elegant Katherine and Petruchio." We suspect we do not understand this word *elegant* in the sense that many people do. But in our sense of the word, we should call Lucentio's description of the mistress elegant.

Tranio, I saw her coral lips move,
And with her breath she did perfume
  the air:
Sacred and sweet was all I saw in her.

When Biondello tells the same Lucentio for his encouragement, "I knew a wench married in an afternoon as she went to the garden for parsley to stuff a rabbit, and may you, sir"—there is nothing elegant in thus, and yet we hardly know which of the two passages is best.

The Taming of the Shrew is a play within a play. It is supposed to be acted for the benefit of Sly the tinker, who is made to believe himself a lord, when he wakes after a drunken brawl. The character of Sly and the remarks with which he accompanies the play are as good as the play itself. His answer when he is asked how he likes it, "Indifferent well; 'tis

a good piece of work, would 'twere done," is in good keeping, as if he were thinking of his Saturday night's job. Sly does not change his tastes with his new situation, but in the midst of splendor and luxury still calls out lustily and repeatedly "for a pot o' the smallest ale." He is very slow in giving up his personal identity in his sudden advancement.—"I am Christophero Sly, call not me honour nor lordship. I ne'er drank sack in my life: and if you give me any conserves, give me conserves

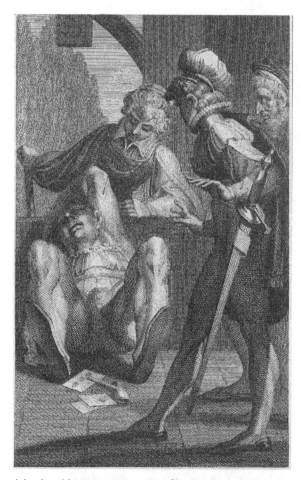

A lord and his men come upon Sly, the peasant, in Induction, Scene 1 of *The Taming of the Shrew*, in this print published by F. & C. Rivington in 1803. *(Illustration by Henry Fuseli; engraving by Charles Turner Warren)*

of beef: ne'er ask me what raiment I'll wear, for I have no more doublets than backs, no more stockings than legs, nor no more shoes than feet, nay, sometimes more feet than shoes, or such shoes as my toes look through over-leather.—What would you make me mad? Am not I Christophero Sly, old Sly's son of Burton-heath, by birth a pedlar, by education a card-maker, by transmutation a bear-herd, and now by present profession a tinker? Ask Marian Hacket, the fat alewife in Wincot, if she know me not; if she say I am not fourteen-pence on the score for sheer ale, score me up for the lying'st knave in Christendom."

This is honest. "The Slies are no rogues," as he says to himself. We have a great predilection for this representative of the family; and what makes us like him the better is, that we take him to be of kin (not many degrees removed) to Sancho Panza.

George Bernard Shaw (1856–1950) [From a letter Shaw wrote to *The Pall Mall Gazette* (1888). The great playwright George Bernard Shaw was frequently critical of Shakespeare. He said readers who idolized Shakespeare were guilty of "Bardolatry." In this letter, Shaw pretends to be a woman, offended by a certain performance of *The Taming of the Shrew*. He finds the taming of Katherina despicable.]

Sir, they say that the American woman is the most advanced woman to be found at present on this planet. I am an Englishwoman, just come up, frivolously enough, from Devon to enjoy a few weeks of the season in London, and at the very first theatre I visit I find an American woman playing Katharine in *The Taming of the Shrew*—a piece which is one vile insult to womanhood and manhood from the first word to the last. I think no woman should enter a theatre where that play is performed; and I should not have stayed

to witness it myself, but that, having been told that the Daly Company has restored Shakespear's version to the stage, I desired to see with my own eyes whether any civilized audience would stand its brutality. . . .

The gentleman who plays Petruchio at Daly's—I neither know nor desire to know his name—does what he can to persuade the audience that he is not in earnest, and that the whole play is a farce, just as Garrick before him found it necessary to do; but in spite of his fine clothes, even at the wedding, and his winks and smirks when Katharine is not looking, he cannot make the spectacle of a man cracking a heavy whip at a starving woman other than disgusting and unmanly. In an age when woman was a mere chattel, Katharine's degrading [obedience] speech . . . might have passed with an audience of bullies. But imagine a parcel of gentlemen in the stalls at the Gaiety Theatre, half of them perhaps living idly on their wives' incomes, grinning complacently through it as if it were true or even honourably romantic. I am sorry that I did not come to town earlier that I might have made a more timely protest. In the future I hope all men and women who respect one another will boycott *The Taming of the Shrew* until it is driven off the boards.

MODERN CRITICISM AND CRITICAL CONTROVERSIES

Like critics of earlier eras, modern critics of *The Taming of the Shrew* have found themselves wrestling with major issues in the play, including whether the play carries a serious message about women's roles or, rather, whether it is simply a farce. The use of the Induction raises questions, as does the catalyst for Katherina's behavior; but the most popular topic for critics remains Kate's "taming" and her famous obedience speech at the close of the play.

A. D. Nuttall, in *Shakespeare the Thinker*, calls *The Taming of the Shrew* a "bombshell" (70), suggesting that its plot and themes incite conversation and strong reactions from readers and viewers. Harold Goddard, in *The Meaning of Shakespeare*, attempts to quell some of the outrage about the play by reminding readers that "We must never for a moment allow ourselves to forget that *The Taming of the Shrew* is a play within a play, an interlude put on by a company of strolling players at the house of a great lord for the gulling of Christopher Sly" (69). Goddard, however, falls into the minority of critics who attempt to defend the play's content by emphasizing *The Taming of the Shrew* really is only a play within a play. Most other critics suggest the message of the play (regardless of the "play within a play" framework) resounds seriously with its audience because of its furthering of patriarchal themes so prevalent in the Renaissance.

For instance, in "'Kate of Kate Hall': The Taming of the Shrew," Ruth Nevo claims that "A more gentlemanly age than our own was embarrassed by *The Shrew*" (253), and Nuttall feels unsettled by his observation that "*The Taming of the Shrew* is now, what it was not in the 1590s, a black comedy. Yet even today it is somehow not as black as it should be. The audience comes out smiling" (71). Shakespearean feminist scholar Penny Gay finds the play very troubling, claiming, "The play enacts the defeat of the threat of a woman's revolt: it does so in comic form, and often with apparent good humour—thus it offers the audience the chance to revel in and reinforce their misogyny while at the same time feeling good" (86). Gay also writes, "*The Taming of the Shrew* argues that the cruel treatment is for the victim's good, to enable her to become a compliant member of patriarchal society" (86). Similarly, in her seminal work *Shakespeare: After All*, Marjorie Garber observes that "Questions of women's rights, women's independence, and cultural and political feminism arising long after the initial writing and staging of *Taming* will, inevitably, have changed the expectations and responses of audiences—and of actors" (67). Gay complements Garber's claim: "The story implied by its title is more thoroughly rooted in a medieval and Elizabethan way of thinking about women and their relation to the patriarchy than any other of

Shakespeare's plays (excluding the histories)" (86). In an effort to explain why many Shakespearean critics feel so deeply troubled by *The Taming of the Shrew*, Garber argues the following: "Part of the problem, if it is a problem, is that many modern readers do not want Shakespeare to hold, or to have held, views that are socially or politically incompatible with their own; this is 'our Shakespeare,' who seems to know us better than we know ourselves, since, in a way, he, or his plays, have made us who and what we are" (67). General readers and critics alike feel troubled that Shakespeare, considered the greatest writer in the English language and the writer best able to capture human nature, could and would write a play suggesting that women must do no more than serve and obey the men in their lives.

One element of the play critics find most intriguing is the Induction. Though inductions were not uncommon in the Renaissance, the Induction in *Taming of the Shrew* poses significant problems because Shakespeare never revisits Sly or the lord playing the trick on him; nor do the players performing for Sly make any commentary on their performance. By the end of *The Taming of the Shrew*, many readers tend to forget the play even opened with an induction and the tale concerning Katherina, Petruchio, Bianca, Lucentio, and the rest was nothing more than a play being performed for an audience. Regardless of Shakespeare failing to include any more information about Sly at the close of the play (What was Sly's reaction to the performance? What happened when Sly discovered he was still only a drunken tinker rather than a nobleman?), Garber notes the Induction's significance, explaining, "Some larger themes of dream, impersonation, transformation, and disguise, initiated in the Induction, carry through and unify the entire play" (58), and adds that "the play-before-the-play, introduces and mirrors all the major issues that will preoccupy the actors in the main drama to come" (59).

Once the play commences, all attention turns to Katherina the shrew and her relationship with Petruchio. Katherina, at first meeting, serves as one of Shakespeare's most unlikable female characters. Several modern critics have worked to discover what exactly transformed Katherina into the angry, hardened young woman readers and viewers meet at the beginning of the play. Goddard argues that Katherina's catalyst for evolving into the famous shrew of Padua concerns her father: "It is the inevitable result of her father's gross partiality toward her sister and neglect of herself, plus the repercussions that his attitude has produced on Bianca and almost everyone else in the region" (69). Similarly, Nuttall's claim that "Kate's father, for all his feebleness, has great power over the women in his house and uses it with repellent entrepreneurial skill" (71) suggests that Baptista's rule of the Minola family shaped, even if indirectly, the woman Katherina became. Nevo explores Katherina's tendency for violence (noting the elder daughter's torture and handtying of Bianca, and also when Katherina strikes Petruchio during their first conversation), claiming that the way in which Baptista and many citizens of Padua treat Katherina serves as the root of her violent temper. Baptista's rule that Bianca cannot marry until Katherina does, Nevo argues, creates a "trap" for Katherina, who "has become nothing but an obstacle or a means to her sister's advancement. Even the husband they seek for her is in reality for her sister's sake, not hers" (256). Regardless of the motives for their marriage, Nuttall adds that Katherina and Petruchio develop an "alliance" simply because Petruchio is "the anti-type of her father and of the world her father ruled, so [by the end of the play] they work together" (81).

The plot component most ripe for critical exploration concerns Katherina as well: Petruchio's taming of her. Goddard, perhaps to defend Shakespeare from some of the unflattering accusations already explored here, argues that Petruchio does not actually tame Katherina, but rather that Katherina masters Petruchio. Goddard argues, "For surely the most psychologically sound as well as the most delightful way of taking *The Taming of the Shrew* is the topsy-turvy one. Kate, in that case, is no shrew at all except in the most superficial sense," and adds further that "the play ends with the prospect that Kate is going to be more nearly the tamer than the tamed, Petruchio more nearly the tamed than the tamer, though his wife naturally will keep the true station under cover" (68). Like Garber's comment about readers being troubled by *The Taming of the Shrew* because Shakespeare, "or his plays, have made us who and what we are," Goddard argues that his interpretation of Petruchio becoming the tamed instead of the tamer "has the advantage of bringing the play into line with all the other Comedies in which Shakespeare gives a distinct edge to his heroine. Otherwise it is an unaccountable exception and regresses to the wholly un-Shakespearean doctrine of male superiority, a view which there is not the slightest evidence elsewhere Shakespeare ever held" (68).

Though Goddard's interpretation may provide some readers with a reason that alleviates Shakespeare from appearing as a misogynist, other critics, namely Nuttall, consider Goddard's interpretation as ludicrous: Nuttall writes that "Katherina and Shakespeare mean every word [of the obedience speech]. To turn Katherina into a sly manipulator of her husband, as Goddard did, is to turn Katherina into Bianca. There could be no greater insult" (80). Unlike Goddard, Nuttall simply acknowledges that *The Taming of the Shrew* is a story about a woman being tamed, plain and simple. Exploring this problematic theme further, Nuttall writes, "Shakespeare's word, to be sure, is 'taming,' but what is our other word for taming, say, a horse? It is 'breaking.' Within the play Shakespeare is thinking all the time not of horse-breaking but of falconry, the training of a hawk." Nuttall provides more evidence for his interpretation that the play most definitely revolves around Katherina's taming by researching the methods of taming hawks (to which Petruchio compares his role with Katherina): "The classic modern text on this subject is T. H. White's *The Goshawk* (1951). White explains the training of a hawk as a protracted battle of wills; the hawk is systematically deprived of sleep (but the falconer must also stay awake) until the bird's resistance cracks. Sleep deprivation figures prominently in the breaking of Katherina."

Perhaps the greatest evidence of Katherina's taming is the speech she gives at the end of the play, commonly referred to as the "obedience speech." Garber refers to the speech as a "love test, a wager about wifely obedience entered upon by characters who believe that the risks and dangers of courtship are past, so that they may now take pleasure in their newly married condition," adding that "such premature overconfidence on the part of Shakespearean lovers will show itself toward the close of many of his romantic comedies" (65). While Garber seems to argue that the context for the final speech is lighthearted, Nuttall believes otherwise. He says, in fact, that "Today the actor is virtually compelled to deliver these lines ironically, if the audience is not to break out in its own open rebellion" (79) and notes that in Katherina's speech "things are being said that we do not wish to hear. Most of us now believe that men and women are equal" (80). Though he openly acknowledges the uncomfortable theme furthered in *The Taming of the Shrew* about the roles of men and women, Nuttall also encourages his readers to consider the practicality of Katherina's obedience speech as well: in a society with "no effective police force" in which Katherina would "have no option but marriage and will be utterly dependent on whatever husband they can get, her suggestion that men are the protectors of the weak women may cease to seem wholly absurd" (80).

Whether the relationship between Katherina and Petruchio delights or disgusts readers and viewers, it continues to engage them and likewise encour-

Petruchio strives to embarrass Katherina during their wedding, in this 19th-century depiction of Act III, Scene 2 of *The Taming of the Shrew. (Illustration by M. Paul Destez)*

ages them to question the dynamics and intentions of both characters. In *Shakespeare: The Invention of the Human,* Harold Bloom suggests, "The swaggering Petruchio provokes a double reaction in [Kate]: outwardly furious, inwardly smitten. The perpetual popularity of *Shrew* does not derive from male sadism in the audience but from sexual excitation of women and men alike" (29). Though, as Garber argues, we may feel uncomfortable with some of the messages Shakespeare's *The Taming of the Shrew* sends, we cannot help becoming engrossed in the sexually charged and witty battle between a shrew and the man who attempts to tame her.

THE PLAY TODAY

The Taming of the Shrew remains popular today, with frequent theater renditions and even a loose modern film adaptation, *Ten Things I Hate About You,* along with the television series of the same name. Perhaps one reason for the play's wild appeal is that Katherina and Petruchio's courtship reminds many readers of contemporary romantic comedies, a connection the critic Harold Bloom also makes: "The *Shrew* is as much a romantic comedy as it is a farce. The mutual roughness of Kate and Petruchio makes a primal appeal, and yet the humor of their relationship is highly sophisticated" (29).

No pair of Shakespearean romantic comedy actors (perhaps with the exception of Kenneth Branagh and Emma Thompson as Benedick and Beatrice in *Much Ado About Nothing*) rival Elizabeth Taylor and Richard Burton as Katherina and Petruchio in Zeffirelli's 1967 film version of *The Taming of the Shrew.* Married in real life during the filming and debut of the film, Burton and Taylor delighted audiences by playing the parts of the two stubborn lovers. Famous for her sexuality and strength, Taylor captured Katherina's spirit (as she would also do in her role as the sensual Egyptian queen in *Cleopatra*), emphasizing her independence and feistiness, especially at the close of the film.

Though general readers and critics tend to struggle with the seemingly blatant misogynistic themes in the play, *The Taming of the Shrew* remains a favorite of Shakespeare's canon for its humor and exploration of themes relatable to all readers, women and men alike.

FIVE TOPICS FOR DISCUSSION AND WRITING

1. **The use of an induction:** *The Taming of the Shrew* is the only Shakespearean play with an induction. Why is this significant? The induction focuses on how Christopher Sly is tricked into thinking he is a lord. Discuss the importance of this ruse. Examine the significance of why Shakespeare never completes Christopher Sly's story—did Shakespeare simply forget about Sly's existence, or is there a reason why Shakespeare does not inform readers of Sly's further experiences?

2. **Play within a play:** The main plot thread of *The Taming of the Shrew* is merely a play being performed for the drunken Christopher Sly and those trying to fool him. Analyze the implications of Katherina's taming if it happens during a play within a play—making it all a staged performance, a farce—versus if that extra layer distancing the main plot from the audience did not exist.

3. **Shakespeare a misogynist?:** Though some critics claim that Shakespeare simply reflects the expectations concerning gender roles in Elizabethan England in *The Taming of the Shrew,* others have accused him of being sexist and misogynistic because of his portrayal of women in this comedy (Katherina, specifically). Analyze whether Shakespeare's depiction of females in this play is unfair and damaging or playful and positive.

4. **Manipulation:** Readers have always questioned whether Katherina's taming is genuine. Does she behave as an obedient wife because Petruchio has manipulated her into believing she should, or does she become an obedient wife only to manipulate Petruchio into thinking he has tamed her? Also consider the way in which Bianca manipulates Lucentio. Does Shakespeare suggest that all romantic entanglements involve some degree of manipulation?

5. **Greed and money:** Petruchio agrees to marry Katherina before he even meets her, simply

because she carries a large dowry. Similarly, Baptista considers Tranio/Lucentio a suitable match for his youngest daughter since Tranio/Lucentio is wealthy. Marriages are made based on money rather than emotion. Why is this significant?

Bibliography

Asimov, Isaac. *Asimov's Guide to Shakespeare*. New York: Wings Books, 1970.

Aspinall, Dana E., ed. The Taming of the Shrew*: Critical Essays*. New York: Routledge, 2002.

Bamber, Linda. *Comic Women, Tragic Men: A Study of Gender and Genre in Shakespeare*. Stanford, Calif.: Stanford University Press, 1982.

Bean, John C. "Comic Structure and the Humanizing of Kate in *The Taming of the Shrew*." In *The Woman's Part: Feminist Criticism of Shakespeare*, 65–79. Urbana: University of Illinois Press.

Berek, Peter. "Text, Gender, and Genre in *The Taming of the Shrew*." In *"Bad" Shakespeare: Revaluations of the Shakespeare Canon*, edited by Maurice Charney, 91–104. Rutherford, N.J.: Fairleigh Dickinson University Press, 1988.

Berggren, Paula S. "The Woman's Part: Female Sexuality as Power in Shakespeare's Plays." In *The Woman's Part: Feminist Criticism of Shakespeare*, 17–34. Urbana: University of Illinois Press.

Berry, Ralph. *Shakespeare's Comedies*. Princeton, N.J.: Princeton University Press, 1972.

Bloom, Harold. *Shakespeare: The Invention of the Human*. New York: Riverhead Books, 1998.

Bonazza, Blaze O. *Shakespeare's Early Comedies: A Structural Analysis*. New York: Mouton, 1965.

Brunvand, Jan H. "The Folktale Origin of *The Taming of the Shrew*." *Shakespeare Quarterly* 17.4 (August 1966): 345–359.

———. The Taming of the Shrew: *A Comparative Study of Oral and Literary Versions*. New York: Garland, 1991.

Callaghan, Dympna, ed. *A Feminist Companion to Shakespeare*. Oxford: Blackwell, 2000.

Coleridge, Samuel Taylor. *Lectures and Notes on Shakespeare and Other Dramatists*. Oxford: Oxford University Press, 1931.

Collins, Michael J., ed. *Shakespeare's Sweet Thunder: Essays on the Early Comedies*. Newark: University of Delaware Press, 1997.

Crystal, David, and Ben Crystal. *The Shakespeare Miscellany*. Woodstock, N.Y.: Overlook Books, 2005.

Dessen, Alan C. "The Tamings of the Shrews." In *Shakespeare's Sweet Thunder: Essays on the Early Comedies*, edited by Michael J. Collins, 35–49. Newark: University of Delaware Press, 1997.

Diamond, Arlyn, and Lee Edwards, eds. *The Authority of Experience: Essays in Feminist Criticism*. Amherst: University of Massachusetts Press, 1977.

Dolan, Frances E., ed. *The Taming of the Shrew: Texts and Contexts*. Boston: Bedford, 1996.

Dusinberre, Juliet. *Shakespeare and the Nature of Women*. New York: Barnes and Noble Books, 1975.

Evans, Malcolm. "Deconstructing Shakespeare's Comedies." In *Alternative Shakespeares*, edited by John Drakakis. London: Routledge, 2002.

Garber, Marjorie. *Shakespeare: After All*. New York: Pantheon Books, 2004.

Gay, Penny. "*The Taming of the Shrew:* Avoiding the Feminist Challenge." In *As She Likes It: Shakespeare's Unruly Women*, 86–119. London: Routledge, 1994.

Giese, Loreen L. *Courtships, Marriage Customs, and Shakespeare's Comedies*. New York: Palgrave, 2006.

Goddard, Harold C. *The Meaning of Shakespeare*. Chicago: University of Chicago Press, 1951.

Hazlitt, William. *The Characters of Shakespeare's Plays*. London: Oxford University Press, 1947.

Heilman, Robert B. "The *Taming* Untamed, or, The Return of the Shrew." *Modern Language Quarterly* 27 (1966): 147–161.

Hosley, Richard. "Sources and Analogues of *The Taming of the Shrew*." *Huntington Library Quarterly* 27 (1964): 289–308.

Johnson, Samuel. *Johnson on Shakespeare*. Oxford: Oxford University Press, 1908.

Khan, Coppélia. "The Taming of the Shrew: Shakespeare's Mirror of Marriage." *Modern Language Studies* 5 (1975): 88–102.

Leggatt, Alexander, ed. *Shakespearean Comedy*. Cambridge: Cambridge University Press, 2002.

————. *Shakespeare's Comedy of Love*. London: Routledge, 1974.

LoMonico, Michael. *The Shakespeare Book of Lists*. Franklin Lakes, N.J.: New Page Books, 2001.

Marvel, Laura, ed. *Readings on* The Taming of the Shrew. San Diego, Calif.: Greenhaven, 2000.

Miller, Stephen Roy, ed. The Taming of a Shrew: *The 1594 Quarto*. Cambridge: Cambridge University Press, 1998.

Miola, Robert S. "The Influence of the New Comedy on *The Comedy of Errors* and *The Taming of the Shrew*." In *Shakespeare's Sweet Thunder: Essays on the Early Comedies,* edited by Michael J. Collins, 21–34. Newark: University of Delaware Press, 1997.

Muir, Kenneth. *The Sources of Shakespeare's Plays*. New Haven, Conn.: Yale University Press, 1978.

Nevo, Ruth. *Comic Transformations in Shakespeare*. London: Routledge, 1980.

Novy, Marianne. "Shakespeare's Female Characters as Actors and Audience." In *The Woman's Part: Feminist Criticism of Shakespeare*, edited by Carolyn Ruth Swift Lenz, Gayle Greene, and Carol Thomas Neely, 256–270. Urbana: University of Illinois Press, 1983.

Nuttall, A. D. *Shakespeare the Thinker*. New Haven, Conn.: Yale University Press, 2007.

Partridge, Eric. *Shakespeare's Bawdy*. London: Routledge, 1968.

Rutter, Carol. "Kate, Bianca, Ruth, and Sarah: Playing the Woman's Part in *The Taming of the Shrew*." In *Shakespeare's Sweet Thunder: Essays on the Early Comedies,* edited by Michael J. Collins, 176–215. Newark: University of Delaware Press, 1997.

Sallinger, Leo. *Shakespeare and the Traditions of Comedy*. Cambridge: Cambridge University Press, 1974.

Schroeder, John W. "A New Analogue and Possible Source for *The Taming of the Shrew*." *Shakespeare Quarterly* 10, no. 2 (Spring 1959): 251–255.

Shaheen, Nasseb. *Biblical References in Shakespeare's Comedies*. Newark: University of Delaware Press, 1993.

Shaw, Bernard. *Shaw on Shakespeare: An Anthology of Bernard Shaw's Writings of the Plays and Production of Shakespeare*. Edited by Edwin Wilson. Freeport, N.Y.: E. P. Dutton & Co., 1961.

Spurgeon, Caroline. *Shakespeare's Imagery and What It Tells Us*. Cambridge: Cambridge University Press, 1935.

Stone, Lawrence. *The Family, Sex, and Marriage in England, 1500–1800*. New York: Harper and Row, 1977.

Swift Lenz, Carolyn Ruth, Gayle Greene, and Carol Thomas Neely, eds. *The Woman's Part: Feminist Criticism of Shakespeare*. Urbana: University of Illinois Press, 1983.

Tillyard, E. M. W. *The Elizabethan World Picture*. New York: Vintage, 1966.

————. *Shakespeare's Early Comedies*. New York: Barnes and Noble, 1965.

Waller, Gary, ed. *Shakespeare's Comedies*. London: Longman, 1991.

FILM AND VIDEO PRODUCTIONS

Badel, Pierre, dir. *La mégère apprivoisée*. With Bernard Noël and Rosy Varte. RTF, 1964.

Collins, Edwin J., dir. *The Taming of the Shrew*. With Lauderdale Maitland and Dacia Deane. British and Colonial Kinematograph, 1923.

Frusta, Arrigo, dir. *La bisbetica domata*. With Eleuterio Rodolfi and Gigetta Morano. Società Anonima Ambrosio, 1913.

Junger, Gil, dir. *Ten Things I Hate About You*. With Julia Stiles and Heath Ledger. Touchstone Pictures, 1999.

Miller, Jonathan, dir. *The Taming of the Shrew*. With John Cleese and Sarah Badel. BBC, 1980.

Richards, Dave, dir. *ShakespeaRe-told: The Taming of the Shrew*. With Shirley Henderson and Rufus Sewell. BBC, 2005.

Sidney, George, dir. *Kiss Me Kate*. With Kathryn Grayson and Fred Graham. MGM, 1953.

Zeffirelli, Franco, dir. *The Taming of the Shrew*. With Elizabeth Taylor and Richard Burton. F.A.I., 1967.

—Karley K. Adney

The Tempest

INTRODUCTION

One could say that *The Tempest* stands both first and last in the canon of Shakespeare's plays. It is first because that is the place given to it in the First Folio collection of Shakespeare's plays, published in 1623 by his fellow actors John Heminges and Henry Condell, something of which we are reminded in Peter Greenaway's film based on the play, *Prospero's Books,* in which we see a copy of the First Folio with 19 pages left blank at the beginning. It is last, because the play is generally regarded as the last play that Shakespeare wrote on his own. This chronology is not absolutely certain—it is not inconceivable that *The Winter's Tale* was written later than *The Tempest* (McMullan 2007: 79)—and it was certainly not the last play on which he ever worked, since he went on to coauthor three plays with John Fletcher, *The Two Noble Kinsmen, Henry VIII,* and the now lost *Cardenio. The Tempest* has, however, become commonly and popularly identified as "Shakespeare's last play," and the role of Prospero, the magus who at the end of the play says farewell to his books, has become associated not only with the figure of Shakespeare himself, retreating to Stratford, but also with a great actor taking his leave of his audience (as in John Gielgud playing Prospero for one last time in *Prospero's Books*).

The Tempest is also the Shakespeare play that most clearly spans the poles of first and last. For only the second time in his career (the first being *The Comedy of Errors,* which was perhaps his first play), Shakespeare here obeys the classical, Aristo-telian unities of time, place, and action (something from which he notably deviates in *The Winter's Tale,* where we fast-forward 16 years in time after the second act). The entirety of *The Tempest* takes place in one day and on one island, with no sub-plot. And yet the play is both deeply rooted in the past—it is heavily indebted to Virgil's *Aeneid*—and at the same time invested in imagining the future, as illustrated by its use as the basis of Aldous Huxley's futuristic novel *Brave New World* and Fred M. Wilcox's classic sci-fi film *Forbidden Planet,* not to mention the various uses made of it in *Star Trek.*

For many readers, *The Tempest* is the culmination of Shakespeare's artistic achievement. Not only does Shakespeare manipulate the 24 hours of the play to reach into both the past and the future, but he makes its setting, a single unnamed island, richly suggestive of many places (including America), and he also makes the apparently simple plot touch on a range of issues, including the nature and purpose of different styles of drama, the relative merits of different types of government, the relationship between nature and nurture, the nature of forgiveness and of freedom, and far-reaching questions of race and colonialism.

BACKGROUND

On November 1, 1611, the feast of All Hallows was marked at the court of King James I of England at Whitehall by a performance of *The Tempest.* It must have been a success, because it was performed again in early 1613 as part of the celebrations for the wedding of King James's only daughter Eliza-

Ferdinand and Miranda playing chess in Act V, Scene 1 of *The Tempest*. This is a print from the Boydell Shakespeare Gallery project, which was first conceived in 1786 and lasted until 1805. *(Painting by Francis Wheatley; engraving by Caroline Watson)*

has been seen as influenced by the growing prominence of James's own daughter, Princess Elizabeth, whose beauty, vivacity, and devout Protestantism made her an extremely popular figure (after the brief elevation of her husband, Frederick, to the throne of Bohemia, she was to become known sometimes as the Queen of Hearts, though she was more commonly referred to as the Winter Queen). Moreover, shortly before Elizabeth's marriage, her beloved brother Henry, Prince of Wales, James's older son, died unexpectedly at the age of 19 (probably of typhus), leaving as heir to the throne his much younger brother, Charles, who had been worryingly slow in learning both to walk and to speak. This might have come to look like the story of *The Winter's Tale*, where the young, beloved prince dies and the princess marries, although *The Winter's Tale* was written before the death of Prince Henry. It is certainly possible to relate Shakespeare's plays to the history of the royal family—the two dukes in *King Lear*, for instance, bear the titles of Albany and Cornwall, which were also two of the titles of James's two sons, and the prominence of Wales in *Cymbeline* should certainly be seen in relation to the installation of Henry as Prince of Wales—but it would be unwise to make too much of it. Nevertheless, it is worth noting that when the play was performed at the marriage of Princess Elizabeth, her new husband, the elector palatine, would certainly have been an interested spectator, for Prague, where he would later briefly be crowned king, was the home of magic in Europe and had been visited by Elizabeth I's "wizard," Dr. John Dee, whom some have seen as the original of Prospero; moreover, as Michael Wood observes, "The story of a deposed duke was current news in the summer of 1611 when the play was first shown: the overthrow of the scholarly Rudolph of Prague had aroused great interest in London" (323).

The Tempest, like the rest of the "last plays," has also been read in relation to Shakespeare's own family. Like King James, Shakespeare, too, had three children: First came a daughter, Susanna, and then twins, Hamnet and Judith, who were named after the Shakespeares' friends and neighbors

beth to Frederick, elector palatine of Bohemia. (When Derek Jarman came to make his film of *The Tempest* and chose Stoneleigh Abbey in Warwickshire as the setting, he was delighted to discover that there was a portrait of Elizabeth in the house, which he felt tied his own version of the play to its origins.) Along with the other Shakespearean "last plays" *Cymbeline, The Winter's Tale,* and *Pericles, The Tempest* has sometimes been read in terms of the king and his family, for all these plays place considerable emphasis on the relationships between fathers and daughters—Pericles and Marina in *Pericles,* Cymbeline and Innogen in *Cymbeline,* Leontes and Perdita in *The Winter's Tale,* and Prospero and Miranda in *The Tempest.* That focus

Hamnet and Judith Sadler. However, Hamnet, Shakespeare's only son, died young, something which biographically minded critics have seen as underlying the shift in his career from comedy to tragedy, begun, of course, with a play named *Hamlet*. There is some evidence to suggest that both his younger daughter Judith and her husband, Thomas Quiney, were a disappointment to Shakespeare, but Susanna's husband, John Hall, was a respectable doctor (he lived at Hall's Croft, still to be seen in Stratford-upon-Avon), and the centrality of father-daughter relationships in the late plays has therefore been related to Shakespeare's presumed feelings for Susanna. Again, though, it would seem unwise to push this far, since it is essentially based on speculation and inference.

A more immediate and tangible stimulus for the change in style, which so many critics have found in Shakespeare's late plays, surely comes from a change in circumstances for the theater company for which he wrote, the King's Men. Since 1599, they had been playing at the Globe, a large open-air theater on the south bank of the Thames, of which a good idea can now be obtained from the reproduction of it built in London late in the last century, close to the original site. Around 1608, though, they also obtained use of the Blackfriars, a converted monastery on the much more central and fashionable north side of the river. This was much smaller than the Globe, and it was also, significantly, an indoor theater, allowing for experiments with lighting, music, and special effects that had simply not been possible at the Globe. The effects of this can be clearly seen in *The Tempest*, though they do not work in the way we might expect. The opening scene is unusual for Shakespeare in that it allows—perhaps even calls for—what we might now think of as "special effects" to create the impression of a storm and shipwreck. Then, in the next scene, Prospero comes on, tells his daughter that everything she has just seen was an illusion, and simply talks and talks and talks in the manner familiar from the older, simpler Globe, almost as though Shakespeare were pitting the two styles against each other and suggesting that it is

the older and simpler that offers us the more trustworthy access to reality.

The theater was not the only aspect of the dramatic scene that had changed. When Shakespeare began to write, the other major dramatist was Christopher Marlowe. Marlowe exerted a considerable influence on Shakespeare's early career, and traces of two of his plays, *Doctor Faustus* and *Dido, Queen of Carthage,* can still be seen in *The Tempest.* But Marlowe died in 1593, and not long before Shakespeare wrote *The Tempest,* two very different authors erupted on the London dramatic scene. Their names were Francis Beaumont and John Fletcher, and after having each written a single-handed play that failed (*The Knight of the Burning Pestle* in the case of Beaumont and *The Faithful Shepherdess* in the case of Fletcher), they rather improbably teamed up to become an instant success. Their play *Philaster* is closely comparable to Shakespeare's *Cymbeline,* though it is not clear which came first, and many of the changes in Shakespeare's style visible in his late plays can be related to the new fashions brought in by Beaumont and Fletcher (indeed Shakespeare's three last plays of all, *Henry VIII, The Two Noble Kinsmen,* and the now lost *Cardenio,* were written in collaboration with Fletcher, who was also responsible for *The Tamer Tamed,* a "sequel" and corrective to *The Taming of the Shrew*). Beaumont and Fletcher valued surprise, suspense, and dramatic effect more than consistent character development, and in their play *The Maid's Tragedy* they both included and subverted a masque-within-a-play, as Shakespeare does in *The Tempest.*

Finally, *The Tempest* was also influenced by what looked at the time like an accident and perhaps even a dead end but which has since come to look like an important stage in a hugely significant development. In July 1609, an English ship called *The Sea Venture* was shipwrecked off the then uninhabited coast of Bermuda (a sea chest from the ship can still be seen in the museum in Hamilton, the capital of Bermuda). The event was recounted in the "True Reportory of the Wracke, and Redemption of Sir Thomas Gates" by William

THE TEMPEST.

Actus primus, Scena prima.

A tempestuous noise of Thunder and Lightning heard: Enter a Ship-master, and a Botes-waine.

Master.

Ote-swaine.

Botes. Heere Master: What cheere?

Mast. Good: Speake to th'Mariners: fall too't, yarely, or we run our selues a ground, bestirre, bestirre. *Exit.*

Enter Mariners.

Botes. Heigh my hearts, cheerely, cheerely my harts: yare, yare: Take in the toppe-sale: Tend to th'Masters whistle: Blow till thou burst thy winde, if roome enough.

Enter Alonso, Sebastian, Anthonio, Ferdinando, Gonzalo, and others.

Alon. Good Boteswaine haue care: where's the Master? Play the men.

Botes. I pray now keepe below.

Anth. Where is the Master, Boson?

Botes. Do you not heare him? you marre our labour, Keepe your Cabines: you do assist the storme.

Gonz. Nay, good be patient.

Botes. When the Sea is: hence, what cares these roarers for the name of King? to Cabine; silence: trouble vs not.

Gon. Good, yet remember whom thou hast aboord.

Botes. None that I more loue then my selfe. You are a Counsellor, if you can command these Elements to silence, and worke the peace of the present, wee will not hand a rope more, vse your authoritie: If you cannot, giue thankes you haue liu'd so long, and make your selfe readie in your Cabine for the mischance of the houre, if it so hap. Cheerely good hearts: out of our way I say. *Exit.*

Gon. I haue great comfort from this fellow: methinks he hath no drowning marke vpon him, his complexion is perfect Gallowes: stand fast good Fate to his hanging, make the rope of his destiny our cable, for our owne doth little aduantage: If he be not borne to bee hang'd, our case is miserable. *Exit.*

Enter Boteswaine.

Botes. Downe with the top-Mast: yare, lower, lower, bring her to Try with Maine-course. A plague——

A cry within. Enter Sebastian, Anthonio & Gonzalo.

vpon this howling: they are lowder then the weather, or our office: yet againe? What do you heere? Shal we giue ore and drowne, haue you a minde to sinke?

Sebas. A poxe o' your throat, you bawling, blasphemous incharitable Dog.

Botes. Worke you then.

Anth. Hang cur, hang, you whoreson insolent Noyse-maker, we are lesse afraid to be drownde, then thou art.

Gonz. I'le warrant him for drowning, though the Ship were no stronger then a Nutt-shell, and as leaky as an vnstanched wench.

Botes. Lay her a hold, a hold, set her two courses off to Sea againe, lay her off.

Enter Mariners wet.

Mari. All lost, to prayers, to prayers, all lost.

Botes. What must our mouths be cold?

Gonz. The King, and Prince, at prayers, let's assist them, for our case is as theirs.

Sebas. I'am out of patience.

An. We are meerly cheated of our liues by drunkards, This wide-chopt-rascall, would thou mightst lye drowning the washing of ten Tides.

Gonz. Hee'l be hang'd yet, Though euery drop of water sweare against it, And gape at widst to glut him. *A confused noyse within.* Mercy on vs. We split, we split, Farewell my wise, and children, Farewell brother: we split, we split, we split.

Anth. Let's all sinke with' King

Seb. Let's take leaue of him. *Exit.*

Gonz. Now would I giue a thousand furlongs of Sea, for an Acre of barren ground: Long heath, Browne firrs, any thing; the wills aboue be done, but I would faine dye a dry death. *Exit.*

Scena Secunda.

Enter Prospero and Miranda.

Mira. If by your Art (my deerest father) you haue Put the wild waters in this Rore; alay them: The skye it seemes would powre down stinking pitch, But that the Sea, mounting to th' welkins cheeke, Dashes the fire out. Oh! I haue suffered With those that I saw suffer: A braue vessell

A (Who

Title page of the First Folio edition of *The Tempest*, published in 1623

Strachey, who seems to have known a number of London dramatists, possibly including Shakespeare, and Strachey's account is clearly the source of some of the details and language found in *The Tempest*. *The Sea Venture* had been on its way to the English colony in Jamestown, which had been founded only two years previously, and one of those on board was John Rolfe, later to become famous as the husband of Pocahontas; Rolfe's daughter Bermuda, by his first wife, was born on the island, and when Miranda speaks of a "Brave new world" (5.1.183) it is impossible not to think of America, which was indeed the brave new world for Shakespeare's England and the destination of *The Sea Venture*. *The Tempest,* then, is not only both the first and the last play in the Shakespeare canon, it is also the only American one.

SYNOPSIS
Brief Synopsis

Prospero, a magician, was once the duke of Milan, but his brother, Antonio, deposed him with the aid of King Alonso. He and his young daughter Miranda were abandoned at sea and came to live on an island far from civilization. As the play opens, Prospero has raised a storm to shipwreck his old enemies and bring them to the island.

Prospero summons his servant, a sprite named Ariel, who reports that he has dispersed the vessel's passengers around the island. Later, Ariel brings Ferdinand, the son of King Alonso. Miranda is amazed at seeing Ferdinand, who is equally charmed to encounter her. Prospero observes in an aside that they are already in love, as he has planned. To ensure that Ferdinand will not take Miranda lightly, he pretends to distrust the young man and imprisons him.

Ariel, traveling around the island, puts King Alonso and his counselor Gonzalo to sleep. Antonio suggests to Sebastian, who is the king's brother, that they should kill the sleeping men and make Sebastian king. Sebastian agrees, but as they draw their swords, Ariel awakens Gonzalo and the king. The four men go off in search of Ferdinand.

Caliban, a native of the island and Prospero's half-human slave, encounters Trinculo, who has survived the shipwreck. Frightened by thunder, Trinculo takes refuge under Caliban's cloak. Another survivor, Stephano, appears, drunk on salvaged wine. He feeds Caliban wine, hoping to tame the monster. Caliban is delighted with his first taste of wine and tipsily volunteers to serve the two men if they will give him more.

Meanwhile Ferdinand labors under Prospero's orders. When Miranda appears, they confess their love for each other and agree to marry.

While Caliban, Stephano, and Trinculo squabble comically, Caliban convinces Stephano to kill Prospero and steal his magic books.

Prospero causes a magical banquet to appear. King Alonso, his brother Sebastian, and his friend Antonio step forward greedily, but the banquet disappears. Ariel, disguised as a Harpy, declares that destiny has stranded them on this island and taken Alonso's son because they are evil men. Alonso leaves, declaring that he will find his dead son and die beside him. Sebastian, Antonio, and Gonzalo follow him.

Prospero consents to the engagement of Miranda and Ferdinand. He calls on Ariel to provide entertainment to celebrate the betrothal. Prospero, recalling Caliban and Stephano's plot, sends Ariel to gather some fine clothes he has prepared, which are hung in full view. Trinculo and Stephano, seeing the fine clothes, cannot resist trying them on. Spirits chase the villains away.

Ariel reports that the captive Alonso, Sebastian, and Antonio are insane, while Gonzalo is grief-stricken. After sending Ariel to fetch them, Prospero asserts that he will renounce magic once he has cured his victims. He exchanges his magician's robes for the garments he wore as duke of Milan, and as the victims recover their senses, they recognize him. He forgives their offenses, and they concede him his duchy. Prospero then reveals Miranda and Ferdinand. The boatswain and the captain of the king's ship report that the vessel has been miraculously restored to shipshape condition. Prospero sends Caliban, Stephano, and Trinculo to restore the stolen clothes to his closet. He then invites the king and his followers indoors, to hear the story of his time on the island.

Act I, Scene 1

In one sense, what happens in this scene is simple: A ship carrying, among others, the king and the prince of Naples is struck by a storm and appears to be on the point of sinking. In another sense, however, it is anything but simple. As already mentioned, this is an uncharacteristic opening scene for a Shakespeare play. Indeed it can in many respects be characterized as a deliberate false start, since it contains two characters, the Master and the Boatswain (this is pronounced "bosun"), whom we will not see again until the last scene, and then only briefly. It contains what would have been even for Shakespeare's original audience difficult technical vocabulary, in the form of references to a ship and its rigging, and rather than trying to get to grips with this, it is probably best to regard it as being there primarily to create atmosphere and a general sense of being at sea. Most of all, we are at sea in more senses than one, because this scene is deceptive: Like the Dover Cliff scene in *King Lear*, it encourages us to believe that an event has taken place when, in fact, it has not, for despite all the frantic cries of "We split!" the ship does not actually go down, and no one is hurt. There is indeed a stark contrast between what we think we see happening here and what we hear in the next scene actually has happened. Thus, this can be seen as evidence of an interest on Shakespeare's part in different ways of representing things in the theater, and indeed it can be related to a wider debate about whether one went to "see" a play or to "hear" a play, as well as contrasting with the very different representational mode of the masque, which we will encounter later on in the action. It is also worth noting that in the general sense of chaos that the scene works so hard to create, an issue that will be increasingly important in the play begins quietly to make itself heard: The Boatswain's question "What cares these roarers for the name of king? (1.1.16–17) is the first hint of the play's concerted investigation into authority and the basis of rule.

Act I, Scene 2

As already stated, this scene is a complete contrast to the first. Whereas we can effectively disregard all the information we are offered in the first scene, it is essential to understand and remember what we are told in the second scene, or the play will simply not make sense. Its importance can be seen in the first-ever film adaptation of *The Tempest*, directed by Percy Stow in 1908, in which the first four scenes (the entire film being only 12 minutes long) all cover events that occurred before the play started (indeed the amount of "backstory" represents a challenge for film adaptations of the play in general).

In this scene, we meet for the first time all of the principal characters in the play, starting with Prospero, the exiled duke of Milan, and his daughter, Miranda. They are the only European inhabitants of a small island on which they have been living for the past 12 years, having been washed ashore when Miranda was not yet three years old. Prospero now explains to her for the first time the circumstances that led to this. He himself had always been more interested in his studies than in ruling his duchy and had gradually allowed his younger brother, Antonio to take over more and more of his duties, until eventually Antonio conspired with the king of Naples to seize power totally, the price of the king's help being that the previously independent duchy of Milan should acknowledge the overlordship of Naples. Prospero and his small daughter (presumably, we must assume that his wife is dead [Orgel 1984]) were put in a boat and set adrift, since Antonio did not dare to kill them outright, and one of the Neapolitan lords, Gonzalo, took pity on them and supplied them with food, water, clothes, and some of Prospero's books (Gonzalo's charity is mirrored in this scene by that of Miranda, who begs her father to take pity on a ship that she has just seen in trouble). Some of those books seem to have been books of magic, for Prospero, we learn, is a magician, and by his art he has learned that his enemies are close at hand.

Having told Miranda all this, Prospero puts her into a magic sleep, and summons Ariel, a spirit who serves him. During their conversation, we learn that it was Ariel who, following Prospero's orders, was responsible for creating the storm (the precise details of how he did this are closely modeled on the Strachey letter). In the time that has elapsed since the end of the scene, Ariel has brought the ship and all the mariners safely to shore, taking particular care of the king's son Ferdinand, while the rest of the king's fleet are on their way home to Naples under the impression that he is dead. Prospero tells Ariel that he has done well but that there is still more work to do, and when Ariel protests at this, Prospero launches into a further slice of "backstory," reminding Ariel that when Prospero and Miranda arrived on the island, they discovered Ariel trapped in a cloven pine tree, in which he had been imprisoned by a witch called Sycorax who had been exiled to the island from Algiers, where she had committed such serious crimes that she would have been executed if she had not been pregnant. Prospero freed Ariel from the tree in exchange for his service and also enslaved the fourth and last inhabitant of the island, Caliban, the son whom Sycorax bore on the island before she died there.

Having reminded him of his obligation, Prospero dispatches Ariel to disguise himself as a sea nymph, wakes Miranda, and takes her to visit Caliban. Caliban reproaches Prospero with steal-

Prospero and Miranda meet Ferdinand in Act I, Scene 2 of *The Tempest.* This is a plate from *Retzsch's Outlines to Shakespeare: The Tempest,* published in 1841. *(Illustration by Moritz Retzsch)*

ing the island from him, while Prospero in turn accuses him of having attempted to rape Miranda. Prospero sends Caliban to fetch wood, and Ariel, now invisible, returns with Prince Ferdinand, who is following the song that Ariel is singing even though he cannot see where the sound is coming from, and who is lamenting the supposed loss of his father. Miranda, who cannot remember seeing any man but her father and Caliban, is very impressed by Ferdinand, and he returns the compliment. This is exactly what Prospero wants, but he resolves to put obstacles in the way of it so that Ferdinand does not regard Miranda as easily won. He therefore accuses Ferdinand of lying when he says that he is now the king of Naples and threatens to put him in chains. When Ferdinand attempts to resist, Prospero casts a spell to prevent him from moving. Miranda pleads for Ferdinand, but Prospero is unmoved. This scene closes with Prospero leading Ferdinand off to captivity.

Act II, Scene 1

In this scene, we meet the rest of the Neapolitans, from whom Ariel has deliberately kept Ferdinand apart. The king is inconsolable for the supposed death of his son. Gonzalo, the lord who assisted Prospero and Miranda so long ago, tries to comfort him, but Prospero's brother Antonio and the king's own brother Sebastian are callously indifferent to his suffering and keep up a running commentary on Gonzalo's remarks. Though their purpose is entirely frivolous, a serious and interesting fact emerges: Their perception of the island is totally different from his, for where he sees lush green grass about him, they see much less fertile-looking territory (ll. 55–59). This motif of variable perceptions and responses will be developed throughout the play; it is partly this which led the director Michael Powell to make intermittent attempts from 1969 to 1979 to film a version of *The Tempest* that would have been explicitly set wholly inside Prospero's head, as his perceptions were dominant. Gonzalo's words also reveal to the audience that the Neapolitan party is returning from the marriage of the king's daughter (and

Ferdinand's sister) Claribel to the king of Tunis (whom we can assume to be black), although Claribel did not enter into the marriage willingly. Gonzalo points out in the process that present-day Tunis was once the great classical city of Carthage, where Dido lived. Antonio and Sebastian make flippant jokes about this, but any educated member of Shakespeare's audience would have been extremely familiar with the story of Dido as recounted in Virgil's *Aeneid* and would have recognized the significance of this information. (Aeneas, after all, can in a way be seen as the first colonizer, and Dido as the first victim of colonialism.) Gonzalo also develops the theme of rule by speculating on what he would do if he were the king of the island. While he is talking, Ariel enters unseen, playing music that apparently puts Gonzalo and the king into an enchanted sleep and then leaves again. Seeing them helpless, Antonio urges Sebastian to kill his brother and take the crown for himself. Both draw their swords, but Prospero, alerted by magic, sends Ariel to wake Gonzalo and the king. Sebastian and Antonio pretend that the sound of lions made them draw their swords, and the king sets off to continue the search for his son Ferdinand.

Act II, Scene 2

This scene opens with Caliban alone, bemoaning his treatment by Prospero. (It is worth noting that this soliloquy allows Caliban to develop a relationship with the audience.) He is joined by Trinculo, the king of Naples's jester, and Stephano, the king's drunken butler. When he first sees Trinculo, Caliban hides himself under his cloak, and Trinculo, having first thought Caliban to be a monster, joins him under the cloak to shelter from an approaching storm, so that Stephano at first thinks there is a four-legged monster under it. He gives Caliban alcohol; Caliban drinks and declares his devotion to Stephano, who tells him he has fallen from the moon and, assuming everyone else to be drowned, declares himself and Trinculo the rulers of the island. Caliban vows that they will be his masters instead of Prospero.

Miranda offers to carry Ferdinand's logs while Prospero looks on in Act III, Scene 1 of *The Tempest*. This is a plate from *Retzsch's Outlines to Shakespeare: The Tempest,* published in 1841. *(Illustration by Moritz Retzsch)*

Act III, Scene 1

This scene opens with Ferdinand carrying logs, on Prospero's orders. Miranda joins him while Prospero, unnoticed by either of them, looks on. Miranda offers to help with the log carrying, but Ferdinand will not allow it. They reveal their love to each other while Prospero privately rejoices.

Act III, Scene 2

Caliban, Stephano, and Trinculo are now all completely drunk. Ariel, who is invisible again, enters to spy on them, echoing the surveillance motif of the previous scene, and sows discord among them by imitating Trinculo's voice (Shakespeare had already used this technique in *A Midsummer Night's Dream* when Puck imitates the voices of Demetrius and Lysander). Caliban suggests that Stephano should kill Prospero while he sleeps and then claim Miranda as his wife. Ariel allows them to hear him playing music, and they are alarmed but resolve to carry out Caliban's plan.

Act III, Scene 3

Now we rejoin the king and his courtiers, who have been looking for Ferdinand. The king despairs of finding him, and Sebastian and Antonio privately agree to make another attempt to kill the king and seize his power. Suddenly, several of Prospero's supernatural servants enter carrying a banquet, watched by Prospero himself, who has made himself invisible. The Neapolitans try to eat the food, but Ariel, disguised as a harpy (a mythical monster, half bird and half woman), lands on the table and, in another "special effect," the banquet vanishes. The Neapolitans draw their swords but are powerless to do anything. Ariel tells the king, Sebastian, and Antonio that their treatment of Prospero is responsible for their present plight, and that they are doomed. The spirits reappear to remove the table. Antonio, Sebastian, and the king run madly off the stage, and Gonzalo leads the other Neapolitans in pursuit of them.

Act IV, Scene 1

Casting off his previous pretense of hostility, Prospero now gives Miranda to Ferdinand and explains the motive for his earlier behavior. He warns them, though, against consummating the relationship before they are married. Prospero sends Ariel to fetch the other spirits to perform an entertainment in celebration of the wedding, and they put on a masque featuring the classical goddesses Iris, Ceres, and Juno. They are joined by some dancing nymphs and reapers, but the masque ends abruptly when Prospero suddenly remembers the plot against him hatched by Caliban, Stephano, and Trinculo. Prospero sends Ferdinand and Miranda to his cave and summons Ariel, who explains that he led the three conspirators on a merry dance and left them up to their necks in a filthy pool. Prospero sends Ariel, still invisible, to fetch some gaudy clothes from his cave and hang them up where Caliban and his new friends will see them. The conspirators enter, see the clothes, and start putting them on. While they are distracted, Prospero's spirits enter in the shape of dogs. Urged on by Prospero and Ariel, they chase Caliban, Stephano, and Trinculo off the stage.

Act V, Scene 1

Prospero and Ariel take stock of the situation, noting that the Neapolitans are all being held prisoner, and that the king, Sebastian, and Antonio are now completely out of their minds. Moved to forgiveness, Prospero sends Ariel to release them and resolves that he will henceforth renounce magic. Ariel returns with the Neapolitans, and Prospero removes the spell that holds them and sends Ariel to the ship to wake the sailors from an enchanted sleep. Coming to himself, the king immediately offers Prospero his dukedom back. Prospero observes privately to Sebastian and Antonio that he could reveal their treachery if he wished, though he will not do so at the moment, and tells Antonio that he forgives him for his earlier treachery. He then reveals Ferdinand and Miranda, who are playing chess inside his cave. Ariel arrives with the Master and Boatswain, who explain that the ship is fully seaworthy. Prospero promises to explain everything in due course and sends Ariel to fetch Caliban, Stephano, and Trinculo, then promises Ariel that he will be free once he has seen them all safely to Naples.

CHARACTER LIST

Alonso, king of Naples He holds the highest rank in the play. He is the father of Ferdinand and of Claribel (whom we never see) and older brother of Sebastian. Twelve years before the play began, he was partly responsible for deposing Prospero as duke of Milan.

Sebastian Younger brother of Alonso and uncle of Ferdinand. He is friendly with Prospero's

Prospero brings the king to Ferdinand and Miranda in Act V, Scene I of *The Tempest*. This is a plate from *Retzsch's Outlines to Shakespeare: The Tempest*, published in 1841. (*Illustration by Moritz Retzsch*)

brother Antonio and conspires with him to kill Alonso.

Prospero   The rightful duke of Milan, who was exiled from Milan 12 years before with his infant daughter, Miranda, and has since been living on a small island with her, Caliban, and Ariel. Prospero is a powerful magician who can call on the services of a number of spirits.

Antonio   Prospero's brother, who was responsible for deposing him and has since been ruling as duke of Milan in his place.

Ferdinand   Heir to the throne of Naples. He is not implicated in his father's or his uncle's wrongdoing and indeed is not really associated at all with the rest of the Neapolitans. He falls in love with Miranda, and they will rule as both king and queen of Naples and duke and duchess of Milan.

Gonzalo   Twelve years earlier, Gonzalo took pity on Prospero and supplied him and Miranda with food, drink, and clothes for their journey, as well as some of Prospero's books. On the island, he invariably takes a more positive view than anyone else, whether it is of their surroundings or of the people they encounter.

Adrian and Francisco   Two Neapolitan lords.

Caliban   Described in the First Folio as "a savage and deformed slave," by the Neapolitans as a fish and a monster, and by Prospero as a demi-devil and a thing of darkness, Caliban has been variously interpreted on stage and screen and in criticism as a Native American, as Irish, as black, and as the power of the id.

Trinculo   The king of Naples's jester, who becomes involved with Caliban and Stephano in a plot to kill Prospero.

Stephano   The king's butler, who comes safely ashore with his own private supply of wine and gives some to Caliban, who thereafter follows him slavishly.

The Master of the Ship   He spends most of the play in an enchanted sleep.

The Boatswain   He is also cast into an enchanted sleep for most of the play.

Mariners   These are seen only in the first scene of the play.

Miranda   Prospero's daughter. Uniquely in Shakespeare, Miranda is the only female character whom we meet in the play. Having lived on the island since she was nearly three, she is completely innocent of the world beyond. She falls in love with Ferdinand and sails away at the end of the play to become queen of Naples and duchess of Milan.

Ariel   A spirit, whom Prospero found imprisoned in a cloven pine tree when he arrived on the island and who has since served him until he is released at the end of the play. In the masque, Ariel takes the role of Ceres.

Two other characters who are never seen should also be mentioned:

Claribel   Daughter of the king of Naples, from whose wedding to the king of Tunis the Neapolitans are returning when they are shipwrecked.

Sycorax   Witch from Algiers and mother of Caliban, she imprisoned Ariel in the tree before she died on the island.

CHARACTER STUDIES
Prospero

Prospero exerts an enormous degree of control over the action of the play, to the extent that he has often been identified as a representation (and representative) of the dramatist himself. It is he who raises the tempest that gives the play its name, and which brings the Neapolitan characters to the island. He seems to have total control over both Caliban and Ariel, though it is unclear whether his control over Ariel is a simple matter of power or due in any part to Ariel's gratitude to Prospero for his release from the cloven pine in which Sycorax had imprisoned him. Prospero manipulates Miranda's perceptions by putting her into an enchanted sleep when he wishes to speak to Ariel, and indeed it is not actually clear whether Miranda is even aware of Ariel; she is certainly never seen speaking to him. Prospero also plays games with Ferdinand by deliberately putting unnecessary obstacles in the way of his courtship of Miranda, and he can perhaps be

Prospero threatens Ferdinand while Miranda protests in Act I, Scene 2 of *The Tempest*. This is a plate from *Retzsch's Outlines to Shakespeare: The Tempest*, published in 1841. *(Illustration by Moritz Retzsch)*

seen as doing something similar when he warns Antonio and Sebastian that he could tell the king of their treachery if he so chose. Moreover, in two separate scenes, he spies invisibly on what people are doing. This is something that he has in common with Vincentio, the duke in the problem play *Measure for Measure*, whose description as an "old fantastical duke of dark corners" (4.3.155–156) might well be thought applicable to Prospero too.

One of the fascinating things about criticism of *The Tempest* is how differently critics of different periods have responded to this degree of control. For the Victorians, Prospero was two things, which were subtly interlinked. First, he was a self-portrait of Shakespeare, manipulating the action and ultimately laying down his art supposedly as Shakespeare decided to retire to Stratford, and second, he was a type of the wise, benevolent colonial master, patiently exercising paternalistic control over his "native" servants much as British imperial administrators dealt firmly but for their own good with "natives" in India and Africa. Prospero's relationship with Caliban might indeed lie behind Rudyard Kipling's famous description of the relationship between colonial master and servant in his 1899 poem "The White Man's Burden":

Take up the White Man's burden—
Send forth the best ye breed—
Go bind your sons to exile
To serve your captives' need;
To wait in heavy harness,
On fluttered folk and wild—
Your new-caught, sullen peoples,
Half-devil and half-child.

A good example of this view of Prospero as wholly benevolent can be see in the first film version of *The Tempest,* directed by Percy Stow in 1908, in which Prospero with his long white hair and beard strongly resembles Father Christmas.

In the 20th century, however, far less positive views of the British Empire began to emerge, and with them came a sea change in critics' and directors' views of Prospero: as Philip Mason, an Englishman, put it in 1962, "In my country until a generation ago we liked Prospero; [now] some of us are beginning not to like him" (qtd. in Vaughan and Vaughan 1991: 162). This came about not least because of the numerous reworkings of and allusions to *The Tempest* from colonized or previously colonized countries such as Octave Mannoni's *Psychology of Colonization* (1950), Frantz Fanon's *Black Skin, White Masks* (1952), George Lamming's *The Pleasures of Exile* (1960) and *Water with Berries* (1971), Aimé Césaire's *A Tempest* (1969), Roberto Fernández Retamar's *Caliban* (1971), and Ngugi wa Thiong'o's *A Grain of Wheat* (1968). The degree of control Prospero exercises began to look sinister rather than benevolent, and it began to seem possible, as it never would have to the Victorians, that Caliban's complaint that Prospero had stolen the island from him might have some force to it. Critics also began to notice that Prospero seems extremely interested in his daughter's chastity, something that looked particularly suggestive as psychoanalysis emerged as an increasingly influential force in literary criticism. Prospero repeatedly exhorts Ferdinand not to sleep with Miranda before they are married, and one might well notice too his reply to Miranda when she asks in surprise if he is not her father, "Thy mother was a piece of virtue, and / She said thou wast my daughter" (1.2.56–57). One might well think that this is a joke in poor taste when talking to a teenage girl, and the suggestion of something slightly sinister here, of something of an obsession with women's sexuality and sexual behavior, is strongly developed in *Forbidden Planet:* One critic refers to "the scientist Dr. Morbius and his daughter Altaira, played with an Electral affection by Walter Pidgeon and Anne Francis" (Knighten 1994: 36).

It is also the issue of control that is at the heart of the Foucaultian reading of Prospero advanced by Richard Wilson:

> Prospero embraces his foes . . . because the
> modern prince exerts no corporal dominion,
> but fabricates each a position in the order
> of discourse, breaking his staff to signify
> that "they shall be themselves" . . . his role
> nears its end as the discipline he instituted
> is disseminated. For historically this duke is
> what Foucault calls a "Napoleonic character";
> a "Great Observer," such as Bacon heralded,
> who stands at the juncture of ritual sovereignty
> and invisible repression. He is "the individual
> who looms over everything with a single gaze,
> at one and the same time the bearer of the
> ancient sword and the organiser of the new
> state, who combines in a single, symbolic
> figure . . . the vigilance which would soon
> render useless both the scaffold and the
> throne. (156)

For Wilson, Prospero is thus effectively a direct development of the "old fantastical duke of dark corners" (4.3.155–156) of *Measure for Measure,* who literally spies on his subjects until he has so effectively implanted in them the idea of his powers of surveillance that they will have internalized them and will no longer need actual watching.

Caliban

It is not really possible to consider Prospero in isolation from other characters, and his relationship with Caliban is particularly important in this

respect. Caliban has the second-largest speaking part in the play (though it is dwarfed by the size of Prospero's—653 lines to 177, giving Prospero 29.3 percent of all the lines in the play and Caliban roughly 8.4 percent [Vaughan and Vaughan 1991: 7]), and in recent years, Caliban has grabbed much of the attention devoted to the play, despite the difficulty of defining who and what he actually is; for Supriya Chaudhuri, indeed he is "a kind of absence," a figure who should be seen as "inhabiting a space made available by the logic of erasure, as the term of what is missing" (225), while Robert Graves wrote that

> Caliban is partly Afagddu in the *Romance of
> Taliesin;* partly Ravaillac, the Jesuit-prompted
> murderer of Henry IV; partly an Adriatic devil
> in Calahorra's romance; partly a sea monster,
> "in shape like a man," seen off Bermuda
> during Admiral Sommers' stay there; partly
> Shakespeare's own *malus angelus* [evil angel].
> (qtd. in Vaughan and Vaughan 1998: 56–57)

In 1875, Edward Dowden, listing interpretations current in his own day, observed that, for at least some of his contemporaries, "Caliban is the colony of Virginia. He is the untutored early drama of Marlowe" or "He is Understanding apart from Imagination" (424).

It is part of the extraordinary suggestiveness and power of Shakespeare's art that he often underwrites characters and events, telling us just enough to pique our interest and never quite enough to satisfy it, and this is rarely more true than in the case of Caliban. It is almost impossible to say anything definitive about Caliban. The First Folio describes him as a "savage and deformed slave," though it should be stressed that we have no way of knowing whether we owe this description to Shakespeare himself or to his fellow actors Heminges and Condell, who collected the plays together to form the First Folio. Even if we accept it as in any sense authoritative, though, it still offers no clue about what Caliban's deformity might be (and it is worth remembering that the character must have been played by a member of Shakespeare's company, the King's Men, and there is no indication that any of them had any kind of deformity, so we need to be thinking about something that can be acted, as Richard III's deformity is, rather than any actual physical malformation). In the past, he has been staged as a tortoise, a snake, a giant fish, a missing link, and a monster; on stage in recent years, Caliban has often been black (or, at a time, covered from head to foot in blue body paint), though the closest we come to this in the text is that the sight of him makes Trinculo think of "a dead Indian" (2.2.32), that is, a Native American—and Shakespeare might have known what Native Americans could look like, for in 1586, Thomas Hariot brought back two, Manteo and Wanchese, from the ill-fated English colony on Roanoke.

If the "deformed" is uncertain, so, too, is the "savage," at any rate for modern readers and audience members, who find it difficult to see Prospero as an uncomplicatedly wise and benevolent ruler against whom it is wicked to rebel. In *Forbidden Planet,* for instance, Caliban is actually a part of Prospero's own psyche, and in many of the numerous rewritings of *The Tempest* originating from formerly colonized countries, Caliban, not Prospero, is the focus of interest. The big problem with this is Caliban's apparent attempt to rape Miranda, since it is impossible to condone that act even given his tentative attempt to suggest that it was part of a strategy to outnumber his would-be colonizers.

Despite—or perhaps because of—the uncertainties surrounding him, Caliban has proved one of the most provocative and intriguing of all Shakespeare's characters. Theories about the origins of his name abound: Is it an anagram of cannibal, does it derive from Carib, or is it from the Romany *caulibon* (meaning something black or dark), is it Irish, or should we trace it to the Arabic *kalebón,* meaning "vile dog" (Vaughan and Vaughan 1999: 27–33)? Is it significant that he gives the name Setebos to the god his mother worshipped, and that this name was mentioned in Antonio Pigafetta's account of Magellan's circumnavigation as that of a deity worshipped in Patagonia (Vaughan and Vaughan 1999: 38)? Two

books have been focused solely on Caliban, Alden T. Vaughan and Virginia Mason Vaughan's *Shakespeare's Caliban: A Cultural History* (Cambridge: Cambridge University Press, 1991) and Nadia Lie and Theo D'haen's edited collection *Constellation Caliban: Figurations of a Character* (Amsterdam: Rodopi, 1997), and he has proved to be extraordinarily versatile. On January 24, 1863, for instance, the satirical English magazine *Punch* depicted Caliban as black "Sambo" to whom Abraham Lincoln, wearing the uniform of a Union officer, is handing the Emancipation Proclamation (Vaughan and Vaughan 1998: 107), though not until 1945 did a black actor, Canada Lee, represent him on stage. In 1878, Ernest Renan cast him as a symbol of the Paris Commune (Vaughan and Vaughan 1998: 111); in the 1890s, Frank Benson acted him as "half monkey, half coco-nut" (Vaughan and Vaughan 1998: 185). In 1918, Sir Walter Raleigh, professor of English at the University of Oxford, equated him with the German army—"the monster, and the mooncalf, as who should say Fritz, or the Boche" (qtd. in Vaughan and Vaughan 1998: 127); for a journalist in 1930s South Africa, he represented Dutch Afrikaners (Vaughan and Vaughan 1998: 158); for Philip Mason, who became director of the Institute of Race Relations in the United Kingdom, Caliban in 1960s Britain was a much more generic figure—"the bad native, the nationalist, the extremist—the man who will be Prime Minister after independence" (Vaughan and Vaughan 1998: 161); in 1974, Max Dorsinville used him to figure the Québecois (Vaughan and Vaughan 1998: 170). Caliban, then, is the classic Other, able to stand as the opposite term of almost anything, but extraordinarily difficult to define on his own terms.

Ariel

Who or what is Ariel? That is no easier to answer than who or what is Caliban, and indeed in some productions the two questions are inextricably interlinked, because Ariel becomes essentially the opposite of whatever the director chooses to make his Caliban (in Jonathan Miller's famous 1970 production, for example, Caliban was a poor and recalcitrant black, while Ariel was also black but was much more biddable and willing to collude with the white masters). This is often the case in criticism too, as when Derek Traversi declares that "In contrast to Caliban as spirit to body, liberty to servitude, 'grace' to nature, stands the figure of Ariel" (237). Ariel has also been imagined primarily in relation to Prospero, as an emanation of Prospero's psyche, as in *Forbidden Planet* where the Ariel character is Robby the Robot, who exists only to do Morbius's bidding.

There are, though, questions about Ariel that are quite separate from the issues raised by Caliban and Prospero: first, which gender is Ariel, and

Ariel plays music and sings behind Ferdinand in Act I, Scene 2 of *The Tempest*. This illustration was designed for a 1918 edition of Charles and Mary Lamb's *Tales from Shakespeare*. (*Illustration by Louis Rhead*)

second, what happens to him/her at the end of the play? The "-el" suffix at the end of Ariel's name is that found in the names of spirits and angels (e.g., Gabriel, Michael, Raphael, Uriel), beings who theoretically transcended gender, though they are conventionally understood as male and are certainly so represented in art and usually in literature (Milton's long disquisition on their sexlessness aside). On the Victorian stage, Ariel was almost invariably played by a woman, but in modern stage and screen, he is generally male; critics generally refer to the character as "he," but in the play Ariel is addressed only in the second person and twice takes on female roles (Ceres and the harpy) as well as twice appearing as a nymph. (Though this does not necessarily indicate anything about his "underlying" gender: Boy actors habitually took the roles of women, as Francis Flute in *A Midsummer Night's Dream* acts Thisbe.) As for what happens to Ariel at the end of the play, that is no easier to answer. As Prospero has repeatedly promised, Ariel will finally be "free," but what does freedom mean for a spirit? Perhaps all we can really say is that the future we are asked to imagine for Ariel is something we *cannot* really imagine.

One thing that we perhaps can say about Ariel is that he appears to be associated with art. Cynthia Lewis suggests that

> Some attribute of Prospero's art . . . lies beyond his ability to corrupt it or to contain it; it is that principle that permits his artistry to intersect with Providence, to instill virtue, and to awaken both conscience and compassion in folly-fallen humanity.
>
> Such words come as close as I can force them to describing Ariel. . . . Many of Ariel's traits delineate him as the pure idea, spirit, of art in nature. (171)

Art was a matter of concern to Shakespeare throughout his career, but particularly so in his late plays. *The Winter's Tale,* for instance, contains a long discussion about the relative merits of art and nature in the production of flowers and shows us an apparent statue that ultimately proves to be alive. Ariel is at the least the instrument of Prospero's art and may well be of its essence, and as such it is perhaps not surprising that the keynote of his character should seem to be about eluding control, just as Shakespeare may well have felt that his own art was indeed something at least partly outside his own conscious control.

Miranda and Ferdinand

Finally, there are the young lovers, the two characters who might in another play have been the hero and heroine but who here are relegated to rather marginal roles. Ferdinand, like most of the young men in Shakespeare's late romances, is a fairly colorless figure, though at least he is not prone to blind jealousy like Postumus in *Cymbeline,* does not visit a brothel like Lysimachus in *Pericles,* and does not deceive his father like Florizel in *The Winter's Tale.* Like the other three heroines of the "last plays," Miranda's name offers us a pointer to how to read her: It is Latin, and it means "to be admired," which is why Ferdinand, when he hears it, says "Admired Miranda! / Indeed the top of admiration" (3.1.37–38). Despite Ferdinand's comment, though, Miranda is really more characterized by her admiring rather than being admired, as is seen in her most famous lines, "How beauteous mankind is! O brave new world / That has such people in't" (5.1.183–184). Miranda is like Gonzalo, charitable and inclined to see the best in everything and everyone, and she is also an interesting study of a personality completely innocent and untouched by civilization (something of the same effect can be seen in the Monster in Mary Shelley's *Frankenstein,* a book much influenced by *The Tempest*). Indeed, in some respects, Miranda can hardly be said to be a character at all; she is rather a blank canvas, a sounding board, an attempt to imagine what human nature might be like before it has been touched and shaped by experience, and as such she can also be seen as a powerful emblem of the mutual wonderment felt in the initial encounters between English explorers and Native Americans at the end of voyages such

Nora Kerin as Miranda and Basil Gill as Ferdinand in Act IV, Scene 1 of *The Tempest,* in this photograph of a 1904 production at His Majesty's Theatre. *(Photograph by J. & L. Caswall Smith; published by Virtue & Company)*

as that on which *The Sea Venture* was embarked at the time of the shipwreck.

DIFFICULTIES OF THE PLAY

The Tempest is not in general one of Shakespeare's more difficult plays, but one aspect modern audiences are likely to find confusing is the masque performance in Act IV, Scene 1. We are accustomed to the use of the play-within-a-play from earlier plays such as *A Midsummer Night's Dream,* but there is clearly something rather different going on in this play. In fact, this is one aspect of *The Tempest*'s sensitivity to changing theatrical tastes, because the masque, which had barely existed at the court of Elizabeth I, had in the decade since her death emerged as a vibrant, important and increasingly codified art form. The essential difference between masques and plays was that masques were performed at court, with courtly performers, usually including the queen, Anna of Denmark herself, accompanied by her ladies. Elaborately costumed, they would dance and speak their lines on stage and then at the end of the performance involve the courtly audience in the dancing. Masques generally centered on complex allegorical material and often involved extensive use of personification and symbolism. In the early years of King James's reign, they were often the joint production of Ben Jonson, who was responsible for the words, and Inigo Jones, who designed the elaborate scenery and costumes, but Jonson and Jones disagreed with increasing bitterness about the relative importance of these two elements until Jones eventually triumphed, establishing the masque as a predominantly visual genre. The presence of a masque in *The Tempest* can thus be clearly related to the play's wider interest in different modes of representation. Did one go to see a play or, as Shakespeare often puts it, to hear a play? Which was the more effective and interesting way of conveying information, the effects-based mode of Act I, Scene 1 or the simpler narrative one of Act I, Scene 2?

It is also important to note that the masque was a genre designed to reflect and enhance the idea of royal power. As part of his work on masques, Inigo Jones brought perspective scenery to the English stage for the first time, but the auditorium was arranged in such a way that only the king had a perfect view of it, underlining the importance of the royal gaze. A similar logic could also be seen at work in the context of some masques. In *The Masque of Blackness,* for instance, the daughters of the king of Niger are told that their supposedly disfiguring blackness will be "cured" if they journey to the court of a king whose country name ends in -tania, and they duly travel to Britannia, though in fact a technical hitch meant that it proved impossible to remove the black coloring with which the queen and her ladies had smeared their faces and arms, and the "happy ending" therefore had to be

deferred until *The Masque of Beauty* two years later. *The Tempest,* too, asks questions about the nature of rule and authority, and though its answers to these are much less clear-cut than those of the masque, its use of the masque form is an important part of the enquiry.

There are two additional aspects of the play that might present problems to a modern audience, though neither would have done so for Shakespeare's original audience. The first is the extent and significance of the debt to classical literature; Margaret Tudeau-Clayton suggests that *The Tempest* stages the disruption of the old world by the new:

> The dis-location of Old World forms and visions is dramatised by the dis-rupture of Prospero's masque, which is marked by "*confused noise*" and which points up the radical negativity at once of history, individual subjectivity and a nature indifferent to the forms received from the ancients, the "fathers of knowledge," and, specifically, Virgil.

She observes that, for example, the

> description of Caliban as "*dis*proportioned" recalls the figure, within Prospero's masque, of "dusky Dis" (iv.i.89), likewise a "thing of darkness" (v.i.275) and likewise a figure "from below," specifically from the Virgilian underworld. (199)

Vaughan and Vaughan further suggest that Caliban recalls another figure from an epic, the giant Polyphemus in Homer's *Odyssey* (Vaughan and Vaughan 1998: 57–58), and Jonathan Bate notes that Ovid, too, is important: "*The Tempest* alludes crucially to the story that was the subject of Ovid's only play; Shakespeare ended his career by collaborating with Fletcher, but his last solo performance was a kind of collaboration with Ovid" (239). Stephen Orgel confirms this, observing that "In giving up his magic, Prospero speaks as Medea" in Ovid's representation of her (11).

The second unfamiliar aspect is the complex hierarchy that exists among the European characters, something that is likely to be totally lost on modern audiences who will probably think of all the Europeans as Italian. This is, however, not strictly true. The Milanese characters—Prospero, Miranda, and Antonio—are Italian and have Italian names, but the Neapolitan characters are in fact Spanish in origin, for the kingdom of Naples had in Shakespeare's time been colonized by the Spanish under the leadership of the House of Aragon (much is made of this in Webster's *The Duchess of Malfi,* where the Spanish-born duchess's reliance on her Italian steward is greeted by her aristocratic brothers rather as a British memsahib's relationship with an Indian might have been viewed in the days of the Raj). The Neapolitans then have in fact already been acting in effect as colonizers before they even land on the island.

KEY PASSAGES
Act I, Scene 2, 121–132

PROSPERO. This King of Naples, being an
  enemy
To me inveterate, hearkens my brother's suit,
Which was that he, in lieu o'th premises
Of homage, and I know not how much tribute,
Should presently extirpate me and mine
Out of the dukedom and confer fair Milan,
With all the honours, on my brother.
  Whereon—
A treacherous army levied—one midnight
Fated to th'purpose did Antonio open
The gates of Milan and i'th'dead of darkness
The ministers for th'purpose hurried thence
Me and thy crying self.

Prospero's account to Miranda of how they came to be exiled on the island is presumably intended to elicit sympathy and to present himself in a good light, as indeed most people's accounts of unfortunate events in their past are usually intended to do. Nevertheless, it is worth noting some potentially troubling features of what he says. First, we are told merely that the king of Naples was "an enemy / To

Prospero explains to Miranda how they came to live on an island in Act I, Scene 2 in this illustration in a 1893 edition of *The Tempest. (Illustration by Walter Crane)*

me inveterate," but we might perhaps feel inclined to wonder why this was, especially because the king of Naples as we see him in the play does not seem a notably unjust or unreasonable man (it is true that he married Claribel to the king of Tunis essentially against her will, but there might have been compelling political reasons for that). Second, Prospero does not know how much tribute Antonio has agreed to pay, confirming the impression of a lack of interest in the practicalities of rule, which might well make one question his fitness and aptitude to exercise power. Finally, it is worth noting Prospero's description of the night on which he and Miranda were expelled from Milan as "Fated to th' purpose," because to suggest that something was fated can often function as a highly effective way of disclaiming any personal responsibility for it. There is something of a suggestion of the expulsion from the Garden of Eden about Prospero's account of how he and Miranda came to be exiled, and given that Adam and Eve bore some responsibility for their fate, perhaps Prospero did too.

Act I, Scene 2, 196–206

ARIEL. I boarded the King's ship: now on the
  beak,
Now in the waist, the deck, in every cabin
I flamed amazement. Sometime I'd divide
And burn in many places—on the topmast,
The yards and bowsprit would I flame
  distinctly,
Then meet and join. Jove's lightning, the
  precursors
O'th'dreadful thunderclaps, more momentary
And sight-outrunning were not; the fire and
  cracks
Of sulphurous roaring the most mighty
  Neptune
Seem to besiege and make his bold waves
  tremble,
Yea, his dread trident shake.

This is the passage that makes plainest Shakespeare's debt to William Strachey's account of the wreck of *The Sea Venture,* for Strachey had reported that

> on the Thursday night, Sir George Summers
> being upon the watch, had an apparition of a
> little round light, like a faint star, trembling,
> and streaming along with a sparkling blaze,
> half the height upon the mainmast, and
> shooting sometimes from shroud to shroud,
> tempting to settle as it were upon any of the
> four shrouds.

Strachey also seems to lie behind Caliban's reference to "Water with berries in't" (1.2.335), since he speaks of "the berries whereof our men, seething, straining, and letting stand some three or four days, made a kind of pleasant drink" (24).

Collectively, these echoes serve firmly to situate the play in the context of the Jamestown colony and the burgeoning British engagement with empire.

Act I, Scene 2, 226–237

ARIEL. Safely in harbour
Is the King's ship, in the deep nook where
  once
Thou called'st me up at midnight to fetch dew
From the still-vexed Bermudas; there she's hid,
The mariners all under hatches stowed,
Who, with a charm joined to their suffered
  labour,
I have left asleep. And for the rest o'th'fleet,
Which I dispersed, they all have met again,
And are upon the Mediterranean float,
Bound sadly home for Naples,
Supposing that they saw the King's ship
  wrecked
And his great person perish.

In this speech of Ariel's, we confront head on the complex question of the geographical positioning of *The Tempest.* We have just seen a passage that forcibly reminds us that part at least of the origin of *The Tempest* lies in accounts of the wreck of *The Sea Venture* on the coast of Bermuda (a connection that was first noticed by Edmond Malone in 1808); but if Prospero has sent Ariel "to fetch dew / From the still-vexed Bermudas" then they cannot be *in* the Bermudas. Indeed a quite different location is suggested when Ariel says that the remaining ships "are upon the Mediterranean float," as would indeed be logical for a party returning from Tunis to Naples, who would have to be very lost indeed before they found themselves anywhere near Bermuda. This is a play that may suggest several locations, but it commits to none.

Act I, Scene 2, 330–344

CALIBAN. I must eat my dinner.
This island's mine by Sycorax, my mother,
Which thou tak'st from me. When thou cam'st
  first

Thou strok'st me and made much of me;
  wouldst give me
Water with berries in't, and teach me how
To name the bigger light and how the less
That burn by day and night. And then I loved
  thee
And showed thee all the qualities o'th'isle:
The fresh springs, brine pits, barren place and
  fertile.
Cursed be I that did so! All the charms
Of Sycorax—toads, beetles, bats—light on
  you,
For I am all the subjects that you have,
Which first was mine own king; and here you
  sty me
In this hard rock, whiles you do keep from me
The rest o'th'island.

Part of what makes Caliban so haunting a character is the unusual combination of simplicity and lyricism in his speeches. From the prosaic and unpromising beginning of "I must eat my dinner," he opens up to us a powerfully imagined vision of what it might be like not to have words for things and to have all one's experiences and expectations overturned. It is also worth noting that Caliban's are the classic experiences of the colonized native: He is taught the new master's language and he is also enslaved by the new master's intoxicating drink, the "water with berries in't," which is surely either wine or spirits. At the same time, though, we are also made powerfully aware of both the seductiveness and the essential hollowness of the idea of rule: Before Prospero came, Caliban was king, but he was king only of himself. Finally, notice the rough versification of Caliban's lines: Though they follow the basic iambic pentameter pattern that is effectively the natural language of Shakespeare's characters, at least the well-born or well-spoken ones, his purchase on it is notably perilous, with the line beginning "Cursed be I that did so" having only eight syllables instead of the 10 it should have. This suggests both that Caliban's discourse is not like that of those around him and also that it does have a distinctive rhythm of its own.

Prospero and Miranda visit Caliban in his cave in Act I, Scene 2 of *The Tempest*. This is a print from the Boydell Shakespeare Gallery project, which was first conceived in 1786 and lasted until 1805. *(Painting by Henry Fuseli; engraving by B. Smith)*

Act I, Scene 2, 352–362

MIRANDA. Abhorred slave,
Which any print of goodness wilt not take,
Being capable of all ill; I pitied thee,
Took pains to make thee speak, taught thee
  each hour
One thing or other. When thou didst not,
  savage,
Know thine own meaning, but wouldst gabble
  like
A thing most brutish, I endowed thy purposes
With words that made them known. But thy
  vile race
(Though thou didst learn) had that in't which
  good natures
Could not abide to be with; therefore wast
  thou
Deservedly confined into this rock,
Who hadst deserved more than a prison.

Although *The Tempest* is a very "clean" text that is found only in the First Folio, meaning that there is no competing quarto version or versions as there is for, say, *Hamlet, Othello* and *King Lear,* this speech has proved controversial, for although the

First Folio clearly assigns it to Miranda, Victorian editors were uncomfortable with the suggestion that the young and virtuous heroine might have been responsible for teaching Caliban language, since he himself specifically says that one of the main things the acquisition of language has given him is the ability to curse, and that is definitely not something a nice girl like Miranda should have been teaching him. The speech was, therefore, generally assigned to Prospero during that period, and you may still find that in some modern editions, though this is increasingly unusual. Interestingly, both the disputed passages in *The Tempest* raise issues of gender, since there was a longstanding debate about whether Ferdinand says "So rare a wondered father and a wise / Makes this place paradise" (4.1.123–124) or "So rare a wondered father and a *wife*." (This was finally resolved when the original reading was shown to be "wife" [Roberts 1978].)

Apart from this, there are two aspects of the speech itself that are worth noting. First, Miranda's description of Caliban as "gabbling like a thing most brutish" may look like a classic instance of the colonial master refusing to accept the legitimacy of the indigenous language, but it also carries something of a sting in its tail, because the supposed foundation of Britain by Brutus, great-grandson of Aeneas, meant that the British were always potentially susceptible to a pun on *Brutish*: as Samuel Purchas was to ask in 1625, "Were not Caesar's Britons as Brutish as Virginians?" (qtd. in Wymer 1999: 4). Second, it is worth noting the way in which Miranda equates race and nature and effectively writes Caliban off as ineducable, since she identifies what she sees as defective in him as the product of nature rather than of nurture. The relative importance of nature and nurture is something to which Shakespeare pays considerable attention, particularly in the later part of his career.

Act II, Scene 1, 150–167

GONZALO. I'th'commonwealth I would by
   contraries
Execute all things, for no kind of traffic

Would I admit; no name of magistrate;
Letters should not be known; riches, poverty
And use of service, none; contract, succession,
Bourn, bound of land, tilth, vineyard—none;
No use of metal, corn, or wine or oil;
No occupation, all men idle, all;
And women too, but innocent and pure;
No sovereignty—

SEBASTIAN. Yet he would be king on't.

ANTONIO. The latter end of his
   commonwealth forgets the beginning.

GONZALO. All things in common nature
   should produce
Without sweat or endeavour; treason, felony,
Sword, pike, knife, gun, or need of any engine
Would I not have; but nature should bring
   forth
Of its own kind all foison, all abundance,
To feed my innocent people.

SEBASTIAN. No marrying 'mong his
   subjects?

ANTONIO. None, man, all idle—whores and
   knaves.

GONZALO. I would with such perfection
   govern, sir, T'excel the Golden Age.

This passage offers the fullest development both of the play's utopian theme and of the antinomies and tensions inherent in the idea of rule. Gonzalo begins by imagining a topsy-turvy state governed on something of the same principle that informed carnivalesque festivities such as those that traditionally attended the celebration of *Twelfth Night,* when the social hierarchy was temporarily inverted and those who were normally at the bottom of it were briefly allowed to preside at the top. He therefore purposes to strip away what we might regard as some of the key structures of society and civility, and yet as he goes on, what he is describing comes to sound not really like a state of anarchy but more and more like one of innocence (indeed the word *innocence* is twice mentioned)—one might even say, Edenic. It is certainly a landscape characterized both by lack of violence and lack of the need to work, two pillars of the prelapsarian state as generally envisaged (one also gets glimpses here of how important the discourse of the pastoral is to the ways *The Tempest* does and does not talk about its island). Just as one might begin to think this, however, Gonzalo introduces a new concept, one that does not sit altogether comfortably with that of the Edenic—the classical idea of the Golden Age, a time in the past when men were better, happier, and closer to the gods. Like *Dr. Faustus* before it, then, *The Tempest* puts classical and Christian values directly alongside each other in a way that may not make it easy for its audience to make a straightforward choice between them.

Act III, Scene 2, 144–152

CALIBAN. Be not afeard. The isle is full of
  noises,
Sounds and sweet airs that give delight and
  hurt not.
Sometimes a thousand twangling instruments
Will hum about mine ears; and sometimes
  voices,
That if I then had waked after long sleep,
Will make me sleep again; and then in
  dreaming,
The clouds, methought, would open and show
  riches
Ready to drop upon me, that when I waked
I cried to dream again.

Leslie Fiedler, in his book *The Stranger in Shakespeare* (1973), called Caliban's lines "No more dams I'll make for fish . . ." "the first American poem" (qtd. in Palmer 1991: 172). He might equally have remarked on this extraordinary vision of Caliban's, in which he displays a perhaps unexpected quality that Shakespeare and his audience seem to have valued very highly, a susceptibility to music. In *The Merchant of Venice*, we read that

The man that hath no music in himself,
Is fit for treasons, stratagems and spoils,
The motions of his spirit are dull night,
And his affections dark as Erebus.

           (5.1.83–87)

In *Pericles,* another of the late plays, we see one of the reasons for the importance that Shakespeare and his culture attached to music when Pericles, reunited with the daughter he had believed dead, thinks he hears "The music of the spheres! List, my Marina!" (5.1.229). The nine planetary spheres were indeed said to make music as they moved on their great dance through the heavens, in testimony to the divine harmony and order by which the universe was governed, and earthly music could thus be imagined as a reflection, however pale, of that cosmic song. That idea might well be present here too, and in a return to the play's interest in the Edenic, we might also wonder whether Caliban does not seem to be afforded something like a glimpse of heaven when the clouds part to show him things. As has often been observed, Gonzalo's Utopia speech is heavily influenced by Montaigne's essay *Of the Caniballes,* which stresses the innocence of New World natives, saying of the indigenous inhabitants of Brazil that "I finde (as farre as I have been informed) there is nothing in that nation, that is either barbarous or savage, unlesse men call that barbarisme, which is not common to them" (qtd. in Vaughan and Vaughan 1999: 303). This passage with its lyrical, haunting final line certainly makes it very difficult to read Caliban simply as a monster, a savage, a creature with an incurably bad nature for whom neither nurture nor civilization could ever do anything—and indeed one might well wonder whether he did not have something to offer to civilization.

Act IV, Scene 1, 14–24

PROSPERO. Then as my gift and thine own
  acquisition
Worthily purchased, take my daughter. But
If thou dost break her virgin-knot before
All sanctimonious ceremonies may

With full and holy rite be ministered,
No sweet aspersion shall the heavens let fall
To make this contract grow; but barren hate,
Sour-eyed disdain and discord shall bestrew
The union of your bed with weeds so loathly
That you shall hate it both. Therefore take
  heed,
As Hymen's lamps shall light you.

Prospero's stark warning to Ferdinand here has
led many critics to wonder what his problem is, and
whether there is not something slightly sinister
about his interest in his daughter's chastity. It is also
worth noting the natural imagery he uses to depict
the union of Ferdinand and Miranda: The "bed"
of which he speaks is literally their marriage bed,
but the mention of "weeds" makes it sound more
like a garden bed, so that the man-made institution
of marriage is here presented as something natural
rather than cultural. The reference to weeds also
recalls the Renaissance practice of strewing the bed
of a newly married couple with flowers, as indeed
happened at the wedding of Princess Elizabeth to
the elector palatine as part of the celebrations for
which *The Tempest* was performed. Finally, it recalls
the link in *A Midsummer Night's Dream* of the discord between Titania and Oberon and disruption
in the natural world, and may therefore remind us
that behind that speech in *A Midsummer Night's
Dream* lay genuinely severe weather conditions that
had caused a series of bad harvests culminating in
grain riots not long before *The Tempest* was written. These lines would therefore have been powerfully resonant for Shakespeare's original audience.

Act IV, Scene 1, 146–163

PROSPERO. You do look, my son, in a moved
  sort,
As if you were dismayed. Be cheerful, sir.
Our revels now are ended. These our actors,
As I foretold you, were all spirits and
Are melted into air, into thin air;
And—like the baseless fabric of this vision—
The cloud-capped towers, the gorgeous
  palaces,

The solemn temples, the great globe itself,
Yea, all which it inherit, shall dissolve,
And like this insubstantial pageant faded,
Leave not a rack behind. We are such stuff
As dreams are made on, and our little life
Is rounded with a sleep. Sir, I am vexed;
Bear with my weakness; my old brain is
  troubled.
Be not disturbed with my infirmity.
If you be pleased, retire into my cell
And there repose. A turn or two I'll walk
To still my beating mind.

This great speech is in some ways more like a
masque than the actual masque in the play, for like
the moment at the end of a masque when the actors
collapse the distinction between stage and reality
by dancing with the audience, so, too, this speech
cuts through the illusion of the play and reminds
us of reality. The reference to "revels" would for
Shakespeare's original audience evoke the Master
of the Revels, the official responsible for the licens-
ing of plays, and we also hear of actors and of the
"great globe" itself, the name of Shakespeare's

Prospero fetches spirits to dance for Ferdinand and
Miranda on their wedding day in Act IV, Scene 1 of *The
Tempest*. This is a print from the Boydell Shakespeare
Gallery project, which was first conceived in 1786 and
lasted until 1805. *(Painting by Joseph Wright; engraving by
Robert Thew)*

theater. Even the reference to Prospero's "cell" might point in a similar direction, because the other venue in which the King's Men performed, the Blackfriars theater, was a former monastery. At the same time, though, the speech also calls reality into question, since "We are such stuff / As dreams are made on," and Prospero's thoughts seem to be turning to whatever may lie beyond the natural, visible world.

DIFFICULT PASSAGES
Act II, Scene 1, 74–85

ADRIAN. Tunis was never graced before with such a paragon to their queen.

GONZALO. Not since widow Dido's time.

ANTONIO. Widow? A pox o'that. How came that widow in? Widow Dido!

SEBASTIAN. What if he had said widower Aeneas too? Good lord, how you take it!

ADRIAN. Widow Dido, said you? You make me study of that. She was of Carthage, not of Tunis.

GONZALO. This Tunis, sir, was Carthage.

ADRIAN. Carthage?

GONZALO. I assure you, Carthage.

All the characters involved seem to find this discussion of great interest, but a modern audience may well feel puzzled about *why* they do. Basically what happens here is that Adrian declares that Tunis has never had such a queen as Claribel, but Gonzalo counters by reminding his companions that the modern Tunis was the classical Carthage, and that Dido was once queen there. The story of Dido and Aeneas was one of great interest to Shakespeare's culture for a number of reasons. First, Aeneas was supposedly the ancestor of the Tudors and Stuarts, while Dido's other name of Elissa made her

a potentially useful figure for referring not only to Queen Elizabeth but also the late queen's young namesake, Princess Elizabeth, at whose wedding *The Tempest* was performed. Second, Dido was the subject of a play by Shakespeare's exact contemporary Christopher Marlowe, *Dido, Queen of Carthage*. Marlowe had died in 1593, but Shakespeare had not forgotten him, and of all Marlowe's plays, *Dido, Queen of Carthage* is perhaps the one that exerted most influence on Shakespeare's work: He remembered it in *A Midsummer Night's Dream*, he remembered it in *Hamlet,* and here he seems to be remembering it in *The Tempest* too. His characteristic attitude in these recollections of Marlowe's play is one of amused affection: In *Hamlet,* it is remembered as an old play that did not find favor with the general public but which Hamlet himself liked; in *A Midsummer Night's Dream*, Dido and Aeneas are mocked as Titania and any-ass; and in *The Tempest,* too, the recollection of Marlowe's play inspires humor, in the shape of the wordplay about the widow Dido. Thus the recurrent metatheatrical note in the play is quietly sounded here, along with a reminder of the importance of the classical world and the role it played in providing a critical paradigm for the exploration and settlement of new territories: Arthur B. Ferguson observes that "Richard Eden . . . noticed, in the course of his translation of Peter Martyr's *Decades of the Newe Worlde,* that the origin myths nourished by the Indians were 'fables much like Ovid his transformations'" (57), Juan Luis Vives found the Indians similar to the Greeks at the time of their mythmaking, and Thomas Hobbes was simultaneously translating Thucydides and investing in the Virginia and Summer Island Companies, while Richard Hakluyt's "Epistle Dedicatory to Sir Walter Raleigh" (1587) exhorted him, "Let the doughty deeds of Ferdinand Cortés, the Castilian, the stout conqueror of New Spain, here beautifully described, resound ever in your ears and let them make your nights not less sleepless than did those of Themistocles the glorious triumphs of Miltiades." Classical comparisons were not, however, chosen at random; Joan Pong Linton points out that "the four mythological heroes most frequently associated with the period's travelers to the New World are Jason, Theseus, Aeneas, and Odysseus: inconstant lovers to the mistresses of their travels because they would be true husbands" (10). Finally, Shakespeare's audience would have been aware that the House of Aragon had indeed attempted to make an alliance with the rulers of Tunis, since they feared that the city might otherwise be used as a bridgehead for the invasion of Spain from the Islamic world.

Act V, Scene 1, 34–57

PROSPERO. Ye elves of hills, brooks, standing
  lakes and groves,
And ye that on the sands with printless foot
Do chase the ebbing Neptune, and do fly him
When he comes back; you demi-puppets that
By moonshine do the green sour ringlets
  make,
Whereof the ewe not bites; and you whose
  pastime
Is to make midnight mushrooms, that rejoice
To hear the solemn curfew, by whose aid—
Weak masters though ye be—I have bedimmed
The noontide sun, called forth the mutinous
  winds,
And 'twixt the green sea and the azured vault
Set roaring war; to the dread-rattling thunder
Have I given fire and rifted Jove's stout oak
With his own bolt: the strong-based
  promontory
Have I made shake, and by the spurs
  plucked up
The pine and cedar; graves at my command
Have waked their sleepers, ope'd and let 'em
  forth
By my so potent art. But this rough magic
I here abjure; and when I have required
Some heavenly music (which even now I do)
To work mine end upon their senses that
This airy charm is for, I'll break my staff,
Bury it certain fathoms in the earth,
And deeper than did ever plummet sound
I'll drown my book.

Prospero's speech starts by evoking a world of nature and nature spirits that might at first seem to take us back to the joyous magic of *A Midsummer Night's Dream,* with its fairies and folk customs. The reference to raising the dead, however, moves us into very different territory and takes us well beyond the love potions and semi-transformations of the fairies in *A Midsummer Night's Dream* to something extremely sinister-sounding, which surely savors of black magic rather than white. Is that what Prospero actually means, though, or could he be imagined rather as Shakespeare speaking here, and referring to the fact that his plays— most notably his histories, which made up nearly a third of his output—have brought long-dead characters "alive" in front of audiences, as Thomas Nashe said he had done in the *Henry VI* plays when he made the great hero Talbot "come alive" again? This speech has certainly been central to those readings of the play that have taken Prospero as a self-portrait of Shakespeare. Finally, something that modern audiences will be unlikely to realize but which at least some members of Shakespeare's original audience would certainly have noticed is that this speech is a close translation of a speech in Ovid, Shakespeare's favorite Roman author, where the lines are spoken by the witch Medea and are addressed to Hecate, queen of the witches. Prospero throughout the play has presented his own magic as the polar opposite of that of the witch Sycorax, Caliban's mother, but here a witch is exactly what he sounds like, and soon he will say of Caliban "This thing of darkness I acknowledge mine," perhaps suggesting that one of the reasons he proves able to forgive the frailties of others is that he is at last beginning to come to terms with his own.

CRITICAL INTRODUCTION TO THE PLAY

The Tempest may well have been the last play that Shakespeare wrote single-handedly, and it has, as many critics have pointed out, some notable family resemblances with what are usually classed as Shakespeare's other "late" plays, *Cymbeline, Pericles,* and

The Winter's Tale. In some ways, though, what is even more striking is its resemblance to works from the very early part of Shakespeare's career, almost as if he were deliberately looking back and recapitulating. *The Comedy of Errors,* which may well have been his first play, also featured magic and shipwreck, and the two have something else in common in that *The Comedy of Errors* is Shakespeare's shortest play and *The Tempest* his second shortest. Both, too, observe the three unities of time, place, and action. Shipwreck is important too in *Twelfth Night,* where Viola escapes from the sea as Ferdinand does, to be reunited with her brother as Ferdinand is with his father (and *Twelfth Night,* like *The Tempest,* has an associated pair of characters, Sebastian and Antonio). Magic was important too in *A Midsummer Night's Dream,* and in many ways Ariel is very like Puck.

This element of revisiting motifs that Shakespeare had already used before is part of the profound narrative and artistic self-consciousness of *The Tempest,* and it is this, together with the fact that Prospero is an older man with a very significant relationship with his daughter, which has made critics so ready to view Prospero as in effect a self-portrait of Shakespeare, aging, tired, and ready to renounce his art as soon as he has finished this one final exhibition of it. In recent years, the idea that Shakespeare is here telling us something about himself has taken a new twist with the growing interest in the idea that Shakespeare might have been a Catholic, since Prospero's references to "indulgence" and his "cell" and to the putting of hands together in his final address to the audience might seem to point in this direction: Richard Wilson speaks of

the theological tenor of the play's epilogue, which ends with what seems to be a heartfelt repetition of the Catholic commemoration of "the souls of the Faithful Departed, for whose release from purgatory prayers are at this time [Hallowmas Night, the date of the first known court performance] offered and masses performed." For when Prospero begged

them to grant an "indulgence," they would have heard not just a breach of the Anglican Thirty-Nine Articles, which condemned the "Romish Doctrine concerning purgatory and pardons" as "a fond thing vainly invented, and grounded upon no warranty of Scripture," but the most positive affirmation ever made on an English Renaissance stage of the Catholic belief in the power of intercessory prayer to the Saints and Virgin: "Which pierces so that it assaults / Mercy itself and frees all faults" (Epi, 17–18) . . . *The Tempest* thus closes with a clear petition to its Whitehall audience, on the day of the Saints, for an act of religious toleration. (206)

It is also conceivable that the mention of "Mistress Line" in the exchange between Caliban, Stephano, and Trinculo (4.1.236) could refer to the Catholic martyr Anne Line, who has been linked by some critics to Shakespeare's strange poem "The Phoenix and the Turtle": Richard Wilson suggests that "Shakespeare associated martyrdom with conspiracy, and in *The Tempest* even draped Caliban's plot in the 'trumpery' left hanging by 'Mistress Line.' Anne Line was the Jesuits' aged landlady, hanged for hiding priests" (201), and he relates this to the possibility that we should understand Shakespeare's strange poem "'The Phoenix and the Turtle' as a funeral elegy . . . for the Catholic martyr Anne Line" (298). We are, however, on speculative ground here.

Less speculative and ultimately more critically rewarding is to consider the nature of the art explored in the play. Obviously, there is the element of self-referential meta-theatricality mentioned earlier, but the specific form that Prospero's own "art" takes is magic. In this, Shakespeare is clearly revisiting not so much his own early work as that of Christopher Marlowe, whose *Dido, Queen of Carthage* told the story of Dido and Aeneas, to which *The Tempest* refers, and whose *Doctor Faustus* tells the story of a magician whose name, like Prospero's, can be translated as "fortunate," though in the case of *Doctor Faustus* that is obviously ironic, since at the end of the play, he is taken away to hell.

Faustus, though, sold his soul to the devil to obtain his magic powers, and there is certainly no suggestion that Prospero has done this (though perhaps Sycorax did). Instead, he seems to be a very different sort of magician, one much more in tune with the High Renaissance aims and ideals of an Italian humanist such as Pico della Mirandola, for whom magic was essentially on a continuum with science rather than a dabbling with dark powers, though this was not always a distinction well understood by the church. Both *Doctor Faustus*

and *The Tempest* do raise questions, though, about the extent to which things are predestined: Stephen Orgel argues that "If Antonio is not forced by Prospero to propose the murder, he is certainly acting as Prospero expects him to do, and as Ariel says, Prospero 'through his art foresees' that he will" (12), raising some of the same kinds of issues as the issue of predestination does in *Doctor Faustus*.

The play's interest in magic also relates to at least two others of its concerns. First, we are reminded in *Doctor Faustus* that the famous Roman poet Virgil, author of the *Aeneid*, had reputedly been a magician (Faustus refers to him

Prospero conjures a storm to wreck the ship of King Alonso in Act I, Scene 1 of *The Tempest*. This is a print from the Boydell Shakespeare Gallery project, which was first conceived in 1786 and lasted until 1805. *(Painting by George Romney; engraving by B. Smith)*

here by his surname, his full name being Publius Virgilius Maro):

> There saw we learnèd Maro's golden tomb,
> The way he cut an English mile in length,
> Through a rock of stone in one night's space.
> (A-text, 3.1.13–15)

As we have already seen, Virgil is very important in *The Tempest,* and indeed Ferdinand's first words to Miranda, "Most sure, the goddess . . . ," are a direct translation of the first words spoken in Virgil's poem by Aeneas when he makes landfall in Africa, "O dea certe" (literally, "O goddess surely"). Virgil, whose works formed the backbone of every schoolboy's education in Elizabethan and Jacobean England, was far from being just a long-dead Roman poet to Shakespeare and his audience. For one thing, the story that he told in the *Aeneid* was directly pertinent to England itself. According to the *Aeneid,* Aeneas, a Trojan nobleman, was one of the few Trojans to escape from the city of Troy when it was sacked by the Greeks, taking with him his father Anchises and his son Ascanius, but mislaying his wife Creusa in the course of the escape. Aeneas was able to do this because of the power of his mother Venus, who told him that he must make his way to Italy and found a new Troy in the city that would eventually become known as Rome. Aeneas got lost on his journey and landed in Africa, where he met the Carthaginian queen Dido, but when the god Mercury reminded him of his duty, he resumed his travels, leaving a distraught Dido to commit suicide. He duly founded the new Troy (Rome), but two generations later, his great-grandson Brutus accidentally shot his father dead with an arrow and had to flee into a further exile. Brutus journeyed until he found an uninhabited island that he named after himself—Britain. His descendants prospered and in due course, via King Arthur, became the ancestors of the Tudor dynasty and hence, rather less directly, of the Stuart dynasty, which was occupying the throne at the time when Shakespeare wrote. The idea that the rulers of Britain were thus pos-

sessed of the prestige and cultural authority of first Troy and subsequently Rome was known as the *translatio imperii,* literally, the "translation of empire" from its original capital city of Troy to its new one of London, which was sometimes called "Troynovaunt" or "New Troy."

For Shakespeare's audience, then, the story told by the *Aeneid* was in an important sense a sort of family history, and though we have largely lost sight of this story today, it was one of which Shakespeare's original audience would have been well aware, even if they did not necessarily believe that it represented actual historical truth. Elizabeth I had been painted with the figure of her supposed ancestor Aeneas clearly visible on a column in the background, and Marlowe's *Dido, Queen of Carthage* makes much play of the connections between the long-dead queen and the contemporary one (something which it was easy to do because in classical mythology Dido's other name, by which she was often known, was Elissa). Of particular importance was the fact that Aeneas was in a sense the first colonist, and his story was of great interest in the context of the nascent British colonial enterprise (Christopher Hodgkins, for instance, has written interestingly about the ways in which the story of the *Aeneid* provided a paradigm for understanding and recounting the story of Powhatan, his daughter Pocahontas, and first John Smith and then John Rolfe [1998]).

Magic, colonialism, and an interest in history were all also found in another figure who may have been of interest to the play, Dr. John Dee, Elizabeth I's professional "wizard," whom she commissioned to predict the most auspicious date for her coronation and whose supposed conversations with a spirit named Uriel may have inspired the name of Ariel. Dee made persistent attempts to speak to "angels" and traveled to Prague, where the Habsburg emperor Rudolph II was fascinated by magic and had collected around him all the "wizards" that he could. Dee was also interested in the attempt to establish a British colony in America. Welsh himself, Dee unearthed from Welsh history the figure of the legendary Prince

Madoc, who was supposed to have discovered America in the 11th century. Indeed it is Dee who is credited with coining the phrase "the British Empire" and who assured Queen Elizabeth that her supposed ancestor King Arthur had traveled extensively, conquering various lands as he went, and that she was therefore fully entitled to lay claim to them.

If one conquered new lands, though, how was one to rule them? This is a question in which *The Tempest* is interested, from the moment in the opening scene in which it is brought home to us that the rank of king means nothing on board a ship, where the Master's word must be law, but where everyone is in any case subject to the elements. Later, Gonzalo discusses how he would rule the island in terms that are clearly reminiscent of the discourse of Utopianism inaugurated by Sir Thomas More in 1516 (in a work directly stimulated by the discovery of America). Another important author recalled in the play is the French essayist Michel de Montaigne, who had written about the New World and, unusually for a writer of the period, was just as interested in how Europeans might appear to the inhabitants of the New World as in how the inhabitants of the New World might appear to Europeans. Everyone who lands on this island wishes to be its king, but the play itself seems unsure about the nature and value of kingship.

Where exactly is this island that everyone wants to rule? Perhaps that is the most puzzling question of all. The Neapolitans are on their way home after the wedding of Claribel in Tunis, so logically it ought to be in the Mediterranean, since they are sailing from Africa to Italy. However, Ariel mentions the Bermudas, and we can hear the echo of an account of a shipwreck off the Bermudas in the language of the play. Finally, many modern critics of the play have been prompted to think of either America or of Ireland (Baker 1997, Callaghan 2000). As mentioned previously, the play obeys the unities of time, place, and action, but just as it defies the unity of time by parading its Virgilian origins, so, too, it defies the unity of place by being suggestive of such very different locations.

Another category that transcends all these is that of genre, and in that respect, too, *The Tempest* is problematic. Jonathan Bate calls the play "a metamorphic romance" (240), but in the First Folio, it heads up the comedies, and Derek Traversi introduces his discussion of the last plays by referring to them as "The last comedies" (1). For Edward Dowden in 1875, *The Tempest* had so much the feel of a last play that he was not particularly concerned about whether it actually was or not:

in The Tempest we find the ideal expression
of the temper of mind which succeeded his
mood of indignation,—the pathetic yet
august serenity of Shakspere's final period. For
the purposes of such a study as this we may
look upon The Tempest as Shakspere's latest
play. Perhaps it actually was such; perhaps A
Winter's Tale or Cymbeline, or both, may have
followed it in point of time. It does not matter
greatly for the purposes of the present study,
which preceded and which succeeded . . . it
is The Tempest which gives its most perfect
expression to the spirit that breathes through
these three plays which bring to an end the
dramatic career of Shakespere; and therefore
for us it is Shakspere's latest play. (380)

In the 20th century, a special category was effectively invented for *The Tempest, Cymbeline, The Winter's Tale,* and *Pericles,* but one that has no certain name, being referred to variously as "romance," "late romance," and "last play," the last being a term that exists solely to denote these four generic puzzles.

There is, then, no general agreement about the generic affiliations of *The Tempest.* This is not an unfamiliar phenomenon in Shakespeare; indeed few of his plays can be easily pigeonholed as belonging wholly and exclusively to one particular genre. *Hamlet, Macbeth,* and *King Lear* are all clearly tragedies, but all also have comic characters in them; *A Midsummer Night's Dream* is a comedy, but it is haunted throughout by a potentially tragic outcome. Particularly pertinent in this respect are the so-called "problem plays," for these, like the last plays, form a distinctively Shakespearean genre so unlike anything else that a special term has had to be coined for it. Indeed the problem plays are in some ways rather like the last plays, but at the same time they are also distinctively different. Both mix elements of tragedy and comedy, and a comic ending of sorts is always supplied, but despite this apparent likeness, the two types of play are a long way apart in feel. "Problem play" is in itself a problematic and contested term in that there is no universal agreement about which actually *are* the problem plays, but *Measure for Measure* and *All's Well That Ends Well* lie at the heart of all definitions and groupings, and both those plays feature a prim young man who both dislikes and lusts after women. In each case, the young man is ultimately induced into a respectable marriage, but in each case, this is brought about only by a "bed-trick"— that is, by the young man being deceived because he thinks he has made a bargain to sleep with the girl he lusts after, but in fact another girl takes her place without his noticing, and by the time he discovers the deception, he finds he has no choice but to accept a marriage with the girl he has slept with rather than pursuing the one he initially desired. It is impossible to feel much confidence in the likely future of marriages founded on such a basis, and many modern female readers in particular will probably feel in any case that nothing would induce them to spend their lives shackled to one of these shallow, bitter young men. These marriages feel contrived and tawdry, rough and ready pairings-up, which are the best solution available in an obviously imperfect world.

The last plays, by contrast, offer us miracles. Contrived they may be, at least when it comes to their plots, but there is certainly nothing tawdry about them. Here we find real magic rather than the crude deception of the bed-trick, and a smack of the pastoral rather than the whiff of city corruption that taints the societies of *Measure for Measure* and *All's Well That Ends Well*. Above all, what last plays offer is romance, in the technical sense of a narrative filled with fantastic and improbable incidents, and usually episodic in form. The magic in itself is of course an important ingredient of the improbability, but so, too, are the shipwrecks, the way in which the heroes first lose and then find again members of their family, and the sense of the long sweeping arc of the story. Romance as a genre can also be seen as inherently reassuring, since part of its logic is that most of the things and people apparently lost or damaged during the course of the narrative are restored by the end, while the marriages that tend to occur among the young characters offer hope for the future. Perhaps this, above all, is what sets the last plays apart from the problem plays and accounts for the very significant difference in tone.

Perhaps above all, romance offers what might be called a depth of perspective, in the temporal rather than in the landscape sense. Perspective scenery had first appeared on the English stage in Inigo Jones's masque sets, and Shakespeare was clearly fascinated by the effect, as we can see in *King Lear,* where the effects of visual perspective are minutely described for the first time in English literature:

How fearful
And dizzy 'tis to cast one's eyes so low!
The crows and choughs that wing the midway
  air
Show scarce so gross as beetles; half way down
Hangs one that gathers sampire, dreadful trade!
Methinks he seems no bigger than his head.
The fishermen that walk upon the beach
Appear like mice, and yond tall anchoring bark
Diminish'd to her cock, her cock a buoy
Almost too small for sight.

(4.6.11–20)

The last plays deploy a similar phenomenon, but they apply it to time rather than distance. In *The Winter's Tale,* the first and second halves of the play are separated by a gap of 16 years; *Pericles* lasts long enough for Marina, who is born toward the beginning of the play, to be marriageable by the end of it. In *The Tempest,* this is achieved by the sense of

Prospero and Miranda go to meet Caliban in Act I, Scene 2 of *The Tempest*. This illustration was designed for a 1918 edition of Charles and Mary Lamb's *Tales from Shakespeare*. *(Illustration by Louis Rhead)*

depth of the past evoked by the Virgilian framework. This allows for events to be seen *sub specie aeternatis* (in the perspective of eternity) rather than just in the here and now, and allows us a viewpoint in which the importance of individual joys and sorrows diminish.

The Tempest has proved to be equally suggestive in the strikingly different things it has been made to mean in the centuries since Shakespeare wrote it. For the Victorians, Prospero might be the epitome of benevolent paternalism, which they liked to think characterized their own brand of colonialism and imperialism, but Caliban spoke

to a rather different discourse, though one that, to many Victorian minds, was interconnected with that of imperialism—the theory of evolution. Almost as soon as the idea of a "missing link" between man and the apes was mooted, Caliban was identified as the ideal candidate, most notably in Daniel Wilson's book *Caliban: The Missing Link* and not least because of lines such as those expressing his fear that he, Stephano, and Trinculo will "all be turned to barnacles, or to apes / With foreheads villainous low" (4.1.248–249), skull height and shape being crucial to Victorian theories of race and species. When the famous actor Frank Benson played the part, he prepared for it by going to London Zoo to study the apes and modeled his mannerisms on theirs. Of particular interest in the light of this is the way in which all the major classificatory mechanisms of race, species, and gender are blurred by the play: Ariel might be either male or female, Caliban can be understood with equal ease as either white or black, and the references to him by other characters as a fish, a monster, and a demi-devil also suggest that his actual species might be in question (not to mention the complex issue of Ariel's status as a spirit and his/her appearance as a harpy, a creature who is half human and half bird).

The theory of evolution was not the only idea to which Caliban proved adaptable; indeed in the sense of the classic Other, he can be used in a variety of situations and paradigms. For Fred M. Wilcox, director of *Forbidden Planet*, Caliban was the embodiment of the psychoanalytic concept of the id; for a number of writers from formerly colonized countries, such as Aimé Césaire or George Lamming, Caliban was a representative of the archetypal native; for J. R. R. Tolkien, Caliban was the figure who lay behind *Lord of the Ring*'s Gollum (Carpenter 1981: 77). For if Prospero represents Art, Caliban by contrast is surely Nature, and nature, as Shakespeare delights to show, is of infinite variety.

Indeed, perhaps the idea of nature lies at the heart of this play as it does in *The Winter's Tale*, where Perdita speaks of "great creating Nature"—

and nature was important, too, in *King Lear,* where the relationship between Lear and Cordelia is to some extent reprised in that of Prospero and Miranda. Nature, however, is not something uniformly positive in Shakespeare, for it can be cruel as well as kind, and it tends to be pitted against not only art but also nurture: Caliban is a "devil, upon whose nature / Nurture can never stick" (4.1.188–189). Modern criticism has also made us see that nature also is an idea that can be deployed in sinister ways, since a rhetoric of the natural can be used to legitimize particular perspectives and to stigmatize others as "unnatural." (One might note here the way in which Prospero's elision of the marriage bed and a garden bed works to pass monogamous, heterosexual marriage off as natural and normal and by implication to suggest that other modes of structuring human relationships run counter to nature.) Perhaps *The Tempest*'s greatest sleight-of-hand is to use its art to stage some very probing questions about what constitutes the "natural" in human power relations, as its apparently simple desert island is revealed as both an island of the mind and a microcosm of a society at the dawn of the colonial enterprise.

EXTRACTS OF CLASSIC CRITICISM

Ben Jonson (1572–1637) [From *Bartholomew Fair* (1614), Induction, l. 100–111. Shakespeare's friend and colleague Ben Jonson was one of the first to comment on *The Tempest*. Although he referred in the First Folio to "my beloved, the Author Master William Shakespeare," he pokes gentle fun here at *The Tempest*, along with *The Winter's Tale,* for the improbability of the events they stage, contrasting this with his own more realist drama.]

The author doth promise a strutting hourse-courser with a leer drunkard, two or three to attend him, in as good equipage as you would wish. And then for Kindheart, the tooth-drawer, a fine oily pig-woman with her tapster to bid you welcome, and a consort of roarers for music. A wise Justice of Peace *meditant,* instead of a juggler with an ape. A civil cutpurse *searchant.* A sweet singer of new ballads *allurant,* and as fresh an hypocrite as ever was broached *rampant.* "If there be never a servant-monster i'the Fair, who can help it?' he says, "nor a nest of antics?' He is loath to make nature afraid in his plays, like those that beget *Tales, Tempests,* and such like drolleries, to mix his head with other men's heels.

Samuel Pepys (1633–1703) [From his diary entry for November 7, 1667. Pepys, the famous 17th-century diarist and an indefatigable playgoer, was not particularly impressed when he saw *The Tempest.*]

At noon resolved with Sir W. Pen to go see "The Tempest," an old play of Shakespeare's . . . The house mighty full; the King and Court there: and the most innocent play that ever I saw; and a curious piece of musique in an echo of half sentences, the echo repeating the former half, while the man goes on to latter; which is mighty pretty. The play [shows] no great wit, but yet good, above ordinary plays.

John Dryden (1631–1700) [From his preface to *Troilus and Cressida* (1679). Himself a playwright who in fact produced a rewriting of *The Tempest* as well as other Shakespeare plays, was one of the first to comment on the originality of Caliban as a dramatic creation.]

No man ever drew so many characters, or generally distinguished 'em better one another, excepting only *Johnson:* I will instance but in one, to show the copiousness of his invention; 'tis that of "Calyban," or the monster in "The Tempest'. He seems there to have created a person which was not in Nature, a boldness which at first sight

Ariel tricks Caliban, Stephano, and Trinculo in a 19th-century illustration of Act IV, Scene 1 of *The Tempest*.

would appear intolerable; for he makes him a species of himself, begotten by an "Incubus" on Witch . . . the Poet has most judiciously furnish'd him with a person, a language, and a character which will suit him both by his Father's and Mother's side: he has all the discontents and malice of a Witch, and of a Devil; besides a convenient proportion of the deadly sins; Gluttony, Sloth, and Lust, are manifest; the dejectedness of a slave is likewise given him, and the ignorance of one bred up in a Desart Island. His person is monstrous, as he is the product of unnatural lust; and his language is as hobgoblin as his person; in all things he is distinguished from other mortals.

Samuel Johnson (1709–1784) [From *General Observations on Shakespeare's Plays* (1768). The great critic Samuel Johnson, who wrote extensively on Shakespeare, disagreed with Ben Jonson completely—he found *The Tempest* to be if anything true to nature rather than flying in the face of it.]

Whatever might be Shakespeare's intention in forming or adapting the plot, he has made it instrumental to the production of many characters, diversified with boundless invention, and preserved with profound skill in nature, extensive knowledge of opinions, and accurate observation of life. In a single drama are here exhibited princes, courtiers, and sailors, all speaking in their real characters. There is the agency of airy spirits, and of an earthly goblin; the operations of magic, the tumults of a storm, the adventures of a desert island, the native effusion of untaught affection, the punishment of guilt, and the final happiness of the pair for whom our passions and reasons are equally interested.

William Hazlitt (1778–1830) [From *Characters of Shakespear's Plays* (1817). Hazlitt is arguably one of the most important Shakespearean critics of the 19th century. This is an early example of an imagination-oriented critic registering the power and strangeness of Caliban.]

The character of Caliban is generally thought (and justly so) to be one of the author's masterpieces. It is not indeed pleasant to see this character on the stage any more than it is to see the god Pan personated there. But in itself it is one of the wildest and most abstracted of all Shakespear's [*sic*] characters, whose deformity whether of body or mind is redeemed by the power and truth of the imagination displayed in it. It is the essence of grossness, but there is not a particle of vulgarity in it. Shakespear has described the brutal mind of Caliban in contact with the pure and original forms of nature; the character grows out of the soil where it is rooted, uncontrouled [sic], uncouth and wild, uncramped by any of the meanness of custom . . . It seems almost to have been dug out of the ground, with a soul instinctively superadded to it answering to its wants and origin.

Anna Jameson (1794–1860) [From *Characteristics of Women* (1832). The critic Anna Jameson is here enthusiastic about Miranda. The piece also reveals something of the mentality that made editors of her time remove the "learning to curse" speech from the supposedly innocent Miranda and assign it instead to Prospero.]

The character of Miranda resolves itself into the very elements of womanhood. She

Miranda in *The Tempest*. (Painting by G. W. Conarroe; engraving by Samuel Sartain)

is beautiful, modest, and tender, and she is these only; they comprise her whole being, external and internal. She is so perfectly unsophisticated, so delicately refined, that she is all but ethereal. Let us imagine any other woman placed beside Miranda—even one of Shakespeare's own loveliest and sweetest creations—there is not one of them that could sustain the comparison for a moment, nor one that would not appear somewhat coarse or artificial when brought into immediate contact with this pure child of nature, this "Eve of an unchanted Paradise." What, then, has Shakespeare done?—"O wondrous skill and sweet wit of the man!"—he has removed Miranda far from all comparison with her own sex; he has placed her between the demi-demon of earth and the delicate spirit of air. The next step is into the ideal and supernatural, and the only being who approaches Miranda, with whom she can be contrasted, is Ariel. Beside the subtle essence of this ethereal sprite, this creature of elemental light and air . . . Miranda herself appears a palpable reality, a woman, "breathing thoughtful breath," a woman, walking the earth in her mortal loveliness, with a heart as frail-strung, as passion-touched, as ever fluttered in a female bosom.

Samuel Taylor Coleridge (1772–1834) [From "The Moved and Sympathetic Imagination" (1836). The great poet Coleridge's response to the second scene of the play is a classic example of what we might call Prospero-centric criticism.]

In the second scene, Prospero's speeches, till the entrance of Ariel, contain the finest example I remember of retrospective narration for the purpose of exciting immediate interest, and putting the audience in possession of all the information necessary for the understanding of the plot. Observe, too, the perfect probability of the moment chosen by

Prospero (the very Shakespeare himself, as it were, of the tempest) to open out the truth to his daughter, his own romantic bearing and how completely any thing that might have been disagreeable to us in the magician, is reconciled and shaded in the humanity and natural feelings of the father. In the very first speech of Miranda the simplicity and tenderness of her character are at once laid open;—it would have been lost in direct contact with the agitation of the first scene.

Thomas de Quincey (1785–1859) [From "Shakespeare," Note 25 (1838). The essayist (and famous opium addict) Thomas de Quincey here offers an early example of a critic who can see some good in Caliban.]

Caliban has not yet been thoroughly fathomed. For all Shakspeare's great creations are, like works of nature, subjects of inexhaustible study. It was this character of whom Charles I and some of his ministers expressed such fervent admiration; and, among other circumstances, most justly they admired the new language almost with which he is endowed for the purpose of expressing his fiendish and yet carnal thought of hatred to his master. Caliban is evidently not meant for scorn, but for abomination mixed with fear and partial respect. He is purposely brought into contract with the drunken Trinculo and Stephano, with an advantageous result. He is much more intellectual than either,—uses a more elevated language not disfigured by vulgarisms, and is not liable to the low passion for plunder, as they are. He is mortal, doubtless, as his "dam" (for Shakspeare will not call her mother) Sycorax. But he inherits from her such qualities of power as a witch could be supposed to bequeath. He trembles indeed before Prospero; but that is, as we are to understand, through the moral superiority of Prospero in Christian wisdom, for, when

he finds himself in the presence of dissolute and unprincipled men, he rises at once into the dignity of intellectual power.

Daniel Wilson (1816–1892) [From *Caliban: The Missing Link* (1873). In 1859, Charles Darwin published *On the Origin of Species by Means of Natural Selection* and plunged the 19th century into a turmoil of doubt and fear about the question of man's origins and destiny. Shakespeare often provided a reassuring presence in this debate, not least

On Prospero's command, Ariel chases Caliban, Stephano, and Trinculo in Act IV, Scene 1 of *The Tempest*, in this print published by Freemantle & Company in 1901. *(Illustration by Robert Anning Bell)*

because he could be used to suggest that Englishmen at least had unquestionably evolved to a very high standard, as in *Coombs' Popular Phrenology* (1865), where a portrait of a suitably high-browed Shakespeare is compared with that of "A Cannibal New Zealand Chief" who is declared "Deficient . . . in all the Intellectual Organs." This passage offers a classic instance of the ways in which the name of Shakespeare could be evoked to make this alarming new theory seem safer and more acceptable.]

Shakespeare, in the Caliban of his "Tempest," anticipates and satisfies the most startling problem of the 19th century . . . It will need no apology to the appreciative student of Shakespeare that "the missing link" in the evolution of man should be sought for in the pages of him "whose aim was to hold as 'twere the mirror up to nature;" nor, if it is to be recovered anywhere, will he wonder at its discovery there.

Robert Browning (1812–1889) [From "Caliban upon Setebos: Or, Natural Theology in the Island" (1864). Although not strictly speaking criticism, the poet Robert Browning's dramatic monologue "Caliban upon Setebos; Or, Natural Theology in the Island," described by Vaughan and Vaughan as "a satire on Victorian theologians" (109), represents one of the 19th century's finest insights into the play and arguably inaugurates the emergence of Caliban rather than Prospero as a focus of critical interest and imaginative response, as well as offering another instance of the post-Darwinian reinterpretation of Caliban. It is a long poem, and space does not permit of reprinting it in full, but below is its opening section.]

"Thou thoughtest that I was altogether such a
   one as thyself.'
                                        (David, Psalms 50.21)

['Will sprawl, now that the heat of day is best,
Flat on his belly in the pit's much mire,
With elbows wide, fists clenched to prop his
   chin.
And, while he kicks both feet in the cool slush,
And feels about his spine small eft-things course,
Run in and out each arm, and make him laugh:
And while above his head a pompion-plant,
Coating the cave-top as a brow its eye,
Creeps down to touch and tickle hair and beard,
And now a flower drops with a bee inside,
And now a fruit to snap at, catch and crunch,—
He looks out o'er yon sea which sunbeams
   cross
And recross till they weave a spider-web
(Meshes of fire, some great fish breaks at times)
And talks to his own self, howe'er he please,
Touching that other, whom his dam called God.
Because to talk about Him, vexes—ha,
Could He but know! and time to vex is now,
When talk is safer than in winter-time.
Moreover Prosper and Miranda sleep
In confidence he drudges at their task,
And it is good to cheat the pair, and gibe,
Letting the rank tongue blossom into speech.]

Setebos, Setebos, and Setebos!
'Thinketh, He dwelleth i' the cold o'the moon.

'Thinketh He made it, with the sun to match,
But not the stars; the stars came otherwise;
Only made clouds, winds, meteors, such as that:
Also this isle, what lives and grows thereon,
And snaky sea which rounds and ends the same.

'Thinketh, it came of being ill at ease:
He hated that He cannot change His cold,
Nor cure its ache. 'Hath spied an icy fish
That longed to 'scape the rock-stream where
   she lived,
And thaw herself within the lukewarm brine
O' the lazy sea her stream thrusts far amid,
A crystal spike 'twixt two warm walls of wave;
Only, she ever sickened, found repulse
At the other kind of water, not her life,
(Green-dense and dim-delicious, bred o' the
   sun)

Flounced back from bliss she was not born to
  breathe,
And in her old bounds buried her despair,
Hating and loving warmth alike: so He.

Edward Dowden (1843–1913) [From "The
Serenity of *The Tempest*" (1875). The critic Dowden
here presents the classic statement of the Prospero-
is-Shakespeare view.]

It is not chiefly because Prospero is a great
enchanter, now about to break his magic
staff, to drown his book deeper than ever
plummet sounded, to dismiss his airy spirits, and to return to the practical service of
his Dukedom, that we identify Prospero in
some measure with Shakspere [*sic*] himself.
It is rather because the temper of Prospero,
the grave harmony of his character, his calm
validity of will, his sensitiveness to wrong,
his unfaltering justice, and with these, a
certain abandonment, a remoteness from the
common joys and sorrows of the world, are
characterics of Shakspere as discovered to us
in all his latest plays.

James Russell Lowell (1819–1891) [From
"Shakespeare Once More" (1868–90). The American poet, critic, and editor James Russell Lowell
exerted an enormous influence on the literature of
his day. Here, he gives an early example of an allegorical interpretation of *The Tempest*.]

If I read it rightly, it is an example of how
a great poet should write allegory,—not
embodying metaphysical abstractions, but
giving us ideals abstracted from life itself,
suggesting an under-meaning everywhere,
forcing it upon us nowhere, tantalizing the
mind with hints that imply so much and tell
so little, and yet keep the attention all eye
and ear with eager, if fruitless, expectation.
Here the leading characters are not merely

typical, but symbolical—that is, they do not
illustrate a class of persons, they belong to
universal Nature.

George Saintsbury (1845–1933) [From *A
Short History of English Literature* (1898). The critic
George Saintsbury also saw *The Tempest* in allegorical terms and followed Dowden in reading Prospero
as Shakespeare.]

The splendour of sunset in "The Tempest"
can escape no one, and the sternest opponent of guesswork must admit the probable
presence of a designed allegory in the figure
of Prospero and the burying of the book,
the breaking of the staff, at the close. Even
if this be thought too fanciful, nowhere has
Shakespeare been more prodigal of every
species of his enchantment. The exquisite
but contrasted grace of Miranda and Ariel,
the wonderful creation of Caliban, the varied human criticism in Gonzalo and the bad
brothers, the farce-comedy of Stephano and
Trinculo, do not more show the illimitable
fancy and creative power of the master in
scene and character than the passages, not so
much scattered as showered over the whole
play, show his absolute supremacy in poetry.
Both in the blank verse and the lyrics, in the
dialogue and the set tirades, in long contexts
and short phrases alike, he shows himself
absolute, with nothing out of reach of his
faculty of expression and suggestion, with
every resource of verbal music and intellectual demonstration at his command.

A. C. Bradley (1851–1935) [From *Shakespearean Tragedy* (1904). We can see Edward Dowden's
idea being developed in A. C. Bradley's comments
on the speech with which Prospero breaks off the
masque. This piece also illustrates the extent to
which Prospero tended to be the focus of Victorian
and Edwardian criticism (especially since Bradley

Prospero (William Haviland) and Miranda (Nora Kerin) with Caliban (Herbert Beerbohm Tree) and Ferdinand (Basil Gill) in Act I, Scene 2 of *The Tempest*. This is an illustration of the 1904 production at His Majesty's Theatre. *(Illustration by A. M. Faulkner)*

focuses in general on the heroes of Shakespeare's tragedies rather than on a tragicomedy/romance such as *The Tempest*).]

We seem to see here the whole mind of Shakespeare in his later years. That which provides in Prospero first a "passion" of anger, and, a moment later, that melancholy and mystical thought that the great world must perish utterly and that man is but a dream, is the sudden recollection of gross and apparently incurable evil in the "monster" whom he had tried in vain to raise and soften, and in the monster's human confederates. It is this, which is but the repetition of his earlier experience of treachery and ingratitude, that troubles his old brain, makes his mind "beat," and forces on him the sense of unreality and evanescence in the world and the life that are haunted by such evil. Nor, though Prospero can spare and forgive, is there any sign to the end that he believed the evil curable in either the monster, the "born devil," or in the more monstrous villains, the "worse than devils," whom he so sternly dismisses. But he has learned patience, has come to regard his anger and loathing as a sign of weakness or infirmity, and would not have it disturb the young and innocent.

MODERN CRITICISM AND CRITICAL CONTROVERSIES

Recent criticism of *The Tempest* has comprehensively reversed the polarities and overturned the priorities of 19th-century discussion of the play. In the first place, undoubtedly the biggest question for critics in the 20th century was to what extent the play should be read in terms of colonialism. Prospero is no longer seen as a benevolently paternalistic figure, second in wisdom only to Shakespeare himself; instead, he becomes the archetypal colonialist, a sinister rather than a kindly presence whose control of the lives of those around him comes to seem troubling and questionable. There have been many critical interventions in this debate, the most notable of which are listed in the bibliography, but two in particular stand out. The first is Paul Brown's analysis from the classic 1985 collection *Political Shakespeare,* a book that revolutionized the study of Shakespeare and acted effectively as a manifesto for cultural materialism:

> *The Tempest* is not simply a reflection of colonialist practices but an intervention in an ambivalent and even contradictory discourse. This intervention takes the form of a powerful and pleasurable narrative which seeks at once to harmonise disjunction, to transcend

irreconcilable contradictions and to mystify the political conditions which demand colonialist discourse. Yet the narrative ultimately fails to deliver that containment and instead may be seen to foreground precisely those problems which it works to efface or overcome. The result is a radically ambivalent text which exemplifies not some *timeless* contradiction internal to the discourse by which it inexorably undermines or deconstructs its "official" pronouncements, but a moment of *historical* crisis. This crisis is the struggle to produce a colonialist discourse adequate to the complex requirements of British colonialism in its initial phase. (48)

For Brown, then, *The Tempest* is not an innocent document produced in a hermetically sealed aesthetic vacuum but a text irremediably imbricated in the cultural and political discourses of the historical moment in which it was produced. Such an approach is of course typical of cultural materialism, but the ways in which *The Tempest* borrows from and intersects with the language of exploration makes it particularly responsive to such treatment, and other critics were quick to follow Brown's lead. However, not everyone agreed. In an essay first published in 1989 in *Shakespeare Quarterly,* Meredith Anne Skura declared that

> The revisionist impulse has been one of the most salutary in recent years in correcting New Critical "blindness" to history and ideology. . . . But here, as critics have been suggesting about new historicism in general, it is now in danger of fostering blindness of its own. Granted that something was wrong with a commentary that focused on *The Tempest* as a self-contained project of a self-contained individual and that ignored the political situation in 1611. But something seems wrong now also, something more than the rhetorical excesses characteristic of any innovative critical movement. The recent criticism not only flattens the text into the mold of colonialist discourse and eliminates

what is characteristically "Shakespearean" in order to foreground what is "colonialist," but it is also—paradoxically—in danger of taking the play further from the particular historical situation in England in 1611 even as it brings it closer to what we mean by "colonialism" today. (292–293)

Skura's has, however, remained a minority opinion, and *The Tempest* is now firmly established as Shakespeare's colonial play.

In this context, it is not surprising that the characters over whom Prospero has power have attracted considerable critical attention. Miranda, who to earlier critics was little more than a typically virtuous daughter figure, has received much more probing analysis in recent years. In the groundbreaking 1980 collection *The Woman's Part,* for instance, Lorie Jerrell Leininger concludes her analysis of *The Tempest* with a battle cry that would have both mystified and appalled 19th-century commentators on the play:

> Let us invent a modern Miranda, and permit her to speak a new Epilogue:
>
> "My father is no God-figure. No one is a God-figure. My father is a man, and fallible, as I am. Let's put an end to the fantasy of infallibility.
>
> "There is no such thing as a 'natural slave.' No subhuman laborers exist. Let's put an end to *that* fantasy. I will not benefit from such a concept represented in any guise, be it Aristotelian, biblical, allegorical, or Neoplatonic. . . .
>
> "I cannot give assent to an ethical scheme that locates all virtue symbolically in one part of my anatomy. My virginity has little to do with the forces that will lead to good harvest or greater social justice.
>
> "Nor am I in any way analogous to a foot. . . . Neither my father, nor my husband, nor any

Miranda in *The Tempest*. This is a print from Charles Heath's 1848 edition of *The Heroines of Shakspeare: Comprising the Principal Female Characters in the Plays of the Great Poet*. (Painting by John Hayter; engraving by W. H. Mote)

one alive has the right to refer to me as his foot while thinking of himself as the head. . . .

"Will I succeed in creating my 'brave new world' which has people in it who no longer exploit one another? I cannot be certain. I will at least make my start by springing the 'Miranda-trap,' being forced into unwitting collusion with domination by appearing to be a beneficiary. I need to join forces with Caliban—to join forces with all those who are exploited or oppressed—to stand beside Caliban and say,

As we from crimes would pardon'd be,

Let's work to set each other free."
(Leininger 1980: 291–292)

Rather more surprisingly, considering that they never appear on stage, some of the other female characters in the play have also attracted attention. Stephen Orgel observes that

> The absent presence of the wife and mother in the play constitutes a space that is filled by Prospero's creation of surrogates and a ghostly family. . . . The space is filled, too, by a whole structure of wifely allusion and reference: widow Dido, model at once of heroic fidelity to a murdered husband and the destructive potential of erotic passion; the witch Medea, murderess and filicide; three exemplary goddesses, the bereft Ceres, nurturing Juno and licentious Venus; and Alonso's daughter, Claribel, unwillingly married off to the ruler of the modern Carthage, and thereby lost to her father forever.

Described in this way, the play has an obvious psychoanalytic shape. (2)

Ania Loomba's discussion of the play has a section entitled "Sycorax," which includes the observation that

> Sycorax is also Prospero's "other"; his repeated comparisons between their different magics and their respective reigns of the island are used by him to claim a superior morality, a greater strength and a greater humanity, and hence legitimise his takeover of the island and its inhabitants; but they also betray an anxiety that Sycorax's power has not been fully exorcised. (152)

She concludes that "Prospero as colonialist consolidates power which is specifically white and male, and constructs Sycorax as a black, wayward and wicked witch in order to legitimise it" (152).

Loomba also discusses Miranda's mother and Claribel (155), and it is also worth considering in this context Peter Greenaway's film *Prospero's Books,* in which Claribel actually appears, pictured as bitterly unhappy in her forced marriage to an African prince who abuses and neglects her.

Caliban in particular has been the focus of sustained critical attention that is very different in tone from the earlier comments made about the character. Dympna Callaghan, for instance, reads him squarely in the light of one particular recipient of the attentions of would-be English colonizers, Ireland. Of Miranda's statement that Caliban gabbles, Callaghan observes that "The first use of the word *gabble* recorded in the *OED* is from Palesman Richard Stanihurst's *Description of Ireland* in Holinshed's *Chronicles* (1.4), a text which argues that three things should accompany conquest," "law, *language,* and clothing" (italics in original) (Callaghan 2000: 117). As she notes, "*gabble* is not an English word but, to quote Spenser, 'a word mingled out of Irish and English together'" (117), and she also compares Caliban's gaberdine to the Irish mantle (131). Ania Loomba, meanwhile, reads Prospero's accusation that Caliban tried to rape Miranda in relation to the "myth, which derives from the idea that, aware of the damage they can do by making sexual advances towards white women, black men have all conceived 'a peculiar lust for white womanhood'" (150).

As well as the very different view of Caliban brought about by the collapse of colonialist ideologies, understanding of the character was also inflected by other considerations. When *Forbidden Planet* turned its version of Caliban into the Prospero-character's id, it offered merely an extreme example of a growing tendency to read the play in psychoanalytic terms. From 1969 to 1979, for example, the director Michael Powell made intermittent attempts to film a version of *The Tempest* that would both have found Caliban more sympathetic than Prospero and have been explicitly set inside Prospero's head. Attention has inevitably focused particularly on the psyche

of Prospero himself, not least the close interest he takes in the relationship of Ferdinand and Miranda. So, for instance, Stephen Orgel, comparing Prospero's tenuous grip on authority to King James I's (8–9), observes that Prospero "has been banished by his wicked, usurping, possibly illegitimate younger brother, Antonio. This too has the shape of Freudian fantasy: the younger child *is* the usurper in the family, and the kingdom he usurps is the mother. On the island, Prospero undoes the usurpation, recreating kingdom and family with himself in sole command" (4). David Sundelson, discussing what he sees as "Prospero's—and the play's—paternal narcissism" (37), says of Prospero's account of the usurpation:

> The language hints at sexual uncertainties that underlie the conflict about power, at a fantasy that Duke Prospero was both mother and father, but doubly vulnerable rather than doubly strong. Antonio was "the ivy which had hid my princely trunk / And suck'd my verdure out on't" (1.2.86–87). The metaphor makes Prospero androgynous: the second clause suggests a mother drained by an insatiable child, while the hidden "princely trunk" is an image of male strength defeated or replaced. This is not the only hint of impotence. (35)

Coppélia Kahn suggests along similar lines that "The island setting of *The Tempest* and the centrality of Prospero as demiurge make it a fantasy of omnipotence" (236).

In the closing years of the 20th century, other concerns came to the fore. For one thing, *The Tempest* came to be seen as a text of particular relevance in the light of the growing interest in Shakespeare's religious affiliations. Another, more distinctively modern concern is revealed by Gabriel Egan in his book *Green Shakespeare;* Egan suggests that to read the play in an ecocritical light shows us the importance of its "recurrent arboreal imagery" and reveals that "Prospero's main activity since

his arrival on the island has been its deforestation" (155). Furthermore, "Shakespeare's play proleptically links colonization, deforestation, and extreme weather in ways that can now be seen as prescient" (171).

More recently, Gordon McMullan, in *Shakespeare and the Idea of Late Writing: Authorship in the Proximity of Death,* has addressed the vexed question of *The Tempest*'s generic affiliations and their relationship (or lack of it) to its chronological place in his career. Since Dowden, *The Tempest* has often been afforded special status as a "late play," but McMullan challenges the whole idea of "lateness" and all that it has come to imply:

> We must not . . . be fooled by late-play mythologising into thinking that Shakespeare would have understood that he was carving out what Henry James would in due course, with only partial irony, call "a certain splendid 'late manner.'" The image of Shakespeare's serene and comfortable retirement to Stratford, free from the impositions of professional theatre and surrounded by his loving family, is profoundly false as an objective correlative for the late style. I have argued that, prior to the latter years of the eighteenth century, the idea of late writing as we understand it now did not exist, that it was invented as a by-product of the emergence of the Romantic idea of individual stylistic development and thus of the newly reconstructed direct relationship between life and work. Neither Steevens nor Malone would have recognised as anything other than fanciful Dowden's account of late Shakespearean serenity. Still less could Shakespeare himself have had in mind anything approximating the concept of late style as it later emerged: the idea, bluntly, postdates him by nearly two centuries. (192)

Four hundred years after it was first written, then, *The Tempest* continues to be the subject of vibrant critical debate.

THE PLAY TODAY

The Tempest continues to be of great interest to critics, partly because of its seemingly modern concerns with such issues as imperialism, colonialism, the environment, and gender roles. More traditional critics also find much to discuss in the play today, particularly regarding its (somewhat contested) status as Shakespeare's "last" play.

The play also has a lively production history. Here are just a few examples: In 2001, Vanessa Redgrave played Prospero at Shakespeare's Globe. In 2006, Rupert Goold transplanted the play to the Arctic for a Royal Shakespeare Company production, with Patrick Stewart as Prospero, shaman-like, wearing a bearskin costume and reindeer-skull headdress; Goold thought of the play in terms of the TV series *Lost,* which he saw as inspired by *The Tempest,* and tried to create a terrifying opening scene in order to evoke the sense of fear he had felt as a child on cross-channel ferries (Bate and Rasmussen 2008: 128). In 1988, Jonathan Miller's production had an Ariel who was both female and black, while Sam Mendes put his Ariel (Simon Russell Beale) into a Chairman Mao suit. Julie Taymor's recent film version featured Helen Mirren as a female Prospero (here called "Prospera") and several other famous actors in the traditional roles, including the comedian Russell Brand as Trinculo.

The Tempest has also been much adapted, starting in 1667 with Dryden's *The Tempest: Or, the Enchanted Island,* which gave Miranda a sister named Dorinda and Prospero a foster son, Hippolito, the rightful duke of Mantua (always acted by a girl dressed as a man). Since then, creative rewritings of it have flourished. In particular, few Shakespearean plays have been more frequently or more freely adapted for the screen than *The Tempest.* Since the first surviving adaptation of it in 1908, Percy Stow's silent version, it has been transported to outer space in *Forbidden Planet,* recast as a western in William Wellman's *Yellow Sky,* and transposed to an English country house in Derek Jarman's *The Tempest,* to a Greek island in Paul Mazursky's *Tempest,* and to a fantasy High

Renaissance island constructed by a digital paint-box in Peter Greenaway's *Prospero's Books*.

Less well known than most of these but also worth noting is Jack Bender's 1998 PG-rated made-for-TV version of *The Tempest*, which is set in the Mississippi bayous during the Civil War, though the stories of both the war and *The Tempest* have been altered in a number of ways. The opening scenes are set on a financially troubled plantation that is faintly reminiscent of *Gone with the Wind*, where the only link with *The Tempest* is that the ranch has "Prosperity" written above it; it then moves to an island in the bayou, and a number of crucial elements of the play are dislocated. Azaleigh, the mambo priestess who teaches "Houngan" Gideon Prosper (Peter Fonda) voodoo, is black, and so, too, is her son Ariel (Harold Perrineau, Jr., of *William Shakespeare's Romeo + Juliet* fame). Azaleigh is a good character, and yet she is also structurally much more like Sycorax than any other character in *The Tempest*; Ariel, too, is a good character, but unlike his counterpart in the original text, he challenges not only Prospero's personal authority over him, or his response to a specific situation such as his meeting with his brother, but also, and much more fundamentally, his entire moral code and governing principle of action. Caliban is a poor white named Gatorman who says "Before they came, this was my bayou." One of the incidental consequences of all this is that Prospero cannot drown his books because there are none—here magic is strictly an oral tradition, as voodoo was for African-American slaves, while Anthony (the Antonio character, played by John Glover) says to his brother, "Gideon, you're sounding more like one of those Yankee abolitionists every day," while Ariel—who does not want freedom, just to get to General Grant's headquarters to help him—wants to fight for the Union because of Lincoln's Emancipation Proclamation. Finally, Gideon comes to help disguised as an American eagle and provides the film's clarification of its own theme when he says "North and South. Brother killing brother," an interesting example of what *The Tempest* can be made to mean today.

FIVE TOPICS FOR DISCUSSION AND WRITING

1. **Art and nature:** How are nature and art presented in the play? Is either seen as a stronger force than the other? Are the two in opposition, or is there a relationship between them?

2. **Modes of representation:** What ways of representing events are given prominence in the play? Is any of them shown as especially effective or especially problematic?

3. **Ways to rule:** What ideas does the play offer about how territories might be ruled? Does it appear to endorse any of them? Might it ever be possible to achieve an ideal system of rule or is every possible system actually or potentially problematic?

4. **Optimism versus cynicism:** What examples does the play show us of optimistic views or of pessimistic/cynical ones? Does it suggest that either of these perspectives has greater validity? Is there any evidence for whether a tendency to optimism or pessimism is a product of nature or of nurture?

5. **The old world versus the new:** What clues do we have about where *The Tempest* is set? Are we more strongly invited to read it in terms of the Old World or in terms of the New? To what extent is each of those two polarities implicated in early modern constructions of the other?

Bibliography

Babula, William. "Claribel, Tunis and Greenaway's *Prospero's Books*." *Journal of the Wooden O Symposium* (2001): 19–25.

Baker, David J. "Where Is Ireland in *The Tempest*?" In *Shakespeare and Ireland: History, Politics, Culture*, edited by Mark Thornton Burnett and Ramona Wray, 68–88. Basingstoke, England: Palgrave, 1997.

Barker, Francis, and Peter Hulme. "Nymphs and Reapers Heavily Vanish: The Discursive Con-texts of *The Tempest*." In *Alternative Shakespeares*, edited by John Drakakis, 191–205. London: Methuen, 1985.

Bate, Jonathan. *Shakespeare and Ovid*. Oxford: Clarendon, 1993.

Bate, Jonathan, and Eric Rasmussen, eds. *The Tempest*. London: Macmillan, 2008.

Brotton, Jerry. "'This Tunis, sir, was Carthage': Contesting Colonialism in *The Tempest*." In *Post-Colonial Shakespeares,* edited by Ania Loomba and Martin Orkin, 23–42. London: Routledge, 1998.

Brown, Paul. "'This thing of darkness I acknowledge mine': *The Tempest* and the Discourse of Colonialism." In *Political Shakespeare,* edited by Jonathan Dollimore and Alan Sinfield, 48–71. Manchester, England: Manchester University Press, 1985.

Bruster, Douglas. "The Postmodern Theater of Paul Mazursky's *Tempest*." In *Shakespeare, Film, Fin-de-Siècle,* edited by Mark Thornton Burnett and Ramona Wray, 26–39. Basingstoke, England: Macmillan, 2000.

Buchanan, Judith. "*Forbidden Planet* and the Retrospective Attribution of Intentions." In *Retrovisions: Reinventing the Past in Film and Fiction,* edited by Deborah Cartmell, I. Q. Hunter, and Imelda Whelehan, 148–162. London: Pluto, 2001.

Callaghan, Dympna. *Shakespeare without Women*. London: Routledge, 2000.

Carpenter, Humphrey. *The Letters of J. R. R. Tolkien*. London: George Allen & Unwin, 1981.

Cartelli, Thomas. "Prospero in Africa: *The Tempest* as Colonialist Text and Precept." In *Shakespeare Reproduced,* edited by Jean E. Howard and Marion F. O'Connor, 99–115. London: Methuen, 1987.

———. *Repositioning Shakespeare: National Formations, Postcolonial Appropriations*. London: Routledge, 1999.

Chaudhuri, Supriya. "The Absence of Caliban: Shakespeare and Colonial Modernity." In *Shakespeare's World: World Shakespeares: Proceedings of the VIII World Shakespeare Congress 2006,* edited by R. S. White, Christa Jansohn, and Richard Fotheringham, 223–236. Newark: University of Delaware Press, 2008.

Demaray, John G. *Shakespeare and the Spectacles of Strangeness*. Pittsburgh, Pa.: Duquesne University Press, 1998.

Donaldson, Peter. "Digital Archives and Sibylline Fragments: *The Tempest* and the End of Books." *Postmodern Culture* 8.2 (January 1998). Available online (subscription only). URL: http://muse.jhu.edu/journals/postmodern_culture/toc/pmc8.2.html.

———. "Shakespeare in the Age of Post-Mechanical Reproduction: Sexual and Electronic Magic in *Prospero's Books*." In *Shakespeare, the Movie: Popularizing the Plays on Film, TV, and Video,* edited by Lynda E. Boose and Richard Burt, 169–185. London: Routledge, 1997.

Dowden, Edward. *Shakspere: A Critical Study of His Mind and Art*. London: Routledge & Kegan Paul, 1875.

Egan, Gabriel. *Green Shakespeare*. London: Routledge, 2006.

Elliott, J. H. *The Old World and the New, 1492–1650*. 1970. Reprint, Cambridge: Canto, 1992.

Ferguson, Arthur B. *Utter Antiquity: Perceptions of Prehistory in Renaissance England*. Durham, N.C.: Duke University Press, 1993.

Gordon, D. J. "Poet and Architect: The Intellectual Setting of the Quarrel between Ben Jonson and Inigo Jones." In *The Renaissance Imagination: Essays and Lectures by D. J. Gordon,* edited by Stephen Orgel, 77–101. Berkeley: University of California Press, 1975.

Greenaway, Peter. *Prospero's Books: A Film of Shakespeare's* The Tempest. London: Chatto & Windus, 1991.

———. *Prospero's Subjects*. Kamakura: Yobisha Co. Ltd, 1992.

Greenblatt, Stephen. "Invisible Bullets: Renaissance Authority and Its Subversion: *Henry IV* and *Henry V*." In *Political Shakespeare,* edited by Jonathan Dollimore and Alan Sinfield, 18–47. Manchester, England: Manchester University Press, 1985.

———. *Marvelous Possessions*. Oxford: Clarendon, 1991.

Griffiths, Trevor R. "'This Island's Mine': Caliban and Colonialism." *The Yearbook of English Studies* 13 (1983): 159–180.

Hart, Jonathan. *Columbus, Shakespeare, and the Interpretation of the New World*. New York: Palgrave, 2003.

Haspel, Paul. "Ariel and Prospero's Modern-English Adventure: Language, Social Criticism, and Adaptation in Paul Mazursky's *Tempest.*" *Literature/Film Quarterly* 34, no. 2 (2006): 130–139.

Hodgkins, Christopher. "The Nubile Savage: Pocahontas as Heathen Convert and Virgilian Bride." *Renaissance Papers* (1998): 81–90.

Hopkins, Lisa. *Shakespeare's The Tempest: The Relationship between Text and Film.* London: New Mermaids, 2008.

Hulme, Peter. *Colonial Encounters: Europe and the Native Caribbean, 1492–1797.* London: Methuen, 1986.

———. "Stormy Weather: Misreading the Postcolonial *Tempest*" *Early Modern Culture* 1, no. 3. Available online. URL: http://eserver.org/emc/1–3/hulme.html. Accessed May 3, 2010.

Jolly, John. "The Bellerophon Myth and *Forbidden Planet.*" *Extrapolation* 27, no. 1 (1986): 84–90.

Kahn, Coppélia. "The Providential Tempest and the Shakespearean Family." In *Representing Shakespeare: New Psychoanalytic Essays,* edited by Murray M. Schwartz and Coppélia Kahn, 217–243. Baltimore: Johns Hopkins University Press, 1980.

Knighten, Merrell. "The Triple Paternity of *Forbidden Planet.*" *Shakespeare Bulletin* 12, no. 3 (Summer 1994): 36–37.

Lanier, Douglas. "Drowning the Book: *Prospero's Books* and the Textual Shakespeare" In *Shakespeare on Film: Contemporary Critical Essays,* edited by Robert Shaughnessy, 173–195. Basingstoke, England: Palgrave, 1998.

Leininger, Lorie Jerrell. "The Miranda Trap: Sexism and Racism in Shakespeare's *Tempest.*" In *The Woman's Part: Feminist Criticism of Shakespeare,* edited by Carolyn Ruth Swift Lenz, Gayle Greene, and Carol Thomas Neely, 285–294. Urbana: University of Illinois Press, 1980.

Lerer, Seth. "*Forbidden Planet* and the Terrors of Philology." *Raritan* 19, no. 3 (Winter 2000): 73–86.

Lewis, Cynthia. *Particular Saints: Shakespeare's Four Antonios, Their Contexts, and Their Plays.* Newark: University of Delaware Press, 1997.

Lie, Nadia, and Theo D'haen, eds. *Constellation Caliban: Figurations of a Character.* Amsterdam: Rodopi, 1997.

Linton, Joan Pong. *The Romance of the New World: Gender and the Literary Formations of English Colonialism.* Cambridge: Cambridge University Press, 1998.

Loomba, Ania. *Gender, Race, Renaissance Drama.* Manchester, England: Manchester University Press, 1989.

Loomba, Ania, and Martin Orkin, eds. *Post-Colonial Shakespeares.* London: Routledge, 1998.

Martin, Sara. "Classic Shakespeare for All: *Forbidden Planet* and *Prospero's Books,* Two Screen Adaptations of *The Tempest.*" In *Classics in Film and Fiction,* edited by Deborah Cartmell, I. Q. Hunter, Heidi Kaye, and Imelda Whelehan, 34–53. London: Pluto, 2000.

McCombe, John P. "'Suiting the Action to the Word': The Clarendon *Tempest* and the Evolution of a Narrative Silent Shakespeare." *Literature/Film Quarterly* 33, no. 2 (2005): 142–155.

McMullan, Gordon. *Shakespeare and the Idea of Late Writing: Authorship in the Proximity of Death.* Cambridge: Cambridge University Press, 2007.

Miller, Anthony. "'In this last tempest': Modernising Shakespeare's *Tempest* on Film." *Sydney Studies in English* 23 (1997): 24–40.

Montrose, Louis. "The Work of Gender in the Discourse of Discovery." *Representations* 33 (Winter 1991): 1–41.

Morse, Ruth. "Monsters, Magicians, Movies: *The Tempest* and the Final Frontier." *Shakespeare Survey* 53 (2000): 164–174.

Orgel, Stephen. "Prospero's Wife." *Representations* 8 (Autumn 1994): 1–13.

Orr, John. "The Art of National Identity: Peter Greenaway and Derek Jarman." In *British Cinema, Past and Present,* edited by Justine Ashby and Andrew Higson, 327–338. London: Routledge, 2000.

Palmer, D. J., ed. *Shakespeare: The Tempest. A Casebook.* Rev. ed. Basingstoke: Palgrave, 1991.

Roberts, Jeanne Addison. "'Wife' or 'Wise'—*The Tempest* l. 1786." *University of Virginia Studies in Bibliography* 31 (1978): 203–208.

Schneider, Ben Ross, Jr. "'Are We Being Historical Yet?': Colonialist Interpretations of Shakespeare's *Tempest.*" *Shakespeare Studies* 23 (1995): 120–145.

Shakespeare, William. *The Tempest.* Edited by Virginia Mason Vaughan and Alden T. Vaughan. London: Thomas Nelson, 1999.

Skura, Meredith Anne. "Discourse and the Individual: The Case of Colonialism in *The Tempest.*" In *The Tempest: A Case Study in Critical Controversy,* edited by Gerald Graff and James Phelan, 286–322. Basingstoke, England: Macmillan, 2000.

Stalpaert, Christel, ed. *Peter Greenaway's Prospero's Books: Critical Essays.* Ghent: Academia Press, 2000.

Strachey, William. *"A True Reportory. . . ."* In *A Voyage to Virginia in 1609: Two Narratives: Strachey's "True Reportory,"* Jourdain's Discovery of the Bermudas. Charlottesville: University Press of Virginia, 1964.

Sundelson, David. "'So rare a wonder'd father': Prospero's *Tempest.*" In *Representing Shakespeare: New Psychoanalytic Essays,* edited by Murray M. Schwartz and Coppélia Kahn, 33–53. Baltimore: Johns Hopkins University Press, 1980.

Thompson, Ann. "'Miranda, where's your sister?': Reading Shakespeare's *The Tempest.*" In *Feminist Criticism: Theory and Practice,* edited by Susan Sellers, 45–55. Hemel Hempstead, England: Harvester Wheatsheaf, 1991.

Traversi, Derek. *Shakespeare: The Last Phase.* London: Hollis & Carter, 1953.

Tudeau-Clayton, Margaret. *Jonson, Shakespeare, and Early Modern Virgil.* Cambridge: Cambridge University Press, 1998.

Vaughan, Alden T., and Virginia Mason Vaughan. *Shakespeare's Caliban: A Cultural History.* Cambridge: Cambridge University Press, 1991.

Warlick, M. E. "Art, Allegory and Alchemy in Peter Greenaway's *Prospero's Books.*" In *New Directions in Emblem Studies,* edited by Amy Wygant, 109–136. Glasgow: Glasgow Emblem Studies, 1999.

Willis, Deborah. "Shakespeare's *Tempest* and the Discourse of Colonialism." *Studies in English Literature 1500–1900* 29 (1989): 277–289.

Willoquet-Maricondi, Paula. "Aimé Césaire's *A Tempest* and Peter Greenaway's *Prospero's Books* as Ecological Rereadings and Rewritings of Shakespeare's *The Tempest.*" In *Reading the Earth: New Directions in the Study of Literature and Environment,* edited by Michael P. Branch, Rochelle Johnson, Daniel Patterson, and Scott Slovic, 209–224. Moscow: University of Idaho Press, 1998.

Wilson, Richard. *Secret Shakespeare: Studies in Theatre, Religion and Resistance.* Manchester, England: Manchester University Press, 2004.

———. *Will Power.* Hemel Hempstead, England: Harvester Wheatsheaf, 1993.

Wood, Michael. *In Search of Shakespeare.* London: BBC Worldwide, 2003.

Wymer, Rowland. *Derek Jarman.* Manchester, England: Manchester University Press, 2005.

———. "*The Tempest* and the Origins of Britain." *Critical Survey* 11, no. 1 (1999): 3–14.

—Lisa Hopkins

Timon of Athens

INTRODUCTION

Timon of Athens, probably written in collaboration with Thomas Middleton, is one of Shakespeare's most enigmatic works. Rather like its hero, it emerged seemingly from nowhere. It was placed in the First Folio edition of Shakespeare's works between *Romeo and Juliet* and *Julius Caesar* to fill the gap left by the temporary absence of *Troilus and Cressida* when the printers ran into problems reproducing that play. It has since proved to be one of the most divisive of Shakespeare's works, with critics disagreeing over such issues as its date and authorship and even whether the play constitutes a complete work or not. These issues may have alienated many potential critics or performers of the play. Nonetheless, the play, though certainly not one of Shakespeare's finest, has its rewards.

It is arguably one of Shakespeare's most intensely pessimistic tragedies. The hero never experiences the "middle of humanity," only "the extremity of both ends" (4.3). He begins the play as a major proponent of the essential goodness of human nature and as a benevolently wealthy citizen of Athens before declining into an uncompromisingly misanthropic existence as a hermit in the woods outside the city. Timon's decline is arguably the most rapid and the most dire of all Shakespeare's tragic heroes. Many critics have been blinded to the play's virtues by the apparent inhumanity of the protagonist, arguing that his extreme misanthropy fails to evoke any sympathy in the reader. Others, such as G. Wilson Knight and William Hazlitt see in the play a

tragic intensity that rivals Shakespeare's other plays in the genre.

Perhaps the most notable of *Timon*'s admirers is Karl Marx, who believed that many of the play's central premises corresponded with his own views on politics and the economy. He paid particular attention to Timon's soliloquy on gold that occurs in the fourth act. For Marx, gold is here exposed as both the "visible deity" that can corrupt human virtue and invert it to its opposite, and as the "universal whore, the universal pander between men and nations." Marx's appreciation provides the reader with a key to the play and a means of finding many contemporary relevancies within it. Timon's downfall is effectively caused by his failure to come to terms with an early incarnation of the modern capitalist economy, based upon credit and debt. The tendency for many 20th-century productions of the play to perform the text in modern dress indicates the contemporary significance that can be perceived in the text. Timon's experiences of economic boom and bust resonate with many modern concerns about our unstable economic system.

Timon of Athens is, without doubt, a challenging play. It is unique in the Shakespearean canon for representing an entirely solitary hero who lacks any kind of familial relations or any love interest. The play's dual authorship has also been seen as a problem by many critics. It does however, reveal two distinct insights and approaches to the drama. Scholars believe they can distinguish between the portions written by Shakespeare and

Timon gives his gold to the prostitutes in Act IV, Scene 3 of *Timon of Athens*. This is a print from the Boydell Shakespeare Gallery project, which was first conceived in 1786 and lasted until 1805. *(Painting by John Opie; engraving by Robert Thew)*

those by Middleton. Shakespeare, on the whole, seems to concentrate upon the human tragedy of Timon's decline, while Middleton generally prefers to take advantage of the material's potential for social drama. The two approaches do not, in general, impede the overall dramatic coherence and unity of the end product. *Timon of Athens* therefore presents the reader with a number of potential approaches to the events it dramatizes and, like the best of Shakespearean drama, resonates with many universal issues and many of the concerns that are likely to be felt by a modern readership.

All textual citations refer to Anthony B. Dawson and Gretchen E. Minton's Arden edition of *Timon of Athens* (2008). Note that act and scene divisions do tend to vary in modern editions of the play.

BACKGROUND

The play's plot derives from a number of sources available to Shakespeare, including various accounts of a figure named Timon, a man famed for misanthropy. The principal source for the play is a brief digression that gives an account of the life of

Timon in the biography of Antony in Sir Thomas North's translation of Plutarch's *Lives of the Noble Grecians and Romans*. This makes it quite possible that *Timon* was written around the same time as *Antony and Cleopatra*. The chief elements of the play extracted from Plutarch's account relate to Timon's misanthropy and his association with Alcibiades, who he believed would one day pose a threat to the city of Athens. Plutarch also provides a source for Timon's epitaph, which is quoted in 5.4 and 5.5, as well as Timon's invitation to the citizens of Athens to hang themselves from a tree near his cave (5.2). Plutarch's account of the life of Alcibiades in the same work also provides the basis for some aspects of the play's action, most notably Timon's meeting with Alcibiades in the woods, in which he introduces himself as "Misanthropos" (4.3), a hater of mankind. Another major source for *Timon of Athens* is Lucian's *Timon, or the Manhater,* which provides a precedent for Timon's discovery of the gold in the woods (4.3) and for the fickle friends who visit Timon and attempt to benefit from his wealth. Lucian's text is also notable for the inclusion of Plutus, the god of gold, whom one of the lords in the Shakespearean text describes as "but his steward" (1.1). Certain sections of the text may well have been influenced by Matteo Boiardo's 15th-century Italian verse comedy, *Timone,* an adaptation and expansion of Lucian's text. Many critics have argued that much of the imagery relating to beasts in *Timon of Athens* is derived from this text. Another possible, and more contemporary, source of inspiration for this play is an anonymous comedy, simply entitled *Timon* (ca. 1601–05), although some critics have argued for a date that places it after the Shakespearean text. Unlike many of the other sources, *Timon* dramatizes episodes from the period before Timon's self-imposed exile from society. The comedy provides a possible model for the character of Flavius in the form of Laches, a servant who is aware of the possible consequences of Timon's reckless spending. *Timon* also contains a scene similar to the mock banquet in which the main character drives out his false friends by throwing stones at them (3.7). Although Apemantus is mentioned in Plutarch, the characterization of him is most probably influenced by the character of Diogenes in John Lyly's court comedy, *Campaspe* (1579), particularly his cynical rhetoric.

The Athens depicted in this play owes more to Jacobean England than to the Athens described in many classical narratives. The city scenes in the first three acts, especially with their uncompromising creditors, are not unlike those a contemporary audience might have expected from one of the popular urban comedies that were regularly featured on the Jacobean stage. The range of possible dates of composition all situate this play within the first five years of the reign of James I. During this time, the new king's command of the national budget was being called increasingly into question. Like Timon, James was known for his reckless spending, his extravagant gifts to his favorites at court, and for the debts he incurred. It is estimated that in his first five years alone as king, during which time England was at peace, his government accrued six times the amount of debt racked up by Elizabeth's government during 15 years of war. The similarities Timon bears to the monarch, and his attitude regarding money, go some way toward indicating the political context that informed this play.

Date and Text of the Play

Timon of Athens is a play about which very little is certain. It was probably never performed during Shakespeare's lifetime. This means that many of the usual sources that can help to ascertain a play's date of composition (such as entries in the Stationer's Register and accounts of public performances in letters or diary entries) are not available for this play. The dating of this text is therefore a complex issue. Estimates for the date of composition range from as early as 1605 to as late as 1608, which places the play somewhere in the midst of the period from which many of Shakespeare's great tragedies, such as *King Lear, Macbeth, Othello,* and *Antony and Cleopatra,* emerged.

The text of the play has also raised a number of questions. The problems with the text, including

continuity errors, apparently incomplete scenes, and faulty lineation, led many early critics to conclude that *Timon* was an inferior or unfinished work. Modern critics, however, have tended to explain these inconsistencies as the result of dual authorship. The critical consensus points to the dramatist Thomas Middleton as Shakespeare's collaborator. *Timon of Athens* emerges from the early point of Middleton's career; he would later become famous for tragedies including *Women Beware Women, The Changeling,* and *The Revenger's Tragedy* and city comedies including *A Trick to Catch the Old One* and *A Chaste Maid in Cheapside* as well as his controversial but extremely popular satire, *A Game at Chess.* Critics have tended to view the division of labor between the authors of this text as follows:

1.1	Primarily Shakespeare, possibly with some input from Middleton
1.2	Middleton
2.1	Shakespeare
2.2	Shakespeare and Middleton
3.1–3.6	Middleton
3.7	Shakespeare and Middleton
4.1	Shakespeare
4.2	Shakespeare and Middleton
4.3–5.1	Primarily Shakespeare, with some input from Middleton
5.2–5.5	Shakespeare

While the idea of dual authorship has not received universal acceptance as an explanation for the inconsistencies in the text, it has certainly achieved a broad critical consensus.

SYNOPSIS
Brief Synopsis

The wealthy Timon of Athens is too generous with his money. A variety of people attempt to please him and expect money in return. Only the philosopher Apemantus refuses to seek gifts from Timon, because it would be sinful to encourage the nobleman's fondness for flattery. Timon hosts a great banquet at which he gives away an enormous

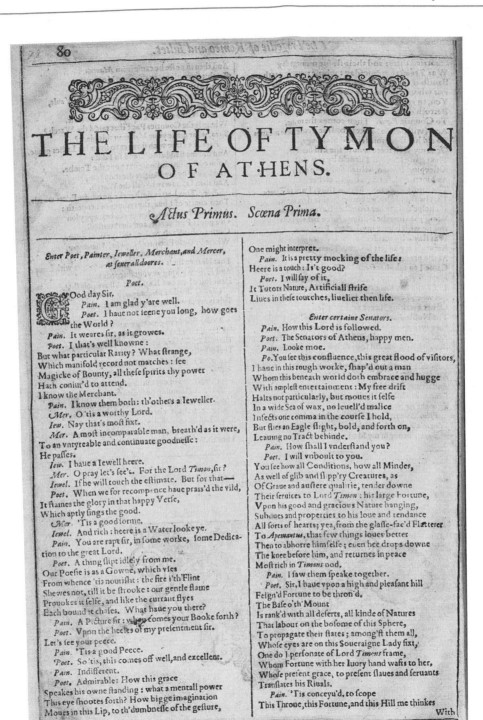

Title page of the First Folio edition of *Timon of Athens*, published in 1623

amount of money, though his steward says he is bankrupt.

A senator who knows of Timon's excessive generosity decides to send his servant, Caphis, to collect the debt Timon owes him before it is too late. When Caphis arrives, Timon is astonished, but his steward points out that he has refused to oversee his accounts despite all urging, and now the debts caused by his generosity cannot be paid. Hoping to borrow money from his friends, Timon sends Flaminius, Servilius, another servant, and the steward to Lucius, Lucullus, Sempronius, and Ventidius, respectively.

Lucullus and Lucius refuse to lend money to Timon. Timon's servant tells Sempronius that his master's other friends have refused to lend money, whereupon Sempronius claims to be offended that he was not asked first and therefore refuses to help.

Lucius's servant meets Titus, Hortensius, Philotus, and the Servants of Varro, all of whom hope to collect money from Timon. Timon appears in a rage and insists that they will have to cut up his body as payment. He then tells the steward to send out messages to all of his friends inviting them to an immense banquet.

Alcibiades seeks mercy from the senators for a friend who has killed someone in a fight. They refuse. When he continues to argue, the senators, offended that he will not accept their decision, banish him from Athens. Alcibiades vows to take revenge on the city with his army.

At Timon's banquet, the guests make excuses for not assisting Timon, who curses them and drives them away.

Timon, alone in the wilderness, denounces humanity. As he digs for roots, he finds gold. Alcibiades appears with his concubines Phrynia and Timandra. Timon rejects Alcibiades' offer of friendship but is pleased to hear of his plan to conquer Athens. Alcibiades departs, and Apemantus arrives. The two misanthropes remark on the faults of humanity and then fall into an exchange of insults. As Apemantus leaves, a group of thieves arrives. Timon sarcastically praises them for taking what they want and gives each gold.

The Poet and the Painter have heard that Timon has gold, and they seek him in the woods. They intend to promise him great works so that he will give them gifts. Timon overhears their plans and pretends to trust them. He gives them gold as he denounces them and drives them away. Two senators arrive and offer to restore Timon's wealth if he will return to Athens and help them against Alcibiades. Timon refuses.

As he seeks Timon with a message from Alcibiades, a soldier finds a bitter note that announces Timon's death. He also sees a gravestone inscribed in a language he cannot read. He makes a copy of it to take to Alcibiades.

A delegation of senators seeks mercy from Alcibiades, and he promises that he will take revenge only on the few people who had offended him. The soldier arrives with the gravestone text, which restates Timon's hatred of humanity. Alcibiades mourns for his friend's state of mind at death, as he enters the city and vows to make a lasting peace in Athens.

Act I, Scene 1

The play begins at Timon's estate where a large group of citizens from various aspects of Athenian life have gathered to await Timon's arrival. Among those who have assembled are a poet, a painter, a jeweller, and a merchant, all of whom intend to bestow gifts upon the host, in the hope of being rewarded in turn. The poet states that he has dedicated his most recent work to Timon and describes an allegory in which Timon climbs to the top of a hill where the goddess of fortune is waiting for him, overcoming the challenges posed by other rivals who become pacified by the approval he has gained from Fortune. Timon will inevitably fall, however, and his former rivals will do nothing to prevent it.

Timon then enters, having just been informed that his friend Ventidius has been imprisoned for debt. He immediately sends the messenger back to confirm that he will pay the ransom so that his friend can be freed and sends word that Ventidius should make his way to the estate as soon as he is able. Timon is then approached by an old Athenian who tells him that Lucilius, one of Timon's servants, has been attempting to woo his daughter. The old man objects that because the servant is too poor, he will not approve of the match. Timon calls forth the servant and, satisfied that he truly loves the old man's daughter, gives his servant a gift of three talents to persuade the old man to approve the match. The old man consequently waives his objections to the marriage.

Timon then receives the offerings of the Poet and the Painter and inspects the Jeweller's stone. Apemantus appears and asserts that he will only return a polite greeting when Timon is turned into a dog, an occurrence as unlikely as his flatterers showing signs of honesty. He then goes on to goad various visitors and dismisses the offerings of the Painter and the Jeweller. He also mocks the merchant for his dependence upon shipping weather and criticizes the poet for the deceitfulness of his work.

Alcibiades then arrives and enters the banqueting hall, along with several lords. As the guests begin to file out, Apemantus reveals his scorn and contempt for the artificiality of the gathering in an aside and confides to some of the lords that he is merely there to observe the display of artificial flattery. He then joins the others, leaving the lords to comment on the seemingly inexhaustible bounty of their host.

Act I, Scene 2

As the banquet is being served, Ventidius enters and thanks Timon for paying his ransom, vowing to repay Timon double the amount from an inheritance left by his recently deceased father. Timon refuses to take up this offer, asserting that it was a gift to his friend. Timon then welcomes Apemantus, who rebukes him and states that he is there merely to observe. He takes his place apart from the rest of the guests and says his own "grace" in which he repudiates the artificial nature of the feast and vows that he will never trust anyone except himself. Timon then makes a speech reflecting upon how fortunate he is to have so many friends and is so moved by the thought that he begins to weep.

An impromptu masque is held in Timon's honor introduced by a figure representing Cupid and performed by a group of ladies dressed as Amazons. Apemantus criticizes the spectacle. Timon then invites the participants in the masque to help themselves to the banquet that has been laid out. He then sends Flavius to bring his casket. Flavius obeys but expresses his misgivings about Timon's spending privately before he leaves. Timon presents one of his guests with a jewel from the box. Flavius then attempts to have a private word with Timon who is too busy entertaining his guests to agree. Timon is then told he has been presented with gifts from his friends, including four milk-white horses from Lucius and two pairs of greyhounds from Lucullus. Flavius then confides in an aside that Timon is bankrupt and that every gift he gives is plunging him further into debt. Unaware of this, Timon continues to bestow gifts upon his guests before they depart, leaving Timon and Apemantus alone. Timon tells Apemantus that if he were more agreeable, he, too, would benefit from his generosity. Apemantus declares that he will not be bribed and warns Timon that eventually he will sign himself away as a gift to someone. Timon also departs, leaving Apemantus to ponder on man's tendency to ignore good advice and pay more attention to flattery.

Act II, Scene 1

This short scene begins with a senator remarking upon the heavy debts Timon has recently incurred and criticizing his irresponsible attitude toward money, complaining that any gift given to Timon is returned with another gift worth 20 times the original. He then calls his servant, Caphis, and orders him to go to Timon's estate and press him for his debts. He emphasizes that Caphis must not be fooled by the courteousness of Timon's behavior. The senator also complains that his own credit and reputation are suffering as a result of Timon's debts.

Act II, Scene 2

This scene, which takes place at Timon's house, begins with a short speech by Flavius, who expresses his exasperation at the failure of his master, who is out hunting at that moment, to realize the full extent of his financial woes. The scene progresses with the appearance of three servants including Caphis and representatives from Isidore and Varro, all with the intention of collecting debts from Timon and all evidently with the same instructions to tolerate no protests from the debtor. Flavius persuades the servants to defer their discussions with Timon until after dinner. The servants are briefly entertained by a hired Fool, who comments upon their occupation as servants of creditors.

Timon reenters and asks Flavius why he did not relate to him the state of his finances. Flavius replies that he had attempted to do so on numerous occasions and warns him that his current assets will barely meet half his debts. He goes on to warn his master that the friends and flatterers he had previously entertained will no doubt desert him now that his riches have gone. Timon still believes otherwise and dispatches three servants respectively to Lucius, Lucullus, and Sempronius to request a loan of 50 talents from each. Timon then orders Flavius to petition the senators for a loan of 1,000 talents to which Flavius replies that he had already taken the liberty of doing so and was greeted with a flat refusal. Timon condemns the senators for their refusal and instructs Flavius to go to Ventidius, who has recently inherited a great estate after his father's death, and request he repay the five talents Timon had paid for his ransom and to use the money to pay the servants who have just arrived. Timon then announces his faith in the loyalty of his friends, a view that is not shared by Flavius.

Act III, Scene 1

Flaminius, one of Timon's servants, arrives at the house of Lucullus who, suspecting he bears a gift from his master, allows him to enter. Flaminius then requests of Lucullus the 50 talents Timon requires. Lucullus refuses, arguing that he has warned Timon about his frivolity on the numerous occasions when he has dined with him. Lucullus then attempts to bribe Flaminius to deny that he had spoken to him about the potential loan. Fla-

minius throws the money back at Lucullus and curses him for his lack of constancy toward his friend.

Act III, Scene 2

Lucius is in a public place discoursing with three strangers to Athens. The strangers relate to Lucius the financial difficulties Timon is facing and the refusal of Lucullus to provide him with financial assistance. Lucius pronounces that he would not repudiate such a request had he been treated as generously by Timon as Lucullus had. Servilius then enters, handing a note to Lucius asking for 50 talents, a request that is initially greeted with credulity. Lucius then tells Servilius that he is unable to provide Timon with the money he requires, making the excuse that he was intending to ask Timon for a loan himself. After Lucius and Servilius have departed, the first stranger condemns the way in which Lucius has taken advantage of Timon's wealth but now refuses to help him when he is in need.

Act III, Scene 3

The third of Timon's servants arrives at the house of Sempronius, who asks the servant why Timon has not asked favors of Lucius, Lucullus, or Ventidius, who, he argues, all owe their fortunes to Timon. The servant then tells Sempronius that the three men have already denied Timon's requests. This prompts Sempronius to launch into a resentful tirade in which he states that he should have been approached first as he was the first to benefit from Timon's gifts. He asserts that, had he been the first person Timon approached, he would willingly have given over three times the amount he requested, but as a response to what he perceives as an insult, he refuses to provide Timon with any money. The servant condemns Sempronius and laments that he was Timon's last hope of financial assistance.

Act III, Scene 4

A group of servants to a number of Timon's creditors assemble outside his house, all with the intention of collecting the debts Timon owes to their masters. The servants are beginning to discuss the extent of Timon's debts when Flavius enters, attempting to pass unseen with his cloak covering his head. The servants manage to waylay him and announce the purpose of their visit. Flavius then scorns the hypocrisy of their masters and leaves them. Servilius approaches the servants and requests they return later, as Timon is unwell, an appeal that fails to satisfy them. A furious Timon then appears from the house and is horrified by the spectacle he witnesses. After he returns to the house, Hortensius expresses his doubt that their masters will ever retrieve their debts.

Act III, Scene 5

Timon, having returned to the interior of his house, calls for Flavius and instructs him to invite his friends to the house for one final feast. Flavius objects that there is not enough left to provide even a modest meal for his guests. Timon ignores the objections of his steward and insists that he shall provide the meal.

Act III, Scene 6

An assembly of Athenian senators is set to take place in which the fate of a friend of Alcibiades, who has apparently committed murder, will be determined. While the senators seem to favor a rigorous punishment for the felony, Alcibiades speaks in favor of his friend and tries to persuade them to be lenient toward him. He also speaks of his friend's valiant military career. When he sees the senators are unmoved by his appeal, he asks them to consider his own services to Athens. The first senator is angered by Alcibiades's persistence and banishes him from Athens before ordering that his friend be executed. Alcibiades curses the senators for their action and vows to have vengeance upon the city from which he has just been banished.

Act III, Scene 7

This scene takes place at Timon's house where his false friends are beginning to arrive. The promise of a feast has led two lords to suspect that the requests for a loan were merely a test of their friendship. Both lords also comment upon the emphatic nature of their invitations. Timon appears and greets the lords shortly before the banquet, represented by a number of covered dishes, is brought in. One lord relates to the others the news of Alcibiades' banishment but is unable to elaborate further as Timon begins to speak to his guests. Timon recites his own mock grace, similar to that delivered by Apemantus in the first act, and invites his guests to uncover their dishes to reveal that they are merely filled with tepid water. He then berates his guests for their lack of loyalty and hypocrisy toward him before launching into a frenzied attack upon them, throwing water in their faces along with any other objects close at hand. The guests hurriedly leave while Timon announces his contempt for Athens and humanity in general. After Timon has left the room, a number of the lords return to retrieve items of clothing they were forced to leave behind. All of them announce their perplexity at their host's behavior.

Act IV, Scene 1

This short scene takes place outside the walls of Athens shortly after Timon has been forced to leave the city. Here Timon launches into an embittered tirade against humanity in which he wishes that civilization will destroy itself and descend into anarchy. He begins tearing off various items of clothing to symbolize his rejection of Athenian civilization.

Act IV, Scene 2

Flavius gathers together the servants at Timon's old house and confirms that their master has left, prompting a series of laments about Timon's plight and the fickle nature of his friends. Flavius then divides a share of money among the servants before watching them leave. He also conveys his own regrets about the downfall of Timon but pledges that he will remain Timon's steward as long as there is money to manage and announces his intention to seek out his former master.

Act IV, Scene 3

Timon has now left the city to lead a troglodyte existence in the woods. Here, he speaks of his contempt for the composition of Athenian society before proceeding to dig for root vegetables. While digging, he inadvertently unearths a trove of gold, which leads him to apostrophise the substance for the way it inverts natural order and to make negative things seem favorable to the individual. He is interrupted in his musings by the sound of a war drum, which prompts him to hide the gold again. Alcibiades then appears with a drum and fife accompanied by two prostitutes, Phrynia and Timandra. At first the two men do not recognize each other. Timon introduces himself to Alcibiades as Misanthropos, hater of mankind, and treats the party with contemptuous disinterest, insulting one of the prostitutes by suggesting she is a harborer of venereal disease. Timon's interest is suddenly aroused, however, by Alcibiades speaking in passing of his intention to invade Athens. Timon unearths some of the gold he has buried and offers to fund Alcibiades' coup, providing his soldiers are ruthless in their conquest and do not succumb to external signs of innocence or virtue in the civilians. Timon also offers money to the prostitutes on the condition that they retain their current profession and spread the sexually transmitted diseases he suspects they carry among their clients. Alcibiades takes his leave of Timon saying he will accept his money, if not his advice.

Timon continues digging in the earth, hoping it will send forth vicious or venomous creatures rather than proud and conceited animals. Apemantus then appears, confessing he is intrigued by reports that Timon is apparently imitating his own misanthropic outlook. He advises him instead to imitate his flatterers who are at that moment leading very comfortable existences. Apemantus doubts how successfully Timon will adapt to his new existence after having experienced such luxury, while Timon, in turn, doubts the veracity of Apemantus's misanthropy as he has not undergone the ordeals that Timon has experienced. The two then engage in a philosophical argument in which

Apemantus comments that if he had control of the world, he would relinquish it to the beast. Timon argues that this is a foolhardy ambition and that the natural world is in a constant state of chaos in which one creature is always another's prey. Apemantus remarks that such a vision has already been realized in Athens. The two exchange insults before Timon orders Apemantus to leave, throwing a rock at him.

Timon is then visited by a group of thieves to whom he also offers gold, providing, in a demand similar to that he imposed upon Alcibiades and the prostitutes, that they continue to spread fear and chaos in their chosen mode of existence. The departure of the thieves is followed by the arrival of Flavius, who laments the sorry state in which he has found his former employer. He continually asserts his loyalty in the face of Timon's misanthropic outbursts. Timon is obviously moved by Flavius's loyalty but implies that the goodness of one man has not swayed his misanthropic stance. Timon then bestows a substantial sum of gold upon his former steward and bids him leave, instructing him to isolate himself from other men and avoid the corrupting influence of society. He then withdraws into his cave.

Act V, Scene 1

The final act begins in exactly the same way as the first, with the Poet and the Painter preparing to present their work to Timon. After having heard of Timon's recent generosity toward Alcibiades, Flavius, Phrynia, and Timandra, they suspect that his poverty is merely a ruse through which he could discover who were his true friends and that giving gifts to Timon at this time would be rewarded when the recipient is restored to his former opulence. Timon appears from his cave unseen and overhears the two artists discussing their gifts. He forces the two to admit they have heard of his recent acquisition of gold. However, the Painter protests it was not their motivation for visiting him. During his discussion with the two opportunists, Timon gets increasingly angry before driving them away by throwing stones at them.

Two senators entreat Timon to return to Athens, only to be rebuffed, in Act V, Scene 2 of *Timon of Athens*. This illustration was designed for a 1918 edition of Charles and Mary Lamb's *Tales from Shakespeare*. (*Illustration by Louis Rhead*)

Act V, Scene 2

Flavius has conducted to Timon's cave two senators who, in spite of the steward's warnings about his current attitude toward humanity, insist upon seeing him. The senators greet Timon and attempt to persuade him to return to Athens by offering to cancel his debts and to make him a captain in the army to help counter the threat posed by Alcibiades. Timon toys with the senators, making his initial utterances imply he will help them, but he eventually reveals that he is unconcerned about the fate of Athens and suggests that any citizen wishing to avoid the wrath of Alcibiades should hang himself from a tree near his cave before he has the chance to chop it down. He then continues his labor of digging his own grave, leaving the two senators to return dejectedly to the city.

Act V, Scene 3

Outside the city, Alcibiades and his army are poised to advance, while two senators are listening to the report of a messenger who has brought them discouraging news. One of the senators observes that the army will only be pacified if Timon agrees to return. The messenger then comments that he encountered a soldier from Alcibiades's army who was in the act of conveying a letter to Timon attempting to persuade him to join his campaign against Athens. The two senators then return from Timon, one of whom imparts the disappointing news that Timon will not return and advises the others to return to the city and prepare for the advance of Alcibiades and his army.

Act V, Scene 4

A soldier appears in the woods searching for Timon but instead discovers that Timon is dead and has been buried near his cave. The tomb bears an inscription that the soldier is unable to decipher. He makes a wax copy of it in the hope that his captain will be able to make sense of it.

Act V, Scene 5

Alcibiades and his troops are outside the walls of Athens preparing to attack the city. A number of senators appear on the walls, to whom Alcibiades announces that the people are tired of their regime and are ready to revolt against them. The senators attempt to avert the attack by protesting that they made their best efforts to make amends with Timon and asserting that innocent people, with whom they should have no quarrel, will be harmed in the fighting. Alcibiades hears their request that they should negotiate and attempt to find a peaceful solution to their quarrels and agrees to speak with them, hoping that he can persuade them that those who betrayed Timon should be punished. While he is waiting for the senators to come down to meet him, a soldier conveys to Alcibiades the news of Timon's death and presents him with the copy of the epitaph he made. Alcibiades agrees to enter the city and attempt to negotiate a peaceful solution, although his final command for the soldiers to strike up their drums provides a note of ambiguity to the play's conclusion.

CHARACTER LIST

Timon Widely regarded for his immense wealth and lavish generosity toward others, Timon basks in what is later revealed to be the false friendship offered by his fellow citizens. When it is revealed that Timon's wealth has evaporated, those who had previously benefited from his generosity fail to exercise the same benevolence during his hour of need. Timon's resultant retreat from society to lead a pitiful existence as an embittered misanthrope in the wilderness, and his offer to fund a military coup led by Alcibiades, emphasize the extent to which his faith in human nature is corroded by this process.

Apemantus A cynical and outspoken philosopher with a deeply pessimistic view of human nature, Apemantus repeatedly scorns Timon for his hubristic and short sighted attitude.

Alcibiades A captain in the Athenian army who is banished from Athens after angering the senators while appealing for their clemency toward one of his friends who has been sentenced to death. As revenge, he intends to launch a military coup upon Athens, which Timon offers to fund with the money he accidentally finds in the woods. As a fellow outcast and victim of the ingratitude of others, Alcibiades's plight is comparable to that of Timon.

Flavius Timon's steward, whose unwavering loyalty toward his master, even after the loss of his fortune, marks him as a foil to the ingratitude and inconstancy of Timon's false friends and flatterers. He is rewarded after Timon discovers the gold in the wood.

Lucilius One of Timon's servants. Timon's gift to him of three talents enables him to marry the woman he loves and overcome her father's objections that he is too poor for his daughter.

Flaminius and Servilius Timon's loyal servants.

Servants More members of Timon's household staff.

Ventidius One of Timon's false friends. Timon pays a ransom to release him from prison. Ventidius does not return the favor when Timon is in need despite his recent acquisition of a substantial inheritance after his father's death.

Lucullus, Lucius, and Sempronius Timon's false friends who fail to come to his assistance when he is in debt.

The Poet and the Painter Two guests at Timon's feast who intend to present their works to their host in order to profit from his generosity. They also visit Timon in the woods but are driven away when he sees through their cynical ploy to endear themselves to him.

The Jeweller and the Merchant Guests at Timon's feast.

Messenger

Old Athenian Visits Timon complaining of the attentions Lucilius has been lavishing upon his daughter.

Cupid Presenter of the masque held at Timon's estate.

Amazon women Participants in the masque.

Senators Governors of Athens, many of whom are creditors to Timon.

Lords Among the guests and false friends gathered at Timon's banquets.

Caphis A servant of one of the senators to whom Timon is debt.

Isidore's servant and two servants of Varro Servants of Timon's creditors.

Fool Professional entertainer to one of the women in the area.

Strangers Friends of Lucius who have never been entertained by Timon. They express disapproval at Lucius's reluctance to offer assistance to Timon.

Titus, Hortensius, and Philotus More servants of Timon's creditors.

Timandra One of the two prostitutes who accompany Alcibiades when he encounters Timon in the woods. Her name, which derives from the Greek phrase "honor of the husband," provides a touch of irony.

Phrynia The other prostitute accompanying Alcibiades. Her name probably alludes to the land of Phrygia where Alcibiades was killed.

Thieves This group encounters Timon in the woods. He gives them money on the condition that they continue to exist as thieves and spread panic across the city.

Soldiers Among the forces assembled by Alcibiades.

CHARACTER STUDIES
Timon

Timon is one of Shakespeare's most challenging tragic protagonists. His excessive and hubristic benevolence in much of the first three acts is quickly replaced by his ruthless and uncompromising misanthropy in the scenes near his cave. It is this experience of, and response to, the two extremes of fortune that make him such an interesting character.

Timon, unlike many of the other opulent figures who populated the Renaissance stage, is motivated neither by the acquisition of gold nor by any kind of zealous impulse to preserve his wealth. His wealth is instead a means of achieving the kind of social interaction he craves and that he intends to gain by holding lavish banquets for the people of Athens and by bestowing extravagant gifts upon them. Apemantus cynically views the gift-giving as a form of bribery and comments that "there would be none left to rail upon thee and then thou wouldst sin the faster" (1.2) if he, too, were to share Timon's bounty. This idea of bribery is reflected by the appearance of the prostitutes in the fourth act and Timon's remark to them that "they love thee not that use thee" (4.3). This statement could be applied in equal measure to Timon, suggesting that his false friends were essentially prostituting their friendship.

There is also no evidence to suggest that Timon has contact with any kind of familial relations. This is one of the factors that contributes to the enigmatic nature of the character. Very little is suggested about Timon's past, although the senators in the fifth act allude to some past civic duty Timon performed, and there is no hint of the source of his immense wealth. He disappears from the play in similarly mysterious circumstances with his death, the cause of which is never made clear, taking place offstage and being accidentally discovered by a soldier who stumbles upon his grave.

It is implied that money, or at least the occasions for social contact it precipitates, is a means for Timon to compensate for the lack of contact with his fellow citizens. The Poet's comment that

Timon presents Alcibiades with gold as a sign of his support for the invasion of Athens in Act IV, Scene 3 of *Timon of Athens*. This illustration was designed for a 1918 edition of Charles and Mary Lamb's *Tales from Shakespeare*. *(Illustration by Louis Rhead)*

Timon appeals to the "glass-faced flatterer" (1.1) is a telling one and reveals a great deal about that which proves to be his fatal flaw. Timon sees that which he wants to see in the false friends and flatterers who gather at his estate, rather than their true greedy and opportunistic natures.

Timon's downfall proves to be his overindulgent role in the economy of usury and gift-giving that is taking place in Athens. One of Timon's guests remarks that Timon will repay a gift "Sevenfold above itself" (1.1) and that "no gift to him / But breeds the giver a return exceeding / All use of quittance" (1.1). This point is reinforced by a senator's comments about Timon's spending. The senator claims, "If I want gold, steal but a beggar's dog / And give it to Timon, why, the dog coins gold" (2.1). This was also indicated in the first act when Timon instructs his servants that the gifts from the lords are to be "received / Not without fair reward" (1.2). The gifts are given freely by Timon's guests, but presumably on the understanding that Timon will give them a greater gift in return. Timon's gift-giving is therefore a process of multiplication and one in which he is not willing for other people to engage. He refuses to accept Ventidius's offer to repay him double the ransom money on the grounds that "there's none / Can truly say he gives if he receives" (1.2). The folly of this approach is not lost on a number of the characters. Flavius, Apemantus, and, in an allegorical warning in his new work, the Poet are all doubtful that his friends will remember his former kindness if he ever needed their assistance.

After the betrayal by his friends, Timon leaves Athens to lead a hermit's existence in the woods outside the city where he chooses to be known as "Misanthropos" who "hates mankind" (4.3). He begins devoting himself to the twin purposes of hating and making himself hated. He also becomes obsessed with the prospect of Athens disappearing in apocalyptic tribulation. As he leaves the city, he wishes that the fortifications surrounding it would fall into the sea and that the gods will "confound" (4.1) the place, thus allowing anarchy and disorder to prevail. With the exception of Flavius who is rewarded for his loyalty and virtuous good service, the people to whom Timon gives money in the woods can all be seen as potential contributors to his apocalyptic vision. He funds the military coup Alcibiades plans to organize in the hope that he will prove "a planetary plague" (4.3) upon the city and that he will not let his "sword skip one" (4.3), no matter how outwardly virtuous they may seem. He then gives money to Timandra and Phrynia on the condition that they remain prostitutes and spread throughout the city the venereal diseases Timon believes they carry. He also imposes a similar condition upon the group of thieves who

pass by. His offer of money is on the condition that they "Rob one another," "Cut throats," and "Break open shops" (4.3), thereby spreading confusion throughout the city.

In the final act, Timon's ambitions seem to change. He ignores the pleas of the senators for him to assist against the threat posed by Alcibiades, asserting he would rather spend his time engaged in the task of digging his grave, hoping that people will visit it and let his gravestone be their "oracle" (5.2). This is the last appearance of Timon in the play. The circumstances of his death are unclear and are only noted when a soldier stumbles upon his grave and copies the epitaph for Alcibiades to read: *Here lie I, Timon, who alive all living men did hate, / Pass by and curse thy fill, but pass and stay not here thy gait"* (5.5). Despite Timon's conviction that he was universally hated, Alcibiades still refers to him as "noble Timon, of whose memory / Hereafter more" (5.5). It seems Alcibiades would prefer the positive aspects of Timon to be remembered, rather than his "latter spirits" (5.5).

Timon's transition from benevolence to misanthropy is almost instant. This makes *Timon of Athens* a play in which the central character is exposed only to the extremes of human experience. Perhaps the most succinct and deft assessment of Timon in the play is provided by Apemantus who comments that Timon has never experienced the "middle of humanity," only the "extremity of both ends" (4.3).

Apemantus

Apemantus is a professional philosopher belonging to the cynical school of thought. He is most representative of the misanthropic aspects of the philosophy, continually insulting and criticizing the characters and humanity in general. His first appearance, for example, sees him dismiss the entire population of Athens as "knaves" (1.1). He also sees the folly of Timon's indulgent lifestyle and his tendency to repeatedly give away extravagant and excessive gifts to his followers. While the masque at Timon's banquet is taking place, he comments that he "should fear those that dance before me now / Would one day stamp upon me"

(1.2). He also refuses to partake of any of Timon's benevolence for fear he should be "bribed," with "none left to rail upon thee" (1.2). Apemantus therefore seems to value the privilege of being able to criticize other men above any potential material gain.

The word *cynic* was erroneously thought to have been derived from the Greek word for "dog-like." Despite the error, this etymology remains a firm influence upon the characterization of Apemantus, who is described or insulted as a dog on several occasions throughout the play, including Timon's remark that Apemantus was "bred a dog" (4.3). While the canine imagery repeatedly suggests the idea of snarling at humanity, as Apemantus does frequently, some critics have also noticed an element of doglike loyalty in Apemantus who, despite his vocal disdain for society, still seems to be a familiar guest at Timon's gatherings. This is evidenced by the Poet's remark that Timon is able to attract a host of people "from the glass-faced flatterer / To Apemantus" (1.1) and Varro's servant's worry that "he'll abuse us" (2.2) when the servants happen to encounter him. He therefore appears to be well-known across all aspects of Athenian society.

Apemantus claims that the main reason for his presence at Timon's gatherings is purely to view and criticize the social customs taking place. He asserts that he wants "to see meat fill knaves and wine heat fools" (1.1) and that he has "come to observe" (1.2). When the feast begins, Timon orders that Apemantus "have a table by himself, / For he does neither affect company / Nor is he for't indeed" (1.2), an arrangement that seems to suit Apemantus who is quite content to separate himself from the gathering and dine on root vegetables and water rather than the meat that is being served to the rest of the guests. Apemantus's deliberate self-exclusion, as well his choice of roots and water as a means of sustenance, provides a grim foreshadowing of Timon's departure from the city.

Apemantus is also one of the succession of people to visit Timon when he leaves the city to lead a troglodyte existence in the woods. Apemantus

has obviously heard reports of Timon's conversion to misanthropy and is clearly intrigued to see for himself the truth behind the words of the people who "report / Thou dost affect my manners and dost use them" (4.3). He clearly sees Timon's misanthropic stance as little more than an imitation of his own. He then begins to argue with Timon about the authenticity of the respective shows of misanthropy they exhibit. He argues that Timon's recent hatred of humanity is "in thee a nature but affected, / A poor unmanly melancholy sprung / From change of fortune" (4.3). He doubts the veracity of Timon's stance as he has adopted it "enforcedly" (4.3). Timon retorts by asserting that Apemantus has never known any better than the base condition in which he currently exists and that, unlike himself, he has never been subjected to such a rapid decline in fortune.

While many of the observations and criticisms Apemantus makes appear fair, as does his lack of faith in the veracity of the friendship offered by Timon's flatterers and followers, he himself is not above criticism. He seems to regularly attend various social occasions, in spite of his very vocal disdain for such gatherings. He also appears to gain a considerable amount of satisfaction from observing the kind of practices he finds distasteful. The Poet comments that Apemantus "few things loves better / Than to abhor himself" (1.1), suggesting that he gains a kind of perverse pleasure from making himself objectionable to others. This hints that he is guilty of the same kind of self-indulgence of which he repeatedly implies that Timon is culpable.

Alcibiades

Alcibiades is very much a marginal character for much of the first half of the play and only begins to exert any significant influence over the plot after his banishment from Athens toward the end of the third act. In spite of this, however, he remains a significant presence throughout the play. Like Timon, Alcibiades is a victim of ingratitude at the hands of the people whom he has previously assisted. His exile as a result of this ingratitude serves to mirror the experiences of Timon and provide an echo of the main plot. There is very little mentioned about his past. He mentions past "victories" (3.6) and instances in which he defended the Athenian people and "kept back their foes" (3.6), suggesting he has obviously had a successful military career. He is also known for his erudition, as indicated by the soldier's decision to make a copy of Timon's epitaph for him to decipher. The soldier goes on to say that he "hath in every figure skill, / An aged interpreter though young in days" (5.4), which seems to suggest he is a significantly educated man.

The first appearance of Alcibiades takes place just before the banquet is held. It seems, judging by the discourse between him and Timon, that the two are long-standing acquaintances and that Alcibiades regularly appears at the feasts hosted by Timon. His comment that Timon has "saved my longing" (1.1), as well as being a mark of courtesy and respect, also suggests a sense of familiarity between the two men. As a captain in the Athenian army, Alcibiades stands out significantly from the rest of the guests at Timon's estate, most of whom are lords or other citizens seeking some kind of patronage. Timon remarks upon how distinctive Alcibiades is in the company of his fellow guests when he suggests that he "had rather be at a breakfast of enemies than a dinner of friends" (1.2), implying that he seems more suited to the battlefield than a social gathering.

As well as marking Alcibiades as a distinctive presence at the feast, this comment also raises questions about the soldier's ability to adjust to civilian life that reemerge toward the end of the third act.

The play's subplot, in which Alcibiades is the key participant, is initiated when one of his former comrades has been sentenced to death for murder. Although the exact details of the incident, and indeed the identity of the accused man, remain sketchy, it seems that he killed his victim in a duel while defending his honor. Alcibiades comments that the action was motivated by the accused "Seeing his reputation touched to death" (3.6). Alcibiades also points out that the man "might have died in war" (3.6), thus allowing him to die in honorable circumstances and at the service of those who now

sentence him to death. The senators are unmoved by Alcibiades' pleas. One of them comments that the man is a "sworn rioter" and that he is a dangerously subversive influence.

Alcibiades attempts to save his comrade's life by reminding the senators of his own victories and the military services he has performed for Athens. He announces his intention to "pawn my victories" for the sake of the condemned man. That he uses a financial metaphor is significant, particularly when one compares this character to Timon. It is implied that they are both victims of the same self-interested economic agendas that are so prevalent in the city of Athens depicted in this play. Alcibiades raises this issue when he comments that he has "kept back their foes / While they have told their money and let out / Their coin upon huge interest" (3.6). This seems to suggest that Alcibiades has been disengaged from the Athenian economy, a view that is complemented by his observation that he is "Rich only in large hurts" (3.6) and Timon's comment that he is a soldier and "therefore seldom rich" (1.2). His lack of finances means that he is dissociated from the policy makers of the city.

After having been forced to leave Athens by the senators, Alcibiades has a chance encounter with Timon in the woods in which he mentions his desire to lay "proud Athens on a heap" (4.3). This prompts Timon to fund Alcibiades' proposed invasion on the condition that he does not let his "sword skip one" (4.3), despite how innocent they may appear. He is also instructed to "Make large confusion" (4.3) in the city. However, Alcibiades suggests that he will not inflict the unbridled destruction that Timon imagines upon the city. He accepts the gold Timon offers, remarking that he will "take the gold thou givest me, / Not all thy counsel" (4.3). He wishes to punish only those who caused grievances to himself and to Timon and is eventually persuaded to spare the innocent rather than leading a ruthless killing spree. In his final speech, he claims he "will use the olive with my sword" (5.5) and "Make war breed peace" (5.5), thus asserting himself as an agent of harmony, rather than destruction.

Flavius

While the role of the play's moralizing voice would initially seem more fitting to Apemantus, the professional philosopher, it is in fact Flavius who fulfills the role. While Apemantus does make several attempts to alert Timon to the folly of his susceptibility to the false friends and flatterers he entertains, it is difficult to divorce these interjections from Apemantus's broader misanthropic worldview while Timon's actions seem to justify this stance. It seems that it is only Flavius and the other servants who truly have Timon's interests at heart.

Flavius is Timon's steward, a role that puts him in charge of Timon's rapidly dwindling finances. He represents a marked contrast to the words of one of the lords at Timon's feast who remarks that "Plutus, the god of gold, / Is but his steward" (1.1).

Timon gives Flavius a bag of gold for his loyalty in Act IV, Scene 3 of *Timon of Athens,* in this print published by D. Appleton and Company in the 19th century. (*Painting by Henry Wallis; engraving by Charles Cousen*)

In reality, Timon's actual steward presents quite a different picture. Throughout the banquet, he can only look on in exasperation as Timon plunges himself deeper into debt. His comments upon Timon's spending are confined to personal asides as his master will not spare a moment to listen to his advice. Timon, he observes, is giving gifts out of "an empty coffer" (1.2), and "what he speaks is all in debt—he owes / For every word" (1.2). When the extent and consequences of Timon's prodigality become clear, Flavius rightly protests that he made numerous attempts to warn Timon about his extravagant spending.

While Flavius's views about Timon's irresponsibility and his lack of faith in Timon's followers may coincide with the views of Apemantus, Flavius does remain loyal to his master. His remark "I bleed inwardly for my lord" (1.2) suggests that he feels the pain against which Timon seems to have desensitized himself. After the wealth has diminished, Flavius describes his fellow servants as "broken implements of a ruined house" (4.2) and is left to utter the proverbial maxim, "We have seen better days" (4.2). He shares out some money among the servants and goes to seek out Timon in the woods, vowing, "Whilst I have gold, I'll be his steward still" (4.2). He professes to Timon that "Ne'er did poor steward wear a truer grief / For his undone lord than mine eyes for you" (4.3). He continually asserts his loyalty to Timon throughout his appearance in this scene and vows to administer even the remnants of his former master's fortune. Timon confesses that Flavius's loyalty "almost turns my dangerous nature mild" (4.3) and describes him as a "singly honest man" (4.3). He then gives Flavius a gift of gold and warns him to stay clear of the corrupting influence of other men.

As the only character who can truly be considered a friend to Timon, Flavius represents a foil to the self-interest and opportunism of the other characters who attempt to exploit Timon's generosity. He therefore provides a marked contrast to the lapsed humanity of the other characters in the play.

DIFFICULTIES OF THE PLAY

Many of the difficulties in understanding the play are based on its problematic text. Critics have frequently debated whether *Timon of Athens* is the work of two authors or whether it is an unfinished piece. It is even possible that both these explanations are true. Nevertheless, for whatever reason, the state of the text poses a number of questions.

Many of these problems are exemplified by the character of Ventidius. Although this character only appears once to utter a handful of lines, he is mentioned several other times. The first reference to him takes place just as Timon makes his first appearance in the play. A messenger informs him that his friend was imprisoned for failing to pay his debts and petitions Timon to provide him with financial assistance. Timon willingly agrees to this offer and requests that Ventidius should join him as soon as he is free. In the next scene, Ventidius appears, having been released from prison, and informs Timon that his father has recently died and left him a large estate. He therefore offers to repay the ransom Timon provided and double it as a gesture of his gratitude. The key question this episode poses is why, if he, or at least his father, was in a stable financial position, he needed to plead for Timon's assistance. This is compounded by the premise that he is able to offer Timon double the amount he received for his ransom. The next reference to Ventidius occurs at the end of the second act when he is listed as one of the friends upon whom Timon thinks he can rely to assist him with his financial difficulties. Timon orders Flavius to go and collect the five talents he was paid. However, unlike the servants' attempts at petitioning the other lords, this meeting is never dramatized in the play. The final reference to Ventidius occurs during the meeting with Sempronius in which Timon's servant comments that he is one of the friends who had been "touched and found base metal" (3.3). Ventidius therefore represents something of a dead end in terms of plot development. This continuity error is possibly a result of inconsistencies between the two collaborating authors or an indication that the text was left unfinished.

Another continuity error takes place in the fourth act during Apemantus's meeting with Timon. During his discourse with Timon that takes place in the middle of the scene, Apemantus observes the Poet and the Painter heading toward Timon's cave, seemingly suggesting that their arrival is imminent. However, neither character appears until the beginning of the next act, during which time Timon is visited by Flavius and the thieves. This seems a clear inconsistency in the development of the play's action.

There is also the baffling appearance of the Fool in the second act who briefly entertains the servants of Timon's creditors along with Apemantus. One of the servants refers to the Fool's "mistress" (2.2), which, considering the only female characters in the play are the two prostitutes who appear with Alcibiades in the fourth act, makes his appearance all the more puzzling. There are, however, a number of jokes that seem to depend upon the fact that the Fool's mistress is a prostitute, suggesting that it could be Phrynia or Timandra. The short sequence also contains the appearance of a page who delivers some letters addressed to Timon and Alcibiades. The content of these letters is never revealed, nor is there any future reference to them as the plot develops. The sequence is therefore somewhat awkwardly integrated into the play. The possibility that it was included as a means to distract the audience's attention from Timon and Flavius is called into question by the fact that, when the focus returns to them, their discourse seems to be a direct continuation of the conversation they were having before the appearance of the Fool. A possible explanation for the perplexing appearance of the Fool and the page, and for Apemantus's premature observation of the arrival of the Poet and Painter in the fourth act is the possibility that the play was never performed during Shakespeare's lifetime. An attempt to mount a production of the text would possibly have highlighted the inconsistencies and continuity problems and prompted some authorial revision.

Another inconsistency that could also be explained by dual authorship relates to the value of money as understood in various parts of the text. Four different types of currency seem to be circulating in the Athens of this play: the talent, the doit, the crown, and the solidare, as well as various unspecified "pieces" and other sums. The talent was a high value denomination of currency, thought to be worth the equivalent of 6,000 drachmas. The values that are quoted do not reflect this. The reader may wonder why Timon is bothering to request that Ventidius repay the five-talent ransom when the senator has estimated his debts to be the sum of 25,000. The discrepancies between the values of the currencies of which the characters speak demonstrates another problem in the coherence and consistency of the play. It is also quite possible that the varying values and currencies are yet another symptom of collaborative authorship, with Shakespeare's references appearing fairly accurate and Middleton frequently underestimating the value of the talent and often switching among various currencies. A number of critics have, however, dismissed the problem of the monetary values expressed in the text, suggesting that it would not have posed such a great barrier to understanding and appreciation for a contemporary audience or readership. It does, nevertheless, pose a significant inconsistency in the development of the play as a whole and is a potential source of confusion for modern readers and performers.

KEY PASSAGES
Act I, Scene 1, 64–94

POET. Sir, I have upon a high and pleasant hill
Feigned Fortune to be throned. The base o'th'
    mount
Is ranked with all deserts, all kinds of natures
That labour on the bosom of this sphere
To propagate their states. Amongst them all
Whose eyes are on this sovereign Lady fixed,
One do I personate of Lord Timon's frame,
Whom fortune with her ivory hand wafts to
    her,
Whose present grace to present slaves and
    servants
Translates his rivals.

PAINTER. 'Tis conceived to scope.
This throne, this Fortune and this hill,
    methinks,
With one man beckoned from the rest below
Bowing his head against the steepy mount
To climb his happiness, would be well
    expressed
In our condition.

POET. Nay, sir, but hear me on:
All those which were his fellows but of late—
Some better than his value—on the moment
Follow his strides, his lobbies fill with
    tendance,
Rain sacrificial whisperings in his ear,
Make sacred even his stirrup and though him
Drink the free air.

PAINTER. Ay, marry, what of these?

POET. When Fortune in her shift and change
    of mood
Spurns down her late beloved, all his
    dependants,
Which laboured after him to the mountain's
    top
Even on their knees and hands, let him slip
    down,
Not one accompanying his declining foot.

PAINTER. 'Tis common:
A thousand moral paintings I can show
That shall demonstrate these quick blows of
    Fortune's
More pregnantly than words. Yet you do well
To show Lord Timon that mean eyes have seen
The foot above the head.

This passage, which occurs near the beginning of the play, evidences a common feature in Shakespearean tragedy in which a small group of minor characters engage in debate about the deeds of the major figures. This feature also takes place in *King Lear, Hamlet, Antony and Cleopatra*, and, perhaps most notably, *Macbeth* in which the three witches initiate the action of the play. The exchanges between the Poet and the Painter take place at Timon's estate while guests are beginning to gather for the banquet and await the arrival of their host. The Poet and the Painter both intend to present Timon with one of their works as a gift, most likely in the hope that they will gain some form of patronage from their host in return. The Painter has already shown the work he intends to present to Timon, which he confidently claims is a "pretty mocking of the life" of his subject.

This passage is influenced strongly by the *paragone* tradition in Renaissance culture. The *paragone,* translated as "competition," was a debate attempting to affirm whether poetry or painting was the superior form of artistic expression in the Renaissance. The intensity of the debate in this scene appears obvious just by looking at the layout of the speeches and the abundance of half lines in the exchange. Half lines often appear as an indicator of intimacy between characters; here, however, they are expressive of the rivalry between the two men and the rapidity of their retorts. This rivalry is also shown by the Painter's interjections during the Poet's attempt to explain the contents of his new work. At one point, the Painter comments that the subject matter "would be well expressed / In our condition" and later concludes that he could provide a "thousand moral paintings" that would exhibit the same features as the poem "More pregnantly than words."

The dispute also highlights the perceived differences between the two forms of artistic endeavor. The Painter has already commented that he has made a "pretty mocking of the life" of Timon, thus alluding to the idea of mimesis, the tradition in which, to borrow the old phrase, art imitates life. The Painter therefore hints that his work is an attempt to provide an accurate representation of the subject. The Poet, on the other hand, comments that he has "*Feigned* Fortune to be throned," thus suggesting his work is a fiction. The idea that poetry is essentially fictitious is also suggested by Apemantus later in this scene when he accuses the Poet of being a liar. This view is influenced by a common debate that was taking place in Renaissance England about the idea of poetry and its apparently artificial nature.

The idea of rivalry also emerges in the matter of the Poet's work, which makes these exchanges an important part of the play. He describes his work as an allegory about the progress of Timon toward fortune, which will be followed by a fall in which he will be unaided by anyone he encounters. The Poet has placed the figure of Fortune "upon a high and pleasant hill." This is one of the less common realizations of Fortune, as the image of the wheel of fortune and the idea of Fortune smiling upon certain people were far more frequently appropriated. However, this choice of realization proves suitable within the context of the play. In the Poet's work, Timon, like many other people, is attempting to climb the hill to reach Fortune at the top. When Timon does finally achieve this goal, the Poet comments that Fortune "to present slaves and servants / Translates his rivals." The rivals will apparently be so enamoured of Timon after his acquisition of Fortune's favor that they will "Follow his strides," "Rain sacrificial whisperings in his ear" and "Make sacred even his stirrup." However, as is common in realizations of Fortune, she is portrayed by the Poet as fickle and subject to a "shift and change of mood" in which she "Spurns down her late beloved." In the Poet's work, Timon's former rivals will "let him slip down, / Not one accompanying his declining foot." Essentially, the Poet has placed himself in the same position as the dramatist giving his audience an idea of the events that take place in their work. The Poet's work can therefore be viewed alongside the warnings advanced to Timon by Apemantus and Flavius about the reliability of his friends. Ironically, however, the Poet emerges as one of the opportunists who attempts to benefit from Timon's benevolence and can also be likened to one of the figures who allows Timon to fall down the hill without offering any help. This is indicated by the fact that his only other appearance in the text occurs after he has heard rumors that Timon is solvent again, prompting him to make another cynical attempt to profit from his wealth.

Act IV, Scene 1, 1–41

TIMON. Let me look back upon thee. O thou
  wall
That girdles in those wolves, dive in the earth
And fence not Athens! Matrons, turn
  incontinent;
Obedience, fail in children; slaves and fools,
Pluck the grave wrinkled senate from the
  bench
And minister in their steads. To general filths
Convert o'th' instant, green virginity,
Do't in your parents' eyes. Bankrupts, hold
  fast;
Rather than render back, out with your knives
And cut your trusters' throats! Bound servants,
  steal:
Large-handed robbers to your grave masters
  are
And pill by law. Maid, to thy master's bed,
Thy mistress is o'th' brothel. Son of sixteen,
Pluck the lined crutch from thy old limping
  sire,
With it beat out his brains. Piety and fear,
Religion to the gods, peace, justice, truth,
Domestic awe, night-rest and neighbourhood,
Instruction, manners, mysteries and trades,
Degrees, observances, customs and laws,
Decline to your confounding contraries—
And let confusion live! Plagues incident to
  men,
Your potent and infectious fevers heap
On Athens, ripe for stroke. Thou cold sciatica,
Cripple our senators that their limbs may halt
As lamely as their manners; lust and liberty,
Creep into the minds and marrows of our
  youth
That 'gainst the stream of virtue they may
  strive
And drown themselves in riot. Itches, blains,
Sow all th'Athenian bosoms, and their crop
Be general leprosy; breath infect breath,
That their society, as their friendship, may
Be merely poison. Nothing I'll bear from thee
But nakedness, thou detestable town.
Take that too, with multiplying bans.

Timon will to the woods, where he shall find
Th'unkindest beast more kinder than mankind.
The gods confound—hear me, you good gods
  all!—
Th'Athenians both within and out that wall,
And grant as Timon grows his hate may grow
To the whole race of mankind, high and low!
Amen. [*Exit*]

After his banishment, Timon tears off his clothes and rejects Athenian civilization in Act IV, Scene 1 of *Timon of Athens,* in this print published by F. & C. Rivington in 1803. *(Illustration by Henry Fuseli; engraving by Robert Hartley Cromek)*

This is the first of Timon's major soliloquies in which he rails against the nature of mankind. The speech is delivered outside the city walls shortly after Timon has decided to leave as a result of the failure of his false friends to help him meet his debts. It is often compared to a scene in *King Lear* in which Lear, having suffered the ingratitude of his two daughters, retreats to the wilderness. In the previous scene, Timon had issued the statement, "henceforth hated be / Of Timon man and all humanity" (3.7). It is this kind of rhetoric that provokes the tirade he delivers at the beginning of the fourth act.

He begins by wishing that the fortifications surrounding the city could sink into the earth. This is in contrast to Timon's wish in the previous scene that the entire city would sink. The city walls, however, are characterized by Timon as containing the malevolent influence of the Athenian people inside the city rather than protecting them from the threats posed by the outside world. This point is emphasized when Timon claims the wall in fact "girdles in those wolves," the people of Athens, suggesting that the city walls are a means of imprisonment rather than protection. He ends the speech by announcing his wish that the gods would exact tribulation upon "Th'Athenians both within and out that wall." This line, in particular, indicates the extent to which Timon's attitudes have changed toward his fellow Athenians. In the play's first scene, Apemantus dismisses all Athenians as "knaves," on the logical basis that they are knaves because they are Athenian. Timon also seems to have adopted a similar logic. He, however, seems to have taken it to its most extreme conclusion.

As Timon's speech continues, he starts to unveil his vision of the city in chaos and disorder. He wishes to see the civilization there contribute to its own destruction and for the values of order and discipline to fail. In his vision of a city in chaos, chaste married women would turn to sexual promiscuity, and children and slaves would rebel against the authority that has made them servile. He also invites the bankrupts of the city to keep the money they owe and to cut the throats of their creditors. He then rhetorically challenges the servants of the city to steal from their masters who, he implies, are little more than respectable thieves themselves, and baits the city youths into overthrowing their elders.

Timon's invective is then directed against various concepts such as domestic order, piety, and the influence of religion. He challenges these concepts to "Decline to your confounding contraries— / And let confusion live!" He therefore wishes to see the corrosion of the values that stabilize and maintain the balance of power in Athens.

The speech then sees the initiation of the motif of disease, which recurs throughout many of Timon's subsequent speeches. He wishes that "cold sciatica" will "Cripple our senators" and that "Itches, blains, / Sow all th'Athenian bosoms, and their crop / Be general leprosy." The symptoms to which Timon alludes were often associated with venereal disease and syphilis. The idea of venereal diseases spreading throughout Athens recurs in the fourth act when Timon encounters the prostitutes Phrynia and Timandra in the woods with Alcibiades. Timon clearly associates disease with his apocalyptic vision and seems to view venereal disease as the one that will spread the most rapidly, possibly as a result of the lapsed sexual morals he hopes will take effect.

Timon begins the final part of his speech by saying he will bear nothing from Athens but nakedness. According to directorial choice, this could take on a literal realization with Timon beginning to remove his clothes. The phrase "Take thou that too" would certainly imply that this is a possibility. This provides another point of comparison with *King Lear* in which Lear begins to strip off his clothes while speaking during the storm as he enters the wilderness.

The speech is concluded with Timon uttering an "Amen." This provides closure to the religious dimensions that were initiated with his direct addresses to the gods at various points during the speech. The use of the phrase also links it to the mock grace intoned by Apemantus in the first act. This speech is therefore important for exemplifying

Timon's disaffection with the human and initiating the apocalyptic imagery with which he becomes obsessed later in this act.

Act IV, Scene 3, 25–49

TIMON. What is here?
Gold? Yellow, glittering, precious gold?
No, gods, I am no idle votarist—
Roots, you clear heavens! Thus much of this
  will make
Black white, foul fair, wrong right,
Base noble, old young, coward valiant.
Ha, you gods, why this? What this, you gods?
  Why, this
Will lug your priests and servants from your
  sides,
Pluck stout men's pillows from below their
  heads.
This yellow slave.
Will knit and break religions, bless th'accursed,
Make the hoar leprosy adored, place thieves
And give them title, knee and approbation
With senators on the bench. This is it
That makes the wappered widow wed again,
She whom the spittle-house and ulcerous sores
Would cast the gorge at, this embalms and
  spices
To th'April day again. Come, damned earth,
Thou common whore of mankind that puts
  odds
Among the rout of nations, I will make thee
Do thy right nature. *March afar off.*
Ha? A drum? Thou'rt quick
But yet I'll bury thee. Thou'lt go, strong thief,
When gouty keepers of thee cannot stand.
Nay, stay thou out for earnest. [*Keeps some
  gold.*]

Timon's lengthy apostrophe to gold is notable for attracting the attention of the political and economic theorist, Karl Marx, who was also an admirer of this play. For Marx, this passage revealed the potential for money to achieve that of which humans alone are incapable and alludes to its ability to invert natural qualities.

In the context of the play, this speech represents the crowning ironical twist instigated by fortune. Timon's discovery of a large trove of gold occurs just as he has abandoned the society in which it is such an essential commodity. The irony is also provided by the fact that the discovery of the gold thwarts Timon's attempts to dig for root vegetables in the earth. His plea to the gods, "Roots, you clear heavens!" remains unanswered. In fact, Timon interprets his failure to find the root vegetables he seeks as a sign that the gods are unconvinced by his

Alcibiades and two prostitutes, Phrynia and Timandra, come upon Timon as he is digging for gold in Act IV, Scene 3 of *Timon of Athens,* in this print published by Jacob Tonson in 1709.

prayers, leading him to assert to the gods that he is "no idle votarist." In other words, his pleas are in earnest. This scene therefore goes some considerable way toward emphasizing the fickle workings of fortune, which is one of the play's principal themes.

Timon goes on to discuss gold's ability to invert natural order and make that which would normally be perceived as negative seem desirable. As well as being able to disguise the negative aspects of human experience, Timon also attributes to gold the ability to disrupt social order. This is manifested through the way in which it apparently "Will lug your priests and servants from sides." The allure of gold therefore presents a challenge to the status of the subjugated servant in society, as well as a challenge to the authority of the church, one of the major sources of power in the early modern era. Timon's comment that gold will also "Pluck stout men's pillows from below their heads," a practice that apparently speeded up the process of death for people on their sickbeds, suggests that gold can also motivate the basest instincts in humanity.

The tone of the speech then shifts. While the previous lines suggested gold was an autonomous element that could consciously subvert concepts of order, Timon goes on to describe it as a "yellow slave." As well as being a corrupting influence upon people, gold can also be used as a means for people to achieve their own personal ambitions. The reference to thieves gaining "title, knee and approbation / With senators on the bench" shows how the substance can be used as a means of self-advancement. Timon goes on to claim that gold is also beneficial to the "wappered widow" whose financial state could make her seem sexually attractive and allow her to "wed again." The same is true of "She whom the spittle-house and ulcerous sores / Would cast the gorge at." These references contribute to Timon's recurring references to venereal disease and leprosy. The "spittle-house" was a kind of hospital devoted to the care of the poor, particularly those infected with leprosy. The spittle-house was also associated with sufferers of venereal disease. Gold, Timon implies, "embalms and spices" these sufferers "To th'April day again." Here gold

provides a literal gloss that deflects attention away from the feelings of disgust and distaste that the sight of these people would usually provoke, in the view of Timon.

Timon then shifts his bile toward the earth, which he terms the "common whore" because it is available for all men to defile and exploit. His wish to "make thee / Do thy right nature" and provide him with the roots for which he is searching reiterates the irony of the whole episode. It also provides a point of comparison between Timon and Apemantus who, in the first act, consciously opted to avoid the luxury and opulence of Timon's feast and instead dine on root vegetables.

Timon is prompted to bury most of the gold again when he hears the sound of Alcibiades' drums in the distance. While gold was previously attributed to have supernatural qualities, it is here given very human traits. Timon comments "Thou'rt quick / But yet I'll bury thee." Timon sees the gold as a "quick," or living, corporeal entity. He also suggests the gold will outlive those who claim ownership of it when he argues, "Thou'lt go, strong thief, / When gouty keepers of thee cannot stand." The use of the word "thief" also marks a change in tone from Timon's initial reference to it as a "slave." This passage is therefore significant in terms of the play's examination of the uses of money and its resonance in the world of the play.

Act IV, Scene 3, 425–463

1 THIEF. We cannot live on grass, on berries, water,
As beasts and birds and fishes.

TIMON. Nor on the beasts themselves, the birds and the fishes—
You must eat men. Yet thanks I must you con
That you are thieves professed, that you work not
In holier shapes, for there is boundless theft
In limited professions. Rascal thieves,
Here's gold. Go, suck the subtle blood o'th' grape
Till the high fever seethe your blood to froth,

And so scape handing. Trust not the
  physician—
His antidotes are poison and he slays
More than you rob. Take wealth and lives
  together,
Do villainy, do, since you protest to do't
Like workmen. I'll example you with thievery:
The sun's a thief and with his great attraction
Robs the vast sea; the moon's an arrant thief
And her pale fire she snatches from the sun;
The sea's a thief whose liquid surge resolves
The moon into salt tears; the earth's a thief
That feeds and breeds by a composture stol'n
From general excrement. Each thing's a thief.
The laws, your curb and whip, in their rough
  power
Has unchecked theft. Love not yourselves;
  away!
Rob one another— there's more gold. Cut
  throats,
All that you meet are thieves. To Athens go,
Break open shops, nothing can you steal
But thieves do lose it. Steal less for this I give
  you,
And gold confound you howsoe'er. Amen.
  [*Withdraws.*]

3 THIEF. He's almost charmed me from my
  profession by persuading me to it.

1 THIEF. 'Tis in the malice of mankind that
  he thus advises us, not to have us thrive in
  our mystery.

2 THIEF. I'll believe him as an enemy and
  give over my trade.

1 THIEF. Let us first see peace in Athens;
  there is no time so miserable but a man may
  be true.
  Exeunt Thieves.

This passage is again delivered during Timon's
self-imposed exile from the city of Athens and
exists as another example of the misanthropic
vision to which he wishes the city would succumb.
Previously in the same scene, he donates money to
Alcibiades so he can lead a violent coup in the city,
and he also provides gifts for the prostitutes Phrynia and Timandra, in the hope that they will spread
venereal diseases throughout the city. His gift of
gold to the thieves will, he hopes, motivate them to
spread fear and disorder throughout Athens. The
speech also acts as a means of exemplifying his own
disaffection with, and contempt for, civilization.

Timon begins his defense of the thieves' chosen means of existence by asserting that they "must
eat men." This exemplifies the recurring imagery
of cannibalism throughout the text as a metaphor
for the consumer society that is beginning to flourish in Athens, in which people can profit from the
demise of other men. He then begins his attempt
to persuade the thieves to continue their lives of
crime. He acknowledges the paradoxical honesty of
the thieves who do not attempt to mask the acts of
dishonesty they perpetrate behind "holier shapes"
and comments that the culture of theft is an integral part of Athenian society, arguing that "there
is boundless theft / In limited professions." He
instructs the thieves, in a manner reminiscent of
his wishes that Alcibiades will prove to be a self-
depleting force of destruction, to overindulge in
consumption of wine, or "suck the subtle blood
o'th' grape," which, he hopes, will give them a fatal
illness, allowing them to "scape hanging" and thus
avoid punishment for their crimes.

Timon then moves on to "example you with
thievery," asserting that all the natural processes
of the world are essentially acts of theft. The sun's
heat has the potential to make parts of the sea evap-
orate, and the moon is accused of stealing its "pale
fire" from the sun. The sea is also said to be complicit in this cycle of theft, robbing the moon of its
"salt tears." In other words, the sea was thought to
draw much of its moisture from the moon. Whereas
the sun, moon, and sea are all represented as both
perpetrator and victim in this cycle of theft, Timon
argues that the earth steals from itself, sustaining itself on a "composture stol'n / From general
excrement."

After having acknowledged that the natural order of the world is based upon a cycle of theft, Timon gives gold to the thieves and tells them to "Cut throats" and "Break open shops," as they are merely part of this natural cycle, and assures them that "nothing can you steal / But thieves do lose it." He concludes his views on theft with an "Amen," as he did in his misanthropic tirade at the beginning of the fourth act. This also places it alongside Apemantus's mock grace at the banquet in the first act.

After having spoken these words, Timon withdraws to his cave, leaving the thieves to debate how they will act upon his words. One comments that Timon "almost charmed me from my profession by persuading me to it." The first thief recognizes they are merely being used as part of Timon's apocalyptic agenda for the city when he comments that it is "in the malice of mankind that he thus advises us, not to have us thrive in our mystery." Nevertheless, he seems quite content to follow Timon's words, at least until peace is restored in the city.

This is another important example of Timon's misanthropic vitriol. It also provides a view of the world that is built upon theft. It is not merely those at the top of the Athenian hierarchy who are complicit in these deeds. As far as Timon is concerned, their role is merely a reflection of the cycle that balances the natural order of the world.

DIFFICULT PASSAGES
Act II, Scene 1, 1–27

SENATOR. And late five thousand; to Varro
  and to Isidore
He owes nine thousand, besides my former
  sum,
Which makes it five and twenty. Still in motion
Of raging waste? It cannot hold, it will not.
If I want gold, steal but a beggar's dog
And give it to Timon, why, the dog coins gold.
If I would sell my horse and buy twenty more
Better than he, why, give my horse to Timon—
Ask nothing, give it him—it foals me straight
And able horses. No porter at his gate,
But rather one that smiles and still invites
All that pass by. It cannot hold; no reason
Can sound his state in safety. Caphis, ho!
Caphis, I say!
Enter Caphis.

CAPHIS. Here, sire, what is your pleasure?

SENATOR. Get on your cloak and haste you
  to Lord Timon.
Importune him for my moneys; be not ceased
With slight denial, nor then silenced when
"Commend me to your master," and the cap
Plays in the right hand, thus. But tell him
My uses cry to me, I must serve my turn
Out of mine own, his days and times are past,
And my reliances on his fracted dates
Have smit my credit. I love and honour him,
But must not break my back to heal his finger.
Immediate are my needs, and my relief
Must not be tossed and turned to me in words,
But find supply immediate.

The challenge of this passage lies in the difficulty of some of its metaphors and allusions as well as the complexity of some of the economic issues to which the senator repeatedly refers. Such complexities are reflected in his summary of the problematic financial situation in which Timon has become involved. It is this summary of the problems that also makes this passage an important one.

This speech occurs shortly after the cracks in Timon's show of wealth and luxury are beginning to show, thanks to the repeated warnings of Flavius, who was exasperated at Timon giving out gifts from "an empty coffer." It is in this passage that the true extent of Timon's debts is revealed. Despite owing a sum of twenty-five thousand to various people, the senator suspects that Timon is "Still in motion / Of raging waste," or still in the process that will lead to his inevitable undoing.

The passage also indicates Timon's tendencies to play an excessive role in the culture of gift-giving. He suggests stealing a beggar's dog and giving it to Timon as a means of gaining a hefty financial reward for a crude gift. In other words, "the dog coins gold." This process of multiplication is also shown by the idea of the gift of a horse producing more horses for whoever provided the initial gift. He also hints at the indiscriminate nature of Timon's generosity when he observes that instead of having someone to turn visitors away, Timon employs someone who "smiles and still invites / All that pass by."

The senator also exposes the workings of the Athenian economy of credit and usury. Timon's irresponsible attitude toward money clearly has an effect upon the others who are involved in this cycle of giving and receiving. The senator's comment, "My uses cry to me," suggests that he himself is in debt and raises the possibility that the money he lent Timon was not his own to give. He complains that Timon's "fracted dates / Have smit my credit," indicating the far-reaching effects of Timon's spending. The senator has relied upon Timon repaying his money, while he, in turn, has allowed others to rely upon his own repayments for which he would require Timon to return the money he owes. His view that he risks breaking his back "to heal his finger" shows the effects of Timon's failure to adhere to the system upon which the Athenian economy is based.

Act V, Scene 5, 64–85

SOLDIER. My noble general, Timon is dead,
Entombed upon the very hem o'th' sea,
And on his gravestone this insculpture, which
With wax I brought away, whose soft impression
Intercepts for my poor ignorance.

ALCIBIADES. *(Reads the epitaph.) Here lie I,*
Timon, who alive all living men did hate,
Pass by and curse thy fill, but pass and stay not
here thy gait.
These well express in thee thy latter spirits.
Though thou abhorred'st in us our human griefs,
Scorned'st our brains' flow and those our droplets which
From niggard nature fall, yet rich conceit

Taught thee to make vast Neptune weep for aye
On thy low grave, on faults forgiven. Dead
Is noble Timon, of whose memory
Hereafter more. Bring me into your city,
And I will use the olive with my sword,
Make war breed peace, make peace stint war, make each
Prescribe to other, as each other's leech.
Let our drums strike.
Exeunt.

The final scene of the play has baffled many readers with its apparent ambiguity. Taking place outside the city walls, where Alcibiades and his troops are ready to strike the city, and where the city's senators are attempting to avert the catastrophe, Alcibiades is informed of Timon's death. The soldier's observation that he is "Entombed upon the very hem o'th' sea" confirms that Timon has achieved his wish that "once a day with his embossed froth / The turbulent surge shall cover" his grave (5.2). There is also a possible allusion to the Poet's reference to a "wide sea of wax" (1.1) in the first act, an image that also predicts the soldier's action of creating a wax impression of Timon's epitaph for Alcibiades to decipher. The imagery of the sea is also complemented by Alcibiades' observation that "rich conceit / Taught thee to make vast Neptune weep for aye / On thy low grave, on faults forgiven." This image suggests that the sea is formed by the tears of Neptune, the god of the sea. Because the tide will regularly cover Timon's grave, Neptune is characterized as Timon's chief mourner. The idea of the atonement for "faults forgiven" is slightly more ambiguous. It remains unclear whether it refers to the faults of Timon or those of Alcibiades who, by considering showing mercy and aborting his invasion of the city, has gone against Timon's instructions and let the city go unpunished for its crimes.

The epitaph expresses Timon's "latter spirits," believing that he was hated by all men, in spite of assistance offered by the likes of Alcibiades and Flavius. Alcibiades suggests that by making "Neptune weep for aye," Timon has achieved something far greater than inspiring the grief of any mortal human mourners. He has created a situation whereby he has overcome the "niggard nature" of humanity and attained a far superior memorial.

The play ends with Alcibiades preparing to enter the city in a spirit of peaceful negotiation and compromise rather than one of destruction and carnage as Timon had hoped. The popular image of the olive branch as a symbol of peace is mingled with that of the sword in an attempt to achieve Alcibiades' wish to "Make war breed peace, make peace stint war, make each / Prescribe to other, as each other's leech." Alcibiades therefore characterizes himself as a stabilizing influence upon the city with acts of war being justified by the arrival of the peace that must follow. The medical imagery of the physicians and the leeches suggests that Alcibiades intends to adopt a role as healer of the city's wrongs. However, the image of the two physicians prescribing each other's treatments and the leeches gaining mutual sustenance suggests that the mutually dependent Athenian economy of which Timon fell foul will continue under the rule of Alcibiades. This provides the play with a rather pessimistic conclusion.

CRITICAL INTRODUCTION TO THE PLAY

The historical Timon lived during the Peloponnesian War, which took place between 431 B.C.E. and 404 B.C.E., thus setting the play at the height of the classical era in ancient Greece's history. This period is characterized by a major surge of cultural endeavors, resulting in the production of some of the finest and most revered works of classical art and architecture, most notably the Parthenon. The historical setting, however, has very little impact upon the action that unfolds. Effectively, the play has a kind of universal and timeless quality about it that renders the temporal and geographical locations of the action fairly unimportant. Shakespeare and Middleton are much more interested in the central character of Timon and his fall into poverty. The historical Timon was well-known for his

misanthropy and solitude. In Plutarch's account of Antony, it is made clear that after his defeat at Actium, Antony intended to withdraw from society and emulate Timon's period of self-imposed exile in the woods. Timon was therefore a familiar figure in classical history and one who enabled the authors to explore a number of key themes and ideas at the core of the play.

Themes and Symbols

With the exception of *The Merchant of Venice*, this is the only Shakespearean text in which the principal theme is an economic one. Indeed, *Timon of Athens* revisits many of the prominent issues dramatized in *The Merchant of Venice*. Like Antonio, Timon falls foul of a system of interest and usury. Whereas Antonio is almost undone by one reckless act of generosity, Timon's problems are the culmination of a long-term and habitual prodigality.

The central plot development of the play is, of course, Timon's transition from a period of wealth and luxury to an existence of abject penury in the woods. This is due to his failure to comprehend the economic system that is in place in Athens in which he plays a grossly overindulgent part. He is frequently shown to donate gifts to others of markedly higher value than anything he receives. One guest comments that any gift to Timon will be repaid "Sevenfold" (1.1). This is also implied when he receives a gift of two pairs of greyhounds and orders that they "be received / Not without fair reward" (1.2). One of Timon's creditors comments that even a gift as crude as a "beggar's dog" (2.1) will prompt him to repay the giver with an excessive gesture of thanks. As the senator comments, the "dog coins gold" (2.1). Timon's role in this process of gift-giving and receiving is therefore disproportionate to say the least.

The Athenian economy is based on a system of usury in which money is lent to various parties with a charge of interest imposed upon it. Money is therefore seen to circulate from hand to hand in an ongoing process. It seems Timon is unwilling to be the privileged party in this process, as shown by his refusal to accept Ventidius's offer of double the ransom money that was paid on his behalf. Timon's conviction that "there's none / Can truly say he gives if he receives" (1.2) proves to be unfortunately misguided in this kind of environment. The prevalence of the system is suggested by Alcibiades' complaints directed at the senate that he has "kept back their foes / While they have told their money and let out / Their coin upon large interest" (3.6). Unlike Timon, Alcibiades seems to understand the system. His offer to "pawn my victories" (3.6) in order for his comrade to be released suggests that even this appeal is understood to be a kind of financial transaction. This suggests that the accumulation of money is the key concern for the governors of Athens. It is not until his self-imposed exile in the woods that Timon realizes the workings of the Athenian economy, which he regards as a process of circulation in which each participant is in turn both a thief and a victim of theft. He argues that it can be likened to a natural cycle:

> The sun's a thief and his great attraction
> Robs the vast sea; the moon's an arrant thief
> And her pale fire she snatches from the sun;
> The sea's a thief whose liquid surge resolves
> The moon into salt tears.
>
> (4.3)

Each participant in this self-perpetuating cycle stands both to gain and lose by it. Timon also goes on to characterize the earth as a self-sustaining element, nourishing itself upon "composture" formed from "general excrement" (4.3). This speech provides a metaphorical view of an economy based upon mutual dependence.

Timon's extravagant gift-giving represents an obstacle to the delicate equilibrium in which this economy functions. These issues are raised by Flavius who despairs that the money that is providing the gifts Timon provides for his guests is not his own. They are given from an "empty coffer" (1.2), and all that Timon "speaks is all in debt—he owes / For every word" (1.2). This process also has a knock-on effect upon others. The problem is summarized by the senator to whom Timon

owes money who appears at the beginning of the second act. The senator comments that Timon's "fracted debts / Have smit my credit" (2.1) and complains that his "uses cry to me," that his needs are "Immediate" and that he is unwilling to "break my back to heal his finger" (2.1). The problem is also indicated in the third act when Timon is beset by servants of creditors demanding the money he owes them. Timon's false friends also realize the folly of his spending habits but were clearly willing to take advantage of them all the same. Lucullus, for instance, recalls how he often went "to supper to him of purpose to have him spend less" (3.1), thus ironically benefiting from Timon's generosity at the same time as he is supposedly warning against it. The participants in the Athenian economy are therefore self-interested and unwilling to cooperate or take any overt action when an imbalance emerges in it. The Poet's description of his work that represents a group of rival men attempting to reach the top of the hill and gain the favor of Fortune, each benefiting from another's fall, seems an apt metaphor for the economy of Athens.

It is not until Timon's retreat into the wilderness that he recognizes the corrupting nature of the pursuit of gold. His accidental discovery of the trove of gold emphasizes the cathartic process he has undergone. His recognition that gold can make "Black white, foul fair, wrong right, / Base noble, old young, coward valiant" indicates that he is now aware of the negative effects gold can have upon the individual. This point is also emphasized in Timon's reply to Apemantus's objection that the wilderness offers "no use for gold." Timon argues that it in fact offers the "best and truest, / For here it sleeps and does no hired harm" (4.3), further emphasizing his recognition of the evil properties of the substance.

The folly of Timon's previously overemphatic generosity is also highlighted by Apemantus who informs Timon that his former flatterers "yet wear silk, drink wine, lie soft, / Hug their diseased perfumes and have forgot / That ever Timon was" (4.3). Timon himself has realized that his false friends offered nothing more than "A usuring

Timon presents a guest with one of his jewels during the banquet in Act I, Scene 2 in this illustration in an 1802 edition of *Timon of Athens*.

kindness," and one in which they give gifts "Expecting in return twenty for one" (4.3). This echoes the words of the senator to whom Timon is in debt that he could "sell my horse and buy twenty more" in the process of giving and receiving in which Timon was the principal participant (2.1). Flavius confirms his former master's earlier naïveté and reasserts the warnings he attempted to convey to him, arguing that Timon "should have feared false times when you did feast, / Suspect still comes where an estate is least" (4.3). He also expresses his wish that Timon "had power and wealth" to repay his services by "making rich yourself" again (4.3). The implication is that he can now profit from the system after having realized the way in which it

truly works, a point that echoes Apemantus's earlier view that Timon should learn the art of flattery and lead a privileged existence similar to that of his former friends. Despite his new awareness of the nature of the Athenian economy, Timon chooses to remain absent from the process and lead his misanthropic existence in the woods. He would rather the civilization of Athens collapse altogether than remain available for him to exploit in the future.

In the light of the emphasis upon economic imperatives, the play's conclusion appears decidedly pessimistic, as indicated by the rise to power of Alcibiades. While Timon had hoped he would be like "a planetary plague" inflicted upon Athens, he eventually agrees to enter the city in peace and attempt to find a peaceful and diplomatic solution to the quarrel. He announces his intention to "Make war breed peace, make peace stint war, make each / Prescribe to other, as each other's leech" (5.5). The image of the two leeches gaining nourishment from each other suggests a return to the economic system based upon the cycle of mutual dependence. Alcibiades therefore has a containing influence upon the play rather than a subversive one. The imagery he appropriates in his final speech suggests that under his leadership, the Athenian authorities will once again allow the perpetuation of the system of credit and usury that led to the downfall of Timon.

Another major recurring feature in the play is food, which takes on a considerable symbolic significance in this play and complements the themes of economics and consumerism that are at the heart of the play. Food is initially seen as a means of social intercourse. Before one of the lords enters Timon's banqueting hall, he anticipates that he and the others will "taste Lord Timon's bounty" (1.1). The use of the metaphor of consumption in this phrase confirms that food provides the prevailing corporeal image of Timon's offerings. This point is inverted toward the end of the third act in which Timon invites his guests to a mock banquet, consisting of tepid water in covered dishes, commenting that "Smoke and lukewarm water / Is your perfection" (3.7). Apemantus observes that a typical occurrence at Timon's estate would be to see "meat fill knaves and wine heat fools" (1.1). This indicates the importance of food as a means of engaging in sociability.

Apemantus's decision to absent himself from the rest of the guests by sitting at his own table consuming water and root vegetables therefore emerges as a deliberate effort to repudiate the social gathering taking place. This is confirmed by his assertion that "I scorn thy meat, 'twould choke me 'fore I should e'er flatter thee" (1.2). Apemantus's choice of roots and water also predicts Timon's rejection of Athenian civilization in favor of an existence in the woods where he seeks sustenance in the form of roots. Even when Timon accidentally stumbles upon the buried gold in the fourth act, he still demands of the gods, "Roots, you clear heavens!" (4.3). The discovery of the gold thwarts his wish to uncover roots in the soil, thus emphasizing his rejection of society. This is also conveyed in his refusal to accept Alcibiades' gold, as he "cannot eat it" (4.3). Food therefore acts as a means of representing one's engagement with society and, by extension, one's status within it.

While the eating of root vegetables represents a rejection of organized society, the consumption of meat suggests that the individual ranks highly in the hierarchy of Athenian society. This idea is also suggested by the references to hunting. In Jacobean England, the hunt was an important part of court life, representing a means of enforcing one's martial prowess, and was one of the favorite pastimes of James I. In the first act, Timon is presented with "two brace of greyhounds" and "four milk-white horses trapped in silver" and is invited to hunt with some of the other lords, an activity in which he is engaging when his house is visited by the servants of the creditors. This represents food, and the pursuit of it, as a means of social interaction and as a representation of the social status of the individuals.

The importance of food and consumption is also suggested by the recurring motif of cannibalism in the play. Throughout the first act, the imagery of cannibalism is appropriated to convey the under-lying rivalry of the Athenian society that depends upon the disintegration of one man in order for the others to benefit. Apemantus views the feast in the first act as an opportunity to see "so many dip their meat in one man's blood" (1.2). The image emphasizes the opportunism of the other characters who are seen to be sustaining themselves upon their host. This allusion is also exemplified in the third act when one of the strangers comments that "For mine own part, / I never tasted Timon in my life" (3.2). The idea of benefiting from Timon's hospitality is therefore expressed as a means of feeding upon Timon himself. Timon only realizes he had placed himself in this vulnerable position after he has suffered from the ingratitude of his former friends. Timon insists that the thieves who visit him "must eat men" (4.3) or sustain themselves upon the losses of others. The cannibalistic imagery therefore serves a very specific purpose as a metaphorical representation of a faction-ridden society in which the individual can benefit from the downfall of other rivals that is allegorized in the Poet's description of his work. Timon's participation in the economy of Athens is therefore seen as a process in which he effectively offers himself as a sacrifice in order for others to benefit. This is also indicated in the third act, when Timon is bombarded with requests from the servants of his ruthless creditors and rhetorically concludes that the only way he can satisfy their demands would be to bleed himself, when he demands they "Tell out my blood" (3.5).

Timon's downfall as a result of the failure of his friends to help him when he was in need acts as the root cause for his misanthropy. The misanthropic persona Timon develops is mirrored by Apemantus who seemingly makes a career from this stance. The two misanthropes encounter each other in the fourth act in which Apemantus observes that Timon "dost affect my manners and dost use them" (4.3). They then engage in a bitter debate about which of the two is more authentic in his misanthropy. Apemantus believes his is superior because it was adopted by choice, while Timon comments that his downfall and experiences of betrayal give him more reason to hate mankind. The key difference between their outlooks is that Apemantus is quite content to remain in the city and provide critiques of the behavior he witnesses, whereas Timon chooses to absent himself from human company altogether. The consistent imagery of nature and beasts throughout the play also emphasizes the distance of Timon and Apemantus from those circulating in Athenian society. Other characters repeatedly refer to Apemantus as a dog, a trait that represents his detachment from humanity. This animal imagery, however, is inverted in the fourth act. Apemantus comments that if he possessed the world he would "Give it to the beasts and be rid of men," an action that Timon perceives would lead to Apemantus having himself "fall in the confusion of men and remain a beast with the beasts" (4.3). Timon then goes on to illustrate how all beasts are prey to another larger creature in the cycle of nature. Apemantus replies that this vision has already been realized as the "commonwealth of Athens is become a forest of beasts" (4.3). This point was also suggested in Timon's soliloquy that initiates the fourth act in which he claims that the function of the city's walls is to keep in "those wolves" (4.1), or the citizens of Athens, thus protecting the natural world from them. Rather than being likened to beasts themselves, in this case the human inhabitants of Athens are characterized as beasts in order to express the difference between them and the misanthropes.

Timon also goes to the extreme of wishing for a kind of apocalyptic punishment to fall upon the city. He reveals this in his soliloquy at the beginning of the fourth act in which he prays for anarchy in the city and begins shedding his clothes as a symbol of his rejection of the values of civilization. He also seeks to express his inhumanity, a conceit that is evidenced by renaming himself "Misanthropos," hater of mankind (4.3).

The recipients of the gold he finds in the woods are of considerable significance in terms of the apocalypse. Timon hopes Alcibiades will spread war throughout the city, while Timandra and Phrynia will, he believes, spread the various diseases they harbor throughout the city in their profession as prostitutes. He also gives money to the thieves under the condition that they remain thieves, a situation that is motivated by their want of food. Plague, famine, and warfare, three of the four factors associated with the apocalypse as represented in the Bible by the four horsemen, are therefore represented in these characters.

Structure

Timon of Athens can be divided into two distinct halves. While charges of structural incoherence have often been leveled at the play, there is a certain asymmetrical coherence that links the two halves. The first half of the play comprises the first three acts and follows Timon's gradual slump from prosperity to debt, highlighting the unwillingness of his friends to help him through these difficulties. The second half consists of the play's final two acts, which take place almost entirely outside the boundaries of the city of Athens. The focus for these final acts is upon the self-imposed exile of the misanthropically enraged Timon and the imminent invasion of the city by Alcibiades.

At the core of the play's second half is the lengthy third scene of the fourth act, which also addresses many of the play's key issues. In many ways, this scene parodies the action of the first act. In both cases, Timon is visited by a succession of guests to whom he offers money. However, he has different reasons for offering gold to his "guests" in the fourth act. The first act portrays the luxury offered by Timon's hospitality, shown by the references to pomp and wealth and most notably by the impromptu masque that is held during the banquet. From the onset of the fourth act, only one scene takes place in Timon's estate, and even then, it is with the reminder that Timon's staff have seen "better days" and that they represent the "broken implements of a ruined house" (4.2). For the majority of the final two acts, Athens is represented only by the city's walls, as most of the action takes place in the woods outside Timon's cave. The final act of the play begins in exactly the same way as the first, with the Poet and Painter preparing to present their works to Timon in the hope of gaining some reward, underlining the contrast in detail. Whereas the first scene takes place amid the "Magic of bounty" (1.1) that represents Timon's luxurious estate, the analogous episode in the final act occurs outside the cave where Timon now lives. This parallelism represents the contrasting emphases of the two distinct halves of the play and indicates the asymmetrical nature and the overall cohesion of these two facets of the text.

Language and Style

The prevalence of the play's economic theme inevitably impacts the language of the play, with gold and wealth becoming two of the text's most significant recurring motifs. The Poet views the gatherings at Timon's estate as a product of the "Magic of bounty" (1.1), while one of the lords comments that "Plutus, the god of gold, / Is but his steward" (1.1). The talk of the multiplication of gifts and gold in this act takes on a supernatural resonance. There is talk of Timon's generosity being multiplied "Sevenfold" (1.1), which contributes to the supernatural imagery. The senator, on the other hand, sees Timon's giving as a natural process, arguing that if he were to give Timon a horse he would receive twenty more and enter a situation whereby the original horse "foals me straight / And able horses" (2.1).

The language of the play emphasizes the luxury offered at Timon's home. References to jewels, meat, and wine all contribute to the image of Timon's wealth and generosity. There are also references to prized animals such as the "four milk-white horses, trapped in silver" and the "two brace of greyhounds" Timon receives as gifts from his false friends (1.2). This microcosm of luxury is filled out by the masque scene in which the guests dance with the Amazonians. It is only at the end of the first act that the imagery of plenty is offset by Flavius's observation that Timon is giving his gifts from "an empty coffer" and that "he owes / For every word" (1.2). However, the luxurious imagery does not subside completely after the first act. In the third act, for example, Lucullus comments that he "dreamt of a silver basin and ewer" and demands his servant pour him some wine (3.1). This emphasizes the self-interested cupidity of the false friends and flatterers who contributed to Timon's downfall.

As the play progresses, gold is associated with negative features. It is a "yellow slave" (4.3) that can be used to invert natural order with the ability to make "Black white, foul fair, wrong right, / Base noble, old young, coward valiant" (4.3), despite the apparent tribute of Timon's description of it as "glittering, precious gold" (4.3). It is a "strong thief" that is "quick," or living (4.3). The negative representation of gold is also apparent in Flaminius's curse upon Lucullus that "molten coin" shall be his "damnation" (3.1). This image gives a clear indication of the shift of imagery toward gold and wealth that begins to occur after the play's earlier scenes. It is not just the imagery of gold that represents the permeation of the economic theme into the language of the play. There are numerous references to the bureaucratic rather than the material side of the economic theme. Money and debt is also manifested in the paperwork, as shown by the succession of servants to Timon's creditors presenting him with their bills. The messenger, to whom Timon gives the news that he will help Ventidius, states that "Your lordship ever binds him" (1.1), thereby making use of an economic metaphor in relation to friendship. Apemantus warns Timon he may "give away thyself in paper shortly" (1.2). Alcibiades also engages in these references to other aspects of the economy, when he offers to "pawn my victories" (3.6) to the senators in order to help his friend. It is therefore acknowledged through the play's language that it is not just the receipt of gold and gifts that motivates the Athenian economy but also debt and exchange.

The play is also notable for the regular use of certain stylistic features. One of the most effective and frequently appropriated devices is that of apostrophe, the lengthy oratorical meditation upon a certain subject or object. The most heightened examples of this feature occur in the fourth act. Timon's departure from the city is complemented by a lengthy soliloquy in which he wishes the walls surrounding the city would "dive in the earth" and "fence not Athens" (4.1). He then conveys his ideal vision of an Athens beset by disorder and anarchy in which the servile and the downtrodden rebel against their oppressors and such features as "Piety and fear / Religion to the gods, peace, justice, truth, / Domestic awe, night-rest and neighbourhood" should fail and thus contribute to the problems he hopes Athens will face. He begins the lengthy third scene of the fourth act by apostrophizing civilization again, particularly the culture whereby anyone with money can command influence and respect to the extent that the "learned pate / Ducks to the golden fool" (4.3). Timon then concludes that "All's obliquy" (4.3). The discovery of the gold then prompts a shift in the focus of his musings to the negative potential of the substance to invert social and moral order. Later in the same scene, he goes on to characterize the process of nature as a cycle of theft that reflects the workings of the Athenian economy. He appropriates the moon, the sea, and the sun and argues that they all stand to benefit and suffer from this process as both thief and victim. The various apostrophic speeches are often examples of the play's language at its best and at its most powerful, exemplifying some of the most startling imagery in the text.

EXTRACTS OF CLASSIC CRITICISM
Samuel Johnson (1709–1784) [Excerpted from his *General Observations on Shakespeare's Plays* (1768). As one of Shakespeare's earliest editors, Johnson is now regarded as one of the most eminent pre-20th-century authorities on Shakespeare's works.]

The play of Timon is a domestick tragedy, and therefore strongly fashions on the attention of the reader. In the plan there is not much art, but the incidents are natural, and the characters various and exact. The catastrophe affords a very powerful warning against that ostentatious liberality, which shatters bounty, but confers no benefits, and buys flattery, but not friendship.

In this tragedy, are many passages perplexed, obscure, and probably corrupt, which I have endeavoured to rectify, or explain, with due diligence; but having only one copy, cannot promise myself that my endeavours shall be much applauded.

William Hazlitt (1778–1830) [Excerpted from *Characters of Shakespear's Plays* (1817). Hazlitt was one of the most observant and lucid of Shakespeare's early critics.]

TIMON OF ATHENS always appeared to us to be written with as intense a feeling of his subject as any one play of Shakespear. It is one of the few in which he seems to be in earnest throughout, never to trifle nor to go out of his way. He does not relax in his efforts, nor lose sight of the unity of his design. It is the only play of our author in which spleen is predominant feeling of mind. It is as much a satire as a play: and contains some of the finest pieces of invective possible to be conceived, both in the snarling, captious answers of the cynic Apemantus, and in the impassioned and more terrible imprecations of Timon. The latter remind the classical reader of the force and swelling impetuosity of the moral declamations in *Juvenal*, while the former have all the keenness and caustic severity of the old Stoic philosophers. The soul of Diogenes appears to have been seated on the lips of Apemantus. The churlish profession of misanthropy in the cynic is contrasted with the profound feeling of it in Timon, and also with the soldierlike and determined resentment of Alcibiades against his countrymen, who have banished him, though this forms only an incidental episode in the tragedy.

The fable consists of a single event—of the transition from the highest pomp and profusion of artificial refinement to the most abject state of savage life, and privation of all social intercourse. The change is as rapid as it is complete; nor is the description of the rich and generous Timon, banqueting in gilded palaces, pampered by ever luxury, prodigal of his hospitality, courted by crowds of flatterers, poets, painters, lords, ladies who:

> Follow his strides, his lobbies fill with
>   tendance,
> Rain sacrificial whisperings in his ear;
> And through him drink the free air—

more striking than that of the sudden falling off of his friends and fortune, and naked exposure in a wild forest digging roots from the earth for his sustenance, with a lofty spirit of self-denial, and bitter scorn of the world, which raise him higher in our esteem than the dazzling gloss of prosperity could do. He grudges himself the means of life, and is only busy in preparing his grave. How forcibly is the difference between what he was and what he is described in Apemantus's taunting questions, when he comes to reproach him with the change in his way of life!

> —What, think'st thou,
> That the bleak air, thy boisterous
>   chamberlain,
> Will put thy shirt on warm? will these
>   moist trees
> That have out-liv'd the eagle, page thy
>   heels,
> And skip when thou point'st out? will
>   the cold brook,
> Candied with ice, caudle thy morning
>   taste
> To cure thy o'er-night's surfeit? Call the
>   creatures,
> Whose naked natures live in all the
>   spight
> Of wreakful heav'n, whose bare
>   unhoused trunks,

> To the conflicting elements expos'd,
> Answer mere nature, bid them flatter
>   thee.

The manners are everywhere preserved with distinct truth. The poet and painter are very skilfully played off against one another, both affecting great attention to the other, and each taken up with his own vanity, and the superiority of his own art. Shakespear has put into the mouth of the former a very lively description of the genius of poetry and of his own in particular.

> —A thing slipt icily from me.
> Our poesy is as a gum, which issues
> From whence 'tis nourish'd. The fire i'
>   th' flint
> Shows not till it be struck: our gentle
>   flame
> Provokes itself—and like the current flies
> Each bound it chafes.

The hollow friendship and shuffling evasions of the Athenian lords, their smooth professions and pitiful ingratitude, are very

A poet and a painter bring gifts to Timon in Act V, Scene I of *Timon of Athens,* in this print published by Cassell & Company in the 19th century. *(Painting by John Ralston; engraving by Georg Goldberg)*

satisfactorily exposed, as well as the different disguises to which the meanness of self-love resorts in such cases to hide a want of generosity and good faith. The lurking selfishness of Apemantus does not pass undetected amidst the grossness of his sarcasms and his contempt for the pretensions of others. Even the two courtezans who accompany Alcibiades to the cave of Timon are very characteristically sketched; and the thieves who come to visit him are also "true men" in their way.—And exception to this general picture of selfish depravity is found in the old and honest steward, Flavius, to whom Timon pays a full tribute of tenderness. Shakespear was unwilling to draw a picture *"all over ugly with hypocrisy."* He owed his character to the good-natured solicitations of his Muse. His mind was well said by Ben Jonson to be the "sphere of humanity."

The moral sententiousness of this play equals that of Lord Bacon's *Treatise on the Wisdom of the Ancients,* and is indeed seasoned with greater variety. Every topic of contempt or indignation is here exhausted; but while the sordid licentiousness of Apemantus, which turns everything to gall and bitterness, shows only the natural virulence of his temper and antipathy to good or evil alike, Timon does not utter an imprecation without betraying the extravagant workings of disappointed passion, of love altered to hate. Apemantus sees nothing good in any object, and exaggerates whatever is disgusting: Timon is tormented with the perpetual contrast between things and appearances, between the fresh, tempting outside and rottenness within, and invokes mischiefs on the heads of mankind proportioned to the sense of his wrongs and of their treacheries. He impatiently cries out, when he finds the gold,

> This yellow slave
> Will knit and break religions; bless the
>   accurs'd;

Make the hoar leprosy ador'd; place
   thieves,
And give them title, knee, and
   approbation,
With senators on the bench; this is it,
That makes the wappen'd widow wed
   again;
She, whom the spital-house
Would cast the gorge at, *this embalms
   and spices*
To th' April day again.

One of his most dreadful imprecations is that which occurs immediately on his leaving Athens.

> Let me look back upon thee, O thou wall,
> That girdlest in those wolves! Dive in
>   the earth
> And fence not Athens! Matrons, turn
>   incontinent;
> Obedience fail in children; slaves and
>   fools
> Pluck the grave wrinkled senate from the
>   bench,
> And minister in their steads. To general
>   filths
> Convert o' th' instant green virginity!
> Do't in your parents' eyes. Bankrupts,
>   hold fast;
> Rather than render back, out with your
>   knives,
> And cut your trusters' throats! Bound
>   servants, steal:
> Large-handed robbers your grave mas-
>   ters are,
> And pill by law. Maid, to thy master's
>   bed:
> Thy mistress is o' th' brothel. Son of
>   sixteen,
> Pluck the lin'd crutch from thy old limp-
>   ing sire,
> And with it beat his brains out! Fear and
>   piety,
> Religion to the Gods, peace, justice, truth,

Domestic awe, night-rest, and
  neighbourhood,
Instructions, manners, mysteries and
  trades,
Degrees, observances, customs and laws,
Decline to your confounding contraries;
And let confusion live!—Plagues, inci-
  dent to men,
Your potent and infectious fevers heap
On Athens, ripe for stroke! Thou cold
  sciatica,
Cripple our senators, that their limbs
  may halt
As lamely as their manners! Lust and
  liberty
Creep, in the minds and manners of our
  youth,
That 'gainst the stream of virtue they
  may strive,
And drown themselves in riot! Itches,
  blains,
Sow all th' Athenian bosoms; and their
  crop
Be general leprosy; breath infect breath,
That their society (as their friendship) may
Be merely poison!

Timon is here just as ideal in his passion for ill as he had before been in his belief of good. Apemantus was satisfied with the mischief existing in the world, and with his own ill-nature. One of the most decisive intimations of Timon's morbid jealousy of appearances is in his answer to Apemantus, who asks him:

What things in the world can'st thou
  nearest compare with thy flatterers?

TIMON. Women nearest: but me, men
  are the things themselves.

Apemantus, it is said, "loved few things better than to abhor himself." This is not the case with Timon, who neither loves to abhor himself nor others. All his vehement misan-thropy is forced, up-hill work. From the slippery turns of fortune, from the turmoils of passion and adversity, he wishes to sink into the quiet of the grave. On that subject his thoughts are intent, on that he finds time and place to grow romantic. He digs his own grave by the sea-shore; contrives his funeral ceremonies amidst the pomp of desolation, and builds his mausoleum of the elements.

Come not to me again; but say to
  Athens,
Timon hath made his everlasting
  mansion
Upon the beached verge of the salt
  flood;
Which once-a-day with his embossed
  froth
The turbulent surge shall cover.—
  Thither come,
And let my grave-stone be your oracle.

And again, Alcibiades, after reading his epitaph, says of him:

These well express in thee thy latter
  spirits:
Though thou abhorred'st in us our
  human griefs,
Scorn'd'st our brain's flow, and those our
  droplets, which
From niggard nature fall; yet rich conceit
Taught thee to make vast Neptune weep
  for aye
On thy low grave—

thus making the winds his funeral dirge, his mourner the murmuring ocean; and seeking in the everlasting solemnities of nature oblivion of the transitory splendour of his lifetime.

Charles Knight (1791–1873) [Excerpted from *Studies of Shakespere* (1849). Most famous for producing an illustrated edition of Shakespeare's plays, Knight was one of the earliest critics to cast doubt over Shakespeare's sole authorship of the play, a view that has had a lasting effect upon criticism of *Timon of Athens*.]

The disguises of the ancient text, which have been so long accepted without hesitation, have given to the "Timon of Athens" something of the semblance of uniformity in the structure of the verse; although in reality the successive scenes, even in the modern text, present the most startling contrarieties to the ear which is accustomed to the versification of Shakespere. The ordinary explanation of this very striking characteristic is, that the ancient text is corrupt. This is the belief of the English editors. Another theory, which has been received in Germany, is, that the "Timon," being one of the latest of Shakespere's performances, has come down to us unfinished. The conviction to which we have ourselves arrived neither rests upon the probable corruption of the text, nor the possibility that the poet has left us only an unfinished draft of his performance; but upon the belief that the differences of style, as well as the more important differences in the cast of thought, which prevail in the successive scenes of this drama, are so remarkable as to justify the conclusion that it is not wholly the work of Shakespere. We think it will not be very difficult to exhibit these differences in detail as to warrant us in requesting the reader's acquiescence in the principle which we seek to establish, namely, that the "Timon of Athens" was a play originally produced by an artist very much inferior to Shakespere, and which probably retained possession of the stage for some time in its first form; that it has come down to us not only re-written, but so far re-modelled that entire scenes of Shakespere have been substituted for entire scenes of the elder play; and lastly, that this substitution has been almost wholly confined to the char-

acter of Timon, and that in the development of that character alone, with the exception of some few occasional touches here and there, we must look for the unity of the Shakesperean conception of the Greek Misanthropos—the Timon of Aristophanes and Lucian and Plutarch—"the enemy of mankind," of the popular story books—of the "Pleasant Histories and excellent Novels," which were greedily devoured by the contemporaries of the boyish Shakespere.

The contrast of style which is to be traced throughout this drama is sufficiently striking in the two opening scenes which now constitute the first act. Nothing can be more free and flowing than the dialogue between the Poet and the Painter. It has all the equable graces of Shakespere's facility, with occasional examples of that condensation of poetical images which so distinguishes him from all other writers. For instance:—

> "All those which were his fellows but of
> late,
> (Some better than his value,) on the
> moment
> Follow his strides, his lobbies fill with
> tendance,
> Rain sacrificial whisperings in his ear,
> Make sacred even his stirrup, and
> through him
> Drink the free air."

The foreshadowing of the fate of Timon in the conclusion of this dialogue is part of the almost invariable system by which Shakespere very early infuses into his audience a dim notion of the catastrophe,—most frequently indeed in the shape of some presentiment. When Timon enters, we feel certain that he is the Timon of Shakespere's own conception. He is as graceful as he is generous; his prodigality is without the slightest particle of arrogance; he builds his munificence upon the necessity of gratifying without restraint the deep sympathies which he cherishes to all of the human family. He is the very model too of patrons, appearing to receive instead of to confer a favor in his reward of art,—a complete gentleman even in the act of purchasing a jewel of a tradesman. That the Apemantus of this scene belongs wholly to Shakespere is not to our minds quite so certain. There is little of wit in any part of his dialogue; and the pelting volley of abuse between the Cynic, the Poet, and the Painter, might have been produced by any writer who was not afraid of exhibiting the *tu quoque* style of repartee which distinguishes the angry rhetoric of fish-wives and school-boys. Shakespere, however, has touched upon the original canvas;—no one can doubt to whom these lines belong:—

> "So, so; there!—
> Aches contact and starve your supple
>   joints!—
> That there should be small love 'mongst
>   these sweet knaves
> And all this court'sy! The strain of man's
>   bred out
> Into baboon and monkey."

These lines in the original are printed as prose; and they continued so to be printed by Theobald and the editors who succeeded him, probably from its not being considered that *aches* is a dis-syllable. This circumstance is a confirmation to us that the dialogue with Apemantus is not entirely Shakespere's; for it is a most remarkable fact that, in all those passages of which there cannot be a doubt that they were *wholly* written by our poet, there is no confusion of prose for verse,—no difficulties whatever in the metrical arrangement,—no opportunity presented for the exercise of any ingenuity in "regulation." It was this fact which first led us to perceive, and subsequently to trace, the differences between particular scenes and pas-

sages. Wherever the modern text follows the ancient text with very slight changes, there we could put our finger undoubtingly upon the work of Shakespere.

A. C. Bradley (1851–1935) [Excerpted from *Shakespearean Tragedy* (1904). Arguably the most eminent of Shakespeare's early-20th-century critics, Bradley's *Shakespearean Tragedy* has proved to be an enthusiastic and influential summary of Shakespeare's works in the tragic genre.]

When we turn from *Othello* to *Timon of Athens* we find a play of quite another kind, *Othello* is dramatically the most perfect of the tragedies. *Timon,* on the contrary, is weak, ill-constructed and confused; and, though care might have made it clear, no mere care could make it really dramatic. Yet it is undoubtedly Shakespearean in part, probably in great part; and it immediately reminds us of *King Lear.* Both plays deal with the tragic effects of ingratitude. In both the victim is exceptionally unsuspicious, soft-hearted and vehement. In both he is completely overwhelmed, passing through fury to madness in the one case, to suicide in the other. Famous passages in both plays are curses. The misanthropy of Timon pours itself out in a torrent of maledictions on the whole race of man; and these at once recall, alike by their form and their substance, the most powerful speeches uttered by Lear in his madness. In both plays occur repeated comparisons between man and the beasts; the idea that this bestial degradation will end in a furious struggle of all with all, in which the race will perish. The "pessimistic" strain in *Timon* suggests to many readers, even more imperatively than *King Lear,* the notion that Shakespeare was giving vent to some personal feeling, whether present or past; for the signs of his hand appear most unmistakably when the hero begins to pour the vials of wrath upon mankind. *Timon,* lastly, in some of the unquestionably Shakespearean part, bears (as it appears to me) so strong a resemblance to *King Lear* in style and in versification that it is hard to understand how competent judges can suppose that it belongs to a time at all near that of the final romances, or even that it was written so late as the last Roman plays. It is more likely to have been composed immediately after *King Lear* and before *Macbeth.*

MODERN CRITICISM AND CRITICAL CONTROVERSIES

Timon of Athens has had a somewhat turbulent critical history. Many scholars have been alienated by a number of aspects of the play, most notably the textual difficulties it poses. As Frank Kermode explains, "a strong sense of its oddity has deflected critical interest; apart from *Titus Andronicus* it is probably the least admired of Shakespeare's tragedies." Critics have also shown the tendency to compare it unfavorably to the roughly contemporary *King Lear,* with which it shares many thematic similarities. These critics have included A. C. Bradley and John Dover Wilson who described the play as "the stillborn twin of *Lear.*" Derek Traversi, however, argues against reading *Timon of Athens* in relation to *King Lear,* insisting instead that it is possible to view "Shakespeare not engaged in repeating himself, but in contriving a new kind of dramatic action, an experiment which, though not entirely successful, is nonetheless the work of a great poet writing at the height of his unique powers."

The *King Lear* comparisons have contributed to the status of *Timon of Athens* as one of Shakespeare's lesser tragedies. The most notable scholar to go against this grain was G. Wilson Knight who gave an enthusiastic and strongly appreciative reading of the play in his book on Shakespearean tragedy, *The Wheel of Fire.* For Knight, *Timon of Athens* represented "the nature of a tragic movement more precipitous and unimpeded than any other in Shakespeare; one which is conceived on a scale even more tremendous than that of *Macbeth*

and *King Lear;* and whose universal tragic significance is of all most clearly apparent." Knight also comments upon Timon's transition from a universal lover to a universal hater, commenting that there exists "no tragic movement so swift, so clean-cut, so daring and so terrible in all Shakespeare as this of Timon. We pity Lear, we dread for Macbeth: but the awfulness of Timon, dwarfing pity and out-topping sympathy, is as the grandeur and menace of a sky-lifted mountain, whither we look and tremble." For Knight, then, *Timon of Athens* represents Shakespeare's most remarkable achievement in the tragic genre.

The chief cause of disagreement amongst modern critics of *Timon of Athens* is the issue of authorship. The play's inconsistencies have often been explained with the theory that *Timon* is an incomplete play or that its current incarnation represents an early draft or a reworking of an existing play that was previously abandoned. The prevailing modern view, however, is that most of the textual problems are due to the fact that *Timon of Athens* is a collaborative work, with Thomas Middleton as Shakespeare's coauthor. The recognition and acceptance of Middleton's hand in the text has not by any means been an easy or straightforward process. Charles Knight's examination of the text in his *Studies of Shakespeare* in 1849 was one of the earliest critical works to challenge Shakespeare's sole authorship of the play. While many of Knight's theories have been rejected over time, his study of the play remains influential for its rejection of Shakespeare's sole contribution to the play, an idea that has retained an integral place in subsequent criticism, raising many issues and provoking a number of lines of critical enquiry.

A note by the critic William Wells, published in 1920, proposed Middleton as the author of a sequence of scenes from Act II, Scene 2 to Act III, Scene 3. This was a turning point in the gradual process by which Middleton has come to be regarded by many as the play's second author. This notion has been corroborated by a series of detailed stylistic tests performed upon the play, which compared various features such as versification and recurring use of certain words and expressions with examples from Middleton's other works.

In spite of the apparent conclusiveness of the various authorship tests applied to the text, the so-called "orthodox view," which states that Shakespeare was the play's sole author, still persisted throughout the 20th century. E. K. Chambers commented that the play's inconsistencies can be explained by the fact that "it is unfinished still. The passages of chaotic verse, in particular, look very much like rough notes, hastily jotted down to be worked up later." The view that the play is unfinished and that many of the passages constitute a rough draft has never quite been eradicated. As late as the 1980s and early 1990s, critics such as A. D. Nuttall and Lois Potter still aligned themselves with the orthodox view of the text's history. Nuttall, for example, observed that an article by Una Ellis-Fermor, published in 1942, is "widely regarded as having finally routed the disintegrators," or those who argue in favor of *Timon of Athens*'s status as a collaborative text. Nuttall goes on to comment that the "arguments for regarding *Timon of Athens* as a collaboration are too strong to be ignored," but he remains tentative when it comes to endorsing such arguments. The text, he argues, constitutes "one play not two, superficially disfigured by technical inconsistencies but conceptually and imaginatively coherent." In an edition of the play published in 2001, Karl Klein also revealed his skepticism about the possibility that *Timon of Athens* was a collaborative effort. This indicates that the issue of collaboration has not been universally accepted in scholarship upon *Timon of Athens*.

In spite of the views of the proponents of the "orthodox theory" of the play's authorship, Middleton's role as Shakespeare's collaborator has gained a widespread acceptance among critics of the play. Brian Vickers concludes his summary of the collaboration debate by going as far as to state that the various stylistic tests to which the play has been subject "agree in assigning to Middleton a substantial part of *Timon,* and Shakespearians who continue to deny this point risk forfeiting their scholarly credibility." John Jowett has been particularly influential in emphasizing Middleton's hand in the play and viewing the place of *Timon of Athens* within the context of Middleton's other works. This process culminated in the appearance of an edition of *Timon of Athens* produced by Jowett in the Oxford publication of *The Collected Works* by Thomas Middleton in 2007.

While the issue of authorship has exerted considerable influence over criticism on *Timon of Athens,* it has by no means been the only avenue of critical enquiry to have been explored. The character of Timon, for example, has provoked a great many critical responses. It has already been noted that G. Wilson Knight was fascinated by the character's rapid transition from "universal lover" to the dedicated misanthrope. However, Timon's misanthropy has alienated many readers who have found him a character with whom it is difficult to engage due to the degree to which his humanity has been corroded. John Russell Brown, for example, sees the misanthropic Timon as "self-centred and irresponsive to offers of help and good advice." While Timon is acknowledged as a flawed and irresponsible hero, if one can call him as much, some critics have also commented that he commands our sympathy. Nuttall sums up the views of H. J. Oliver and J. C. Maxwell, both editors of significant editions of the text, by revealing an attitude whereby "we pity Timon despite his faults." Janette Dillon argues that during his solitude Timon "remains totally outside any community, an outlaw in the most explicit sense, and his only contact with other men is forced on him by the visits others pay him in his solitude." Paradoxically, however, Timon exhibits a need to communicate his misanthropy to his visitors, thereby suggesting he does not completely reject any kind of contact with other people. The character of Timon has therefore provoked a range of critical response. Some adopt a course of sympathetic engagement with Timon, who is regarded as a victim, either of the nascent consumer society taking root in Athens, or of human cruelty. Others view him with a sense of detachment and regard his fate as punishment for the hubris and cupidity he exhibited in the first act.

A horrified Flavius asserts his loyalty to Timon in Act IV, Scene 3 of *Timon of Athens*. This illustration was designed for a 1918 edition of Charles and Mary Lamb's *Tales from Shakespeare*. (*Illustration by Louis Rhead*)

The absence of any kind of family or love interest for Timon has also provoked a number of responses. The unexplained absence of any kind of maternal figure has been especially significant. Coppélia Kahn's influential essay, "'Magic of bounty': *Timon of Athens*, Jacobean Patronage, and Maternal Power," argues that the figure of Fortune in the Poet's explanation of his work

acted as a kind of surrogate mother who had the maternal powers to both embrace and reject her subjects. Kahn's essay also viewed *Timon* against the social backdrop of the Jacobean culture of patronage. Kahn comments that the play "explores the lethal ambiguities underlying the gifts and loans through which power was brokered in the courts of Elizabeth and James." John Jowett also views Timon as a kind of Jacobean patron, suggesting that "within the aesthetic economy of the play as a tragedy it is Timon who occupies the initial position of a king." Jowett goes on to point out that "kings too had to petition for money. Debt was one of the most fundamental characteristics of the Renaissance court and its economy." The play therefore raises important issues relating to the contemporary concerns of the financial policies of the Jacobean court and the system of debt and credit in which it was engaged.

Kahn's view of *Timon of Athens* as a response to the culture of Jacobean patronage also influenced critical readings by Andrew Hadfield and David Bevington and David L. Smith, which link Timon to James I and the Jacobean court. Hadfield argues that various aspects of *Timon of Athens* are influenced by a popular anecdote that was circulating regarding the king's spending habits and his liberality toward his favorites. According to this anecdote, James I ordered a payment in the sum of £20,000 to his favorite, Robert Carr, which prompted the lord treasurer, Sir Robert Cecil, to lay out this money on the floor of a room the king would pass. The king passed the room, noticed the piles of money, and enquired to whom it belonged. Cecil replied that it was the king's before he gave it away. This apparently sent the king into a sudden hysteria in which he cast himself on the ground and began scrabbling through the gold, eventually limiting his donation to half the initial amount. Whether or not this anecdote is true is debatable, yet for Hadfield, it does reflect the popular view of James's failure to grasp the value of money and provides an important context for *Timon of Athens*. He even argues that the image of Timon digging for roots acts as a parody of the image of James scrabbling through the pile of gold. These approaches confirm that *Timon of Athens* can be viewed as an emphatically topical play and indicates the extent to which its critical reputation has benefited from the increased prominence of political and historicist theoretical approaches to the text.

Timon of Athens has therefore provoked a rich range of critical responses that examine the play from various points of view. The healthy body of criticism confirms the importance of the place of *Timon of Athens* in both the Shakespearean and the Middletonian canons.

THE PLAY TODAY

While *Timon of Athens* may not be considered to be of the same artistic caliber of Shakespeare's great tragedies, it has inspired many imaginative and powerful interpretations as well as a fairly robust and wide ranging body of scholarship. It is however performed and studied with considerably less frequency than many of Shakespeare's other tragedies.

The play was probably never performed during Shakespeare's lifetime and was very rarely performed on stage before the onset of the 20th century. During the Restoration era, it was adapted by Thomas Shadwell as *The History of Timon of Athens the Man-Hater* and was subject to frequent revivals until as late as the 1740s. Adaptation of Shakespeare's plays was a common practice during the Restoration, as much of the contents of his works were not conducive to the prevailing vogue for neoclassical decorum. Records do not indicate that the authentically Shakespearean version was performed in England at all during the 18th century and only a handful of performances are recorded throughout the 19th century.

The play in performance had better fortunes throughout the 20th century, receiving a great many significant and imaginative interpretations. Modern dress performances have been a commonplace since the late 1940s and have allowed directors to take advantage of the play's potential for political and satirical comment. A notable example

of this occurred in Michael Langham's 1963 production at Stratford, Ontario. The use of modern dress as a means of providing a critique of Western capitalism was made most apparent by the realization of Alcibiades as a revolutionary guerrilla reminiscent of such contemporary figures as Che Guevara and Fidel Castro. This production also had the meeting with Lucius in the third act take place in a steam bath where he was receiving treatment.

The play's frequent association with *King Lear* has also had an effect upon the performance of the play. An essay on *King Lear* in Jan Kott's influential book *Shakespeare Our Contemporary* likened the play to the endeavors of the theater of the absurd, particularly Samuel Beckett's play *Endgame*. The absurdist influence upon performances of *King Lear* is exemplified by Peter Brook's film version, which starred Paul Scofield and spread to theatrical productions of the play, including Brook's own production at Les Bouffes du Nord. Other significant stage versions include John Schlesinger's 1965 production at Stratford-upon-Avon starring Paul Scofield and an acclaimed realization of Timon from Richard Pasco in a production directed by Ron Daniels and staged at Stratford-upon-Avon in 1980. The play was also adapted into a one-man version by the critic G. Wilson Knight, which he continued to perform until he was well into his 80s. This version became notorious due to the fact that Knight would apparently strip completely naked during the performance to represent the hero's "severance from humanity." Knight did, however, caution that the lights should remain dim below his waist.

The only filmed version of the play was produced as part of the BBC's Complete Works series and was first transmitted on British television in April 1981. In common with the other productions in this strand, *Timon of Athens* was entirely studio-bound and recorded on videotape. This production was initially to have been directed by the celebrated and at times controversial theater director Michael Bogdanov. However, Bogdanov's vision of a modern-dress version with an Oriental theme proved to be at odds with the general brief for the series as a whole. Directorial duties then passed to the series producer Jonathan Miller, who directed a version in which the characters all wore anachronistic Elizabethan period dress rather than authentic ancient Athenian apparel. Jonathan Pryce stars as Timon who, in the early scenes, appears shy and soft spoken before erupting into the intense rages characteristic of the later scenes. Another significant piece of casting is that of the comic duo John Bird and John Fortune as, respectively, the Painter and the Poet. That this partnership was primarily associated with topical and satirical humor suggests a satirical swipe at the culture of patronage, thus possibly serving a similar purpose to their representation in the original text.

Timon of Athens has failed to permeate the popular consciousness to the extent of many of Shakespeare's other works. Nevertheless, it did provide the inspiration for the title of Vladimir Nabokov's 1962 novel, *Pale Fire*. The novel consists of a long poem by a fictitious author, supplemented by a foreword and a commentary compiled by the late poet's former friend and editor. The title alludes to Act IV, Scene 3, in which Timon proclaims that "the moon's an arrant thief / And her pale fire she snatches from the sun." The idea at the core of this quote is reflected in one of the principal premises of the novel, the reliance of the editor upon the work of the late poet in order to ignite his own "pale fire." This notion is also reflected in Timon's likening of himself to a moon that had run out of suns from which to borrow light (4.3). *Timon of Athens* is thus a significant motif throughout Nabokov's novel.

In spite of its rather shaky critical reputation, and its often scant performance history, *Timon of Athens* remains a work of relevance, perhaps even more so for readers and spectators of today than for the original audience and readership. The dramatization of Timon's descent from fabulous wealth to debt-ridden poverty has added resonance at a time when such issues as debt and financial strife have gained great prominence in a world subject to an unstable economy.

FIVE TOPICS FOR DISCUSSION AND WRITING

1. **The tragic hero:** Can Timon be considered a "hero" by definition? What is the effect of his sudden fall from prosperity? Discuss his rapid transition from extreme benevolence to dedicated misanthropy and how this is represented in the play.

2. **Gold and money:** How does gold figure in this play? What functions does it perform? How is it represented? In what ways does the desire for it impact the actions of the various characters in the play? Does the play hint at the potential for any positive uses for it?

3. **The natural world:** What uses do the authors of this play make of natural imagery? What issues are raised by Timon's conscious decision to abandon Athenian civilization and lead a wild existence in the woods? How does the natural world exist in relation to the urban environment of Athens? What purpose does the imagery of beasts serve?

4. **Friendship:** Discuss the representations of friendship in the play. Do any of the play's characters exhibit behavior that is not motivated by self-interest? How do the false friends and flatterers exploit Timon's perception of friendship? Can anyone in the play be considered a true friend to Timon?

5. **Human nature:** What view of human nature and behavior is represented in the play? What comments are made on the subject by the play's characters and how does this relate to their own actions and behavior? Does the play offer any redeeming images of, or faith in, human nature?

Bibliography

Berry, Edward. *Shakespeare and the Hunt: A Cultural and Social Study.* Cambridge: Cambridge University Press, 2001.

Bertram, Benjamin. *The Time Is out of Joint: Skepticism in Shakespeare's England.* Cranbury, N.J.: Associated University Presses, 2004.

Bevington, David, and David L. Smith "James I and *Timon of Athens.*" *Comparative Drama* 33, no. 1 (1999): 56–87.

Brown, John Russell. *Shakespeare: The Tragedies*. Basingstoke, England: Palgrave, 2001.

Bullough, Geoffrey, ed. *Narrative and Dramatic Sources of Shakespeare*. Vol. 6, *Other "Classical" Plays*. London: Routledge, 1965.

Dillon, Janette. *Shakespeare and the Solitary Man*. London: Macmillan, 1981.

Egan, Gabriel. *Shakespeare and Marx*. Oxford: Oxford University Press, 2004.

Empson, William. *The Structure of Complex Words*. London: Chatto and Windus, 1964.

Garner, Shirley Nelson, and Madelon Sprengnether. *Shakespearean Tragedy and Gender*. Bloomington: Indiana University Press, 1996.

Hadfield, Andrew. *Shakespeare and Renaissance Politics*. London: Thomson Learning, 2004.

Jowett, John, ed. *Timon of Athens*. Oxford: Oxford University Press, 2004.

Kermode, Frank. *Shakespeare's Language*. London: Penguin, 2000.

Klein, Karl, ed. *Timon of Athens*. Cambridge: Cambridge University Press, 2001.

Knight, G. Wilson. *The Wheel of Fire: Interpretations of Shakespearean Tragedy*. London: Methuen, 1965.

Kott, Jan. *Shakespeare Our Contemporary*. Translated by Boleslaw Taborski. London: Methuen, 1967.

Marx, Karl. *Selected Writings in Sociology and Social Philosophy*. Translated by T. B. Bottomore. New York: MacGraw-Hill, 1964.

Nuttall, A. D. *Timon of Athens*. Hemel Hempstead, England: Harvester Wheatsheaf, 1989.

Spencer, T. J. B., ed. *Shakespeare's Plutarch*. Harmondsworth, England: Penguin, 1964.

Traversi, Derek. *An Approach to Shakespeare*. Vol. 2, Troilus and Cressida *to* The Tempest. London: Hollis and Carter, 1968.

Vickers, Brian. *Shakespeare, Co-Author*. Oxford: Oxford University Press, 2002.

Willis, Susan. *The BBC Shakespeare Plays: Making the Televised Canon*. Chapel Hill: University of North Carolina Press, 1991.

Wilson, John Dover. *The Essential Shakespeare*. 1932. Reprint, Cambridge: Cambridge University Press, 1967.

Woodbridge, Linda, ed. *Money and the Age of Shakespeare: Essays in New Economic Criticism*. Basingstoke, England: Palgrave Macmillan, 2003.

FILM AND VIDEO PRODUCTION

Miller, Jonathan, dir. *Timon of Athens*. With Jonathan Pryce. BBC, 1981.

—Daniel J. Cadman

Titus Andronicus

INTRODUCTION

Titus Andronicus has suffered from its long-standing reputation as Shakespeare's worst play. Indeed, many critics thought it was so bad that Shakespeare could not have possibly written it, arguing that perhaps his contemporary George Peele was the author. Other critics agreed that it was bad but claimed that since Shakespeare wrote it at the beginning of his career he should be excused, as he was still developing his creative powers. Questions about the authorship of the play continue to provoke debate among Shakespeare scholars.

Nonetheless, *Titus Andronicus* occupies an important position in Shakespeare's canon and in the history of Elizabethan theater. It was Shakespeare's first tragedy and the first of Shakespeare's plays to be printed. The only surviving contemporary sketch of a scene from a Shakespeare play is of the opening scene from *Titus Andronicus*. Known as the Peacham Drawing, it shows Tamora kneeling before Titus, with her sons and Aaron standing behind her. The figures wear a mixture of Roman and Elizabethan costumes. Titus is identified by the laurel wreath he wears on his head, his costume combines a toga and breastplate while he carries a decorated ceremonial staff to celebrate his victory over the Goths. The Roman soldiers behind Titus are dressed as Elizabethan men-at-arms carrying halberds.

The reasons behind the play's dubious reputation are precisely the reasons for its continuing interest and relevance to a modern audience or reader. The play is a revenge play, concerned with those very powerful emotions of anger, grief, and a desire for retribution. Through its examination of revenge, the play also considers the related subjects of violence and human suffering. Its depiction of mutilation, rape, and murder prompted critics to condemn it as a play simply designed to satisfy Elizabethan appetites for blood and gore. The play certainly *is* violent, with at least a dozen killings, and yet at the heart of the play is a father and war hero who makes terrible mistakes but goes on to command our sympathies partly because of the cruel attacks against him and his family. Recent stage productions and films of the play make it clear through the use of modern dress and set design that, while the play is set in the ancient past, its interest in the relationship between an individual and society and in society's attitudes toward violence and cruelty continues to resonate in the 21st century.

BACKGROUND

Titus Andronicus is set in imperial Rome but is not related to a specific historical emperor or set of events. The play takes place at a time, probably around the late fourth century C.E., when the empire was threatened by its enemies the Goths and was on the brink of collapse. Shakespeare uses the Roman setting to examine how the values that had made Rome great also contributed to its decline. By locating the play in the past in ancient Rome, Shakespeare was also able to use his play

In 1595, Henry Peacham drew the only surviving contemporary sketch of a scene from a Shakespeare play. Known as the Peacham Drawing, it depicts the opening scene of *Titus Andronicus*. The figure on the right is Aaron the Moor.

to comment on the present. This was a strategy frequently used by Elizabethan and Jacobean dramatists as it allowed them to engage with contemporary concerns without incurring the disapproval of the authorities. *Titus Andronicus* is thought to have been written between 1592 and 1594, during the final decade of the reign of Elizabeth I, and the play considers political and social issues that would have been relevant to its audience. One such issue dealt with in the opening scene of the play is the political turmoil prompted by the rival claims of Saturninus and Bassianus for the emperorship. Throughout the reign of Elizabeth, the question of who would succeed the queen when she died remained a live issue. When it was clear by the early 1580s that Elizabeth would not marry and produce an heir of her own, the focus shifted to possible claimants to the throne from abroad, including James IV of Scotland. Elizabeth refused until her death in 1603 to specify who would succeed her, and so the anxiety about who might take the English throne was the subject of intense speculation, particularly in the final years of her reign. *Titus Andronicus* rehearses contemporary debates about what kind of claimant would make the best ruler: Should power be given based on the law of primogeniture as Saturninus argues, or should it be based on merit and suitable qualities as argued by Bassianus? Rome and its models of government

were frequently used by the Elizabethans to shape their own ideas about England and the concept of nationhood. It was thought that Rome had a particular connection with Britain through the theory of the translation of the empire, or *translatio imperii*, which argued that history consists of a gradual westward shift of the greatest imperial power, starting with Troy, moving to Rome, and then to Britain. In *Titus Andronicus*, this theory is alluded to when a Roman lord refers to "Our Troy, our Rome." Here the play makes the connection between the ancient city of Troy and Rome, and the career of the Trojan prince Aeneas, whose destiny it was to escape the city of Troy before its destruction and to found the city of Rome. British writers developed this idea and claimed that Aeneas's great grandson Brutus fled from Rome and was responsible for founding Britain. One of the names used for London to make this imperial genealogy explicit was Troynovant, or New Troy, and this idea was used to promote England's imperial aspirations during the 16th and 17th centuries. The story of Aeneas and his descendants was frequently referred to in Elizabethan literature and is alluded to throughout *Titus Andronicus*, either through the choice of names for characters, such as the epithet Pius for Titus, which was also for Aeneas. Lavinia is also a significant name since it belonged to the wife of Aeneas and daughter of the king of Latium, whose descendants established the Roman Empire.

Titus Andronicus, unlike the later Roman plays such as *Antony and Cleopatra*, does not rely on a single specific source for its narrative such as Plutarch's *Lives of the Noble Grecians and Romans*. Instead, Shakespeare draws upon ideas generated by existing Elizabethan plays that were being performed at the Rose theater and by his own poetry such as *Venus and Adonis* and *The Rape of Lucrece*. The two plays that influenced *Titus Andronicus* were Thomas Kyd's *The Spanish Tragedy* (1587–90) and Christopher Marlowe's *The Jew of Malta* (1589–90). The plot of *The Spanish Tragedy* offers clear parallels with that of *Titus*, as both are concerned with quest for justice and with revenge. Hieronimo, the play's protagonist, is a magistrate, and yet when his son Horatio is murdered by a member of the royal family, Hieronimo quickly finds that his attempts to have the murderers brought to justice are thwarted by the villainous Lorenzo. Hieronimo experiences bouts of madness as his grief threatens to overwhelm him, but he recovers his wits to exact his revenge. The long, stylized speeches in the play quickly became famous, and their influence can be seen in the speeches of the grieving Titus. The plot is violent and sensational, as Hieronimo invites his enemies to act in a play he has written for performance at court. He pretends that the daggers used in the play-within-the play will be props, but in fact both Hieronimo and his daughter Bel-Imperia use real daggers upon their enemies. With his revenge complete, Hieronimo refuses to speak further and bites out his own tongue. The second play that influenced Shakespeare's *Titus* is Marlowe's *The Jew of Malta*. This is not, strictly speaking, a revenge play, but rather a series of plots and revenges executed by different groups of characters on the island of Malta. The play's protagonist, the Jew and outsider Barabas, provided Shakespeare with a template for his villain Aaron. Barabas, like Aaron, is evil and an audience is aware that they should condemn them both, but each villain is charming, charismatic, with speeches designed to entrance an audience with their poetry and to make them laugh with their outrageous claims.

Other influences upon Titus come from Shakespeare's poem *The Rape of Lucrece*, which was also published in 1594 and narrates the rape of Lucrece by Tarquin and how it eventually led to the downfall of the king and the establishment of a republic. In *Titus Andronicus*, Lavinia's brother Lucius compares her to Lucrece when he promises to overthrow Saturninus. Another classical source that provided an analogy for the story of Lavinia was that of Philomel, found in Ovid's *Metamorphoses*, a popular Latin text that was used to teach translation in Elizabethan schools. *Titus Andronicus* is a play in which the characters like to read

classical stories and indeed the rape of Lavinia is explained through using Young Lucius's copy of *Metamorphoses*.

Date and Text of the Play

Titus Andronicus is thought to have been written in the early 1590s. The play was entered in the Stationers' Register on February 6, 1594, with the first quarto of the play published later that year. The title page of the first quarto gives the play's title in full together with details of the theater companies who had performed the play: "THE MOST Lamentable Romaine Tragedie of Titus Andronicus: As it was Plaide by the Right Ho-

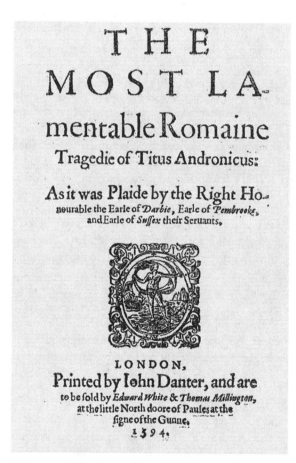

Title page of the first quarto of *Titus Andronicus*, published in 1594

nourable the Earle of Darbie, Earl of Pembrooke and Earl of Sussex their seruants." The play was popular on the stage and continued to be so until at least 1614, when a character in Ben Jonson's *Bartholomew Fair* refers to those audience members who "will swear, *Jeronimo,* or *Andronicus* are the best plays . . . whose judgement shows it is constant, and hath stood still, these five and twenty or thirty years." Here, Jonson is poking fun at those audience members who have continued to enjoy what by 1614 would be considered old-fashioned plays such as *The Spanish Tragedy (Jeronimo)* and *Titus Andronicus,* but the gibe also indicates that while they may be old, they were still popular and continued to be performed.

SYNOPSIS
Brief Synopsis

Titus Andronicus returns from a successful war against the Goths. Lucius, one of his sons, declares that their religion demands a human sacrifice, and he nominates Alarbus, a son of Tamora, the captive Queen of the Goths. Alarbus is killed. When asked to choose a new emperor, Titus chooses Saturninus over his brother, Bassaianus. Saturninus declares that he will marry Titus's only daughter, Lavinia. Bassianus claims Lavinia as his own betrothed, and Titus's sons back him. Saturninus seizes on the chance to reject Titus, whose popularity he fears. The emperor then declares his intention to marry Tamora, who recommends that he take revenge later. Saturninus therefore pretends to forgive Titus and his family. A double wedding is proposed.

Aaron, a Moor in Tamora's court, exults in his mistress's newly exalted position, for he knows she loves him completely. Tamora's sons Demetrius and Chiron enter, arguing over Lavinia, whom each desires. Aaron suggests that they rape Lavinia during the next day's festive hunt.

Titus and his sons and Saturninus and his court go to the hunt. The two couples, Saturninus and Tamora and Bassianus and Lavinia, are married. Aaron arranges an encounter in which Demetrius and Chiron kill Bassianus and carry Lavinia off to rape her. Then, he frames Martius and Quintus, sons of Titus, for the murder. Saturninus decrees that the sons shall be executed.

Chiron and Demetrius cut off Lavinia's tongue and hands before abandoning her to be discovered by Marcus Andronicus, Titus's brother.

Martius and Quintus are on their way to be executed when Marcus appears with Lavinia. Aaron announces that Titus's severed hand will be accepted as ransom for the lives of the two sons. Titus lets Aaron cut off his hand and take it away. Soon afterwards, Titus receives the heads of his two sons, accompanied by his own hand, and he realizes that Aaron has tricked him. Titus sends Lucius to the Goths to raise an army.

Mute Lavinia conveys to Titus and Marcus that she wants them to consult Ovid's *Metamorphoses*, where she directs them to the tale of the rape of Philomel. They deduce that her case is the same, and they have her write the names of her attackers in the sand with a wooden staff.

Chiron and Demetrius receive a gift of weapons from Titus, with verses that hint at vengeance. A Nurse enters holding the black infant just born to Tamora. She tells Aaron that the empress wants him to kill it so that no one knows of her adultery. Aaron kills the Nurse and sends Chiron and Demetrius to buy a white baby and take it to Tamora to be passed off as the child of Saturninus.

Titus persuades a Clown to deliver two pigeons as an offering to the emperor. Included with the birds is a message wrapped around a dagger. The Clown presents the pigeons and Titus's message to Saturninus, who orders the Clown hanged and vows to execute Titus personally. Aemilius appears, reporting that a Gothic army under Lucius is approaching. Aemilius is then sent to arrange a parley with Lucius at Titus's house.

Aaron, who has been captured with his child, is brought before Lucius, who decrees that both be hanged. Aaron says that he will confess the truth about all his misdeeds if Lucius will spare the child. When Lucius agrees, Aaron brags of his evil actions. Aemilius arrives with the offer of a parley, and Lucius accepts.

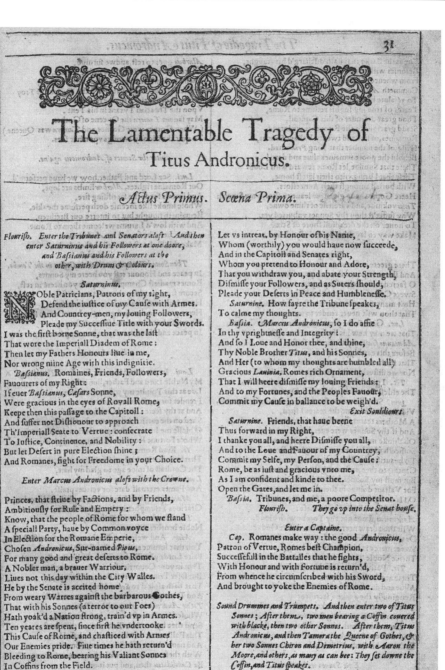

Title page of the First Folio edition of *Titus Andronicus*, published in 1623

Tamora and her sons, in disguise, approach Titus's house. Titus recognizes them, but he pretends to be taken in. Tamora proposes to bring Saturninus to a banquet, where Titus can wreak his vengeance. She goes, leaving behind Chiron and Demetrius, whose throats Titus cuts.

Lucius, arriving at Titus's house for the parley, turns Aaron over to Marcus. Saturninus and Tamora arrive, and all are seated at the banquet table. Titus welcomes them, dressed as a cook. Referring to a famous legend of a father who killed his raped daughter to remove his family's shame, he kills Lavinia before the horrified guests. He declares that she had been raped by Chiron and Demetrius. He reveals their heads baked in a meat pie, which Tamora has already sampled, and then he stabs Tamora to death. Saturninus promptly kills him and is himself immediately dispatched by Lucius. The assembled nobles declare Lucius to be the new emperor. Aaron is brought forward and sentenced by Lucius to be buried to his neck and starved. He responds with a last boastful refusal to repent.

Act I, Scene 1

The opening of the play consists of a single extended scene of nearly 500 lines. The scene can be divided into six sections. The action throughout the first act takes place in Rome on the Capitol before the Senate. The first section of this scene is concerned with the political turmoil prompted by the death of the emperor and the competing claims of his sons Saturninus and Bassianus for the title of emperor. Saturninus claims his right based on the laws of inheritance as the eldest son, whereas Bassianus makes his claim based on his own qualities and talents, which would make him a good leader. The two rivals are persuaded by Marcus Andronicus to dismiss their crowds of supporters and allow his brother Titus Andronicus, who has just returned to Rome, to arbitrate in the dispute.

The second section is marked by the entrance of the Roman warrior Titus Andronicus, who has just returned from a successful military campaign against the Goths. Titus is both a triumphant soldier and a grieving father, since he has lost 21 of his 25 sons during the campaign. Titus's first concern is to bury his dead sons in the family tomb, a ritual that he argues requires human sacrifice, and he selects Alarbus, the eldest son of Tamora, queen of the Goths, as the necessary victim. Despite Tamora's pleas for mercy and her appeal to Titus as a parent, Titus remains resolute in his decision, and Alarbus is taken away to be killed. As a consequence of Titus's actions, Tamora and her sons Chiron and Demetrius swear vengeance against Titus and his family. The bodies are buried in the family tomb, and Titus is greeted by his daughter Lavinia.

The third section returns to the political question of the succession. Marcus Andronicus brings news that the people of Rome have nominated Titus as emperor in recognition for his service to the state. Titus, however, is unwilling to accept the position, suggesting he is too old and, as a soldier, is not suited to politics. Titus uses his influence with the people to confirm Saturninus as emperor, arguing that the traditions of inheritance by the first-born son should be honored. Saturninus begins his reign by making a number of important declarations. First, he honors Titus by offering to make Titus's daughter Lavinia his empress. Unbeknownst to either Titus or Saturninus, Lavinia is already betrothed to Bassianus, who intervenes when Saturninus proposes marriage to claim Lavinia as his bride. Since Titus is clearly unaware of this betrothal between Bassianus and Lavinia, he regards it as the theft of his daughter, an insult to his family, and, more important, an act of disobedience. Titus's remaining sons help Bassianus and Lavinia to leave the stage, and Titus regards their behavior as an act of treachery. In a fit of anger, Titus draws his sword and kills his son Mutius, who was guarding the door to prevent his father from pursuing the lovers.

The response of Saturninus to the loss of Lavinia as his bride forms the focus for the next section of this scene. The emperor rebukes Titus and his family for their involvement in Bassianus's abduction of Lavinia and, having freed the Goths, proposes marriage to Tamora, their queen.

Attention then turns to Titus who is rejoined by his three remaining sons and his brother Marcus, who are confronted with the murdered body of Mutius. Titus initially refuses their request to have Mutius buried in the Andronici tomb but eventually capitulates in the face of their pleas.

The action of the scene then turns to the figure of Tamora and her relationship with Saturninus. Saturninus threatens to be avenged on Bassianus for claiming Lavinia as his bride, but Tamora encourages Saturninus to forgive his brother and restore the Andronici to favor. In an aside, Tamora reveals her true motives for appearing as a peacemaker since she plans to avenge herself on Titus and his family for murdering her son Alarbus and for humiliating Tamora before the Romans. The scene concludes with Saturninus appearing to be reconciled with Bassianus and Titus. Titus invites the emperor and his bride to join him and his family on a hunting expedition the following day.

Act II, Scene 1

In a soliloquy, Tamora's lover, Aaron, describes her advancement from prisoner to empress. The speech uses lyrical language as Aaron expresses his love for Tamora, but he is interrupted by the arrival of Tamora's sons Chiron and Demetrius, who are both quarrelling over their own desire for Lavinia. In order to put a stop to their heated disagreement, Aaron proposes a plan that will allow the brothers an opportunity to satisfy their lust for Lavinia. Using the occasion of the hunt arranged by Titus, Aaron suggests that Lavinia can easily be separated from the hunting party in the wood, making her an easy target for the rape planned by Chiron and Demetrius.

Act II, Scene 2

This brief scene establishes that it is the morning of the hunt. Titus and his sons, together with his brother Marcus, are joined by Saturninus, Tamora, Chiron, and Demetrius together with Lavinia and Bassianus.

Act II, Scene 3

In a wood outside Rome, Aaron appears, burying a bag of gold, which he explains is part of his wider plot for the destruction of the Andronici family. He is joined by Tamora, who hopes to use the encounter in the wood as an opportunity

Martius discovers Bassianus's body while Quintus leans over the pit in Act II, Scene 3 in *Titus Andronicus,* in this print published by F. & C. Rivington in 1804. *(Painting by Henry Fuseli; engraving by J. Dadley)*

for lovemaking with Aaron, but Aaron quickly explains his plans for revenge include the murder of Bassianus and the rape of Lavinia. Aaron also gives Tamora a letter to deliver to the emperor. The lovers are interrupted by the arrival of Bassianus and Lavinia, who rebuke Tamora for her relationship with Aaron. Aaron leaves to fetch Chiron and Demetrius, and upon their return, the two brothers begin by stabbing Bassianus and then reveal their intention to rape Lavinia. Lavinia appeals to Tamora for mercy but without success. Chiron and Demetrius throw Bassianus's body into a pit before dragging Lavinia away.

Aaron returns to the clearing in the wood with Titus's sons Quintus and Martius and leads them to the pit on the pretext of having trapped a panther. Martius falls into the pit and discovers the body of Bassianus, and in his efforts to pull Martius out, Quintus also falls into the hole. Aaron returns with Saturninus, Tamora, Titus, and Marcus. The emperor opens the letter delivered by Tamora, which appears to contain details of a plot by Martius and Quintus to murder Bassianus. Saturninus believes that the letter is proof of their guilt and orders their immediate execution.

Act II, Scene 4

Having raped Lavinia, Chiron and Demetrius also cut off her hands and tongue to prevent her from identifying her attackers. Lavinia is found by her uncle Marcus, and in a lyrical speech, he attempts to come to terms with the horrific sight of Lavinia's mutilated body.

Act III, Scene 1

Martius and Quintus are sentenced to death for the murder of Bassianus. Titus appeals to the judges, tribunes, and senators for mercy but without success. Titus is overwhelmed by grief and falls to the floor. Lucius, the only son Titus now has left, reveals he has been banished by the emperor for attempting to free his brothers. Titus's grief is increased by the arrival of Marcus and Lavinia. Aaron the Moor brings a message

from the emperor offering to ransom the two condemned sons in exchange for the hand of one of the remaining Andronici family. Both Marcus and Lucius offer their hands, but while they leave the stage to find an axe, Titus asks Aaron if he will cut off Titus's hand. In an aside, Aaron reveals that Titus's hand will not be exchanged for his sons, but instead the emperor will send him their heads. Aaron returns from the emperor with the heads of Martius and Quintus and with Titus's own hand. From this point on, Titus resolves to be avenged upon his enemies and advises his son Lucius to join forces with the Goths and raise an army to march on Rome.

Act III, Scene 2

The scene takes place at Titus's house where the remaining Andronici family eat a meal together.

Act IV, Scene 1

Lavinia uses the story of Philomel in her nephew's copy of Ovid's *Metamorphoses* to try to explain to her father and uncle what has happened to her. Titus encourages Lavinia to reveal the name of her attackers by using a staff held in her mouth to write their names in the dust. Lavinia uses the staff to write the names of Chiron and Demetrius.

Act IV, Scene 2

Titus sends his grandson Lucius to visit Chiron and Demetrius with a bundle of weapons with Latin verses written upon them. These verses indicate that Titus has discovered that they are responsible for the rape of Lavinia. While neither Chiron nor Demetrius properly translates the verses and understands their meaning, Aaron realizes that Titus has identified Tamora's sons as his enemies.

Aaron reveals that Tamora is pregnant with his child and is about to give birth. Shortly afterwards a nurse enters with the child and delivers the message that Tamora wishes that the child be killed to conceal the pregnancy. Aaron refuses to kill the child and instead kills the nurse. He plans to also

Aaron kills the nurse in order to protect his child with Tamora in Act IV, Scene 2 of *Titus Andronicus*. This is a plate from the 1744 edition of the play edited by Sir Thomas Hanmer. *(Illustration by Francis Hayman; engraving by Hubert Gravelot)*

kill the midwife and give the child to a Moorish family in order to keep it safe.

Act IV, Scene 3

Titus, during a fit of grief-induced madness, orders his grandson Lucius to shoot a series of arrows into the sky. The arrows contain messages calling upon the gods to intervene since justice cannot be found on earth. In a moment of comic timing, Titus's calls for divine intervention are juxtaposed with the arrival on stage of a clown, whom Titus mistakes as a god or one of the messengers of the gods.

Titus uses the clown as a messenger to deliver his pleas for justice to the emperor. This scene demonstrates Titus's increasing grief and frustration as he realizes that personal revenge is the only means by which he will secure justice for the wrongs he has suffered.

Act IV, Scene 4

Saturninus has received the arrows that Lucius fired into the emperor's palace and is angry that Titus's demands for justice and his grief at the loss of his sons and the mutilation of Lavinia will increase public sympathy for him. The Clown brings Titus's petition to Saturninus wrapped around a knife, indicating that Titus is warning the emperor that he is Titus's enemy. Saturninus orders the Clown to be hanged and to have Titus brought before him to explain his actions. A messenger brings the news that the Goths, led by Lucius, Titus's son, are marching on Rome. Saturninus fears that Lucius's popularity as Titus's son will threaten his position as emperor. Tamora persuades Saturninus to arrange a meeting with Lucius at Titus's house.

Act V, Scene 1

Lucius gathers with the Goth army at the gates of Rome. A Goth soldier finds Aaron and his child at the city walls. Lucius recognizes Aaron and prepares to hang him from a tree but first gives the Moor an opportunity to confess his wicked deeds. Aaron goes on to explain that the child is the product of his union with Tamora and that it was Chiron and Demetrius who were responsible for the attack upon Lavinia and the murder of Bassianus. Aaron also explains how he tricked Martius and Quintus into discovering the body of Bassianus in order that they might be blamed for the murder. Aaron concludes by revealing that he fabricated the story that Martius and Quintus could be ransomed in exchange for an Andronici hand. Lucius resolves that hanging is too easy a death for the villainous Moor and allows him to live for the moment. A messenger from the emperor brings his request that

Lucius and the Goths should meet with Saturninus for a parley at Titus's house.

Act V, Scene 2

Tamora, disguised as Revenge, arrives at Titus's house with Chiron and Demetrius who are disguised as Rape and Murder. Titus sees through their costumes, recognizing each of them, but plays along with their story. Tamora as Revenge promises to bring the emperor and all of Titus's enemies to the house. Titus requests that Rape and Murder be left behind with him. When Tamora leaves, Titus has Chiron and Demetrius bound and gagged and explains that he intends to use their blood and heads to make a pie that he will serve to Tamora and the emperor. Titus concludes his speech by cutting their throats, while Lavinia catches their blood in the basin she holds between her arms.

Act V, Scene 3

Lucius and the Goths, together with Saturninus and Tamora, gather at Titus's house. Titus dressed as a cook welcomes his visitors to his banquet. Titus begins the banquet by killing Lavinia. When asked for an explanation of his actions by Saturninus and Tamora, he recounts the story of her rape. Titus then stabs Tamora, and in response, Saturninus stabs and kills Titus. Lucius avenges his father's murder by killing the emperor and then tells the story of what has befallen the Andronici family to the Romans who have gathered at the house.

Lucius is proclaimed emperor, and the play concludes by outlining the punishment decided upon for Aaron. He is to be buried up to his chest and left to starve. Titus and Lavinia are to be buried in the family tomb, while Tamora's corpse is to be thrown outside the city walls for animals to feed upon.

CHARACTER LIST

Saturninus The eldest son of the dead emperor, who succeeds his father when Titus Andronicus endorses his claim to the emperorship. Saturninus fears and resents Titus who has the support of ordinary Romans, and he plots with Tamora, the queen of the Goths, to avenge himself on the Andronici family for the humiliation he feels he suffers at their hands.

Bassianus The younger brother of Saturninus, who is secretly betrothed to Titus's daughter Lavinia. Bassianus is murdered by Tamora's sons, Demetrius and Chiron.

Titus Andronicus A Roman general whose victories against the Goths have made him famous. While Titus embodies the qualities of military valor and loyalty to Rome, he is a flawed character whose pride, concern with a strict code of honor, and failure to be merciful trigger a series of events that result in the decimation of the Andronici family.

Marcus Andronicus The brother of Titus Andronicus and a tribune, who intervenes in the conflict between Saturninus and Bassianus to present the people's view that Titus should serve as emperor. In the final scene of the play, he serves as chorus to explain to Lucius, Titus's only remaining son, who returns to liberate Rome, what has happened during his absence.

Lucius The eldest surviving son of Titus Andronicus, who is sent by his father to raise a Goth army to liberate Rome from Saturninus and Tamora, and who is nominated as emperor at the play's conclusion.

Quintus and Martius The two sons who are blamed for the murder of Bassianus through the plotting of Aaron, Tamora, and her sons Chiron and Demetrius. They are executed on the orders of Saturninus without a trial.

Mutius The youngest son of Titus, who supports the union between Bassianus and Lavinia when Saturninus offers to marry Lavinia himself. When he ensures the lovers escape and defends Bassianus, Titus kills him in a fit of rage.

Lavinia The daughter of Titus and wife of Bassianus, who is raped and mutilated by Chiron and Demetrius.

Young Lucius The son of Lucius and grandson of Titus, he remains with his grandfather when Lucius leaves Rome.

Publius   The son of Marcus.

Sempronius   A relative of Titus.

Caius   A relative of Titus.

Valentine   A relative of Titus.

Emillius   A Roman.

A Clown   A simple man who delivers Titus's letter to Saturninus that demands justice.

Tamora   The queen of the Goths who becomes the wife of the emperor Saturninus. Tamora is stabbed by Titus at his banquet, where he first feeds Tamora a pie containing her sons Chiron and Demetrius.

Alarbus   The eldest son of Tamora, who is sacrificed by Titus and his sons as part of the burial rites for their dead relatives.

Demetrius and Chiron   The surviving sons of Tamora, who rape and mutilate Lavinia. Titus avenges himself upon them by killing them and then serves their heads and blood in a pie to their mother.

Aaron   An evil Moor who is Tamora's lover. Their union produces a baby that Aaron protects from being murdered by Tamora's sons. Aaron is buried alive at the play's conclusion.

CHARACTER STUDIES
Titus Andronicus

Titus, the great general and head of the Andronici family, embodies those Roman qualities of valor, honor, military success, and a devotion to the state. It is Titus's belief in these Roman values that establishes both the strengths of his character and also some of its weaknesses. It is through his protagonist that Shakespeare examines the ways in which Rome and its virtues have become corrupted.

In the first scene of the play, Titus's reputation and behavior provoke a series of contradictory responses in the audience. On the one hand, he is to be admired as a conqueror and is hailed as war hero by fellow soldiers and family as he returns to Rome after a successful campaign against the Goths. He is "Renowned Titus" and "Rome's best champion," and he is also celebrated for his integrity as a "Patron of virtue." Titus describes his service to the state using an elaborate metaphor in which he presents himself as a merchant ship returning after a dangerous voyage and bringing back a rich cargo:

> Lo, as the bark that hath discharged his fraught
> Returns with precious lading to the bay
> From whence at first she weighed her
>   anchorage
> Cometh Andronicus, bound with laurel
>   boughs,
> To re-salute his country with tears,
> Tears of true joy for his return to Rome.

Titus presents his victory against the Goths and his prisoners as a tribute to his city. Titus's reputation as a successful military leader makes him the people's candidate to become the emperor: "A nobler man, a braver warrior / Lives not this day within the city walls." On the other hand, this portrait of Titus established in the first part of the opening scene of the play is then contrasted with a series of decisions made by Titus that immediately calls into question the values of the man who has just been celebrated. Titus's triumphant entrance into the city of Rome is tempered by the knowledge that the war has cost him 21 of his 25 sons and that his first concern is to perform the proper burial rites for his dead children. Before interring his sons in the family tomb, Titus explains that tradition requires the sacrifice of one of his enemies, and for that purpose, he selects Alarbus, the eldest son of Tamora, queen of the Goths. Despite his position as a grieving father who should perhaps have encouraged sympathy for Tamora, Titus is impassive as she begs him to spare her son:

> Stay, Roman brethren, gracious conqueror,
> Victorious Titus, rue the tears I shed,
> A mother's tears in passion for her son;
> And if thy sons were ever dear to thee,
> O, think my son to be as dear to me.

The appeal for mercy is disregarded by Titus, and his rigid adherence to the performance of a human sacrifice immediately complicates the view of Titus presented so far, since here he appears unbending and without compassion. This decision calls into the question the reputation of Rome and its inhabitants as civilized and cultured in comparison with the wild, barbarous Goths.

When the tribunes offer Titus the emperorship, he refuses to accept it, arguing that he is a soldier rather than a politician:

> Rome, I have been thy soldier forty years,
> And led my country's strength successfully,
> And buried one and twenty sons,
> Knighted in field, slain manfully in arms,
> In right and service of their noble country.
> Give me a staff of honor for mine age,
> But not a sceptre to rule the world.

Titus uses the support he has to persuade the people to follow his choice of Saturninus as emperor. Once again, Titus supports tradition, favoring primogeniture, the law of inheritance that favors the inheritance of the eldest son. Titus, therefore, supports Saturninus instead of Bassianus, who argues that unlike his elder brother he has the qualities and virtues that would make him an effective leader rather than simply having the advantage of being the first born.

The relationship between the individual and the state is brought under further scrutiny through Saturninus's decision to honor the Andronici family by selecting Lavinia as his new bride. Titus is clearly flattered by the decision—"I hold me highly honoured of your grace"—but his joy quickly turns to anger when Bassianus reveals that Lavinia is already betrothed to him and that the proposed marriage has the support of Titus's sons. This challenge to both Titus's position as Lavinia's father and to Saturninus as emperor is too much for Titus; he brands his sons traitors and reacts to Mutius's decision to help the lovers escape by killing him. Here Titus's behavior underlines the ways in which he privileges loyalty to the state and concern for family honor above paternal feelings for his own son or daughter. As a result of these feelings, Titus initially refuses to allow Mutius to be buried in the family tomb until his brother Marcus reminds him:

"Thou art a Roman, be not barbarous." These lines serve to emphasize the ways in which Roman values have degenerated, so that it becomes difficult to believe that the Romans do have a clear code of virtuous principles. When Saturninus rejects the Andronici family for their part in publicly humiliating him through their support for Bassianus, Titus is dismayed that the emperor, whom he has just helped secure the election, is able to dismiss him so quickly and he exclaims: "These words are razors to my heart." By the end of Act I, Titus appears to combine a series of contradictory qualities. He is brave, with a reputation that inspires loyalty, yet he acts in a cruel and merciless way against Alarbus, Tamora's son, and against his own son Mutius, ordering the killing of one son and, more shockingly still, stabbing the other with his own sword. Titus's failure to heed Tamora's pleas for mercy precipitates the revenge plot against Titus and his family, as Tamora seeks to avenge herself for the killing of her son. The decision to support Saturninus also backfires on Titus as the emperor frees the Goths and makes his enemy, Tamora, his empress.

Certainly Titus makes a number of mistakes in the first scene, but as the play progresses and the revenge plot against him swings into action our feelings toward him turn to pity as we see the ways in which Tamora's revenge exceeds all expectations. The first part of that revenge plot focuses on the framing of Martius and Quintus for the murder of Bassianus. Titus is keen that his sons be given a fair trial and be able to answer the accusations leveled against them, but Saturninus refuses and orders their execution without delay. In Act III, Scene 1, Titus is forced to plead to the tribunes for his sons' lives:

> O reverend tribunes! O gentle, aged men!
> Unbind my sons, reverse the doom of death,
> And let me say (that never wept before)
> My tears are now prevailing orators.

Titus's situation here recalls Tamora's position in the opening scene of the play as she attempted to appeal for mercy, and like Tamora, his calls go unheeded, and he concludes: "Rome is but a wilderness of tigers / Tigers must prey, and Rome affords no prey but me and mine." This imagery is important as it emphasizes the way in which the city under Saturnine's command has become wild and uncivilized.

In Act III of the play, Titus's grief is intensified by the appearance of Lavinia, and he is overwhelmed with emotion:

> For now I stand as one upon a rock,
> Environed with a wilderness of sea,
> Who marks the waxing tide grow wave by wave,
> Expecting ever when some envious surge
> Will in his brinish bowels swallow him.

He still believes, however, that these horrific crimes against him and his children will not go unheeded by the gods:

> For heaven shall hear our prayers,
> Or with our sighs we'll breathe the whelkin
>   dim
> And stain the sun with fog, as sometime
>   clouds
> When they do hug him with their melting
>   bosoms.

His faith in the gods and their ability to intervene in the lives of men is tested by the return of his own severed hand and his sons' heads. Titus responds to these escalating horrors with laughter, and when Marcus asks "Why dost thou laugh? It fits not with this hour," Titus explains that he can no longer grieve and shed tears for what has happened:

> Why, I have not another tear to shed.
> Besides this sorrow is an enemy,
> And would usurp upon my wat'ry eyes,
> And make them blind with tributary tears;
> Then which way shall I find Revenge's cave?

The laughter is unexpected and, as Marcus suggests, is an inappropriate response that seems to jar in the face of these events. Titus's laughter and his explanation, however, suggests that the situa-

tion is so extreme that grief no longer seems the appropriate response; the killings and mutilation have almost become absurd. It is at this point in the play that Titus decides he must take revenge rather than simply stand by and grieve. Titus's grief now manifests itself in moments of black humor when he makes jokes about the loss of his own and Lavinia's hands. He tells his brother Marcus:

> O, handle not the theme, to talk of hands,
> Lest we remember that we have none.
> Fie, fie, how frantically I square my talk,
> As if we should forget we have no hands,
> If Marcus did not name that word of hands!

When Titus discovers that Chiron and Demetrius are responsible for the attack on Lavinia, he begins to plot his revenge against them and their mother. He begins by sending Chiron and Demetrius weapons wrapped in a Latin poem that indicates he has identified them as his enemy. Although Titus takes some pleasure in displaying his cunning as a revenger, his behavior in Act IV also indicates that he is torn between securing justice for himself and his family via the law and taking revenge that involves stepping outside the law. In Act IV, Scene 3, Titus fires arrows to the gods in an attempt to secure justice from the gods. One of the arrows carries the Latin motto *"Terras Astraea reliquit,"* which means "Astraea the goddess of justice has left the earth," so Titus appeals to gods to intervene in the affairs of men. When the gods appear deaf to Titus's pleas, he continues with his own efforts to secure his own justice through revenge. Like many revenge heroes including Hieronimo in *The Spanish Tragedy* and Hamlet, Titus chooses to execute his revenge using a theatrical device, in this case he invites his enemies to a banquet that he as the chef has carefully stage-managed. Since it is the story of Philomel that has provided the means by which Lavinia's rape is explained, Titus chooses to use the story of the revenge exacted by Philomel and her sister Progne upon her rapist, Tereus. The two sisters invited Tereus to a feast, and they feed Tereus a pie that contains the body of his son. Tereus only realizes what the pie contains when Progne throws his son's head at him while he is eating. Titus explains the appropriateness of the manner of their death to Chiron and Demetrius:

> Hark, villains, I will grind your bones to dust,
> And with your blood and it I'll make a paste,
> And of the paste a coffin I will rear,
> And make two pasties of your shameful heads,
> And bid that strumpet, your unhallowed dam,
> Like to the earth swallow her own increase.
> This is the feast that I have bid her to,
> And this the banket she shall surfeit on,
> For worse than Philomel you us'd my
>   daughter,
> And worse than Progne I will be reveng'd.

In the final scene of the play, audience response to Titus is once again complicated by his role as revenger. On the one hand, the audience is part of the plot against Tamora and Saturninus as we know what the pie is made of and can derive some satisfaction from the appropriate nature of their killing. On the other hand, it is also apparent that Titus has become obsessed by his quest for revenge and that events are spiraling out of control. In one final shocking moment, Titus considers the story of Virginius, a Roman centurion, and his daughter Virginia, whom he killed to prevent her rape by Appius Claudius. Titus suggests that the story has parallels with his own and kills Lavinia explaining: "I am as woeful as Virginius was, / And have a thousand times more cause than he / To do this outrage." Although the killing of Lavinia does not prevent her rape as it did in the case of Virginia, it underlines Titus's continuing concern with family honor and the belief that a raped daughter is a symbol of shame. Titus, having first stabbed Tamora, is then killed by Saturninus. The play's conclusion offers a bleak view of Titus's experience as we are left to ponder whether he had in fact learned anything. The killing of Lavinia seems difficult to reconcile with the earlier scenes in the play when Titus appeared as a father caring for his daughter. Titus seems even at the end to adhere to those Roman values that have been shown to be so destructive.

Lavinia

Lavinia's function in the play is to be gazed upon, first as an object of desire and later as an object of pity. Lavinia is defined by her relationships with her father and husband, and in this way, the play examines the role of women in Rome and the effects of a patriarchal society upon the relationships between men and women. In the opening scene of the play, Bassianus describes Titus's daughter as "Gracious Lavinia, Rome's rich ornament," while Titus calls her "The cordial of mine age to glad my heart." Lavinia as Titus's daughter is an object of exchange between her father and other men in the play, and the proposed marriage between Lavinia and Saturninus is used to cement the bonds between the new emperor and his supporter and to confer honor upon the Andronici family: to advance / Thy name and honourable family / Lavinia will I make my empress, Rome's royal mistress, mistress of my heart." The secret betrothal of Lavinia to Bassianus suggests that Titus has neglected to properly police his daughter's affections. When Bassianus lays his claim to Lavinia and reveals they are in fact betrothed, the relationship is described in terms that suggest both rape and theft. Titus exclaims "Treason my lord! Lavinia is surprised," while Saturninus warns his brother, "Thou and thy faction shall repent this rape." Here, the term *rape* is used to suggest theft or abduction rather than sexual attack, but nevertheless the play invites comparison between the ideas of marriage expressed in the play and the different meanings of the word *rape*. Lavinia's value is as the chaste daughter of Titus whose marriage will increase the family honor. Lavinia's reputation as a virgin provides Tamora with the means by which she can attack Titus and begin her campaign of vengeance, since an attack on Lavinia is an attack upon her father. Aaron describes Lavinia in the context of the story of Lucrece, who like Lavinia was noted for her chastity and was raped by the lustful Tarquin: "Lucrece was not more chaste / Than this

Lavinia." Later in the wood, Lavinia goads Tamora by alluding to her affair with Aaron, and Demetrius resolves to punish Lavinia by destroying her reputation: "This minion stood upon her chastity, / Upon her nuptial vow, her loyalty / And with that painted hope braves your mightiness; / And shall she carry this unto her grave?"

Critics such as Alexander Legatt have examined the symbolic nature of location in the play to examine the relationship between the Andronici tomb and the pit in the wood. Leggatt argues that just as the distinction between civilized Roman and barbarous Goth begin to break down in the play, so the tomb, which should represent order and family honor, becomes tainted by the sacrifice of Alarbus and the killing of Mutius. Tamora

Lavinia in *Titus Andronicus*. This is a print from Charles Heath's 1848 edition of *The Heroines of Shakspeare: Comprising the Principal Female Characters in the Plays of the Great Poet. (Painting by J. W. Wright; engraving by W. H. Mote)*

begs Titus "stain not thy tomb with blood," but is ignored. The boundaries or differences between the Andronici tomb and the pit also begin to blur. The pit is described in terms that suggest it is a sexual image. As the rape cannot be shown, the play provides a verbal analogy using the description of the pit by Quintus and Martius. Quintus asks:

> What subtle hole is this,
> Whose mouth is covered with rude-growing
>   briers,
> Upon whose leaves are drops of new-shed
>   blood
> As fresh as morning dew distilled on flowers.

Martius begs his brother to rescue him from "this unhallowed and bloodstained hole." Like the family tomb, the pit becomes a bloody hole, and this blurring of the two images is used to suggest the breakdown of Rome and its values, from symbols of family and wider social order to the horror and chaos of the pit in the woods.

After the rape and mutilation, Lavinia becomes ever more reliant upon her father and family, depending upon them to interpret and speak for her. Titus's description of his role as interpreter underlines the violence that has already been done to Lavinia's body and which the act of interpreting or reading her body reenacts:

> Speechless complainer, I will learn thy
>   thought.
> In thy dumb action will I be as perfect
> As begging hermits in their holy prayers.
> Thou shalt not sigh, nor hold thy stumps to
>   heaven,
> Nor wink, nor nod, nor kneel, nor make a sign,
> But I of these will wrest an alphabet
> And by still practice learn to know thy
>   meaning.

The descriptions of Lavinia's suffering, however, tend to emphasize its effect upon the male speaker. For example, when Titus first sees his daughter, the sight of her severed limbs causes him to reflect upon Rome's ingratitude toward him:

> Speak Lavinia, what accursed hand
> Hath made thee handless in thy father's sight?
> . . .
> Give me a sword, I'll chop off my hands too;
> For they have fought for Rome and all in vain
> . . .
> 'Tis well, Lavinia, that thou hast no hand,
> For hands to do Rome service is but vain.

Although the rape reinforces Lavinia's powerless position within Roman society, she does perhaps gain a certain amount of control or agency as she contributes to the revenge plot against Chiron and Demetrius, but Titus's decision to compare the story of Lavinia to the story of Virginia, who was killed by her father to prevent her from being raped and thus to preserve the family honor, offers a bleak view of the position of women in Roman society.

Aaron

In the character of Aaron, Shakespeare presents a complex portrait of villainy. The Moor clearly delights in his own cunning and the evil plots he lays against the Andronici family, and yet his cruelty is tempered by his own display of paternal care for his child by Tamora. The enjoyment Aaron derives from his own evil behavior as well as his intimate relationship with the audience indicate that his character was influenced by the stage tradition of the Vice from medieval morality plays. Vice was a popular character, often depicted as a devilish tempter of innocent souls, whose role involved entertaining the audience with tales of his wickedness. Aaron is also often referred to as a Stage Machiavel, a term that refers to a character type found in Elizabethan and Jacobean plays, who acts according to the principles suggested by the Italian political theorist Niccolò Machiavelli in his treatise on statecraft. It was thought that Machiavelli's ideas encouraged ruthless, unprincipled behavior based on the idea that success or power should be achieved by any means. Other examples of the

Elizabethan Stage Machiavel included the scheming and unscrupulous Barabas in Christopher Marlowe's *The Jew of Malta* and Lorenzo in Thomas Kyd's *The Spanish Tragedy*. Shakespeare would go on to develop this role in subsequent plays such as *Richard III* in his portrait of the dangerous yet charismatic Richard of Gloucester and in the characters of Iago in *Othello* and Edmund in *King Lear*. Stage Machiavels have a special relationship with the audience, as they frequently make use of the soliloquy or the comic aside to draw the audience into their confidence and implicate them in their plans. Shakespeare makes use of the soliloquy in *Titus Andronicus* when Aaron describes his relationship with Tamora in Act II, Scene 1 and later to explain why he is burying the bag of gold in the forest clearing in Act II, Scene 3. When Aaron brings news in Act III, Scene 1, that Martius and Quintus are to be ransomed in exchange for a hand of one of the Andronici family, Titus immediately places his trust in Aaron's words, overjoyed at the news that his sons might be spared despite the physical cost to himself: "With all my heart I'll send the Emperor my hand," but through the use of the aside the audience is made aware that this offer of hope is a diabolical lie:

> I go Andronicus; and for thy hand
> Look by and by to have thy sons with thee.
> *(Aside)* Their heads I mean. O, how this
>   villainy
> Doth fat me with the thought of it!
> Let fools do good and fair men call for grace;
> Aaron will have his soul black like his face.

This knowledge makes the return of the hand seem even more cruel as we know how disappointed and grieved Titus is destined to be.

Aaron is an outsider in Rome due to his identity as a Moor. He is the first of three Moorish characters that Shakespeare includes in his plays. The other examples are the Prince of Morocco in *The Merchant of Venice,* who comes to Belmont as one of Portia's suitors, and the other is the heroic military general Othello who marries Desdemona,

Illustration of Ira Aldridge as Aaron in the Britannia Theatre's 1852 production of *Titus Andronicus*. This is a plate from Tallis's *Shakespeare Gallery of Engravings*.

a white Venetian woman. Moors were members of the Berber and Arab tribes who lived in Morocco and North Africa. Often the term *Moor* was used by the Elizabethans to refer to someone who was black and non-Christian and to suggest that they were less than human. We can see these attitudes at work in *Titus Andronicus* when Aaron is referred to as "misbelieving Moor," while his black skin is regarded as the outward sign of his evil nature, so he is compared to devils and dogs: "incarnate devil," "so foul a fiend," and "hellish dog." While Aaron seems to conform to the stereotype of an evil Moor, Shakespeare problematizes our response to him, partly by making him so charismatic, but also by the way in which he makes him a caring father. When the Nurse brings Aaron's son to him, she describes the baby's appearance: "As loath-

some as a toad / Amongst the fair-faced breeders of our clime." Aaron immediately challenges her: "Zounds ye whore! Is black so base a hue? / Sweet blowse, you are a beauteous blossom sure." In a surprise reversal of his usually murderous behavior, Aaron is contrasted with Tamora and Titus in the way that he offers care and affection toward his child. At the beginning of the play, Aaron seems to be motivated in his revenge plots by his loyalty to Tamora, but as the play progresses, Aaron's motivation becomes less clear; the audience senses that he simply enjoys boasting of his evil deeds and his own cleverness in their execution. In the final scenes of the play, he recounts a catalog of different crimes:

> Oft have I digged up dead men from their
> graves,
> And set them upright at their dear friends'
> door,
> Even when their sorrows almost was forgot,
> And on their skins, as on the barks of trees,
> Have with my knife carved in Roman letters
> 'Let not your sorrow die, though I am dead.'

His only regret is that "I cannot do ten thousand more." Lucius's punishment of Aaron in the final scene of the play with a slow death leaves a feeling of unfinished business at the end of the play, since Aaron's voice is not finally silenced, suggesting that there will always be evil characters like him for Lucius to deal with.

Tamora

Tamora, is the queen of the Goths and the mother of Alarbus, Chiron, and Demetrius. Since their defeat by the Romans, Tamora and her children are at the mercy of their Roman captors. The play immediately begins to challenge audience expectations of the differences between Romans and Goths when Titus and his sons propose a human sacrifice of Alarbus, Tamora's eldest son, and the queen begs for his life:

> Victorious Titus, rue the tears I shed,
> A mother's tears in passion for her son;

And if thy sons were ever dear to thee,
O, think my son to be as dear to me!

Tamora's speech is eloquent and invites Titus to consider their mutual role as parents and in particular her position as a mother. Tamora's cries for mercy are contrasted with Titus's lack of compassion and human feeling. Demetrius, Tamora's son, provides his mother with a classical precedent for seeking her revenge against Titus when he recalls the story of Hecuba, the queen of Troy, who exacted her revenge against Polymnestor, the king of Thrace, for the killing of her son Polydorus by killing Polymnestor's sons:

The self-same gods that arm'd the Queen of
  Troy
With opportunity of sharp revenge
Upon the Thracian tyrant in his tent
May favour Tamora, the Queen of Goths.

Saturninus's decision to marry Tamora in place of Lavinia provides the Gothic queen with the opportunity to act against the Andronici family with impunity:

I'll find a day to massacre them all,
And raze their faction and their family,
The cruel father and his traitorous sons,
To whom I sued for my dear son's life;
And make them know what 'tis to let a queen
Kneel in the streets and beg for grace in vain.

Tamora's role as an outsider is underlined by her association with another outsider, Aaron. During her clandestine meeting with Aaron, she compares them with a famous pair of lovers from classical myth, Dido, the queen of Carthage and Aeneas, the Trojan prince:

Aaron, let us sit,
And, whilst the babbling echo mocks the
  hounds,
Replying shrilly to the well-tuned horns,
As if a double hunt were heard at once,

Let us sit down and mark their yelping noise;
And, after conflict such as was supposed
The wandering prince and Dido once enjoy'd,
When with a happy storm they were surprised
And curtain'd with a counsel-keeping cave,
We may, each wreathed in the other's arms,
Our pastimes done, possess a golden slumber

The comparison that Tamora makes between herself and Dido is important, as it underlines her identity as a foreign queen, an outsider in Rome. Dido fell in love with Aeneas and attempted to keep him with her in her kingdom, but since Aeneas's destiny was to found Rome, he eventually left Dido and when he did so the queen took her own life. By looking back to stories of Rome's founding father, the play seems to be remembering threats to empire that came in the form of a foreign

Tamora watches as Chiron and Demetrius drag Lavinia away in Act II, Scene 3 of *Titus Andronicus*. *(Illustration by John Thurston; engraving by Allen Robert Branston)*

queen. This speech is used to suggest that Rome under Saturninus becomes weakened through its association with Tamora and her offspring.

Although Tamora is described by other characters as lascivious—Lavinia, for example, calls her Semiramis, the name of the Assyrian queen who was known for her lusty reputation—the play invites its audience to compare the weaknesses in her character with those of the other male characters such as Titus. In Act II, Scene 3, Tamora explains that her refusal to show pity to Lavinia is a direct response to Titus's own behavior:

> Remember, boys, I pour'd forth tears in vain
> To save your brother from the sacrifice,
> But fierce Andronicus would not relent,
> Therefore away with her, and use her as you will;
> The worse to her, the better lov'd of me.

Later in the play, Tamora believes that she, like Aaron, can out-jest Titus when she decides to disguise herself as the figure of Revenge. She hopes that she can manipulate Titus's obsession with revenge for her own ends and thwart the invasion by Lucius and his Gothic forces. Unfortunately, Tamora underestimates Titus, believing that he is mad, and allows Titus to hijack her role as stage dramatist. Titus goes on to put on the banquet where he feeds Tamora her sons in a pie before stabbing her to death.

DIFFICULTIES OF THE PLAY

Titus Andronicus offers a number of challenges to both the reader and the theatergoer. The first of these is the number of classical allusions in the play that may be unfamiliar to a modern audience, including references to the stories of Philomel and Lucrece as well as Coriolanus, Dido, and Aeneas. Furthermore, the repeated use of such references contributes to the play's highly artificial rhetorical style. Often audiences have been baffled by the stylized poetic language used by characters as they bear witness to scenes of human suffering and misery. The best example of this is Marcus's response to his niece in Act II, Scene 4. Many critics have

insisted that his metaphorical language distances Marcus from the horror before him. Others have suggested that the lengthy, elaborate speech is used to signal the failure of language to accurately describe or simply put into words what can be seen.

In addition to the different styles of writing found in the play, there is also the issue of how to respond to the violence itself. S. Clark Hulse has provided the following list of atrocities in the play: "14 killings, 9 of them on stage, 6 severed members, 1 rape (or 2, depending on how you count), 1 live burial, 1 case of insanity and 1 of cannibalism—an average of 5.2 atrocities per act, or one for every 97 lines."

In her discussion of violence in Shakespeare's plays, Deborah Cartmell pinpoints one of the major stumbling blocks for a modern audience in responding to *Titus Andronicus:* "Arguably the most filmic of all Shakespeare plays is *Titus Andronicus;* a play which resembles Quentin Tarantino's *Reservoir Dogs* (1992) or *Pulp Fiction* (1994) in its unnerving blend of violence and humour."

As a revenge tragedy, the play mixes comedy and tragedy. Moments of black comedy are often used, not to provide some relief to the audience, but rather to reinforce the pathos of particular scenes and make more acute the suffering of particular characters. In Act II, Scene 4, for example, Chiron and Demetrius mock Lavinia, but the effect here is to underline their barbarity:

> DEMETRIUS. So, now go tell, and if thy
>   tongue can speak,
> Who 'twas that cut thy tongue and ravished
>   thee
>
> CHIRON. Write down thy mind, bewray thy
>   meaning so,
> And if thy stumps will let thee, play the scribe.

Aaron also engages in macabre humor as he mimics the sound made by the Nurse as he murders her:

> The empress, the midwife and yourself.
> Two may keep counsel when the third's away.

Go to the empress, tell her this I said:
[*He kills her*]
'Wheak, wheak!'—so cries a pig prepared to
the spit.

Aaron's role as the stage villain complicates the audience's position in relation to the acts of violence he commits, since his brand is seductive and we laugh when we know we ought not to. The play also draws attention to the absurdity of the situation in which Titus, Marcus, and Lucius all compete to cut off their own hand:

AARON. Nay, come, agree whose hand shall
go along
For fear they die before their pardon come

MARCUS. My hand shall go.

LUCIUS. By heaven it shall not go.

Jokes about the loss of hands recur throughout the play. They often serve to underline the fragmented nature of Rome and question the services performed by individuals in the name of the state. The amount of laughter the play inspires depends on how its violence is staged. See the Modern Criticism and Critical Controversies section.

KEY PASSAGES
Act I, Scene 1, 104–130

TAMORA. Stay, Roman brethren! Gracious
conqueror,
Victorious Titus, rue the tears I shed,
A mother's tears in passion for her son;
And if thy sons were ever dear to thee,
O, think my son to be as dear to me!
Sufficeth not that we are brought to Rome,
To beautify thy triumphs, and return
Captive to thee and to thy Roman yoke;
But must my sons be slaughtered in the streets,
For valiant doings in their country's cause?
O, if to fight for king and commonweal
Were piety in thine, it is in these.
Andronicus, stain not thy tomb with blood!

Wilt thou draw near the nature of the gods?
Draw near them then in being merciful:
Sweet mercy is nobility's true badge:
Thrice-noble Titus, spare my first-born son!

TITUS ANDRONICUS. Patient yourself,
madam, and pardon me.
These are their brethren, whom you Goths
beheld
Alive and dead, and for their brethren slain
Religiously they ask a sacrifice:
To this your son is mark'd, and die he must,
T' appease their groaning shadows that are gone.

LUCIUS. Away with him, and make a fire
straight,
And with our swords, upon a pile of wood,
Let's hew his limbs till they be clean consum'd.
Exeunt Titus' sons with Alarbus

TAMORA. O cruel, irreligious piety!

This important passage is the moment in the play when Titus agrees to sacrifice Alarbus, the eldest son of Tamora, queen of the Goths, thus precipitating the revenge plot that culminates in the decimation of the Andronici family. The play opens with a series of public rituals, including the election of the emperor and the return of the triumphant Roman army led by Titus, who brings with him not only the Goth prisoners but also the bodies of his dead sons for burial in the family tomb. The opening scene would therefore appear to underline the clear differences between Romans and Goths, and yet Shakespeare immediately disrupts the sense of civilized and barbarous characters through Titus's disregard for Tamora's pleas that her son be spared, in order to scrutinize the values that underpin Rome and its sense of identity. Titus's dramatic entrance in his chariot, together with the accounts of his bravery as "Rome's best champion," indicates that he exemplifies the Roman concepts of *virtus* and *pietas,* which refer to the masculine qualities of valor, military prowess, and loyalty to the state. Titus's rigid adherence to these values has in fact had a negative effect, upon Titus as an individual and more widely upon Rome itself. As a father who is grieving for the loss of 21 sons, Titus could demonstrate compassion in this situation, but he does not, and is ruthless in his dismissal of Tamora's call for mercy. The blind adherence to barbaric human sacrifice to appease the ghosts of his dead sons and fulfill a bloody ritual out of a sense of honor is the first example we are given that Titus is suffering from a moral blindness and is a flawed Roman hero. Tamora's oxymoron "O cruel irreligious piety" indicates that the murder of Alarbus cannot be excused as a ritual killing.

Lucius's description of the sacrifice, "Alarbus' limbs are lopped," foreshadows the later rape and mutilation of Lavinia. Tamora does not simply avenge herself upon Titus by murdering Titus's children but chooses to increase his suffering by the grotesque manner of their torture and deaths.

Act II, Scene 3, 10–50

TAMORA. My lovely Aaron, wherefore look'st thou sad,
When every thing doth make a gleeful boast?
The birds chant melody on every bush,
The [snake] lies rolled in the cheerful sun,
The green leaves quiver with the cooling wind
And make a chequer'd shadow on the ground.
Under their sweet shade, Aaron, let us sit,
And whilst the babbling echo mocks the hounds,
Replying shrilly to the well-tun'd horns,
As if a double hunt were heard at once,
Let us sit down and mark their yelping noise;
And, after conflict such as was suppos'd
The wand'ring prince and Dido once enjoyed,
When with a happy storm they were surpris'd
And curtain'd with a counsel-keeping cave,
We may, each wreathed in the other's arms,
(Our pastimes done), possess a golden slumber,
Whiles hounds and horns and sweet melodious birds
Be unto us as is a nurse's song
Of lullaby to bring her babe asleep.

AARON. Madam, though Venus govern your desires,
Saturn is dominator over mine:
What signifies my deadly-standing eye,
My silence, an' my cloudy melancholy,
My fleece of woolly hair that now uncurls,
Even as an adder when she doth unroll
To do some fatal execution?
No, madam, these are no venereal signs.
Vengeance is in my heart, death in my hand,
Blood and revenge are hammering in my head,
Hark, Tamora, the empress of my soul,
Which never hopes more heaven than rests in thee,
This is the day of doom for Bassianus:
His Philomel must lose her tongue to-day,
Thy sons make pillage of her chastity,
And wash their hands in Bassianus' blood.
Seest thou this letter? take it up, I pray thee,
And give the King this fatal-plotted scroll.
Now question me no more, we are espied.
Here comes a parcel of our hopeful booty,
Which dreads not yet their lives' destruction.

This scene signals the shift from the Capitol in Rome, which served as the backdrop for the first act of the play, to the countryside and the wood where Titus has invited the emperor and his wife to hunt with him as a sign of the amity between them. The wood is initially characterized as a positive greenwood world by Titus as he prepares for the hunt: "The hunt is up, the morn is bright and grey / The fields are fragrant and the woods are green." These lines are imbued with a sense of irony as the audience is aware that Chiron and Demetrius have plotted to rape Lavinia in the wood during the hunt:

The forest walks are wide and spacious
And many unfrequented plots there are,
Fitted by kind for rape and villainy.

Aaron explains that unlike the emperor's palace, which is "full of tongues, of eyes and ears," the woods will provide a suitable spot for their plans since it is "ruthless, dreadful, deaf and dull." In this scene, Tamora also regards the wood as a place of concealment and therefore an appropriate place for an assignation with her lover, Aaron. Tamora's lyrical description of the woods as a pastoral idyll is ironic, since it will be a place of rape and violation rather than of passion between two lovers. While Tamora alludes to the meeting in a wood of the famous classical lovers Dido and Aeneas to figure her meeting with Aaron, the Moor also draws upon a classical story, but in Aaron's case, he recounts the rape of Philomel taken from Ovid's *Metamorphoses.* The story describes how Tereus, the king of Thrace, marries Progne, but he also lusts after Progne's sister Philomel and satisfies his desire by raping Philomel in a wood. To conceal his identity and the crime, Tereus cuts out Philomel's tongue. The crime is discovered when Philomel sews the event onto a sampler and identifies her rapist. The two sisters Philomel and Progne then avenge themselves upon Tereus by killing his son Itys and serving him in a pie to Tereus. Aaron's use of Philomel as a classical analogy for Lavinia serves to build the dramatic tension before the rape of Lavinia, while also anticipating the ways in which the crime perpetrated against Lavinia will be exposed and avenged by Titus. Lavinia uses the story of Philomel in Ovid to communicate what has happened to her in Act IV of the play while Titus draws on the strategies of revenge employed by Progne and Philomel, since he, too, serves a pie containing the heads of Demetrius and Chiron to Tamora and Saturninus.

Act III, Scene 1, 81–137

LUCIUS. Speak, gentle sister, who hath martyr'd thee?

MARCUS ANDRONICUS. O, that delightful engine of her thoughts,
That blabb'd them with such pleasing eloquence,
Is torn from forth that pretty hollow cage,
Where, like a sweet melodious bird, it sung
Sweet varied notes, enchanting every ear!

LUCIUS. O, say thou for her, who hath done this deed?

MARCUS ANDRONICUS O, thus I found her, straying in the park,
Seeking to hide herself, as doth the deer
That hath received some unrecuring wound.

TITUS ANDRONICUS. It was my dear, and he that wounded her
Hath hurt me more than had he kill'd me dead:
For now I stand as one upon a rock,
Environ'd with a wilderness of sea,
Who marks the waxing tide grow wave by wave,
Expecting ever when some envious surge
Will in his brinish bowels swallow him.
This way to death my wretched sons are gone,
Here stands my other son, a banish'd man,
And here my brother, weeping at my woes;
But that which gives my soul the greatest spurn,
Is dear Lavinia, dearer than my soul.
Had I but seen thy picture in this plight,
It would have madded me; what shall I do
Now I behold thy lively body so?
Thou hast no hands, to wipe away thy tears,
Nor tongue, to tell me who hath mart'red thee.
Thy husband he is dead, and for his death
Thy brothers are condemn'd, and dead by this.
Look, Marcus! ah, son Lucius, look on her!
When I did name her brothers, then fresh tears
Stood on her cheeks, as doth the honey-dew
Upon a gather'd lily almost withered.

MARCUS ANDRONICUS. Perchance she weeps because they kill'd her husband,
Perchance because she knows them innocent.

TITUS ANDRONICUS. If they did kill thy husband, then be joyful,
Because the law hath ta'en revenge on them.

No, no, they would not do so foul a deed;
Witness the sorrow that their sister makes.
Gentle Lavinia, let me kiss thy lips,
Or make some sign how I may do thee ease.
Shall thy good uncle, and thy brother Lucius,
And thou, and I, sit round about some
    fountain,
Looking all downwards to behold our cheeks,
How they are stain'd, as meadows yet not dry,
With miry slime left on them by a flood?
And in the fountain shall we gaze so long
Till the fresh taste be taken from that
    clearness,
And made a brine-pit with our bitter tears?
Or shall we cut away our hands, like thine?
Or shall we bite our tongues, and in dumb
    shows
Pass the remainder of our hateful days?
What shall we do? Let us, that have our
    tongues,
Plot some deuce of further misery,
To make us wonder'd at in time to come.

LUCIUS. Sweet father, cease your tears; for, at
    your grief,
See how my wretched sister sobs and weeps.

This passage comes from another long scene in the play, which is made up of 300 lines and can be divided into a clearly marked sequence of actions and events. It is a pivotal scene that charts the relentless buildup of horrific acts aimed at Titus and his children. The opening of the scene witnesses the rejection by the tribunes of Titus's pleas for justice and mercy for his sons Martius and Quintus, who have been condemned to death for the murder of Bassianus, and his son Lucius has been banished from Rome for attempting to rescue them. His grief is increased by the arrival of Marcus and the maimed figure of his daughter Lavinia. The passage opens with Lucius's enquiry "Speak, gentle sister, who hath martyr'd thee?" and the passage is punctuated throughout with questions as Lavinia's relatives try to make sense of what has happened to her and who might be responsible. In response to

Lucius's question, Marcus explains that Lavinia's tongue has been cut out, but again as in the previous scene when he first encounters his niece, his language is poetic, making use of metaphor to describe Lavinia's loss of her voice and tongue rather than employing prosaic straightforward terms to identify the injuries she has suffered. Marcus compares Lavinia's tongue to a bird and her voice to its song:

O, that delightful engine of her thoughts
That blabb'd them with such pleasing
    eloquence,
Is torn from forth that pretty hollow cage,
Where, like a sweet melodious bird, it sung
Sweet varied notes, enchanting every ear!

As a consequence of her injuries, Marcus cannot answer Lucius's demand for the identity of her attackers, although Marcus's comparison between Lavinia and an injured deer immediately recalls the scenes in the wood of the hunt and the language of Chiron and Demetrius who refer to Lavinia as their prey. Titus puns on the word "deer" when he refers to his daughter as "my dear" and later in the same speech calls her "dear Lavinia, dearer than my soul." The sight of Lavinia threatens to overwhelm Titus with grief and sorrow, and his swelling emotions give way to a memorable description of Titus as isolated:

For now I stand as one upon a rock
Environed with a wilderness of sea,
Who marks the waxing tide grow wave by
    wave,
Expecting ever when some envious surge
Will in his brinish bowels swallow him.

Titus reflects on his situation and lists the wrongs he has suffered through the treatment of his children. When Lavinia begins to weep, each of the men attempt to read and interpret her body language in the hope that it provide a clear sign or answer to their questions. Marcus for example, wonders: "Perchance she weeps because they kill'd her husband; / Perchance because she knows them innocent." Titus is desperate for Lavinia to communicate clearly with him; "Gentle Lavinia, let me kiss thy lips. / Or make some sign how I may do thee ease." His suggestion that the family contemplate their grief by gazing on their tear-stained reflections in a fountain's pool recalls the image used by Marcus to describe Lavinia's bleeding mouth in the previous scene:

Why dost not speak to me?
Alas, a crimson river of warm blood,
Like to a bubbling fountain stirr'd with wind,
Doth rise and fall between thy rosed lips.

The sight of Lavinia prompts contemplation, but it also indicates the breakdown of communication.

Act III, Scene 1, 235–288

Enter a MESSENGER, with two heads and a hand.

MESSENGER. Worthy Andronicus, ill art thou repaid
For that good hand thou sent'st the emperor.
Here are the heads of thy two noble sons,
And here's thy hand, in scorn to thee sent back -
Thy grief their sports! thy resolution mock'd!
That woe is me to think upon thy woes,
More than remembrance of my father's death.
[*Exit.*]

MARCUS ANDRONICUS. Now let hot Aetna cool in Sicily,
And be my heart an ever-burning hell!
These miseries are more than may be borne.
To weep with them that weep doth ease some deal;
But sorrow flouted at is double death.

LUCIUS. Ah, that this sight should make so deep a wound,
And yet detested life not shrink thereat!
That ever death should let life bear his name,
Where life hath no more interest but to breathe!

[*Lavinia kisses Titus.*]

MARCUS ANDRONICUS. Alas, poor heart, that kiss is comfortless
As frozen water to a starved snake.

TITUS ANDRONICUS. When will this fearful slumber have an end?

MARCUS ANDRONICUS. Now farewell, flattery; die, Andronicus.
Thou dost not slumber: see, thy two sons' heads,
Thy warlike hand, thy mangled daughter here,
Thy other banish'd son, with this dear sight
Struck pale and bloodless, and thy brother, I,
Even like a stony image, cold and numb.
Ah, now no more will I control thy griefs.
Rend off thy silver hair, thy other hand
Gnawing with thy teeth; and be this dismal sight
The closing up of our most wretched eyes.
Now is a time to storm; why art thou still?

TITUS ANDRONICUS. Ha, ha, ha!

MARCUS ANDRONICUS. Why dost thou laugh? It fits not with this hour.

TITUS ANDRONICUS. Why, I have not another tear to shed.
Besides, this sorrow is an enemy,
And would usurp upon my wat'ry eyes,
And make them blind with tributary tears;
Then which way shall I find Revenge's cave?
For these two heads do seem to speak to me,
And threat me I shall never come to bliss
Till all these mischiefs be return'd again,
Even in their throats that have committed them.
Come, let me see what task I have to do.
You heavy people, circle me about,
That I may turn me to each one of you,
And swear unto my soul to right your wrongs.
The vow is made. Come, brother, take a head,

And in this hand the other I will bear;
Lavinia, thou shalt be employ'd;
Bear thou my hand, sweet wench, between thy
  teeth.
As for thee, boy, go get thee from my sight;
Thou art an exile, and thou must not stay.
Hie to the Goths, and raise an army there,
And, if ye love me, as I think you do,
Let's kiss and part, for we have much to do.

This passage traces the responses of Titus, his brother Marcus, and Lavinia to the cruel deception by Aaron in which he promised that Titus's sons could be exchanged for his hand. In this section of the scene, a messenger from Saturninus returns both Titus's hand and the heads of his sons to him. The horror of the situation is emphasized by the response of the messenger, who despite being a stranger remarks, "woe is me to think upon thy woes / More than remembrance of my father's death." Marcus also indicates that the horror of the sight of these severed heads and hand is agonizing, "These miseries are more than can be borne." The play's intense scrutiny of human suffering in this scene, and the way in which the revenge exacted by Tamora and her confederates Saturninus and Aaron far exceeds Titus's own faults, anticipates Shakespeare's continued interest in these themes in his later tragedies, such as *King Lear*. Titus's initial response is that the return of the hand and heads is a vision or bad dream, "When will this fearful slumber have an end?" Marcus, however, rather than attempting to assuage Titus's grief suggests that the only response is to howl with rage at the injustice of their situation:

Ah, now no more will I control thy griefs:
Rend off thy silver hair, thy other hand
Gnawing with thy teeth; and be this dismal
  sight
The closing up of our most wretched eyes;
Now is a time to storm; why art thou still?

Titus's reaction, however, to this impassioned speech from his brother is to laugh, which seems incongruous both as a response to his brother's words and also to his situation. This laughter marks a pivotal point in the play, as it pinpoints the moment when Titus shifts from a tragic protagonist to that of a revenger. He explains that laughter is an appropriate reaction since tears prevent him from seeing clearly, and now he must act rather than lament: "which way shall I find Revenge's cave?" The mixing of comedy and tragedy in this section of the scene is used to underline the horror of Titus's situation, since the laughter emphasizes the extreme nature of his situation and the feeling that it cannot possibly get any worse. The laughter also signals the play's interest in the failure of language to adequately express intense emotion. Here laughter, rather than more words or speeches, provides the best expression of Titus's feelings at this point in the play. The scene concludes with another instance of grotesque humor when Titus and Marcus leave the stage each carrying one of his son's heads and Titus instructs Lavinia "Bear thou my hand sweet wench, between thy teeth." Critics and theater audiences have often been revolted by Titus's treatment of Lavinia at this point and have argued that it is a sign of Titus's madness and unstable mental state. Other critics have suggested that Titus's symbolic gesture recalls the earlier rape of Lavinia by Chiron and Demetrius, with the hand acting as another example of phallic penetration. Jonathan Bate and Coppélia Kahn have argued that since Titus and the Andronici family have just pledged to act together to avenge themselves on their enemies, by giving Lavinia his hand Titus gives her an active role in his plans for revenge. This is borne out in the preparations for the banquet when Lavinia holds the basin to catch the blood of Chiron and Demetrius.

DIFFICULT PASSAGES
Act II, Scene 4, 11–57
MARCUS. Who is this? my niece, that flies
  away so fast!
Cousin, a word; where is your husband?
If I do dream, would all my wealth would
  wake me!

If I do wake, some planet strike me down,
That I may slumber in eternal sleep!
Speak, gentle niece, what stern ungentle hands
Have lopp'd and hew'd and made thy body
  bare
Of her two branches, those sweet ornaments,
Whose circling shadows kings have sought to
  sleep in,
And might not gain so great a happiness
As have thy love? Why dost not speak to me?
Alas, a crimson river of warm blood,
Like to a bubbling fountain stirr'd with wind,
Doth rise and fall between thy rosed lips,
Coming and going with thy honey breath.
But, sure, some Tereus hath deflowered thee,
And, lest thou shouldst detect him, cut thy
  tongue.
Ah, now thou turn'st away thy face for shame!
And, notwithstanding all this loss of blood,
As from a conduit with three issuing spouts,
Yet do thy cheeks look red as Titan's face
Blushing to be encountered with a cloud.
Shall I speak for thee? shall I say 'tis so?
O, that I knew thy heart; and knew the beast,
That I might rail at him, to ease my mind!
Sorrow concealed, like an oven stopp'd,
Doth burn the heart to cinders where it is.
Fair Philomela, she but lost her tongue,
And in a tedious sampler sew'd her mind:
But, lovely niece, that mean is cut from thee;
A craftier Tereus, cousin, hast thou met,
And he hath cut those pretty fingers off,
That could have better sew'd than Philomel.
O, had the monster seen those lily hands
Tremble, like aspen-leaves, upon a lute,
And make the silken strings delight to kiss
  them,
He would not then have touch'd them for his
  life!
Or, had he heard the heavenly harmony
Which that sweet tongue hath made,
He would have dropp'd his knife, and fell
  asleep
As Cerberus at the Thracian poet's feet.
Come, let us go, and make thy father blind;

For such a sight will blind a father's eye:
One hour's storm will drown the fragrant
  meads;
What will whole months of tears thy father's
  eyes?
Do not draw back, for we will mourn with
  thee
O, could our mourning ease thy misery!

Part of the difficulty of this scene is that Lavinia's appearance is so shocking. The stage directions describe her entry onto the stage: "Enter the Empress' sons [DEMETRIUS and CHIRON] with LAVINIA, her hands cut off, and her tongue cut out, and ravish'd." What readers have frequently found difficult to reconcile is the image of Lavinia and the way in which her uncle Marcus responds to her in this speech. The speech is over 40 lines long and is one of the longest in the play. Its stylized poetic language seems completely at odds with the shocking nature of what Marcus is seeing.

At first, Marcus struggles to come to terms to with what he is seeing and wonders if it is real or simply a bad dream "If I do dream, would all my wealth would wake me! / If I do wake, some planet strike me down, / That I may slumber an eternal sleep!" Then Marcus addresses each of Lavinia's injuries in turn starting with her arms and then her tongue using the poetic device called a *blazon*, which was traditionally used in Elizabethan love poetry, particularly the sonnets where the physical features of a woman such as her eyes, lips, and hair would be listed and celebrated in detail. The metaphor that describes Lavinia's hands and arms as tree branches has two important effects. First, when Marcus asks "what stern ungentle hands / Hath lopp'd and hew'd, and made thy body bare / Of her two branches," the use of the forestry imagery to describe the cutting away of Lavinia's arms or "branches" recalls the killing of Alarbus in the opening scene of the play, whose "limbs are lopp'd" as part of the burial rites for Titus's dead sons. It is his decision to allow the sacrifice of Alarbus that precipitates Tamora's revenge plot against Titus and his children.

Marcus's description of Lavinia's arms as "those sweet ornaments / Whose circling shadows kings have sought to sleep in" also underlines the ways in which Lavinia has been an object of desire to be exchanged and fought over, first by Saturninus and Bassianus and later by Chiron and Demetrius. Marcus's blazon then moves on to describe her tongue, "a crimson river of warm blood, / Like to a bubbling fountain stirr'd with wind, / Doth rise and fall between thy rosed lips, / Coming and going with thy honey breath." As Marcus struggles to comprehend the horror of Lavinia's injuries, he recalls the story of the rape of Philomel by Tereus, which helps him to understand what has happened to Lavinia. The story of Philomel is found in Book 6 of Ovid's *Metamorphoses* and becomes an important motif during the course of the play. The story is briefly as follows: The Thracian king Tereus is married to Progne, but he lusts after his wife's sister Philomel. Tereus rapes Philomel and cuts out her tongue to keep the crime secret. He then tells Progne that her sister is dead, but Philomel weaves a tapestry detailing the crime and sends it to her sister. Progne rescues Philomel, and she vows to take revenge against her husband and does so by murdering her son by Tereus, Itys, and serving the son to her husband for dinner. When Philomel throws Itys's head at Tereus during the meal, he realizes what has happened. When he pursues the two sisters to kill them, all three are changed into birds.

The characters of *Titus Andronicus* are familiar with the story, including Aaron the Moor, who is the first to link Lavinia with Philomel when he outlines the plot against Lavinia and Bassianus to Tamora:

This is the day of doom for Bassianus:
His Philomel must lose her tongue to-day,
Thy sons make pillage of her chastity,
And wash their hands in Bassianus' blood
                (2.2.42–45).

Marcus in his speech considers how Lavinia's injuries offer a further twist on the story of Philomel, since Philomel did not lose her hands and was therefore able to use her tapesty to identify her attacker:

Fair Philomela, why, she but lost her tongue,
And in a tedious sampler sewed her mind;
But lovely niece, that mean is cut from thee.
A craftier Tereus, cousin hast thou met,
And he hath cut those pretty fingers off
That could have better sew'd than Philomel.

Later, in Act IV of the play, Lavinia uses her nephew's copy of Ovid's *Metamorphoses* and the story of Philomel to suggest to Titus and her uncle what has happened to her.

Lavinia, were thou thus surprised, sweet girl,
Ravished and wronged as Philomela was,
Forced in the ruthless, vast and gloomy woods?

This classical story then provides Titus with his own model for revenge since he uses Progne's method of revenge against Tamora, when he feeds her the pies made from the heads of her two sons, Chiron and Demetrius, in the final act of the play. In this scene of discovery, however, Marcus's recourse to lyrical language and classical myth creates a deliberate gap between the language used and the realities he is attempting to describe. It suggests that there is a failure of language to articulate the horror of the scene before him and that Marcus tries to make sense of it by using existing stories and poetic imagery.

Act IV, Scene 3, 77–120

Enter a Clown, with a basket, and two pigeons in it

TITUS ANDRONICUS. News, news from heaven! Marcus, the post is come. Sirrah, what tidings? have you any letters? Shall I have justice? what says Jupiter?

CLOWN. O, the gibbet-maker! he says that he hath taken them down again, for the man must not be hanged till the next week.

TITUS ANDRONICUS. But what says Jupiter, I ask thee?

CLOWN. Alas, sir, I know not Jupiter; I never drank with him in all my life.

TITUS ANDRONICUS. Why, villain, art not thou the carrier?

CLOWN. Ay, of my pigeons, sir; nothing else.

TITUS ANDRONICUS. Why, didst thou not come from heaven?

CLOWN. From heaven! alas, sir, I never came there God forbid I should be so bold to press to heaven in my young days. Why, I am going with my pigeons to the tribunal plebs, to take up a matter of brawl betwixt my uncle and one of the emperial's men.

MARCUS ANDRONICUS. Why, sir, that is as fit as can be to serve for your oration; and let him deliver the pigeons to the emperor from you.

TITUS ANDRONICUS. Tell me, can you deliver an oration to the emperor with a grace?

CLOWN. Nay, truly, sir, I could never say grace in all my life.

TITUS ANDRONICUS. Sirrah, come hither: make no more ado,
But give your pigeons to the emperor:
By me thou shalt have justice at his hands.
Hold, hold; meanwhile here's money for thy charges.
Give me pen and ink. Sirrah, can you with a grace deliver a supplication?

CLOWN. Ay, sir.

TITUS ANDRONICUS. Then here is a supplication for you. And when you come to him, at the first approach you must kneel, then kiss his foot, then deliver up your pigeons, and then look for your reward. I'll be at hand, sir; see you do it bravely.

CLOWN. I warrant you, sir, let me alone.

TITUS ANDRONICUS. Sirrah, hast thou a knife? come, let me see it.
Here, Marcus, fold it in the oration;
For thou hast made it like an humble suppliant.
And when thou hast given it the emperor,
Knock at my door, and tell me what he says.

CLOWN. God be with you, sir; I will.

The challenge facing the reader of this section of the scene is how to account for the inclusion of the Clown at this point in the play's action. The Clown has frequently been dismissed as simply as a device to provide comic relief after the murder of the Nurse in the previous scene by Aaron and in the face of Titus's apparent decline into madness. The figure of the Clown, however, is an integral part of the play's overall dramatic structure since it permits the continued examination of the themes of revenge, the quest for justice, and the corruption of the state. This use of the Clown anticipates other examples of Shakespeare's use of the Clown in plays such as *Othello, Julius Caesar,* and *Anthony and Cleopatra.*

Titus exhibits his frustration that justice cannot be secured through the legal mechanisms of the state, since they are ultimately controlled by the emperor and Titus's enemies. The act of writing his woes and attaching them to arrows to shoot into the skies to the gods also indicates his feelings of isolation since the gods also seem deaf to his cries for justice. Titus mistakes the Clown as a messenger from the gods when he asks "Sirrah, what tidings? Have you any letters? / Shall I have justice? What says Jupiter?" The Clown's misunderstanding of Titus's reference to the king of the gods as "the gibbet-maker" and his assertion "Alas sir, I know not Jupiter; I never drank with him in all my life" serves to reinforce the sense of the failure of communication. Titus either cannot get people to listen to his calls for justice or, in the case of the Clown, he is unable to make them understand him. It is possible to establish similarities between the Clown and Titus, since the Clown is on his way to visit the Senate to offer a bribe of two pigeons to settle a dispute concerning his uncle and a brawl with one of the emperor's men. Marcus suggests that the Clown could also be used to present Titus's case before the emperor. The Clown is willing after he receives payment to bring Titus's "supplication" before Saturninus. When the Clown presents the letter from Titus to the emperor in 4.4, Saturninus immediately orders that he should be hung without trial or explanation: "Go take him away and hang him presently." The death of the Clown provides another example of the suffering of innocent bystanders in the play.

CRITICAL INTRODUCTION TO THE PLAY
Romans and Goths

While a Roman setting allowed Shakespeare's play to engage with contemporary political debates concerning the issue of the succession, for example, the imperial backdrop for the play also reflected a wider interest in classical cultures during the Renaissance. As a revenge play, *Titus* is influenced by the drama of Seneca, but it is also indebted to the work of the Roman poet Ovid. Shakespeare would have been familiar with Ovid's poetry from his schooldays, as those works made up the translation exercises performed by Elizabethan schoolchildren; indeed the play shows us the Young Lucius reading Ovid's *Metamorphoses*. So, for Shakespeare and his contemporaries, Rome was a great source of literature and culture, but in *Titus Andronicus,* Shakespeare interrogates the ways in which that sophisticated culture and source of learning fell into decay. The story of Philomel found in Ovid's *Metamorphoses* is used as a motif throughout the play, a parallel for the story of Lavinia and for the revenge exacted by Titus upon Tamora, Chiron, and Demetrius, but the repeated use of this story also seems to suggest

Marcus Andronicus tells Lucius not to fear Lavinia, who has been running after Lucius, in Act IV, Scene 1 of *Titus Andronicus*. This is a print from the Boydell Shakespeare Gallery project, which was first conceived in 1786 and lasted until 1805. *(Painting and engraving by Thomas Kirk)*

that the wealth of literature and learning in Rome has been reduced to this story and that its place in Roman society is to provide the inspiration for rape and revenge.

While Elizabethan histories of Rome provided accounts of her achievements, they also detailed her vices, thus encouraging varied ideas and opinions on the subject. In *Titus Andronicus,* the apparently straightforward opposition between Romans and Goths becomes blurred. The reputation of Rome as the model for any civilized city quickly begins to unravel as its inhabitants behave in ways more barbarous than those of their enemies the Goths. In the opening scene of the play, the corruption of Roman values is signaled by Titus's decision to permit his son Lucius to demand the sacrifice of Alarbus:

> That we may hew his limbs, and on a pile
> *Ad manes fratrum* sacrifice his flesh
> Before the earthly prison of their bones,
> That so the shadows be not unappeas'd,
> Nor we disturbed with prodigies on earth.

Despite Tamora's eloquent pleas for mercy, Titus is unyielding, placing his own rigid beliefs in the gods and the performance of ritual above human compassion. The bloody nature of that ritual is underlined by Lucius's account of it:

> See, lord and father, how we have performed
> Our Roman Rites: Alarbus' limbs are lopped
> And entrails feed the sacrificing fire,
> Whose smoke like incense doth perfume the
>   sky

The killing of Alarbus is described by Tamora as "cruel irreligious piety," while Chiron, her son, adds "Was never Scythia half so barbarous," suggesting that the behavior of the Romans is worse than that of the Scythians. The Scythians were a nomadic tribe who roamed across northern Europe and Asiatic Russia and were reputed to be bloodthirsty and barbaric.

Titus's adherence to traditional Roman values, including absolute unquestioning loyalty to the state and the belief in primogeniture, are shown to be problematic, since they prompt him to support Saturninus's claim. While his role as arbiter between the two brothers prevents civil war, his choice of Saturninus indicates that he is a poor judge of character, since Saturninus quickly establishes himself as a Roman tyrant. Once Saturninus becomes emperor, he quickly forgets the loyalty and service of the Andronici family to Rome and instead begins his reign by plotting his own revenge against them with Tamora's help. He is weak-willed, cowardly, and jealous of the loyalty that the Andronici family inspire in the common people. He fails therefore to fulfill his duty to uphold law and order and administer justice, and when Quintus and Martius are accused of Bassianus's murder, he responds by condemning them to death without a trial.

The corruption of Rome under Saturninus's rule is emphasized by Titus's description of the city when his own request for justice for his sons is denied. Rome, the model of civilization, has become a wilderness, a city that feeds on its own offspring:

> Rome is but a wilderness of tigers.
> Tigers must prey, and Rome affords no prey
> But me and mine: how happy are thou
>   [Lucius], then,
> From these devourers to be banished!

Titus responds by turning against the city and sends his exiled son Lucius to the Goths to raise an army that will overthrow Saturninus, so that the Andronici can "with revengeful war / Take wreak on Rome for this ingratitude, / And vengeance on the traitor Saturnine."

Critics have frequently been revolted and disturbed by the violence in *Titus Andronicus*. In addition to at least 13 deaths, the play also depicts the maimed bodies of Titus and Lavinia as well as an assortment of severed hands, heads, and tongues. The violence, however, is not simply gratuitous or used for shock value but rather it contributes to the exploration of a number of important themes. The mutilated bodies of both Titus and Lavinia are used symbolically to examine the political decline of Rome under Saturninus and the effect of Roman values upon the relationships between men and women and parents and children in the play.

The play's interest in the relationship between the individual and the state is signaled from the beginning through the images employed to describe the city of Rome. In the opening scene of the play, the city of Rome is presented using two images, both of which are important to our understanding of the play's interest in violence, particularly violence perpetrated against the human body. The first set of images present the city as female during the dispute between Saturninus and Bassianus. Each brother uses the image of the city with a boundary or threshold to be protected or penetrated. Bassianus, for example, suggests he will protect Rome and its political institutions and "will not suffer dishonour to approach / The imperial seat." Saturninus also appeals to Rome as a female figure, suggesting the paternal role he will take on, which will complement the maternal identity of the city:

> Rome be as just and gracious unto me
> As I am confident and kind to thee.
> Open the gates and let me in.

The next set of images used to describe the city draws in a more explicit fashion on the metaphor of the city as a body. This idea draws upon the political concept of the body politic, a medieval idea that refers to the institutions that make up the state, including the monarchy and the elected body of representatives. When Marcus offers his brother Titus the title of emperor to resolve the threat of civil war between Saturninus and Bassianus, he suggests that what Rome needs is a leader, someone who will become the head of the state "and set a head upon headless Rome." Titus declines the offer and puns upon the idea of the figurative or symbolic head of a state and his own head: "A better head her glorious body fits / Than his that shakes for age and feebleness." Titus selects Saturninus as emperor and also agrees to hand over his daughter Lavinia to the emperor to be his bride. The conflict between the brothers over the city of Rome has only just been settled, but now disagreement breaks out between them again as Bassianus claims that he is already betrothed to Lavinia and that she belongs to him. Saturninus regards Bassianus's escape with Lavinia as theft:

> Traitor, if Rome have law or we have power,
> Thou and thy faction shall repent this rape.

There is a clear symmetry between the action of the first and final acts of the play as both are concerned with the election of an emperor. In Act V, Scene 3, Marcus returns to the image of Rome as both female and as a mutilated body when he appeals for calm after the bloody outcome of the banquet and once again attempts to prevent civil war:

> O let me teach you how to knit again
> This scattered corn into one mutual sheaf
> These broken limbs again into one body;
> Lest Rome be a bane unto herself,
> And she whom mighty kingdoms cur'sy to,
> Like a forlorn and desperate castaway,
> Do shameful execution on herself.

Critics have disagreed about the final message that the play offers about the future of Rome under Titus's son Lucius. Ronald Broude argues that by combining with the Goths, Lucius and his followers will bring about the necessary reform and regeneration of the Roman Empire. The Goths, far from simply embodying a savage race, offer further lessons to the Romans in civilization. Molly Easo Smith offers a much less optimistic reading of the play's conclusion, as she considers the character of Lucius and what kind of emperor he is likely to make. On the one hand, Lucius brings about the overthrow of Saturninus and Tamora, and his acceptance of the emperorship prevents civil unrest, on the other hand, Lucius's return to Rome at the head of an army and his election as emperor with the support of the tribunes recalls Titus's entry into the city at the start of the play. Just as the opening scene of the play invites the audience to consider which of the two brothers would make the best ruler, so here we are reminded of Lucius's initial role as a revenger who demanded the sacrifice of one of Tamora's sons. Lucius therefore is tainted by his involvement in that first killing, which set in motion the first revenge plot. At the play's conclusion, his first action as emperor involves the burial of his father and sister and the sentence of death upon Aaron. This final act of revenge requires Lucius to proclaim, "If anyone relieves or pities him, / For the offence he dies," suggesting perhaps that Aaron could inspire sympathy and that the cycle of murder and revenge could erupt again at anytime.

Revenge

Titus Andronicus belongs to a group of plays known as revenge tragedies that were popular on the Elizabethan and Jacobean stage. These plays were influenced by the plays of the Roman dramatist Seneca, including *Medea* and *Agamemnon*, violent stories of passion and murder involving the revenge of characters such as Medea and Clytemnestra for the crimes committed against them. Early Elizabethan examples of revenge tragedy included Thomas Kyd's *The Spanish Tragedy*, Christopher Marlowe's *The Jew of Malta*, and, later, Shakespeare's *Hamlet*.

A revenge tragedy can be broadly characterized as follows: The plot will trace the actions of the protagonist as they pursue revenge for the murder of a loved one. The murder is often revealed through the visitation of a ghost who demands vengeance. This process will include the contemplation of the moral implications of taking revenge and a period of delay as the murderer's identity or guilt is confirmed. The emotional pressures may cause the protagonists to fall prey to temporary bouts of madness or to feign madness in the pursuit of his enemies. The final execution of the revenge plot may involve the revenger using a disguise or costume and employing a theatrical device such as a play-within-a-play or a banquet. At the play's bloody conclusion, the revenger and his enemies will be killed.

The popularity of revenge plays was partly due to the way in which the scenes of blood and gore appealed to an Elizabethan theater audience in a similar way to present-day horror or violent action films, they wanted to be shocked and entertained by what they saw. In *The Spanish Tragedy,* for example, the hero Hieronimo stabs his enemies and then bites out his own tongue. Although the violence of these revenge plays gave the audiences what they wanted, it also had another important

role to fulfill, since the plays allowed dramatists and their audiences to consider a range of related issues, including the breakdown of law and order in society and the corruption of legal and political institutions.

The moral dilemma facing each revenge hero was the question of whether he should take revenge himself or leave it to God to punish his enemy. Christian teaching on this subject was quite clear, it was God's role to judge and punish sinners. In the Old Testament, this idea was expressed through the following phrase "Vindicti Mihi" and means "Vengeance is mine saith the Lord I will repay." Hieronimo uses the phrase "Vindicti Mihi" at the start of a long soliloquy in Kyd's play to underline the difficulty of his situation as the father of a murdered son. While Christian teaching on the subject of revenge and murder was quite clear, the audience response to the protagonist is complicated by the emotional response to their predicament. Audience sympathies for the revenger would be particularly high in cases of the murder of a loved one, where the victim or relative is unable to obtain legal redress and if the murder had been committed in a treacherous manner.

An important source of Elizabethan ideas about revenge can be found in an essay by Sir Francis Bacon, first published in 1597 and entitled "Of Revenge." In this essay, Bacon famously described revenge as "a kind of wild justice" that helps to sum up some of the complexities of the relationship between justice and revenge. If revenge is "a kind of wild justice," it means that revenge cannot be controlled, it is ungovernable, destructive, and once unleashed it cannot be recalled. Revenge, unlike justice in the strict legal sense of the word, exists and operates outside the controls and perimeters of the law, which exists to keep society safe. Bacon explains that taking revenge is problematic since it means that the individual is in fact taking the law into his or her own hands, undermining those laws and institutions that are designed to maintain law and order. This is what Bacon is referring to when he explains: "As for the first wrong, it doth but offend the law; but

Lavinia begs Tamora for mercy as Chiron and Demetrius drag her away in this 19th-century depiction of Act II, Scene 3 of *Titus Andronicus. (Engraving by Edward Smith)*

the revenge of that wrong putteth the law out of office." If you take revenge, Bacon suggests you will set off a domino effect, a chain reaction that will contribute to the breakdown of the law, so it is vital to seek redress through the established legal channels. During the rest of the essay, Bacon puts forward the Christian teaching of forgiving your enemies and provides examples from the Bible to support his point. Midway through the essay, however, Bacon considers an exception to the rules he has been examining and indicates that there might be one scenario when revenge is acceptable: "The most tolerable sort of revenge is for those wrongs which there is no law to remedy." Here, he highlights the dilemma posed when the crime is perpetrated by the source of law and order, the figure at the top of the social and legal system: the

king himself. In this case, Bacon explains that the revenger is doubly at a disadvantage, since he or she cannot seek justice through the legal channels because the wrong-doer is the law, that is, the king, and by pursuing revenge, he or she will break the law and so can be punished by the law for that revenge. Bacon then turns his attention to the psychology of the revenger and those who meditate on revenge: "A man that studieth revenge keeps his own wounds green, which otherwise would heal and do well." The problem with becoming a revenger then is that by focusing exclusively upon the wrongs committed against you, it is likely that your desire for revenge will become an obsession and have a negative effect upon your personality. Finally, Bacon considers the differences between public and private revenge. He argues that public revenge is "fortunate," and here he seems to be making the radical suggestion that revenge can be committed against a ruler who is corrupt, since their removal will have a positive effect on the state, whereas private revenge is condemned, as individuals act from a mixture of selfish or malicious motives.

Titus Andronicus certainly engages with the issues outlined above in Bacon's essay and contains many of the features of a revenge play. Audience responses to Titus are complicated by his own actions in the opening scene of the play when he sets in motion Tamora's revenge plot against him, but by the end of Act III, he certainly commands audience sympathies for his own quest for revenge because of the atrocities committed against him and his family by Tamora through her relationships with both Saturninus and Aaron. Tamora's revenge does not simply exact the killing of one of Titus's children for the loss of Alarbus, instead it is the scale of her revenge and the way it involves innocent bystanders such as Lavinia that encourages our pity for Titus.

Titus makes repeated attempts to secure justice through the legal institutions when Martius and Quintus are accused of the murder of Bassianus, but the tribunes refuse to listen to his pleas, and Saturninus orders their execution without a trial. Later, Titus's attempt to ransom his sons in exchange for his hand is revealed to be a grotesque charade on the part of Aaron. So here Titus has made some efforts to obtain redress via the law, but only when he sees that Saturninus is not concerned with dispensing the law fairly and makes a mockery of Titus's willingness to save his sons at the expense of his own hand does he consider taking revenge. Even after the remaining members of the Andronici family have pledged to exact their revenge, Titus's behavior continues to underline the dilemma of whether revenge should be left to a divine power. In Act IV, Scene 3, for example, Titus uses the messages tied to arrows to try and rouse the gods to assist him in his search for justice:

> sith there's no justice in earth nor hell,
> We will solicit heaven and move the gods
> To send down justice for to wreak our wrongs.

It seems, however, that the gods are deaf to his calls to intervene in his affairs, and so he must pursue his own course of action to achieve satisfaction. Since it is the emperor and empress who are Titus's enemies, his circumstances fall under Bacon's description of an instance of the "most tolerable sort of revenge" when there is "no law to remedy." Shakespeare returns to this dilemma in *Hamlet*, when Hamlet is placed in a comparable position by his suspicions that Claudius, the king, has murdered his father.

By the final act of the play, Titus takes on the role of author and director of his revenge, even choosing to dress as chef to serve his pie with characteristic black humor. "I'll play the cook." Titus's obsession with planning his revenge invites the audience to consider how Titus, rather like Aaron, has come to revel in the details of his plans and has lost sight perhaps of why he chose to exact his revenge in the first place. The killing of Tamora and Saturninus could be regarded as the kind of public revenge advocated by Bacon and that their removal offers hope for the future of Rome under its new emperor, Lucius, although any optimism is qualified by the way in which Lucius rejects pity in favor of harsh punishment, which serves to maintain rather than halt the cycle of revenge.

EXTRACTS OF CLASSIC CRITICISM

Edward Ravenscroft (fl. 1659–1697) [Excerpted from the Address to the Reader in *Titus Andronicus, or The Rape of Lavinia. Acted at the Theatre Royall, A Tragedy. Alter'd from Mr Shakespears Works, by Mr Edw. Ravenscroft* (1687). *Titus Andronicus,* like many of Shakespeare's plays, including *King Lear,* was adapted for the Restoration stage when the theaters were reopened in 1660. This adaptation is significant for two reasons, first it develops the character of Aaron and gives him a more prominent role, accentuating his villainy, and second, in his Address to the Reader, Ravenscroft raises doubts about the authorship of the play, kick-starting a debate that continues to exercise critics. Critics such as Jonathan Bate have recently suggested that there is no evidence for Ravenscroft's claim and that he probably invented the story that Shakespeare was the "improver" of the play to "give precedent and warrant for his own practice as improver."]

I have been told by some anciently conversant with the Stage, that it was not Originally his, but brought by a private Author to be Acted, and he only gave some Master-touches to one or two of the Principal Parts or Characters; this I am apt to believe, because 'tis the most incorrect and indigested piece in all his Works; It seems rather a heap of Rubbish then a Structure.—However as if some great Building had been design'd, in the removal we found many Large and Square Stones both usefull and Ornamental to the Fabrick, as now Modell'd.

Samuel Johnson (1709–1784) [Excerpted from the notes to *The Plays of William Shakespeare* (1765). Johnson's comments about the play's style would prove to be influential. He, too, was skeptical about Shakespeare's involvement as its author. He also contributed to what would become an established strand of criticism of the play, which dismissed the violence within *Titus* as simply gratuitous.]

The editors and critics agree with Mr. Theobald in supposing this play spurious. I see no reason for differing from them; for the colour of the stile is wholly different from that of the other plays, and there is an attempt at regular versification, and artificial closes, not always inelegant, yet seldom pleasing. The barbarity of the spectacles, and the general massacre, which are here exhibited, can scarcely be conceived tolerable to any audience; yet we are told by Jonson, that they were not only borne, but praised. . . .

The testimony produced at the beginning of this play, by which it is ascribed to Shakespeare, is by no means equal to the argument against its authenticity, arising from the total difference of conduct, language, and sentiments, by which it stands apart from all the rest. Meres had probably no other evidence than that of a title-page, which, though in our time it be sufficient, was then of no great authority; for all the plays which were rejected by the first collectors of Shakespeare's works, and admitted in later editions, and again rejected by the critical editors, had Shakespeare's name on the title, as we must suppose, by the fraudulence of the printers, who, while there were yet no gazettes, nor advertisements, nor any means of circulating literary intelligence, could usurp at pleasure any celebrated name. Nor had Shakespeare any interest in detecting the imposture, as none of his fame or profit was produced by the press.

Ravenscroft, who in the reign of Charles II, revised this play, and restored it to the stage, tells us, in his preface, from a theatrical tradition, I suppose, which in his time might be of sufficient authority, that this play was touched in different parts by Shakespeare, but written by some other poet. I do not find Shakespeare's touches very discernible

William Hazlitt (1778–1830) [Excerpted from *Characters of Shakespeare's Plays* (1817). Hazlitt also doubts that Shakespeare could in fact be the play's author, based on its violence, characterization, style, and grammar. Hazlitt seems to counter the suggestion made by other critics that perhaps *Titus,* a play that comes early in Shakespeare's career, demonstrates his immaturity as a writer. Hazlitt argues that the play is simply the work of another dramatist. One of the effects of this position is that *Titus* is discussed in isolation from Shakespeare's other tragedies.]

Titus Andronicus is certainly as unlike Shakespear's usual style as it is possible. It is an accumulation of vulgar physical horrors, in which the power exercised by the poet bears no proportion to the repugnance excited by the subject. The character of Aaron the Moor is the only thing which shews any originality of conception; and the scene in which he expresses his joy "at the blackness and ugliness of his child begot in adultery," the only one worthy of Shakespear. Even this is worthy of him only in the display of power, for it gives no pleasure. Shakespear managed these things differently. Nor do we think it a sufficient answer to say that this was an embryo or crude production of the author. In its kind it is full grown, and its features decided and overcharged. It is not like a first imperfect essay, but shews a confirmed habit, a systematic preference of violent effect to everything else. There are occasional detached images of great beauty and delicacy, but these were not beyond the powers of other writers then living. The circumstance which inclines us to reject the external evidence in favor of this play being Shakespear's is, that the grammatical construction is constantly false and mixed up with vulgar abbreviations, a fault that never occurs in any of his genuine plays.

Gulian Crommelin Verplanck (1786–1870)

[Excerpted from *The Illustrated Shakespeare*, vol. 3 (1847). This American scholar holds the opposing view to Hazlitt and suggests that the play was written to satisfy contemporary audience demands for sensational, gory plots. Verplanck argues that the play's sensational nature and its characterization are the work of a young, naive playwright.]

Critics have vied with one another in loading this play with epithets of contempt; and indeed, as compared with the higher products of dramatic poetry, it has little to recommend it. But in itself, and for its times, it was very far from giving the indication of an unpoetical or undramatic mind. One proof of this is that it was long a popular favorite on the stage. It is full of defects, but these are precisely such as a youthful aspirant, in an age of authorship, would be most likely to exhibit such as the subjection to the taste of the day, good or bad, and the absence of that dramatic truth and reality which some experience of human passion and observation of life and manners, can alone give the power to produce.

Edward Dowden (1843–1913)

[Excerpted from *Shakspere, A Critical Study of His Mind and Art* (1875). Dowden is another critic who attributes the play to a period of apprenticeship by Shakespeare.]

That tragedy belongs to the pre-Shaksperian school of bloody dramas. If any portions of it be from Shakspere's hand, it has at least this interest it shows that there was a period of Shakspere's authorship when the poet had not yet discovered himself, a period when he yielded to the popular influences of the day and hour; this much interest, and no more.

George Wyndham (1863–1913)

[Excerpted from *The Poems of Shakespeare* (1898). Wyndham makes a case for the importance of *Titus Andronicus* in the face of an established school of criticism that disliked its characters and atrocities.]

Our loss is great indeed if an impertinent solicitude for Shakespeare's morals, an officious care for his reputation as a creator of character, lead us to pass over "Titus Andronicus."

MODERN CRITICISM AND CRITICAL CONTROVERSIES

During the first half of the 20th century, *Titus Andronicus* continued to provoke largely negative responses from critics, with T. S. Eliot in 1932 describing it as "one of the stupidest and most uninspired plays ever written." John Dover Wilson, the editor of the 1948 Cambridge edition of the play, criticized the play's style, structure, and characterization. Wilson described *Titus* as:

A strange play, with something odd or baffling about it. If not the crudest of its kind, it is less homogenous in style, and more ramshackle in structure than most, while its incidents are often merely absurd.

Wilson describes the figure of Lavinia as "ludicrous" and dismisses the play as a grotesque experiment:

In a word, *The Most Lamentable Romaine Tragedie of Titus Andronicus* seems to jolt and bump along like some broken-down cart, laden with bleeding corpses from an Elizabethan scaffold, and driven by an executioner from Bedlam dressed in cap and bells.

Attitudes toward the play began to improve during the second half of the 20th century, due in part to a number of significant stage productions of *Titus Andronicus* and as a result of new critical approaches to the play, including feminist criticism, discussion of source materials, and more subtle readings of the play's overall tone. Criticism of *Titus Andronicus* at last began to move away from simple outraged dismissal of the play's style and content, which had characterized the critical response to the play for so long.

The turning point in the critical reception of *Titus Andronicus* came in 1955, with Peter Brook's production of the play in Stratford, starring Laurence Olivier as Titus and Vivien Leigh as Lavinia. Performance criticism on *Titus,* in particular the work of G. Harold Metz and Alan Dessen, which discussed the stage history of the play, have provided another approach to the play and allowed readers to consider some of the practical difficulties facing a director when planning a production of the play. By examining the decisions made by a director, it is possible to reconsider the criticism leveled at the play that has suggested that it is unperformable in front of a modern theater audience. Peter Brook made two important decisions concerning his production in 1955. First, he tackled the issue of how to stage the violent scenes by opting for a stylized approach to the blood and gore. When Lavinia was discovered by her uncle, the blood was symbolized by red streamers or ribbons. Richard David, who reviewed the production, described Lavinia's appearance on stage after the rape to the sound of "slow plucking harp-strings, like drops of blood falling into a pool." Lavinia stands motionless, her "right arm outstretched and head drooping away from it, left arm crooked with the wrist at the mouth. Her hair falls in disorder over face and shoulders, and from wrist and wrist-and-mouth trail scarlet streamers, symbols of her mutilation." Olivier's portrait of Titus was not as a conquering hero but as an exhausted man: "He was a veteran white-haired warrior, a man desperately tired. All the lines of his body drooped; his eyes among the seamed crowsfeet, were weary. Standing in midstage like some crumbling limestone crag, he greeted Rome because it was a thing of custom, but there was no spring in his voice, no light. . . . Presently we understood that the man we had seen at Olivier's entrance was a close relative of the Lear we had known long before: the old man on the edge of the gulf. Lear became identified with the storm in his mind, Titus with the sea."

In addition to this, Brook also decided to cut more than 650 lines from the play, including Marcus's long formal speech to Lavinia. The effect of removing this speech altogether was to suspend time and to force the audience to gaze upon the figure of Lavinia and to contemplate her suffering. In 1987, the director Deborah Warner was determined to challenge the criticism that some of the play's scenes did not work in performance. Warner's production at the Swan in Stratford performed the play in full without a single cut. This meant that Marcus's speech in 2.4 was delivered in full, but because the production made only sparing use of blood, the images of conduits and fountains pouring with blood used to describe Lavinia worked to create an image in the mind's eye of the audience.

In 1957, Eugene Waith published a seminal essay on *Titus* in which he considered the importance of Ovid's *Metamorphoses,* specifically the story of Philomel, in attempting to understand the relationship between the violence in the play and the manner in which it is described. Waith argues that the violence of the play serves as an emblem of the moral and political disorder in Rome. Waith's essay challenges the long-held view of earlier critics, such as Samuel Taylor Coleridge, that the play was "obviously intended to excite vulgar audiences by its scenes of blood and horror—to our eyes shocking and disgusting." The frequent criticism leveled at the speech made by Marcus upon encountering Lavinia is that the form and style of the speech are at odds with what he is describing and therefore seems absurd. D. J. Palmer argues, however, that the stylized language of the play reflects the play's interest in ceremony and ritual. In the case of Marcus's speech to Lavinia, for example, he suggests that "here and throughout the play, the response to the intolerable is ritualized, in language and action, because ritual is the ultimate means by which man seeks to order and control his precarious and unstable world."

During the 1980s and 1990s, criticism on the play reflected the upsurge in feminist criticism of Shakespeare's plays more generally, with particular attention paid to the treatment of female characters in the play. Some critics sought to complicate the existing stereotypes of Lavinia as a passive victim and Tamora as a merciless witch. Coppélia Kahn's *Roman Shakespeare: Warriors, Wounds and Women,* published in 1997 was the first book-length study of Shakespeare's Roman plays by a feminist critic. In the chapter on *Titus Andronicus,* Kahn examines the effect of the Roman concept of masculinity upon the family, focusing on both the men and women of the play. New Historicist criticism also discussed the play in the context of Elizabethan rituals of violence, such as public execution, performed as part of the state's mechanism of control. Molly Easo Smith, for example, argues that "*Titus* more than any other of Shakespeare's plays dwells on the spectacle of dismemberment and mutilation, a reliance that may have much to do with popular Tudor practices."

THE PLAY TODAY

One of the most important consequences of the recent criticism on *Titus Andronicus* has been to underline its relevance for a modern audience. It is increasingly seen as not simply a gory relic from the Elizabethan past but as a play whose bloodshed and relentless cruelty speaks forcefully to audiences worldwide who are familiar with accounts of atrocities in places such as Rwanda and Iraq, as well as much closer to home.

The continuing popularity of *Titus Andronicus* during the last decade is demonstrated by the number of productions of the play for the stage and screen. In 1999, Julie Taymor released her film version of *Titus Andronicus,* which had grown out of her off-Broadway production of the play in 1994. In an interview, Taymor described why she believed that the play was still important for an audience at the end of the 20th century: "*Titus Andronicus* speaks directly to a time whose audience feeds daily on tabloid sex scandals, teenage gang rape, high school gun sprees."

The film drew repeated parallels between ancient Rome and modern times through its blend of ancient and modern costuming and design. The first set of parallels is established through a framing device that begins the film by focusing on a young boy who plays violent war games with his toy soldiers on a kitchen table, using tomato ketchup to provide the necessary gore. The boy is interrupted by a small explosion that heralds the arrival of a leather-clad man who transports the boy to the world of Rome and its returning hero.

The Roman army is an eclectic mix of chariots and motorbikes, while the Colosseum in the film's opening sequence underlines the violent element of ancient and modern forms of entertainment as the arena also recalls a wrestling or boxing ring. The young boy from the opening sequence goes on to play the part of Titus's grandson Lucius, and events are frequently seen through his eyes. The position of the child in the film invites the audience to consider how the violent scenes he witnesses might affect him and more generally what kind of effect might a violent society have upon its children.

During the scenes of the election, the followers of Saturninus dressed in black trench coats and waving red and multicolored flags established a connection between Rome under Saturninus and later Fascist Italy under Mussolini. Tamora and the Goths were presented with blond hair and elaborate tattoos, while Tamora wore a gold breastplate and later a gold lamé dress, while the Romans were distinguished by dark hair and clothing. The figure of Lavinia after her rape and maiming is presented with bundles of twigs where her hands should be, in a cinematic nod to Edward Scissorhands. Other moments of cinematic intertextuality included casting Anthony Hopkins as Titus, drawing on Hopkins's fame for his role as Hannibal Lecter, the serial-killer cannibal in *The Silence of the Lambs* (1991).

In 2006 alone, it was possible to see two very different stage productions at Stratford and at the Globe in London. The production of *Titus* performed at Stratford as part of the Complete Works Festival in 2006 was directed by the Japanese director Yukio Ninagawa. The production looked back to the stylized direction of Peter Hall, since it made use of red silk thread to symbolize the blood, and a set design and costuming predominantly white. The backdrop for the set was a huge marble statue of Romulus and Remus being suckled by a she-wolf. Here the production alludes to another of the myths of the founding of Rome. The quarrel between the two brothers over who would rule over the city of Rome led to the murder of Remus by Romulus. The statue provided a clever visual link with that example of sibling rivalry, which neatly anticipated the clash between Bassianus and Saturninus. The Globe's production of the play in the same year, directed by Lucy Bailey, went for a more realistic approach to the play's bloody scenes, with Lavinia drenched in blood from her freshly severed limbs, prompting reports that the production had audience members fainting and even walking out. As Taymor rightly suggests, the play's meditation on violence provides its audience with an opportunity to scrutinize their own society's notions of what constitutes civilized or barbarous behavior.

FIVE TOPICS FOR DISCUSSION AND WRITING

1. **Revenge tragedy:** How helpful is the idea of the tragic hero when considering the figure of Titus? How far is he responsible for the revenge plots that are laid against him? Why is Titus forced to seek redress outside of the law? Francis Bacon said "a man that studieth revenge, keeps his own wounds green." How does Shakespeare indicate that Titus's quest for justice has become an obsession? Does the play offer an optimistic outlook for the future of Rome under the rule of Lucius?

2. **Romans and Goths:** How is Rome characterized in the first and final scenes of the play? How does Shakespeare raise doubts about Rome's reputation as a civilized city of culture? How is reading and storytelling used in the play and to what effect? Consider the figure of Aaron—what is his role in the play? Is he simply the epitome of evil?

3. **Staging the play:** If you were to direct your own production of *Titus Andronicus,* what decisions would you make in relation to the staging of violent or disturbing scenes such as Act II, Scene 4? How would you depict the figure of Lavinia here? Compare two productions of the play to help you with your decisions—for example, the BBC production directed by Jane Howell and the 1955 stage production directed by Peter Brook, or the film *Titus* directed by Julie Taymor.

4. **Comedy:** Although the play is a tragedy, it includes a number of comic characters and comic moments. Select some examples of comedy in the play and consider how the comedy relates to the themes and issues under discussion. What is the function of the character of the Clown in the play?

5. **Mutilation:** Give examples from the play where hands, heads, and other body parts are discussed. Consider how these body parts may be used symbolically within the play. Consider the problems posed by these body parts if you were staging a production of the play. Are the hands and heads, for example, simply comic props or can they be used in a more meaningful way?

Bibliography

Aebischer, Pascale. "Shakespeare, Sex and Violence: Negotiating Masculinities in Branagh's *Henry V* and Taymor's *Titus*." In *The Concise Blackwell Companion to Shakespeare on Screen,* edited by Diana Henderson. Oxford: Blackwell, 2005.

————. *Shakespeare's Violated Bodies: Stage and Screen Performance.* Cambridge: Cambridge University Press, 2004.

Bacon, Francis. Essays of Francis Bacon. "Of Revenge." Available online. URL: http://www.authorama.com/essays-of-francis-bacon-5.html. Accessed June 16, 2011.

Barker, Francis. *The Culture of Violence: Essays on Tragedy and History.* Chicago: University of Chicago Press, 1994.

Bassnett, Susan. *Shakespeare: The Elizabethan Plays.* Houndmills, England: Macmillan, 1993.

Bate, Jonathan, ed. *Shakespeare and Ovid.* Oxford: Oxford University Press, 1993.

————, ed. *Titus Andronicus.* London: Thomson Learning, 2006.

Billington, Michael. Review of *Titus Andronicus* at the Globe Theatre. The Guardian Newspaper Online. Available online. URL: http://www.guardian.co.uk/stage/2006/jun/22/theatre.rsc. Accessed March 10, 2011.

Billington, Michael. Review of the Yukio Ninagawa production of *Titus Andronicus.* The Guardian Newspaper Online. Available online. URL: http://www.guardian.co.uk/stage/2006/jun/22/theatre.rsc. Posted June 22, 2006.

Bowers, Fredson. *Elizabethan Revenge Tragedy.* Princeton, N.J.: Princeton University Press, 1940.

Braden, Gordon. "Shakespeare's Roman Tragedies." In *A Companion to Shakespeare's Works: The Tragedies,* edited by Richard Dutton and Jean E. Howard. Oxford: Blackwell, 2003.

Brooke, Harold. *Shakespeare's Early Tragedies.* London: Routledge, 1968.

Broude, Ronald. "Roman and Goth in *Titus Andronicus.*" *Shakespeare Studies* 6 (1970): 27–34.

Buchanan, Judith. *Shakespeare on Film.* Harlow, England: Pearson Education, 2005.

Charney, Maurice. *Shakespeare's Roman Plays: The Function of Imagery in the Drama.* Cambridge, Mass.: Harvard University Press, 1961.

Cartmell, Deborah. *Interpreting Shakespeare on Screen.* Houndmills, England: Palgrave Macmillan, 2000.

Cohen, Derek. *Shakespeare's Culture of Violence.* Houndmills, England: Macmillan, 1993.

Dessen, Alan C. *Shakespeare in Performance: Titus Andronicus.* Manchester, England: Manchester University Press, 1989.

Dillon, Janette, ed. *Cambridge Introduction to Shakespeare's Tragedies.* Cambridge: Cambridge University Press, 2007.

Donaldson, Peter S. "Game Space/Tragic Space: Julie Taymor's *Titus.*" In *A Companion to Shakespeare and Performance,* edited by Barbara Hodgdon and William B. Worthen. Oxford, England: Wiley Blackwell, 2005.

Findlay, Alison. *A Feminist Perspective on Renaissance Drama.* Oxford, England: Blackwell, 1999.

Fisher, Philip. Review of *Titus Andronicus* at the Globe, 2006. *The British Theatre Guide.* Available online. URL: http://www.britishtheatreguide.info/reviews/titusglobe-rev.htm.

Foakes, R. A. *Shakespeare and Violence.* Cambridge: Cambridge University Press, 2003.

Green, Douglas E. "Interpreting 'her martyr'd signs': Gender and Tragedy in *Titus Andronicus.*" *Shakespeare Quarterly* 40 (1989): 317–326.

Hamilton, A. C. "*Titus Andronicus:* The Form of Shakespearean Tragedy." *Shakespeare Quarterly* 3 (1963): 201–213.

Hancock, Brecken Rose. "Roman or Revenger?: The Definition and Distortion of Masculine Identity in *Titus Andronicus.*" *Early Modern Literary Studies* 10, no. 1 (May 2004). Available online. URL: http://extra.shu.oc.uk/emls/10–1/hancroma.htm. Accessed June 16, 2011.

Hopkins, Lisa, and Matthew Steggle. *Renaissance Literature and Culture.* New York: Continuum, 2006.

Hulse, S. Clark. "'Wrestling the Alphabet': Oratory and Action in *Titus Andronicus.*" *Criticism* 21 (1979): 106–118.

Johnson, Samuel. *The Plays of William Shakespeare.* Vol. 3, *The Tragedies.* 1765.

Kahn, Coppélia. *Roman Shakespeare.* London: Routledge, 1997.

Kerrigan, John. *Revenge Tragedy: Aeschylus to Armageddon.* Oxford, England: Clarendon Press, 1996.

Kingsley-Smith, Jane. "*Titus Andronicus:* A Violent Change of Fortunes." *Literature Compass* 5, no. 1 (2008): 106–121. Available online. URL: http://www.blackwell-compass.com/subject/literature/article_view?article_id=lico_articles_bpl510. Accessed June 16, 2011.

Kolin, Philip C., ed. *Titus Andronicus: Critical Essays.* New York: Garland Publishing, 1997.

Leggatt, Alexander. *Shakespeare's Tragedies: Violation and Identity.* Cambridge: Cambridge University Press, 2005.

Marlowe, Sam. Review of *Titus Andronicus* at the Globe Theater. *The Times Newspaper.* Available online. URL: http://entertainment.timesonline.co.uk/tol/arts_and_entertainment/article670088.ece. Accessed June 16, 2011.

McCandless, David. "A Tale of Two Tituses: Julie Taymor's Vision on Stage and Screen." *Shakespeare Quarterly* 53 (2002): 486–510.

Mehl, Dieter. *Shakespeare's Tragedies: An Introduction.* Cambridge: Cambridge University Press, 1986.

Metz, Harold G. "Stage History of *Titus Andronicus.*" *Shakespeare Quarterly* 28 (1977): 154–169.

Miola, Robert S. *Shakespeare's Rome.* Cambridge: Cambridge University Press, 1983.

Mohler, Tina. "'What Is Thy Body but a Swallowing Grave . . . ?': Desire Underground in *Titus Andronicus.*" *Shakespeare Quarterly* 57 (2006): 23–44.

Palmer, D. J. "The Unspeakable in Pursuit of the Uneatable: Language and Action in *Titus Andronicus.*" *Critical Quarterly* 14 (1972): 320–339.

Ravenscroft, Edward. *Titus Andronicus or The Rape of Lavinia.* London: n.p., 1687.

Secher, Benjamin. Review of *Titus Andronicus,* directed by Yukio Ninagawa. The Telegraph Newspaper Online. Available online. URL: http://www.telegraph.co.uk/culture/theatre/drama/3653023/Death-mutilation-and-not-a-drop-of-blood.html. Accessed June 16, 2011.

Smith, Ian. "Titus Andronicus: A Time for Race and Revenge." In *A Companion to Shakespeare's Works: The Tragedies,* edited by Richard Dutton and Jean E. Howard. Oxford, England: Blackwell, 2003.

Smith, Molly Easo. "Spectacles of Torment in *Titus Andronicus.*" *Studies in English Literature* 36 (1996): 315–331.

Starks, Lisa S. "Cinema of Cruelty: Powers of Horror in Julie Taymor's *Titus.*" In *The Reel Shakespeare: Alternative Cinema and Theory,* edited by Lisa S. Starks and Courtney Lehmann, 121–142. London: Associated University Presses, 2002.

Taylor, A. B. *Shakespeare's Ovid: The Metamorphoses in the Plays and Poems.* Cambridge: Cambridge University Press, 2000.

Taylor, Paul. Review of *Titus Andronicus,* directed by Yukio Ninagawa. The Independent Newspaper. Available online. URL: http://www.independent.co.uk/arts-entertainment/theatre-dance/reviews/titus-andronicus-royal-shakespeare-theatre-stratforduponavon—none-onestar-twostar-threestar-fourstar-fivestar-405029.html. Posted June 22, 2006.

Thompson, Ann. "Philomel in *Titus Andronicus* and *Cymbeline.*" *Shakespeare Studies* 31 (1978): 23–32.

Titus. Fox Searchlight official Web site for Julie Taymor's film. Available online. URL: http://www.foxsearchlight.com/titus/#.

Tricomi, Albert H. "The Aesthetics of Mutilation in *Titus Andronicus.*" *Shakespeare Survey* 27 (1974): 11–19.

Waith, Eugene, ed. *Titus Andronicus.* Oxford: Oxford University Press, 1998.

Wells, Stanley. "Shakespeare Performances in London and Stratford-upon-Avon 1986–87." *Shakespeare Survey* 41 (1988): 159–182.

Willbern, David. "Rape and Revenge in *Titus Andronicus.*" *English Literary Renaissance* 8 (1978): 159–182.

Willis, Deborah. "'The Gnawing Vulture': Revenge, Trauma Theory and *Titus Andronicus.*" *Shakespeare Quarterly* 53 (2002): 21–52.

Wilson, John Dover, ed. *Titus Andronicus.* 1948. Reprint, Cambridge: Cambridge University Press, 1968.

FILM AND VIDEO PRODUCTIONS

Dunne, Christopher, dir. *Titus Andronicus.* With Robert Reece, Richard Porter, and Alex Chew. Joe Redner Film and Productions, 1999.

Griffin, Richard, dir. *Titus Andronicus*. With Nigel Gore, Zoya Pierson, and John Capalbo. South Main Street Productions, 2000.

Howell, Jane, dir. *Titus Andronicus*. With Trevor Peacock, Eileen Atkins, and Edward Hardwicke. BBC, 1985.

Patton, Pat, dir. Titus Andronicus 1986. A video-taping of the Oregon Shakespeare Festival performance June 24, 1986. TOFT archival copy available at Lincoln Center.

Taymor, Julie, dir. *Titus*. With Anthony Hopkins, Jessica Lange, and Jonathan Rhys Meyers. Walt Disney Studios Home Entertainment, 1999.

—Annaliese Connolly

Troilus and Cressida

INTRODUCTION

William J. Rolfe's single-sentence preface to his 1882 edition of *Troilus and Cressida* for the English Classics series must rank among the briefest, and most negative, written for any of Shakespeare's plays: "As this play, like *Timon of Athens,* is not suitable for school use or for social reading, the text is given without expurgation." Despite the fact that the play seems to have been written while Shakespeare was at the very height of his powers, coming midway between such undisputed masterpieces as *Hamlet* and *Othello,* the play's pessimistic, even nihilistic, tone was so little appreciated that as late as 1923 (the year of the play's first modern professional stage production), critic Agnes Mackensie pronounced it "the work of a man whose soul is poisoned with filth." Disdain for this seemingly sordid tale of a one-night stand gone bad, set against the backdrop of an equally sordid war going even worse, was so thorough, for so long, that it seems to have gone nearly three centuries without having been given a single performance. Although the title page on the initial quarto publication of the play suggests that it had been performed by Shakespeare's company, there is no definite record of any performance before 1898, and that one was an amateur production in Germany with two-thirds of the play cut. In that very year, however, George Bernard Shaw made the claim that *Troilus and Cressida* was one of the plays that showed that Shakespeare was "ready and willing to start at the 20th century if the seven-teenth would only let him." Shaw proved correct, and over the course of the 20th century, the play grew steadily in critical and popular esteem to such a degree that during the 1990s it became the single most frequently performed of Shakespeare's plays. In the 21st century, *Troilus and Cressida* has cemented its status as one of the most fascinating and elusive plays in Shakespeare's canon, and the one that may speak the most directly to the temper of our time. It is now seen as a worthy companion to the great works written around it, and Virgil Whitaker speaks for many critics in suggesting that this highly philosophical play serves as "the keystone in the arch of Shakespeare's intellectual development."

BACKGROUND

The myth that Britain had been founded by, and named for, a Trojan (Aeneas's grandson Brutus) and that London was originally created as a New Troy had been common currency in England at least since Geoffrey of Monmouth's version of the island's story in his *Historia Regum Britanniae* (1136). In addition to lending antiquity and nobility to the national narrative, the myth also played into the twin traditions of *translatio imperii* and *translatio studii,* according to which world history, properly understood, revealed the progression of empire and of learning steadily westward from its origins in Greece, and development in Rome, toward its final fulfillment in Britain. This tradition simultaneously established not just cultural but spiritual ascendancy, since that patently purposive history revealed divine preference for the nation. While not all authorities accepted the myth uncritically, it was sufficiently widely held that Elizabeth had deemed it worthwhile to trace her ancestry back to Aeneas, and James I had claimed descent from Trojans on both sides. Adaptations of stories based on the Trojan War had proven durably popular fare, including a *Troilus and Cressida* play written by Henry Chettle and William Dekker for a rival company, The Admiral's Men, in 1599, just a few years earlier.

The plot of that part of Shakespeare's play that treats of the Trojan War is largely based upon Homer, which Shakespeare could have known from a variety of Latin and French sources (though not directly from Homer). Of particular importance as impetus and inspiration is George Chapman's English translation of Homer's *Iliad* (dedicated to the earl of Essex as a new Achilles): The first installment, comprising seven books, had just appeared in 1598. For those critics who see Chapman as the chief "rival poet" in the *Sonnets* sequence, one might add competitive rivalry as another interest in Chapman's work. The great editor F. J. Furnivall speculated that Shakespeare's envy of Chapman had motivated his own "deliberate debasing of the heroes" to create his "repulsive picture of the Trojan and Grecian war" in opposition to Chapman's hero-worship of them. Other important sources include William Caxton's version of *The Recuyell of the Historyes of Troye* (translated by 1471, published by 1474—possibly the first English-language book to be printed in England—and reissued in 1596), probably supplemented in places by John Lydgate's *The Troy Book* (1513), especially in the portrait of Ajax or the late battle scenes in which Hector kills a man for his armor and Achilles has his Myrmidons brutally murder the unarmed Hector.

The love story between Troilus and Cressida was widely known in Shakespeare's time, with Cressida already a byword for the unfaithful lover. His treatment of the lovers is largely derived from Chaucer's *Troilus and Criseyde* (ca. 1382), though sufficiently altered at some points that many critics used to be skeptical that he had even had firsthand knowledge of Chaucer's poem, much less been influenced by it. As is often the case, he seldom seems to have had his source in front of him, working rather with remembered bits and pieces from it than substantial passages: There are almost no direct verbal borrowings or even close echoes. Robert Henryson's *Testament of Cresseid* (ca. 1490) is a continuation of Chaucer's work (normally printed with it beginning with Thynne's 1532 edition), in which the abandoned and promiscuous Cresseid has been stricken with leprosy (generally considered in the later Middle Ages to be a venereal disease) and reduced to begging. While the poem provides no clear plot parallels to Shakespeare's version, its emphasis on her crime and punishment seems to have served as a counterweight to Chaucer's highly sympathetic portrayal of Cressida, helping to establish a generally negative view of her character, and it may also have contributed to the frequent use of the imagery of venereal disease in Shakespeare's play.

Date and Text of the Play

F. J. Furnivall declared in 1877 that "this is the most difficult of all Shakespeare's plays to deal with, as well for date as position." The dating of *Troilus* depends primarily upon how one interprets two key pieces of evidence. On February 7, 1603, an entry appears in the *Stationers' Register* that would permit James Roberts "to print, when he has gotten sufficient authority for it, the book of Troilus and Cressida as it is acted by my Lord Chamberlain's Men." Despite a good deal of speculation and discussion, there is no critical consensus as to whose authority would have been required, or how serious Roberts was in his intention to publish the play, or how closely this play might have resembled the one we read today. While there is no direct evidence of public performance, several lines in Thomas Middleton's *The Family of Love* (1602) appear to parody Ulysses' discourse on order, which implies that he must have known Shakespeare's play, probably, though not certainly,

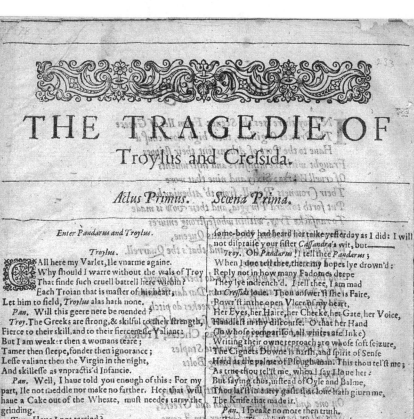

THE TRAGEDIE OF
Troylus and Cressida.

Actus Primus. Scæna Prima.

Enter Pandarus and Troylus.

Troylus.

CAll here my Varlet, Ile vnarme againe.
Why should I warre without the wals of Troy
That finde such cruell battell here within?
Each Troian that is master of his heart,
Let him to field, *Troylus* alas hath none.

Pan. Will this geere nere be mended?

Troy. The Greeks are strong, & skilful to their strength,
Fierce to their skill, and to their fiercenesse Valiant:
But I am weaker then a womans teare;
Tamer then sleepe, fonder then ignorance;
Lesse valiant then the Virgin in the night,
And skillesse as vnpractis'd Infancie.

Pan. Well, I haue told you enough of this: For my
part, Ile not meddle nor make no farther. Hee that will
haue a Cake out of the Wheate, must needes tarry the
grinding.

Troy. Haue I not tarried?

Pan. I the grinding; but you must tarry the bolting.

Troy. Haue I not tarried?

Pan. I the boulting; but you must tarry the leau'ing.

Troy. Still haue I tarried.

Pan. I, to the leauening: but heeres yet in the word
hereafter, the Kneading, the making of the Cake, the
heating of the Ouen, and the Baking; nay, you must stay
the cooling too, or you may chance to burne your lips.

Troy. Patience her selfe, what Goddesse ere she be,
Doth lesser blench at sufferance, then I doe:
At *Priams* Royall Table doe I sit;
And when faire *Cressid* comes into my thoughts,
So (Traitor) then she comes, when she is thence.

Pan. Well:
She look'd yesternight fairer, then euer I saw her looke,
Or any woman else.

Troy. I was about to tell thee, when my heart,
As wedged with a sigh, would riue in twaine,
Least *Hector* or my Father should perceiue me:
I haue (as when the Sunne doth light a-scorne)
Buried this sigh, in wrinkle of a smile:
But sorrow, that is couch'd in seeming gladnesse,
Is like that mirth, Fate turnes to sudden sadnesse.

Pan. And her haire were not somewhat darker then
Helens, well go too, there were no more comparison betweene the Women. But for my part she is my Kinswo-
man, I would not (as they tearme it) praise it, but I wold

some-body had heard her talke yesterday as I did: I will
not dispraise your sister *Cassandra's* wit, but———

Troy. Oh *Pandarus*! I tell thee *Pandarus*;
When I doe tell thee, there my hopes lye drown'd:
Reply not in how many Fadomes deepe
They lye indrench'd. I tell thee, I am mad
In *Cressids* loue. Thou answer'st she is Faire,
Powr'st in the open Vlcer of my heart,
Her Eyes, her Haire, her Cheeke, her Gate, her Voice,
Handlest in thy discourse. O that her Hand
(In whose comparison, all whites are Inke)
Writing their owne reproach, to whose soft seizure,
The Cignets Downe is harsh, and spirit of Sense
Hard as the palme of Ploughman. This thou tel'st me;
As true thou tel'st me, when I say I loue her:
But saying thus, instead of Oyle and Balme,
Thou lai'st in euery gash that loue hath giuen me,
The Knife that made it.

Pan. I speake no more then truth.

Troy. Thou do'st not speake so much.

Pan. Faith, Ile not meddle in't: Let her be as shee is,
if she be faire, 'tis the better for her, and she be not, she
ha's the mends in her owne hands.

Troy. Good *Pandarus*: How now *Pandarus*?

Pan. I haue had my Labour for my trauell, ill thought
on of her, and ill thought on of you: Gone betweene and
betweene, but small thankes for my labour.

Troy. What art thou angry *Pandarus*? what with me?

Pan. Because she's Kinne to me, therefore shee's not
so faire as *Helen*, and she were not kin to me, she would
be as faire on Friday, as *Helen* is on Sunday. But what
care I? I care not and she were a Black-a-Moore, 'tis all
one to me.

Troy. Say I she is not faire?

Troy. I doe not care whether you doe or no. Shee's a
Foole to stay behinde her Father: Let her to the Greeks,
and so Ile tell her the next time I see her: for my part, Ile
meddle nor make no more i'th'matter.

Troy. *Pandarus*? *Pan.* Not I.

Troy. Sweete *Pandarus*.

Pan. Pray you speake no more to me, I will leaue all
as I found it, and there an end.   *Exit Pand.*

Sound Alarum.

Tro. Peace you vngracious Clamors, peace rude sounds,
Fooles on both sides, *Helen* must needs be faire,
When with your bloud you daily paint her thus.
I cannot fight vpon this Argument:

Title page of the First Folio edition of *Troilus and Cressida*, published in 1623 by means of a public performance. On January 28, 1609, another entry appears, registering to Richard Bonian and Henry Walley "a book called the History of Troilus and Cressida." They did indeed have the play printed (by George Eld, who also printed the *Sonnets* in that same year), and the resulting 1609 quarto exists in two states. The first calls the play "The History of Troilus and Cressida" and assures readers that it appears "As it was acted by the King's Majesty's servants at the Globe." The second state has a different title page, identifying itself as "The Famous History of Troilus and Cressida, excellently expressing the beginning of their loves, with the conceited wooing of Pandarus, Prince of Licia," and includes an "Epistle" to the reader implying that it is a new play, and one that has never been performed. It seems, then, that a version of the play must have existed and had probably been performed no later than 1602, and possibly a year or two earlier, but it is not certain that it is exactly the same play as the one published in 1609.

The text of the play is similarly difficult to pin down, as the two states of the quarto (Q) and the version in the First Folio (F, 1623) have each been seen by different editors to be the most authoritative copy-text upon which to base modern editions. Even though almost all modern editions finally take Q as their control-text (only the Oxford edition takes F as its control), this near-unanimity should not be thought of as an indication that there is no controversy. In fact, the decision is sufficiently complex that it has been proposed that the best solution might be to edit both the Q and F texts separately and print them together on facing pages. The first three pages of the F text are a reprint of Q, but the remainder derives from Q as supplemented and corrected with reference to some other text, presumably a manuscript. The traditional consensus had long been that the manuscript was Shakespeare's own working draft of the play (his so-called "foul papers"). But because the stage directions, including those for sound effects, are more complete in F, recent studies have speculated that the additional manuscript may have been a the-

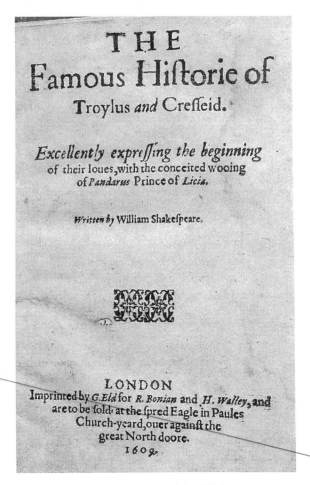

Title page of the second state of the 1609 quarto publication of *Troilus and Cressida*

atrical promptbook, a playhouse copy that would have been marked up for performance. There are some 5,000 total variants between Q and F, mostly in spelling and punctuation, but there are also several hundred substantive variants, and F contains a prologue and 45 lines of text, occurring in 19 separate passages, that are not included in Q. The sheer number of changes suggests to many editors that Shakespeare himself may have revised the play, perhaps in stages over a period of years, but close scrutiny has not revealed any consistent pattern that would prove one version more reliable than another. The differences most often come down to individual word choices, however, and despite the great difficulty the play poses for editors, the differences are not likely to cause confusion for the reader or playgoer, or to alter seriously their overall interpretations of characters or actions.

SYNOPSIS
Brief Synopsis

The play covers a period of three days during the seventh year of the Trojan War, in which the Greek armies, led by Agamemnon, are attempting to retrieve Helen, his brother Menelaus's wife, from her abductor and current lover, Paris, son of King Priam of Troy. The Greeks are concerned that their seven-year siege has accomplished so little and strategize to get their greatest warrior, Achilles, back to the battlefield, which he has avoided partly from his love for Priam's daughter Polyxena and partly from his contempt for the Greek leaders. They see their opportunity when the Trojans deliver a challenge to combat from Hector, their greatest warrior; by sending Ajax instead of Achilles to meet him, they hope to rouse Achilles' anger and lust for battle. The Trojans, similarly frustrated by the protracted war, debate whether it would be wiser to return Helen and end the war. Although Hector argues persuasively that reason and justice dictate returning her to her husband, the demands of honor and glory, most strongly pressed by Priam's son Troilus, eventually lead them to decide to continue the war.

Interspersed with these military and political events are scenes devoted to the love story between Troilus and Cressida, which is even more tightly compressed in time: They have their first meeting in the evening, spend that night together, and are separated by circumstance the next morning; that same night, Cressida takes a new lover. The play opens as Troilus, in love with Cressida, pleads with her uncle Pandarus to help him gain her heart. Neither man is aware that Cressida, who has carefully hidden her feelings, has also fallen in love with Troilus. Pandarus does get them together, and they quickly reach an understanding and spend the night together. The two plots of love and war intersect when Cressida's father Calchas, a prophet who has foreseen the Greek victory and deserted to their camp, persuades the Greek commanders to exchange Antenor, a captured Trojan, for his daughter. The next morning, as Troilus and Cressida emerge from their first night together, the exchange is made, and the lovers are parted after exchanging vows to remain faithful to one another. Although the end of the war is not included in the action of the play, the audience would know that Antenor, ironically, will be the traitor who causes the destruction of Troy.

By that evening, Cressida has resigned herself to her separation from Troilus and transferred her love to the dynamic Greek warrior Diomedes. Troilus, who has observed the scene between them while hidden, vows revenge on Diomedes. The next day consists largely of a series of battle scenes. Hector kills Patroclus, Achilles' beloved friend, which brings him back into the battle. He and his soldiers surround and brutally murder the unarmed Hector, virtually guaranteeing the downfall of Troy. Troilus resolves to fight on nevertheless, rejecting Pandarus and Cressida in favor of violence and revenge.

Prologue

The play opens with a prologue delivered by an "arm'd" character—presumably dressed as a warrior—explaining the background to the story: The Greeks have sailed to Troy to wage war against the Trojans to retrieve Menelaus's wife, Helen, from Paris, with whom she had eloped. The prologue alerts the audience that the play will begin in the middle of the wars rather than at the beginning. Somewhat oddly, it contains no reference to the story of Troilus and Cressida.

Act I, Scene 1

In Troy, before King Priam's palace, Troilus complains to his friend Pandarus that his secret love for Pandarus's niece Cressida has made him unequal to his duties as a soldier and member of the royal

A 16th-century depiction of the abduction of Helen *(Painting by Francesco Primaticcio)*

family. Pandarus pretends to be unsympathetic and declares that he will meddle no more in their relationship. He exits, and then Aeneas enters and persuades Troilus to accompany him to join the battle against the Greeks.

Act I, Scene 2

In a street in Troy, Cressida and her servant Alexander exchange small talk about a recent encounter on the battlefield between Ajax, one of the leading Greek warriors, and Troilus's brother Hector, the greatest Trojan warrior. Pandarus enters and attempts to turn the conversation from Hector's merits to those of Troilus. He relates an anecdote demonstrating Helen's esteem for Troilus by way of baiting Cressida into a jealous reaction, but she deflects his gambit with clever wordplay and feigned misunderstandings. Several of the most renowned Trojan soldiers return from the battle and file past them, Pandarus comparing each of them unfavorably to Troilus, and Cressida mocking his comments. She pretends not to admire or even recognize Troilus when he finally passes, but after Pandarus is called away by a servant to meet with

Troilus, she reveals her love for him in a soliloquy. She explains that her pretended disdain is a strategy to maintain control of their relationship, fearing that a woman who surrenders too easily will be little prized by her lover.

Act I, Scene 3

In the Greek camp, King Agamemnon and his generals debate why, after seven years of the siege, Troy still stands unbeaten. Agamemnon speculates that the gods are testing the Greek warriors by denying them victory, and the elderly adviser Nestor agrees. Ulysses, however, argues that discord and factionalism within the Greek ranks is the cause and not the will of the gods or the great strength of Troy. Specifically, Ulysses blames the refusal of Achilles, their greatest warrior, to take orders and follow Agamemnon into battle. Instead, he lies in his tent mocking the Greek leadership, as his friend Patroclus parodies their words and appearances. Nestor notes that other warriors have been infected by their disrespectful attitude, including Ajax, whose servant Thersites similarly slanders the Greek generals. The Trojan warrior Aeneas arrives with a message for the king. Whether innocently or as an insult—Agamemnon is unsure how to take his ceremonious behavior— he is slow to recognize that Agamemnon is the king, taking him for a common soldier. Aeneas transmits Hector's challenge to the Greeks, putting his honor and the beauty of his wife up against the honor of the Greeks and the beauty of their women. Agamemnon accepts the challenge on behalf of the Greeks and invites Aeneas to feast with them. Ulysses and Nestor remain behind as the others leave the stage. They recognize that the challenge from Hector, the greatest Trojan warrior, is undoubtedly aimed at Achilles, the greatest Greek warrior. But rather than make the obvious response by choosing Achilles to represent them, Ulysses explains the advantages of sending Ajax instead. Not only will the choice rebuke Achilles' insolence and pride, but it will allow them to sustain Greek morale and honor even if Ajax were to lose the battle, since everyone knows that he

is not really their most able warrior. They agree to choose Ajax as their champion by means of a rigged lottery.

Act II, Scene 1

At the Greek camp, Ajax questions his servant Thersites about the proclamation regarding Hector's challenge, but Thersites responds only with verbal abuse until finally Ajax begins to beat him. Achilles and Patroclus appear, are similarly insulted by Thersites, and then tell Ajax of Hector's challenge and the proposed lottery.

Act II, Scene 2

In Troy, Priam reads to his sons (Hector, Troilus, Paris, and Helenus) a letter from Nestor demanding Helen's release, in return for which the Greeks will return home. Hector argues that reason dictates

The Love of Helen and Paris (1788) *(Painting by Jacques-Louis David)*

letting her go, since she is of no value to the Trojans that could justify further loss of lives. Helenus agrees, but Troilus mocks their reliance on mere reason, asserting that manhood and honor are higher principles than reason and that their honor, even more than Helen, is the crucial thing to be defended. He reminds them that Paris's abduction of Helen was originally undertaken in revenge for the Greeks' refusal to return Priam's sister Hesione after her own earlier abduction by the Greeks, and that they had all consented to it beforehand. At the peak of their debate, Priam's daughter Cassandra, a mad prophetess, runs through the scene declaring that Troy will burn unless Helen is returned to the Greeks. Troilus dismisses her prophecy as brain sick raving, and Paris declares his determination to retain Helen. Hector insists again that they are arguing out of passion and appetite rather than logic, and that the dictates of law as well as of reason demand that Helen be returned. Nevertheless, he agrees to support them and to uphold their collective honor by continuing the fight against the Greeks.

Act II, Scene 3

Thersites, having switched his allegiance and service from Ajax to Achilles, rants against the Greeks, then insults Achilles and Patroclus when they come out of their tent. Agamemnon approaches with several of his generals to meet with Achilles, but upon seeing them, Achilles retreats into his tent with Thersites. Patroclus tells them that Achilles is too sick to meet with them, but they correctly attribute his refusal to his pride. Patroclus and Ulysses enter the tent to persuade Achilles to come out, while Agamemnon works to flatter Ajax and arouse his anger against Achilles. Ulysses returns to confirm Achilles' refusal to speak with the Greek leaders. He, Nestor, and Diomedes join Agamemnon in lavishly praising Ajax at Achilles' expense, playing on Ajax's pride and ambition to convince him that they all regard him as Achilles' superior in every way. All the while, they amuse themselves with mocking asides on his gullibility and stupidity.

Act III, Scene 1

In Troy, Pandarus, after some verbal byplay with Paris's witty servant, tells Paris and Helen that Troilus will not be able to have supper at the palace that evening. Paris quickly suspects that a meeting with Cressida is the explanation for his absence. The three chat about love, and Pandarus sings a song before leaving.

Act III, Scene 2

Pandarus meets Troilus in Calchas's orchard and goes to fetch Cressida, while Troilus rhapsodizes about his love. He brings Cressida forth, but the lovers are shy and speak in generalities about love and lovers, while he goes back inside the house to build a fire. After Pandarus returns, Cressida is sufficiently emboldened to admit she has loved Troilus for many months, breaking her vow to herself to hide her emotions. They kiss, but then Cressida's doubts seem to renew themselves, as she questions both her own motives and Troilus's love. Troilus reassures her and predicts that the phrase "As true as Troilus" will become a cliché for describing constancy in love. Cressida oddly, and ominously, focuses on her own potential for deceit, claiming that if she should ever be untrue, her identifying phrase will be "As false as Cressid." Pandarus characterizes himself as their go-between and sums up by declaring that if they prove false, "Let all constant men be Troiluses, all false women Cressids, and all brokers-between Pandars." He then shows them to a bed chamber where they will consummate their love.

Act III, Scene 3

At the Greek camp, Cressida's father, the traitor Calchas, who had gone over to the Greek side when his gift of prophecy showed him that they would be victorious in the war, requests that Agamemnon and the Greek leadership exchange their recently captured Trojan prisoner, Antenor, for his daughter. Agamemnon grants the request, asking Diomedes to conduct the exchange and to notify Hector that Ajax will be his opponent in the battlefield challenge. Achilles and Patroclus step out of their tent as Diomedes and Calchas leave, and Ulysses suggests that they all walk past Achilles' tent and either ignore him completely or greet him with disdain. Achilles first reacts with reflections upon the transience of fortune but then assures himself that his own position is still secure. He accosts Ulysses, who is pretending to be engrossed in reading about the very topic on Achilles' mind. Ulysses explains that a man's merits and virtues are only widely appreciated when exercised on behalf of others. He then remarks upon the opportunity that Ajax will soon have to gain glory by meeting Hector in single combat. Feigning sympathy for Achilles, he reminds him that such renown will effectively erase the Greeks' memory of Achilles' own exploits, especially since he has entombed himself in his tent. Not only does Ulysses point out that all of the Greek leaders are already fawning over Ajax, but he also reveals his knowledge of Achilles' passion for Priam's daughter Polyxena and speculates on the relative degree of reputation to be won between the warrior who defeats the mighty Hector and the warrior who merely conquers Hector's sister. When Ulysses leaves, Patroclus, who has overheard the entire conversation, convinces Achilles that his reputation is at stake, especially since many of the Greeks believe that Achilles' absence from the battlefield is caused in part by his love for the effeminate Patroclus. Achilles resolves to send Thersites to invite the Trojan leaders to his tent after the combat between Ajax and Hector. Thersites enters and gives them a satirical report on Ajax's vainglory and imitates his speech and actions for their amusement.

Act IV, Scene 1

The four early scenes of Act IV are all extremely short and follow one another rapidly, emphasizing the rapidity and abruptness of the lovers' separation. Diomedes, arriving in Troy with Antenor, Deiphibus, and Paris, meets Aeneas, who has been sent by Priam to assist with the exchange of Cressida for Antenor. Diomedes greets Aeneas as a respected and worthy adversary, but once Aeneas leaves them to give notice to Cressida and Troilus of her imminent departure, Diomedes insults Paris, calling him a lecher and Helen a whore.

Act IV, Scene 2

At Calchas's house, Cressida and Troilus have emerged after their first night together. Pandarus shows up and embarrasses them with bawdy comments about sleeping together. Cressida coaxes Troilus back into her chamber just before Aeneas arrives. Pandarus claims that Troilus is not there, but then Troilus emerges and is informed of the exchange of Cressida for Antenor. Troilus goes with Aeneas to meet Diomedes and the others, leaving Pandarus to give Cressida the news. She is distraught and reenters the house with Pandarus, resolving that she will not leave Troy.

Act IV, Scene 3

Diomedes and the Trojans reach Calchas's house, and Troilus offers to fetch Cressida. Paris, who like Aeneas suspects Troilus's attachment to her, takes the men to another room.

Act IV, Scene 4

Troilus joins Pandarus and the grieving Cressida within and confirms that she must depart "From Troy and Troilus." Both promise to stay faithful during their separation and offer tokens of their love, as Troilus gives Cressida his sleeve, and she gives him her glove. Troilus tells her of his fear that the Greeks will win her away from his love and repeats his own vow of constancy. Diomedes enters with the rest of the men, and Troilus courteously asks him to look after Cressida. Diomedes' insolent response is to flirt with Cressida, provoking Troilus to anger and threats, which he casually dismisses. As Troilus and Cressida leave hand in hand, accompanied by Diomedes, Aeneas and the others recall that this will be the day of the combat between Ajax and Hector.

Act IV, Scene 5

In the Greek camp, the armed Ajax and the Greek generals are waiting for his battle with Hector when Diomedes arrives with Cressida. Agamemnon welcomes her, and without uttering a word,

Cressida kisses Agamemnon, Nestor, Achilles, and Patroclus (twice). When Menelaus and then Ulysses demand kisses, however, she replies with wordplay and riddles and refuses them. After she leaves with Diomedes, Nestor remarks upon her quick wit, but Ulysses dismisses her as a sluttish and promiscuous "daughter of the game." Aeneas, Troilus, Paris, Helenus, and other Trojans arrive with Hector to watch the fight with Ajax. Aeneas, noting that Ajax is half-Trojan and a relative of Hector's (Priam's sister Hesione was his mother and Hector's aunt), wonders whether the fight will be to the death or only until one man has the advantage. They begin fighting as Diomedes returns, and the issue is left to him and Aeneas, who ask the combatants to stop. Ajax wishes to continue, but Hector refuses to fight further against his cousin. They embrace, and the Greeks and Trojans vie with one another in graciously praising their enemies. Hector agrees to feast with Agamemnon and Ulysses, although before they depart in harmony, Achilles and Hector exchange threats to kill each other the next time they meet in battle. Troilus holds Ulysses behind as the rest leave to discover where Calchas, and therefore Cressida, can be found. Ulysses, unaware of Troilus's love for Cressida, reveals that Diomedes seems intent on winning her love. He agrees to take Troilus to their tent after their feast with Agamemnon.

Act V, Scene 1

Before Achilles' tent in the Greek camp, Thersites brings Achilles a letter from Troy and berates Patroclus on the basis of gossip that he is Achilles' "masculine whore," eliciting counter-insults from Patroclus. The letter from Queen Hecuba, with a token from her daughter Polyxena, reminds Achilles of his vow not to fight, which he resolves to keep, despite his recent threats to Hector. The Greek generals bring Hector and Troilus to the tent, but when Diomedes leaves, Ulysses and Troilus follow him, followed in turn by Thersites.

Act V, Scene 2

At Calchas's tent, Cressida and Diomedes, after considerable vacillation on her part, pledge their hearts to one another. She gives him Troilus's sleeve as a token of her love, delivering a brief farewell soliloquy to Troilus after Diomedes leaves, then retreating into her tent. Unknown to her, Troilus and Ulysses have witnessed the entire scene and commented upon it, from a distance, while Thersites has observed all four of the other parties and provided his own cynical commentary. Troilus first reacts with disorientation and disbelief, then with anger at Diomedes, whom he vows to kill in battle. Aeneas approaches to send Troilus back to Troy, who leaves after he says his own farewell to Cressida's memory. Thersites resolves that he will recommend Cressida to Patroclus, who is always looking for another easy whore like her.

Act V, Scene 3

In Troy, Hector's wife Andromache, who has had ominous dreams of slaughter, and his sister Cassandra persuade Hector to stay away from the battle that day. When Troilus enters, Hector advises him to stay away as well, but Troilus, bent on revenge against Diomedes, berates Hector for his decision and faults him generally for his noble and chivalric approach to war. Priam enters and reveals that his wife has had similar visions of disaster, but Troilus has successfully convinced Hector that his duty is to fight. After all but Troilus leave, Pandarus brings him a letter from Cressida. He dismisses the letter as "mere words" and tears it up.

Act V, Scene 4

The final seven scenes of the play are all very brief and follow one another rapidly—in many productions these are treated virtually as a single continuous scene. In the battlefield between Troy and the Greek camp, Troilus and Diomedes fight while Thersites observes and mocks them for what he calls their lechery.

Act V, Scene 5

Diomedes, having captured Troilus's horse, tells his servant to take it to Cressida, perhaps as (false) proof that Troilus is dead. A series of Greek warriors pass over the stage in succession, each providing information about the battle: Agamemnon alerts Diomedes that the battle is going against them and that reinforcements are needed; Nestor confirms that Patroclus is among the many Greeks killed by Hector, and that his body has been taken to Achilles; and Ulysses reports that Achilles has vowed revenge against Hector, as has Ajax against Troilus, who has killed one of his friends. Ajax and Achilles cross the stage raging for blood.

Act V, Scene 6
Ajax and Diomedes meet with Troilus and exit fighting. Hector gains the advantage fighting against Achilles but chivalrously lets him go unharmed. Troilus returns to announce that Ajax has captured Aeneas and leaves to rescue him. Hector pursues a Greek warrior for his splendid armor.

Act V, Scene 7
Achilles exhorts his personal troops, the Myrmidons, to help him find and kill Hector. Menelaus and Paris cross the stage fighting, as Thersites insults them. Margarelon chases the cowardly Thersites off the stage.

Act V, Scene 8
While Hector rests unarmed, Achilles and his Myrmidons surround and kill him. Achilles orders them to spread the word that he killed Hector himself and to tie Hector's body behind his horse so he can drag it through the battlefield.

Act V, Scene 9
The Greek generals and soldiers rejoice at the news of Hector's death, which ensures the inevitable defeat of the Trojans.

Act V, Scene 10
The Trojans, still in possession of the field, learn of Hector's death from Troilus, who vows to continue fighting despite the ruinous consequences sure to follow the loss of Hector. Pandarus enters, to be rebuked and slapped by Troilus. Left alone, Pandarus addresses the audience as bawds and frequenters of brothels and vows to bequeath them his venereal diseases.

Achilles drags Hector's corpse to the front gates of Troy in this 19th-century fresco from the main hall of the Achilleion at Corfu. (*Painting by Franz Matsch*)

CHARACTER LIST

A Prologue An actor personifying the Prologue delivers the opening speech to the audience. The part is often played by Pandarus or Thersites in modern productions, but it was played by Ulysses in the BBC film version and by Helen in the 2008 production at London's Barbican Theatre.

THE TROJANS:

Troilus A son of Priam, the king of Troy, in love with Cressida.

Cressida (Cressid) In love with Troilus, she is the daughter of Calchas, who has left Troy to join the Greeks in the war, and the niece of Troilus's friend Pandarus.

Pandarus A lord, Cressida's uncle, who will serve as the go-between to bring the lovers together.

Hector A son of Priam and the greatest and most chivalrous of the Trojan warriors.

Cassandra Daughter of Priam who has the power of prophecy but is condemned to never be believed.

Andromache Hector's wife.

Priam The king of Troy.

Paris A son of Priam, he abducted Helen from her husband, Menelaus, the event that triggered the Trojan War. The Trojans, however, see this act as revenge for the earlier abduction of Priam's sister Hesione by the Greeks.

Calchas A Trojan priest and soothsayer. Having prophesied the Greeks' victory, he deserts Troy and joins the Greek camp. His desire to be reunited with his daughter, Cressida, dooms her love affair with Troilus.

Aeneas A Trojan commander.

Antenor A Trojan commander. He has been captured by the Greeks and will be returned to Troy in exchange for Cressida. Ironically, his treason will eventually give the Greeks their victory, so the outcome of the romantic plot will prove decisive for the determination of the military plot.

Deiphibus A son of Priam.

Helenus A son of Priam and a priest of Troy.

Margarelon A bastard son of Priam.

Alexander A witty servant to Cressida.

Servant and Boy In Troilus's service.

Servant In Paris's service.

THE GREEKS:

Ulysses A Greek commander and their chief strategist.

Thersites Ajax's servant; deformed and scurrilous Greek. He provides a cynical running commentary on the characters on both sides and on the love and war stories.

Achilles The greatest of the Greek warriors. He has promised not to participate in the war because of his love for Polyxena, a daughter of King Priam and Queen Hecuba of Troy.

Agamemnon The general commander of the Greek army and Menelaus's brother.

Menelaus The King of Sparta, brother of Agamemnon, and husband of Helen.

Helen Menelaus's wife, now Paris's lover in Troy.

Nestor An elderly Greek commander.

Ajax A fatuous and self-important Greek commander, who considers himself in a rivalry with Achilles for the reputation as the Greeks' greatest warrior.

Diomedes (Diomed) A cynical Greek commander who will succeed Troilus as Cressida's lover after she is sent to the Greek camp.

Patroclus A Greek commander and beloved friend of Achilles. His death at the hands of Hector will incite Achilles to break his vow not to fight and return to battle.

Servant In Diomedes' service.

CHARACTER STUDIES
Troilus

Most early criticism saw Troilus as noble and honorable but inexperienced and naive, a faithful lover who is seduced and disillusioned by a manipulative and fickle Cressida. His first appearance in English in Chaucer's *Troilus and Criseyde* had immediately established his role as the quintessential, tormented Petrarchan courtly lover. Oscar J. Campbell (1938) first proposed the interpretation that he was portrayed rather as a sensualist, established in the debate scene as "a warrior who makes a virtue of emancipating his will from the control of his reason." In this reading, his passion for Cressida is read as merely eroticism and lust rather than as courtly love. For such critics, his soliloquy about Cressida that imagines "Her bed is India, there she lies, a pearl / . . . / Ourself the merchant" (1.1.100, 103) reveals not only his lofty pretensions but also his predatory instincts: While he may at one level praise her as a "pearl," he also reduces her to an object, places her in a bed, and thinks of himself as buying her. He will also call Helen a "pearl" in the council scene and assess her "price," one of several connections that show the two women as linked in his mind. This view, it is argued, makes the abrupt dismissal of his passion, or rather its sudden transmutation into bloodlust, even more psychologically convincing. Ulysses' description of Troilus's military prowess offers a confirmation of his susceptibility to passion, as the war plot once again echoes the love plot: "he in heat of action / Is more vindicative than jealous love" (4.5.106–107).

Several of his extravagant speeches have proven similarly susceptible of reinterpretation, revealing his self-absorption rather than a genuine love for Cressida. His surprisingly understated reaction to the news of Cressida's exchange for Antenor is a touchstone for such readings, which see him as almost indifferent to her once he has achieved his sexual ends. After asking for confirmation of the news, his only reaction is to exclaim "How my achievements mock me!" (4.2.69) and to run off to meet the Greeks without even speaking to her. While his silence and abrupt departure might be interpreted as signs of acute emotional turmoil, the repetition of the term "achievement" from Cressida's earlier soliloquy cannot help but suggest a confirmation of the fear she had expressed that for men "Achievement is command" (1.2.293) and what all men truly desire is physical consummation rather than love.

David Kaula (1961) offers a middle path between these two opposed views, locating his ambivalent character between the extremes of idealist and sen-sualist, believing in the ideal but unable to find it in a degenerate world. The two distinct strands of imagery that pervade Troilus's speeches about his love are appropriate to this ambivalent perspective: For every reference to beauty, heaven, and light, one can point to a reference to appetite, hot blood, and madness. One might well complicate the matter further by arguing that Troilus develops during the course of the play from being relatively more idealistic, albeit with a fair share of youthful passion, to relatively more animalistic, albeit always with a keen sense of honor.

Cressida (Cressid)

Even though her name appears in the title of the play, the role of Cressida was usually considered a minor and even shallow one, until the latter part of the 20th century. While legendary contrarian George Bernard Shaw famously declared Cressida to be "most enchanting" and called her "Shakespeare's first real woman," most critics, for most of the play's history, had been vociferous in condemning her outright for her betrayal of Troilus, seeing her not so much as a victim of Fortune but as an embodiment of Fortune in her fickleness and instability. None of Shakespeare's sources leave us with so apparently negative a view of Cressida, who finally condemns herself, offering no excuse but her own weakness for her inconstancy. Even in Robert Henryson's late medieval version, which reduced her to a leprous beggar, Cressida was allowed a period of repentance and eventual redemption.

Much of the critical disapproval derived from comparison to Chaucer's Criseyde, whose character and actions were long understood as more admirable, or at least less culpable. The vastly different fictional time frames of the two works have inevitably influenced some of these judgments as well. Chaucer's heroine takes an unspecified but extended period to fall in love with Troilus, stays with him as a true lover for some three years, and only falls in love with Diomedes very gradually over another unspecified but extended period. In addition, Chaucer's highly sympathetic narrator defends her at every point, as does Troilus, whose love con-

Cressida in *Troilus and Cressida,* in this print published by Sampson Low, Marston, Searle & Rivington in 1888 *(Painting by Edward J. Poynter; engraving by Goupil & Cie)*

Donaldson's comparative analysis of Criseyde and Cressida in 1985, however, definitively changed the terms of that discussion, demonstrating that both characters should be read as more nuanced and ambiguous than had been assumed, emphasizing Criseyde's calculating nature and Cressida's vulnerability and youth.

Another problem in interpreting Cressida's character is the relative lack of evidence to work with, as her role is not a large one in terms of lines spoken and appearances on stage. She appears in only six of the play's 24 scenes, and her speaking role is relatively small: She speaks 152 times, but 128 of her speeches are of less than 20 words, 93 of them less than 10 words. Furthermore, some 30 percent of her speeches are, or contain, questions, especially early in the play—there is only one line in her opening conversation with her servant Alexander that is not a question. Not surprisingly, these short and often evasive speeches and this preponderance of questions reveal different patterns to different critics: for some, a pattern of deception and misdirection consistent with her calculating nature; for others, the effect is to illustrate her youth and inexperience, implying that she may be fearful and unsure of herself; for others, at least some of her questions should be seen as elements of a conscious discursive strategy, demonstrating her desire to question masculine authority and her power to seize control of situations and to introduce new subjects into discussions.

While earlier critics almost always interpreted such ambiguous indicators as though they were unambiguously negative, more recent critics, beginning with stage versions in the 1960s but especially during and after the dominance of feminist criticism since the 1980s, have tended to interpret these ambiguities in more positive ways. Rather than dismissing Cressida as a cynical and manipulative character who shares Pandarus's eagerness to get the affair consummated, her defenders emphasize that she has resisted the affair with appropriate caution "for many weary months" (3.2.124), during which time Troilus has found her consistently "stubborn-chaste against all suit" (1.1.97).

tinues even after she abandons him. And finally, Chaucer emphasizes the real dangers that Criseyde faces as a woman on her own, with no male protection, in a military camp, including the possibility of rape. Shakespeare's heroine, on the other hand, first speaks to Troilus on one day, spends that night with him, and has a new lover by the next night. Rather than having the Chaucerian narrator to defend her, Cressida is surrounded by a chorus of verbal abusers, from Ulysses to Thersites to, eventually, Troilus himself. Finally, the play offers little explicit evidence to suggest that she is anything but safe and even pampered in her new surroundings, with her father clearly a man of influence among the Greeks, King Agamemnon himself assuring her that she is "Most dearly welcome," and his generals literally lining up to get a kiss from her. E. Talbot

Suzanne Burden's performance in the 1981 film version keeps multiple interpretive options open in presenting her as a chameleon who changes her hues as her companions and circumstances are altered (this came about in part as an accident, as she and director Jonathan Miller had very different ideas about how to play the character). In Troy, she is witty and confident with Pandarus, thoughtful and clear-sighted in her soliloquies, and awkward and embarrassed when Troilus is around; in both of her scenes in the Greek camp, she begins hesitantly but quickly figures out how to cope with the generals and Diomedes. Such readings quite plausibly take her repeated vacillations between fear and desire to be genuine rather than insincere rhetorical displays, and to emphasize the desperate circumstances into which she is thrown as a young woman sent to a camp full of violent foreign men. Obviously taking such feminist readings to extremes can easily rob her of autonomy, resulting in a Cressida who is merely the innocent and passive victim of an oppressive patriarchy, with little more depth than the comparably one-dimensional flirt of the earliest critics. But most contemporary criticism has avoided overreaction, and she is now widely read in more balanced terms, as a truly enigmatic and perhaps even tragic figure, both a victim of circumstance and an active agent who bears responsibility for the results of her decisions.

Ulysses
According to Richard Grant White (1877):

Ulysses is the real hero of the play; the chief, or, at least, the great purpose of which is the utterance of the Ulyssean view of life; and in this play Shakespeare is Ulysses, or Ulysses Shakespeare. In all his other plays Shakespeare . . . lost his personal consciousness in the individuality of his own creations. . . . But in Ulysses, Shakespeare . . . drew a man of mature years, of wide observation, of profoundest cognitive power, one who knew all the weakness and all the wiles of human nature, and yet who remained with blood

unbittered and soul unsoured—a man who saw through all shams, and fathomed all motives, and yet who was not scornful of his kind, not misanthropic, hardly cynical except in passing moods; and what other man was this than Shakespeare himself?

After Troilus, Ulysses speaks the most lines, and in a play seemingly in need of a hero, he has often been seen as the likeliest candidate for the role. Modern critics have gradually grown more skeptical about Ulysses, however, often noting that his inspirational speeches on Order and Time are undercut by their immediate contexts, as both function in the development and execution of his plot to deceive and provoke Achilles into combat. The pendulum had swung to the other end of its arc by 1965, when Joseph Papp's production in New York's Central Park depicted Ulysses as the villain of the play because of his detachment and manipulative nature. This dismissal of the second-largest role in the play can create severe problems in performance, however, as directors and actors sometimes awkwardly struggle to find ingenious ways to caricature his genuinely eloquent speeches as vapid propaganda.

Thersites
One might well sketch a fair amount of the critical history of this play by comparing Richard Grant White's question about Ulysses with the question that Edward Dowden asked himself five years later (1882): "But can Shakspere's view of things be the same as that of Thersites? . . . Now such a mood of contemptuous depreciation of life may have come over Shakspere, and spoiled him, at that time, for a writer of comedy. . . . At this time, *Troilus and Cressida* may have been written, and then Shakspere, rousing himself to a deeper insight into things, may have passed on to his great series of tragedies. Let us call this, then, the comedy of disillusion." White himself, though far from approving of Thersites' "insight," did appreciate his humor: "the railings of this deformed slave are splendid. Thersites is almost as good as Falstaff." To the extent that Thersites' role is to provide comic relief, he serves

some of the same functions as Falstaff and the various fools appearing in *King Lear* and other plays, who are charged with unmasking the hypocrisies and delusions of the higher-ranking characters. In "Elizabethan" period productions, he is often costumed as a fool and shares with them the same protection from the direst consequences of his honesty: When Patroclus objects to Thersites' insults in Act II, Scene 3, Achilles tells him that Thersites should be allowed to speak freely, because "He is a privileg'd man" (l. 56).

Productions set in more modern periods, especially since Michael Macowan's influential 1938 production, tend to make Thersites a sympathetic character whose comments are to be taken as serious expressions of a point of view that the play demonstrates to be valid, rather than as primarily comic relief. He is often presented as intelligent but powerless and frustrated, a working-class hero whose honesty is meant to be favorably contrasted to the overblown rhetoric and hypocrisies of both the lovers and the corrupt officers. If in the army, he is usually played as a low-ranking soldier in the Greek army; if a civilian, he has often been a reporter, emphasizing his role as an outside commentator. In the homoerotic interpretations that have come to dominate the play since the late 1960s, he is often played as a homosexual and/or transvestite: in the 2008 Barbican Theatre production, for example, he plays one scene in a blond wig and a copy of Helen's ball gown. In performances, at least half of Thersites' lines are addressed directly to the audience, reinforcing the suggestion that his perspective is wider and thus more reliable than that of the other characters. His dominance in Act V also may contribute to the perception that he has, if not literally the last word, at least a disproportionately large share of the last words; in fact some modern productions bring him onstage during Pandarus's final speech as if to emphasize that he has survived, while so many heroes have died.

Pandarus

A Trojan nobleman, Cressida's uncle and Troilus's friend, he serves as the go-between in their love affair to help them get together. Many readers see his intense interest in the love affair as going well beyond the limits of friendly matchmaking and verging on pimping, as his concern seems to be exclusively with getting the young couple into bed, with never a mention of marriage as a goal. Both of the lovers adopt that same view, one early and one late: Cressida may be jesting when she calls Pandarus a bawd in the first act of the play, but Troilus is certainly serious in the final act when he strikes him and curses him to live forever with his name (*pander* was already a synonym for *pimp* in Shakespeare's time). He is often played in modern productions as an elderly gay man who is strongly attracted to Troilus and who takes vicarious pleasure by having his niece function as a sort of sexual surrogate in his homosexual fantasies about Troilus. While Thersites often speaks to the audience, only Pandarus explicitly breaks the convention of theatrical illusion and twice shows his awareness that he is addressing an audience in a theater, first directly after the lovers exit to Cressida's bedroom ("And Cupid grant all maidens *here* [in the theater] / Bed, chamber, Pandar to provide this gear" [3.2.207]), and in the final epilogue ("As many as be *here* of Pandar's hall" [5.10.47]). In both instances, he breaks not only a theatrical but historical frame, as he shows his awareness that his name has become the common noun for a pimp. Directors frequently extend this privilege by having him perform as the Prologue as well, which creates a symmetrical series of addresses at the beginning, the exact middle, and the end of the play. Such framing necessarily foregrounds his role and implies that his mocking and irreverent perspective constitutes a broader, and hence perhaps more comprehensive and reliable, frame than the historical and tragic perspectives contained within it.

Hector

Hector's traditional role as the greatest and most chivalrous of the Trojan warriors is largely retained by Shakespeare from his sources, but even his noble character is complicated and compromised by being embedded within the generally skeptical

Andromache and Cassandra beg Hector not to enter the battlefield in Act V, Scene 3 of *Troilus and Cressida*. This is a print from the Boydell Shakespeare Gallery project, which was first conceived in 1786 and lasted until 1805. *(Painting by Thomas Kirk; engraving by James Fittler)*

view of human nature that dominates the play. In a sense, he exemplifies the strengths and weaknesses of Troy itself, an implication developed by Ulysses when he visits the Greek camp: "I wonder now how yonder city stands / When we have here her base and pillar by us" (4.5.211–212). He is first mentioned by Cressida's servant Alexander, who in one breath establishes him as a soldier "whose patience / Is as a virtue fix'd" (1.2.4–5), and yet in the next reveals that he has scolded his wife, struck his armorer, and gone to the battlefield in wrath (1.2.11) and shame (1.2.34). His role in the Trojan council scene is similarly inconsistent, as he

first presents a compelling argument for returning Helen and ending the war but then finishes his speech by not only agreeing to keep her but revealing that he had already offered the Greeks a challenge that would guarantee further combat (although here one might concede that Shakespeare's sources leave him little choice but to have Hector come around, since the war does indeed go on). His final appearances in the play also seem to offer contradictory views of his character within a single scene (5.6), as he displays the height of knightly courtesy in sparing the defeated Achilles' life on the battlefield but then, six lines later resolves to kill a fleeing Greek warrior because he covets his beautiful armor, the act that results in his ignoble death. While he remains one of the most admirable characters in this fallen world, his end diminishes what might otherwise have lent a tragic ending to the play.

DIFFICULTIES OF THE PLAY

Troilus and Cressida is among Shakespeare's longest and most densely poetic plays, with more than its share of long-winded oratory; in performance, it is usually heavily cut. F. S. Boas, in *Shakspere and his Predecessors* (1896), made the famous observation that *Troilus and Cressida,* along with *Hamlet, All's Well That Ends Well,* and *Measure for Measure,* presents unusual difficulties to the reader: "Throughout these plays we move along dim untrodden paths, and at the close our feeling is neither of simple joy nor pain; we are excited, fascinated, perplexed, for the issues raised preclude a completely satisfactory outcome, . . . and we are left to interpret their enigmas as best we may. Dramas so singular in theme and temper cannot be strictly called comedies or tragedies. We may therefore borrow a convenient phrase of to-day and class them together as Shakspere's problem-plays."

As the quotation from Boas suggests, many of the difficulties that the play presents for readers are tied to uncertainty about its genre: Is it a history play, a tragedy, a comedy, or a satire? The quarto title pages refer to the play as a History, but the Epistle to the reader in the second state of Q repeatedly refers to it as a Comedy, while the First Folio title page calls it a Tragedy. The ordering of the First Folio originally positioned it with the Tragedies, between *Romeo and Juliet* and *Julius Caesar,* but finally placed it between the last of the Histories *(Henry VIII)* and the first of the Tragedies *(Coriolanus)* without committing to classifying it as either: The table of contents does not list it at all. Earlier critics took these mixed signals as evidence that even Shakespeare's friends and fellow actors had no idea how to label the play, but now we know that these anomalies are due to accidents during the printing of the volume. For some reason, a satisfactory text of the play apparently was not available until the very last stages of production, and the compositors' work was disrupted, so the play is the only one in the Folio that does not have page numbers throughout. Nevertheless, the coincidence has proven to be an appropriate sign of the play's undeniable slipperiness in terms of genre.

A similar degree of interpretive difficulty is presented by the characters in the play: Virtually every major character (with the possible exception of the consistently misanthropic Thersites) is presented as a blend of positive and negative qualities jostling one another in an unstable balance. Even a buffoon like Ajax may be portrayed as noble and chivalrous in his meeting with Hector, and Achilles is capable of both philosophical debate with Ulysses and cold-blooded murder.

The Language of the Play

Having been published in the same year as the Sonnets, it should not be surprising that *Troilus* displays considerable complexity and density in its poetic diction and imagery. Almost every extended speech requires close attention to unravel its implications. Even those early critics who were disgusted by the plot and characters found much to praise in the poetry and the wisdom of individual speeches (especially Ulysses' oration on degree), agreeing with Swinburne that "of all Shakespeare's offspring it is the one whose best things lose least by extraction and separation from their context." The strained, often Latinate diction is difficult even by Shakespeare's standards, with numerous unusual coinages like "abruption," "conflux," "impressure," "oppugnancy," "persistive," "propend," "protractive," "tortive," and "violentith." Such language forces readers to struggle to understand the play's meaning at the fundamental level of words and sentences, much as the comparably disruptive obstacles at higher levels cause them to struggle to understand the play's genre, themes, and character portrayals. As Jane Adamson has pointed out, a high proportion of the vocabulary in the play contributes to these larger issues of conflict, negation, and cancellation in various ways: She highlights the number of words with "dis" and "un" as prefixes ("disunite," "dispraise," "unplausive,"

An 18th-century study of Ajax's head *(Illustration by John Flaxman)* "unrespective," "untasted," "unsecret") or "less" as a suffix ("characterless," "handless"), as well as "an awesome array" of unusual words for violent acts ("deracinate," "frush"). Thomas McAlindon has identified several kinds of "stylistic dissonance" as characters lose their grip on the style appropriate to their situation, in a linguistic equivalent to the loss of order and degree analyzed in Ulysses' oration. Yet another linguistic approach notes the extraordinary number of questions in the play (approximately 400 of them, many of them significantly never answered), a stylistic device well-suited to the play's pervasively skeptical and interrogative mode. The language of the play, together with the presence of formal debates and rhetorical displays, prompted Peter Alexander to hypothesize in 1929 that it may originally have been written for a private performance before an audience of lawyers and Clerks at the Inns of Court rather than a public one at the Globe, though this theory has been drawing less and less support among recent critics.

Prose and Poetry

Prose in Shakespeare is generally the verbal medium of comical and lower-class characters, and Pandarus, as befits his role as a pimp for his own niece, speaks almost entirely in prose. He does have a rhyming couplet to end Act II, Scene 2, often taken to be the end of the first half of the play, and speaks again in rhyming verse at the very end of the play, but in both instances, the formal "rule" that sections end with rhyme overrides the behavioral "rule" that such an ignoble character speaks in prose. The other primary speaker of prose in the play is, of course, Thersites, who has nine of the play's 14 soliloquies, and whose satiric asides are rendered even more discordant when contrasted with the lofty rhetoric of the characters he comments upon. Thersites speaks only once in verse, with his rhymed couplet (rhyming, predictably enough, on the word "whore") following Cressida's final speech. Conversely, the romantic Troilus speaks only once in prose, when he and Cressida first meet (3.2.53ff.), presumably an indicator of the emotional turmoil disrupting his normally

elegant speech. Cressida, on the other hand, is highly adaptable to the verbal context: In her first scene, for example, she speaks in prose when conversing with her servant Alexander and with her uncle Pandarus but then shifts to rhyming couplets when she focuses on her love for Troilus—one might interpret this switching either as a sign of her intelligence and versatility or as a foreshadowing of her fickleness. This frequent juxtaposition of verse and prose (the play contains more than 1,000 lines of prose) has also been cited by some recent scholars in connection with the debate over the play's genre, as one of the key identifying features of Menippean satire.

KEY PASSAGES
Act I, Scene 2, 273–321

PANDARUS. Well, well! Why, have you any discretion? have you any eyes? do you know what a man is? Is not birth, beauty, good shape, discourse, manhood, learning, gentleness, virtue, youth, liberality, and suchlike, the spice and salt that season a man?

CRESSIDA. Ay, a minc'd man, and then to be bak'd with no date in the pie, for then the man's date's out.

PANDARUS. You are such a woman, a man knows not at what ward you lie.

CRESSIDA. Upon my back, to defend my belly, upon my wit, to defend my wiles, upon my secrecy, to defend mine honesty, my mask, to defend my beauty, and you, to defend all these; and at all these wards I lie, at a thousand watches.

PANDARUS. Say one of your watches.

CRESSIDA. Nay, I'll watch you for that; and that's one of the chiefest of them too. If I cannot ward what I would not have hit, I can watch you for telling how I took the blow—

unless it swell past hiding, and then it's past watching.

PANDARUS. You are such another!

Enter [Troilus's] Boy

BOY. Sir, my lord would instantly speak with you.

PANDARUS. Where?

BOY. At your own house, there he unarms him.

PANDARUS. Good boy, tell him I come. [*Exit Boy.*] I doubt he be hurt. Fare ye well, good niece.

CRESSIDA. Adieu, uncle.

PANDARUS. I will be with you, niece, by and by.

CRESSIDA. To bring, uncle?

PANDARUS. Ay, a token from Troilus.

CRESSIDA. By the same token, you are a bawd.

[*Exit Pandarus.*]

Words, vows, gifts, tears, and love's full
  sacrifice,
He offers in another's enterprise,
But more in Troilus thousandfold I see
Than in the glass of Pandar's praise may be;
Yet hold I off. Women are angels, wooing:
Things won are done, joy's soul lies in the
  doing.
That she belov'd knows nought that knows not
  this:
Men prize the thing ungain'd more than it is.
That she was never yet that ever knew

Love got so sweet as when desire did sue.
Therefore this maxim out of love I teach:
Achievement is command; ungain'd, beseech;
Then though my heart's content firm love doth
  bear,
Nothing of that shall from mine eyes appear.
Exit [with Alexander]

Cressida, pretending to be indifferent as Pandarus praises Troilus's virtues, engages in a series of flippant replies calculated both to keep her love for Troilus secret and also to protect herself from

Pandarus compares the passing Trojan soldiers to Troilus during his conversation with Cressida in Act I, Scene 2 of *Troilus and Cressida*. This is a print from the Boydell Shakespeare Gallery project, which was first conceived in 1786 and lasted until 1805. *(Painting by Thomas Kirk; engraving by Charles Warren)*

the pressure her uncle is putting on her to accept Troilus as a lover. At least part of the difficulty in assessing her character lies in how one reads her frequently ambiguous wordplay in these replies, which constitute her first introduction to the audience. Just before these lines, as soon as her servant Alexander tells her that Pandarus is approaching, Cressida has praised Hector's gallantry aloud: Does this line imply that she is a sophisticated tease, intent upon mocking her uncle when he (inevitably) begins praising Troilus's prowess, or that she is a lovesick girl, hoping to incite him to conversation about her beloved Troilus? When Pandarus relies on a metaphor from cookery (one of several dozen in the play) in enumerating Troilus's virtues as though they were the ingredients in a recipe, she picks up on his metaphor and wittily suggests that Troilus would be an unappealing dish, missing a key ingredient for sweetness and flavor (dates) and also stale (out of date). Modern editors routinely provide a footnote to these lines asserting the existence of sexual imagery here—the lack of dates, they claim, implies that Troilus is impotent—but it hardly seems obvious that one must interpret a date as a phallic image, especially since the passage makes perfect sense without that strained additional meaning. Do we take the passage as an indication of her spirit, intelligence, and independence or, as most editors seem to imply, of her vulgarity and promiscuity? How a reader handles such local interpretive decisions has much to do with how he or she will view Cressida generally (and vice versa).

The famous speech following, in which she picks up on Pandarus's metaphor from fencing (*ward* is the technical term for the fencer's positions, perfectly appropriate for the verbal fencing that the two are engaged in), is also regularly cited as evidence of her crudely bawdy disposition, with its mention of her "belly" and the suggestion of pregnancy as the cause of that belly to "swell." But again the passage may be just as easily read in a positive light, as a demonstration of her shrewd awareness that she is under attack by Troilus and Pandarus (whom she correctly identifies as a "bawd"), who have blatantly sexual designs on

her that she needs to defend herself against (there is no suggestion that Troilus is even considering marriage). Just as lying on her back cannot help her defend her belly or honesty, neither can relying on Pandarus—in fact, her commentary suggests that she has no reliable defenses at all beyond a state of always being on the alert, "at a thousand watches."

Similarly, her "maxim of love," which asserts that "once a man has achieved his goal of sexual access to a woman, he can control her, but until then he must serve her," has seemed unduly cynical to many critics but may also be read as evidence of her insecurity. Interestingly, this comment is surrounded by quotation marks in both the quarto and Folio texts, indicating that at least the original compositors, if not the author, interpreted the line approvingly as an instance of proverbial wisdom. Indeed, the truism does seem to be borne out by the events of the play, as she does lose control of her situation after she yields to Troilus, and she will clearly have no control over Diomedes once she yields to him. One might well argue that her recognition of the mechanisms that drive her male-dominated world only makes her more clear-sighted, not less of a victim forced to conform to that world. Does one read her soliloquy as a touching profession of love by a self-possessed but vulnerable young woman in a precarious position or as the exploitative manifesto of a cunning politician? Perhaps the best a reader can do is to recognize that all of these aspects are potentially relevant at different points and to keep all of these potential versions of Cressida in mind.

Act I, Scene 3, 75–137

ULYSSES. Troy, yet upon his bases, had been down,
And the great Hector's sword had lack'd a master,
But for these instances.
The specialty of rule hath been neglected:
And look how many Grecian tents do stand
Hollow upon this plain, so many hollow factions.

When that the general is not like the hive
To whom the foragers shall all repair,
What honey is expected? Degree being
  vizarded,
Th' unworthiest shows as fairly in the mask.
The heavens themselves, the planets, and this
  centre
Observe degree, priority, and place,
Insisture, course, proportion, season, form,
Office, and custom, in all line of order;
And therefore is the glorious planet Sol
In noble eminence enthron'd and spher'd
Amidst the other; whose med'cinable eye
Corrects the [ill aspects] of [planets' evil],
And posts like the commandment of a king,
Sans check to good and bad. But when the
  planets
In evil mixture to disorder wander,
What plagues and what portents, what mutiny!
What raging of the sea, shaking of earth!
Commotion in the winds! frights, changes,
  horrors
Divert and crack, rend and deracinate
The unity and married calm of states
Quite from their fixure! O, when degree is
  shak'd,
Which is the ladder to all high designs,
The enterprise is sick! How could
  communities,
Degrees in schools, and brotherhoods in cities,
Peaceful commerce from dividable shores,
The primogenity and due of birth,
Prerogative of age, crowns, sceptres, laurels,
But by degree stand in authentic place?
Take but degree away, untune that string,
And hark what discord follows. Each thing
  [meets]
In mere oppugnancy: the bounded waters
Should lift their bosoms higher than the shores
And make a sop of all this solid globe;
Strength should be lord of imbecility,
And the rude son should strike his father dead;
Force should be right, or rather, right and
  wrong;
(Between whose endless jar justice resides)

Should lose their names, and so should justice
  too!
Then every thing include itself in power,
Power into will, will into appetite,
And appetite, an universal wolf
(So doubly seconded with will and power),
Must make perforce an universal prey,
And last eat up himself. Great Agamemnon,
This chaos, when degree is suffocate,
Follows the choking,
And this neglection of degree it is
That by a pace goes backward with a purpose
It hath to climb. The general's disdain'd
By him one step below, he by the next,
That next by him beneath; so every step,
Exampled by the first pace that is sick
Of his superior, grows to an envious fever
Of pale and bloodless emulation,
And 'tis this fever that keeps Troy on foot,
Not her own sinews. To end a tale of length,
Troy in our weakness stands, not in her
  strength.

Ulysses' speech comes in the longest scene of the play, and one that forms a distinct contrast to the lighter romantic scenes that precede it. In one of the key passages for modern study of the Elizabethan conception of the "Great Chain of Being," he describes eloquently the established ideological values that are consistently violated in the actions of the play, and he has often been seen as a spokesman for the author's own beliefs. His claim that all order depends upon subordination within a nested series of rigid and interdependent hierarchies (from the universe down through states, cities, schools, families, and individual lives) may seem dogmatic and repressive to some modern audiences, but was a widely approved commonplace during the Elizabethan period (and long after). A. L. Rowse, for instance, argued that "Of all Shakespeare's characters Ulysses is the one who most completely expresses his creator's views: indeed he hardly speaks anything else." The image of Order as a musical instrument that unworthy behavior may "untune" to produce "discord" rather than the harmonious music that should rule all of these spheres is characteristically associated with positive elements in Shakespeare's practice in other contexts. Even the lofty diction of the speech, with such neologisms as "insisture," "deracinate," and "oppugnancy," may serve as markers of Ulysses' prudence and judgment.

Apart from the general intellectual import of the argument, Ulysses offers more specific analyses of Greek policy, including implicit criticism of Agamemnon himself, who has not proven a capable leader ("the general is not like the hive," "The general's disdain'd"), although he does not make the application explicit, and Agamemnon appears to ignore his meaning. Here, Ulysses may be seen to agree with Thersites' judgment that Agamemnon "has not so much brain as ear-wax" (5.1.52–53). In the BBC film version, Agamemnon's obtuseness is partly a matter of his constant inebriation: He always has a goblet in his hand (once even a pitcher) to sip from throughout each scene. The implication that Agamemnon is not a true leader is raised again shortly after this speech, when Aeneas enters to deliver a challenge through Agamemnon, but takes him to be a common soldier, seeing no signs of greatness about him (or, perhaps, contemptuously pretending not to).

Other critics, however, read the speech as an implicit critique of Ulysses himself as well as of the Greek cause and emphasize the Machiavellian ends to which he will finally put his noble philosophizing. Despite his astute diagnosis of the problem, the solution he will subsequently propose (using the fake lottery to coerce Achilles by promoting Ajax over him) is not only dishonest and unethical but will prove ineffective and even farcical. Appointing Ajax to fight Hector not only fails to provoke Achilles to fight but does not even succeed in getting Ajax to fight Hector, as their combat will be stopped almost before it begins. Only the death of Patroclus will incite Achilles to action, and that result pushes the action further into the realm of chaos than into a more stable order. More broadly, the passage may be read not only for its characterization and critique of the Greek leadership but as part of the larger theme of the incommensurability of philosophy and history, theory and practice: Ulysses' ideals may all be valid in the abstract, but in practice they do not prove to be viable guides to human conduct, which will always find its appetite and will to be sufficiently powerful to overcome justice.

Act IV, Scene 5, 15–64

AGAMEMNON. Is not yond Diomed, with Calchas' daughter?

ULYSSES. 'Tis he, I ken the manner of his gait,
He rises on the toe. That spirit of his
In aspiration lifts him from the earth.

AGAMEMNON. Is this the Lady Cressid?

DIOMEDES. Even she.

AGAMEMNON. Most dearly welcome to the Greeks, sweet lady.
[*Kisses her.*]

NESTOR. Our general doth salute you with a kiss.

ULYSSES. Yet is the kindness but particular,
'Twere better she were kiss'd in general.

NESTOR. And very courtly counsel. I'll begin.
So much for Nestor.
[*Kisses her.*]

ACHILLES. I'll take that winter from your lips, fair lady;
Achilles bids you welcome.
[*Kisses her.*]

MENELAUS. I had good argument for kissing once.

PATROCLUS. But that's no argument for kissing now,
For this popp'd Paris in his hardiment,

And parted thus you and your argument.
[*Kisses her.*]

ULYSSES. O deadly gall, and theme of all our
  scorns,
For which we lose our heads to gild his horns!

PATROCLUS. The first was Menelaus' kiss,
  this, mine;
Patroclus kisses you.
[*Kisses her again.*]

MENELAUS. O, this is trim!

PATROCLUS. Paris and I kiss evermore for
  him.

MENELAUS. I'll have my kiss, sir. Lady, by
  your leave.

CRESSIDA. In kissing, do you render or
  receive?

PATROCLUS. Both take and give.

CRESSIDA. I'll make my match to live,
The kiss you take is better than you give;
Therefore no kiss.

MENELAUS. I'll give you boot, I'll give you
  three for one.

CRESSIDA. You're an odd man, give even or
  give none.

MENELAUS. An odd man, lady? Every man
  is odd.

CRESSIDA. No, Paris is not, for you know 'tis
  true
That you are odd, and he is even with you.

MENELAUS. You fillip me a'th' head.

CRESSIDA. No, I'll be sworn.

ULYSSES. It were no match, your nail against
  his horn.
May I, sweet lady, beg a kiss of you?

CRESSIDA. You may.

ULYSSES. I do desire it.

CRESSIDA. Why, beg then.

ULYSSES. Why then for Venus' sake, give me
  a kiss
When Helen is a maid again and his.

CRESSIDA. I am your debtor, claim it when
  'tis due.

ULYSSES. Never's my day, and then a kiss of
  you.

DIOMEDES. Lady, a word. I'll bring you to
  your father.
[*Exit with Cressida.*]

NESTOR. A woman of quick sense.

ULYSSES. Fie, fie upon her!
There's language in her eye, her cheek, her lip,
Nay, her foot speaks; her wanton spirits look
  out
At every joint and motive of her body.
O, these encounterers, so glib of tongue,
That give a coasting welcome ere it comes,
And wide unclasp the tables of their thoughts
To every ticklish reader! set them down
For sluttish spoils of opportunity,
And daughters of the game. Flourish.

ALL. The Troyans' trumpet.

This passage has always been a touchstone for
the interpretation of Cressida's character. As E.
Talbot Donaldson remarked, "Until recently the
weightiest critics of the play seem to have been followers of Ulysses, the first high-minded intellectual

to settle Cressida's business by calling her a slut." After the first 12 lines of the scene establish that the Greek commanders are awaiting the imminent arrival of Hector to meet the Greek champion in single combat, the sudden appearance of Cressida seems at first to be almost humorously anticlimactic. Cressida's departure in mid-scene will be followed by the arrival of the Trojans and the armed Hector, who are introduced in a parallel fashion to Cressida's introduction before beginning the battle. The long-awaited battle, however, is ended almost before it begins (only four lines of dialogue are uttered during it), creating an even more pronounced anticlimax.

Much depends upon the actors and direction here: Is the scene imagined as a friendly welcoming party and her arch responses as appropriately witty teasing, as in Caxton, where she receives gifts and "all of the greatest that were there promised to keep her and hold her as dear as their daughter," or is Cressida a stranger in danger, being treated aggressively and roughly? The kissing scene had always been handled sedately and even politely in early productions, but more contemporary ones have often made the scene a highly threatening sexual assault. In the previous scene, just minutes before, a "woeful" Cressida was being led away by Troilus to leave for the Greek camp. How had the actress decided to portray her for that scene, and how has her demeanor changed (if at all) for this scene? Twenty-three lines are spoken by six different men after her entrance before she speaks a word, having already been kissed five times by four of those men, and even then she speaks only to ask a question (indeed, she had spent the final 47 lines of the prior scene in silence—what has she been doing on stage during all that time?). The portrayal of Cressida here is closely tied to how one interprets the portrayal of Ulysses. Does his final speech represent a genuine insight into her true nature that will shortly be proven correct in her next scene with Diomedes? Or is it more significant that the general kissing-game is proposed by Ulysses himself, who after all does beg her (unsuccessfully) for a kiss? Simply on the basis that

she speaks no lines at all before the kissing begins, one might well discount Ulysses' claim that she has given a "welcome" to this accosting before it comes. His further claim, that she is prone to freely unclasping her thoughts, may be similarly questioned—if anything, her remarks seem calculated to conceal her true thoughts rather than to reveal them. Assuming that these emphases are justified, it makes sense to attribute his verbal abuse to his resentment at being outwitted by a girl. Indeed, given that no more kissing follows after she begins to talk back, one might well look at this effect in speculating about the cause and conclude that she finally speaks in self-defense to extricate herself from a difficult and unwelcome, if not actually dangerous situation, rather than, as has often been claimed, to extend the flirtation with the Greek commanders.

Suzanne Burden's ambiguous performance in the most readily available film version allows the audience to read the scene in both ways. An initially frightened Cressida comes into the scene closely hemmed in by a crowd of dirty and unruly men, but they back off quickly as Agamemnon greets her graciously and gives her a thoroughly nonthreatening kiss on the hand. She visibly gains confidence in her ability to control them as the scene progresses. One final subtle comment on the issue lies in the minor bit of wordplay after Ulysses' dismissal: Productions often have the actors call out "The Troyan strumpet" instead of "The Troyans' trumpet," as though they were bidding Cressida a demeaning farewell as they prepared finally to meet Hector.

Act V, Scene 2, 64–146
Enter CRESSID.

THERSITES. Now the pledge, now, now, now!

CRESSIDA. Here, Diomed, keep this sleeve.

TROILUS. O beauty, where is thy faith?

ULYSSES. My lord—

TROILUS. I will be patient, outwardly I will.

CRESSIDA. You look upon that sleeve, behold it well.
He lov'd me—O false wench!—Give't me again.

DIOMEDES. Whose was't?

CRESSIDA. It is no matter now I ha't again.
I will not meet with you to-morrow night.
I prithee, Diomed, visit me no more.

THERSITES. Now she sharpens. Well said, whetstone!

DIOMEDES. I shall have it.

CRESSIDA. What, this?

CRESSIDA. O all you gods! O pretty, pretty pledge!
Thy master now lies thinking on his bed
Of thee and me, and sighs, and takes my glove,
And gives memorial dainty kisses to it,
As I kiss thee. Nay, do not snatch it from me.
He that takes that doth take my heart withal.

DIOMEDES. I had your heart before, this follows it.

TROILUS. I did swear patience.

CRESSIDA. You shall not have it, Diomed, faith, you shall not.
I'll give you something else.

CRESSIDA. It is no matter.

DIOMEDES. Come, tell me whose it was.

CRESSIDA. 'Twas one's that lov'd me better than you will.
But now you have it, take it.

DIOMEDES. Whose was it?

CRESSIDA. By all Diana's waiting-women yond,
And by herself, I will not tell you whose.

DIOMEDES. To-morrow will I wear it on my helm,
And grieve his spirit that dares not challenge it.

TROILUS. Wert thou the devil, and wor'st it on thy horn,
It should be challeng'd.

CRESSIDA. Well, well, 'tis done, 'tis past.
And yet it is not;
I will not keep my word.

DIOMEDE. Why then farewell.

CRESSIDA. You shall not go. One cannot speak a word
But it straight starts you.

DIOMEDES. I do not like this fooling.

THERSITES. Nor I, by Pluto; but that that likes not you pleases me best.

CRESSIDA. Ay, come—O Jove!—do come.—I shall be plagued.

DIOMEDES. Farewell till then.

CRESSIDA. Good night. I prithee come.
[*Exit Diomedes.*]
Troilus, farewell! one eye yet looks on thee,
But with my heart the other eye doth see.
Ah, poor our sex! this fault in us I find,
The error of our eye directs our mind.
What error leads must err; O then conclude
Minds sway'd by eyes are full of turpitude.
[*Exit*].

THERSITES. A proof of strength she could not publish more,
Unless she said, "My mind is now turn'd whore."

ULYSSES. All's done, my lord.

TROILUS. It is.

ULYSSES. Why stay we then?

TROILUS. To make a recordation to my soul
Of every syllable that here was spoke.
But if I tell how these two did [co-act],
Shall I not lie in publishing a truth?
Sith yet there is a credence in my heart,
An esperance so obstinately strong,
That doth invert th' attest of eyes and ears,
As if those organs [had deceptious] functions,
Created only to calumniate.
Was Cressid here?

ULYSSES. I cannot conjure, Troyan.

TROILUS. She was not, sure.

ULYSSES. Most sure she was.

TROILUS. Why, my negation hath no taste of
madness.

ULYSSES. Nor mine, my lord: Cressid was
here but now.

TROILUS. Let it not be believ'd for womanhood!
Think we had mothers, do not give advantage
To stubborn critics, apt without a theme
For depravation, to square the general sex

ULYSSES. What hath she done, Prince, that
can [soil] our mothers?

TROILUS. Nothing at all, unless that this
were she.

THERSITES. Will 'a swagger himself out on's
own eyes?

TROILUS. This she? no, this is Diomed's
Cressida.

If beauty have a soul, this is not she;
If souls guide vows, if vows be sanctimonies,
If sanctimony be the gods' delight,
If there be rule in unity itself,
This was not she. O madness of discourse,
That cause sets up with and against itself!
Bi-fold authority, where reason can revolt
Without perdition, and loss assume all reason
Without revolt. This is, and is not, Cressid! . . .

In terms of stagecraft, this climactic episode has
been praised by Kenneth Muir as "the most complex
scene in all of Shakespeare's works, and one which
demands to the full the exercise of multi-conscious-
ness." Troilus, intent upon keeping his word that
he will visit Cressida in the Greek camp, has asked
Ulysses to help him find her. Ulysses, unaware that
Troilus was Cressida's lover, informs him that Diomedes has been pursuing her. They thus follow Diomedes' torch (because all performances would have
been during the day, the playwright needs to remind
the audience that it is a dark night, and thus remind
them why the separate groups of characters will
be invisible to each other) to the tent where Cressida is staying. Thersites has in turn followed them,
apparently expecting to see, and enjoy, evidence of
Diomedes' false-heartedness. Cressida presumably
emerges from one of the curtained doors at the back
of the stage to speak with Diomedes, or perhaps on
the balcony above, while Troilus and Ulysses might
be toward the front of the stage, at the opposite
side from Thersites. The scene thus presents the
negotiation between Cressida and Diomedes as
watched, overheard, and commented upon by the
concealed Troilus and Ulysses (who is also observing Troilus's behavior closely); all four parties are
in turn observed, overheard, and commented upon
by Thersites, who is hidden from those four; and all
five characters, with their multiple conversations and
comments, are observed and overheard by the audience. The film version takes advantage of lighting
and camera positions to have Diomedes and Cressida in a tent lighted by a torch within, so that Troilus, Ulysses, and Thersites can see their silhouettes
and overhear them without being seen.

Ulysses holds Troilus back from killing Diomedes, who shares an intimate moment with Cressida, in this 1789 depiction of Act V, Scene 2 of *Troilus and Cressida. (Painting by Angelic Kauffmann; engraving by Luigi Schiavonetti)*

As A. P. Rossiter has remarked, Troilus's final attempt to hold on to his illusions about Cressida repeats a pattern found in other speeches in the play (including his own earlier speech on value): "The sudden shift from some particular question to an appeal to, or discussion of, the widest and most universal principles. . . . He is being made to think philosophically by Shakespeare, and his assumptions are those of Ulysses in his speech about 'Degree.'" His rational assumption that the universe is ordered and ruled by natural law seems entirely at odds with his experience of that universe. As not only the characters' comments but the very staging of the scene make clear, there are at least as many Cres-

sidas as there are observers, and in fact more, since both Troilus and Cressida herself (symbolized by the actions of her two contradictory eyes) see her as divided and multiple. The stoically rational Ulysses serves here as one foil to Troilus's impetuosity and hyperbolic reaction, advising patience and asking such sensible questions as "What hath she done, Prince, that can soil our mothers?" On the other hand, Thersites' own brand of cynical rationality provides another contrast to Troilus: He sees only one Cressida, the "whetstone" whose "mind is now turn'd whore." Troilus simply cannot hold these multiple and contradictory points of view at once: In Rossiter's pithy formulation, he "has a mind incapable of irony." The scene demands, however, that the audience be capable of irony and of holding simultaneously all of these formulations in their minds for a correct response and interpretation. As throughout the play, this scene provides no single reliable observer to serve as a chorus for the audience: None of the images held by the characters is adequate, and each spectator must decide how much to accept and reject from each of these disjointed and contradictory images of Cressida. In the film of the play, Suzanne Burden again plays a conflicted Cressida right down the middle, never allowing the audience to be sure how much of her hesitancy with Diomedes is genuine remorse at leaving Troilus and how much is an attempt (largely unsuccessful) to gain command of Diomedes, to whom she is genuinely attracted but who is proving much harder to manage than the inexperienced young Troilus. In first offering, and then refusing, to give him Troilus's sleeve, for example, she initiates a tug-of-war that ends as she lies back on her couch and pulls Diomedes down on top of her—is she giving in to him or enticing him?

DIFFICULT PASSAGES
Act II, Scene 2, 51–193

HECTOR. Brother, she is not worth what she doth cost
The keeping.

TROILUS. What is aught, but as 'tis valued?

HECTOR. But value dwells not in particular will,
It holds his estimate and dignity
As well wherein 'tis precious of itself
As in the prizer. 'Tis mad idolatry
To make the service greater than the god,
And the will dotes that is attributive
To what infectiously itself affects,
Without some image of th' affected merit.
Tro. I take to-day a wife, and my election
Is led on in the conduct of my will.
My will enkindled by mine eyes and ears,
Two traded pilots 'twixt the dangerous [shores]

Of will and judgment: how may I avoid
(Although my will distaste what it elected)
The wife I chose? There can be no evasion
To blench from this and to stand firm by honour.
We turn not back the silks upon the merchant
When we have soil'd them, nor the remainder viands
We do not throw in unrespective sieve,
Because we now are full. It was thought meet
Paris should do some vengeance on the Greeks.
Your breath with full consent bellied his sails;
The seas and winds, old wranglers, took a truce,
And did him service; he touch'd the ports desir'd,
And for an old aunt whom the Greeks held captive,
He brought a Grecian queen, whose youth and freshness
Wrinkles Apollo's, and makes pale the morning.
Why keep we her? The Grecians keep our aunt.
Is she worth keeping? Why, she is a pearl,
Whose price hath launch'd above a thousand ships,
And turn'd crown'd kings to merchants.
If you'll avouch 'twas wisdom Paris went—
As you must needs, for you all cried "Go, go"—
If you'll confess [he] brought home worthy prize—
As you must needs, for you all clapp'd your hands,
And cried "Inestimable!"—why do you now
The issue of your proper wisdoms rate,
And do a deed that never Fortune did,
Beggar the estimation which you priz'd
Richer than sea and land? O theft most base,
That we have stol'n what we do fear to keep!
But thieves unworthy of a thing so stol'n,
That in their country did them that disgrace,
We fear to warrant in our native place!
[*Cassandra rushes in and interrupts the debate at this point; ll. 97–162 are omitted.*]

HECTOR. Paris and Troilus, you have both
   said well,
And on the cause and question now in hand
Have gloz'd, but superficially, not much
Unlike young men, whom Aristotle thought
Unfit to hear moral philosophy.
The reasons you allege do more conduce
To the hot passion of distemp'red blood
Than to make up a free determination
'Twixt right and wrong; for pleasure and
   revenge
Have ears more deaf than adders to the voice
Of any true decision. Nature craves
All dues be rend'red to their owners: now,
What nearer debt in all humanity
Than wife is to the husband? If this law
Of nature be corrupted through affection,
And that great minds, of partial indulgence
To their benumbed wills, resist the same,
There is a law in each well-order'd nation
To curb those raging appetites that are
Most disobedient and refractory.
If Helen then be wife to Sparta's king,
As it is known she is, these moral laws
Of nature and of nations speak aloud
To have her back return'd. Thus to persist
In doing wrong extenuates not wrong,
But makes it much more heavy. Hector's
   opinion
Is this in way of truth; yet ne'er the less,
My spritely brethren, I propend to you
In resolution to keep Helen still,
For 'tis a cause that hath no mean dependance
Upon our joint and several dignities.

Cassandra prophesies the burning of Troy in Act II, Scene 2 of *Troilus and Cressida*. This is a print from the Boydell Shakespeare Gallery project, which was first conceived in 1786 and lasted until 1805. *(Painting by George Romney; engraving by Francis Legat)*

More than any other of Shakespeare's plays, *Troilus and Cressida* is filled with long formal speeches and debates. Rossiter offers the following paraphrase of what he calls Hector's "extremely difficult" lines: "The willful inclination of an individual cannot of itself confer value: it depends on intrinsic merit, as well as on being precious to someone . . . ; and the will which ascribes value to what attracts it (and infectiously) is a *doting* will, if it sees imaginary excellences in the object of its affection. . . . Statute law exists to curb willful people who are as blind to right and wrong as you are." Hector's reference to Aristotle's philosophy was long mocked as an anachronism, but critics have recently argued for the importance of his *Nicomachean Ethics* as a source for this argument, in its linkage of the psychology of emotional young men to their incapacity to make rational ethical choices. Hector's speech clearly parallels Ulysses' speech on order in the previous act. Both make the case for the importance of adhering to ethical principles as dictated by reason and order, and both prove to have no effect on the action or outcome of the play. As Robert Kimbrough has argued, Hector's words offer a unifying theme that can be applied to all three of the main plotlines: "Troilus dotes on an unworthy object, the Greek host is on the edge of chaos because will has asserted itself over reason . . . , and the Trojans defend Helen who has little intrinsic worth."

If Hector is usually seen as exemplifying the principle of intrinsic value, in which things are impartially assessed according to their inherent worth, Troilus exemplifies an extrinsic model, in which value is purely subjective, to be conferred by individual evaluators. In this play at least, such subjectivity is inevitably distorted by the baser passions and impulses that ensure the violation of these principles. Troilus may argue that "the remainder viands / We do not throw in unrespective sieve, / Because we now are full," but later he will use precisely the same metaphor of discarded leftovers in rationalizing his own casting off of Cressida to Diomedes: "The fragments, scraps, the bits and greasy relics / Of her o'er-eaten faith, are given to Diomed" (5.2.159–160).

CRITICAL INTRODUCTION
TO THE PLAY
Themes

Two of the play's major themes are explicitly raised in the first two acts by means of two long didactic speeches: Ulysses' oration on the importance of order and degree (1.3) and Hector's argument in the Trojan debate on value (2.2), both of which are briefly discussed above.

A third important theme, that of time, is outlined in a key speech in the third act, again by Ulysses (3.3.145–190), who is trying to convince Achilles that he needs to return to battle to retain his reputation, since his past glories are quickly being forgotten. While many of the sonnets, probably completed before *Troilus and Cressida* was written, had confidently offered a vision of true love that might overcome time's decay, the opposite vision is delineated here. Ulysses' analysis, which asserts the mutability and impermanence of all human relationships, appears to contradict the position developed in his first great speech,

in which he had asserted that permanently stable human relationships are a norm dictated by the immutable laws of the universe. In both of his two oratorical showpieces, as with Hector's in between, the context complicates the thematic message but does not necessarily invalidate it: The acute reader should be able to appreciate Ulysses' manipulative stratagem while also contemplating seriously the conception of time that he proposes. Ulysses begins by declaring that "Time hath, my lord, a wallet at his back, / Wherein he puts alms for oblivion, / . . . Those scraps are good deeds past, which are devour'd / As fast as they are made, forgot as soon / As done" (3.3.145–150). The traditional use of this common image assumed that the "scraps" going into the bag symbolize things ill-done and better forgotten (and hence carried behind the back); Shakespeare's version claims instead that good deeds are the first to be forgotten. The passage goes on to lament that "beauty, wit, / High birth, vigor of bone, desert in service, / Love, friendship, charity, are subjects all / To envious and calumniating Time" (3.3.171–175). Virtue not only fails to stand the test of time, it is the first casualty of time, which aggressively attacks the memory and reputation of the virtuous rather than serving to spread their fame. Here, Ulysses seems to anticipate the harsh treatment that the mythic heroes of the Trojan War are to undergo at the hands of Shakespeare himself in this very play. As so often happens in *Troilus and Cressida*, the characters seem self-conscious about how their own portrayal will be managed in subsequent stories about them (as when Troilus, Cressida, and Pandarus coin slogans for themselves for later writers to refer to them by). The failure of romantic love in particular to withstand the passage of time is most acutely anticipated in Troilus's many images of time and its depredations. When Cressida complains on the morning after their meeting that the night has been too brief, he personifies it as a witch who "flies the grasps of love / With wings more momentary-swift than thought" (4.2.13–14) and then, having learned of her imminent departure to the Greek camp, as a thief stealing away their period for leave-taking: "Injurious time now with a robber's haste / Crams his rich thiev'ry up, he knows not how" (4.4.42–43).

Intricately related to the themes of order, value, and time is an exploration of the nature of personal identity, with its frequently alleged capacity for nobility, constancy, and wholeness and its just as frequently demonstrated liability to degeneration, mutability, and fragmentation over time. One of Shakespeare's most striking methods of undercutting his characters' reliability or fixity in this play is by presenting them as divided within, and against, themselves. Characters frequently speak of individuals as fixed and stable unities, but their actions in the play prove them to be changeable and conflicted. Troilus, for example, claims to be the very benchmark for unity and coherence in an individual: "I am as true as truth's simplicity, / And simpler than the infancy of truth" (3.2.169–170), but when he sees Cressida with Diomedes, he is forced to recognize that human nature can often be contradictory and "Bi-fold," a word that Shakespeare apparently coined for this passage (5.2.144). Even his own inner being seems strangely divided by the shock as he vacillates back and forth, displaying his own internal contradictions: He concedes that "Within my soul there doth conduce a fight" (5.2.147) but then, a few lines later, insists again that "Never did young man fancy / With so eternal and fix'd a soul" (5.2.167–168), in effect denying that any change in his feelings is possible while he is in the very process of changing them completely. He is anguished and baffled when confronted with evidence that Cressida's character has proven ambiguous ("This is, and is not, Cressid"), but virtually the same observation was made of him near the beginning of the play:

PANDARUS. Well, I say Troilus is Troilus.

CRESSIDA. Then you say as I say, for I am sure he is not Hector.

PANDARUS. No, nor Hector is not Troilus in some degrees.

CRESSIDA. 'Tis just to each of them; he is himself.

PANDARUS. Himself? alas, poor Troilus, I would he were! . . .
Himself? no! he's not himself. Would 'a were himself!

(1.2.66–76)

While Pandarus is playing on the sense that the lovesick Troilus is not behaving entirely normally, there does seem to be a deep divide between the idealistic lover and the ruthless fighter that parallels the divide in Cressida between her deep love for Troilus and the seemingly shallow opportunism of her liaison with Diomedes. She demonstrates her own awareness of this instability even as she commits herself to Troilus, confessing (and accurately predicting) that she has "a kind of self resides with you; / But an unkind self, that itself will leave / To be another's fool" (3.2.148–150). Indeed, if Cressida's final exit will confirm her fears about her divided nature, Troilus had unwittingly made much the same point about himself in the opening lines of the play: "Why should I war without the walls of Troy, / That find such cruel battle here within?" (1.1.2–3). Achilles is similarly depicted as a microcosm of a human city-state engaged in a civil war with himself, "That 'twixt his mental and his active parts / Kingdom'd Achilles in commotion rages, / And batters down himself" (2.3.73–75). Other self-divided characters would include Hector and Ajax, who are both described by Aeneas as split into halves by a combination of mixed ancestry and mixed feelings: "This Ajax is half made of Hector's blood, / In love whereof, half Hector stays at home; / Half heart, half hand, half Hector comes to seek / This blended knight, half Troyan and half Greek" (5.5.83–86).

Structure

While it is difficult to imagine that a famous and commercially successful author such as Shakespeare would have written a play without ever producing it, no English-language production can be documented before 1907, and no professional production until 1923. As Robert Kimbrough has observed, "This theatrical indifference is an impressive kind of unrecorded criticism," and *Troilus and Cressida* has often been regarded as a "closet play" that works better for a reader of the text than for a spectator at a performance of it. The play seems to have no natural beginning and no definite ending: not only the war but the love between Troilus and Cressida are already far advanced when the action starts in medias res, and the play also ends in the middle of things, trailing off with Troilus's desire to continue the battle and get his revenge on the next day. As a result, the overall structure of the play has often been severely criticized as confused and chaotic: Dryden felt obliged to remodel the play by combining scattered scenes into blocks, to avoid leaping back and forth from Troy to the Greek camp, and dismissed the end of the play as "nothing but a confusion." The imbalance between the war and love stories has also attracted commentary, as only about one-third of the play is concerned directly with the lovers as lovers: Troilus does have the largest number of lines in the play, but only by a slim margin over Ulysses, and despite sharing the play's title, Cressida appears in only six scenes, and she and Troilus only speak to each other in three of the play's 24 scenes (they each have a scene in which they observe the other from a slight distance). Furthermore, both title characters wind up most oddly as lovers who have given up on each other and as loose ends whose ultimate fates we never do learn—we last see Cressida as she reenters her tent after Act V, Scene 2, and leave Troilus at the end of the play heading home with hopes of further revenge.

But if the play seems to lack structure in some ways, it seems very tightly structured in others. The scenes alternate in a fairly symmetrical pattern among the multiple centers of interest, rotating between the Greek military camp and locations in Troy (for the love story, Pandarus's and Cressida's houses, and for the war story, Priam's palace). The play begins, for example, with two scenes in Troy, one with Troilus and one with Cressida, then fea-

tures two scenes in the Greek camp, one elevated and one comical, then one in Priam's palace. Each of these five scenes introduces, and presents the viewpoint of, one of the key characters in the play: Troilus, then Cressida (both of these including Pandarus), followed by Ulysses, Thersites, and Hector. Scenes within this linear sequence may also parallel or echo each other, as Achilles' speech on degree and order (1.3) is balanced by Hector's speech on ethics to the Trojans (2.2). Most modern directors produce an additional symmetry by placing the single intermission after Act III, Scene 2, with the result that both "halves" of the play end with speeches by Pandarus to the audience (although this does reduce the dramatic effect of immediately following the lovers' union with Calchas's request for Cressida's exchange, and thus their disunion). By the end of the play, the major plotlines and characters have all been brought together and most of the final act takes place on a new location, the battlefield.

Another structural issue has been the difficulty of finding a protagonist around whom the play revolves. While there is no single starring role that the play centers on (Reuben Brower called it "*Hamlet* without Hamlet"), there are several substantial roles that function by parallelism or antithesis. Cressida is obviously paired with Helen, for example, as indicated by Pandarus's comparisons of them in the opening scene (1.1.41–42, 74–76). Such pairings also inevitably thrust the characters into larger patterns: the Helen-Menelaus-Hesione-Paris quadrangle mirrors the Cressida-Troilus-Antenor-Diomedes group (with the Greek and Trojan affiliations reversed). Both women are tokens to be exchanged in the war, as each is taken from one nation to the other to redeem a previous transfer (Helen for Hesione, Cressida for Antenor), causing both to leave their first love (Menelaus and Troilus) for a new lover in the opposite camp (Paris and Diomedes). Both are alternately worshipped and reviled by the men who speak of them both as a "pearl" (1.1.100, 2.2.81) and a "whore" (4.2.67, 5.2.14), and both remain ultimately ambiguous and open to varying interpretations.

The one element that cannot be effectively undercut, however, is the unalloyed pessimism of the ending of the play, in which every honorable or vulnerable character has been killed or otherwise defeated and disillusioned, and the unethical and brutal characters have clearly won the battle and will surely win the war.

Style and Imagery

Criticism of the style of *Troilus* has reflected a wide range of reactions. Early critics and editors often found much of the writing so deplorable that they could not accept that it was all by Shakespeare: Furnivall, approvingly citing Dyce, considered it "unquestionable that parts of the play as we have it, 'particularly toward the end, are from the pen of a very inferior dramatist.'" Mark Van Doren (1939) argued that Shakespeare in this play "either lacks feeling or cannot control the feeling he has; and he cannot control the style which, however amazing in its volume and perhaps admirable in its invention, certainly runs loose." For Van Doren, the characters all "rave at the tops of their never modulated voices," and their all-too-frequent mannerism and prolixity produces little effect in the audience beyond boredom and impatience. The style is, as he does recognize, appropriate for people who are "all guile and raillery, all vanity and contempt." But, as he points out, the characters are already so degraded by their own actions and words that the internal criticism provided of it in different registers is rendered ineffectual: the abuse of Thersites, for example, or the frivolity and shallowness of Pandarus, are simply redundant. A. P. Rossiter has emphasized the variety of styles encountered in the play, which include not just Pandarus's buffoonery and Thersites' invective but also the military-heroical rhetoric of the Prologue, Troilus's hyperbolic rhapsodizing, and Cressida's witty chat and double entendres.

Several clusters of imagery are prevalent enough to have invited extended analysis by numerous critics, all of whom are indebted to Caroline Spurgeon's groundbreaking work in cataloging Shakespeare's imagery (1935). She devoted a separate chart at the end of her book to highlight the dominating images in *Troilus and Cressida* and *Hamlet*, revealing the unusually high frequency with which images of the body (sickness, disease, and medicine) and of eating (food, drink, and cooking) appear in these two closely related plays. While the imagery of disease is more prevalent in *Hamlet*, the amount of food imagery in *Troilus and Cressida* is overwhelmingly dominant, occurring more than twice as often as any other pattern of imagery occurs in any other play. Spurgeon counts 44 images of food in the play, used by 14 different characters, including allusions to or descriptions of 12 different processes of cooking. Productions often underscore this imagery with frequent displays of food to be eaten on stage.

This abundance of food imagery is clearly appropriate to the play's topics and themes, most obviously through the love story: Food may readily be linked to sex, in that humans have appetites for both, and of course both appetites have the apparently paradoxical quality of fading with their satisfaction. The idealistic early stages of love are imagined in terms of tasting: Immediately before his first meeting with Cressida, Troilus wonders "What will it be, / When that the wat'ry palates taste indeed / Love's thrice-repured nectar?" (3.2.18–20). How will his inexperienced senses, used to milder emotions (imagined as watered-down beverages), handle the intense "sweetness" (3.2.22) of true love? Or is the imagery rather a somewhat less romantic image of his mouth watering in anticipation of feasting on Cressida? As with many of Shakespeare's images, more than one reading is possible. In fact, the word *sweetness* just cited occurs in the phrase "tuned too sharp in sweetness," mixing a musical image of over-tightening the strings on an instrument with the food image of sweet nectar, suggesting not only his anticipation of sweetness but also how tightly Troilus's nerves are wound up. At the end of their brief affair, having witnessed Cressida's betrayal, Troilus is driven to find other images to describe their love, as he bitterly declares that the "scraps, the bits and greasy relics / Of her o'er-eaten faith, are given to Diomed" (5.2.166–167). The image still compares Cressida to a banquet but reduced now to a plate of leftover scraps, already chewed on and discarded. Ironically, he had earlier adopted the same food metaphor in comparing another woman, in that case Helen, to leftovers thrown into a basket, but to a different conclusion, his point then being that no honorable person would behave so: "nor the remainder viands / We do not throw in unrespective sieve" (2.2.70–71). Similarly, Diomedes derides Menelaus's desire to recover his wife as an urge to "drink up / The lees and dregs."

The connection of love and war is perhaps inevitable in a war caused by Paris's elopement with Helen, and just as much of the food imagery occurs in the war scenes as in the love scenes, especially when it is to be applied to men rather than to women. Thersites, although he is seeking Troilus and Diomedes in the middle of a battle, knows that their motivation is their rivalry over Cressida rather than any military objectives: He lumps them together as "wenching rogues" and suggests that they may "have swallow'd one another . . . in a sort lechery eats itself." Much like the instances in which Troilus and Diomedes speak of Cressida and Helen as food to be tasted, Achilles speaks of the murdered Hector as though he had been a meal: "My half-supp'd sword that frankly would have fed, / Pleas'd with this dainty bait, thus goes to bed" (5.8.19–20). Ulysses' speech on order sums up the entire image cluster: "Power into will [a synonym for "lust" in Elizabethan English], will into appetite, / And appetite, an universal wolf / . . . / Must make perforce an universal prey, / And at last eat up himself" (1.3.120–124).

As the symbol of the devouring wolf suggests, animal imagery provides another of the major patterns. Dozens of comparisons throughout the play insist upon the inevitable ascendancy of our baser animal impulses over our humanistic ideals. To cite only a few examples, beef-witted Ajax is an ass, bear, dog, elephant, horse, land-fish, lion, mongrel cur, monster, and peacock; Achilles a cur

and dog-fox; Menelaus a herring and louse. These images are primarily applied to the Greek camp, one of the reasons that so many critics have seen the Trojans depicted as at least marginally superior in terms of their ethical conduct to the "bestial" Greeks; on the other hand, the majority of these images are supplied by Thersites, whose positioning within the Greek camp naturally limits his opportunities to comment on the Trojans (with the exception of a few insults directed toward the naïveté of Troilus's love). However much a given reader might discount Thersites' judgment, the cumulative weight of this imagery can hardly fail to create a powerful effect: as Muir puts it, "some of the mud he throws is bound to stick." The devaluation of the human to the level of animals, or even beneath that level, is implied in Troilus's striking challenge of Diomedes on the battlefield, just a few brief scenes after witnessing his seduction of Cressida: "turn thy false face, thou traitor, / And pay thy life thou owest me for my horse" (5.6.6–7), as though the loss of the horse were more important than, or perhaps interchangeable with, the loss of Cressida.

Finally, *Troilus and Cressida*'s imagery also includes a comprehensive survey of varieties of diseases, including ague, running biles, bone-ache, catarrhs, cold palsies, itch, leprosy, lethargies, plague, red murrain, ruptures, and scabs. One might also include the unheroic body-parts that are infected by them: belly, raw eyes, guts, bowels, sinews, blood. Some are associated with sex, others more generally with human behavior, as in Ulysses' use of the metaphor of sickness to describe the anarchy in the Greek camp. The diseases are at once individual, collective, and universal, located in persons, political states, or even in the heavens, dependent upon the level of microcosm or macrocosm invoked. Thersites is frequently shown as sickly and covered with sores and scabs in modern performances, as is Pandarus. The disease imagery has the final word in the play, both literally—the very last word spoken is in fact "diseases"—and metaphorically, as Pandarus vows to infect the audience with venereal disease.

A 17th-century illustration depicting a battle between Aeneas and Diomedes. *(Illustration by Wenzel Hollar)*

EXTRACTS OF CLASSIC CRITICISM

John Dryden (1631–1700) [Excerpted from the preface to his 1679 adaptation of Shakespeare's play. Dryden's concern over Shakespeare's failure to observe the "three unities" of plot, time, and place, and his belief that the play demanded consistently elevated poetic diction, are characteristic of much neoclassical criticism of the period. Dryden's assumption that the play was a tragedy also led him to make significant plot changes. Considering that a tragedy must end with the protagonist's death, he rejected Shakespeare's inconclusive ending and made Cressida a faithful lover who commits suicide when Troilus mistakenly believes that she has betrayed him for Diomedes.]

. . . it must be allow'd to the present Age, that the tongue in general is so much refin'd since *Shakespeare's* time, that many of his words, and more of his Phrases, are scarce intelligible. And of those which we understand some are ungrammatical, others coarse; and his whole stile is so pester'd with Figurative expressions, that it is as affected as it is obscure. 'Tis true, that in his later Plays he had worn off somewhat of the rust; but the Tragedy which I have undertaken to correct, was, in all probability, one of his first endeavours on the Stage.

. . . For the Play itself, the Author seems to have begun it with some fire; the Characters of *Pandarus* and *Thersites,* are promising enough; but as if he grew weary of his task, after an Entrance or two, he lets 'em fall: and the later part of the Tragedy is nothing but a confusion of Drums and Trumpets, Excursions and Alarms. The chief persons, who give name to the Tragedy, are left alive: *Cressida* is false, and is not punish'd. Yet after all, because the Play was *Shakespeare's,* and that there appear'd in some places of it, the admirable Genius of the Author; I undertook to remove that heap of Rubbish, under which many excellent thoughts lay wholly bury'd. Accordingly, I new model'd the Plot; threw

out many unnecessary persons; improv'd those Characters which were begun, and left unfinish'd: as *Hector, Troilus, Pandarus* and *Thersites;* and added that of *Andromache.* After this, I made with no small trouble, and Order and Connexion of all the Scenes; removing them from the places where they were inartificially set: and though it was impossible to keep 'em all unbroken, because the Scene must be sometimes in the City, and sometimes in the Camp, yet I have so order'd them that there is a coherence of 'em with one another, and a dependence on the main design: no leaping from Troy to the Grecian Tents, and thence back again in the same Act; but a due proportion of time allow'd for every motion.

Charlotte Lennox (ca. 1729–1804) [Excerpted from *Shakespear Illustrated* (1753–54), in which she analyzes Shakespeare's use of his sources. She follows Dryden in censuring the faults of the plot ("if that can be called a Plot which is only a Succession of Incidents without Order, Connexion, or any Dependance upon each other") and in lamenting the lack of clear ethical and poetic justice but defends the consistency of Shakespeare's development of the title characters.]

Troilus and Cressida give Name to the Tragedy, and by Consequence are the most considerable Persons in it; yet *Troilus* is left alive, and *Cressida,* too scandalous a Character to draw our Pity, does not satisfy that Detestation her Crimes raise in us by her Death, but, escaping Punishment, leaves the Play without a Moral and absolutely deficient in poetical Justice.

The Manners of these two Persons, however, ought to escape the general Charge of Inequality.

Troilus, who is drawn exactly after *Chaucer,* is every where consistent with his Character of a brave Soldier and a passionate and

Cressida in Act IV, Scene 4 of *Troilus and Cressida*. This is a print from Charles Heath's 1848 edition of *The Heroines of Shakspeare: Comprising the Principal Female Characters in the Plays of the Great Poet.* (Painting by K. Meadows; engraving by W. H. Mote)

faithful Lover. From *Cressida*'s first and second Appearance we may easily guess what her future Conduct will be. The deep Art with which she conceals her Passion for *Troilus,* her loose Conversation with her Uncle, her free Coquetry with the Prince, and her easy yielding to his Addresses prepare us for her Falsehood in the succeeding Part of the Play, and all together make up the Character of a compleat Jilt. Her not being punished is indeed an unpardonable Fault and brings the greatest Imputation imaginable upon *Shakespeare*'s Judgment, who could introduce so vicious a Person in a Tragedy and leave her without due Reward of her Crimes.

The Character of *Cressida* is much more consistent in *Shakespeare* than in *Chaucer;* the latter represents her wise, humble, and modest, nicely sensible of Fame, fond of her Country, not easily susceptible of Love, hard to be won, and rather betrayed than yielding to the Desires of her Lover. With all these amiable Qualities to engage our Esteem and those alleviating Circumstances that attended her Fall with *Troilus,* we cannot, without Surprize, see her so soon changing her Love, violating her Vows, and basely prostituting her Honour to *Diomede.* The inequality of her Manners here is very observable; but *Shakespeare* in drawing her Character has avoided falling into the same Fault by copying *Chaucer* too closely, and *Cressida* throughout the Play is always equal and consistent with herself.

Samuel Johnson (1709–1784) [Excerpted from his landmark edition of Shakespeare's plays (1765). Johnson remains one of the most influential Shakespearean critics.]

This play is more correctly written than most of Shakespeare's compositions, but it is not one of those in which either the extent of his views or elevation of his fancy is fully displayed. As the story abounded with materials, he has exerted little invention; but he has diversified his characters with great variety, and preserved them with great exactness. His vicious characters sometimes disgust, but cannot corrupt, for both Cressida and Pandarus are detested and contemned. The comick characters seem to have been the favourites of the writer, they are of the superficial kind, and exhibit more of manners than of nature, but they are copiously filled and powerfully impressed.

William Hazlitt (1778–1830) [Excerpted from his *Characters of Shakespear's Plays* (1817). The important essayist and critic Hazlitt here provides one of the earliest and most insightful comparative analyses of Shakespeare's reworking of Chaucer's poem.]

This is one of the most loose and desultory of our author's plays: it rambles on just as it happens, but it overtakes, together with some indifferent matter, a prodigious number of fine things in its way. Troilus himself is no character: he is merely a common lover: but Cressida and her uncle Pandarus are hit off with proverbial truth. By the speeches given to the leaders of the Grecian host, Nestor, Ulysses, Agamemnon, Achilles, Shakespear seems to have known them as well as if he had been a spy sent by the Trojans into the enemy's camp—to say nothing of their affording very lofty examples of didactic eloquence. . . .

The characters of Cressida and Pandarus are very amusing and instructive. . . . Both characters are originals, and quite different from what they are in Chaucer. In Chaucer, Cressida is represented as a grave, sober, considerate personage . . . ; Shakespear's Cressida is a giddy girl, and unpractised jilt, who falls in love with Troilus, as she afterwards deserts him, from mere levity and thoughtlessness of temper. She may be wooed and won to any thing and from any thing, at a moment's warning; the other knows very well what she would be at, and sticks to it, and is more governed by substantial reasons than by caprice or vanity. . . . The difference of the manner in which the subject is treated arises perhaps less from intention, than from the different genius of the two poets. . . . We see Chaucer's characters as they saw themselves, not as they appeared to others or might have appeared to the poet. He is as deeply implicated in the affairs of his personages as they could be themselves. . . . Shakespear never committed himself to his characters. . . . His genius was dramatic, as Chaucer's was historical. He saw both sides

of a question, the different views taken of it according to the different interests of the parties concerned. . . . If any thing, he is too various and flexible: too full of transitions, of glancing lights, of salient points. . . .

Chaucer attended chiefly to the real and the natural. . . ; Shakespear exhibited also the possible and the fantastical,—not only what things are in themselves, but whatever they might seem to be, their different reflections, their endless combinations. He lent his fancy, wit, invention, to others, and borrowed their feelings in return. . . . Chaucer's mind was consecutive, rather than discursive. He arrived at truth through a certain process; Shakespear saw everything by intuition. . . . What is the most wonderful thing in Shakespear's faculties is their excessive sociability, and how they gossiped and compared notes together.

Samuel Taylor Coleridge (1772–1834)
[Excerpted from the published notes for a lecture he gave on February 25, 1819. Coleridge is better known as the poet who wrote "Kubla Khan" and "The Rime of the Ancient Mariner," but he was also an important critic. Here, he largely eschews the discussions of plot, the unities, and morality that had been crucial for neoclassical critics in favor of a focus on psychological analyses of characters.]

Indeed, there is none of Shakespeare's Plays harder to characterize. The name and the remembrances connected with it prepare us for the representation of attachment no less faithful than fervent on the side of the youth, and of sudden and shameless inconstancy on the part of the Lady. And this indeed is the gold thread on which the scenes are strung, tho' often kept out of sight and out of mind by gems of greater value than itself. But as Shakespeare calls forth nothing from the Mausoleum of History or the Catacombs of Tradition without giving or eliciting some permanent and general interest, brings forward no subject which he does not moralize or intellectualize, so here he has drawn in Cressida the Portrait of a vehement *Passion* that, having its true origin and proper cause in warmth of temperament, fastens on, rather than fixes to, some one Object by *Liking* and temporary Preference. This he has contrasted with the profound Affection represented in Troilus, and alone worthy of the name of Love, Affection, passionate indeed, swoln from the confluence of youthful instincts and youthful Fancy, glowing in the radiance of Hope newly risen, in short enlarged by the collective sympathies of Nature; but still having a depth of calmer element, in a will stronger than Desire, more entire than Choice, and which gives permanence to its own act by converting it into Faith and Duty. Hence with excellent Judgement and with an excellence higher than mere Judgement can give, at the close of the Play, when Cressida has sunk into infamy below retrieval and beneath a hope, the same Will, which had been the substance and the basis of his Love, while the restless Pleasures and Passionate Longings, like Sea-waves, had tossed but on its surface, the same moral energy snatches him aloof from all neighbourhood with her Dishonor, from all lingering Fondness and languishing Regrets, while it rushes with him into other and nobler Duties, and deepens the Channel which his heroic Brother's Death had left empty for its collected flood. Yet another secondary and subordinate purpose he has inwoven with the two characters, that of opposing the inferior civilization but purer morals of the Trojans to the refinements, deep policy, but duplicity and sensual corruptions of the Greeks.

To all this, however, there is so little comparative projection given, nay, the masterly Group of Agamemnon, Nestor, Ulysses, and still more in advance, of Achilles, Ajax, and Thersites, so manifestly occupy the foreground, that the subservience and vassalage of Strength and animal Courage to Intellect and Policy seem to be the Lesson most often in our Poet's View, and which he has taken little pains to connect with the former more interesting Moral impersonated in the titular Hero and Heroine of the Drama. But I am half inclined to believe that Shakespeare's main object, or shall I rather say that his ruling impulse, was to translate the poetic Heroes of Paganism into the not less rude but more intellectually vigorous, more *featurely* Warriors of Christian Chivalry, to substantiate the distinct and graceful Profiles or Outlines of the Homeric Epic into the flesh and blood of the Romantic Drama—in short, to give a grand History-piece in the robust style of Albert Durer.

The character of Thersites well deserves a more particular attention—as the Caliban of Demagogues—the admirable Portrait of intellectual power deserted by all grace, all moral principle, all not momentary purpose, just wise enough to detect the weak head and fool enough to provoke the armed fist of his Betters, whom Malcontent Achilles can inveigle from Malcontent Ajax, under the one condition that he shall be called on to do nothing but to abuse and slander and that he shall be allowed to abuse as much and as purulently as he likes—that is, as he can—in short, a mule—quarrelsome by the original discord of its Nature, a slave by tenure of his own baseness made to bray and be brayed, to despise and be despicable.

Heinrich Heine (1797–1856) [Excerpted from *Shakespeare's Girls and Women* (1839; translated by C. G. Leland, 1891). Heine was one of the great German poets of his time, in addition to an influential critic.]

Those critics who judged *Troilus and Cressida* according to the rules drawn by Aristotle from the best Greek plays, must often have fallen into the greatest perplexities, if not into the most ridiculous blunders. As a tragedy the play did not seem to them earnest and pathetic enough; because everything in it came to pass just as naturally as with us; and the heroes behaved as foolishly, perhaps even as barbarously, as they would now; the hero in chief is a lout and the heroine is a common wench, such as we can find in plenty among our acquaintance . . . and even the most honored names, celebrities of the heroic age, for example the great Achilles, brave son of Peleus and Thetis, how wretched do they seem here? Conversely, the play could not be interpreted as comedy, for it streamed with blood, and resounded with the loftiest and lengthiest pronouncements of wisdom, such as for example the reflections of Ulysses on the necessity of authority, which to this day merit close attention. . . . No, *Troilus and Cressida* is neither a comedy nor a tragedy in the usual sense; it belongs to no special kind of poetry, and still less can it be judged by any received standard: it is Shakespeare's most characteristic creation.

Algernon Charles Swinburne (1837–1909) [Excerpted from *A Study of Shakespeare* (1880). Despite his sensitive appreciation of some aspects of this "mysterious and magnificent monster of a play," the poet Swinburne here finally adheres to the typically moralistic Victorian dismissal of the work on the basis of its "realism and obscenity."]

This wonderful play, one of the most admirable among all the works of Shakespeare's immeasurable and unfathomable intelligence, as it must always hold its natural high place among the most admired, will always in all probability be also, and as naturally, the least beloved of all. . . . What ailed the man or any man to write such a manner of dramatic poem at all? . . .

Alike in its most palpable perplexities and in its most patent splendours, this political and philosophic and poetic problem, this hybrid and hundred-faced and hydra-headed prodigy, at once defies and derides all definitive comment. This however we may surely and confidently say of it, that of all Shakespeare's offspring it is the one whose best things lose least by extraction and separation from their context. That some cynic had lately bitten him by the brain—and possibly a cynic himself in a nearly rabid stage of anthropophobia—we might conclude as reasonably from consideration of the whole as from examination of the parts more especially and virulently affected: yet how much is here also of hyper-Platonic subtlety and sublimity, of golden and Hyblfan eloquence above the reach and beyond the snap of any cynic's tooth! Shakespeare, as under the guidance at once for good and for evil of his alternately Socratic and Swiftian familiar, has set himself as if prepensely and on purpose to brutalise the type of Achilles and spiritualise the type of Ulysses. . . . It is true, if that be any little compensation, that Hector and Andromache fare here hardly any better than [Achilles]: while of the momentary presentation of Helen on the dirtier boards of a stage more miry than the tub of Diogenes I would not if I could and I must not though I would say so much as one single proper word. The hysterics of the eponymous hero and the harlotries of the eponymous heroine remove both alike beyond the outer pale of all rational and manly sympathy; though Shakespeare's self may never have exceeded or equaled for subtle and accurate and bitter fidelity the study here given of an utterly light woman, shallow and loose and dissolute in the most literal sense, rather than perverse or unkindly or unclean; and though Keats alone in his most perfect mood of lyric passion and burning vision as full of fragrance as of flame could have matched and all but overmatched those passages in which the rapture of Troilus makes pale and horrible by comparison the keenest raptures of Romeo.

Georg   Brandes (1842–1927) [Excerpted from *William Shakespeare: A Critical Study* (1895; translated by W. Archer et al., 1898). Brandes, an important Danish scholar, wrote extensively on Shakespeare's plays.]

It was a curious coincidence that Shakespeare should lay hands on this material just at the most despondent period of his life; for nowhere could we well receive a deeper impression of modern crudeness and decadence, and never could we meet with a fuller expression of German-Gothic barbarism in relation to Hellenism than when we see this great poet of the Northern Renaissance make free with the poetry of the old world. . . . In the *Iliad* these forms represent the outcome of the imagination of the noblest people of the Mediterranean shores, unaffected by religious terrors and alcohol; they are bright, glad, reverential phantasies, born in a warm sun under a deep blue sky. From Shakespeare they step forth travestied by the gloom and bitterness of a great poet of a Northern race, of a stock civilised by Christianity, not by culture; a stock which, despite all the efforts of the Renaissance to give new birth to heathendom, has become, once for all, disciplined and habituated to look upon the senses as tempters which lead down into the mire; to which the pleasurable is forbidden and sexual attraction is a disgrace.

. . . It reads like the invention of a medieval barbarian. But Shakespeare is neither medieval nor a barbarian. No, he has written it down out of a bitterness so deep that he has felt hero-worship, like love, to be an illusion of the senses. As the phantasy of first love is absurd, and Troilus's loyalty towards its object ridiculous, so is the honour of our forefathers and of war in general a delusion . . . the melancholy of Shakespeare's natural perception sets its iron tooth in everything at this period of his life, and he looks upon absorption in love as senseless and laughable . . . he shows it without sympathy, coldly. Therefore the play never once arouses any true emotion, since Troilus himself never really interests. The piece blazes out, but imparts no warmth. Shakespeare wrote it thus, and therefore, while *Troilus and Cressida* will find many readers who will admire it, few will love it.

MODERN CRITICISM AND CRITICAL CONTROVERSIES

The selective list in Frances A. Shirley's "Shakespeare in Production" volume on the play records only 29 theatrical productions in English from 1602–1950, but then 85 productions from 1950–2004. In the 21st century, *Troilus* has become securely established as one of the most widely discussed, debated, and performed plays in Shakespeare's canon. In addition to the influential discussions of the play's sources, textual history, and imagery summarized above, modern criticism has changed its course, or at least its emphasis, in two key areas: the assessment of the play's theme, especially regarding the war plot, and the tendency to reinterpret key characters by the light of contemporary cultural discussions of gender and sexuality.

Most early critics would have accepted G. Wilson Knight's 1930 assessment (following Coleridge) that the "Trojan party stands for human beauty and worth, the Greek party for the bestial and stupid elements of man, the barren stagnancy of intellect divorced from action." While Knight did see the play as pessimistic and notes that the handing over of Cressida from the Trojans to the Greeks as "the pivot incident of the play, [and] has thus a symbolic suggestion," he claims that the human failings depicted do not negate the genuine human values with which they are contrasted. Modern theatrical productions have usually endorsed this slant at least implicitly by costuming the Greeks in darker and drabber shades and the Trojans in lighter and more colorful clothes. The 1981 BBC film version, however, helps make clear that there are realistic, as opposed to strictly thematic, explanations for the difference in appearance: The grubby Greeks have been living in crude tents on a muddy field for seven years, unlike the manicured and coiffed Trojans, who after all are still living comfortably in their palaces.

Una Ellis-Fermor's "The Universe of *Troilus and Cressida*" (1945) altered this pro-Trojan bias by developing the watershed interpretation, highly original at the time and now virtually taken for granted, that the play was not a failed though interesting experiment (nor, as some would have it, evidence of clinical depression in the author) but in fact a highly accomplished and successful rendering of a depressing and chaotic world. Critics used to consider Ulysses and Hector as spokesmen for Shakespeare's own positions in their long speeches on order and reason, and Troilus to be unambiguously the image of the heroic soldier and perfect courtly lover. Ellis-Fermor contends that the audience gradually comes to reject both camps and learns to side with Thersites as he rails against the actions and delusions of the other characters. The war is not, as Troilus would have it, evidence of a noble commitment to principles of "Manhood and honor" (2.2.47) but rather, as Thersites more honestly explains, "All the argument is a whore and a cuckold, a good quarrel to draw emulous factions and bleed to death upon" (2.3.72–74). Her explanation for the failure of earlier criticism to emphasize this negative reading lies essentially in the fact that those previous critics had not lived though World War II and had not shared her "actual experience of disintegration and disruption, so unlike that of any age in between." Later readers, many of whom would assert that they have lived through comparably disjointed times, have generally followed her lead in seeing *Troilus* as a carefully unified play depicting disharmony and collapse, "the unilluminated wreckage of the universe of vision," and to see Thersites—often in conjunction with Pandarus—as the dominant voice of the play. The play

was accordingly read primarily as an antiwar statement, an approach that became dominant during the 1960s and 1970s in the context of the Vietnam War, and has continued with recent productions that draw parallels with the war on terror. The play has been adapted to other political contexts as well, though. An American production in 1961, marking the centenary of the Civil War, cast the play in costumes of that period, with the Greeks as the North in blue and the Trojans as the South in gray, with Priam made up to resemble Robert E. Lee and Agamemnon as Ulysses S. Grant. Other productions sought to create contemporary resonances by such devices as dressing Achilles' Myrmidons as Ku Klux Klansmen during the civil rights turmoil in 1963. Trevor Nunn's 1999 National Theatre production suggested an allegory of imperialism and colonialism by casting the white-robed Trojans primarily with black actors and the Greeks, clad in black leather, with white actors.

While Ellis-Fermor's pessimistic reading proved enormously influential for later critics, it also shifted interest in the play toward the war plot at the expense of the love plot. Not surprisingly, the unanimous condemnation of Cressida by the earliest critics was significantly moderated by those of later generations, perhaps beginning with E. K. Chambers in 1926, whose sympathetic reading saw her as a basically good but unheroic woman who was put into a difficult position that demanded more of her than she could handle. The gradual recuperation of the character of Cressida would help shift the focus back to the lovers, a shift accelerated by the rise of feminism in the 1960s. In fact, her relatively small role would often come to be seen as central to interpretation of the play. Although the 1960 production at Stratford (codirected by John Barton and Peter Hall) still presented an unambiguously sensual Cressida with a definite erotic interest in both Troilus and Diomedes, she would soon come to be played as a sympathetic victim of circumstance. A 1963 production included Cassandra in its general valorization of the female characters, making her not the traditional prophetess whose apparently uncontrol-

An 18th-century portrait of Cassandra, from John Hamilton Mortimer's *Shakespeare Characters* series.

lable ravings make it impossible to believe her, but instead as a modern feminist and political leader of the Trojan peace movement. Jan Kott, in 1964, declared that "Cressida is one of the most amazing Shakespearian characters, perhaps just as amazing as Hamlet. And like Hamlet, she has many aspects and cannot be defined by a single formula. . . . She is our contemporary because of this self-distrust, reserve, and need of self-analysis. She defends herself by irony." Joseph Papp's 1965 production saw Cressida as a victim "of men, their wars, their desires, and their double standards," and academic criticism of the 1970s and 1980s would follow the lead of these and other directors and actors who reinvented Cressida's role. Helen Mirren, in a 1968 Royal Shakespeare Company (RCS) production, played Cressida neither as a victim nor a villain but as an intelligent woman who realized exactly how her very attractiveness made her both powerful and vulnerable under the circumstances of the war. The other side of the coin of character analysis has been to more closely interrogate the male characters in the play, especially Troilus. The sympathetic promotion of Cressida's role proportionately diminished Troilus's standing, as her exoneration in feminist-influenced productions was often transformed into his culpability.

While most productions until the late 1960s were content to present a generalized atmosphere of decadence and sexual license (especially in England, where laws against same-sex relationships were more vigorously enforced), more permissive times resulted in a foregrounding of the homosexual elements implicit in the play. John Barton, who saw *Troilus and Cressida* as "perhaps the most modern play in the canon," directed the 1968 RSC production that is usually cited as the first major version to foreground the homoerotic and homosexual interpretation of the play and subordinate the heterosexual content (an especially daring move considering that the play opened the month before British censorship of stage plays officially ended). In this highly influential staging, Achilles and Patroclus openly flaunted their homosexuality. Barton had Achilles enter after the duel between Ajax and Hector on Helen's litter, wearing women's clothing, a blond wig, and a veil, flashing his naked body to Hector, and then engaging in suggestive play with Thersites' prominent codpiece. The warriors would strip to loincloths for the battle scenes, which were played as violent mating rituals. The heterosexual romance, on the other hand, was downplayed, with a brief scene affirming Troilus's reverence for her eliminated (4.3) and a somewhat old-fashioned emphasis on Cressida's coarse sexuality and his confused innocence. Subsequent productions immediately followed Barton's lead and searched for ways to add new layers to the now-standard homosexual interpretation. Some chose to costume the characters as transvestites: In the 1973 New York Shakespeare Festival production, Diomedes wore a black negligee, Achilles a bikini, and Nestor had prosthetic breasts.

The strongest textual warrant for these gay readings lies in Thersites' calling Patroclus Achilles'

Achilles tends to a wounded Patroclus in this vase from the 5th century B.C.E.

"masculine whore" (5.1.17): As Alfred Harbage has noted, this phrase is indeed "the only indubitable allusion to homosexuality in Shakespeare." But, sodomy, as it would have been called, was a serious crime in Shakespeare's time (punishable by death), and as Harbage has demonstrated, references to it, even joking ones, are extremely rare in Elizabethan public theaters. Shakespeare's allusions to homosexuality in the play are understandably cautious. Thersites' claim is meant as an offensive slander, and Patroclus takes it as such and insults him back. Furthermore, Shakespeare (following Caxton) has explicitly provided Achilles with a female lover in Hector's sister Polyxena and taken care to remind the audience of her importance to him by making that his chief motivation is to keep away from the battle, unlike in his other sources (and even in Caxton, Achilles' love for Polyxena only begins a year after Hector's death). Thersites' next reference to Patroclus's sexuality—perhaps to be taken as more reliable, since it is made when the stage is empty and Patroclus is not there to react to an insult—is his resolve to tell him that Cressida is a whore, since no one will give more to get "a commodious drab" than Patroclus would (5.2.189–192). Cast-

ing aspersions on a man's masculinity has always been a common form of crude humor—Ajax had earlier insulted Thersites himself by calling him "Mistress Thersites" (2.1.37)—and Thersites' other insults are surely not to be taken as literal truth (even as Cressida is not literally a whore). Patroclus admits that some think him "effeminate" (3.3.218) because of his refusal to engage in the battle, but clearly heterosexual characters such as Romeo and Prince Hal are called "effeminate" as well, and Troilus, Hector, and Achilles also compare themselves to women in this play (1.1.9, 2.2.11, 3.3.237). Of course, most directors quite properly feel that part of their job is to make the plays relevant and responsive to the cultural context of the performance, rather than merely attempt to recover Shakespeare's original intentions and staging: Such immediacy of engagement can often provoke audiences into seeing the plays with fresh eyes and renewed interest, as it did in this case for a generation of academic critics.

THE PLAY TODAY

The modernist response of discouragement or despair over the play's themes of fragmentation, disorder, and the loss of stable ethical values has been largely transmuted into a cheerful and playful welcoming of the good news on the part of poststructuralist critics, for whom such developments are seen as positive attributes to be celebrated rather than mourned. Similarly, the antiwar theme that was so powerful during and shortly after the Vietnam era has ceased to be such a challenging or subversive proposition during the most recent period of cultural history: Directors are now more apt to take for granted audiences' widespread opposition to any and all wars, along with their readiness to accept the cynical deglamorizing of all heroes. The current consensus is that no character in the play is free of contradictions and weaknesses, and that there is no one unassailable position that represents an authorial viewpoint or even authorial approval. As tempting as it may be to choose sides, the play seems content to present multiple points of view virtually kaleidoscopically. Shakespeare's rhetorical and stylistic resources are sufficiently powerful to present every point of view as at least provisionally viable, yet each is just as effectively undercut.

Earlier trends that have continued in contemporary productions of the play include the convention of presenting Achilles and Patroclus (and often Pandarus and Thersites as well) as homosexuals, although the treatments are generally subdued in comparison with those of the late 1960s and 1970s. The 1981 film version is fairly representative of this approach: Pandarus is a gay character who flirts with Paris's servant and makes little effort to conceal his lust for Troilus; Thersites wears a dress throughout his first two scenes and appears with a clinging male lover in a later scene; and Patroclus gives Achilles a romantic back rub. The 1998 RCS touring production hit upon another twist by crosscasting Patroclus, who was played by a woman, creating an additional homosexual perspective when "he" kisses, and then dances sensuously with, Cressida. Reviewers have faulted such productions for "cultural hijacking," arguing that the homosexual presentations are largely dependent upon invented stage business, costumes, and set designs rather than any plausible interpretation of the lines that Shakespeare wrote. Critical enthusiasm has waned as these came to be seen not as principled attempts to shock staid audiences but as commercialized travesties that at best offered a frivolous air of feel-good campiness and at worst identified homosexuality with decadence and perversity, perpetuating and exaggerating a series of offensive gay stereotypes (the *New York Times* actually kept track of the reviews of the flamboyant 1973 production: 10 negative to one positive). Many feminist critics were also nonplussed by the misogyny and regressive treatment afforded to the character of Cressida in such productions, which typically evinced little interest in her role. If political readings have occasionally tended to ignore the love plot, and feminist readings have tended to ignore the war plot, "queering" the play has at times seemed to ignore both plots in favor of flashy stunts adopted for their shock value or political correctness. Despite such critical objections, however, the homosexual reading of the play has remained the usual approach, to

the extent that the 1998 Regent's Park staging of the play by Alan Strachan with heterosexual characters was seen by most reviewers as an innovative departure from the norm.

Another older line of analysis still current has been to mitigate Cressida's personal responsibility in a feminist critique of the male-dominated system that has treated her as little more than property; some productions have extended comparable attention to the minor part of Helen as well, for example by costuming her in golden chains. Although the text of the play offers little direct support for such readings—Cressida herself refuses to offer any such excuses for her behavior—much can be done in performance to activate a feminist subtext. Juliet Stevenson, for example, played her as resistant and even heroic in the kissing scene in the 1985 RSC production. Her vulnerability was initially emphasized by keeping her dressed in her nightgown from the preceding scene, but she quickly showed her determination to resist being manhandled by slapping Agamemnon and wiping the first kiss off her face in disgust, which incited the generals to become even more aggressive. She was barely able to extricate herself from a threat of gang rape before eventually gaining control of the situation, to the extent of addressing Ulysses as a contemptible dog whom she could order to perform tricks (the 2008 Barbican Theatre production adopted the same visual metaphor, with Cressida even making him roll over at command). His final taunting of her was an expression of his anger over being outwitted and humiliated rather than a serious comment on Cressida's behavior, as the other generals exchanged puzzled looks behind his back. Victoria Hamilton (in Ian Judge's 1996 RSC production) gained confidence and power throughout the kissing scene, culminating in her self-assured responses to Menelaus and Ulysses. Instead of immediately exiting, however, Cressida remained onstage, allowing her to hear and react to Ulysses' assessment of her as a "daughter of the game," with a mixture of shock at his response and self-realization of her complicity in provoking that response. The 1999 National Theatre production even moved lines from two earlier scenes to the end of the play so that Cressida could appear in a final tableau with Pandarus, who painted her lips red as the last image in what one reviewer would call "a garish sign of whoredom imposed by masculine power."

Some of the more extreme interpretations have led to complaints that ideologues have distorted the work by reading it as though Cressida were the protagonist rather than a minor character, with the plot focusing on sexual violence that never occurs rather than on an infidelity that does. But while overtly feminist approaches to her character can occasionally seem superficial and anachronistic, Bridget Escolme, in a survey of recent stage treatments of Cressida, concedes that contemporary directors find themselves in an uncomfortable bind: "It seems that, to avoid an embarrassingly anti-feminist reading of the figure, Cressida must be a sympathetic victim of circumstance, with understandable motivations to guess at through the darkness." For most readers, at least, Shakespeare's character is far more interesting and nuanced when conceived as neither the unprincipled harlot of the earliest moralistic critics or the equally flat victim of the most extreme moralistic critics. On the whole, Cressida is more likely now than in even the recent past to be viewed as a complex character combining multiple "Cressidas," which may include at once moral weakness and cultural victimization, youthful romantic love and cynical opportunism. While some critics have complained that such interpretations are conservative and nostalgic rather than challenging and subversive, others have welcomed them as more balanced and moderate interpretations. Frances A. Shirley concludes her own comprehensive survey of the play's production history with a nod to those recent directors "who trust the play," perhaps a sign that a return is under way to a period of more direct engagement with the play on its own terms as a work of imaginative literature.

FIVE TOPICS FOR DISCUSSION AND WRITING

1. **Genre:** From its first publication more than 400 years ago, *Troilus and Cressida* has provoked discussions about its genre. At one time or another,
it has been called a tragedy, history, comedy, satire (including such subtypes as Menippean satire and comical satire), or simply a "problem play." What are the key elements of the play that cause these difficulties in classification? Are these disagreements due primarily to differing critical assumptions and biases or to inherent contradictions within the play itself?

2. **Major characters:** Reuben Brower called this play "*Hamlet* without Hamlet" because of its apparent lack of a single major character around whom the action revolves. In another sense, however, one might argue that this is "*Hamlet* with multiple Hamlets," since so many of the characters in *Troilus and Cressida* have remained mysterious, their motives and integrity obscure and complex enough to be open to widely varying interpretations. Which character do you take to be the most complicated or difficult to pin down, and why?

3. **Gender:** *Troilus and Cressida* presents an overwhelmingly misogynistic view of women, with very few positive images or comments to be found (only *Othello* uses the word "whore" more often). On the other hand, most of that commentary comes from the mouths of characters whose motives and dispositions make us question their reliability and judgment. Furthermore, the images of men presented in the play are arguably just as negative. How would you describe the play's overall treatment of gender?

4. **Speeches:** The long didactic speeches by Ulysses and Hector were almost unanimously acclaimed as the greatest strengths of the play for most of its history but have met with less enthusiasm from modern critics. What did earlier generations of critics believe that these set speeches contributed to the themes and texture of the play? What do you take to be the reasons that admiration of these passages has declined, or at least shifted in emphasis?

5. **Love and war:** The exchange of Cressida for Antenor turns out to be one of the most pivotal events for the downfall of both Troilus and Troy, as Cressida will never be reunited with Troilus, and Antenor will turn out to be a traitor who

eventually betrays his city to the Greeks. How does the play succeed (or, perhaps, fail) in combining the love story and the war story? What other key connections might be made between the two subplots of love and war?

Bibliography

Adamson, Jane. *Troilus and Cressida*. New York: Twayne, 1987.

Apfelbaum, Roger. *Shakespeare's Troilus and Cressida: Textual Problems and Performance Solutions*. Newark: University of Delaware Press, 2004.

Bevington, David, ed. *Troilus and Cressida*. Walton-on-Thames, England: Thomas Nelson, 1998.

Bowen, Barbara E. *Gender in the Theater of War: Shakespeare's Troilus and Cressida*. New York: Garland, 1993.

Brower, Reuben A. *Hero & Saint: Shakespeare and the Graeco-Roman Heroic Tradition*. Oxford: Oxford University Press, 1971.

Burns, M. M. "*Troilus and Cressida:* The Worst of Both Worlds." *Shakespeare Studies* 13 (1980): 105–130.

Butler, Colin. *The Practical Shakespeare: The Plays in Practice and on the Page*. Athens: Ohio University Press, 2005.

Campbell, Oscar James. *Comicall Satyre and Shakespeare's Troilus and Cressida*. San Marino, Calif.: Huntington Library, 1938.

Charnes, Linda. "The Two Party System in *Troilus and Cressida*." In *A Companion to Shakespeare's Work*. Vol. 4, *The Poems, Problem Comedies, Late Plays*, edited by Richard Dutton and Jean E. Howard, 302–315. Malden, Mass.: Blackwell, 2003.

Clark, Ira. *Rhetorical Readings, Dark Comedies, and Shakespeare's Problem Plays*. Gainesville: University Press of Florida, 2007.

Coleridge, Samuel Taylor. *Lectures 1808–1819 on literature II. The Collected Works of Samuel Taylor Coleridge*, edited by R. A. Foakes. Vol. 5, pt. 2. Princeton, N.J.: Princeton University Press, 1987.

Dawson, Anthony B. *Troilus and Cressida*. Cambridge: Cambridge University Press, 2003.

Donaldson, E. Talbot. *The Swan at the Well: Shakespeare Reading Chaucer*. New Haven, Conn.: Yale University Press, 1985.

Ellis-Fermor, Una. *The Frontiers of Drama*. London: Methuen, 1945.

Elton, W. R. "Aristotle's *Nicomachean Ethics* and Shakespeare's *Troilus and Cressida*." *Journal of the History of Ideas* 58, no. 2 (1997): 331–337.

Escolme, Bridget. *Talking to the Audience: Shakespeare, Performance, Self*. Abington: Routledge, 2005.

Freund, Elizabeth. "'Ariachne's broken woof': The Rhetoric of Citation in *Troilus and Cressida*." In *Shakespeare and the Question of Theory*, edited by Patricia Parker and Geoffrey Hartman, 19–36. New York: Methuen, 1985.

Greene, Gayle. "Shakespeare's Cressida: 'A kind of self.'" In *The Woman's Part: Feminist Criticism of Shakespeare*, edited by Carolyn Ruth Swift Lenz, Gayle Greene, and Carol Thomas Neely, 133–149. Urbana: University of Illinois Press, 1980.

Harbage, Alfred. *Shakespeare and the Rival Traditions*. New York: Macmillan, 1952.

Harris, Sharon M. "Feminism and Shakespeare's Cressida: '*If* I be false . . .'" *Women's Studies* 18 (1990): 65–82.

Hazlitt, William. *The Round Table and Characters of Shakespeare's Plays*. Vol. 4. *The Complete Works of William Hazlitt*, edited by P. P. Howe. New York: AMS Press, 1967.

Hillebrand, H. N., ed. *Troilus and Cressida. The New Variorum Shakespeare*. Philadelphia: Lippincott, 1953.

Hodgdon, Barbara. "He Do Cressida in Different Voices." *English Literary Renaissance* 20 (1990): 254–286.

Jensen, Phebe. "The Textual Politics of *Troilus and Cressida*." *Shakespeare Quarterly* 46, no. 4 (1995): 414–423.

Jowitt, J. A., and R. K. S. Taylor, eds. *Self and Society in Shakespeare's Troilus and Cressida and Measure for Measure*. Bradford, England: Bradford Centre Occasional Papers no. 4, 1982.

Kimbrough, Robert. *Shakespeare's "Troilus and Cressida" and Its Setting*. Cambridge, Mass.: Harvard University Press, 1964.

Lenz, Carolyn R. S., Gayle Greene, and Carol Thomas Neely, eds. *The Woman's Part: Feminist Criticism of Shakespeare.* Urbana: University of Illinois Press, 1980.

Loggins, Vernon P. *The Life of Our Design: Organization and Related Strategies in "Troilus and Cressida."* Lanham, Md.: University Press of America, 1992.

Martin, Priscilla, ed. *Troilus and Cressida: A Selection of Critical Essays.* London: Macmillan, 1976.

McAlindon, Thomas. "Language, Style, and Meaning in *Troilus and Cressida.*" *PMLA* 84 (1969): 29–43.

Milowicki, Edward J., and Robert Rawdon Wilson. "A Measure for Menippean Discourse: The Example of Shakespeare." *Poetics Today* 23, no. 2 (2002): 291–326.

Muir, Kenneth. "*Troilus and Cressida.*" *Shakespeare Survey* 8 (1955): 28–39.

———, ed. *Troilus and Cressida.* Oxford: Oxford University Press, 1982.

Nuttal, A. D. *Shakespeare the Thinker.* New Haven, Conn.: Yale University Press, 2007.

Palmer, Kenneth, ed. *Troilus and Cressida.* New York: Methuen, 1982.

Presson, Robert K. *Shakespeare's "Troilus and Cressida" and the Legends of Troy.* Madison: University of Wisconsin Press, 1953.

Rutter, Carol Chillington. "Designs on Shakespeare: Troilus's Sleeve, Cressida's Glove, Helen's Placket." In *Enter the Body: Women and Representation on Shakespeare's Stage,* 104–141. London: Routledge.

Shirley, Frances A. *Troilus and Cressida.* Cambridge: Cambridge University Press, 2005.

Spurgeon, Caroline F. E. *Shakespeare's Imagery and What It Tells Us.* Cambridge: Cambridge University Press, 1935.

Stříbrný, Zdenek. "Time in *Troilus and Cressida.*" *Shakespeare-Jahrbuch* 112 (1976): 105–121.

Swinburne, Algernon Charles. *Prose Works.* Vol. 11, pt. 1, *The Complete Works of Algernon Charles Swinburne,* edited by Sir Edmund Gosse and Thomas James Wise. New York: Russell & Russell, 1925.

Taylor, Gary. "*Troilus and Cressida:* Bibliography, Performance, Interpretation." *Shakespeare Studies* 15 (1982): 99–136.

Thompson, Ann. *Shakespeare's Chaucer: A Study in Literary Origins.* New York: Barnes & Noble, 1978.

Yachnin, Paul. "Shakespeare's Problem Plays and the Drama of His Time: *Troilus and Cressida, All's Well That Ends Well, Measure for Measure.*" In *A Companion to Shakespeare's Work,* Vol. 4, *The Poems, Problem Comedies, Late Plays,* edited by Richard Dutton and Jean E. Howard, 46–68. Malden, Mass.: Blackwell, 2003.

Yoder, R. A. "'Sons and Daughters of the Game': An Essay on Shakespeare's 'Troilus and Cressida.'" *Shakespeare Survey* 25 (1972): 11–25.

FILM AND VIDEO PRODUCTIONS

Brill, Clive, dir. *Troilus and Cressida.* With Norman Rodway (Pandarus), David Troughton (Thersites), Julia Ford (Cressida), Ian Pepperell (Troilus). Arkangel, 1998.

Cellan Jones, James, dir. *Fortunes of War.* A five-minute excerpt from the play appears in this television miniseries. With Kenneth Branagh and Emma Thompson. BBC/WNET, 1987.

Hepton, Bernard, and Michael Croft, dirs. *Troilus and Cressida.* A recording of the National Youth Theatre's touring production. BBC, 1966.

Miller, Jonathan, dir. *Troilus and Cressida.* BBC Shakespeare Plays Series. With Charles Gray (Pandarus), Anton Lesser (Troilus), Suzanne Burden (Cressida), Vernon Dobtcheff (Agamemnon), Benjamin Whitrow (Ulysses), "The Incredible Orlando" [Jack Birkett] (Thersites), Kenneth Haigh (Achilles), John Shrapnel (Hector). BBC/Time-Warner, 1981.

Rylands, George, dir. *Troilus and Cressida.* With Mary Watson (Cressida), John Fraser (Troilus), Richard Wordsworth (Thersites), Frank Pettingell (Pandarus). BBC, 1954.

Troilus and Cressida: War, War, Glorious War. A 23-minute adaptation for the Explorations in Shakespeare series. Ontario Educational Communications Authority, 1969.

—William Nelles

Twelfth Night

INTRODUCTION

Twelfth Night (subtitled "What You Will") is one of Shakespeare's mature comedies, written at about the midpoint of his career as a dramatist. It is one of his most delightful and popular plays, containing laughable and awkward circumstances, as well as clever and ironic statements, many resulting from the character Viola's dressing as a man. Central to the merriment is the presence of one of the most famous professional fools (court jesters or clowns) in Shakespeare's plays. Feste is a classic "wise fool": He is an older character among the many young people in the play and has the most experience in and knowledge of human nature and love. Underneath his fooling is a serious and, at times, melancholy soul. In a sense, he also is in a disguise that hides his real nature.

Twelfth Night pleases the audience because of its apparent light comedy, joy, and general happiness, but it also manages to reflect deeply on serious issues about human nature and life. Feste and Viola are the primary "teachers" or "clarifiers": They teach other characters but also teach us—a fact we do not fully realize until the end of the play.

Shakespeare here gives the audience indeed a comprehensive view of the world and the place of the human in it. He deals with our old and constant enemies—time, age, and mortality. But he also suggests ways to face and contend with them. Furthermore, *Twelfth Night* sheds light on issues that were politically, socially, and morally relevant to Shakespeare's time and continue to be so today.

In particular, some of the satire of the play is aimed at the Puritans of the time—those who, like Malvolio, frowned on fun, celebrations, festivals, and jokes and who wished to impose their own strictures upon all other people and generally to squelch joy. Shakespeare sees the Malvolios of his time (and consequently our own time) as absorbed in self-love and self-concern. They only breed conflict, sadness, and death.

Written probably in 1600 or 1601, *Twelfth Night* ushered in not only a new century but also a decade in which Shakespeare was at the height of his career and wrote his greatest plays. It is an appropriate entrance into the fullness of Shakespeare's dramatic art. The play features such classic lines as "If music be the food of love, play on"; "Then come kiss me sweet and twenty"; and "Some are born great, some achieve greatness, and some have greatness thrust upon them." Joseph H. Summers aptly says, "*Twelfth Night* is the climax of Shakespeare's early achievement in comedy. The effects and values of the earlier comedies are here subtly embodied in the most complex structure which Shakespeare had yet created."

BACKGROUND

The last years of Queen Elizabeth I's reign were marked by increased patriotism. Englishmen were proud of their country and celebrated its new esteem in the eyes of the world. They had little worry at this time about being seriously threatened from any external power: They had taken care

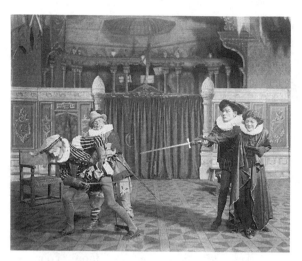

Toby holds Sebastian's arm as he draws his sword after being hit by Andrew in Act IV, Scene I of a 1905 production of *Twelfth Night*. (Photographed by Hall's Studio)

of that menace with the defeat of the prestigious and feared Spanish Armada in 1588. The smaller English naval ships had sent the large warships from Spain limping back to their own country after a battle extending over several days in the English Channel. Queen Elizabeth from then on was seen as a savior figure. But since a storm aided them in this defeat of the Spanish, the English certainly felt also that God himself, with his providential direction, definitely was on their side. Some critics believe that this same feeling of the happy workings of providence is evident in *Twelfth Night*. And generally both the feeling of life's goodness and the celebratory mood prevailing in the English consciousness in the 1590s carry into the moods and actions of this play.

Important also in *Twelfth Night* is the general context of Italy and things Italian, as seen at this time in history. In 16th-century England, there was an attitude of both love and hate for Italian things. On the one hand, there was the association of Italy with greedy, grasping values—reflected, in fact, a few years earlier in Shakespeare's *The Merchant of Venice*. Also through the century, one finds dispar-

aging remarks about Italian fashions being brought into England and snide comments about Italian sexual preferences—for example, John Donne in his "Elegy XVI" of the 1590s advises his lady of the dangers of traveling in Italy while she is disguised as a young man as follows:

> The indifferent Italian, as we pass
> His warm land, well content to think thee
> page,
> Will hunt thee with such lust and hideous rage
> As Lot's fair guests were vexed.

In other words, the Italian man here is seen as perverted and bisexual—"indifferent" as to whether the sexual object is female or male. Italy and the Italians were also associated with the Machiavellian figure, a political leader or governmental ruler who presided as a ruthless tyrant, wielding power without regard for ethics and morals, using anything (even lying and hypocrisy) to gain and hold his position. This figure originated in the Italian work *The Prince*, written by Machiavelli in 1513. This kind of ruler was looked on with great horror and loathing by the Elizabethans, and many of the history plays and tragedies of the period picture him as a political monster: This includes Shakespeare's own *Richard III; Henry IV, Part 1; Henry IV, Part 2; Hamlet;* and others. On the other hand, Italy was the home of Castiglione, the man who wrote *The Courtier*, an idealistic Platonic view of love and beauty. Its assumptions are embodied in Christian Platonism and are diametrically opposed to the view that Italianate matters are physical, monetary, and generally decadent. *The Courtier* was translated into English by Sir Thomas Hoby in 1561 and became one of the most influential books in England under Queen Elizabeth. In fact, it defined and stimulated the whole idea of the Renaissance man, the well-rounded individual who is skilled and adept in many fields—the perfect scholar, musician, writer, soldier, etc. He is pictured in the work as the perfect courtier who can advise the ruler he serves with wisdom and experience. He also is to exemplify the highest intellectual and spiritual values and behave with utmost courtesy and grace. Therefore, again, the attitude toward Italy and Italians was composed of opposites.

So, what does this concern with Italy and views of the Italian have to do with *Twelfth Night*? True, the setting of the play is not specified as Italy. Instead, it is a supposed land called Illyria. Although there was an ancient Adriatic country of Illyria, it nonetheless seems clear that, in Shakespeare's mind and the minds of the members of his audience, Illyria is a fantasy version of Italy. There is a Countess in the play. We also have the term "Madonna" used by Feste. "Viola" is an Italian word. And Viola in the play is in disguise and, in essence, a very wise counselor to the ruler Duke Orsino—she is, then, an embodiment of Castiglione's courtier, but in female form. It is doubly interesting to consider that she also is like Donne's lady in disguise: Her male costume is intended partly to be a device for self-protection. But even more evidence is in the fact that Shakespeare's major source for the play is an Italian comedy titled *Gl' Ingannati*, written in 1537. It also was sometimes called *Inganni*. In fact, John Manningham, in his diary entry in which he mentions the play, says that *Twelfth Night* is "most like and near to that in Italian called *Inganni*." This play includes a woman disguised as a man, and as such she helps the man she loves try to win another woman: This parallels the role of the disguised Viola in *Twelfth Night*. Also, the disguised woman in the Italian play says her name is Cesare: Viola's assumed name is Cesario.

Another major source of the play seems to be "Apolonius and Silla," one of the stories by Barnaby Riche in his *Farewell to Militarie Profession* (1581). It features twins of different sexes, the girl disguised as a man. There is a shipwreck on the coast of a strange land, and the female Silla assumes the appearance and disguise of her brother, just as does Viola. Other possible sources have been proposed for some elements, scenes, and characters of *Twelfth Night*, but it is an extremely complex and indefinite matter.

A full understanding of the play is not possible without an awareness of Puritanism in Queen Elizabeth's reign. The "Puritans" were so-called because they wished to "purify" the English Church. They did not want to break away from that church originally: They wanted Elizabeth as the head of the Church of England to significantly change the church to embody more of their ideas and to eliminate certain elements that they considered to be too Roman Catholic. The attitudes of the Puritans, however, earned them the reputation of being demanding, self-serving, greedy, and generally sour and joyless. Shakespeare is picturing such a person in the character of Malvolio. His name alone means "ill will." Maria refers to him when she says (in Act II, Scene 3), "Marry, sir, sometimes he is a kind of puritan" and also "The dev'l a puritan that he is, or any thing constantly but a time-pleaser, an affection'd ass . . ." Spoilsports similar to Malvolio were common in Shakespeare's time, as they are today. For example, in 1598 at the court, the chief server (Ambrose Willoughby) ordered (and argued with) the earl of Southampton and friends to stop a late-night card game. Malvolio similarly interferes with the revelry of Sir Toby and his friends.

Another key to understanding the play is to have some knowledge of festivals and festive rituals common in the time of Shakespeare. This is related to the matter of Puritans as well, since Puritans loathed festivals and celebrations. In the Middle Ages and Renaissance, there were numerous festivals occurring through each year, and the celebrations of them were major entertainments for the populace. Each festival had certain rituals and customary elements associated with it. Certain of these festivals/holidays were celebrated according to a ritualized pattern of Misrule—they are generally referred to as Misrule celebrations. Shakespeare titles his play *Twelfth Night*, and indeed the holiday so named was one of the highlights of festive celebrations of the year. It is the climax of the 12 days of Christmas: January 6 is Epiphany, the 12th day. That night, Twelfth Night, ended the Christmas revels and was always celebrated by the Misrule ritual. Any group in Shakespeare's time celebrating this festival would elect a person to preside over and guide the celebration: He was known as the Lord of Misrule. His responsibility was to lead the group in misrule and disorder. All normal social and moral strictures, rules, and restrictions are overturned. All ranks and titles are meaningless. Duties and schedules are discarded. Fun and games, eating and drinking prevail. People wear costumes and masks and are not identified until the end of the holiday, when the masks are removed. At the end of the holiday, the followers of the Lord of Misrule enact a ritual rebellion and overthrow of him. Sociologists and anthropologists note that this makes him the scapegoat for the group: They blame him for any sins and wrongs they have committed and thus can enter the everyday world again with a sense of being cleansed. They have enjoyed a period of laxity and release from pressures, duties, and worries and are reinvigorated to take up their normal roles in life after the holiday. In addition, on Twelfth Night gifts are given and an Epiphany cake is made, in which embedded favors were received by lucky individuals as they took a piece of it.

Shakespeare implies that his characters in *Twelfth Night* are in the roles of celebrants in a Misrule festival and in particular the climactic one of Epiphany. Characters are in physical and symbolic disguises; celebrants are rowdy and disorderly and are criticized for this by a Puritanical steward; there is a Lord of Misrule figure; people receive gifts and surprises; and at the end, everyone prepares to reenter the real world beyond the holiday one. The festive pattern of the play is crucial throughout.

Date and Text of the Play

Most scholars agree that Shakespeare wrote the play in 1600 or 1601; however, the first mention of it in writing occurs in the diary of John Manningham, who saw the play on February 2, 1602. He wrote:

> At our feast we had a play called 'Twelve Night, or What You Will,' much like the Comedy of Errors, or Menechmi in Plautus, but most like and near to that in Italian called *Inganni*. A good practice in it to make the

steward believe his Lady widow was in Love with him by counterfeiting a letter as from his lady in general terms telling him what she liked best in him and prescribing his gesture in smiling, his apparel, etc., and then when he came to practice making him believe they took him to be mad, etc.

Although the Lady Olivia in the play is not a widow, there is no doubt that Manningham is referring to Malvolio's ridiculous attempts to woo her. This performance by the theater company in which Shakespeare himself was a shareholder/owner (The Lord Chamberlain's Men) took place in the ornate dining hall at Middle Temple, one of the Inns of Court. This is one of the few places still well-preserved today where we know Shakespeare himself was physically present. It is a site not to be missed by any true Shakespearean visiting London.

The first publication of *Twelfth Night* was in 1623 in the First Folio of Shakespeare's plays, seven years after his death. This first publication is the only authoritative one for this play, and all later editions of the play derive from this one. No previous quarto edition has been discovered. The text of the play presents no major problems or puzzling errors, unlike many of Shakespeare's plays.

SYNOPSIS
Brief Synopsis

Viola is cast upon the shore of Illyria. She thinks her twin brother, Sebastian, has drowned during the great storm at sea. She decides to disguise herself as a man and go to Orsino, the duke of Illyria. Under the name Cesario, she eventually becomes a favorite page at Orsino's court. Orsino sends her to Lady Olivia, with whom he is in love, as a messenger. Although Viola agrees to do her best to woo his lady, she has already fallen in love with Orsino herself.

At Olivia's home, Sir Toby Belch, Olivia's uncle, complains to Maria, Olivia's gentlewoman, about St. Andrew Aguecheek, a wealthy nobleman courting Lady Olivia. Viola (as Cesario) arrives and, after their conversation, Olivia falls in love with Cesario.

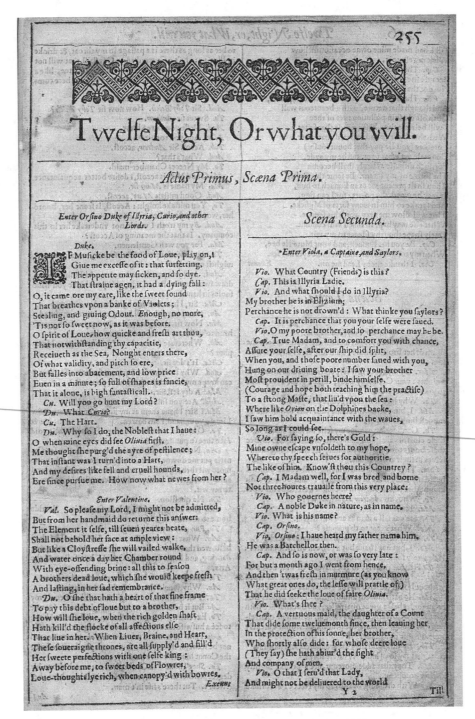

255

TwelfeNight, Or what you will.

Actus Primus, Scæna Prima.

Enter Orſino Duke of Illyria, Curio, and other Lords.

Duke.

IF Muſicke be the food of Loue, play on,
Giue me exceſſe of it : that ſurfetting,
The appetite may ſicken, and ſo dye.
That ſtraine agen, it had a dying fall :
O, it came ore my eare, like the ſweet ſound
That breathes vpon a banke of Violets ;
Stealing, and giuing Odour. Enough, no more,
'Tis not ſo ſweet now, as it was before.
O ſpirit of Loue, how quicke and freſh art thou,
That notwithſtanding thy capacitie,
Receiueth as the Sea, Nought enters there,
Of what validity, and pitch ſo ere,
But falles into abatement, and low price
Euen in a minute ; ſo full of ſhapes is fancie,
That it alone, is high fantaſticall.

Cu. Will you go hunt my Lord?

Du. What *Curio?*

Cu. The Hart.

Du. Why ſo I do, the Nobleſt that I haue :
O when mine eyes did ſee *Oliuia* firſt,
Me thought ſhe purg'd the ayre of peſtilence ;
That inſtant was I turn'd into a Hart,
And my deſires like fell and cruell hounds,
Ere ſince purſue me. How now what newes from her ?

Enter Valentine.

Val. So pleaſe my Lord, I might not be admitted,
But from her handmaid do returne this anſwer :
The Element it ſelfe, till ſeuen yeares heate,
Shall not behold her face at ample view :
But like a Cloyſtreſſe ſhe will vailed walke,
And water once a day her Chamber round
With eye-offending brine : all this to ſeaſon
A brothers dead loue, which ſhe would keepe freſh
And laſting, in her ſad remembrance.

Du. O ſhe that hath a heart of that fine frame
To pay this debt of loue but to a brother,
How will ſhe loue, when the rich golden ſhaft
Hath kill'd the flocke of all affections elſe
That liue in her. When Liuer, Braine, and Heart,
Theſe ſoueraigne thrones, are all ſupply'd and fill'd
Her ſweete perfections with one ſelfe king :
Away before me, to ſweet beds of Flowres,
Loue-thoughts lye rich, when canopy'd with bowres.

Exeunt

Scena Secunda.

Enter Viola, a Captaine, and Saylors.

Vio. What Country (Friends) is this ?

Cap. This is Illyria Ladie.

Vio. And what ſhould I do in Illyria?
My brother he is in Elizium ;
Perchance he is not drown'd : What thinke you ſaylors ?

Cap. It is perchance that you your ſelfe were ſaued.

Vio. O my poore brother, and ſo perchance may he be.

Cap. True Madam, and to comfort you with chance,
Aſſure your ſelfe, after our ſhip did ſplit,
When you, and thoſe poore number ſaued with you,
Hung on our driuing boate : I ſaw your brother
Moſt prouident in perill, binde himſelfe,
(Courage and hope both teaching him the practiſe)
To a ſtrong Maſte, that liu'd vpon the ſea :
Where like *Orion* on the Dolphines backe,
I ſaw him hold acquaintance with the waues,
So long as I could ſee.

Vio. For ſaying ſo, there's Gold :
Mine owne eſcape vnfoldeth to my hope,
Whereto thy ſpeech ſerues for authoritie,
The like of him. Know'ſt thou this Countrey ?

Cap. I Madam well, for I was bred and borne
Not three houres trauaile from this very place :

Vio. Who gouernes heere?

Cap. A noble Duke in nature, as in name.

Vio. What is his name?

Cap. Orſino.

Vio. Orſino : I haue heard my father name him,
He was a Batchellor then.

Cap. And ſo is now, or was ſo very late :
For but a month ago I went from hence,
And then 'twas freſh in murmure (as you know
What great ones do, the leſſe will prattle of,)
That he did ſeeke the loue of faire *Oliuia.*

Vio. What's ſhee ?

Cap. A vertuous maid, the daughter of a Count
That dide ſome tweluemonth ſince, then leauing her
In the protection of his ſonne, her brother,
Who ſhortly alſo dide : for whoſe deere loue
(They ſay) ſhe hath abiur'd the ſight
And company of men.

Vio. O that I ſeru'd that Lady,
And might not be deliuered to the world

Y 2

Til

Title page of the First Folio edition of *Twelfth Night,* published in 1623

After Viola leaves, Olivia sends Malvolio, her steward, to give Cesario a ring and to ask "him" to visit her the next day.

At the seacoast, Sebastian and Antonio come ashore. Sebastian assumes that his twin sister has drowned. Although Antonio has many enemies nearby at Orsino's court, he is determined to follow Sebastian out of the great affection he feels for him.

Malvolio returns the ring that Cesario supposedly left with Olivia. Cesario tells Olivia that it would be better if she loved a dream.

Sir Toby, Sir Andrew, Feste the Clown, and Maria stay up late one night and make so much noise that Malvolio storms into their room. Failing to calm them down, he reports them to Olivia. Maria, in order to get revenge, suggests they trick him.

At his palace, Orsino expresses his feelings for Olivia and presses Cesario to renew his suit. Viola confesses her love for the Duke, but he apparently fails to understand. Cesario returns to Olivia, who now shows hints of her love. Although Viola safely keeps her distance, Olivia bids Cesario to come back again. At Sir Toby's suggestion, a restive Sir Andrew writes a challenge to Cesario.

Sir Toby, Sir Andrew, Maria, and Fabian place a forged love letter, supposedly written by Olivia, before Malvolio. In it, she asks him to wear yellow stockings cross-gartered and to smile constantly in her presence. To the delight of the conspirators, Malvolio is taken in.

In the street, Antonio gives Sebastian his purse. Sebastian goes off to tour the city, while Antonio leaves to find lodging at an inn.

While Olivia waits in her garden for Cesario, Malvolio appears dressed in yellow stockings and answers her questions by quoting sentences from her supposed letter. Olivia thinks he has gone insane. She orders Maria to have her people take special care of him. Sir Toby, Fabian, and Maria have him bound and confined to a dark room.

Sir Toby presses the fearful Sir Andrew and Cesario into a duel. As they unwillingly draw their swords, Antonio enters and, thinking that Viola is Sebastian, goes to rescue his friend. The officers of the Duke enter; one of them recognizes Antonio as an old outlaw, and they arrest him. Antonio asks Cesario for his purse, but Cesario denies any acquaintance with him whatsoever. When Antonio addresses Cesario as Sebastian, Viola is left with the thought that Sebastian might in fact be alive.

Feste, who is sent to find Cesario, instead finds Sebastian. Sir Andrew, Sir Toby, and Fabian enter. Sir Andrew instantly attacks Sebastian, who draws his sword readily and wounds the knight and Sir Toby.

Olivia enters and orders everyone away from Sebastian, whom she also takes to be Cesario. She offers herself to him. Although baffled, Sebastian accepts the offer to marry her. The priest comes and they marry.

In the final scene, Antonio, before the duke, relates his adventures with Sebastian; Olivia enters and claims that Viola, whom she believes is Cesario, is her husband; Sir Toby and Sir Andrew break into the scene and blame Viola for their wounds. When Sebastian makes an entrance, the company realizes that Viola and Sebastian, twin brother and sister, are both alive.

In the end, Orsino marries Viola. We are told that Sir Toby will marry Maria. Malvolio, finally released from his imprisonment, swears vengeance upon them all. Feste's sobering song closes the play.

Act I, Scene 1

The play opens in the palace of Orsino, the duke of Illyria. He is accompanied by musicians. Orsino wants their sweet music, but then suddenly his mood changes, and he wants no music. An attendant, Curio, asks him if he wishes to go hunt, and Orsino answers that he already is hunting Olivia. Valentine then enters with the news that Olivia has rejected Orsino's love suit and that she plans to remain isolated for seven years to mourn and honor her brother who had died. Orsino is surprised at such sisterly devotion, but he hopes that her large capacity for love will eventually come to himself from her.

Viola (Viola Allen) after the shipwreck in Act I, Scene 2 of *Twelfth Night,* in this photograph published by the Byron Company in 1903

Act I, Scene 2

Viola and a captain enter Illyria after a shipwreck. Viola wonders if her brother perished in the wreck, but the captain gives her hope that he might be safe also. The captain's home is Illyria, and he tells Viola that it is governed by a noble duke named Orsino. He also informs her that Orsino is trying to win the beautiful and virtuous Olivia's love but that her father and brother died about a year ago and that Olivia is in seclusion and will not see or receive any men. Viola takes the captain in her confidence and tells him of her plan to disguise herself as a man and seek to serve Orsino. She asks him to introduce her at Orsino's court.

Act I, Scene 3

Olivia's uncle, Sir Toby, complains to Maria, her chambermaid, that Olivia is mourning for her brother's death excessively and to the detriment of her life. Maria tells Toby that Olivia is displeased with his excessive drinking and carousing late into the night. Maria also tells him that Olivia mentioned the foolishness of the knight, Sir Andrew Aguecheek, one that Toby has urged to woo Olivia. Sir Andrew enters and proves his doltish nature in a verbal combat with Maria. Sir Andrew tells

Toby that he plans to leave, since Orsino is courting Olivia, but Toby informs him that Olivia will not accept Orsino. Sir Andrew then decides to stay another month.

Act I, Scene 4

At the Duke's palace, Viola is disguised as a young man named Cesario. The Duke sends Cesario to speak on Orsino's behalf in his continuing suit of Olivia. Despite Cesario's belief that Olivia will not admit him (her), Orsino feels that the youth's adamant request will be heeded. Viola sets off on this mission, even though she acknowledges to herself that she is in the predicament of trying to win another woman for the very man that she herself would like to marry.

Act I, Scene 5

Maria criticizes the court jester (fool, clown) Feste for being absent so long. Olivia then enters in a foul mood and accompanied by Malvolio, her steward. She tells attendants to take away the "fool," Feste. But Feste says that they should take away Olivia, implying that she is really the fool. He then secures her permission to prove to her that she is the fool: He does so by a witty trap in which she admits that she is grieving for her brother who is in heaven. Appreciating Feste's witty catechism of her, Olivia warms into a better mood and admires Feste's ability as a jester. However, Malvolio remains sour and degrading toward him, and Olivia comments that Malvolio is too strict and extreme in his self-love and lack of generosity toward others. Maria comes back in with word of a young emissary from Orsino, who wishes an audience with Olivia. In the face of this young gentleman's insistence, and after hearing a description of Cesario, Olivia agrees to see him. Viola, as Cesario, convinces Olivia of her peaceful mission on Orsino's behalf and praises Olivia's great beauty that should not be left to waste away and to end without being reflected in her children through marriage. Olivia still rejects Orsino, but after Viola leaves, Olivia realizes that she has been attracted to and fallen in love with Cesario.

She sends Malvolio after Cesario with a ring that Olivia claims was left her by Cesario on Orsino's behalf. She says that if Cesario will return tomorrow, she will give her reasons for this.

Act II, Scene 1

Sebastian tells Antonio, a sea captain who rescued him from drowning, that he will go on alone to the court of Orsino: He does not want Antonio to accompany him and become subject to Sebastian's propensity for ill fortune. He tells Antonio that his twin sister (Viola) drowned, and he reveals his grief for her. Sebastian leaves. Antonio then decides to follow Sebastian, despite the fact that he has some enemies in Orsino's court.

Act II, Scene 2

Malvolio overtakes Viola and gives her the ring Olivia sent. After Malvolio leaves, Viola briefly wonders why she is "returning" this ring that was not given to her. Then Viola realizes that Olivia has been "charmed" by Cesario and that this ring is a love token meant to convey this message to Cesario. She summarizes the baffling predicament that exists: Orsino loves Olivia, Olivia loves Cesario, and Cesario/Viola loves Orsino. She feels absolutely helpless and can only trust that time will solve these problems.

Act II, Scene 3

Sir Toby, Sir Andrew, and Feste drink and joke noisily after midnight. Feste sings for the two knights. Maria comes and warns them of carrying on too noisily and notes that Olivia might send Malvolio to quiet them. Indeed, he does appear and rebukes them, but Toby simply mocks Malvolio. Malvolio leaves after warning all of them, including Maria, that their disorder will not be tolerated and that they will answer for it. Maria then hatches a plot to get revenge on the puritanical Malvolio—a scheme in which she will write love letters to him that he will think came from Olivia. The other three are happy to participate in this duping of Malvolio and eagerly anticipate the trap being sprung the next day.

Act II, Scene 4

Orsino wants to hear the song that Feste had previously sung for him. While Curio seeks Feste, Orsino talks to Cesario about love, and Cesario implies that "he" (Cesario) loves one (Orsino assuming that it is a woman Cesario loves) very similar to Orsino. Feste appears and sings the song concerning sad love from a rejecting lady. Orsino then sends Cesario again on an embassy to Olivia to win her heart.

Act II, Scene 5

Maria places a letter in Malvolio's path and has Toby, Andrew, and Fabian hide to observe his reaction. She leaves. Even before he finds the letter, Malvolio arrogantly praises himself and assumes that Olivia admires him. He creates for himself a vision of being her husband with the title of count and of being able to put down Toby. He then finds the letter and, as Maria intended, interprets it as a letter from Olivia that is meant for him. He plans to wear foolish clothing and to smile continually, actions that the letter designates as Olivia's wishes.

Malvolio leaves. Maria returns and finds the three men ecstatic over the success of the scheme. She asks them to follow her to see the outcome when Malvolio approaches Olivia. They vow to follow her wherever she leads.

Act III, Scene 1

At Olivia's home, Viola and Feste spar verbally. Toby and Andrew enter and converse with Viola. Olivia enters and dismisses the others, leaving only Viola/Cesario with her. Viola again tells Olivia that she is there on Orsino's behalf. Olivia says plainly that she has no interest in Orsino but would like to hear Cesario woo her for himself. She hears the clock strike and realizes that she herself is wasting time. She confesses her love for Cesario. Viola says that she cannot respond to her professed love, and she leaves.

Act III, Scene 2

Sir Andrew tells Sir Toby and Fabian that he will give up his attempt to win Olivia, since she obviously is greatly attracted to Cesario and pays no attention to Andrew. Toby and Fabian, however, convince him that Olivia is only trying to make Andrew jealous, and they also talk him into challenging Cesario to a duel. Andrew leaves to write this challenge, and Toby and Fabian anticipate great fun in seeing the outcome of this battle between two cowards. Maria enters. She tells them that Malvolio is dressed and is acting as prescribed in her false letter, and they rush off to enjoy the fun when Olivia encounters him.

Act III, Scene 3

Sebastian thanks Antonio for protectively following him, even though Antonio faces danger from his enemies if discovered. Sebastian leaves to see some of the famous places of the city, while Antonio arranges with him to meet later at the Elephant Inn.

Act III, Scene 4

Maria warns Olivia that Malvolio is acting strangely and seems to verge on madness. After Malvolio enters, Olivia indeed believes her, judging from his odd actions and statements. Word is brought to Olivia that Cesario has arrived. Olivia leaves to receive him but tells Maria to have someone, possibly Toby, care for Malvolio. Maria exits with Olivia and returns with Sir Toby and Fabian. They treat Malvolio as if he is possessed by Satan. Malvolio scoffs and leaves. Toby then says that they will bind him and keep him in a dark room, as mad people were treated. Sir Andrew arrives with his letter of challenge to Cesario. Toby sees that it is too foolish and laughable to be taken seriously, so he tells Andrew that he will deliver it for him. Actually Toby plans to use his own words and not Andrew's. Olivia and Cesario enter, and the others leave. Olivia continues to declare her love for Cesario, while Viola keeps trying to divert her attention to Orsino and his love for Olivia. After Olivia leaves, Toby and Fabian tell Viola of the fierce challenge of Cesario by a gentleman greatly to be feared. Fabian remains with Cesario while Toby goes to Andrew and tells him that Cesario

Malvolio acts strangely in front of Olivia in Act III, Scene 4 of *Twelfth Night*. This illustration is of an 1884 production at the Lyceum. *(Illustration by John Jellicoe)*

is a skilled fighter to be feared. Andrew wants to withdraw his challenge, but Toby says that Cesario will not hear of it. Toby succeeds in bringing the two together, and they draw swords. At that precise moment, Antonio appears and assumes that Cesario is his friend Sebastian, since Viola looks exactly like her twin brother. Antonio defies Andrew and stops the duel. Officers appear and arrest Antonio as an enemy of Orsino. Before he is taken away, Antonio addresses Viola as "Sebastian" and asks for some of the money from the purse that he earlier had given Sebastian. Viola is taken aback, since she does not know Antonio. Antonio, on the other hand, believes Sebastian is an ingrate and liar. After Antonio is taken away,

Viola has hope that her brother is alive, since Antonio told of saving him from the sea and has mistaken her for her brother. Viola leaves. Toby and Fabian convince Andrew that Cesario is a dishonest coward. Andrew is again enkindled to fight with Cesario and leaves to find him. Toby and Fabian follow to see the fun.

Act IV, Scene 1

Feste encounters Sebastian, thinking that he is Cesario. He tries to make him come with him to Olivia, and Sebastian refuses, saying he is not the person Feste wants. Toby, Andrew, and Fabian enter and also think that Sebastian is Cesario. Andrew hits him, and Sebastian fights back and draws his dagger. Toby holds his arm, but Sebastian breaks away and draws his sword. Toby draws his sword, but Olivia arrives and stops the fighting. She sends Toby, Andrew, and Fabian away. She, of course, also thinks that this young man is Cesario. She invites him to her house. Sebastian thinks that he has become mad or is in a dream. Olivia asks him to be ruled by her, and Sebastian agrees and leaves with her.

Sebastian fights with Toby, Andrew, and Fabian in Act IV, Scene 1 of *Twelfth Night*. This is a print from Malcolm C. Salaman's 1916 edition of *Shakespeare in Pictorial Art*. *(Painting by F. Wheatley; engraving by J. R. Smith)*

Act IV, Scene 2

Maria has Feste wear a gown and beard to pose as a priest and visit Malvolio in his dark room. Feste, as Sir Topas, insists to Malvolio that he is certainly mad and is not in a dark room, despite Malvolio's vehement protests. Sir Toby then tells Feste to visit Malvolio as the jester he is and to prepare to end the joke, since he fears more blame and trouble from Olivia. Feste then talks to Malvolio largely as himself (but also voices comments as Sir Topas during the conversation). Finally, Feste agrees to get Malvolio light, pen, and paper so that he can write a message to Olivia to inform her of his dire situation.

Act IV, Scene 3

In a soliloquy, Sebastian tries to grasp the amazing incidents that have occurred and the situation he is in. He concludes that neither he nor Olivia is mad. Olivia enters and asks him to go with her and a priest to be betrothed and become her husband. She tells him that their public wedding will occur later. Sebastian agrees and swears his truth to her.

Act V, Scene 1

The duke, accompanied by Viola and others, arrives at Olivia's home and has Feste go in to tell Olivia of his presence and to bring her out to speak with him. Officers with Antonio appear, and Viola/Cesario tells Orsino that this is the man who rescued her/him. Antonio thinks that she is Sebastian and tells the duke that he saved the young man from drowning, cared for him for three months, defended him in the swordfight, and was surprised that the gentleman denied him the purse he had earlier let him have. The duke tells Antonio that this young gentleman has been attending him for three months. Further discussion of the matter is interrupted by the arrival of Olivia. Olivia again rejects Orsino's overtures. Orsino says that he knows it is Cesario who has stolen Olivia's love and that, despite his own love for Cesario, he will sacrifice him by putting him to death. Cesario Viola says that she is willing to die for her love of Orsino. Olivia then addresses Cesario as *husband,* surprising everyone, including Viola. She calls for the priest who presided at the betrothal, and he verifies Olivia's claim. Orsino then tells Cesario to go to Olivia but to be sure that he never sees Orsino again. Sir Toby, Sir Andrew, and Feste enter at this point and claim that Cesario beat them. Viola claims innocence. Sebastian enters, and everyone is amazed to see these two people who are mirror images of each other. The twins identify each other and are joyously reunited. Orsino takes Viola as his wife. Olivia has Malvolio released from his dark room. He has Olivia read the letter that he believed was from her, but Olivia recognizes that Maria wrote it. Fabian tries to explain the scheme against Malvolio and notes that Toby has married Maria. He says that their injustice to Malvolio only repays his to them. Malvolio, however, will not be reconciled and exits, angrily vowing revenge. Everyone but Feste departs, leaving him to sing a melancholy song but one that promises to please the audience every day with a play.

CHARACTER LIST

Orsino The duke of Illyria. A melancholy romantic who continually tries to win the Countess Olivia's love but is rejected by her. Viola, in disguise as a young man, serves him in his court. Once her disguise is removed, Orsino marries her.

Olivia A rich countess who has lost both her father and brother to death. She is still mourning for her brother and refuses to receive men who wish to court her. She rejects Orsino's overtures of love. But she makes an exception to her rule when she decides to receive the young man Cesario (Viola in disguise) into her presence. She falls passionately in love with Cesario and pursues him. Her problem of wooing a man who actually is a woman is solved when Sebastian, Viola's twin brother, arrives and is mistaken for Cesario. She proposes marriage to him, and he accepts.

Viola A young woman who survives a shipwreck and lands in Illyria. She believes that her twin brother, Sebastian, has perished in the ship-

wreck. She disguises herself as a young man named Cesario and serves in the court of Duke Orsino. She dresses herself to look exactly like her twin brother. Although she herself is in love with Orsino, she must serve as his emissary to woo Olivia on Orsino's behalf. She is unsuccessful in this but ironically attracts Olivia to herself in the guise of Cesario. Her disguise brings several troubles for Viola, but all is solved when it is revealed that her brother is actually alive. They are reunited, with Olivia marrying Sebastian and Viola marrying Orsino.

Sebastian Viola's twin brother who survives a shipwreck, unbeknownst to Viola. Viola in disguise has dressed herself as Sebastian. When they are reunited, their problems in Illyria are solved. He is surprised by Olivia's vows of love for him, since he does not know that she thinks he is Cesario, Viola in disguise. Regardless, he accepts her offer of marriage.

Sir Toby Belch Olivia's uncle, who lives in her home. He is one who lives for good eating and drinking, fun, jokes, general merriment, and a carefree life. He is always at odds with Malvolio, Olivia's steward, who wants no disorder and senseless merriment in the household. Sir Toby and others plot against Malvolio in retribution for his severe treatment of them.

Malvolio Olivia's steward, in charge of managing Olivia's household. He is extremely severe and puritanical in enforcing order and discipline. His sour, condemning attitude creates many enemies in the household.

Feste Olivia's court fool (jester, clown). He has a sharp wit and is adept at verbal combats. He jokes and sings for entertainment and to make his living. He is an enemy to Malvolio, who always belittles and criticizes Feste. Feste joins Sir Toby and others in their plot to embarrass Malvolio and deflate his ego. Despite Feste's comic surface, he actually is a very serious, somber, and wise person.

Maria Olivia's gentlewoman. She is the prime mover in the plot against Malvolio that is

Maria in *Twelfth Night*. This is a print from Charles Heath's 1848 edition of *The Heroines of Shakspeare: Comprising the Principal Female Characters in the Plays of the Great Poet*. (Painting by A. Egg; engraving by W. H. Egleton)

undertaken by Sir Toby and others. She writes the key letter that completely fools Malvolio. Sir Toby marries her.

Sir Andrew Aguecheek Friend to Sir Toby Belch. Dimwitted dupe to Sir Toby, who convinces him that he can win Olivia. Participates in the plot against Malvolio. Is manipulated by Toby into challenging Cesario to a duel—all for the laughs that Toby and Fabian can derive from the situation.

Fabian A servant to Olivia. A prime participant in the plot against Malvolio and in the fun engineered by Toby at Sir Andrew Aguecheek's expense.

Antonio A sea captain who befriends and helps Sebastian after a shipwreck.

Sea Captain Befriends Viola after a shipwreck and keeps her female clothing for her after she disguises herself as a young man.

Valentine A gentleman attending on Duke Orsino.

Curio A gentleman attending on Duke Orsino.

CHARACTER STUDIES
Olivia

We first hear of Olivia in the 18th line of the play: Orsino extravagantly describes her effect on him when he first saw her. He falls in love with her immediately. But quickly thereafter we hear that she will remain veiled and isolated for seven years in order to mourn for her dead brother. In the second scene of the play, the sea captain tells Viola about the "fair Olivia," a "virtuous maid" whom the duke wishes to win. She is a beautiful woman, but she does not plan to bring that beauty to fruition in love and marriage during her lengthy period of mourning. At the beginning of the third scene of the play, we hear Sir Toby, her uncle, complain about Olivia's excessive grieving over her brother's death: He says that "care's an enemy to life." Olivia's character, then, even before she comes on stage, impresses us as being sober, somber, and perhaps devoted too extremely to sadness, melancholy, and death. We wonder if she might be wasting away and not vitally participating in life and joy. She is sought after by men—Orsino, certainly, but also Sir Andrew Aguecheek and even her steward, Malvolio, would like to win her as a wife.

She first appears in 1.5, and our insight into her nature comes sharply into focus. She enters with Malvolio, who at this point reflects her melancholy and sour mood. Feste is present and tries to greet her happily, but she just says, "Take the fool away." Feste persists, however, and implies that she is really the fool that should be taken away. He asks her to be allowed to prove that she is the fool, and she agrees to this. With his wit operative, Feste does prove that she is foolish for mourning a brother who is in heaven. Olivia appreciates Feste's cleverness, and her mood changes to one more receptive of joy. When Malvolio peevishly argues against Feste and his wit, Olivia berates him: She implies that he is a victim of self-love and lacks a generous disposition toward others. We see that Olivia actually is generous, ungrudging, and appreciative of humor herself. This suggests that she does have the capacity and will to give of herself, to break out of her melancholy role, and indeed to truly love another in the future. This is borne out later in this scene when Cesario (Viola in disguise) comes to speak to Olivia on Orsino's behalf. At first, Olivia does not want to hear more about Orsino's offer of love. But when she is told that the messenger is a handsome young man, she lets Cesario come to her. This does suggest that she is indeed receptive to male attention, despite her protests that she will remain in mournful isolation. Viola converses with intelligence and wit and also praises Olivia's great beauty. Viola tells her that she would be cruel to die without leaving the world copies of herself (in children). After Olivia still refuses Orsino, Viola leaves. Olivia immediately sends Malvolio to overtake Cesario, ostensibly to return a ring "he" left. However, no ring was left, and it actually is a message of attraction felt by Olivia for Cesario. Her passionate side has overwhelmed her, and she is coming "out of her shell," so to speak. From this point on, she becomes quite determined and aggressive in her pursuit of Cesario. Ironically, she becomes the thwarted lover, since Viola has to reject her mistaken love for a woman. Her own aggressive pursuit of love is most evident in 4.1 and 4.2: Here, she mistakes Sebastian for Cesario and invites him first to her home and then to accompany her to a priest to be betrothed. Sebastian accepts this good fortune gladly from the beautiful, impressive Olivia.

Olivia also is characterized as extremely peaceful and compassionate. We see this in her when she tries to make peace between Feste and Malvolio in 1.5, but it is most clear when she intervenes to stop the sword fight between Sir Toby and Sebastian in 4.1: She steps in to say (l. 45), "Hold, Toby, on thy life I charge thee hold!" Her compassionate nature also appears near the end of the play when she orders Malvolio released from the dark house in which he has been held as a madman, because of the trick played on him by Maria, Sir Toby, and others. Then she tells Malvolio feelingly, "Alas, poor fool, how have they baffled thee!" (5.1.369).

In sum, Olivia is impressive as a beautiful and independent woman who at first appears to be distinguished, detached, melancholy, and unemotional but who turns out to be very human, compassionate, generous, passionate, and full of vitality.

Olivia in Act I, Scene 5 of *Twelfth Night*. This is a print from Charles Heath's 1848 edition of *The Heroines of Shakspeare: Comprising the Principal Female Characters in the Plays of the Great Poet. (Painting by W. P. Frith; engraving by W. H. Mote)*

Orsino

Orsino, duke of Illyria, characterizes himself immediately: He has the first speech in the play. He calls for music to an excess but then rapidly changes his mind and wants none. Music is "sweet" to him one minute and then is not. He is moody, sentimental, and melancholy. This is enforced later when we hear Orsino say, "I myself am best / When least in company" (1.4.37–38). We learn that he had been attracted to Olivia at first sight and is now pursuing her romantically, despite the fact that she has sworn to receive no men during the lengthy period of mourning for her dead brother. In the second scene, we hear the sea captain tell Viola that Orsino is a "noble duke," both in name and character. Viola recognizes the high respect that Orsino apparently is accorded in general, and she decides to disguise herself as a man and seek a position of service in Orsino's court. Later (1.4), Valentine tells Viola (as Cesario) that Orsino is constant and generous in his favors to those in devoted service to him and that Cesario undoubtedly will be advanced by the duke. So, he is a benevolent and understanding ruler. It is apparent that Orsino is impressive in the goodness of his character when Viola is sent by him on her first embassy as Cesario to woo Olivia on Orsino's behalf and in an aside Viola says, "Whoe'er I woo, myself would be his wife" (1.4.42). After only three days serving him, she already loves him and would like to marry him.

In 2.4, Orsino sends for Feste to sing the old song that he heard from him the previous night. When Feste sings it, we perceive that he actually is mocking with some seriousness the extreme nature of Orsino as a lover of the idealized Olivia. Feste's song pictures a man being "slain by a fair cruel maid" and then almost reveling in the "death" that comes from her rejection. It pictures the male lover as full of self-pity ("my poor corpse") and sighs. These are typical characteristics of the melancholy Petrarchan man, one who woos an idealized lady who never accepts his love. Her rejection is a kind of death to this man. Thus, this is the type of man Orsino is: This is the extreme element in his nature. Feste goes on to say that such a man as he has described is on a "good voyage of nothing." In other words, a man such as Orsino whose goal is an unattainable lady will never reach that port, that goal. He will never find fulfillment for his love and will never enjoy fruition in life. This is the weak, limited side of Orsino's character that is revealed. At this point, Orsino does not have the self-perception to recognize and change this aspect of himself. Feste sees it, and we see it. Eventually, Orsino will give up on the impossible goal of attaining Olivia and will instead love Viola and take her in marriage to lead to a realistic, fulfilling life. Knowing his noble, generous nature, we feel that he ultimately deserves that reward.

Viola

Viola enters in the second scene of the play. She has just escaped the sea after a shipwreck and is conversing with a sea captain. He informs her that this country is Illyria, that he was born here, and that the noble Duke Orsino rules. Viola expresses fear and sorrow that her brother might have drowned in the shipwreck, but she expresses hope that he might have escaped. Regardless, we see that she is a young woman of action who makes unhesitating use, not waste, of time: She immediately decides to try to serve in a position in Orsino's court. She will disguise herself as a young man, and she asks the captain to introduce her at the court. The next we hear of her is in the fourth scene: She has a position as Orsino's page and has served him three days. Valentine implies that she (in her male disguise as Cesario) has impressed the duke and is likely to be rewarded and advanced by him. Then Orsino enters and sends Cesario on a mission to try to woo Olivia on behalf of Orsino. Viola (as Cesario) agrees to do this for him, although she tries to convey to him that his mission is doomed to fail. We see Viola's perceptive and practical nature, in contrast to Orsino's rather extreme impracticality, in matters of love. Viola sees that Olivia will not change her lack of interest in Orsino so easily and rapidly as Orsino thinks and would like. So, Viola is a woman of common sense and shrewd insight into human character and motive. At the same time, she is most complaisant and wanting to please—especially Orsino. She does not pursue her argument at length with him but instead agrees to do his will, and she vows to do her best to woo

Olivia. At this point we also see that Viola is an extremely selfless, self-sacrificing individual. She wants to please others and to make them happy, although it might even work against her own goals and happiness. This is evident in her aside at the end of this scene: She reveals that she will woo another woman for the duke, even though she herself would like to become Orsino's wife.

In 1.5, Viola puts into practice what she promised Orsino. Olivia surprisingly agrees to receive the young man Cesario, after Cesario kept insisting and standing at the door, facing down Malvolio. Once admitted, Cesario/Viola reveals that she is quite qualified to teach others the somber, clear facts of life, beauty, age, and mortality: This, in fact, is what she does with Olivia. She tries to hold up a mirror for Olivia to see herself realistically and to teach her a sensible approach to life and the proper uses of beauty and time. She bluntly tells Olivia (ll. 187–189) that Olivia is overthrowing herself by not giving herself to a husband. She also bluntly tells her that she is the most cruel woman alive, if she lets her beauty die with her, having no children as copies of that beauty left for the betterment of the world (ll. 241–243). Viola tells her that she is too proud, courageously speaking the truth as she sees it. In this manner, she is a major teacher or clarifier of others' natures, trying to point out their limitations and noting how they can improve themselves, to their own advantage. However, Viola also is adept at humor: She easily adapts to and extends extravagant analogies used by others such as Maria and Olivia in this scene to a comic degree. In fact, at one point Olivia asks Cesario if he is a "comedian," an actor. In a sense, she indeed is an actor, using comic and serious assertions. Olivia responds to the vibrant intellect, wit, and emotion of Viola/Cesario: She acknowledges at the end of the scene how she has been trapped by "this youth's perfections."

In 2.2, Viola receives the ring that Olivia has sent by Malvolio. Viola knows that it is not a ring that she left with Olivia: Instead, it is a love token sent as a subtle hint of Olivia's attraction to Cesario. Viola's perceptiveness immediately convinces her that Olivia has fallen for Cesario. She analyzes the predicament that this reveals: Orsino loves Olivia, Olivia loves Cesario, and Cesario (Viola) loves Orsino. Again we see Viola's extremely selfless character as she says (l. 39), "What thriftless sighs shall poor Olivia breathe!" She is more concerned for Olivia's eventual disappointment and frustration than for her own. Viola's reaction to this problematic situation reveals another major facet of her character. She says (ll. 40–41), "O time, thou must untangle this, not I, / It is too hard a knot for me t' untie." She realizes that human will, the free will and power to determine matters, has its limit. She is acutely aware of her own weakness in this area. What she does trust, however, is the power of time itself to solve

Viola in Act II, Scene 2 of *Twelfth Night*. This is a print from Charles Heath's 1848 edition of *The Heroines of Shakspeare: Comprising the Principal Female Characters in the Plays of the Great Poet. (Painting by A. Egg; engraving by B. Holl)*

problems. She is one of the optimists of the world, then, and operates by a personal philosophy that a benevolent, providential force, through time in the universe and life, will make things work out for the good. She simply will let the passage of time solve problems beyond her control, and she trusts that this will indeed come about.

In 3.4, Viola's philosophy is tested. She, as Cesario, is tricked into a duel with Sir Andrew Aguecheek. She is frightened, since she cannot reveal that she is not really a man at all and is not trained for fighting with swords. In an aside, she exclaims "Pray God defend me!" As they draw swords, she states "I do assure you, 'tis against my will." At that precise moment, Antonio (thinking that Cesario is Sebastian, Viola's twin brother) steps in and stops the fight, defying Sir Andrew to fight Antonio instead. Viola's philosophy of God's providential direction and time solving her problems is thus supported. Her own "will," her wish for peace, is brought about by matters beyond her own control. Later in the scene, she feels that Sebastian might be alive, since Antonio mentioned him. She then says that if this is true, "Tempests are kind and salt waves fresh in love" (l. 384). In other words, to Viola even storms at sea and shipwrecks can bring good things: This is her optimistic philosophy about life and time enforced again.

In the last scene of the play, Viola/Cesario accompanies the duke into the presence of Olivia. Orsino discovers that Olivia has been attracted to Cesario and, out of irrational jealousy, threatens to take out his wrath on Cesario. But Viola says, "And I most jocund, apt, and willingly, / To do you rest, a thousand deaths would die" (ll. 132–133). Viola, consistent in her character, is again extremely selfless. With the fortunate appearance of Sebastian shortly after, all problems are solved. As emotions subside, Duke Orsino realizes his love for Viola and offers her marriage—a just reward for the generous, intelligent, and self-giving young lady.

Feste

Feste is a professional fool, a court jester. He also is referred to in the play as a "clown." He is one of the older individuals in Illyria, and he certainly is one of the most experienced. Despite his witty, comic profession, he is really a quite serious and philosophical person—even somewhat world-weary and melancholy. But he undoubtedly is the wisest of the characters and is qualified to be a critic and teacher and clarifier of others. We see him in these capacities through the play. As Viola says about him in 3.1.60, "This fellow is wise enough to play the fool."

We first see Feste in 1.5. He verbally spars with Maria—as we see him later doing with many of the characters. Olivia enters and sourly tells her servants to take away the fool, meaning Feste. But immediately, he says that they are to take away Olivia—clearly implying that she is a "fool" in another sense. He significantly tells her that he does not wear "motley in my brain." "Motley" refers to the varicolored costume that jesters typically would wear, so he is saying that he is only a fool in outer appearance. The implication is that actually he is wise within. He then asks her to give him permission to prove that she is a fool. In a better mood now, and seeing that Feste is inviting her to participate in a game of wit, she agrees. At this point Feste ironically takes on the role of a kind of priest: He puts her through a catechism, just as a priest does children in the church. He will ask her questions, and she is to answer. He leads her into admitting that she mourns for her brother's death and that she knows his soul is in heaven. Feste proves her to be a fool if she is mourning for him while he is in heaven, the place of bliss. We thus experience Feste's fertile and effective wit, and Olivia sees it also and appreciates it. It is evident that she and others respect Feste's comic and critical imagination. We can conclude, in fact, just from this scene that a serious lesson from Feste to Olivia lurks beneath his jesting surface: He implies that she is irrational and excessive in being caught up with death and grief. He implies that she should instead pick up with life again.

Feste shows his continuing concern with Olivia's welfare and that his philosophical seriousness always lies beneath his external joy and humor in 2.3. He sings a song for the entertainment of Sir Toby and Sir Andrew. They are carousing and enjoying themselves: Feste seems to join them in their celebrating spirit with the joy of a song. But we perceive that the song itself is quite somber in theme and is Feste's musing further on Olivia's nature. He begins the song addressing "mistress mine": In one sense, this ambiguous phrase can refer to Olivia, the mistress of the household. Feste asks, "Where are you roaming?" Certainly Feste perceives that she is roaming on the outskirts of love and life and that she needs to enter again the thicket of love and life, participate in the joy of living again, rather than remain in the depth of grief, death, and sadness. In the second stanza, Feste sings that love is not "hereafter": That is where he sees Olivia's mind dwelling, and she will find no love there. He urges her to not "delay" and that youth "will not endure." Feste realizes the truth of the classic carpe diem theme: One must "seize the day," live life fully before age and death come. He sees Olivia wasting her youth: His song mirrors his deep concern for her to learn this valuable lesson of the power of time and death to frustrate life and beauty.

In 2.4, we see this same facet of Feste's philosophical perception and his wish to improve others. Here, he is singing another song, one that Duke Orsino requests. This time his song is a mirror and criticism of the duke's nature, of his imperceptions and excessive traits. Feste sees Orsino wasting precious time and life, just as Olivia is. In fact, Feste implies that Orsino is also caught up in a kind of "death," as long as he lives the role of the Petrarchan man, the lover continually rejected by a proud lady. Her rejection is a "death," and Olivia keeps dealing out this kind of death to Orsino. Irrationally, Orsino keeps pursuing her, despite her cruel rejection. So, Feste, in this song, pictures Orsino as the man "slain" by the "fair cruel maid" and wrapped in a death "shroud." So, central to Feste's character is this basically somber awareness of life's truths, of life versus death. He is admirable for his wish to clarify these truths and the value of asserting vitality for others. His name suggests

festivity, in fact, and this is a preferable view of life over morbidity.

Feste is a participant in jokes and fun himself. He agrees to play a role in the duping of Malvolio. After Toby and Maria have Malvolio locked in a dark house as a madman, they ask Feste to disguise himself as a clergyman and visit Malvolio in his prison. Ironically, Feste is again in the role of a priest, just as he was in his earlier catechism of Olivia. In 4.2, Feste, pretending he is Sir Topas the curate, pays the visit to Malvolio. In this disguise, Feste tries to convince Malvolio that Malvolio really is mad for thinking that he is in a dark room: Sir Topas argues (against the truth) that he is in a room full of light. Then Feste speaks to Malvolio in his own voice as the fool—he agrees to bring Malvolio light, paper, and ink so that he can write Olivia about his predicament. In the final scene of the play, Feste delivers Malvolio's letter to Olivia. After Malvolio is brought into the presence of Olivia and the others, Feste reveals to Malvolio that he was part of the scheme against Malvolio and played the part of Sir Topas. He implies that he only has achieved just revenge against Malvolio for his past treatment of Feste.

Feste remains on stage after all others have left and, in essence, gives the epilogue in the form of a song. This song surveys the various stages of life from childhood through old age. We glimpse here the underlying melancholy of Feste: His picture of life is not as joyous as the play itself has portrayed it. In fact, he notes the entrance of evil and unpleasantness in human nature (thieves, braggarts, drunkards) as one progresses through the stages of life. The refrain of his song, in fact, insists, "For the rain it raineth every day." So, life is not all sunshine, as Feste sees it: Indeed, much of life lacks sunshine. Nevertheless, at the song's end, he promises the audience that, if they come back tomorrow and every day, the actors will try to please them while they are in the theater.

Toby

Sir Toby Belch is Olivia's uncle and thus is one of the older generation in the play. However, his age does not mean that he is more mature in all ways: In fact, he is immature in some ways. For example, he lives for frivolity, jokes, and sensuous pleasures of food and drink. The name "Belch" certainly is Shakespeare's means of emphasizing this last aspect of Toby's character. The extremity in Toby's view of life is embodied in his first speech in the play (1.3.2): "I am sure care's an enemy to life." He is quite carefree, not bending to the rules of order in Olivia's household. Maria warns him in this same scene that Olivia is disturbed by Toby's late hours and his drinking and noisiness with the foolish knight Sir Andrew Aguecheek. Toby is highly amused at Sir Andrew and takes advantage of his foolishness and stupidity to get laughs. He also extracts money from Sir Andrew, since he promises that he will win Olivia for him. A good example of Toby's noisy riotousness is in 2.3: Here, he drinks after midnight with Sir Andrew, pays Feste to sing a song for them, and joins in a song with Sir Andrew and Feste that will "rouse the night-owl" (2.3.58). This motivates Maria to enter and say, "What a caterwauling do you keep here!" (2.3.72). Maria is unsuccessful in quieting the trio, and eventually Malvolio stomps in (2.3.86) and says, "My masters, are you mad? Or what are you? Have you no wit, manners, nor honesty but to gabble like tinkers at this time of night?" Malvolio warns Toby that Olivia will allow him to continue living in her house, if he will rid himself of his "disorders" and "misdemeanors." Otherwise, he might be ejected from the household. After Malvolio further threatens the group, he leaves. It is then that Maria, Toby, and the others plan to get back at Malvolio and his puritanical, egotistical nature by fooling him with a letter Maria will write that will convince Malvolio that the letter comes to him from Olivia. Toby gleefully endorses the plot. In 2.5 Sir Toby, Sir Andrew, Maria, and Fabian observe Malvolio as he finds the supposed letter from Olivia, and they see that their plot to fool him succeeds.

Another plot for amusement that Toby engineers is one involving Sir Andrew. He talks Andrew into challenging Cesario/Viola to a fight with swords.

Toby knows that neither one is of fighting blood and predicts a lot of laughs to come from the reluctant sworders. He succeeds in bringing them to the brink of conflict in 3.4, but Antonio arrives just in time to intervene and prevent the fight: Antonio believes that Viola in disguise is actually Sebastian, her twin and Antonio's friend. After the collapse of this anticipated fun, Toby eggs on Andrew to pursue Cesario and beat him. Sir Toby, Andrew, and Fabian do encounter the one they believe to be Cesario (in 4.1), but actually this time it really is Sebastian, Viola's twin. When they attack him, he is not cowardly and reluctant—to their surprise. He is ready to defend himself, but this time Olivia breaks up the fight, since she thinks Sebastian is her beloved Cesario! So, again, Toby's anticipated fun is spoiled with the foiling of this plot.

Toby's joyous revenge against Malvolio, however, is carried out when he, Maria, and their group have Malvolio locked up as a madman and continue to trick and taunt him. Eventually, though, Toby realizes that he could be in deep trouble with Olivia because of the duping of Malvolio, and he agrees on the releasing of him. At the end of the play, when the plot is revealed to Malvolio, Olivia, and the others, Fabian asserts that the plot was for wrongs committed by Malvolio against Toby and the others. Also, we learn that Toby has married Maria (5.1.364). So, Toby has been tamed and made more orderly—taking a socially acceptable and conforming role through marriage.

Malvolio

Malvolio is Olivia's steward: He manages her household property, provisions, and finances. He is pompous, self-loving, self-important, and dour. He continually criticizes and denigrates Sir Toby and Feste, in particular. His heavy-handed rule of the household and his extremely somber and sour personality make him the natural enemy of the lovers of fun and humor—such as Sir Toby, Feste, and Maria. Thus, when they have the chance, they enact a plot to deflate his ego and make a fool of him.

His first entrance is in 1.5: He accompanies Olivia as she comes into the presence of Feste and

Maria. Olivia's testy mood is reflected, in fact, in the sour Malvolio's presence. When Olivia asks Malvolio's opinion of Feste's jesting, Malvolio only belittles and insults him. Olivia tells Malvolio that he (Malvolio) is "sick of self-love" and implies that instead he should be generous and of free disposition. His unpleasant personality is felt by everyone: This is why Viola in 2.2.23 refers to him as "churlish." In 2.3, Malvolio comes in to chastise Sir Toby, Sir Andrew, Feste, and Maria for the boisterous drinking and fun of the group and threatens them with telling Olivia about their "disorders" and "uncivil rule." After he leaves, Maria refers to him as "a kind of puritan" (2.3.140). Like the Puritans of Shakespeare's day, Malvolio is intolerant of others' festivities and fun and arrogant about his own virtuous and abstemious nature. It is his self-love and false conception of himself that Maria plans to use in her plot to make a fool of him (2.3.147–153). She writes a letter in the handwriting of Olivia and leaves it where Malvolio will find it. We see him discovering it in 2.5 and, just as Maria planned, interpreting everything in the letter as referring to himself as Olivia's desired lover and future husband. Before and after finding the letter, he verbalizes his arrogant assumptions while Maria, Sir Toby, Sir Andrew, and Fabian overhear him. He imagines himself becoming "Count Malvolio" and lording it over Sir Toby in the countess's household. He imagines saying to Toby, "You must amend your drunkenness" (2.5.73). The letter says that Olivia wishes for him to appear in cross-gartered yellow stockings, which Maria knows that Olivia loathes (2.5.198–201). Later, Malvolio will appear in these, since he thinks that Olivia desires him to wear them.

In 3.4, Maria tells Olivia that Malvolio seems to have gone mad, since he has changed his appearance and now continually smiles (which Maria also said in the letter that Olivia wished to see). Olivia concludes that he is indeed mad and tells Maria to have Sir Toby see to some care for him. After pretending that Malvolio is mad, Toby says that they will put Malvolio in a dark room and bind him—a treatment given to mad people at this time.

George Clarke as Malvolio in a late-19th-century production of *Twelfth Night*

When Malvolio is in his dark prison, Maria has Feste visit him (4.2) disguised as the clergyman Sir Topas. Despite Malvolio's protests, Feste continues telling him that he is mad. Malvolio writes Olivia a letter, and it is read to her by Fabian in Act V. She calls for his release. Malvolio shows her the letter that he thinks she wrote to him. Olivia recognizes Maria's handwriting, and the plot against Malvolio is thus revealed. Fabian explains that the plot was arranged in order to repay the wrongs Malvolio had committed against Sir Toby, Maria, and their group. Fabian argues that the injuries against Malvolio equal those against them and that they all should now laugh about it and be friends. However, consistent in his character, Malvolio refuses to be reconciled: He bitterly says, "I'll be revenged on the whole pack of you" and stomps out. He thus remains isolated from the others who are capable of directing love and charity outward: He cannot do this in his unchanged self-love. Appropriately, his name means "ill will."

DIFFICULTIES OF THE PLAY

The first difficulty a modern reader will encounter appears in the first scene of the play and permeates it thereafter—that is, the Petrarchan love convention. This convention would be very familiar to Shakespeare's audience, but not to modern readers. Shakespeare and other 16th- and 17th-century writers frequently use images and metaphors derived from Petrarchan love poetry. (Petrarch [1304–74] was a famous Italian writer of love sonnets.) For example, when Orsino in the first few lines of the play calls for an excess of music and then suddenly wants none, this is quite puzzling unless the reader understands the Petrarchan love convention and recognizes that Orsino is indeed the typical Petrarchan man. As pictured by countless writers that followed this convention after Petrarch introduced it in his sonnets, the man in love is typically moody and extremely changeable in his feelings regarding love. The man also traditionally woos an extremely beautiful but proud and rejecting lady. She always rejects the man, and her rejection many times is called a kind of death. She is pictured as a cruel goddess with the power of "life" (acceptance) and "death" (rejection) over the man.

If a reader is not cognizant of these facts, he or she misses the critical satire directed by Feste at Orsino in the song he sings for him in 2.4. In that song, Feste portrays the man wanting to be laid in "sad cypress" and wrapped in his death "shroud," as well as referring to his own "poor corpse" and his "thousand sighs." All of these are due to his being "slain by a fair cruel maid." Feste is parodying the man he is singing for: Orsino is the Petrarchan man rejected by the cruel and beautiful maid Olivia. Feste pictures him as killed by her rejection. Also, the Petrarchan man's typical sighing and self-pity ("poor corpse") are alluded to

here. Right after Feste's song, Orsino sends Cesario on a mission to try again to win that "sovereign cruelty" (Olivia) for him. In terms of the convention, Olivia is indeed the Petrarchan woman who is extremely beautiful but cruel in her rejection of Orsino. This conventional view of the Petrarchan lady explains why Viola (as Cesario) says the following to Olivia (1.5.250–251): "I see you what you are, you are too proud; / But if you were the devil, you are fair." As she later leaves (1.5.288), Viola calls Olivia "fair cruelty." Thus, Olivia's character, Orsino's character, and numerous statements of the play are not fully understood and appreciated without knowing the elements of the Petrarchan love convention.

The carpe diem theme is another central matter. This classical literary theme was reinvigorated in the English Renaissance, and Shakespeare uses it in this play as its underlying important philosophy. The Latin phrase *carpe diem* literally means "seize the day" and enjoins one to live and love fully, making use of time and life. It primarily is used by poets to urge beautiful young women to respond to overtures of love and not to postpone participating in the activities of love and life to the fullest. One should use youth and beauty, take advantage of them, because time passes rapidly, and aging and death threaten. In a famous song in his play *Volpone*, Ben Jonson, Shakespeare's friend and fellow dramatist, has the male speaker addressing Celia as follows: "Come, my Celia, let us prove, / While we can, the sports of love. / Time will not be ours forever." He is trying to seduce Celia by frightening her with the fleeting nature of time and life. This philosophical context is somberly in the background when Feste sings his essentially carpe diem song in 2.3, obviously having Olivia in mind. Feste says, "What is love? 'Tis not hereafter" and "In delay there lies no plenty, / Then come kiss me sweet and twenty; / Youth's a stuff will not endure." In other words, the frightening power of time to erase youth and bring on age and death should be heeded by Olivia: She should not keep up her excessive dwelling on her brother's death and refusing to pick up with life itself. Feste warns that there is no love in the "hereafter," in the realm of death where Olivia's mind is dwelling, as Feste sees it. This same assumption about the necessity to use time fully underlies some of Viola's comments to Olivia. For example, she says (1.5.241–243), "Lady, you are the cruell'st she alive / If you will lead these graces to the grave, / And leave the world no copy." Viola (as Cesario) is looking at Olivia's beautiful face and means that Olivia should now love a man and have a child. This will leave a copy of her own beauty in the form of her child and thus will be doing the world a favor to leave her beauty for the world to admire. She should "seize the day"—love now and fulfill life. Viola herself has no problem with living by the carpe diem philosophy: She already has fallen in love and would like to act upon it.

Perhaps the largest difficulty for modern readers is the lack of knowledge concerning festivities and the rituals of celebration in Shakespeare's time. *Twelfth Night* is the play most dependent on knowledge about a particular festival and its typical patterns of celebration. If one does not know the elements of the Twelfth Night holiday and of its Misrule pattern of celebration, then one cannot understand major implications, suggestions, and allusions in the play. The title of the play refers to the Christian holiday (January 6) that celebrates the visit of the Magi to the Christ child. It is Epiphany, suggesting the revealing of Christ to the Gentiles. This festival on the night of January 6 ends the Christmas season (the 12 days of Christmas) and was in Shakespeare's time the climax of that season's joy. It was the time of the giving of gifts and of an Epiphany cake with surprises baked inside. Thus, the idea of revelations, surprises, and gifts relate to the revelation of and gift of the Christ child himself. This aura is carried over into the play, since many of the characters receive surprises and gifts (especially in the area of love). Many receive self-revelations, self-epiphanies. The good eating and drinking of the festival is reflected in the play—especially in the character and interests of Sir Toby Belch—to say nothing of his name!

Of even larger significance is the particular pattern of festival celebration employed at this time for this holiday. What is largely known as the Misrule pattern was used on this night. Each group of people celebrating the holiday would elect one person to be the Lord of Misrule: His duty was to lead the participants in a life of misrule during the holiday. In other words, normal order, rules, and so on, were dispensed with. Everyone was to celebrate frivolously without the normal restrictions on behavior. Shakespeare implies that Sir Toby corresponds to the Lord of Misrule. He is the one that drinks and jokes to excess and leads others in his fun-making schemes, and he is also the one criticized by Malvolio of "uncivil rule" and "disorders." At the end of the holiday, the followers would ritualistically overthrow the Lord of Misrule, making him the scapegoat, the recipient of blame for any sins they committed during the festival. Then they all were ready to take up normal roles again in the everyday world. Sir Toby is this scapegoat at the end of the play: The end of the play is like the end of the holiday.

Also essential in celebrating this holiday in Shakespeare's time was the wearing of disguises, costumes, and masks. Some would dress as well-known authority figures and mock and parody those individuals: This was accepted as part of the dispensing with normal rules, decorum, and order during the time of the festivity. Especially important is the fact that people would hide their true identities until the end of the holiday. Then all would remove their masks and reveal who they really were. This certainly is carried into the world of this play by Shakespeare. Viola is literally disguised until the end of the play. The end of the play, therefore, indeed corresponds in another way to the end of the holiday. The characters are placed in the roles of participants in a festival. Even more important than shedding a literal disguise is the fact that several of the characters have an emotional or psychological or other kind of disguise throughout the play that is removed at the end. For example, Olivia's emotional mask as one obsessed by death is removed, as well as her other mask as the Petrarchan lady. She no longer lives those roles. Her real nature is no longer covered by these false faces. Anthropologists and sociologists argue that festivals and holidays such as those celebrated in Shakespeare's time allowed people to experience release from the ordinary pressures of daily life and achieve perhaps some clarification about themselves, about others, about life, and about human nature in general. They then entered the everyday world again with new attitudes and perceptions. Certainly, this is what Shakespeare implies in Olivia's case: She has been clarified about her own limitations and excesses and about love and life. She has grown and matured emotionally and psychologically. Her symbolic masks have been removed. One can say that others' symbolic masks also have been removed. Sir Toby is no longer the extremely irresponsible person, and Orsino is no longer the Petrarchan man. One might also say that Feste wears multiple masks in the play: Appearing as a fool actually hides his truly wise nature, and he plays the role of a priest more than once. Shakespeare, then, embodies much of the meaning of the play in its festive pattern.

KEY PASSAGES
Act I, Scene 5, 57–104

FESTE. The lady bade take away the fool, therefore I say again, take her away.

OLIVIA. Sir, I bade them take away you.

FESTE. Misprision in the highest degree! Lady, *"Cucullus non facit monachum"*: that's as much to say as I wear not motley in my brain. Good madonna, give me leave to prove you a fool.

OLIVIA. Can you do it?

FESTE. Dexteriously, good madonna.

OLIVIA. Make your proof.

FESTE. I must catechize you for it, madonna. Good my mouse of virtue, answer me.

OLIVIA. Well, sir, for want of other idleness, I'll bide your proof.

FESTE. Good madonna, why mourn'st thou?

OLIVIA. Good fool, for my brother's death.

FESTE. I think his soul is in hell, madonna.

OLIVIA. I know his soul is in heaven, fool.

FESTE. The more fool, madonna, to mourn for your brother's soul, being in heaven. Take away the fool, gentlemen.

OLIVIA. What think you of this fool, Malvolio? Doth he not mend?

MALVOLIO. Yes, and shall do till the pangs of death shake him. Infirmity, that decays the wise, doth ever make the better fool.

FESTE. God send you, sir, a speedy infirmity, for the better increasing your folly. Sir Toby will be sworn that I am no fox, but he will not pass his word for twopence that you are no fool.

OLIVIA. How say you to that, Malvolio?

MALVOLIO. I marvel your ladyship takes delight in such a barren rascal. I saw him put down the other day with an ordinary fool that has no more brain than a stone. Look you now, he's out of his guard already. Unless you laugh and minister occasion to him, he is gagg'd. I protest I take these wise men that crow so at these set kind of fools no better than the fools' zanies.

OLIVIA. O, you are sick of self-love, Malvolio, and taste with a distemper'd appetite. To be generous, guiltless, and of free disposition, is to take those things for bird-bolts that you deem cannon-bullets. There is no slander in an allow'd fool, though he do nothing but rail; nor no railing in a known discreet man, though he do nothing but reprove.

Olivia (Tita Brand) speaks with Feste (W. B. Field) in a Royal Botanical Gardens production of *Twelfth Night*. *(Illustration by George Grenville Manton)*

This passage introduces us to the all-important character Olivia. It also reveals to us the complex character of Feste, with his mixture of the humorous and somber elements of his intellect and perspective on life. Especially admirable is his ability to completely transform the sour mood of Olivia into one of happiness and appreciation.

Olivia wants the fool removed from her presence, since she enters in no mood for jokes and humor. But Feste turns the tables on her by saying that she should be taken away, since she is actually the fool, not he. When he tells her (in the Latin phrase) that the cowl does not make the monk, he clearly implies that his outer costume of a court jester does not mean that he actually is a fool within: He tells her that he wears "not motley in my brain." "Motley" is the varicolored costume of a fool. We do see

that actually Feste is wise and serious underneath his outer appearance. But just as important is the clear implication that, although Olivia is dressed in the black clothes of mourning (and indeed is the one who looks like a monk in his cowl), she really is the foolish one beneath her somber appearance. When he cleverly asks her questions and elicits answers from her (just as a priest does in a catechism), he leads her into a trap: He proves that she is a fool, if she is mournful over a brother whose soul is in heaven!

It is apparent after this witty ploy that Olivia is in a much more happy frame of mind. And she even criticizes Malvolio for his bitter and ungenerous attitude toward Feste. She criticizes Malvolio's "self-love," a major flaw in him that we see persisting in the rest of the play.

This passage also implies the belief on Feste's part (as well as on others' in the play) that Olivia needs to stop dwelling on death at some reasonable point and to begin participating in love and life. This is a major concern of Feste's through the play, as well as a major theme in the play.

Act II, Scene 2, 1–42

Enter Viola *and* Malvolio *at several doors.*

MALVOLIO. Were you not ev'n now with the Countess Olivia?

VIOLA. Even now, sir; on a moderate pace I have since arriv'd but hither.

MALVOLIO. She returns this ring to you, sir. You might have sav'd me my pains, to have taken it away yourself. She adds moreover, that you should put your lord into a desperate assurance she will none of him. And one thing more, that you be never so hardy to come again in his affairs, unless it be to report your lord's taking of this. Receive it so.

VIOLA. She took the ring of me, I'll none of it.

MALVOLIO. Come, sir, you peevishly threw it to her; and her will is, it should be so return'd. If it be worth stooping for, there it lies, in your eye; if not, be it his that finds it. *Exit.*

VIOLA. I left no ring with her. What means this lady?
Fortune forbid my outside have not charm'd her!
She made good view of me; indeed so much
That methought her eyes had lost her tongue,
For she did speak in starts distractedly.
She loves me sure, the cunning of her passion
Invites me in this churlish messenger.
None of my lord's ring? Why, he sent her none.
I am the man! If it be so, as 'tis,
Poor lady, she were better love a dream.
Disguise, I see thou art a wickedness
Wherein the pregnant enemy does much.
How easy is it for the proper-false
In women's waxen hearts to set their forms!
Alas, our frailty is the cause, not we,
For such as we are made of, such we be.
How will this fadge? My master loves her dearly,
And I (poor monster) fond as much on him;
And she (mistaken) seems to dote on me.
What will become of this? As I am man,
My state is desperate for my master's love;
As I am woman (now alas the day!),
What thriftless sighs shall poor Olivia breathe!
O time, thou must untangle this, not I,
It is too hard a knot for me t' untie.

This short scene is important in revealing that Olivia indeed is beginning again to participate in love and life, since she has fallen in love with Cesario (Viola in disguise). She is sending the ring to Cesario as a sign of her love: This is apparent to Viola (since she left no ring with Olivia) but is not apparent to Malvolio. This scene also furthers the characterization of Malvolio as "churlish."

This scene sets up the complications to come, since Olivia has actually fallen for a woman, unbeknownst to her. This will lead to many problems for the disguised Viola. She will have to fend off the now-enamored Olivia, as well as combative challenges from Sir Andrew and Sir Toby.

The most important and key element of this scene, however, is in the final statement of Viola's soliloquy. She feels helpless in the face of these difficulties and will rely on "time" to solve her problems. In essence, her overriding philosophy of life is to trust in a benevolent providential force that operates through time to bring about goodness and to solve problems. This is the first time in the play that Viola's philosophy is expressed, but from now on we see that she is supported in it and that it indeed seems to be the major view of life in the play.

Act II, Scene 3, 30–53

SIR ANDREW. Excellent! Why, this is the best fooling, when all is done. Now a song.

SIR TOBY. Come on, there is sixpence for you. Let's have a song.

SIR ANDREW. There's a testril of me too. If one knight give a—

FESTE. Would you have a love-song, or a song of good life?

SIR TOBY. A love-song, a love-song.

SIR ANDREW. Ay, ay. I care not for good life.

Feste sings.
O mistress mine, where are you roaming?
O, stay and hear, your true-love's coming,
That can sing both high and low.
Trip no further, pretty sweeting;
Journeys end in lovers meeting,
Every wise man's son doth know.

SIR ANDREW. Excellent good, I' faith.

SIR TOBY. Good, good.

Feste sings.
What is love? 'Tis not hereafter;
Present mirth hath present laughter;
What's to come is still unsure.
In delay there lies no plenty,

Then come kiss me sweet and twenty;
Youth's a stuff will not endure.

In a play of very important songs by Feste, this particular song is one of the most significant and reflective of a major theme. It can be seen as referring to Olivia. She is the one who has been "roaming" outside of love and life, and as far as Feste knows at this point, she still is. She has been absorbed in mourning and dwelling on death. But the message is that love is "not hereafter": If Olivia (or anyone) wants the joyous participation in love, then it is to be found now in "present mirth" of this life and not in the grave. Olivia should so participate while young and not delay. This is specifically the carpe diem theme that urges one to "seize the day" now. This is a major theme implied all through the play. The song also contains a humorous but accurate prediction that Olivia's "true-love" is coming. It is not Cesario (Viola in disguise) as Olivia currently thinks. However, it will turn out to be Viola's twin brother, Sebastian. Thus, in a sense, her "true-love" can sing "both high and low," since Viola has the high female voice, and Sebastian has the low male voice!

Act V, Scene 1, 216–270

Enter SEBASTIAN.

SEBASTIAN. I am sorry, madam, I have hurt
  your kinsman,
But had it been the brother of my blood,
I must have done no less with wit and safety.
You throw a strange regard upon me, and by
  that
I do perceive it hath offended you.
Pardon me, sweet one, even for the vows
We made each other but so late ago.

DUKE. One face, one voice, one habit, and
  two persons,
A natural perspective, that is and is not!

SEBASTIAN. Antonio, O my dear Antonio!
How have the hours rack'd and tortur'd me
Since I have lost thee!

ANTONIO. Sebastian are you?

SEBASTIAN. Fear'st thou that, Antonio?

ANTONIO. How have you made division of
  yourself?
An apple, cleft in two, is not more twin
Than these two creatures. Which is Sebastian?

OLIVIA. Most wonderful!

SEBASTIAN. Do I stand there? I never had a
  brother;
Nor can there be that deity in my nature
Of here and every where. I had a sister,
Whom the blind waves and surges have
  devour'd.
Of charity, what kin are you to me?
What countryman? What name? What
  parentage?

VIOLA. Of Messaline; Sebastian was my
  father,
Such a Sebastian was my brother too;
So went he suited to his watery tomb.
If spirits can assume both form and suit,
You come to fright us.

SEBASTIAN. A spirit I am indeed,
But am in that dimension grossly clad
Which from the womb I did participate.
Were you a woman, as the rest goes even,
I should my tears let fall upon your cheek,
And say, "Thrice welcome, drowned Viola!"

VIOLA. My father had a mole upon his
  brow.

SEBASTIAN. And so had mine.

VIOLA. And died that day when Viola from
  her birth
Had numb'red thirteen years.

SEBASTIAN. O, that record is lively in my
  soul!

He finished indeed his mortal act
That day that made my sister thirteen years.

VIOLA. If nothing lets to make us happy both
But this my masculine usurp'd attire,
Do not embrace me till each circumstance
Of place, time, fortune, do cohere and jump
That I am Viola—which to confirm,
I'll bring you to a captain in this town,
Where lie my maiden weeds; by whose gentle
  help
I was preserv'd to serve this noble count.
All the occurrence of my fortune since
Hath been between this lady and this lord.

SEBASTIAN. [*To Olivia.*] So comes it, lady,
  you have been mistook;
But Nature to her bias drew in that.
You would have been contracted to a maid,
Nor are you therein, by my life, deceiv'd,
You are betroth'd both to a maid and man.

This passage near the end of the play depicts the
action that the audience has anxiously been hoping and waiting for. Finally Viola and Sebastian
are reunited, and this solves all of the problems of
mistaken identities, miscarried loves, and threats of
danger and death. This is truly the "what you will"
of the play's subtitle for a spectator or reader of the
play. It is what everyone has been wishing would
happen. When Sebastian tells Olivia that she has
been mistaken but that "Nature to her bias drew in
that," he is using a metaphor from bowling. Bowling was on the grass in Shakespeare's time, and if
the ball had a weight added, it would take a curved
path ("bias") to reach its goal. This is what has happened in the world of this play: Things seem to go
awry, but Olivia (as well as others) actually makes a
strike and achieves her goal and success in love and
life. This outcome reinforces the optimistic view
of life inherent in the world of the play from the
time that Viola first voices the philosophy that time
must untangle the knots, the problems, encountered in life. This is precisely what has happened,
as this reunion of brother and sister amply testifies.

DIFFICULT PASSAGES
Act I, Scene 5, 248–282

VIOLA. Good madam, let me see your face.

OLIVIA. Have you any commission from your
lord to negotiate with my face? You are now
out of your text; but we will draw the curtain,
and show you the picture. Look you, sir, such
a one I was this present. [*Unveiling.*] Is't not
well done?

VIOLA. Excellently done, if God did all.

OLIVIA. 'Tis in grain, sir, 'twill endure wind
and weather.

VIOLA. 'Tis beauty truly blent, whose red and
white
Nature's own sweet and cunning hand laid on.
Lady, you are the cruell'st she alive
If you will lead these graces to the grave,
And leave the world no copy.

OLIVIA. O, sir, I will not be so hard-
hearted; I will give out divers schedules of
my beauty. It shall be inventoried, and every
particle and utensil labell'd to my will: as,
item, two lips, indifferent red; *item,* two grey
eyes, with lids to them; *item,* one neck, one
chin, and so forth. Were you sent hither to
praise me?

VIOLA. I see you what you are, you are too
proud;
But if you were the devil, you are fair.
My lord and master loves you. O, such love
Could be recompens'd, though you were
crown'd
The nonpareil of beauty.

OLIVIA. How does he love me?

VIOLA. With adorations, fertile tears,
With groans that thunder love, with sighs of
fire.

OLIVIA. Your lord does know my mind, I
  cannot love him.
Yet I suppose him virtuous, know him noble,
Of great estate, of fresh and stainless youth;
In voices well divulg'd, free, learn'd, and
  valiant,
And in dimension, and the shape of nature,
A gracious person. But yet I cannot love him.
He might have took his answer long ago.

Part of the difficulty in this passage stems from
the extended metaphor of Olivia's face as a picture.
Viola (disguised as Cesario) asks to see Olivia's face
without the veil she is wearing in the prolonged

A disguised Viola asks Olivia to show her face in Act I,
Scene 5 of *Twelfth Night*. This illustration was designed
for a 1918 edition of Charles and Mary Lamb's *Tales
from Shakespeare. (Illustration by Louis Rhead)*

period of mourning over her brother's death.
Olivia agrees to reveal her face: She refers to her
veil as a "curtain" that is covering a "picture" (her
face). Viola says that Olivia's face is well done, "if
God did all," picturing God as the painter of this
picture: By this she means that it is well done if her
face is in its natural state, not enhanced by cosmet-
ics. Olivia asserts that her face is indeed not so arti-
ficially painted when she says, "'Tis in grain, sir."
Viola then praises her beauty and enjoins Olivia to
leave the world a copy of herself. In other words,
she should marry and have a child that will carry on
her beauty beyond her own death.

The other primary difficulty in this passage for
modern readers is that much of it depends upon
familiarity with the Petrarchan love convention. In
this stereotypical view of romantic love between a
man and a woman, the lady is pictured as very beautiful but also proud and rejecting the man wooing her. Since Olivia has been continually rejecting
Orsino in his overtures of love, Viola labels Olivia
as "too proud" but also "fair" (beautiful). The
implication is that she is indeed a Petrarchan lady.
This use of Petrarchan assumptions is continued
when Viola pictures Orsino as loving Olivia "With
adorations, fertile tears, / With groans that thunder love, with sighs of fire." In the Petrarchan convention, the man was always portrayed as adoring
the lady as if worshipping her, as weeping, and as
sighing. So, Viola pictures Orsino as the Petrarchan
man in his wooing of the Petrarchan lady (Olivia).

Act II, Scene 4, 52–81

FESTE. Come away, come away, death,
And in sad cypress let me be laid.
Fly away, fly away, breath,
I am slain by a fair cruel maid.
My shroud of white, stuck all with yew,
O, prepare it!
My part of death, no one so true
Did share it.
Not a flower, not a flower sweet
On my black coffin let there be strown.
Not a friend, not a friend greet
My poor corpse, where my bones

Shall be thrown.
A thousand thousand sighs to save,
Lay me, O, where
Sad true lover never find my grave,
To weep there.

DUKE. There's for thy pains.

FESTE. No pains, sir, I take pleasure in
singing, sir.

DUKE. I'll pay thy pleasure then.

FESTE. Truly, sir, and pleasure will be paid,
one time or another.

DUKE. Give me now leave to leave thee.

FESTE. Now the melancholy god protect thee,
and the tailor make thy doublet of changeable
taffeta, for thy mind is a very opal. I would
have men of such constancy put to sea, that
their business might be every thing and their
intent every where, for that's it that always
makes a good voyage of nothing. Farewell.

This passage, consisting of a song sung by Feste
for Duke Orsino and their conversation following
it, is difficult in a way similar to the preceding passage cited. Its import also depends very much on the
audience or reader being familiar with the elements
of the Petrarchan love convention. The reader must
perceive the ridiculing and critical light being shed
by Feste upon Orsino. Feste is picturing Orsino in
the song as the most extreme type of Petrarchan
man. The lady's rejection in the Petrarchan convention was commonly called "death." The Petrarchan
man is "killed" by her rejection. Feste is portraying Orsino as such a man being repeatedly rejected
by Olivia and thus seems to be a masochist in a
love relationship that will never lead to acceptance.
So, Orsino is wasting his life by reveling in such
"death." Feste pictures, in essence, Orsino (the
Petrarchan man) as the "I" in the song: Orsino is
the one "slain by a fair cruel maid." Olivia, as the

typical Petrarchan lady, is both beautiful ("fair")
and "cruel" in her pride and rejection. The man
in the song is portrayed as preparing and calling
for his own coffin. The Petrarchan man typically
is self-pitying: Thus, the man in the song refers to
his own "poor corpse." The Petrarchan man always
sighs and moans over his sad state: Thus, there is
the reference to the "thousand thousand sighs."

Following the song, Feste gives a kind of satirical benediction to Orsino: He calls for the "melancholy god" to protect Orsino. This would be
the god that Orsino is most devoted to, since he
is always melancholy over his failure to win Olivia
and actually seems to overindulge himself in such
melancholy and to take a perverse pleasure in it.
Feste also says that Orsino should wear "changeable taffeta." This highlights the fact that Orsino
himself, as the Petrarchan man, is so changeable
in his moods and feelings. Taffeta and the opal
both carry the idea of change, since both reflect
light, appearing to quickly change colors. Feste's
final barbed criticism of Orsino is in his reference
to "a good voyage of nothing": In effect, this is the
precise kind of voyage or journey through life that
Orsino is on. As long as he plays at life in the role of
the Petrarchan man, he has no reachable goal and
is doomed to frustration. His whole life is a voyage
of nothingness. Feste clearly implies that Orsino
needs to forsake the present voyage he is on.

Act V, Scene 1, 398–417

FESTE. [*sings*] When that I was and a little
  tine boy,
With hey ho, the wind and the rain,
A foolish thing was but a toy,
For the rain it raineth every day.
But when I came to man's estate,
With hey ho, the wind and the rain,
'Gainst knaves and thieves men shut their gate,
For the rain it raineth every day.
But when I came, alas, to wive,
With hey ho, the wind and the rain,
By swaggering could I never thrive,
For the rain it raineth every day.
But when I came unto my beds,

With hey ho, the wind and the rain,
With toss-pots still had drunken heads,
For the rain it raineth every day.
A great while ago the world begun,
With hey ho, the wind and the rain,
But that's all one, our play is done,
And we'll strive to please you every day. [*Exit.*]

Feste's final song as a kind of epilogue in the play is difficult in that it is subtle in its symbolic or almost allegorical suggestions, but also because its philosophy is such a striking contrast to that of the play that we have just experienced. In essence, the song pictures the stages of one's life from childhood to old age. The first stanza concerns the young boy ("tine" ["tiny"] boy) who lives a carefree life almost outside of time and responsibility. Even acts of mischief in this stage are regarded as foolish and trifling. The second stanza portrays this child grown into manhood, into adulthood. Apparently, he has become a thief and bully: Now his "mischief" is no longer trifling, since it involves robbery and violence. His crimes and vices are not overlooked by others. The third stanza says that when he became even older, he married, but he admits that his bullying led to trouble for him. He could not accomplish any good in this stage of life. The fourth stanza depicts the man in old age and apparently fallen into alcoholism and keeping company with other drunkards ("toss-pots"). In other words, in this last stage of life, he is depressed, feels useless, and escapes from life and his own lack of accomplishment by retreating into drink. A sad and melancholy trek through time is thus traced by this little song. The final stanza implies that this is simply the sad story of human life that has existed from the beginning of the world. All humans from the beginning of humanity are given this pessimistic lot in life, according to this song. What a contrast this is to the joyous, rosy, optimistic view of life that has been pictured in the play itself. In the play, all troubles are resolved and all problems solved. In the play, time works everything out to the good, and with time, age, and maturity comes great happiness in life. Not

so in this song. The conscious contrast between the play and the final song is made specific when Feste says, "But that's all one, our play is done, / And we'll strive to please you every day." In other words, Feste says to the audience that this play, with its most pleasant view of life, has now ended. But if the audience will return each day to see another play, then they will again feel joy at seeing the pleasantness in life pictured in the play. But the clear implication is that real life between plays is not as wonderful as plays such as *Twelfth Night* depict it. In fact, life might be rather harsh, unpleasant, and melancholy—as portrayed in Feste's song. The refrain of each stanza ("For the rain it raineth every day") also points to the depressing, unpleasant nature of life. But, of course, the refrain is an exaggeration: It does not really rain every day. So, the song seems to be Shakespeare's realistic nature moderating somewhat the exaggerated rosiness of life just shown in his own play proper. Shakespeare, then, is saying that life itself has both sunny days and rainy days and that, ironically, one should not expect life always to be as joy-filled as it has been presented here.

CRITICAL INTRODUCTION TO THE PLAY

The overriding topic of *Twelfth Night* is romantic love. The play shows its unpredictable nature and strange manners of development, as well as the various motives and tactics of lovers. For example, we see both love at first sight (Olivia falling for Cesario/Viola) and a most practical love between two who had been acquainted a long time (Sir Toby and Maria). We see lovers fail miserably in their attempts to attract others (Orsino's Petrarchan wooing of Olivia and Malvolio's ridiculous attempts to attract Olivia with outlandish clothing and actions). We also see the good and selfless (such as Viola) succeed in achieving love and marriage. It is almost equally satisfying to witness the self-loving person (such as Malvolio) fail to attract another on the basis of only self-serving motives. The successful relationships of those who learn to give of themselves culminate in marriage.

However, using the backdrop of such romantic loves, Shakespeare reveals even deeper and more significant concerns in his play. Nothing less than somber examinations of time, age, mortality, the nature of the universe, and the nature of life itself subtly permeate the play. These are the elements that must be grasped to understand the play fully.

Setting and Structure

The setting of the play is Illyria, a land that Shakespeare seems to make very much like Italy. However, within this general setting are essentially two major locales in the form of two homes, Olivia's and Orsino's. These provide one essential element of the play's structure, since most of the scenes occur in one or the other home. Or we see people traveling from one to the other. One household is the realm of a Petrarchan lady, and the other is that of a Petrarchan man. Each noble household has residents and servants who figure in important ways in the play. Almost every character in the play owes allegiance in some way to either the master or the mistress of these residences. Thus, the simple use of these two homes provides an effective structural principle for the characters and actions through the play.

Another structural principle is the employment of Shakespeare's typical pattern of comedy. In other words, early in the play we see people encountering various problems and obstacles to happiness: Olivia's brother has died, Viola fears that her brother has drowned, Orsino cannot get Olivia to respond to his offers of love, Viola is in love with Orsino but cannot do anything to declare this love as long as she is in her disguise as a male, and Sir Toby and others are stifled in their joy and put down continually by the sour Malvolio. Additionally, Olivia has a hopeless love for a female in disguise. Images of sterility, grieving, and death abound early in the play. However, in the course of things, fruitful loves develop as problems are overcome: Olivia can love a man after Sebastian appears, Viola can have Orsino after her disguise is removed, and Toby pairs up with Maria. So, sterility and deathlike existences are supplanted by fruitfulness and vitality and life-affirming love. Typical of Shakespearean comedy, the loves lead to multiple marriages at the end of the play. So, the play builds toward love and life and creating life (through children assumed to result from marriage). As problems are solved, love blooms through the play. This is a unifying structural thread in the play.

Related to the comic pattern, however, is another pattern Shakespeare uses in the structure of *Twelfth Night.* This is his embodiment of some conventional elements of the pastoral romance. In pastoral romances (in both poetry and prose) written prior to Shakespeare's play, main characters were usually shepherds and noble people disguised as shepherds. They lived in the natural world of forests and pastures for a time and frequently were separated from other family members—for example, a brother and sister separated by various circumstances for a long time. But in these works, eventually the family members would be reunited in surprising situations. It was common for the two family members to identify one another through moles, birthmarks, and family ancestry. In *Twelfth Night,* Shakespeare has Viola and Sebastian separated from one another through most of the play. With all of the problems accumulating, especially for Viola, the audience is aware that most of them could be solved if only Sebastian could be reunited with Viola. In one sense, this is "what we will," as the play's subtitle implies. We wish for this event to occur, and Shakespeare deliberately creates suspense and anticipation by delaying its occurrence. But near the end, Sebastian strolls into the gathering of Viola and the other major characters. He sees Viola (dressed just like Sebastian) and exclaims the following (5.1.226–231):

Do I stand there? I never had a brother;
Nor can there be that deity in my nature
Of here and every where. I had a sister,
Whom the blind waves and surges have
  devour'd.
Of charity, what kin are you to me?
What countryman? What name? What
  parentage?

Viola answers his queries, and then we have this exchange (5.1.242–248):

VIOLA. My father had a mole upon his brow.

SEBASTIAN. And so had mine.

VIOLA. And died that day when Viola from her birth
Had numb'red thirteen years.

SEBASTIAN. O, that record is lively in my soul!
He finished indeed his mortal act
That day that made my sister thirteen years.

Thus, Shakespeare employs, with some humorous exaggeration, the very elements of a pastoral romance—identification and miraculous reunion of the long-lost brother and sister through family ancestry, names, dates, and moles! This pattern, then, contributes to the comic pattern, heightening the sense of resolution of problems and an outcome of utter joy, surprise, and happiness.

Finally, a major element of the play's structure is its mirroring of the festive pattern of holiday celebration in Shakespeare's time. Shakespeare presents his characters as holiday celebrants—specifically like people using the so-called Misrule pattern of celebration. The festivity of Twelfth Night was celebrated by groups of people wearing masks and/or disguises and led by an elected leader called the Lord of Misrule. This leader was to lead the group in a life of misrule—of disorder, breaking of rules and social restrictions, unbridled eating and drinking, and mocking of figures of authority. Thus, in his play, Shakespeare presents Sir Toby Belch as equivalent to the Lord of Misrule on such a holiday. He blatantly disregards the rules of decorum in Olivia's household, especially those imposed by the puritanical Malvolio. Sir Toby leads Sir Andrew in a life of inebriation, gluttony, debauchery, carefree existence, jokes, tricks, etc. At one point, Malvolio accuses Toby of "disorders" (line 2.3.97) and of "uncivil rule" (2.3.123). The Puritans of Shakespeare's time loathed Misrule festivals and condemned them. The play has characters in disguise, both literally and figuratively. First, in literal disguise is Viola pretending to be the male Cesario. Ironically, Viola at one point tells Olivia that she is disguised: "I am not what I am" (3.1.141). Of course, Olivia cannot perceive this level of meaning in her statement, but Viola and the audience certainly understand it. Her unmasking occurs at the end of the play. Also literally playing another role at one point is Feste: He pretends to be the clergyman Sir Topas when he visits Malvolio locked in the dark room (4.2). A more subtle use of the misrule tradition of masking and disguising, however, is Shakespeare's implication that many other characters are wearing "masks," playing roles, and hiding their true personalities and/or potentials. A prime example is Olivia: She could be said, in fact, to be wearing two masks. She is wearing the mask of the Petrarchan lady and the mask of the extreme connoisseur of grief and melancholy. By the end of the play, she has removed both of these "masks," and her true nature has blossomed. Thus, her true identity appears, just as it would for a festive celebrant of Shakespeare's day who would remove his or her mask at the end of the festival. In addition, one can say that Orsino eventually removes his mask of the Petrarchan man. Feste could be said to be wearing the mask of a court fool, since actually he is a very wise person underneath that mask. In sum, much of Shakespeare's study of human nature and life's serious themes resides in his uses of the festive pattern and the rituals of a misrule celebration.

Themes

Although the most obvious theme of the play is romantic love, with the eventual pairing of members of opposite sexes for marriage, other themes can be seen as subsidiaries of this one. Indeed, other themes are actually even more important and on levels much more serious than just romantic love. The Petrarchan love theme, for example, is one type of romantic love. It involves a Petrarchan man, such as Orsino, who continually and stubbornly woos a Petrarchan lady, such

as Olivia, who never reciprocates his love. Despite the man's exaggerated and flowery descriptions of her, his sighs over her, and his melancholy suffering from her rejections, she proudly and cruelly wants nothing to do with him. Romantic love can only result from this sterile Petrarchan relationship when the two people take other partners that do respond and harmonize as lovers and potential mates. Such is the case with Olivia's eventual pairing with Sebastian and Orsino's eventual choosing of Viola.

The Petrarchan form of "love" in the play, however, leads into one of the most serious and somber themes—one of much greater importance than the mere theme of Petrarchan love in isolation. This is the carpe diem theme—that is, the classical theme of "seize the day," the theme that argues for participation in life and love while one has the chance. Always implied in this theme is the stark fact that every human is continually aging and moving farther from youth into old age and eventual death. The enemy is time. The carpe diem theme argues that one should use time vitally by participating in love and by enjoying life. This is why Shakespeare presents Olivia at first as only dwelling on the death of her brother and not really living and loving: She plays the Petrarchan lady who always rejects love. It is only when she meets Cesario that she is surprised by love and begins to enter life again. Similarly, Orsino is dwelling on "death" in his rejection by Olivia. It is only when this relationship with her becomes impossible that he can begin life with Viola. The lesson of carpe diem is the one that Feste primarily is trying to teach both Olivia and Orsino. He mocks both critically for not really participating in life and instead choosing to remain stagnant, sterile, and in isolation from love and life. Viola also is a teacher of this same lesson, particularly during her missions to Olivia on Orsino's behalf. She pointedly criticizes Olivia for not choosing love and thereby not choosing eventual marriage and children. She tells Olivia, in fact, that Olivia is cruel to the world if she takes her beauty to the grave and leaves no copy of it

(in a child) for humanity. The real and persistent threats of time, age, and death for humans are lurking very somberly beneath the comic surface of *Twelfth Night.*

Related to the carpe diem theme is the theme of festivity in the play. Shakespeare couches the play in festive rituals that his audience would be accustomed to on many holidays through the year. The characters of the play are created by Shakespeare to be like celebrants in a festivity—particularly like those in a Twelfth Night celebration, one of

After the shipwreck, Viola asks the captain about her brother's safety in Act I, Scene 2 of *Twelfth Night.* This illustration was designed for a 1918 edition of Charles and Mary Lamb's *Tales from Shakespeare. (Illustration by Louis Rhead)*

the Misrule celebrations of the year. The sense of festivity, jokes, food, and drink through the play embody the idea of participation in fun and the enjoyment of life, just as the carpe diem theme prescribes. But in these festivals, the celebrants would be disguised and then unmasked at the end of the festival, revealing their true identities. This is precisely what Shakespeare has occur in the play: Viola's literal disguise is removed, and also the symbolic disguises worn by Olivia and Orsino. Also, festivals allow people to get away from the normal routines, duties, problems, and pressures of life for a while. After this period of emotional and psychological release, they are refreshed and prepared to take up their normal roles in the everyday world. This is what Shakespeare implies by the festive pattern in the play: The characters have been clarified, in their relationships with others, in love, in life, and time, age, and death. At the end of the play, they are ready to enter the real world of life with an improved perspective.

Another major theme involves nothing less than an entire philosophy of life, a view of the universe itself. We see this theme primarily through the eyes of Viola. When the problems she faces seem to be beyond her ability to solve them, she says that time must untangle these knots (2.2). She does rely on things working out through time. And they do. Later, when she is being drawn into a fight with Sir Andrew, Antonio walks in at just the right time to save her. Again, at the end of the play, Sebastian appears at just the right time to save her and to solve all of the major problems. So, Viola has a very optimistic philosophy about life and the nature of the universe. Essentially, she believes in a providential, benevolent view in which all will be worked out to the good through time. Shakespeare indeed supports Viola's philosophy by the actions occurring in the play. The realistic Shakespeare does raise some question about this view, however, in Feste's song ending the play. Things do not always work out well, according to the song. This tempers the possibly excessive optimism reflected by the play as a whole. But the play as a whole presents a vision of life, and it is a world in itself. It gives a world view not entirely negated by the concluding song.

Imagery

Permeating the play are specifics of festive images. The title of the play itself alludes to a specific holiday, and we see typical images and hear words associated with this holiday—such as cakes, ale, disorder, songs, surprises, disguises, laughter, and jokes. These convey the sense of activity, vitality, and good will that the play argues are essential in love and life and preferable over excessively dwelling on age and death. On the other hand, images of age and death are present significantly in the play and vividly show their powerful presence in everyone's life. Olivia and others mention her brother's death. Viola fears at first that her own brother died at sea. Feste's song (2.3) mentions that love is "not hereafter" and that "youth's a stuff will not endure." Viola (as Cesario) warns Olivia not to let her beauty die with her in the grave. In his song for Orsino (2.4), Feste saturates it with images of death ("sad cypress," "slain," "shroud," "coffin," "poor corpse") to imply the stagnation of Orsino as the rejected Petrarchan man but also as one only marching toward death, not life, as long as he plays this role. Feste's concluding song pictures some sad effects of time's passing and of one's aging. So, the playing of death against life that is reflected in the imagery enforces the carpe diem argument. Also supportive of this theme and of the theme of the providential nature of the universe are numerous mentions of time and its passing. Interesting as well in this regard are the images and subtle implications of circles. For example, a climactic one is Feste's reference to "the whirligig of time" (5.1.376). This implies that time is like a spinning top, that it takes a circling course. This perfectly supports Viola's philosophy that all eventually works out and is brought to fruition through time. In effect, Feste's concluding song portrays a human's life as a kind of circle—from tiny boy to helpless old man. Youthful joy to melancholy aging to old age and death make up a circle examined by Shakespeare, then, in this ultimately somber comedy.

EXTRACTS OF CLASSIC CRITICISM

William Hazlitt (1778–1830) [Excerpted from *Characters of Shakespeare's Plays* (1817). The influential romantic critic Hazlitt here shows his appreciation of *Twelfth Night* and its characters.]

This is justly considered as one of the most delightful of Shakespear's comedies. It is full of sweetness and pleasantry. It is perhaps too good-natured for comedy. It has little satire, and no spleen. It aims at the ludicrous rather than the ridiculous. It makes us laugh at the follies of mankind, not despite them, and still less bear any ill-will towards them. Shakespear's comic genius resembles the bee rather in its power of extracting sweets from weeds or poisons, than in leaving a sting behind it. He gives the most amusing exaggeration of the prevailing foibles of his characters, but in a way that they themselves, instead of being offended at, would almost join in to humour; he rather contrives opportunities for them to shew themselves off in the happiest lights, rather than renders them contemptible in the perverse construction of the wit or malice of others. There is a certain stage of society in which people become conscious of their peculiarities and absurdities, affect to disguise what they are, and set up pretensions to what they are not. This gives rise to a corresponding style of comedy, the object of which is to detect the disguises of self-love, and to make reprisals on these preposterous assumptions of vanity, by marking the contrast between the real and the affected character as severely as possible, and denying to those, who would impose on us for what they are not, even the merit which they have. This is the comedy of artificial life, of wit and satire, such as we see it in Congreve, Wycherley, Vanbrugh, &c. To

this succeeds a state of society from which the same sort of affectation and pretence are banished by a greater knowledge of the world or by their successful exposure on the stage; and which by neutralizing the materials of comic character, both natural and artificial, leaves no comedy at all but the sentimental. Such is our modern comedy. There is a period in the progress of manners anterior to both these, in which the foibles and follies of individuals are of nature's planting, not the growth of art or study; in which they are therefore unconscious of themselves, or care not who knows them, if they can but have their whim out; and in which, as there is no attempt at imposition, the spectators rather receive pleasure from humouring the incantations of the persons they laugh at, than wish to give them pain by exposing their absurdity. This may be called the comedy of nature, and it is the comedy which we generally find in Shakespear. Whether the analysis here given be just or not, the spirit of his comedies is evidently quite distinct from that of the authors above mentioned, as it is in its essence the same with that of Cervantes, and also very frequently of Moliere, though he was more systematic in his extravagance than Shakespear. Shakespear's comedy is of a pastoral and poetical cast. Folly is indigenous to the soil, and shoots out with native, happy, unchecked luxuriance. Absurdity has every encouragement afforded it; and nonsense has room to flourish in. Nothing is stunted by the churlish, icy hand of indifference or severity. The poet runs riot in a conceit, and idolizes a quibble. His whole object is to turn the meanest or rudest objects to a pleasurable account. The relish which he has of a pun, or of the quaint humour of a low character, does not interfere with the delight with which he describes a beautiful image, or the most refined love. The clown's forced jests do not spoil the sweetness of the character of Viola; the same house is big enough to hold Malvolio, the Countess,

Maria, Sir Toby, and Sir Andrew Aguecheek. For instance, nothing can fall much lower than this last character in intellect or morals; yet how are his weaknesses nursed and dandled by Sir Toby into something "high fantastical," when on Sir Andrew's commendation of himself for dancing and fencing, Sir Toby answers, "Wherefore are these things hid? Wherefore have these gifts a curtain before them? Are they like to take dust like mistress Moll's picture? Why dost thou not go to church in a galliard, and come home in a coranto? My very walk should be a jig! I would not so much as make water but in a cinque-pace. What dost thou mean? Is this a world to hide virtues in? I did think by the excellent constitution of thy leg, it was framed under the star of a galliard!" How Sir Toby, Sir Andrew, and the Clown afterwards chirp over their cups, how they "rouse the night-owl in a catch, able to draw three souls out of one weaver!" What can be better than Sir Toby's unanswerable answer to Malvolio, "Dost thou think, because thou art virtuous, there shall be no more cakes and ale?" In a word, the best turn is given to everything, instead of the worst. There is a constant infusion of the romantic and enthusiastic, in proportion as the characters are natural and sincere; whereas, in the more artificial style of comedy, every thing gives way to ridicule and indifference, there being nothing left but affectation on one side, and incredulity on the other. Much as we like Shakespear's comedies, we cannot agree with Dr. Johnson that they are better than his tragedies; nor do we like them half so well. If his inclination to comedy sometimes led him to trifle with the seriousness of tragedy, the poetical and impassioned passages are the best parts of his comedies. The great and secret charm of *Twelfth Night* is the character of Viola. Much as we like catches and cakes and ale, there is something that we like better. We have a friendship for Sir Toby; we patronize Sir Andrew; we have an understanding with the Clown, a sneaking kindness for Maria and her rogueries; we feel a regard for Malvolio, and sympathise with his gravity, his smiles, his cross garters, his yellow stockings, and imprisonment in the stocks. But there is something that excites in us a stronger feeling than all this—it is Viola's confession of her love.

> *Duke.* What's her history?

> *Viola.* A blank my lord, she never told
>   her love:
> She let concealment, like a worm i' th'
>   bud,
> Feed on her damask cheek: she pin'd in
>   thought,
> And with a green and yellow melancholy,
> She sat like Patience on a monument,
> Smiling at grief. Was not this love
>   indeed?
> We men may say more, swear more, but
>   indeed,
> Our shews are more than will; for still
>   we prove
> Much in our vows, but little in our love.

> *Duke.* But died thy sister of her love, my
>   boy?

> *Viola.* I am all the daughters of my
>   father's house,
> And all the brothers too; and yet I know
>   not.

Shakespear alone could describe the effect of his own poetry.

> Oh, it came o'er the ear like the sweet
>   south
> That breathes upon a bank of violets,
> Stealing and giving odour.

What we so much admire here is not the image of Patience on a monument, which has been generally quoted, but the lines before and after it. They give a very echo to the seat where love is throned. How long ago it is since we first learnt to repeat them; and still, still they vibrate on the heart, like the sounds which the passing wind draws from the trembling strings of a harp left on some desert shore! There are other passages of not less impassioned sweetness. Such is Olivia's address to Sebastian, whom she supposes to have already deceived her in a promise of marriage.

Olivia asks Sebastian to become her betrothed in front of a priest in Act IV, Scene 3 of *Twelfth Night*. This is a print from the Boydell Shakespeare Gallery project, which was first conceived in 1786 and lasted until 1805. *(Painting by William Hamilton; engraving by William Angus)*

> Blame not this haste of mine: if you
>   mean well,
> Now go with me and with this holy man
> Into the chantry by: there before him,
> And underneath that consecrated roof,
> Plight me the full assurance of your faith,
> That my most jealous and too doubtful soul
> May live at peace.

We have already said something of Shakespeare's songs. One of the most beautiful of them occurs in this play, with a preface of his own to it.

> *Duke.* O fellow, come, the song we had
>   last night.
> Mark it, Cesario, it is old and plain;
> The spinsters and the knitters in the sun,
> And the free maids that weave their
>   thread with bones,
> Do use to chaunt it: it is silly sooth,
> And dallies with the innocence of love,
> Like the old age.

> *Song*
> Come away, come away, death,
> And in sad cypress let me be laid;
> Fly away, fly away, breath;
> I am slain by a fair cruel maid.
> My shroud of white, stuck all with yew,
> O prepare it;
> My part of death no one so true
> Did share it.
> Not a flower, not a flower sweet,
> On my black coffin let there be strewn;
> Not a friend, not a friend greet
> My poor corpse, where my bones shall
>   be thrown;
> A thousand thousand sighs to save,
> Lay me, O! where
> Sad true-love never find my grave,
> To weep there.

Who after this will say that Shakespear's genius was only fitted for comedy? Yet after reading other parts of this play, and particularly the garden-scene where Malvolio picks up the letter, if we were to say that his genius for comedy was less than his genius for tragedy, it would perhaps only prove that our own taste in such matters is more saturnine than mercurial.

Enter Maria:

Sir Toby. Here comes the little villain:—How now, my nettle of India?

Maria. Get ye all three into the box-tree: Malvolio's coming down this walk: he has been yonder i' the sun, practicing behavior to his own shadow this half hour: observe him, for the love of mockery; for I know this letter will make a contemplative idiot of him. Close, in the name of jesting! Lie thou there; for here comes the trout that must be caught with tickling.

[*They hide themselves. Maria throws down a letter, and Exit.*]

Enter Malvolio.

Malvolio. 'Tis but fortune; all is fortune. Maria once told me, she did affect me; and I have heard herself come thus near, that, should she fancy, it should be one of my complexion. Besides, she uses me with a more exalted respect than any one else that follows her. What should I think on't?

Sir Toby. Here's an over-weening rogue!

Fabian. O, peace! Contemplation makes a rare turkey-cock of him; how he jets under his advanced plumes!

Sir Andrew. 'Slight, I could so beat the rogue:—

Sir Toby. Peace, I say.

Malvolio. To be Count Malvolio;—

Sir Toby. Ah, rogue!

Sir Andrew. Pistol him, pistol him.

Sir Toby. Peace, peace!

Malvolio. There is example for't; the lady of the Strachy married the yeoman of the wardrobe.

Sir Andrew. Fie on him, Jezebel!

Fabian. O, peace! Now he's deeply in; look, how imagination blows him.

Malvolio. Having been three months married to her, sitting in my chair of state,—

Sir Toby. O for a stone bow, to hit him in the eye!

Malvolio. Calling my officers about me, in my branch'd velvet gown; having come from a day-bed, where I have left Olivia sleeping.

Sir Toby. Fire and brimstone!

Fabian. O peace, peace!

Malvolio. And then to have the humour of state: and after a demure travel of regard,—telling them, I know my place, as I would they should do theirs,—to ask for my kinsman Toby.—

Sir Toby. Bolts and shackles!

Fabian. O, peace, peace, peace! now, now.

Malvolio. Seven of my people, with an obedient start, make out for him; I frown the while; and, perchance, wind up my watch, or play with some rich jewel. Toby approaches; curtsies there to me.

Sir Toby. Shall this fellow live?

Fabian. Though our silence be drawn from us with cares, yet peace.

Malvolio. I extend my hand to him thus, quenching my familiar smile with an austere regard to controul.

Sir Toby. And does not Toby take you a blow o' the lips then?

Malvolio. Saying—Cousin Toby, my fortunes having cast me on your niece, give me this prerogative of speech;—

Sir Toby. What, what?

Malvolio. You must amend your drunkenness.

Fabian. Nay, patience, or we break the sinews of our plot.

Malvolio. Besides, you waste the treasure of your time with a foolish knight.—

Sir Andrew. That's me, I warrant you.

Malvolio. One Sir Andrew—

Sir Andrew. I knew, 'twas I; for many do call me fool.

Malvolio. What employment have we here? [*Taking up the letter.*]

The letter and his comments on it are equally good. If poor Malvolio's treatment

Toby, Andrew, and Fabian observe Malvolio's reaction to Maria's letter, which he believes to be from Olivia, in this 19th-century depiction of Act II, Scene 5 of *Twelfth Night.*

afterwards is a bit hard, poetical justice is done in the uneasiness which Olivia suffers on account of her mistaken attachment to Cesario, as her insensibility to the violence of the Duke's passion is atoned for by the discovery of Viola's concealed love of him.

Charles Lamb (1775–1834) [Excerpted from "On Some of the Old Actors" (1823). Lamb was an early popularizer of Shakespeare. In this essay, he discusses some of the actors who performed in *Twelfth Night* (as well as in other plays), but in the process, he also reveals his interpretations of both the play and the characters.]

The casual sight of an old Play Bill, which I picked up the other day—I know not by what chance it was preserved so long—tempts me to call to mind a few of the players, who make the principal figure in it. It presents the cast of parts in the Twelfth Night, at the old Drury-lane Theatre two-and-thirty years ago. There is something very touching in these old remembrances. They make us think how we once used to read a Play Bill—not, as now peradventure, singling out a favorite performer, and casting a negligent eye over the rest; but spelling out every name, down to the very mutes and servants of the scene;—when it was a matter of no small moment to us whether Whitfield, or Packer, took the part of Fabian; when Benson, and Burton, and Phillimore—names of small account—had an importance, beyond what we can be content to attribute now to the time's best actors,—"Orsino, by Mr. Barrymore."—What a full Shakspearian sound it carries! How fresh to memory arise the image, and the manner, of the gentle actor!

Those who have only seen Mrs. Jordan within the last ten or fifteen years, can have no adequate notion of her performance of such parts as Ophelia; Helena, in All's Well that Ends Well; and Viola in this play. Her voice had latterly acquired a coarseness, which suited well enough with her Nells and Hoydens, but in those days it sank, with her steady melting eye, into the heart. Her joyous parts—in which her memory now chiefly lives—in her youth were outdone by her plaintive ones. There is no giving an account how she delivered the disguised story of her love for Orsino. It was no set speech, that she had foreseen, so as to weave it into an harmonious period, line necessarily following line, to make up the music—yet I have heard it so spoken, or rather read, not without its grace and beauty—but, when she had declared her sister's history to be a "blank," and that she "never told her love," there was a pause, as if the story had ended—and then the image of the "worm in the bud" came up as a new suggestion—and the heightened image of "Patience" still followed after that, as by some growing (and not mechanical) process, thought springing up after thought, I would almost say, as they were watered by her tears. So in those fine lines—

Write loyal cantos of contemned love—
Hollow your name to the reverberate hills—

there was no preparation made in the foregoing image for that which was to follow. She used no rhetoric in her passion; or it was nature's own rhetoric, most legitimate then, when it seemed altogether without rule or law.

Mrs. Powel (now Mrs. Renaud), then in the pride of her beauty, made an admirable Olivia. She was particularly excellent in her unbending scenes in conversation with the Clown. I have seen some Olivias—and those very sensible actresses too—who in these interlocutions have seemed to set their wits at the jester, and to vie conceits with him in downright emulation. But she used him for her sport, like what he was, to trifle a leisure sentence or two with, and then to be dismissed, and she to be the Great Lady still. She touched the imperious fantastic humour of the character with nicety. Her fine spacious person filled the scene.

The part of Malvolio has in my judgment been so often misunderstood, and the *general merits* of the actor, who then played it, so unduly appreciated, that I shall hope for pardon, if I am a little prolix upon these points.

Of all the actors who flourished in my time—a melancholy phrase if taken aright, reader—Bensley had most of the swell of the soul, was greatest in the delivery of heroic conceptions, the emotions consequent upon the presentment of a great idea to the fancy. He had the true poetical enthusiasm—the rarest faculty among players. None that I remember possessed even a portion of that fine madness which he threw out in Hotspur's famous rant about glory, or the transports of the Venetian incendiary at the vision of the fired city. His voice had the dissonance, and at times the inspiriting effect of the trumpet. His gait was uncouth and stiff, but no way embarrassed by affectation; and the thorough-bred gentleman was uppermost in every movement. He seized the moment of passion with the greatest truth; like a faithful clock, never striking before the time; never anticipating or leading you to anticipate. He was totally destitute of trick and artifice. He seemed come upon the stage to do the poet's message simply, and he did it with as genuine fidelity as the nuncios in Homer deliver the errands of the gods. He let the passion or the sentiment do its own work without prop or bolstering. He would have scorned to mountebank it; and betrayed none of that cleverness which is the bane of serious acting. For this reason, his Iago was the only endurable one which I remember to have seen. No spectator from his action could divine more of his artifice than Othello was supposed to do. His confessions in soliloquy alone put you in possession of the mystery. There were no by-intimations to make the audience fancy their own discernment so much greater than that of the Moor—who commonly stands like a great helpless mark set up for mine Ancient, and a quantity of barren spectators, to shoot their bolts at. The Iago of Bensley did not go to work so grossly. There was a triumphant tone about the character, natural to a general consciousness of power; but none of that petty vanity which chuckles and cannot contain itself upon any little successful stroke of its knavery—as is common with your small villains, and green probationers in mischief. It did not clap or crow before its time. It was not a man setting his wits at a child, and winking all the while at other children who are mightily pleased at being let into the secret; but a consummate villain entrapping a noble nature into toils, against which no discernment was available, where the manner was as fathomless as the purpose seemed dark, and without motive. The part of Malvolio, in the Twelfth Night, was performed by Bensley, with a richness and a dignity, of which (to judge from some recent castings of that character) the very tradition must be worn out from the stage. No manager in those days would have dreamed of giving it to Mr. Baddeley, or Mr. Parsons:

when Bensley was occasionally absent from the theatre, John Kemble thought it no derogation to succeed to the part. Malvolio is not essentially ludicrous. He becomes comic but by accident. He is cold, austere, repelling; but dignified, consistent, and, for what appears, rather of an over-stretched morality. Maria describes him as a sort of Puritan; and he might have worn his gold chain with honour in one of our old round-head families, in the service of a Lambert, or of a Lady Fairfax. But his morality and his manners are misplaced in Illyria. He is opposed to the proper *levities* of the piece, and falls in the unequal contest. Still his pride, or his gravity, (call it which you will) is inherent, and native to the man, not mock or affected, which latter only are the fit objects to excite laughter. His quality is at the best unlovely, but neither buffoon or contemptible. His bearing is lofty, a little above his station, but probably not much above his deserts. We see no reason why he should not have been brave, honourable, and accomplished. His careless committal of the ring to the ground (which he was commissioned to restore to Cesario), bespeaks a generosity of birth and feeling. His dialect on all occasions is that of a gentleman, and a man of education. We must not confound him with the eternal old, low steward of comedy. He is master of the household to a great Princess; a dignity probably conferred upon him for other respects than age or length of service. Olivia, at the first indication of his supposed madness, declares that she "would not have him miscarry for half of her dowry." Does this look as if the character was meant to appear little or insignificant? Once, indeed, she accuses him to his face—of what?—of being "sick of self-love,"—but with a gentleness and considerateness which could not have been, if she had not thought that this particular infirmity shaded some virtues. His rebuke to the knight, and his sottish revelers, is sensible and spirited; and when we

Malvolio acts strangely in front of Olivia and Maria while Andrew, Toby, and Fabian watch from behind the screen in Act III, Scene 4 of *Twelfth Night*. This is a print from the Boydell Shakespeare Gallery project, which was first conceived in 1786 and lasted until 1805. *(Painting by John Henry Ramberg; engraving by Thomas Ryder)*

take into consideration the unprotected condition of his mistress, and the strict regard with which her state of real or dissembled mourning would draw the eyes of the world upon her house-affairs, Malvolio might feel the honour of the family in some sort in his keeping; as it appears not that Olivia had any more brothers, or kinsmen, to look to it—for Sir Toby had dropped all such nice respects at the buttery hatch. That Malvolio was meant to be represented as possessing estimable qualities, the expression of the Duke in his anxiety to have him reconciled, almost

infers. "Pursue him, and entreat him to a peace." Even in his abused state of chains and darkness, a sort of greatness seems never to desert him. He argues highly and well with the supposed Sir Topas, and philosophises gallantly upon his straw. There must have been some shadow of worth about the man; he must have been something more than a mere vapour—a thing of straw, or Jack in office—before Fabian and Maria could have ventured sending him on a courting-errand to Olivia. There was some consonancy (as he would say) in the undertaking, or the jest would have been too bold even for that house of misrule.

Bensley, accordingly, threw over the part an air of Spanish loftiness. He looked, spake, and moved like an old Castilian. He was starch, spruce, opinionated, but his super-structure of pride seemed bottomed upon a sense of worth. There was something in it beyond the coxcomb. It was big and swell-ing, but you could not be sure that it was hollow. You might wish to see it taken down, but you felt that it was upon an elevation. He was magnificent from the outset; but when the decent sobrieties of the character began to give way, and the poison of self-love, in his conceit of the Countess's affection, gradually to work, you would have thought that the hero of La Mancha in person stood before you. How he went smiling to himself! with what ineffable carelessness would he twirl his gold chain! what a dream it was! you were infected with the illusion, and did not wish that it should be removed! you had no room for laughter! if an unseasonable reflection of morality obtruded itself, it was a deep sense of the pitiable infirmity of man's nature, that can lay him open to such frenzies—but in truth you rather admired than pitied the lunacy while it lasted—you felt that an hour of such mistake was worth an age with the eyes open. Who would not wish to live but for a day in the conceit of such a lady's love as Olivia? Why, the Duke would have given his principality but for a quarter of a minute, sleeping or waking, to have been so deluded. The man seemed to tread upon air, to taste manna, to walk with his head in the clouds, to mate Hyperion. O! shake not the castles of his pride—endure yet for a sea-son bright moments of confidence—"stand still ye watches of the element," that Malvo-lio may be still in fancy fair Olivia's lord—but fate and retribution say no—I hear the mischievous titter of Maria—the witty taunts of Sir Toby—the still more insupportable

triumph of the foolish knight—the counter-feit Sir Topas is unmasked—and "thus the whirligig of time," as the true clown hath it, "brings in his revenges." I confess that I never saw the catastrophe of this character, while Bensley played it, without a kind of tragic interest. There was good foolery too. Few now remember Dodd. What an Aguecheek the stage lost in him! Lovegrove, who came nearest to the old actors, revived the charac-ter some few seasons ago, and made it suf-ficiently grotesque; but Dodd was *it*, as it came out of nature's hands. It might be said to remain *in puris naturalibus*. In expressing slowness of apprehension this actor surpassed all others. You could see the first dawn of an idea stealing slowly over his countenance, climbing up by little and little, with a painful process, till it cleared up at last to the full-ness of a twilight conception—its highest meridian. He seemed to keep back his intel-lect, as some have had the power to retard their pulsation. The balloon takes less time in filling, than it took to cover the expansion of his broad moony face over all its quarters with expression. A glimmer of understand-ing would appear in a corner of his eye, and for lack of fuel go out again. A part of his forehead would catch a little intelligence, and be a long time in communicating it to the remainder.

MODERN CRITICISM AND CRITICAL CONTROVERSIES

Modern critics of *Twelfth Night* debate the nature of the characters and the moods of the play. They also explore facets such as the imagery and artistic patterns. A major contribution of modern criticism is to increase understanding of the celebrations of festivals and holidays in Shakespeare's time that are reflected in the play.

The critic Mark Van Doren picks up and fur-thers the view of Malvolio first noted by Charles Lamb (see "Extracts of Classic Criticism"). He supports Lamb's view that Malvolio is one with

Another depiction of Malvolio acting strangely in front of Olivia and Maria in Act III, Scene 4 of *Twelfth Night*. This is a print from Malcolm C. Salaman's 1916 edition of *Shakespeare in Pictorial Art*. (Painting by Thomas Stothard)

some dignity and honor and is not just a buffoon that deserves the ill treatment he receives from the vengeful group that tricks and imprisons him. Van Doren implies that the audience should feel some sympathy for the humiliated Malvolio. He points to Olivia's statement that Malvolio "hath been notoriously abused" for support in his interpretation and argues that Malvolio has "an integrity" that "we cannot but respect." To some extent Harold C. Goddard agrees. He accords Malvolio "dignity, decency, decorum, servility and severity in the cause of 'good order.'" Many critics, however, dissent from this view of Malvolio. In fact, the majority of critics might be represented by D. A.

Traversi in this matter. Traversi notes that Malvolio is punished for his self-love and that the darkness in which he is confined reflects his own attitude toward life and his ignorance of reality. Traversi argues that Malvolio sees himself at the center of things and refuses to respond to Orsino's efforts for him to join in a peaceful reconciliation. His bitter cry of "I'll be revenged on the whole pack of you" makes him a "legitimate object for the comic derision which so abundantly overtakes him in the course of the play, and for which we need not pity him."

The imagery of the play has been studied from various perspectives. Caroline Spurgeon examined the imagery in all of Shakespeare's plays. Concerning *Twelfth Night,* she feels that the "types of images reflect subtly and accurately the rather peculiar mixture of tones in the play." She sees music, romance, sadness, and beauty mixed with wit and comedy. Donald A. Stauffer perceives melancholy through the play, especially the repeated melancholy imagery implying that beauty must die. In addition, Stauffer emphasizes the important imagery of music permeating the play: It is the perfect symbol for the exalted view of love and for the harmony achieved through unselfish love.

Joseph H. Summers wrote a very perceptive essay on the importance of the Twelfth Night holiday in understanding the play. He concentrates on the tradition of wearing masks and disguises during this traditional Misrule festival. He contends that every character has a mask. Feste and Viola have masks, but they also have the ability to see through the masks and disguises of others. Summers also proposes that the audience is a participant in the festivity, and as the fictional lovers have unmasked to reveal or realize their true identities, Feste in his final song unmasks the whole play as the imitation of a desired world. The audience must return to the real and harsher everyday world. C. L. Barber also concerns himself with the human experience and truth that Shakespeare treats with the forms of festival, especially that of Misrule on Twelfth Night. Barber notes that the characters are people caught up in delusions or misapprehensions that take them out of themselves, bringing out what they would keep hidden or did not know was there. In other words, the characters are wearing various "masks." The play, Barber says, deals with the folly of misrule. The festive spirit shows the sour vanity of Malvolio's decorum. It also allows us to see the wisdom of Viola as a teacher, given free rein by her disguise. Her constant shifting of tone in response to the situation goes with her manipulation of her role in disguise: Instead of simply listening to her speak, we watch her conduct her speech. We feel her secure sense of proportion and her alert consciousness. Barber argues that the audience, as well as the characters, are moved "through release to clarification."

THE PLAY TODAY

Twelfth Night is today one of the most popular of Shakespeare's comedies. Its timeless theme of young love continues to appeal to today's audiences, all the more so because the seriousness of the theme is moderated by hilarious predicaments and entanglements. In addition, anyone who enjoys seeing a pompous and self-loving hypocrite put down could not ask for a better entertainment than the plot that unfolds against Malvolio.

The accessibility and the appeal of *Twelfth Night* today can be seen many ways. It is often said to be the most-produced of Shakespeare's plays, and it is one of only two Shakespeare plays reprinted in full in the latest edition of the most popular student anthology of English literature, the *Norton Anthology of English Literature* (the other is *King Lear*). It also serves as the basis for the recent popular movie *She's the Man* (2006). In this romantic comedy, Amanda Bynes plays a teenage Viola who tries to convince students at her twin brother's school that she is indeed her brother. Romantic complications ensue, and humor abounds. More traditional screen productions of the play have also been made. A 1996 movie version was directed by Trevor Nunn and features Imogen Stubbs and Steven Mackintosh. In 2003, Tim Supple directed the play for video, with Parminder Nagra, Claire Price, and Ronny Jhutti.

Recent criticism of the play has been lively and pointed. Some recent essays have been concerned with themes of emotional freedom and the purging of self-deception in love, as well as excessive revelry and undesirable activities. Critics also seem increasingly preoccupied with the essentially somber and melancholy air beneath the play's joyous surface; they emphasize the bitter vengefulness of some characters, the role of time as the inevitable destroyer of beauty and indeed life itself, and the unpredictability of life. The comedy may be lighthearted on the surface, but it definitely hints at and foreshadows the darker comedies and tragedies that would follow it over the next few years of Shakespeare's career.

FIVE TOPICS FOR DISCUSSION AND WRITING

1. **Appearance versus reality:** What characters in *Twelfth Night* have "masks"? Are they literal masks? Or symbolic ones? What are the natures of the masks that are removed by the end of the play? What changes or new manifestations in the real natures of certain characters have occurred?

2. **Philosophy of life:** Is there an overall vision of life and the world that is developed in *Twelfth Night*? What is it, and what are its various components? What actions and statements most suggest this vision? What is the importance of Viola in our perception of the metaphysical vision?

3. **Carpe diem:** What is the carpe diem theme? In what ways is it present in *Twelfth Night*? What characters, statements, and actions seem most important in its development? What is the significance of Feste in regard to this theme?

4. **Feast of epiphany:** In what ways is the Twelfth Night celebration reflected literally in *Twelfth Night*? Furthermore, in what ways can this particular yearly festival be applied in symbolic, emotional, and social ways—beyond the literal?

5. **Love:** What are the many varieties of love pictured in *Twelfth Night*? What characters exemplify each type? Who succeeds in love and why? Who fails in love and why?

Bibliography

Arlidge, Anthony. *Shakespeare and the Prince of Love: The Feast of Misrule in the Middle Temple.* London: Giles de la Mare, 2000.

Barber, C. L. *Shakespeare's Festive Comedy: A Study of Dramatic Form and Its Relation to Social Custom.* Princeton, N.J.: Princeton University Press, 1959.

Berry, Ralph. *Shakespeare's Comedies: Explorations in Form.* Princeton, N.J.: Princeton University Press, 1972.

Bloom, Harold, ed. *Modern Critical Interpretations of "Twelfth Night."* New York: Chelsea House, 1987.

Brown, John Russell. *Shakespeare and His Comedies.* London: Methuen, 1957.

Evans, Bertrand. *Shakespeare's Comedies.* Oxford: Clarendon, 1960.

Goddard, Harold C. *The Meaning of Shakespeare.* Chicago: University of Chicago Press, 1951.

Goldsmith, Robert Hillis. *Wise Fools in Shakespeare.* East Lansing: Michigan State University Press, 1955.

King, Walter N., ed. *Twentieth Century Interpretations of "Twelfth Night."* Englewood Cliffs, N.J.: Prentice-Hall, 1968.

Leech, Clifford. *"Twelfth Night" and Shakespearian Comedy.* Toronto: University of Toronto Press, 1965.

Muir, Kenneth, ed. *Shakespeare: The Comedies.* Englewood Cliffs, N.J.: Prentice-Hall, 1965.

Palmer, D. J. *Shakespeare, "Twelfth Night": A Casebook.* London: Macmillan, 1972.

Phialas, Peter G. *Shakespeare's Romantic Comedies.* Chapel Hill: North Carolina University Press, 1966.

Potter, Lois. *"Twelfth Night": Text and Performance.* London: Macmillan, 1985.

Ryan, Kiernan. *Shakespeare's Comedies.* Basingstoke, England: Palgrave Macmillan, 2009.

Schiffer, James, ed. *Twelfth Night: New Critical Essays.* New York: Routledge, 2008.

Spurgeon, Caroline. *Shakespeare's Imagery and What It Tells Us.* Cambridge: Cambridge University Press, 1935.

Stauffer, Donald A. *Shakespeare's World of Images: The Development of His Moral Ideas.* New York: Norton, 1949.

Summers, Joseph H. "The Masks of *Twelfth Night.*" *University of Kansas City Review* 22 (1955): 25–32. Reprint. In *Shakespeare: Modern Essays in Criticism,* edited by Leonard F. Dean. Rev. ed. London and New York: Oxford University Press, 1967, 1969.

Traversi, D. A. *An Approach to Shakespeare.* London: Sands, 1957.

Van Doren, Mark. *Shakespeare.* New York: Henry Holt, 1939.

Welsford, Enid. *The Fool: His Social and Literary History.* London: Faber and Faber, 1935.

FILM AND VIDEO PRODUCTIONS

Dexter, John, and John Sichel, dirs. *Twelfth Night.* With Alec Guinness, Joan Plowright, and Ralph Richardson. Koch Vision, 1969.

Gorrie, John, dir. *Twelfth Night.* With Alec McCowen, Felicity Kendal, and Trevor Peacock. BBC, 1980.

Kafno, Paul, dir. *Twelfth Night.* With Frances Barber and Christopher Hollis. A&E Home Video, 1987.

Nunn, Trevor, dir. *Twelfth Night.* With Imogen Stubbs and Steven Mackintosh. BBC, 1996.

Supple, Tim, dir. *Twelfth Night.* With Parminder Nagra, Claire Price, and Ronny Jhutti. Projector Productions, 2003.

—Robert H. Ray

The Two Gentlemen of Verona

INTRODUCTION

The Two Gentlemen of Verona, an early comedy, is often seen as merely an apprentice work, a foreshadowing of greater plays to come, and indeed it is hardly Shakespeare's finest achievement. However, the play has much to offer on its own terms. In the first place, *The Two Gentlemen of Verona* takes seriously the conflict between homosocial and heterosexual bonds—that is, the conflict between being a good friend to someone of the same sex and being a traditional heterosexual lover. For Shakespeare, as can be seen in the Sonnets, the conflict between these two bonds is a powerful one.

Homosocial relationships, which are not necessarily of a sexual or even erotic nature, refer to the bonds between men that are required in a society run by men (usually referred to as "patriarchal"). Another term for these homosocial bonds is "male friendship." But often our sense of friendship today is insufficient to describe the scope and importance of friendships between men in Shakespeare's time. The conclusion of *The Two Gentlemen of Verona*, in which one friend offers his lover to another, is one of the most striking examples of the sacrifice of one's heterosexual obligations in favor of a homosocial one.

In addition to stressing the conflict between homosocial and heterosexual ties, the play portrays a positive relationship between two women. Frequently in plays of the time, women of marriageable age (and the women who are in charge of them) are either isolated or pitted against other women in the play. In *The Two Gentlemen of Verona*, Julia and Silvia do not fight, and Silvia even feels an obligation to Julia that is certainly stronger than their lack of acquaintance would require. As far as Silvia knows, she has never even met Julia, yet Silvia sympathizes with the lover Proteus has cast off in order to pursue her.

The play also examines the process of becoming a perfect gentleman (or gentlewoman). All four of the main characters go through learning processes over the course of the play that roughly parallel the requirements of the conduct literature of the period. For example, Panthino and Antonio's discussion at Act I, Scene 3 about why Proteus should go abroad takes its material directly from books that taught young gentlemen how to be good young gentlemen. The importance and prominence of such books as *The English Gentleman* (1630, by Richard Braithwaite), *The Book of the Governor* (1531, by Thomas Elyot), and *The Book of the Courtier* (translated into English by Thomas Hoby in 1561, originally in Italian by Baldasare Castiglione) can hardly be exaggerated. Books on self-improvement were omnipresent in the early modern person's library (male and female alike).

While it is not the first play that comes to mind when people mention Shakespeare, *The Two Gentlemen of Verona* is certainly interesting, if at times perplexing. Readers today may want to condemn Valentine for his decisions and urge Silvia to speak up for herself. In many ways, *The Two Gentlemen of Verona* is most interesting for the way it outrages us.

Valentine becomes the leader of a band of outlaws in Act IV, Scene I of *The Two Gentlemen of Verona*. This illustration was designed for a 1918 edition of Charles and Mary Lamb's *Tales from Shakespeare*. (Illustration by Louis Rhead)

BACKGROUND

The major source for the play is *Los Siete Libros de la Diana* written by Jorge Montemayor around 1559. *Diana* was part of (and perhaps even started) a trend of pastoral literature in Spain and Portugal. Quite popular, the work was probably circulating in English in manuscripts long before the first printed English translation by Bartholomew Yong appeared in 1598. The late date of 1598 led many very early critics to argue that *The Two Gentlemen of Verona* could not have been written previously, but most now agree that the manuscript translations were likely to have reached Shakespeare. Others argue further that there is no reason why Shakespeare could not have relied on the Spanish text or an earlier French translation as his source. There is even evidence of an anonymous and now lost English court production of the story entitled *The History of Felix and Philomena*. Moreover, there is some evidence to suggest that the first performance of *The Two Gentlemen of Verona* took place in 1594–95.

The Two Gentlemen of Verona is primarily indebted to *Diana* for the Julia and Proteus plot. In *Diana Enamorada* (one of the seven books), a young woman, Felismena, dresses as a page to follow her love, Feliz, who has left her for another young woman, Celia. Celia falls in love with Felismena, as a page, and dies of a broken heart when Felismena rejects her. Charlotte Porter and Helen A. Clarke summarize the conclusion of *Diana* in their 1908 edition of *The Two Gentlemen of Verona* as follows:

> The conclusion of the story shows Celia's falling in love with the disguised page and dying of grief; Don Felix's anguish and disappearance; and the prowess shown later by the page in a combat with two knights, resulting in the rescue of Don Felix, whom they had fatally wounded; the restoration of Don Felix by magic, and his union with his doughty and faithful Felismena. From all this Shakespeare varies in every particular except the happy ending.

The need for this "happy ending" is in part what leads to the Difficulties of the Play discussed below.

For the Valentine and Proteus plot, scholars usually turn to the story of Titus and Gisippus in Boccaccio's *Decameron*. At least one critic argues that Shakespeare's source is in fact the retelling of the story in the second book of Sir Thomas Elyot's *Book of the Governor* (1531). In this story, Titus and Gisippus have been friends all their lives. When Titus falls in love with Gisippus's betrothed, the latter offers his fiancée to his friend. Gisippus, in return, confesses to a crime of which Titus has been accused. Elyot points to this story as "a right goodly example of friendship."

Date and Text of the Play

The Two Gentlemen of Verona was first published in the 1623 First Folio collection of Shakespeare's plays, compiled by members of Shakespeare's theater company after his death. Because this is the play's first appearance in print, the date when it was written and first performed is even harder than usual to ascertain. Most scholars now agree that the

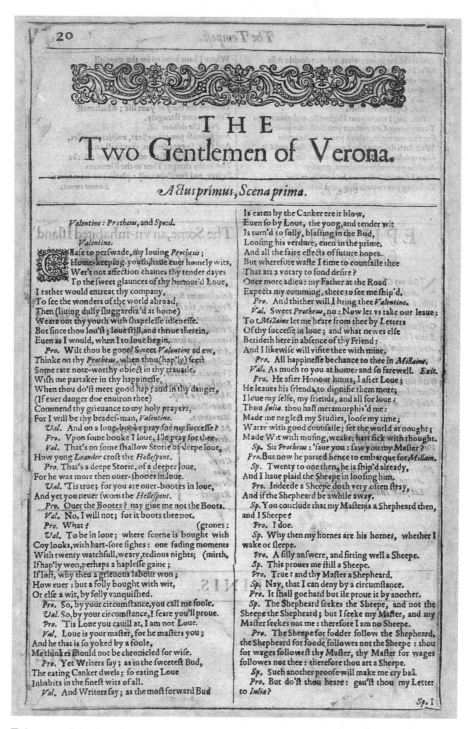

20

THE
Two Gentlemen of Verona.

Actus primus, Scena prima.

Valentine : Protheus, and Speed.

Valentine.

Ease to perswade, my louing *Protheus*;
Home-keeping-youth,haue euer homely wits,
Wer't not affection chaines thy tender dayes
To the sweet glaunces of thy honour'd Loue,
I rather would entreat thy company,
To see the wonders of the world abroad,
Then (liuing dully sluggardiz'd at home)
Weare out thy youth with shapelesse idlenesse.
But since thou lou'st; loue still,and thriue therein,
Euen as I would, when I to loue begin.

Pro. Wilt thou be gone? Sweet *Valentine* adew,
Thinke on thy *Protheus*, when thou(hap'ly) seest
Some rare note-worthy obiect in thy trauaile.
Wish me partaker in thy happinesse,
When thou do'st meet good hap; and in thy danger,
(If euer danger doe enuiron thee)
Commend thy grieuance to my holy prayers,
For I will be thy beadesman, *Valentine.*

Val. And on a loue-booke pray for my successe?
Pro. Vpon some booke I loue, I'le pray for thee.
Val. That's on some shallow Storie of deepe loue,
How yong *Leander* crost the *Hellespont.*
Pro. That's a deepe Storie, of a deeper loue,
For he was more then ouer-shooes in loue.
Val. 'Tis true; for you are ouer-bootes in loue,
And yet you neuer swom the *Hellespont.*
Pro. Ouer the Bootes? nay giue me not the Boots.
Val. No, I will not; for it boots thee not.
Pro. What?   (grones)
Val. To be in loue; where scorne is bought with
Coy looks,with hart-sore sighes : one fading moments
With twenty watchfull,weary,tedious nights; (mirth,
If hap'ly won,perhaps a haplesse gaine ;
If lost, why then a grieuous labour won ;
How euer : but a folly bought with wit,
Or else a wit, by folly vanquished.
Pro. So, by your circumstance,you call me foole.
Val. So, by your circumstance,I feare you'll proue.
Pro. 'Tis Loue you cauill at, I am not Loue.
Val. Loue is your master, for he masters you;
And he that is so yoked by a foole,
Me thinkes should not be chronicled for wise.
Pro. Yet Writers say; as in the sweetest Bud,
The eating Canker dwels; so eating Loue
Inhabits in the finest wits of all.
Val. And Writers say; as the most forward Bud

Is eaten by the Canker ere it blow,
Euen so by Loue, the yong,and tender wit
Is turn'd to folly, blasting in the Bud,
Loosing his verdure, euen in the prime,
And all the faire effects of future hopes.
But wherefore waste I time to counsaile thee
That art a votary to fond desire?
Once more adieu : my Father at the Road
Expects my comming, there to see me ship'd.
Pro. And thither will I bring thee *Valentine.*
Val. Sweet *Protheus*,no : Now let vs take our leaue:
To *Millaine* let me heare from thee by Letters
Of thy successe in loue; and what newes else
Betideth here in absence of thy Friend ;
And I likewise will visite thee with mine.
Pro. All happinesse bechance to thee in *Millaine.*
Val. As much to you at home: and so farewell. *Exit.*
Pro. He after Honour hunts, I after Loue;
He leaues his friends,to dignifie them more;
I loue my selfe, my friends, and all for loue :
Thou *Iulia* thou hast metamorphis'd me :
Made me neglect my Studies, loose my time;
Warre with good counsaile; set the world at nought;
Made Wit with musing,weake; hart sick with thought.
Sp. Sir *Protheus* : 'saue you : saw you my Master?
Pro. But now he parted hence to embarque for *Millain.*
Sp. Twenty to one then, he is ship'd already,
And I haue plaid the Sheepe in loosing him.
Pro. Indeede a Sheepe doth very often stray,
And if the Shepheard be awhile away.
Sp. You conclude that my Master is a Shepheard then,
and I Sheepe?
Pro. I doe.
Sp. Why then my hornes are his hornes, whether I
wake or sleepe.
Pro. A silly answere, and fitting well a Sheepe.
Sp. This proues me still a Sheepe.
Pro. True : and thy Master a Shepheard.
Sp. Nay, that I can deny by a circumstance.
Pro. It shall goe hard but ile proue it by another.
Sp. The Shepheard seekes the Sheepe, and not the
Sheepe the Shepheard; but I seeke my Master, and my
Master seekes not me : therefore I am no Sheepe.
Pro. The Sheepe for fodder follow the Shepheard,
the Shepheard for foode followes not the Sheepe : thou
for wages followest thy Master, thy Master for wages
followes not thee : therefore thou art a Sheepe.
Sp. Such another proofe will make me cry baâ.
Pro. But do'st thou heare? gau'st thou my Letter
to *Iulia*?

Sp. I

Title page of the First Folio edition of *The Two Gentlemen of Verona*, published in 1623 play was likely written very early in Shakespeare's career. Some even argue that it is his very first play. Typically, scholars now date the play sometime from 1590 to 1592, though early critics believed it could not have been earlier than 1598 or after, since the first printed English translation of an important source was published in 1598. However, modern critics believe a translation must have circulated in manuscript form many years before that.

SYNOPSIS
Brief Synopsis

The Two Gentlemen of Verona begins with the parting of two friends—a physical and philosophic parting, since one plans to go abroad to complete his education as a gentleman and the other plans to stay at home and embrace his role as a lover. Valentine heads off to the emperor's court in Milan (though we later find him at the Duke's court there), and Proteus stays home to woo Julia. Antonio has other plans for his son, however, and Proteus soon finds himself sailing to Milan to meet his friend. In Milan, Valentine has himself transformed into a lover and is wooing Silvia, the Duke's daughter. Proteus arrives, and Valentine's praise of Silvia enflames his heart. Soon Proteus has changed his love from Julia to Silvia and vowed to remove Valentine from Silvia's life through a cunning plan. Proteus exposes Valentine and Silvia's elopement plans to the Duke, who banishes Valentine as a result. Valentine leaves Milan and takes up with a band of outlaws in the woods. The outlaws elect Valentine their captain. Meanwhile, Julia has come to Milan dressed as a page named Sebastian in order to be near Proteus. It breaks her heart to hear his vows of love to Silvia, but she is pleased that his love object scorns him because of his inconstancy to Julia. Silvia resolves to follow Valentine into exile, and Proteus follows. When the outlaws capture everyone (except Silvia's companion, Eglamour, who runs away), they take them to their captain (who is really Valentine). Not realizing that Valentine is present but unseen, Proteus attempts to rape Silvia. Valentine reveals himself and chastises Proteus for betraying their friendship.

Proteus apologizes, and as a sign of his acceptance of that apology, Valentine offers Silvia to Proteus. Julia then reveals herself, and Proteus decides she is good enough for him. The play ends with plans for a double wedding and amity between the two couples.

Act I, Scene 1

The play opens with a farewell. In Verona, Valentine is taking leave of Proteus to go abroad to Milan. Proteus desires to stay at home, and Valentine's opening line ("Cease to persuade, my loving Proteus" 1.1.1) suggests that Proteus has just been trying to convince Valentine to stay in Verona. Valentine criticizes Proteus's choice of the position of lover, but it is clear that the two men will not agree. Valentine leaves, Proteus begins to think of himself as changed because of love, and Speed, Valentine's clown, enters with the news that Julia has received Proteus's love letter. In a witty exchange with Proteus, Speed claims that Julia must be a cruel mistress because she failed to pay him for delivering the letter.

Act I, Scene 2

In Julia's home in Verona, Julia and her waiting woman Lucetta discuss falling in love. Julia asks Lucetta's opinion of her many suitors (compare this scene to similar ones in *The Merchant of Venice* and *Romeo and Juliet*). Lucetta claims that she likes Proteus best of all of the suitors and gives Julia the letter Speed has recently delivered from Proteus. Lucetta confesses to receiving the letter on Julia's behalf, revealing that it was she who did not tip Speed (see Act I, Scene 1 above). Playing the role of proper lady, Julia refuses the letter, and Lucetta leaves. While Lucetta is off stage, Julia wonders at her waiting woman's inability to understand what it is her mistress *really* wants—to be coerced into reading the letter. When Lucetta returns, she picks up the letter she had conspicuously dropped in Julia's way, which Julia did not see, and gives it to her mistress. Julia tears the letter and asks Lucetta to leave. While Lucetta is once again off stage, Julia frantically picks up the pieces of the letter in

Julia sends Lucetta away in Act I, Scene 2 of *The Two Gentlemen of Verona,* in this print published by F. & C. Rivington in 1803. *(Illustration by Henry Fuseli; engraving by William Bromley)*

an attempt to reconstruct it. She reads bits of the letter, finding mostly the names "Proteus" and "Julia" and bringing the pieces together to "kiss" one another.

Act I, Scene 3
In Antonio's house in Verona, Panthino and Antonio discuss Proteus's future, and Panthino, supported by a conversation he has recently had with Antonio's brother, argues for sending him abroad like Valentine. Panthino argues that Proteus needs to leave home in order to complete his education as a gentleman. Antonio agrees wholeheartedly and decides to send his son after Valentine. Proteus enters reading Julia's letter but tells his father it is a letter from Valentine. Antonio, believing his son's desires to be in line with his own, reveals the plan to send Proteus abroad. Proteus agrees to go as he is bound by filial obligation, and his attempts to delay are thwarted by Antonio.

Act II, Scene 1
At the Duke's court in Milan, Speed tells Valentine that he is barely recognizable as his master because he has been so changed by love. Valentine talks sincerely of his love for Silvia, while Speed pokes fun at him. Silvia enters and asks for the letter that she has commissioned Valentine to write to her lover. Valentine produces it reluctantly, and she asks him to take it back. Speed comments upon the action in a series of asides that highlight the trick Silvia plays on Valentine in order to declare her love without risking impropriety. Silvia had asked Valentine to write the letter to one she loves, and by asking him to take the letter back, she is giving it to the one she loves. Valentine cannot see through his disappointment to the truth of Silvia's affection, and Speed must explain it to him after she leaves.

Act II, Scene 2
Back in Verona, Julia and Proteus take leave of one another. Proteus calls for Julia's patience in dealing with his absence, and she pledges it. They trade rings as a way to remember one another while they are apart. Proteus pledges "true constancy." Panthino enters to hurry Proteus along.

Act II, Scene 3
Launce reenacts parting from his family in the comic monologue that opens this scene in Verona before the ship's departure for Milan. With his shoes for parents and his staff for a sister, he shows the audience how sad they all were that he would

have to leave with his master Proteus. All except his dog, Crab, whom he portrays as lacking emotion. Panthino enters to hurry Launce along.

Act II, Scene 4

Valentine and Thurio are exchanging witty banter about Thurio's pursuit of Silvia when the Duke announces that Proteus will be joining them in Milan. Valentine praises Proteus to the Duke, claiming to know him as well as he knows himself. Everyone welcomes the newly arrived Proteus. When they are alone, Valentine reveals to Proteus his love for Silvia and tells him of the plan to elope. Proteus, alone, declares in a soliloquy that he loves Silvia even though they have just met, and he is determined to have her in spite of his friend.

Act II, Scene 5

Speed, happy to have news from home, plies Launce for information about Proteus and Julia's wedding plans. Launce plays with his words in reply. Finally, they resolve to go to the alehouse together and get a drink.

Act II, Scene 6

Proteus is alone in this scene, and he shares his plan to win Silvia. By uncovering the elopement plot, he plans to ingratiate himself with the Duke and then gain access to Silvia. Here, Proteus also discusses the competing claims of friendship and love.

Act II, Scene 7

Back in Verona, Julia tells Lucetta that she misses Proteus terribly and plans to dress as a male page to follow him to Milan. Lucetta warns Julia that Proteus may not be as happy to see her as she him, but Julia is resolved to go and recruits Lucetta to help her.

Act III, Scene 1

Proteus, claiming a sense of duty to the Duke, exposes Valentine's plan to elope with Silvia with the use of a rope ladder, but asks that the Duke not make it known that he learned this from Proteus. When Valentine enters, the Duke pretends to need wooing advice. Valentine recommends a ladder hidden under a cloak, and the Duke discovers the ladder Valentine is hiding when he asks to borrow his cloak for the purpose. The Duke banishes Valentine. Proteus encounters Valentine and promises to deliver a letter to Silvia. Launce voices his suspicions in an aside.

Act III, Scene 2

Proteus offers to help win Silvia's affection for Thurio by slandering Valentine. He also advises Thurio to put himself in the position of the poet/lover and woo Silvia with words and promises. As part of this wooing plan, Thurio and Proteus will serenade Silvia at her window that night.

Act IV, Scene 1

Valentine encounters a band of Outlaws in the woods. Rather than reveal the truth of his banishment, he tells the men that he killed someone. The Outlaws offer him the option to become their leader or be killed. He chooses the former.

Act IV, Scene 2

Proteus, alone, complains about his lack of success in wooing Silvia. In particular, it seems that the more she dislikes him, the more he wants her. Thurio meets Proteus under Silvia's window, and the musicians sing her a song. Meanwhile, Julia, dressed as a page named Sebastian, arrives and sees Proteus singing to Silvia. Thurio and the musicians leave Proteus alone beneath Silvia's window. Heartbroken, Julia watches as Proteus pledges his love to Silvia and she rejects him. Silvia promises to send him her picture and asks him to leave. During the exchange, the Host who has accompanied Julia (as Sebastian) falls asleep. She wakes him, and they return to his house where she is staying.

Act IV, Scene 3

Eglamour comes to Silvia at her command, and she tells him her plan to go in search of Valentine in Mantua. He agrees, and they plan to meet at Friar Patrick's cell that evening.

Act IV, Scene 4

This scene opens with Launce's reprimand of Crab for being an unfit gift for Silvia. Crab blatantly ignored Launce's request to model his behavior after his master's. Launce lost the lap dog that Proteus intended to send to Silvia and gave Crab in its place. When Proteus learns about the substitution (which is a big sacrifice for Launce) and Silvia's rejection of the gift, he scolds Launce and sends him to find the original dog. Proteus decides to enlist the help of Sebastian (Julia in disguise) to win Silvia. He begins by offering Silvia the ring that Julia had given him. Sebastian protests that the lady who gave the ring to Proteus is much wronged, but Proteus will hear none of it. Julia brings the ring to Silvia, who refuses it and tears up the letter that Proteus sent with the gift.

Act V, Scene 1

Eglamour and Silvia meet at Friar Patrick's cell and leave for the forest.

Act V, Scene 2

Thurio requests an update from Proteus on his wooing of Silvia on Thurio's behalf. Proteus plays with him, and Julia mocks him in asides. The Duke enters and tells Thurio, Proteus, and Julia (Sebastian) that he believes Silvia and Eglamour have run off in search of Valentine. The group leaves together to retrieve Silvia.

Act V, Scene 3

The Outlaws capture Silvia in the woods, but Eglamour escapes. Carrying her off to their captain, the First Outlaw assures Silvia that she will be safe because the captain is honorable.

Act V, Scene 4

Valentine, alone, praises the life of solitude while yearning to see Silvia again. He withdraws when Proteus, Silvia, and Julia (as Sebastian) enter. Proteus proclaims his love to Silvia and declares that he will save her. Silvia rejects Proteus's rescue and accuses him of being false. At this moment,

Julia, disguised as Sebastian, faints when she hears Valentine offer Silvia to Proteus in this 1834 depiction of Act V, Scene 4 of *The Two Gentlemen of Verona. (Painting by Richard Westall; engraving by William Humphrys)*

Proteus's pursuit turns violent, and he claims he will take her by force. Valentine comes forward to save Silvia from Proteus's attempted rape. He turns on Proteus and charges him with being a terrible friend. Proteus apologizes and, in token of his forgiveness, Valentine offers Silvia to Proteus. Julia (as Sebastian) swoons at this news and then reveals herself as Julia. Proteus realizes his error in chasing after Silvia and chooses to be constant.

The Outlaws enter with the Duke and Thurio. Thurio immediately lays a claim to Silvia, but Valentine effectively challenges him. The Duke is disgusted with Thurio's behavior, praises Valentine, and offers him Silvia in marriage. Valentine successfully petitions for the Outlaws' return from exile, and a double wedding is planned.

CHARACTER LIST

Antonio Proteus's father. On advice from his brother and Panthino, he decides to send Proteus to Milan to complete his education as a gentleman.

Duke of Milan Silvia's father. The Duke originally prefers Thurio to Valentine as a suitor for his daughter. However, by the end of the play, he accepts Valentine in Thurio's place.

Valentine One of the two eponymous gentlemen, Valentine initially rejects the image of a lover only to embrace it while he is in Milan by falling in love with Silvia, the Duke's daughter. For a time, Valentine is the captain of a band of outlaws.

Proteus Valentine's best friend and the other of the two eponymous gentlemen. Proteus proclaims himself a lover at the opening of the play in opposition to Valentine's quest to become a gentleman by going abroad. When he follows Valentine to Milan, he falls in love with Silvia.

Thurio A foolish rival to Valentine, Thurio is wealthy and the Duke prefers him for this reason. He easily gives up his suit when faced with a threat from Valentine at the end of the play, claiming "I care not for her, I" (5.4.133).

Eglamour A gentleman of the Duke's household, Sir Eglamour helps Silvia escape to find Valentine after he is banished. When the band of outlaws appears, Eglamour runs away, leaving Silvia to fend for herself in the woods with the group of strange men.

Host The Host runs the place where Julia (as Sebastian) lodges in Milan. He brings her to see Proteus and falls asleep while Proteus woos Silvia.

Outlaws A group of gentlemen banished for a variety of reasons, the Outlaws have formed a society in the forest. One outlaw is guilty of the same offense as Valentine—trying to steal away with someone's daughter. Valentine becomes their captain.

Speed Valentine's servant, who is a witty clown in the Roman style. Speed often recognizes the truth when his master cannot. In Verona, he runs an errand for Proteus.

Launce Proteus's servant, an unsophisticated clown whose own love story mockingly comments on the main plot.

Panthino A servant to Antonio, Panthino is instrumental in securing Proteus's trip to Milan. Panthino speaks to Antonio's brother, whose opinion Antonio appears to hold in high regard, and carries the brother's suggestion that Proteus go abroad.

Julia Proteus's beloved in the beginning of the play whom he trades for Silvia later. Julia also spends a good portion of the play disguised as Sebastian, a page.

Silvia Valentine's beloved, Silvia is pursued by Proteus and Thurio as well. Silvia is outspoken against Proteus's betrayal of Julia and Valentine in his pursuit of her.

Lucetta A waiting-woman to Julia, Lucetta encourages her to love Proteus.

Servants and Musicians The Musicians are present when Proteus serenades Silvia allegedly in Thurio's name. Proteus's deceit is made visible to Julia at this moment.

CHARACTER STUDIES
Proteus

Proteus's name, which comes from the shape-shifting Greek god, suggests mutability. We are introduced to Proteus as a changeable character from the very first scene of the play. Valentine exits after his unsuccessful attempt to persuade Proteus to come with him to Milan, and Proteus marvels at his own metamorphosis. He talks of himself as a man "metamorphosed" into a lover (1.1.66). However, it is not merely change that marks Proteus; his description of his transformation includes a division of the self from the self: "I leave myself, my friends, and all for love" (1.1.65). In order to love Julia, according to Proteus, he must separate himself from all that has come before—including his former self.

The split between a former Proteus and the changing Proteus becomes even clearer as the play progresses and he becomes determined to take Silvia from Valentine. By separating from himself, he separates from the subject who made the promise in the first place. He claims,

> To leave my Julia, shall I be forsworn;
> To love fair Silvia, shall I be forsworn;
> To wrong my friend, I shall be much forsworn;
> And ev'n that power which gave me my first
> oath
> Provokes me to this threefold perjury.
> Love bade me swear, and Love bids me
> forswear.
>
> (2.6.1–6)

That "power," love, urged him to give an "oath" to Julia that he now plans to forswear (that is, to renounce or abandon). Once he decides to love Silvia, he associates his identity with the self that loves her and not the self that made the promise to Julia. But he recognizes that there is something not quite right with this equation because he calls it a "threefold perjury." Just as he has changed love objects from Julia to Silvia, so must he change allegiances with the competing versions of himself.

In order to justify his actions, Proteus portrays his pursuit of Silvia as loyalty to himself:

> If I keep them, I needs must lose myself;
> If I lose them, thus find I by their loss:
> For Valentine, myself; for Julia, Silvia.
>
> (2.6.20–22)

Proteus exposes Valentine's plan to elope with Silvia to the Duke, as Valentine enters, in Act III, Scene 1 of *The Two Gentlemen of Verona*. This is a plate from Walter Crane's *Eight Illustrations to Shakespeare's Two Gentlemen of Verona*, published in 1894. *(Illustration by Walter Crane)*

To be faithful to Valentine and Julia, he must be unfaithful to himself. Here he also suggests that he will find a better version of himself if he trades his love for Valentine for his love for Silvia: "I cannot now prove constant to myself / Without some treachery used to Valentine" (2.6.31–32). Proteus thus convinces himself that taking Silvia is the best course of action.

Before he metamorphosed into a lover, who was Proteus? Who is this better person he has abandoned in his pursuit of one woman and then another? Valentine gives a glimpse of Proteus's character in a conversation with the Duke in Milan, claiming, "I know him as myself, for from our infancy / We have conversed and spent our hours together" (2.4.60–61). Criticizing himself for being an "idle truant," Valentine praises Proteus to the Duke: "His years but young, but his experience old; / His head unmellowed, but his judgment ripe" (2.4.67–68). According to Valentine, Proteus has experience beyond his years, but he is also close to perfect: "He is complete in feature and in mind / With all good grace to grace a gentleman" (2.4.71–72). Some of this praise may be above what Proteus has actually earned. Antonio was eager to send him to Milan, after all, so at least his father did not think him "complete in feature and in mind." On the other hand, Valentine's portrait of a worthy Proteus is followed directly by his friend's decision to betray Valentine for love. This juxtaposition may be meant to show that Proteus was indeed transformed by love and no longer has complete control over his own actions. It also serves to remind us that his friendship with Valentine, while once quite strong, is currently under strain.

Proteus's least attractive moment as a character is his attempted rape of Silvia in Act V, Scene 4. He begins his case by arguing that Silvia owes him just "one fair look" in recompense for saving her life (5.4.23), but his logic quickly builds through the scene until he asserts that Silvia is a cruel mistress and women are cold and uncaring: "O, 'tis the curse in love, and still approved / When women cannot love where they're beloved" (5.4.43–44). Once he categorizes Silvia as a cruel mistress, he moves seamlessly to sexual violence:

Nay, if the gentle spirit of moving words
Can no way change you to a milder form,
I'll woo you like a soldier, at arm's end,
And love you 'gainst the nature of love—
    force ye.

(5.4.55–58)

The words he has been using to convince Silvia were unsuccessful, and he decides that physical force is his only recourse. The self-justification in which Proteus engages in Act II lays the groundwork for the logic that he uses in this last scene.

After Valentine exposes Proteus and offers him Silvia, Julia reveals her disguise. It is at this moment that Proteus seems to return to some version of himself, as he laments the imperfection of men: "O heaven, were man / But constant, he were perfect!" (5.4.111–112). Proteus figures the inability to be constant as a manly trait—man's one flaw.

Valentine

Valentine's name brings immediately to mind St. Valentine, associated with lovers since at least the 14th century. The Latin root of the name means "worthy, strong, and powerful." If we take just his name, Valentine should be the hero of this play because he is both strong and a lover. Valentine does seem the more reasonable of the two young "gentlemen" of Verona when the play begins. He characterizes Proteus's choice to be in love as a choice to remain "dully sluggardized" and spend his days in "shapeless idleness" (1.1.7–8). The first discussion between the two men portrays Valentine's decision to travel in order to complete his education as a gentleman as active and masculine in contrast to the stereotypical passive and feminine courtly lover Proteus wants to become.

Although Proteus and Valentine were raised together and Valentine claims to know Proteus as he knows himself, the first scene demonstrates that the young men are on very different paths. Valentine will be going abroad to become a gentleman. Traveling, as the conversation between Antonio and Panthino makes clear, is crucial to the development of a young gentleman (see Critical Introduction to the Play); as Proteus says of Valentine after he departs, "He after honor hunts, I after love" (1.1.63).

When next we see Valentine, however, he is much changed. Speed describes his master as having the "special marks" of a lover and being prone to "weep like a young wench that had buried her grandam" (2.1.18, 22–23). Valentine has himself "metamorphosed with a mistress" (2.1.29–30) as Proteus claims he had in Act I, Scene 1. Speed, Valentine's witty servant, jumps at the chance to mock his master for this transformation (2.1).

Valentine's love of Silvia leads him to undermine the authority of the Duke, her father, by making plans to wed her secretly. The poor decision-making leads to Valentine's banishment. In his banishment, we see further mirroring of Proteus's experience because Valentine describes his banishment as a division of his self from his self: "To die is to be banished from myself. / And Silvia is myself; banished from her / Is self from self, a deadly banishment" (3.1.171–173). Valentine considers Silvia and himself to be one, and the Duke's sentence causes a split between those two parts of the self.

Whereas Proteus's split self leads him to treachery, Valentine's leads him to the Outlaws. This group of men, some of them gentlemen, has formed a society in the forest and would like Valentine to be their captain. He accepts an offer he cannot refuse because the Outlaws offer him the choice between ruling them and death (4.1.69). The solitude that the woods offer to Valentine is a welcome one. As he says, "This shadowy desert, unfrequented woods, / I better brook than flourishing peopled towns. / Here can I sit alone, unseen of any" (5.4.2–4).

Silvia

Silvia's name associates her with the forest, giving us a glimpse of the play's pastoral conclusion. Other than finding Valentine in the woods, however, Silvia herself shows little affinity with the outskirts of court. Silvia is witty and urbane. Her intelligence is clear from the first moment we see her in the play in Act II, Scene 1. Silvia's first appearance shows her negotiating expectations of behavior by declaring her love for Valentine through a subtle trick—she asks Valentine to write a letter to her lover and then asks him to take it back. In this way, Silvia can reveal her feelings to Valentine without overstepping the bounds of propriety. This first scene highlights Silvia's intelligence by contrasting it with Valentine's lack of wit. Speed must explain Silvia's subtle trick to Valentine before he understands what is happening.

Silvia, like Julia, is a constant lover, but she is also constant to her own sex. She feels an obligation to defend Julia from Proteus's infidelity even though she believes she has never met her. Silvia balances her position as an ardent defender of Julia with her romantic attachment to Valentine by remaining steadfast in both. Celia, Silvia's analogue in the *Diana*, Shakespeare's major source for the play (see Background above), falls in love with a disguise. Silvia, on the other hand, shows a friendship for the woman under the disguise. When Proteus protests his love, Silvia recommends that he return to Julia: "Return, return, and make thy love amends" (4.2.100–101). Proteus's lie that Julia is dead does

Silvia in *The Two Gentlemen of Verona*. This is a print from Charles Heath's 1848 edition of *The Heroines of Shakspeare: Comprising the Principal Female Characters in the Plays of the Great Poet. (Painting by J. W. Wright; engraving by J. Brown)*

not even sway her commitment to another woman: "Go to thy lady's grave and call hers [her love] thence" (4.2.117). Silvia chastises Proteus for being unfaithful to his love even if she had passed away. Her reprimands of Proteus make Silvia a kind of moral center in the universe of the play.

The Duke does not see his daughter as morally perfect, however. He describes his daughter as petulant and disobedient:

No, trust me, she is peevish, sullen, froward,
Proud, disobedient, stubborn, lacking duty,
Neither regarding that she is my child,
Nor fearing me as if I were her father.

(3.1.68–71)

According to the Duke, Silvia has trouble obeying authority and does not show him the duty he deserves. The power that the Duke tries to exert over Silvia would force her to marry someone she does not love. While the play seems generally to condemn the Duke's tyrannical view of Silvia's marriage choices, the fact that Valentine exercises the same power over her later in the play complicates that view somewhat.

Like Julia, Silvia leaves her father's house to follow the man she loves. Silvia's pursuit of Valentine resembles Juliet's pursuit of Romeo in *Romeo and Juliet* (Silvia meets Eglamour in a friar's cell) and Rosalind's pursuit of Orlando in *As You Like It* (she heads to the woods outside her father's court). Silvia does not dress in man's clothing like Julia or Rosalind, but she does take a companion for her safety, Sir Eglamour. Although his name suggests constancy in love, Eglamour proves to be a poor choice. The Outlaws easily scare him away, and Silvia is left unprotected in the woods.

Julia

Julia, like Silvia, shows significant range in negotiating behavioral expectations. Her first scene in the play demonstrates her skill at this negotiation. Act I, Scene 2 opens with a discussion between Julia and Lucetta about Julia's suitors. Julia asks Lucetta for advice, although in one way it appears that she has an idea of her favorite already. By requesting Lucetta's opinion, Julia expresses an aloofness that does not represent how she really feels but which does look proper. Placing Proteus's name in the middle of her list of suitors, for example, might suggest that she buries his name in order not to appear to privilege it. The 1983 BBC production of *The Two Gentlemen of Verona* plays the scene as if Julia has already decided on Proteus but goes through the motions with Lucetta in order to maintain appearances.

On the other hand, there is the suggestion that Lucetta's favoring of Proteus coupled with his letter increase his worth in Julia's eyes. Julia claims that Proteus "of all the rest, hath never moved me" (1.2.27). This line could just mean that he has

never proposed to her, but it can also mean that he has not moved her fancy. In the same way that Valentine's praise of Silvia seems to encourage Proteus's passion for her, Lucetta's praise of Proteus might do the same for Julia. Lucetta's logic is irrefutable: "I have no other but a woman's reason: / I think him so because I think him so" (1.2.23–24). Lucetta claims that Proteus seems to love Julia best (1.2.28), and she knows this because he expresses it the least: "Fire that's closest kept burns most of all" (1.2.28).

Julia disguises whatever feelings she might have behind an act of propriety when Lucetta is in the room. Julia accuses Lucetta of acting as "a goodly broker" who wishes to "whisper and conspire against [her] youth" (1.2.41, 43). But once Lucetta is off stage, the audience sees Julia's passions: "How angerly I taught my brow to frown, / When inward joy enforced my heart to smile!" (1.2.62–63). With Lucetta in the room again, Julia

Julia tears Proteus's letter in front of Lucetta in Act I, Scene 2 of *The Two Gentlemen of Verona*. This illustration was designed for a 1918 edition of Charles and Mary Lamb's *Tales from Shakespeare*. *(Illustration by Louis Rhead)*

proves her modesty by tearing Proteus's letter to shreds. Lucetta marvels at Julia's over-the-top performance: "She makes it strange, but she would be best pleased / To be so angered with another letter" (1.2.103–104). Here, Lucetta acknowledges that Julia's protestations are nothing but show; she plays the indifferent mistress, but her desire is to hear more from Proteus. Julia reveals this desire to the audience when she is once again alone on stage, picking up the pieces of the letter in an attempt to reconstruct it. She asks the wind to "blow not a word away / Till [she has] found each letter in the letter" (1.2.119–120). She brings together the pieces of the letter that have her name and Proteus's and tells them "Now kiss, embrace, contend, do what you will" (1.2.130).

In the episode with Proteus's letter, Julia disguises her feelings. When she decides to dress as a male page in order to follow Proteus, she disguises her female body (see Critical Introduction to the Play below for a discussion of early modern cross-dressing). As Sebastian, Julia will be able to move in spaces that were not previously safe for her, which links her with such heroines as Viola in *Twelfth Night* and Rosalind in *As You Like It.* Travel is acceptable for young men who wish to become gentlemen, but this is not so for young women. Julia likens being apart from Proteus to starving from want of food (2.7.15). She also suggests that trying to stem her desire to see him only makes that desire stronger: "The more thou dam'st it up, the more it burns" (2.7.24). Julia resolves to satisfy her desire by following Proteus, but she cannot go as herself:

> Not like a woman, for I would prevent
> The loose encounters of lascivious men.
> Gentle Lucetta, fit me with such weeds
> As may beseem some well-reputed page.
>
> (2.7.40–43)

Julia's decision to wear the clothes of a "well-reputed page" suggests that she is still interested in propriety. The decision to dress as a male also reveals the dangers that women faced from "lascivi-

ous men" when traveling alone. Julia's cross-dressing, however, does not necessarily mean that she takes on masculine qualities (as opposed to Portia in *The Merchant of Venice,* for example, who takes on the appearance of a man in order to be allowed to argue in court). She maintains what could be considered stereotypical femininity throughout the portion of the play she spends as Sebastian. For example, when Valentine offers Silvia to Proteus, Julia exclaims "O me unhappy!" (5.4.84) and swoons. She also refers to her disguise as only a change of clothing:

> if shame live
> In a disguise of love.
> It is the lesser blot, modesty finds,
> Women to change their shapes than men their
>   minds.
>
> (5.4.107–110)

Julia's "disguise" is one "of love," and it is merely a "change" of "shape." In opposition to Proteus's inconstancy, Julia has not changed her mind, only her appearance.

The Clowns

Launce and Speed are the two clowns in *The Two Gentlemen of Verona.* They offer both comic relief and commentary upon the main action of the plot. Launce is a country clown in the English native tradition; he is not as urbane and witty as Speed. Launce is Proteus's servant, but does not excel at this job. For example, when Proteus commands him to bring a dog to Silvia, Launce loses the dog and tries to give her his own dog, Crab, as a replacement. Launce is also quite emotional, as can be seen in his first scene on stage in which he describes his leave taking from his family: "Nay, 'twill be this hour ere I have done weeping. All the kind of Launces have this very fault" (2.3.1–2).

Launce's relationship with his dog, Crab, in many ways mirrors the other lovers' in the play. His description of parting from his parents is aimed mostly at criticizing Crab's lack of emotion. Launce accuses Crab of being "the sourest-natured dog that lives" (2.3.5), aligning him with the cruel mistress of courtly love.

Speed is a servant clown in the tradition of Roman comedy—he is witty (often more so than his master) and is often subject to physical violence. An extreme example of this violence can be seen in *The Taming of the Shrew* in the way that Petruchio treats Grumio. In the relationship between Speed and Valentine, it is Speed who helps Valentine come to understanding. For example, when Silvia declares her love for Valentine, Speed must explain to Valentine that what he has just witnessed was in fact a declaration of love (see Difficulties of the Play below for an extended discussion of this scene).

DIFFICULTIES OF THE PLAY

One of the primary difficulties for readers of the play is its ending. Many wonder how Shakespeare could allow Proteus off the hook so easily after his violent treatment of Silvia. The simple answer is that a comedy must end with at least one marriage—but this seems hardly satisfying. Proteus's only punishment is to hear about how poorly he has behaved since his arrival in Milan:

VALENTINE. Come, Proteus, 'tis your
  penance but to hear
The story of your loves discoverèd;
That done, our day of marriage shall be yours:
One feast, one house, one mutual happiness.
                                        (5.4.171–174)

The barely public shaming of Proteus (they are walking back in a group that includes the women and the Duke) hardly seems a just "penance" for his attempt to rape Silvia or, as Valentine figures it, his attempt to harm his friend's property. Today's readers often have trouble reconciling what happens before Valentine quickly forgives Proteus (5.4.77) and the ostensibly happy ending of a double wedding. The concern over the last scene is nothing new for people who encounter the play. Critics have struggled with understanding this scene since at least the 18th century. In particular, the great poet Alexander Pope claimed that Shakespeare could

not possibly have written this scene because not one of the characters seems to be behaving in the way that he or she should.

Part of Valentine's behavior can be explained by cultural differences with regard to behavioral expectations. Sir Thomas Elyot recounts the story on which the Valentine-Proteus-Silvia plot is based (see Background above) as a superior example of male friendship. Elyot introduces the story of Titus and Gisippus as follows:

But now in the middle of my labor, as it were to pause and take a breath, & also to recreate the readers, which fatigate with long precepts, desire variety of matter, or some new pleasant fable or history. I will rehearse a right goodly example of friendship. Which example studiously read, shall minister to the reader's singular pleasure, and also incredible comfort to practice amity.

Here, in the middle of Elyot's treatise on becoming a proper gentleman, he takes pause to share a story of perfect friendship. Sacrificing what one loves most is an important mark of the strong bond required by male-male friendship according to the Titus and Gisippus story Elyot tells. Thus by offering Silvia to Proteus, Valentine is proving that he has become a gentleman and understands the bonds of friendship with Proteus.

Elyot describes Titus (the Proteus character) as having "had the heart pierced with the fiery dart of Cupid: often which wound the anguish was so exceeding and vehement, that neither the study of Philosophy, neither the remembrance of his dear friend Gisippus, who so much loved and trusted him, could anything withdraw from him that unkind [as in unnatural] appetite." Titus is "wounded" by love and cannot make it go away. Gisippus's offer of his beloved is an attempt to heal his friend's wound. His sacrifice has the potential to make Titus's suffering less. Proteus shows in his soliloquies that he does not wish to suffer and will therefore do what it takes to win Silvia, but Valentine does not have access to these speeches.

He believes his friend is suffering and that it is this suffering that leads him to try to force himself on Silvia. We might then consider Valentine's offer of his beloved to be a curative move by him to help his friend.

Anyone who has visited or studied Italy will also be somewhat confused by the topography of Shakespeare's Italy in this play. Editors have long been perplexed by the trip by boat from Verona to Milan. The location of the forest somewhere between Milan and Mantua (or even perhaps Padua) is also puzzling to many. Most reconcile this confusing geography by thinking of the play as taking place in a fictional version of Northern Italy. In this fictional Northern Italy, there is an emperor's court as well as a duke's. Valentine sets off for the emperor's court in Milan, but we later find him at the Duke's court. While this seems to be an error that belies carelessness on Shakespeare's part, the critic George Steevens argued that both an emperor and a duke could have been at Milan simultaneously, and it would not have been unusual for Valentine to find service in the duke's household instead of the emperor's.

There are also two separate Eglamours in the play—one who is a suitor to Julia and the other who helps Silvia escape from the Duke's house to find Valentine in the forest. The two Eglamours are not the same, but the echoing of the name need not necessarily be a mistake. Julia and Lucetta discuss the first Eglamour in their evaluation of Julia's suitor. Lucetta thinks of him "As of a knght well-spoken, neat and fine; / But were I you, he never should be mine" (1.2.10–11). However, we never hear about this Eglamour again. Perhaps the fact that his name suggests either that he is faithful in love or that he is always in love explains why Shakespeare uses this name for one of Julia's suitors. It is also possible that the audience should be making a connection between these two Eglamours. Perhaps Lucetta's rejection of Eglamour, "he never should be mine," should signal that the second Eglamour will prove faulty in some way. Silvia's Eglamour seems at first the perfect companion, as Silvia praises him to be "Valiant, wise, remorseful, well-

accomplished" (4.3.13). Silvia needs a companion to find Valentine because the forest can be dangerous for a woman traveling alone. At the first sign of danger, however, Eglamour runs away. An Outlaw reports, "Being nimble-footed, he hath outrun us" (5.3.7). The echo of the name Eglamour may be intended as a warning to the audience that this seemingly virtuous gentleman is not the ideal companion for Silvia.

KEY PASSAGES
Act II, Scene 1, 18–34

SPEED. Marry, by these special marks: first, you have learned, like Sir Proteus, to wreathe your arms, like a malcontent; to relish a love-song, like a robin-redbreast; to walk alone, like one that had the pestilence; to sigh, like a school-boy that had lost his A B C; to weep, like a young wench that had buried her grandam; to fast, like one that takes diet; to watch like one that fears robbing; to speak puling, like a beggar at Hallowmas. You were wont, when you laughed, to crow like a cock; when you walked, to walk like one of the lions; when you fasted, it was presently after dinner; when you looked sadly, it was for want of money: and now you are metamorphosed with a mistress, that, when I look on you, I can hardly think you my master.

Speed here describes how Valentine has become a stereotypical courtly lover afflicted with love-sickness. The symptoms of lovesickness include decreased appetite, excessive sighing and weeping, and withdrawal from the society of others. The "special marks" Speed lists are characteristics typically associated with the courtly lover, and Speed mentions them in mocking tones. A "malcontent" is a person given to melancholy, one who seems never to be happy. Speed does not just say that his master seems sad, however; he tells Valentine that he has learned to "wreathe [his] arms like a malcontent." The arm-wreathing stands for the state of malcontent and in this case suggests that Valentine's malcontent involves posing. Speed compares Valentine to a robin redbreast, which was especially known for its beautiful warbling song in mating season. Speed infantilizes his master by claiming that he sighs "like a schoolboy." Valentine is prone "to walk alone," and this withdrawal from society is one that implies Valentine's education as a gentleman has come to a halt while he takes on the pose of a lover. His weeping is effeminate, according to Speed, who compares it to "a young wench that had buried her grandam." Valentine's appetite has decreased to the point of fasting. His master's voice has begun to annoy Speed, who compares it to that of a whining beggar.

Speed contrasts these "special marks" to the Valentine he knew before he was struck by love. The original Valentine expressed a very masculine identity: He was proud and confident, he fasted only when he was full, and looked sad only when he was low on money. The "metamorphosed" Valentine exhibits traits that are traditionally associated with a feminine identity: He weeps, sighs, and is withdrawn. Because Speed's mocking tone reveals that he is critical of his master's dedication to love, this speech also relates to the play's treatment of the courtly love tradition more generally. By becoming a lover, Valentine in a way consents to relinquish some portion of his masculinity, and this, according to Speed, reflects badly on his servant. As the opening scene of *Romeo and Juliet* demonstrates, servants' prowess is largely dependent on that of their masters.

Act II, Scene 4, 60–72

VALENTINE. I know him as myself, for from our infancy
We have conversed and spent our hours together;
And though myself have been an idle truant,
Omitting the sweet benefit of time
To clothe mine age with angel-like perfection,
Yet hath Sir Proteus—for that's his name—
Made use and fair advantage of his days;
His years but young, but his experience old;
His head unmellowed, but his judgment ripe;
And in a word—for far behind his worth
Comes all the praises that I now bestow—
He is complete in feature and in mind
With all good grace to grace a gentleman.

In response to the Duke's inquiry about Proteus's character, Valentine praises Proteus for his great wisdom in spite of youth. So highly, in fact, that many readers wonder if Valentine is telling the truth since his praise conflicts with Proteus's behavior throughout the play. Valentine opens by establishing his authority on the subject of Proteus, "I know him as myself," and then proceeds to praise Proteus in contrast to himself. Proteus has "made use and fair advantage of his days," whereas Valentine has "been an idle truant." This is a far cry from Valentine's critique of Proteus in the opening scene of the play, in which he accuses Proteus of staying "dully sluggardized at home" (1.1.7). Perhaps, as is suggested in Character Studies above, Valentine's praise of Proteus is a glimpse into the character before he was "metamorphosed" into a lover. Possibly, Proteus has previously proven himself to be wise beyond his years and capable of gentlemanly behavior.

Valentine may also be engaging in a rhetorical strategy intended to make himself look appealing to the Duke. By praising Proteus so highly, Valentine shows himself to be skilled at the art of male friendship. At the same time, he associates himself intimately with a worthy gentleman. By association, Valentine shows that he, too, is a worthy gentleman. The Duke's favor is in Valentine's best interest since he loves the Duke's daughter.

Act I, Scene 3, 4–16

PANTHINO. He wondered that your lordship
Would suffer him to spend his youth at home,
While other men, of slender reputation,
Put forth their sons to seek preferment out:
Some to the wars to try their fortune there,
Some to discover islands far away,
Some to studious universities.
For any or for all these exercises
He said that Proteus your son was meet,

And did request me to importune you
To let him spend his time no more at home,
Which would be great impeachment to his age
In having known no travel in his youth.

Here, Panthino reports a conversation he has had with Antonio's brother about Proteus. His report reveals not only the brother's expectations of Proteus's education but also the expectations that governed all young men of a certain social standing. Antonio's brother expresses concern for Proteus's development as a gentleman if he "spend[s] his youth at home." Panthino's description makes it clear that a young man was expected to go abroad in order to complete his education as a gentleman. He need not necessarily serve in the court of an emperor, as Valentine had planned, but he must leave home to gain experience. Elyot, in his *Book of the Governor* (see Background above), holds experience very high in his estimation of what it takes to become a gentleman. Cicero, according to Elyot, claims that experience is the "light of virtue" and is thus necessary to becoming a virtuous gentleman.

The call for Proteus to travel and gain experience is at the same time a critique of courtly love. As a male courtly lover, Proteus withdraws from society and puts his education on hold while he "spends his youth." By spending his youth in this way, he wastes it. Continuing in the pose of a lover will be a "great impeachment to [Proteus's] age" because it hinders the education that Proteus must receive in his youth to become a gentleman. Valentine later tells the Duke that Proteus has "all good grace to grace a gentleman" and is "complete in feature and in mind" (2.4.71–72). However, Antonio, his brother, and Panthino, presumably authorities on the subject as they are gentlemen themselves, see Proteus's education as incomplete.

Act II, Scene 4, 192–198

PROTEUS. Even as one heat another heat
  expels,
Or as one nail by strength drives out another,
So the remembrance of my former love
Is by newer object quite forgotten.

It is mine eye, or Valentine's praise,
Her true perfection, or my false transgression,
That makes me reasonless to reason thus.

According to a major medical theory during the early modern period, human bodies were ruled by humors. In humoral theory, gender exists on a continuum: More masculine is hot and dry, and more feminine is cold and moist. Proteus uses extremely masculine images to describe his passion for Silvia: "one heat another heat expels," and "one nail by strength drives out another." The courtly lover is usually highly feminized, and this moment of masculine language suggests a shift in Proteus's approach to love. Later, Proteus says that his "zeal

Valentine introduces Silvia to Proteus in Act II, Scene 4 of *The Two Gentlemen of Verona*. This is a plate from Walter Crane's *Eight Illustrations to Shakespeare's Two Gentlemen of Verona*, published in 1894. *(Illustration by Walter Crane)*

to Valentine is cold" (2.4.201), implying a balance that must be maintained between his bond with Valentine and the love bond. If there is heat in heterosexual desire, then there must be coldness in male-male friendship.

This speech also shows the paradoxical effect of Valentine's friendship on Proteus's emotions. Because of the strength of their bond, Valentine's praise of Silvia may in fact be responsible for Proteus's infatuation with her. Proteus admits that it could be his own "false transgression" that causes him "reasonless to reason thus," but as his speeches here and two scenes later (2.6) demonstrate, Proteus does not feel responsible in any way for his own emotions.

Act II, Scene 7, 24–43

JULIA. The more thou dam'st it up, the more
   it burns.
The current that with gentle murmur glides,
Thou know'st, being stopped, impatiently doth
   rage;
But when his fair course is not hinderèd,
He makes sweet music with th' enameled stones,
Giving a gentle kiss to every sedge
He overtaketh his pilgrimage.
And so by many winding nooks he strays
With willing sport to the wild ocean.
Then let me go and hinder not my course.
I'll be as patient as a gentle stream
And make a pastime of each weary step,
Till the last step have brought me to my love;
And there I'll rest, as after much turmoil
A blessèd soul doth in Elysium.

LUCETTA. But in what habit will you go
   along?

JULIA. Not like a woman, for I would prevent
The loose encounters of lascivious men.
Gentle Lucetta, fit me with such weeds
As may beseem some well-reputed page.

Julia compares her "love's hot fire" (2.7.21) to a current of water. In this extended metaphor (also called a conceit), Julia argues that trying to suppress her desire is like damming up the flow of water that is by nature a "gentle stream." If she is allowed to follow Proteus, her love will not "burn above the bounds of reason," as Lucetta fears (2.7.23). The beautiful imagery of this passage also suggests that being allowed to follow Proteus will open up for Julia a freedom that she will not be able to experience if she must stay at home. The current of water, when it is "not hindered," flows over rocks and barely touches the plants on its banks on its way to the "wild ocean." For Julia, following Proteus will also bring her into the society of people in Milan (an "ocean" of sorts). If allowed to travel to Milan, Julia claims that she will be "patient as a gentle stream," bearing the arduous trip virtuously. Julia implies that her temper will be impatient and difficult if Lucetta, who would bear the brunt of her mistress's raging, does not permit her to leave.

Julia's destination (Proteus) is to her what the afterlife is to a deceased person's "blessèd soul." In a secondary comparison, Julia likens the current's journey to a pilgrimage. Like a pilgrim, then, Julia's aim is to reach a place of worship. Courtly love tropes often use the language of religion to describe the lover's commitment to the beloved and to love more generally. Julia adopts the rhetoric of courtly love in the conceit that governs this passage.

For her journey to be safe, however, Julia must dress in men's clothing. Although she will be patient and gentle, she must not travel "like a woman" because the physical danger from "loose encounters" is too great. The freedom that the current of water feels when it meets with the "wild ocean" can be accessible to Julia only if she dresses as a "well-reputed page." Julia's cross-dressing is an important element of *The Two Gentlemen of Verona*.

DIFFICULT PASSAGES
Act V, Scene 4, 62–72

VALENTINE. Thou common friend, that's
   without faith or love,
For such is a friend now. Treacherous man,
Thou hast beguiled my hopes. Naught but
   mine eye

Could have persuaded me: now I dare not say
I have one friend alive; thou wouldst disprove
  me.
Who should be trusted, when one's right hand
Is perjured to the bosom? Proteus,
I am sorry I must never trust thee more,
But count the world a stranger for thy sake.
The private wound is deepest. O time most
  accurst,
'Mongst all foes that a friend should be the
  worst!

Incongruity and contradiction, as they are
embodied in Proteus's treachery, occupy Valentine
throughout this speech, which often gives people
difficulty not just because of its language but also
because of its own seeming incongruity within the
action of the play. After Proteus's attempted rape of
Silvia, Valentine is most disturbed by his betrayal
of their friendship. The passage explains Valentine's
sense of that betrayal. Proteus has "beguiled [Val-
entine's] hopes" because their friendship is based
largely on faith in one another. Valentine believed
Proteus to be a faithful friend but discovers that
he is not: "Now I dare not say / I have one friend
alive." Not only does Valentine expect good friendship from Proteus, but he is also alone without
him. The significance of this must be understood
in terms of Valentine's relationship to society. Valentine has been banished from the Duke's court.
Banishment works as a punishment because it cuts
him off from the society on which he relies. As a
man in exile, Valentine believes he still has one
link to that society: Proteus. When he, unseen,
witnesses Proteus's betrayal of him through the
attempted rape of Silvia, the full force of his exile
becomes clear. In fact, exile seems to have been
bearable precisely because Valentine could rely
on Proteus's friendship. Once he discovers that
Proteus is unfaithful, he will "count the world a
stranger" because of Proteus.

Valentine thinks of Proteus as such a close friend
that he is part of his body: "one's right hand." Valentine has believed Proteus to be his "right hand"
in the figurative sense, as a person on whom he can

rely, but there is also a sense in this speech that he
means it in a literal way as well. This literalness can
be seen a couple of lines later, as Valentine claims,
"The private wound is deepest." By calling Proteus's betrayal a "private wound," Valentine sets
their friendship in opposition to the community,
effectively merging the two as one. The incongruity of a friend who proves the worst enemy causes
Valentine much grief. He ends the speech with an
exclamation: "O time most accurst, / 'Mongst all
foes that a friend should be the worst!"

Act IV, Scene 1, 129–133

SILVIA. I am very loath to be your idol, sir.
But, since your falsehood shall become you
  well
To worship shadows and adore false shapes,
Send to me in the morning, and I'll send it.
And so, good rest.

Silvia's agreement to give Proteus her picture
often puzzles readers of the play because her language is so filled with contempt for Proteus. Her
promise to send Proteus her picture begins with
the image of an idol. Here, Silvia refers to the biblical injunction against idol worship. Silvia does not
wish to encourage Proteus's breaking of a commandment. She quickly moves from that to an
image that invokes Plato's "Allegory of the Cave"
from his *Republic,* book 7. Idols are untrustworthy
and evil because of their significant remove from
"truth." In the "Allegory of the Cave," Socrates
imagines a scene in which prisoners have lived in
an underground cave looking at "shadows" on a
wall. The prisoners believe the shadows, which are
projected onto the wall as objects pass in front of a
fire behind them, are real and try to glean meaning from them. However, these shadows are "false
shapes." Socrates then contrasts those prisoners
with the philosopher who once was a prisoner but
is now free and can see forms, which are the highest kind of reality. Silvia thus offers her picture to
Proteus as a way of pointing to his status as still a
prisoner who worships shadows removed from reality. In this way, Silvia places her knowledge above

Proteus's, criticizing him in a way that he cannot completely understand.

Act II, Scene 1, 103–142

VALENTINE. Madam and mistress, a
  thousand good morrows.

SPEED. [*Aside*] O, give ye good ev'n! Here's a
  million of manners!

SILVIA. Sir Valentine and servant, to you two
  thousand.

SPEED. [*Aside*] He should give her interest,
  and she gives it him.

VALENTINE. As you enjoined me, I have
  writ your letter
Unto the secret, nameless friend of yours,
Which I was much unwilling to proceed in
But for my duty to your ladyship.
[*Gives a letter*]

SILVIA. I thank you, gentle servant. 'Tis very
  clerkly done.

VALENTINE. Now trust me, madam, it came
  hardly off,
For, being ignorant to whom it goes,
I writ at random, very doubtfully.

SILVIA. Perchance you think too much of so
  much pains?

VALENTINE. No, madam. So it stead you, I
  will write—
Please you command—a thousand times as much.
And yet—

SILVIA. A pretty period! Well, I guess the
  sequel—
And yet I will not name it—and yet I care
  not—
And yet take this again—and yet I thank you,
Meaning henceforth to trouble you no more.

SPEED. [*Aside*] And yet you will; and yet
  another "yet."

VALENTINE. What means your ladyship? Do
  you not like it?

SILVIA. Yes, yes. The lines are very quaintly
  writ,
But since unwillingly, take them again.
Nay take them.
[*Gives back the letter*]

VALENTINE. Madam, they are for you.

SILVIA. Ay, ay, you writ them, sir, at my
  request,
But I will none of them. They are for you—
I would have had them writ more movingly.

VALENTINE. Please you, I'll write your
  ladyship another.

SILVIA. And when it's writ, for my sake read
  it over,
And if it please you, so; if not, why, so.

VALENTINE. If it please me, madam, what
  then?

SILVIA. Why, if it please you, take it for your
  labor—
And so, good morrow, servant.

SPEED. O jest unseen, inscrutable, invisible,
As a nose on a man's face, or a weathercock on
  a steeple!

Readers of the play are often as confused by Silvia's subterfuge as Valentine himself is. Silvia's father, the Duke, has accepted Valentine into his household to attend him. This arrangement puts Valentine at Silvia's disposal. Silvia asked Valentine to write a love letter for her to another man. Valentine wrote the letter, as duty would require him to do, but he did so reluctantly because he himself is in love with Silvia. When he reveals his reluctance to her, she feigns anger and tells him to keep the letter if he wrote it so "unwillingly." In this way, she has delivered the love letter to its intended recipient. But, she goes further and asks him to write another letter and "read it over." This second letter will be the continuation of a communication with her beloved (Valentine). Valentine is fortunate that Speed is present because he explains Silvia's intentions to his master.

This scene also shows the importance of Speed both to Valentine and to the audience. His role in the letter trick is to be sure that the audience understands what Silvia is doing, even though Valentine seems unable to. He uncovers the comedy of the moment: "That my master, being scribe, to himself should write the letter!" (2.1.135). But Speed does not merely comment on the action, as in his "jest unseen" comment, he also criticizes the rhetoric of love in which Valentine and Silvia engage. Speed likens Silvia's doubling of Valentine's "good morrows" to a monetary exchange, where compliments become goods. Speed also mocks Silvia's overuse of "yet," which signals a turn in the speaker's meaning. Because Silvia repeats "yet" over and over, her language is turning around in a circle.

CRITICAL INTRODUCTION TO THE PLAY

The Two Gentlemen of Verona tells the story of two young men who must learn to bring together friendship and romantic love in order to participate fully in their roles as "gentlemen." The concepts that govern the play, such as courtly love, education, and the conflicting demands of friendship and romantic love, are relevant to the journey of becoming a complete gentleman. What follows is a discussion of each of these components, as well as of another crucial feature of the play—cross-dressing.

Courtly Love

Shakespeare often treats the subject of courtly love (other examples are *Romeo and Juliet, A Mid-* *summer Night's Dream, The Merchant of Venice, Twelfth Night,* and the Sonnets), and his take on it is rarely positive. *The Two Gentlemen of Verona* is no exception here. Proteus plays the stereotypical courtly lover in the opening scene of the play—he is "metamorphosed," "over boots in love," neglecting his studies, "Made wit with musing weak, heart sick with thought" (1.1.66, 25, 67, 69). A courtly lover was usually wasting away with hunger, neglectful of his everyday life and friends, and feminized. His love is frequently unrequited, and the mistress is portrayed as cruel. Proteus describes courtly love poetry in his advice to Thurio: "Say that upon the altar of her beauty / You sacrifice your tears, your sighs, your heart" (3.2.72–73).

The poet who exemplifies this tradition is Francesco Petrarch (1304–74), whose *Il Canzoniere* (in English, "Songbook") contains 366 poems in praise of his beloved, Laura. Poets who adopt Petrarchan conceits often do so in praise of a Petrarchan mistress who displays the characteristics associated with this kind of love poetry. In *Romeo and Juliet,* Romeo (in a way that is clearly meant to invite mockery) uses a series of paradoxical Petrarchan conceits when he talks of his love for Rosaline. The Petrarchan mistress has eyes like the sun, rosy cheeks, alabaster skin, flowing locks of hair (usually blond), and beautiful teeth. Mocking this ideal becomes almost as commonplace as the ideal itself was for a short time (as can be seen in the illustration of literal beauty below). In a later play, *As You Like It,* Shakespeare will explore what it means to write bad love poetry as a way of criticizing the tradition. The Sonnets, on the other hand, participate in the tradition even as they critique it (for example, the anti-Petrarchan Sonnet 130 is part of the same sequence as the moving Sonnet 18).

Launce's character is a vehicle for mocking these elements of courtly love. Launce's first complaints about Crab figure the dog as a type of cruel mistress (2.3.1–31). Crab is "the sourest-natured dog that lives" who "has no more pity in him than a dog" (2.3.5–6, 10). In Milan, Launce reveals that he, too, is secretly in love: "He lives not now that knows me to be in love, yet I am in love" (3.1.263–264). Reminding the audience of his relationship with Crab, Launce compares his beloved to a dog: "She hath more qualities than a water spaniel" (3.1.269–270). Love letters are a crucial part of the relationships between the two main sets of lovers (Proteus and Julia and Valentine and Silvia), and Launce's possession of a catalog of the milkmaid's "condition" is a comical interrogation of the meaning of those letters (3.1.272). The excessive praise of courtly love wooing is reduced to an itemized list. Speed reads each "Item" from the list of the milkmaid's characteristics, with witty comments for each one.

In addition to its similarity to a love letter, Launce's paper also connects the courting of a woman to an exchange of goods because it is an itemized list like a catalog of goods. The connection exposes one of the main characteristics of male-female courtship: Among the upper class, when it comes down to it, marriage is primarily a business arrangement. The Duke's interest in Thurio's wealth stems from the expectation that marrying his daughter off should bring with it some benefit. The tradition of courtly love wooing denies this business transaction while at the same time sup-

porting it. Proteus recommends that Thurio court Silvia with "wailful sonnets, whose composèd rhymes / Should be full-fraught with serviceable vows" (3.2.69–70). Thurio will not be successful, Proteus suggests, if he relies merely on the Duke's preference for him. Shakespeare explores the idea of a father's preference in *A Midsummer Night's Dream,* but in that play, the daughter is the one who will be most severely punished for resisting her father's will.

Education of a Gentleman

Panthino outlines the importance of travel to becoming a gentleman in his conversation with Antonio in Act I, Scene 3. Educating sons properly was extremely important to early modern parents, especially because of the way that inheritance worked in early modern England. Since the first-born son was to inherit all of the family's wealth and lands, it was important to ensure his good handling of that inheritance. As discussed above in Key Passages, experience is crucial to the education of a young gentleman. Books such as Thomas Elyot's *Book of the Governor* (see Background above) sought to instruct parents in the raising and education of the future men of power, and these books argue that experience is crucial to that education. In order for a man to become a gentleman in spirit and not only in birth, he must have the experience of history (in other words, he must know about what has come before) and of encounters with the world. Only through this experience will a man be able to know true virtue and embody it. However, the mere fact of travel is not enough to make a man into a gentleman. According to Richard Braithwaite in his 1630 *The English Gentleman* (see Introduction above), travel can help only a man who is willing to make a change in his "disposition." To become a gentleman, a young man must remain open to transformation, weighing virtues against vices. Experience has the potential to show him the difference between virtues and vices, but it is only through the young man's mindful interpretation of experience that the ability to distinguish can be honed.

Speed reads Launce's letter in this 19th-century depiction of Act III, Scene 1 of *The Two Gentlemen of Verona. (Illustration by John Gilbert; engraving by William Luson Thomas)*

While Proteus's transformation from gentleman to lover to deceiver is not necessarily a positive one in the play, there is a sense that change is essential to the human experience. When Valentine leaves to go to Milan, he is determined to gather the experience required to be a gentleman, but he does not permit the possibility that he might change while he is abroad. In the first scene of the play, Valentine worries about his friend's subjection to love: "Love is your master, for he masters you; / And he that is so yokèd by a fool / Methinks should not be chronicled for wise" (1.1.39–41). The next time that Valentine appears on stage, his "life is altered now," as he later tells Proteus (2.4.126). Part of Valentine's education, then, is learning to be open to modification in his behavior. Almost all of the major characters in the play change in some way: Julia dresses as a boy, Proteus is ever changing, and Silvia transforms from a disobedient daughter to an obedient beloved (an example of this is that she does not speak when Valentine offers her to Proteus).

Proteus declares that men are imperfect only in their inconstancy ("were man / But constant, he were perfect!" 5.4.111–112), which suggests that there is something natural about man's inconstancy. Change is part of human experience, and it is a positive part of man's experience (as the discussion of Braithwaite's *English Gentleman* above shows). However, here, Proteus suggests that malleability is man's one flaw. Proteus's claim is surprising because in humoral theory (see Key Passages above), temperamental inconstancy falls on the feminine side of the continuum of gender characteristics. For Aristotle, whose teachings were very influential in Shakespeare's time, constancy is crucial to the practice of virtue. Early modern literature portraying romantic relationships nevertheless frequently explores the concept of man's inconstancy in contrast to woman's constancy. For instance, Amphilanthus, a male character in Lady Mary Wroth's prose romance, *The Countess of Montgomery's Urania,* learns the value of constancy through the constant example of the virtuous woman who loves him, Pamphilia. The implication in *The Two Gentleman of Verona* may be that learning constancy is one of the rarely

discussed steps to becoming a gentleman, but that it is the most important one. After all, as Proteus makes clear, constancy is all that man is missing in his quest for perfection.

Cross-dressing

Cross-dressing in early modern England was particularly controversial in the late 16th and early 17th centuries, and this can be seen in the numerous debates in print about the evils of not dressing in accordance with cultural expectations of a person's gender and class. In this debate, women were accused of seizing masculine power by wearing "breeches," and men were criticized for ceding such power by dressing like "fops." There were sumptuary laws, which were statutes that dictated how subjects should dress according to their class and gender. Additionally, some communities punished any behavior that seemed to cross the boundary between man and woman with public shaming. These codified restrictions suggest that perhaps there were people who were ignoring or flouting the norms. Theater was an unsettling example of dressing outside of one's station, for average men dressed as kings, and boys dressed as women.

Julia dresses as a male page to make her search for Proteus a safe one. Lucetta does not worry that Julia will somehow develop a penchant for inappropriate behavior; she worries only that her poor mistress might have to cut her hair. Julia quells Lucetta's fear, "No, girl, I'll knit it up in silken strings" (2.7.45), and they then begin the process of planning Sebastian's outfit. The purpose of her trip is a heterosexual union with Proteus and therefore is not necessarily an example of seizing masculine privilege. Even though she appears to be a young man by the way she is dressed, Julia remains stereotypically feminine throughout the play. Unlike Portia in *The Merchant of Venice,* who dresses as a man in order that she may have her arguments heard in court, Julia does not have an interest in the masculine privilege of public speech. Julia wants to protect her virginity because it is the most important asset she has as a young gentlewoman. Her behavior throughout her time as Sebastian demonstrates Julia's normative heterosexual desire, as she continually reminds the audience that her heart is breaking as she watches Proteus's treachery.

Conflict between Love and Friendship

The friendship between Proteus and Valentine, based as it is in early modern expectations of the devotion of male friends to one another, is almost destroyed by a conflict over romantic love. Competing demands govern the logic of the connection between romantic, male-female love that leads to marriage and homosocial, male-male friendship that leads to good government. In terms of the worldview of Shakespeare's time, bonds between men are required to make a society ruled by men

work properly, thus male friendship is extremely important to the continued function of that society. Male-female marriage, on the other hand, is required to produce heirs to that society. In order to live up to cultural ideals, these two kinds of human relationship should work in concert. Because male-male friendship requires behavior that is in direct opposition to male-female romance, however, these ideals are difficult to realize.

For instance, Valentine offers Silvia to Proteus as a sign of his true friendship (5.4.83). A friend who offers his beloved, lauded as it is by Thomas Elyot in his *Book of the Governor*'s retelling of "Titus and Gisippus" (see Background above), is entirely consistent with the expectations of friendship between men. Contrarily, Valentine's offer of Silvia does not at all fit with the expectations of the male-female romantic bond. Silvia's silence does not necessarily imply her joyful reaction. As can be seen in Modern Criticism and Critical Controversies below, Shakespeare may in fact be revealing the absurdity of the competition between these social bonds. Making these two competing bonds work together is the challenge that the aspiring gentleman faces, and Shakespeare may hint that it is in fact an insurmountable challenge.

EXTRACTS OF CLASSIC CRITICISM

Alexander Pope (1688–1744) [Excerpted from his edition of Shakespeare's plays (1723–25). Alexander Pope, best known as the poet of "The Rape of the Lock" and other classics, was also a literary critic whose edition of Shakespeare was very influential.]

> It is observable (I know not for what cause,) that the style of this comedy is less figurative, and more natural and unaffected, than the greater part of this author's, though supposed to be one of the first he wrote.

Thomas Hanmer (1647–1746) [Excerpted from his early edition of Shakespeare's plays (1744). The first passage is Hanmer's introductory note to

Julia reveals herself to Proteus, Silvia, and Valentine in Act V, Scene 4 of *The Two Gentlemen of Verona*. This is a print from the Boydell Shakespeare Gallery project, which was first conceived in 1786 and lasted until 1805. *(Painting by Thomas Stothard; engraving by John Ogborne)*

The Two Gentlemen of Verona, and the second is from his discussion of the last scene of the play.]

It may very well be doubted whether Shakespear had any other hand in this play than the enlivening it with some speeches and lines thrown in here and there, which are easily distinguished, as being of a different stamp from the rest.

෫෩ ෫෩ ෫෩

This passage either hath been much sophisticated or is one great proof that the main parts of this Play did not proceed from Shakespear: for it is impossible He could make Valentine act and speak so much out of character; or give to Silvia so unnatural a behavior as to take no notice of this declaration if it had been made.

Samuel Johnson (1709–1784) [Excerpted from the introductory and concluding notes to *The Two Gentlemen of Verona* in *The Plays of William Shakspeare* (1765). Samuel Johnson was crucial both to the preservation of Shakespeare's works and to literary criticism more generally.]

To this observation of Mr. Pope, which is very just, Mr. Theobald has added, that this is one of Shakspeare's *worst plays, and is less corrupted than any other.* Mr. Upton peremptorily determines, *that if any proof can be drawn from manner and style, this play must be sent packing, and seek for its parent elsewhere. How otherwise,* says he, *do painters distinguish copies from originals? And have not authors their peculiar style and manner, from which a true critic can form as unerring judgement as a painter?* I am afraid this illustration of a critic's science will not prove what is desired. A painter knows a copy from an original by rules somewhat resembling those by which critics know a translation, which if it be literal, and literal it must be

to resemble the copy of a picture, will be easily distinguished. Copies are known from originals, even when the painter copies his own picture; so, if an author should literally translate his work, he would lose the manner of an original.

Mr. Upton confounds the copy of a picture with the imitation of a painter's manner. Copies are easily known; but good imitations are not detected with equal certainty, and are, by the best judges, often mistaken. Nor is it true that the writer has always peculiarities equally distinguishable with those of the painter. The peculiar manner of each arises from the desire, natural to every performer, of facilitating his subsequent work by recurrence to his former ideas; this recurrence produces that repetition which is called habit. The painter, whose work is partly intellectual and partly manual, has habits of the mind, the eye, and the hand; the writer has only habits of the mind. Yet, some painters have differed as much from themselves as from any other; and I have been told, that there is little resemblance between the first works of Raphael and the last. The same variation may be expected in writers; and if it be true, as it seems, that they are less subject to habit, the difference between their works may be yet greater.

But by the internal marks of composition we may discover the author with probability, though seldom with certainty. When I read this play, I cannot but think that I find, both in the serious and ludicrous scenes, the language and sentiments of Shakspeare. It is not indeed one of his most powerful effusions; it has neither many diversities of character, nor striking delineations of life; but it abounds in [Greek: gnomahi] beyond most of his plays, and few have more lines or passages, which, singly considered, are eminently beautiful. I am yet inclined to believe that it was not very successful, and suspect that it has escaped corruption, only because, being seldom played, it was less exposed to the hazards of transcription.

☙ ☙ ☙

In this play there is a strange mixture of knowledge and ignorance, of care and negligence. The verification is often excellent, the allusions are learned and just; but the author conveys his heroes by sea from one inland town to another in the same country; he places the emperor at Milan, and sends his young men to attend him, but never mentions him more; he makes Protheus, after an interview with Silvia, say he has only send her picture; and, if we may credit the old copies, he has by mistaking places, left his scenery inextricable. The reason of all this confusion seems to be, that he took his story from a novel, which he sometimes followed, and sometimes forsook, sometimes remembered, and sometimes forgot.

That this play is rightly attributed to *Shakespeare* I have little doubt. If it be taken from him, to whom shall it be given. This question may be asked of all the disputed plays, except *Titus Andronicus;* and it will be found more credible that *Shakespeare* might sometimes sink below his highest flights, than that any other should rise up to his lowest.

George Steevens (1736–1800) [Excerpted from his edition of the plays, *The Works of Shakespeare with the Corrections and Illustrations of Various Commentators* (1773), on which he collaborated with Samuel Johnson.]

Some of the incidents in this play may be supposed to have been taken from *The Arcadia,* Book I. chap. 6. Where Pyrocles consents to head the Helots. (*The Arcadia* was entered on the books of the Stationers' Company, Aug. 23d, 1588.) The love-adventure of Julia resembles that of Viola in *Twelfth Night,* and

is indeed common to many of the ancient novels.

☙ ☙ ☙

Shakspeare has been guilty of no mistake in placing the emperor's court at Milan in this play. Several of the first German emperors held their courts there occasionally, it being, at that time, their immediate property, and the chief town of their Italian dominions. Some of them were crowned kings of Italy at Milan, before they received the imperial crown at Rome. Nor has the poet fallen into any contradiction by giving a duke to Milan at the same time that the emperor held his court there. The first dukes of that, and all the other great cities in Italy, were not foreign princes, as they afterward became; but were merely governors or viceroys, under the emperors, and removable at their pleasure. Such was the *Duke of Milan* mentioned in this play.

William Hazlitt (1778–1830) [Excerpted from *Characters of Shakespear's Plays* (1817). *Characters* was the first affordable full-length criticism of Shakespeare's works. The essayist Hazlitt was one of the most important Shakespearean critics of his time.]

This is little more than the first outlines of a comedy loosely sketched in. It is the story of a novel dramatized with very little labor or pretension; yet there are passages of high poetical spirit, and of inimitable quaintness of humor, which are undoubtedly Shakespeare's, and there is throughout the conduct of the fable, a careless grace and felicity which marks it for his. One of the editors (we believe Mr. Pope) remarks in a marginal note to the *Two Gentlemen of Verona*—"It is observable (I know not for what cause) that the style of this comedy is less figurative, and more natural and unaffected than the greater part of this author's, though supposed to be one of the first he wrote." Yet so little does the editor appear to have made up his mind upon this subject, that we find the following note to the very next (the second) scene. "This whole scene, like many others in these plays (some of which I believe were written by Shakspeare, and others interpolated by players) is composed of the lowest and most trifling conceits, to be accounted for only by the gross taste of the age he lived in: *Populo ut placerent*. I wish I had authority to lease them out, but I have done all I could, set a mark of reprobation upon them, throughout this edition." It is strange that our fastidious critic should fall so soon from praising to reprobating. The style of the familiar parts of this comedy is indeed made up of conceits—low they may be for what we know, but then they are not poor, but rich ones. The scene of Launce with his dog (not that in the second, but that in the fourth act) is a perfect treat in the way of farcical droller and invention; nor do we think Speed's manner of proving his master to be in love deficient in wit or sense though the style may be criticized as not simple enough for the modern taste.

 ✌ ✌ ✌

The tender scenes in this play, though not so highly wrought as in some others, have often much sweetness of sentiment and expression. There is something pretty and playful in the conversation of Julia with her maid, when she shows such a disposition to coquetry about receiving the letter from Protheus; and her behavior afterwards and her disappointment, when she finds him faithless to his vows, remind us at a distance of Imogen's tender constancy. Her answer to Lucetta, who advises her against following her lover in disguise, is a beautiful piece of poetry.

> LUCETTA. I do not seek to quench
> your love's hot fire,
> But qualify the fire's extremest rage,

Lest it should burn above the bounds of reason.

> JULIA. The more thou damm'st it up,
> the more it burns;
> The current that with gentle murmur
> glides,
> Thou know'st, being stopp'd, impa-
> tiently doth rage;
> But when his fair course is not hindered,
> He makes sweet music with th' enamell'd
> stones,
> Giving a gentle kiss to every sedge
> He overtaketh in his pilgrimage.
> And so by many winding nooks he strays,
> With willing sport, to the wild ocean.
> Then let me go, and hinder not my
> course;
> I'll be as patient as a gentle stream,
> And make a pastime of each weary step,
> Till the last step have brought me to my
> love;
> And there I'll rest, as after much
> turmoil,
> A blessed soul doth in Elysium, . . .

If Shakspeare indeed had written only this and other passages in the *Two Gentlemen of Verona*, he would *almost* have deserved Milton's praise of him—

> And sweetest Shakspeare, Fancy's child,
> Warbles his native wood-notes wild.

But as it is, he deserves more praise than this.

Algernon Charles Swinburne (1837–1909)

[Excerpted from *A Study of Shakespeare* (1880). Swinburne, best known as a poet, was also an interesting critic.]

What was highest as poetry in the *Comedy of Errors* was mainly in rhyme; all indeed, we might say, between the prelude spoken by

Ægeon and the appearance in the last scene of his wife: in *Love's Labour's Lost* what was highest was couched wholly in blank verse; in the *Two Gentlemen of Verona* rhyme has fallen seemingly into abeyance, and there are no passages of such elegiac beauty as in the former, of such exalted eloquence as in the latter of these plays; there is an even sweetness, a simple equality of grace in thought and language which keeps the whole poem in tune, written as it is in a subdued key of unambitious harmony. In perfect unity and keeping the composition of this beautiful sketch may perhaps be said to mark a stage of advance, a new point of work attained, a faint but sensible change of manner, signalised by increased firmness of hand and clearness of outline. Slight and swift in execution as it is, few and simple as are the chords here struck of character and emotion, every shade of drawing and every note of sound is at one with the whole scheme of form and music. Here too is the first dawn of that higher and more tender humour which was never given in such perfection to any man as ultimately to Shakespeare; one touch of the by-play of Launce and his immortal dog is worth all the bright fantastic interludes of Boyet and Adriano, Costard and Holofernes; worth even half the sallies of Mercutio, and half the dancing doggrel or broad-witted prose of either Dromio. But in the final poem which concludes and crowns the first epoch of Shakespeare's work, the special graces and peculiar glories of each that went before are gathered together as in one garland "of every hue and every scent."

Edward Dowden (1843–1913) [Excerpted from *Shakespere* (1879). Dowden was a literary critic, poet, and professor of English. He is perhaps most well known for his controversial biography of Percy Shelley and his acquaintance with W. B. Yeats.]

The Two Gentlemen of Verona, though in parts slightly worked out, exhibits an advance on the preceding comedies. The *Errors* was a clever tangle of diverting incidents, with a few passages of lyric beauty, and one of almost tragos pathos; *Love's Labour's Lost* was a play of glittering and elaborate dialogue. In *The Two Gentlemen of Verona* Shakspere struck into a new path, which he was to pursue with admirable results; it is his earliest comedy in which a romantic love-story is told in dramatic form. Here first Shakspere records the tender and passionate history of a woman's heart, and the adventures to which love may prompt her. Julia (who is like a crayon sketch of Juliet, conceived in a way suitable to comedy instead of tragedy) is the first of that charming group of children of Shakspere's imagination which includes Viola, Portia, Rosalind, and Imogen—women who assume, under some constraint of fortune, the disguise of male attire, and who, while submitting to their transformation, forfeit none of the grace, modesty, the sensitive delicacy, or the pretty wilfulness of their sex. Launce, accompanied by his immortal dog, leads the train of Shakspere's humorous clowns: his rich, grotesque humanity is "worth all the bright, fantastic interludes of Boyet and Adriano, Costard and Holofernes," worth all the "dancing doggerel or broad-witted prose of either Dromio." The play contains a number of sketches, from which Shakspere after worked out finished pictures . . . The characters are clearly conceived, and contrasted with almost too obvious a design: The faithful Valentine is set over against the faithless Proteus; the bright and clever Silvia is set over against the tender and ardent Julia; the clown Speed, notable as a verbal wit and nibbler, is set over against the humorous Launce.

The general theme of the play we may define as love and friendship, with their mutual relations. The *dénouement* in act V, if written by Shakspere in the form we now have

Julia in *The Two Gentlemen of Verona*. This is a print from Charles Heath's 1848 edition of *The Heroines of Shakspeare: Comprising the Principal Female Characters in the Plays of the Great Poet*. (Painting by A. Egg; engraving by W. H. Egleton)

it, is a very crude piece of work. Proteus' sudden repentance, Valentine's sudden abandonment to him of Silvia, under an impulse of extravagant friendship ("all that was mine in Silvia I give thee;" 5.4.83), and Silvia's silence and passiveness whilst disposed of from lover to lover are, even for the fifth act of a comedy, strangely unreal and ill-contrived. Can it be that this fifth act has reached us in an imperfect form, and that some speeches between Silvia and Valentine have dropped out? The date of the play cannot be definitely fixed; but its place among the comedies is probably after *Love's Labour's Lost*, and before *A Midsummer Night's Dream*. The language and verse are

characterised by an even sweetness; rhymed lines and doggerel verses are lessening in number; the blank verse is written with careful regularity. It is as if Shakspere were giving up his early licenses of versification, were aiming at a more refined style (which occasionally became a little tame), but being still a novice in the art of writing blank verse, were timid, and failed to write it with the freedom and "happy valiancy" which distinguish his later manner. The story of *The Two Gentlemen of Verona* is identical in many particulars with *The Story of the Shepherdess Felismena*, in the Spanish pastoral romance, *Diana*, by George of Montemayor; but though manuscript translations of *Diana* existed at an earlier date, no translation was published before that of Yonge, in 1598. The story had probably been dramatised before Shakspere's play, for we read in the accounts of the revels of *The History of Felix and Philomena*, acted before her Highness in 1584. Valentine's consenting to become captain of the robbers has been compared with a somewhat similar incident in Sidney's *Arcadia*, but the coincidences are slight, and it may be doubted that Shakspere had any thought of the *Arcadia*.

[Excerpted from *Shakespere: A Critical Study of His Mind and Art* (1875).]

The Two Gentlemen of Verona, a comedy of graceful mirth and sprightly and tender feeling. . . .

In *The Two Gentlemen of Verona*, while Julia standing by disguised hears her faithless lover devoting himself to Silvia, the Host falls sound asleep. This is quite as it should be. The world is not all made for passionate young gentlemen and ladies.

MODERN CRITICISM AND CRITICAL CONTROVERSIES

The Two Gentlemen of Verona does not inspire as much scholarly attention as do some of Shakespeare's other comedies, such as *The Merchant of Venice* and *Measure for Measure*. The attention the play does get tends to concentrate around a few key issues. These include authorship, the play's worth as an object of study, poetry, friendship between males, and cross-dressing.

Authorship

Many early critics concentrate on whether Shakespeare wrote *The Two Gentlemen of Verona*. Some argue that he wrote only parts, while others claim that the text as we have it is a corruption of Shakespeare's now lost original. This tradition in the scholarship is exemplified by the early editor Thomas Hanmer, who claimed, "It may very well be doubted whether Shakespear had any other hand in this play than the enlivening it with some speeches and lines thrown in here and there, which are easily distinguished, as being of a different stamp from the rest." Later critics, such as Edward Dowden, saw in the play early attempts at some of the devices Shakespeare later uses expertly, which suggests that the play must be Shakespeare's in its entirety. While scholars in the late 20th and early 21st centuries rarely doubt that Shakespeare wrote the play, much writing about the play is haunted by allegations of the play's "illegitimacy."

The Play's Worth as an Object of Study

Modern critics have spent quite a bit of energy to rescue the play from earlier critics' negative assessments and, by extension, the fate of obscurity. There are competing visions of the success of this energetic effort. June Schleuter writes, "*The Two Gentlemen* has yet to redeem itself from a largely scornful—even polarizing—critical history, which, from the start, characterized the play as the work of a crude, unpolished youth, who had thematic ideas and dramatic ideals he was as yet unable to realize." Even critics who saw the work as one of Shakespeare's could not attribute to it much more than a few beautiful lines embedded in plot devices that are much more successful in later plays.

Most critics agree that this play serves as a testing ground for many of the themes and situations of Shakespeare's later plays. Julia's cross-dressing seems an early attempt at Rosalind's in *As You Like It*, Silvia and Valentine's elopement resembles the elopement of Romeo and Juliet in *Romeo and Juliet*, the exchange of rings and later betrayal of that exchange brings to mind a similar exchange in *The Merchant of Venice*, Lucetta is a prototype of both Nerissa in *The Merchant of Venice* and the Nurse in *Romeo and Juliet*, and even Launce and Speed can be said to be early tries for the more developed clowns of *The Winter's Tale* and *Twelfth Night*. One can see many of the episodes from *The Two Gentlemen of Verona* in a number of later plays. The mere fact of the repetition of motifs and devices, however, does not necessarily mean that the play is underdeveloped.

Marjorie Garber, for example, warns us not to sell *Two Gentlemen* short, calling it "a lively and often funny play, which contains, among its other assets, a genuinely comic early clown and one of the most beautiful lyric songs in all of Shakespeare" (43–44). Garber's analysis combines many of the positive aspects of the play that are scattered throughout hundreds of years of criticism, and it turns those positive aspects into more than just anomalies.

Poetry

The "beautiful lyric song" to which Garber refers is the song used to serenade Silvia in Act IV, Scene 2: "Who is Silvia? What is she, / That all our swains commend her?" (4.2.39–40). Written in Sicilian Quintains (5-line stanzas, in iambic pentameter, with an ababa rhyme scheme), the song praises Silvia's virtues through a description of her as a Petrarchan mistress who excels even that ideal (see Critical Introduction to the Play for a discussion of Petrarch). The beauty of the song led to its musical setting by Franz Schubert in the 19th century. Some claim that Schubert's 1826 "An Sylvia" "is one of the greatest song settings of Shakespeare."

Frank Kermode echoes early criticisms of the play by calling it "a slight work" and ceding only that "it has many pretty verses." These "pretty verses" are for Kermode the only good thing about the play. He asserts that the characters are nothing more than a series of childish pairs without substance: two lovers, two women, and two servants. Since Shakespeare's language is often Kermode's focus, his assertion that the play contains "pretty verses" seems not the worst verdict. Unfortunately, Kermode's dismissal portrays the "pretty verses" as a peculiar characteristic of an otherwise forgettable play.

Male-Male Friendship

According to many scholars, *The Two Gentlemen of Verona* is primarily concerned with representing the relationship between love and friendship. S. Asa Small, in a 1933 essay about the conclusion of the play, writes, "The friendship theme, though greatly emphasised, is, after all, only a strong framework to motivate the love story." Heterosexual love triumphs over homosocial friendship in the play's central conflict between the two social bonds. Stephen Guy-Bray, on the other hand, sees the romantic relationship as "a function of, and to some extent subordinate to, the homosociality that dominates the world of the play." By the conclusion of the play, according to Guy-Bray, we see that the male-female romantic relationship "takes a great deal of work." The ending, then, is meant to show the tide against which lovers must fight to live up to the ideal of marriage.

Just as students, audiences, and directors struggle with the concluding scene of the play (see Difficulties of the Play and The Play Today), so do scholars. Michael Friedman, in his *The World Must Be Peopled: Shakespeare's Comedies of Forgiveness*, argues

a more complex portrayal of the Forgiven Comic Hero [Proteus], one that gives equal weight to his vices and virtues, can elucidate the ways in which an overvaluation of male bonds creates problems for women in heterosexual relationships, and an ironic attitude toward male follies can also prevent

such an emphasis from becoming oppressive or polemical.

For Friedman, Proteus's complexity is purposeful and should remain. Readers are supposed to feel uncomfortable in the concluding scene so that they can create an ironic distance from the "male follies" the scene shows.

Camille Slights Wells argues that it is in fact a "comic exploration of the nature and function of a gentleman." In her article, she looks at courtesy books from the 16th century as the models from which Shakespeare would have been working in the crafting of these two gentlemen. The conclusion of the play "fills personal emotional needs and indicates their renewed acceptance of their place in civilized society where men are bound together by mutual trust as well as by civil authority." In Wells's argument, then, Valentine and Proteus must reconcile in order to complete their education as gentlemen and become "the two gentlemen of Verona."

Valentine saves Silvia from Proteus's attempted rape while Julia, disguised as Sebastian, looks on in Act V, Scene 4, of *The Two Gentlemen of Verona*. This is a print from the Boydell Shakespeare Gallery project, which was first conceived in 1786 and lasted until 1805. *(Painting by Maria Angelic Kauffmann; engraving by Luigi Schiavonetti)*

Cross-dressing

Writing in 1915, Victor Oscar Freeburg looks to continental and earlier English models for Shakespeare's use of the female character dressed as a male page. The tradition is not only a well-established one, according to Freeburg, but it is also one that enhances the femininity of the character: "Starting from medieval French romance, and threading her way through the novels or plays of Italy, the heroine in doublet and hose at last reached the England of Shakespeare, where she became the most graceful and charming figure on the stage." Jean Howard, in her landmark essay about cross-dressing and early modern theater, does not address Julia's assumption of the clothing of a male page, but her assessment of *Twelfth Night*'s Viola applies here as well. According to Howard, Viola, although dressed as Cesario, displays "a properly feminine subjectivity; and this fact countervails the threat posed by her clothes and removes any possibility that she might permanently aspire to masculine privilege and prerogatives."

Julia's cross-dressing and Silvia's outspokenness are often grouped together in feminist readings of the play. Silvia repels Proteus through the use of assertive speech, which many (including her own father, the Duke) associate with disobedient women. Women who use speech, the argument goes, are like women who seize male privilege and prerogative in other ways. In the world of the play, however, Silvia's speech is heroic because the play (and by extension the audience) agrees with her refusal and chastisement of Proteus.

THE PLAY TODAY

Students and theatergoers today are still disturbed by the play's ending. Performances of the play have dealt with this conclusion in a number of ways. Many productions of the 18th century, for example, left the attempted rape and offer of Silvia out completely. Late-20th-century productions tend to make an attempt to reconcile this disturbing moment with the actions of the play. In describing a 1990 production by Charles Newell, Jean Peterson claims "Julia's appalled, ironic response to their self-absorbed bonding gives release and expression to the audience's own." Newell's production uses Julia to comment on the exchange between Proteus and Valentine, which makes the moment more bearable in some sense.

David Thacker's 1991 Royal Shakespeare Company production of the play, set in the 1930s, also comments on the play's end. Exposing the game of masculinity for what it seems to be, Thacker's production features physical encounters between Proteus and Valentine. In the concluding scene, Valentine wrestles Proteus to stop his rape of Silvia. According to Paul Nelson, this shows "the sporting manners of a class whose clubby members are more concerned with preserving and entertaining themselves than they are with adjudicating matters of morality." Like Newell's, Thacker's production treats the relationship between the two young men as one deserving of a certain amount of contempt. Another way to deal with the problem of this last scene is to deny it importance. Elizabeth Ingram's 2010 production at Syracuse University does this by running through the offer of Silvia fairly quickly.

Newell moves the two gentlemen to the 1950s, and Thacker to the 1930s, but director Arne Pohlmeier takes an entirely different approach by setting the play in Zimbabwe. In her *Vakoma Vaviri Ve Zimbabwe* (2008), Proteus and Valentine court the same woman, and Valentine is banished. This production concentrates on the Proteus/Valentine/Silvia plot as a way of highlighting the strains that can be put on friendship and the experience of exile. Critic Kate Jackson lauds the production for treating "alienation, exile, power struggles and making them resonate anew with the sound of the Zimbabwean experience." Pohlmeier's adaptation of *The Two Gentlemen of Verona* is thus very relevant for Zimbabweans.

Readers tend to feel contempt for Valentine and Proteus in the last scene of the play, but the conflict between homosocial and heterosexual bonds is one that rings true for many of today's students. Popular films and magazines often ask how one can do well at male-male friendship *and* male-female romance simultaneously. For example, the central conflict of the television show *Dawson's Creek* is that between friendship and love for a number of seasons. In 2000, an episode entitled "Two Gentlemen of Capeside" refers directly to *The Two Gentlemen of Verona*, because the two young men in the show are reading it in their high school English class. The episode uses the play as a thematic cipher to highlight the rivalry between the two young men that centers on a young woman.

The play is not as frequently performed in the theater as many of Shakespeare's other plays. The critic Michael Feingold, in a discussion of Kate Marshall's revival of Mel Shapiro and John Guare's musical production of the play in Central Park in 1971, claims, "Nobody has ever been particularly happy with Shakespeare's notoriously flawed early play, a study in the unreliabilities of love and friendship." But, Feingold asserts, the musical is like "cheap champagne" and "can still induce a pleasantly woozy feeling." And for some, the play will still do this as well.

Associating itself with the current vogue for the "bromance," another production of the musical version of *The Two Gentlemen of Verona,* directed by Irene Lewis (2004–05), updated the play to include references to laptops, cell phones, and even former president George W. Bush. Lewis's vision for the musical, which also includes contemporary music, suggests that there is a desire to make the play more relevant for today's audiences.

Shakespeare in Love, the 1998 film directed by John Madden, contains a performance of *The Two Gentlemen of Verona* before Queen Elizabeth I. Much of the action of the scene takes place backstage during the performance, but snippets of the play's language drift in. Viola de Lesseps, the female lead in the film and Will Shakespeare's love interest, is not only visibly moved by Valentine's declaration of love for Silvia after he has been banished by the Duke, but she also seems to know it by heart:

What light is light if Silvia be not seen?
What joy is joy, if Silvia be not by?

Unless it be to think that she is by
And feed upon the shadow of perfection.

(3.1.174–177)

This appearance of the play demonstrates the power of some of its poetry. Viola and her Nurse, in a scene that brings to mind that between Julia and Lucetta, evaluate the performance later that evening: Viola says she dislikes the character of Silvia because a "pipsqueak boy" plays the role.

FIVE TOPICS FOR DISCUSSION AND WRITING

1. **Disguise:** There are a number of different kinds of disguise operating simultaneously in this play. Some examples are that Proteus disguises his true intentions from Valentine, Julia dresses as a male page to follow Proteus, and Silvia and Valentine disguise their love for one another to keep it from her father. Disguise in these cases can function as a means of deceiving another person, but it can also function as a way of discovering the truth about another person. How do the various disguises in the play hide or reveal truths about the characters that don them? What are some of the different kinds of disguises characters use?

2. **Courtly love:** The stereotypical courtly lover wastes away while pining for his (usually unrequited) love; he also sometimes writes poetry expressing his suffering. First Proteus and then Valentine become in some ways stereotypical courtly lovers in this play. However, both of their relationships to the stereotype are fraught with difficulty. For example, Proteus easily transfers his supposed never-ending love from Julia to Silvia, and Valentine does not languish as much as one would expect when he is separated from Silvia. Might each of these characters be a comment on the idea of courtly love? How do Valentine and Proteus wear the concept of the "courtly lover" differently? Is this difference somehow related to their characters more generally?

3. **Friendship:** There are three main sets of friends in the play: Proteus and Valentine, Speed and

Launce, and Julia and Silvia. Proteus and Valentine are the characters in the play with the most standing and the most power. Speed and Launce are surrogates for Valentine and Proteus in one sense because they reflect their masters' power. Julia and Silvia, on the other hand, are friends who are not both aware of their dedication to one another because Silvia knows *of* Julia, but knows only Sebastian. What are some of the characteristics of these different friendships? What role does the gender or social station of these characters play in the kind of friendships in which they engage?

4. **The woods:** When the Duke banishes him, Valentine heads into the woods on his way to Mantua. While he is there, he meets a band of outlaws, who have presumably organized themselves into an ordered society of a sort. What are some of the "ordered" elements of the Outlaws' group? Is there a suggestion that they are not as noble as they present themselves? How does their conscription of Valentine into the role of captain comment on the ways that characters in the play persuade other characters in the play to do things? In what way do Outlaws reflect on the behavior of the Duke's court?

5. **Fathers:** The fathers of this play both loom large and fade into the background. What are some of the similarities and differences between Antonio (Proteus's father) and the Duke (Silvia's father)? What do these similarities and differences tell us about the characters who are the children of these men? What do they tell us about the ways each household functions?

Bibliography

Atkinson, Dorothy F. "The Source of *Two Gentlemen of Verona*." *Studies in Philology* 41 (1944): 223–234.

Bergeron, David Moore. "Wherefore Verona in *The Two Gentlemen of Verona*?" *Comparative Drama* 41, no. 4 (2007): 423–438.

Berggren, Paula S. "'More grace than boy': Male disguise in *The Two Gentlemen of Verona*." In *Love's Labor's Lost; The Two Gentlemen of Verona; The Merry Wives of Windsor,* edited by John Arthos, Bertrand Evans, and William Green, 195–203. New York: Signet, 1988.

Bowden, Betsy. "Latin Pedagogical Plays and the Rape Scene in *The Two Gentlemen of Verona*." *English Language Notes* 41, no. 2 (2003): 18–32.

Bradbrook, M. C. "Courtier and Courtesy: Castiglione, Lyly, and Shakespeare's *Two Gentlemen of Verona*." In *Theatre of the English and Italian Renaissance,* edited by J. R. Mulryne and Margaret Shewring, 161–178. New York: St. Martin's, 1991.

Bradbury, Malcolm, and David Palmer, eds. *Shakespearean Comedy.* Stratford-upon-Avon Studies 14. New York: Cran, Russak, 1972.

Braunmuller, A. R. "Characterization through Language in the Early Plays of Shakespeare and His Contemporaries." In *Shakespeare, Man of the Theater,* edited by Kenneth Muir, Jay L. Halio, D. J. Palmer, and Samuel Schoenbaum, 128–147. Newark; London: University of Delaware Press; Associated University Presses, 1983.

———. "'Second means': Agent and Accessory in Elizabethan Drama." In *The Elizabethan Theatre, XI,* edited by A. L. Magnusson and C. E. McGee, 177–203. Port Credit, Ont.: P. D. Meany, 1990.

Brooks, Harold F. "Two Clowns in a Comedy (to Say Nothing of the Dog): Speed, Launce (and Crab) in *The Two Gentlemen of Verona*." *Essays and Studies* 16 (1963): 91–100.

Carroll, William C. "'And Love You 'gainst the Nature of Love': Ovid, Rape, and *The Two Gentlemen of Verona*." In *Shakespeare's Ovid: The Metamorphoses in the Plays and Poems,* edited by A. B. Taylor, 49–65. Cambridge: Cambridge University Press, 2000.

———. *The Metamorphoses of Shakespearean Comedy.* Princeton, N.J.: Princeton University Press, 1985.

Cole, Howard C. "The 'full meaning' of *The Two Gentlemen of Verona*." *Comparative Drama* 23, no. 3 (1989): 201–227.

Evans, Bertrand. *Shakespeare's Comedies.* Oxford, England: Clarendon, 1960.

Feingold, Michael. "Voices Choices: Theater: Reviving Verona: Guare's 'Two Gentlemen,' 34 Years Later:

Have the Preservatives Done Something to the Flavor?" *Village Voice,* 31 August 2005–6 September 2005, 68.

Freeburg, Victor Oscar. *Disguise Plots in Elizabethan Drama.* New York: Columbia University Press, 1915.

Friedman, Michael. *The World Must Be Peopled: Shakespeare's Comedies of Forgiveness.* Madison, N.J.: Fairleigh Dickinson University Press, 2002.

Garber, Marjorie. *Shakespeare after All.* New York: Random House, 2004.

Gay, Penny. *The Cambridge Introduction to Shakespeare's Comedies.* Cambridge: Cambridge University Press, 2008.

Godshalk, William L. "The Structural Unity of *Two Gentlemen of Verona.*" *Studies in Philology* 66 (1969): 168–181.

Guy-Bray, Stephen. "Shakespeare and the Invention of the Heterosexual." *Early Modern Literary Studies: A Journal of Sixteenth- and Seventeenth-Century English Literature* 16, no. 12 (October 2007): 1–28. Available online. URL: http://purl.oclc.org/emls/si-16/brayshks.htm. Accessed May 10, 2011.

Howard, Jean. "Crossdressing, The Theatre, and Gender Struggle in Early Modern England." *Shakespeare Quarterly* 39 (1988): 418–440.

Kermode, Frank. *The Age of Shakespeare.* Modern Library Chronicles. New York: Modern Library, 2004.

Kiefer, Frederick. "Love Letters in *The Two Gentlemen of Verona.*" *Shakespeare Studies* 18 (1986): 65–85.

Leech, Clifford, ed. *The Two Gentlemen of Verona.* London: Methuen, 1969.

Lenz, Carolyn Ruth Swift, Gayle Greene, and Carol Thomas Neely, eds. *The Woman's Part: Feminist Criticism of Shakespeare.* Urbana: University of Illinois Press, 1980.

Lindenbaum, Peter. "Education in *The Two Gentlemen of Verona.*" *Studies in English Literature* 15 (1973): 229–244.

Partridge, Eric. *Shakespeare's Bawdy.* London: Routledge, 1968.

Pearson, D'Orsay W., and William Godshalk. *Two Gentlemen of Verona: An Annotated Bibliography.* Garland Shakespeare Bibliographies 16. New York: Garland, 1988.

Perry, Thomas A. "Proteus, Wry-transformed Traveller." *Shakespeare Quarterly* 5, no. 1 (1954): 33–40.

Sargent, Ralph M. "Sir Thomas Elyot and the Integrity of *The Two Gentlemen of Verona.*" *PMLA: Publications of the Modern Language Association of America* 65, no. 6 (1950): 1,166–1,180.

Scheye, Thomas E. "Two Gentlemen of Milan." *Shakespeare Studies* 7 (1974): 11–24.

Schlueter, June, ed. *Two Gentlemen of Verona: Critical Essays.* New York: Garland, 1996.

Slights, Camille Wells. "The Two Gentlemen of Verona and the Courtesy Book Tradition." *Shakespeare Studies* 16 (1983): 13–31.

Small, Samuel Asa. "The Ending of *The Two Gentlemen of Verona.*" *PMLA: Publications of the Modern Language Association of America* 48, no. 3 (1933): 767–776.

Tillyard, E. M. W. *Shakespeare's Early Comedies.* New York: Barnes & Noble, 1965.

Weimann, Robert. "Laughing with the Audience: *The Two Gentlemen of Verona* and the Popular Tradition of Comedy." *Shakespeare Survey: An Annual Survey of Shakespeare Studies and Production* 22 (1969): 35–42.

Wells, Stanley. "The Failure of *The Two Gentlemen of Verona.*" *Silliman Journal* 99 (1963): 161–173.

Zimmerman, Susan, ed. *Erotic Politics: Desire on the Renaissance Stage.* London: Routledge, 1992.

FILM AND VIDEO PRODUCTIONS

Dawson's Creek: The Complete Fourth Season. DVD. Sony Pictures Home Entertainment, 2004.

Madden, John, dir. *Shakespeare in Love.* DVD. Miramax Home Entertainment, 1998.

Taylor, John, dir. *The Two Gentlemen of Verona,* DVD. The Complete Dramatic Works of Shakespeare, British Broadcasting Corporation. New York: Ambrose Video Publishing, 2000.

—Jessica C. Murphy

The Two Noble Kinsmen

INTRODUCTION

The Two Noble Kinsmen occupies a curious place in the Shakespeare canon. It is significant in that it contains probably the last words Shakespeare ever wrote for the stage. However, the play is not entirely Shakespeare's own but actually the result of a collaboration with the younger playwright John Fletcher (1579–1625), who was most famous for working with Francis Beaumont on plays such as *Philaster, A King and No King,* and *The Maid's Tragedy. The Two Noble Kinsmen* represents a kind of literary handing over of the reins, as Fletcher would take over Shakespeare's job as playwright for the theater company The King's Men after Shakespeare's retirement. Since the play was not included in Shakespeare's First Folio of 1623, many early critics questioned whether Shakespeare was involved in the play at all, but few scholars today doubt Shakespeare's role.

The play has never been considered Shakespeare's masterpiece, but it is well worth studying. Shakespeare's plays are often talked about in terms of their author's genius, rarity, and exceptional talent—the plays themselves are often read as works of unmatched genius exceeding the artistic expectations of their age and any other. Yet plays like *The Two Noble Kinsmen* allow the readers to see fascinating and often underplayed aspects of Shakespeare's work. Though most of Shakespeare's plays draw from other literary sources, *The Two Noble Kinsmen* is one of the few to draw from another English author whose reputation would have far exceeded that of Shakespeare in Shakespeare's time:

Geoffrey Chaucer (1343–1400). Chaucer was for Renaissance authors the great exemplar of what an English author could hope to be. As one of the first writers in England to actually write in English, and as a pioneer of iambic pentameter, Shakespeare's preferred meter, Chaucer was behind many of the literary innovations that made Shakespeare's work so exceptional within the English literary canon. In *The Two Noble Kinsmen,* Shakespeare takes on one of Chaucer's greatest works, "The Knight's Tale," the first and longest tale in Chaucer's celebrated *Canterbury Tales.* The play, then, represents the literary meeting of two great minds of early English literature.

Furthermore, the play explores many of the political and personal issues that were at the forefront of the Renaissance, such as the nature of political power, romantic love, and same-sex friendship, as well as more abstract concerns, such as the tensions between interiority and exteriority and confinement and freedom. Many critics find the play experimental, somewhat modern, in comparison with Shakespeare's other, earlier works. Rather than offering a dramatic plot driving toward a tragic or comic resolution, the play instead provides a far more ambiguous dramatic experience in which tragedy and comedy become fascinatingly and at times problematically linked.

BACKGROUND

Shakespeare's collaborator on the play, John Fletcher, was an important and revered playwright of his day, but one who is rarely discussed outside

The first page of Chaucer's "The Knight's Tale" from the 14th-century Ellesmere Manuscript

of academic circles these days. He is perhaps most famous for being the playwriting partner to Francis Beaumont. The two men collaborated on many plays, such as *The Maid's Tragedy, A King and No King,* and *Philaster,* which were quite popular in the early decades of the 17th century. On his own, however, Fletcher was also an accomplished writer, writing the unpopular at the time though somewhat revolutionary play *The Faithful Shepherdess* a few years before collaborating with Shakespeare on *The Two Noble Kinsmen.* Fletcher's style in *The Faithful Shepherdess* is fascinating, and he certainly brought some of it into *The Two Noble Kinsmen.* The plot centers around a shepherdess Clorin, who, like Emilia, mourns a dead love and vows never to marry:

> Hail, holy earth, whose cold arms do embrace
> The truest man that ever fed his flocks
> By the fat plains of fruitful Thessaly!
> Thus I salute thy grave; thus do I pay
> My early vows and tribute of mine eyes
> To thy still-lovèd ashes; thus I free
> Myself from all ensuing heats and fires
> Of love . . .
> (*The Faithful Shepherdess* Act I, Scene 1)

Though the Shepherdess grieves for a dead man, not a woman, the thematic parallels between Clorin and Emilia are clear: Both prefer chastity to love, and both in the end become victims to the irrational love and jealousy of male characters around them. Fletcher was himself interested in bringing the stage into a more elevated and moral place. The Renaissance stage was often considered a place of bawdy excess, immoral spectacles of sexuality and violence, and generally an offering for the masses rather than the literary elite. John Fletcher, like Ben Jonson and Shakespeare, wanted to elevate the stage to literary and moral heights it had rarely seen before. This project, reaching its apotheosis in the 1610s, almost certainly includes *The Two Noble Kinsmen* among its ranks.

The exact division of who wrote what scene in the play has been a major critical question for cen-turies. Walter Cohen, in the Norton edition of the play, summarizes what many scholars believe is the best guess:

> Shakespeare probably wrote a little less than half the play: 1.1–2.1 (though some scholars give Fletcher 1.4–1.5), perhaps 2.3, 3.1, perhaps 3.2, perhaps 4.3, 5.1.34–5.3 (although 5.2 is sometimes attributed to Fletcher), and 5.5–5.6. These attributions are necessarily tentative, given the likelihood that the plan of the play changed a bit in the course of the composition and that Fletcher undertook some revisions to bring the play to its final form— perhaps of Shakespeare's text, perhaps of his own in light of Shakespeare's sections. (3211)

This play then is, most likely, at best only half or so the work of Shakespeare. Throughout this entry, one may see phrases such as "Shakespeare writes . . ." or "Shakespeare emphasizes," but one must always remember in dealing with *The Two Noble Kinsmen* that this is a collaborative work, always containing the influence and words of two distinct authors. In the end, the best the scholar or reader can do is appreciate the product of the interplay of these great minds in the absence of being able to definitively separate their work.

The main plot of *The Two Noble Kinsmen* comes quite faithfully from Geoffrey Chaucer's "The Knight's Tale," a work derived its plot from Boccaccio's *Teseida.* Shakespeare and Fletcher most likely read Chaucer's work in a 1598 edition (a revised edition was also available in 1602) entitled *The Workes of Our Antient and Learned English Poet, Geffrey Chaucer* that was edited by Thomas Speght (Waithe 26). The story of Palamon and Arcite in this play and in Chaucer is quite close, with one of the main differences coming in the intensity of Palamon and Arcite's love for each other. In Chaucer, the details of their friendship are not deeply explored, and their major characteristic is their rivalry over Emilia. Shakespeare and Fletcher, then, must have had a special interest in enhancing their friendship in their version, a fact not surprising given the play's profound interest in the politics of same-sex friendship.

Date and Text of the Play

The play is probably the last that can be attributed to Shakespeare, dating from late 1613 to early 1614, just a few years before the playwright's death in 1616. Some scholars believe that the reference to "our losses" in the Prologue (l. 32) is a reference to the burning of the Globe Theater, which occurred on June 29, 1613. Many of the play's generic elements suggest an affinity with the plays in the last phase in Shakespeare's career—a period known less for grand tragedies than comedies and more for tragicomedies, a genre imported from Italy that combined tragic and comedic elements. Often, as is the case with *The Two Noble Kinsmen*, these works feature death and romantic coupling as important plot elements, confusing the boundaries between tragedy (which usually ends in death) and comedy (which usually ends in marriage).

This play does not appear in any 17th-century folios bearing Shakespeare's name. Folio publications were intended to be large collections that would establish an author's reputation by preserving the best copies possible, at least in theory, of an author's work to preserve it for posterity. Ben Jonson, another famous English Renaissance playwright, had famously published a folio of his own work in 1616, and Shakespeare's First Folio had been released in 1623. *The Two Noble Kinsmen*, though performed around 1613 or 1614, does not appear in this publication but did appear in a quarto edition in 1634, with a title page that reads: "THE TWO NOBLE KINSMEN: Presented at the Blackfriers by the Kings Majesties servants, with great applause: Written by the memorable Worthies of their time: Mr. John Fletcher and Mr. William Shakespeare, Gentlemen." In 1679, the play was published in an edition entitled *Fifty Comedies and Tragedies, Written by Francis Beaumont and John Fletcher, Gentlemen*. In this publication, the play is attributed to Fletcher but not to Shakespeare. The basis for most modern editions of the text is the 1634 quarto edition.

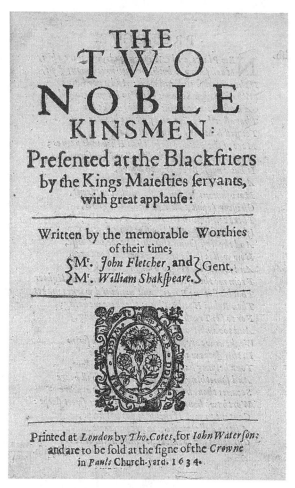

Title page of the 1634 quarto of *The Two Noble Kinsmen*

SYNOPSIS
Brief Synopsis

The play begins with the entrance of the Prologue who compares new plays to maidenheads, noting that both are long sought after by many people at great cost. The Prologue, however, notes that a good play can be renewed again and again while a maidenhead is gone after its first enjoyment. After declaring Geoffrey Chaucer to be the "noble breeder" of the plot of the play, the Prologue declares the bold ambition of undertaking a play based on the work of so noble a poet and hopes that in the end the audience approves of the play.

Act I begins with a wedding procession for Theseus and Hippolyta. The procession is interrupted by three queens whose husbands were killed when they unsuccessfully attacked Thebes, a city led by King Creon. Creon had forbidden the bodies of the slain to be buried, and the Queens ask Theseus to intervene on their behalf. Though wanting originally to wait until after the marriage ceremonies, Theseus is eventually convinced to leave immediately to attack Thebes. The play then shifts to Thebes where Palamon and Arcite are reflecting on how Thebes has decayed since they were young. They blame Creon for this, because of his injustice and cruelty, and resent their familial bond with him. During their critique of Creon, they are interrupted by Valerius who informs them that Thebes is under attack by Theseus and they must rush to fight. The plot then shifts to Emilia who, in chatting with Hippolyta about the friendship between Pirithous and Theseus as well as between Emilia and Flavina, asserts that she will never marry. Back outside Thebes, Theseus has been victorious. As they are celebrating their victory, a herald brings in Palamon and Arcite who, though still breathing, have been badly wounded. Theseus takes them as prisoners back to Athens. Act I ends with the three queens giving their kings the proper funerary rites they had been denied by Creon.

Act II begins with a conversation between Palamon and Arcite's Jailer and a wooer interested in the Jailer's Daughter. As they discuss a possible match, the Jailer's Daughter enters, reporting how noble and impressive she finds Palamon and Arcite, who are rumored to have fought bravely in the battle. Palamon and Arcite are left alone in their cells. In this celebrated and famous scene, the two men discuss their sadness over never being able to leave prison, but they eventually take comfort in their intimate relationship, seeing their close bond as a safe space that will hide them from the corruption of the world. This bond, however, is disrupted when Palamon, and then Arcite, spy Emilia and her servant woman below them. Palamon declares his love for her to Arcite, who falls in love with her himself upon seeing her. As they quarrel, they are interrupted by the Jailer who pulls Arcite out of their prison cell because Pirithous convinced Theseus to banish him forever rather than keep him in prison. Arcite leaves the cell, and Palamon is made to leave the areas near the windows where they saw Emilia. Arcite is next seen alone grieving over his banishment, angry that he will never be able to see Emilia again. Running into some countrymen on their way to perform for the Duke, Arcite decides to go in disguise to the performance so he can see Emilia again. Arcite presents himself as a wrestler and runner to Theseus who is impressed with his service. Meanwhile, the Jailer's Daughter has fallen in love with Palamon and has released him from prison, bringing him out into the woods.

In a forest outside of Athens, Arcite and the newly escaped Palamon run into each other and start quarreling over Emilia. Their fighting is passionate, reflecting both their past affection and their current infatuation with Emilia. The Jailer's Daughter, meaning to bring Palamon a file to get rid of his chains, cannot find him and assumes he has been killed—an assumption that makes her suicidal and insane. Arcite feeds Palamon and brings him files so he can be ready to fight with him to settle the score over Emilia. Meanwhile, the Jailer's Daughter, by this point quite mad, has been found by the schoolmaster and the countrymen who need a woman to perform with them. They all perform for Theseus, Hippolyta, Emilia, and others who are all pleased with it. Palamon and Arcite, elsewhere, are now ready to fight, and though they hear the Duke coming, Palamon is too heated to delay the fight further. They are both caught by Theseus, and the fight is broken up. They ask to be able to fight each other over Emilia and then be allowed to be killed. In the end, however, Emilia seeks further pardon and asks for their lives, eventually agreeing to marry the winner of the fight.

Act IV begins in the prison where the Jailer finds out that he will not be executed for his daughter's allowing Palamon to escape, because Palamon has secured his pardon. However, he discovers how truly mad his daughter has become over her love for Palamon. Emilia, meanwhile, gazes at pictures of Palamon and Arcite, finding that she cannot make a firm choice over which she prefers. They prepare for the fight. Meanwhile, a doctor examining the Jailer's Daughter decides that the wooer must disguise and present himself as Palamon to her in order to win her heart and cure her of her madness.

Act V begins with the preparations for the fight. Arcite leads his three knights in a prayer to Mars, the god of war. Palamon then leads his three knights in a prayer to Venus, the goddess of love. Emilia then enters dressed in white carrying a silver hind full of incense, materials for the prayer she then leads to Diana, the virgin huntress. As the fight begins, initially a cry of "A Palamon" is heard, but in the end, Arcite is the victor and wins Emilia. However, as Palamon grieves that his knights and he lost and must die, news comes that Arcite has fallen off a horse and is near death. Arcite, seeing Palamon, tells him to take Emilia. Arcite dies, Palamon and the others go off to Arcite's funeral and eventually the wedding between Palamon and Arcite. In the end, an Epilogue enters the stage, fearing the audience did not much like this ending but hopes that they in some way were contented with it. The play ends with the Epilogue wishing the audience goodnight.

Prologue

After a flourish, the character who speaks the Prologue, named Prologue in later editions of the play, enters and compares new plays to maidenheads in that they are both pursued for a long time, with a lot of money spent to acquire them. The Prologue states that plays, however, unlike maidenheads can spring back again and again to new life after being purchased as they hope this play will. Continuing the reproductive metaphor, the Prologue asserts that there is a good breeder behind the play, the play's main influence Geoffrey Chaucer, who is "of all admired." The Prologue recognizes the bold ambition of bringing a story from so beloved an author to the stage and admits that if they fail they will have to give up acting.

Act I, Scene 1

A boy in a white robe enters singing, followed by Hymen carrying a burning torch, and after Hymen, a nymph bearing a wheaten garland, making up the beginning of a wedding procession. Theseus, the groom, then enters flanked by nymphs, while Hippolyta, the bride, enters with Pirithous, a friend of Theseus. The boy sings a wedding song. The procession is then interrupted by three Queens who complain that their Kings, slain in a failed attempt to conquer Thebes, have gone unburied because of the cruelty of Creon, the king of Thebes. With some coaxing from Hippolyta and Emilia, Theseus agrees to go immediately to conquer Thebes and redress the wrong done to their husbands.

Act I, Scene 2

Arcite and Palamon are in Thebes, discussing their shame and frustration over the state of the city, which has decayed under the rule of their uncle King Creon. They resent their close relationship to him, with Palamon wishing that "The blood of mine that's sib to him be sucked / From me with leeches. . . ." As they lament the state of Thebes, Valerius, a Theban, enters to tell them that the city is at war with Theseus and they must leave to fight.

Act I, Scene 3

Hippolyta and Emilia send their good wishes to Theseus through Pirithous, who is on his way to join Theseus at Thebes. After he leaves, Emilia and Hippolyta discuss the close friendship that Theseus and Pirithous enjoy. In discussing this friendship, Emilia brings up her own past friendship with Flavina, which, though she admits not as intense as that between Theseus and Pirithous, was still quite intimate. The scene ends with Emilia asserting, despite Hippolyta's doubts, her intentions never to marry.

Act I, Scene 4

After the battle, Theseus enters victorious. The three Queens celebrate, while a Herald enters bringing in Palamon and Arcite, unconscious though alive. Their performance in the battle has been impressive, and Theseus decides that they are more valuable as prisoners than dead, so they are carried back to Athens.

Act I, Scene 5

The three Queens, recently having recovered their husband's bodies, perform the funeral rites for them.

Act II, Scene 1

Palamon and Arcite's Jailer is seen meeting with a wooer who is interested in marrying the Jailer's Daughter. They decide that when he has "full promise of her," her full devotion, they will discuss the details of the marriage. The Jailer's Daughter then enters, explaining how impressed and taken she is with the new prisoners. She seems to fall in love with the image of them as she ends the scene crying out, "It is a holiday to look on them."

Act II, Scene 2

In Palamon and Arcite's jail cell, the two men discover that they are most likely to be prisoners forever. Palamon expresses sadness at their perhaps never seeing Thebes again nor using their celebrated fighting ability. Arcite, in response, laments that they will grow old in the prison cell, never marrying and never having children. They lament that they will never know anything except for one another and "the clock that tells our woes," the sense of the time of their unending sentence passing. Reflecting on these laments, however, the men think on their intimate relationship and the comfort it will offer them during their punishment. Arcite argues that the prison cell will provide safety to them, keeping them safe from war and from danger. He argues that by staying in the cell, they will be wives to each other, birthing love instead of children—and that their isolated status will keep their relationship safe from wives, business, and envy that would otherwise threaten their relationship. This so convinces Palamon that he becomes "almost wanton" with his captivity, and they argue that no one has loved as much as they have.

Emilia and her Woman enter below. Palamon catches sight of her and becomes distracted, urg-

ing Arcite to look. When Arcite sees her, he is also quite impressed with her beauty. Palamon realizes that Arcite has fallen in love with her as well, which angers Palamon because he saw her first. They grow angrier with each other as they fight over Emilia. They are interrupted when the Jailer pulls Arcite out of his cell—Pirithous has awarded him pardon, and he is exiled from Athens rather than made to stay in prison. Palamon is then jealous that Arcite is free, knowing that if he himself were free he would do everything to impress Emilia and make her "seek to ravish" him. The scene ends when the Jailer tells Palamon he is too close to the windows, through which he had seen Emilia, and must be taken away.

Act II, Scene 3

Arcite enters and laments his banishment, which will keep him far away from Emilia—he decides to break the terms of his punishment and not leave the kingdom, but rather dress up in a disguise to see her again. A group of countrymen pass Arcite on their way to perform for the Duke after the games. Arcite decides he will disguise himself to join in the games in Athens so that he "may ever dwell in sight of her."

Act II, Scene 4

The Jailer's Daughter, in a soliloquy, admits that she is in love with Palamon and decides that the only way to let him know she loves him is to set him free in spite of the clear legal consequences of this. She decides that she will do it either that night or the next day.

Act II, Scene 5

Theseus praises Arcite, who is in disguise, for his excellent running and wrestling. Theseus, Hippolyta, Emilia, and Pirithous are all taken with the natural nobility of this new stranger, and to reward him, he is placed in the service of Emilia. Arcite has the honor of leading them all back into the city, and Theseus states that Emilia has an excellent servant, one, that, were he in her position, he would marry. Emilia says that she "hopes too wise" to believe that this could happen.

Act II, Scene 6

The Jailer's Daughter soliloquizes that she has freed Palamon by bringing him a mile outside of town into the woods where he is waiting for her to bring him files and food so he can refresh himself and free himself of the iron braces that the Jailer had put on him. She is concerned that he did not even thank her or kiss her for this service and hopes that she can eventually make him love her. She heads off to see him, knowing that by the time the prison is aware of the loss she will be with Palamon.

Act III, Scene 1

Arcite is alone in the woods and brags about how close Fortune has brought him to Emilia. He imagines that Palamon thinks he is in Thebes when in reality he is very close to her. Right after soliloquizing this, he runs into Palamon who is still wearing his braces from jail. They wish to fight in order to settle their competition over Emilia but agree to do so after Palamon is freed from his braces and has eaten and rested. Throughout this scene, there is a sense that some of their old affection is still present even in the midst of their bitter competition. Arcite runs back to Emilia, a fact that makes Palamon very jealous, and Palamon is left to rest.

Act III, Scene 2

The Jailer's Daughter seeks out Palamon to give him the file to free him from his braces, but she cannot find him. She fears that he has been killed, and her fears over his safety as well as her intense love for him drive her to depression and madness.

Act III, Scene 3

Arcite brings Palamon wine, meat, and files. Palamon eats intensely. There is a warmth between them as Arcite is glad to see Palamon eating so voraciously, and they reminisce about the women they have known. This accord falls apart when Palamon believes that Arcite is sighing for Emilia, breaking their agreement not to mention her, and they go separate ways preparing to fight for Emilia and settle their difference.

Act III, Scene 4

The Jailer's Daughter enters, gripped by madness, stating that Palamon is in heaven and unsure of where she is. She sees images of ships and water and ends the scene singing a suggestive song longing for a man

Act III, Scene 5

The Schoolmaster and some countrymen enter as they prepare their dance to perform before the Duke. As they see what is needed in their performance they realize that they need a woman to perform with them. Realizing that they do not have one, they are fearful that the whole thing will be ruined. At this moment, the Jailer's Daughter enters singing. They lead her to perform with them in front of Theseus, Hippolyta, Pirithous, and Emilia, who all enjoy it.

Act III, Scene 6

Palamon enters to meet Arcite. After some discussion, they select their arms and begin to fight. They are interrupted, however, by horns that announce that the Duke is coming. Arcite urges that they stop and hide, but Palamon says he will no longer hide or delay their fight, which Arcite agrees to, though understanding how dangerous a decision this is. Theseus comes in and stops the fight, ordering that both of them shall die. Palamon asks him to allow them to finish fighting before they are killed. Theseus agrees to this condition, but Emilia and the others intervene, asking that they be banished rather than killed, as long as they agree to never come back to Athens, never know her or fight over her, and never see each other again. Palamon and Arcite reject these terms. Emilia agrees to marry one of them if the other dies but will not choose whom she prefers. As a solution, they must fight, and she will marry the winner while the loser must die.

Act IV, Scene 1

The Jailer and a friend enter while the Jailer asks if his friend has heard anything about Palamon's escape—for which the Jailer was sentenced to die.

While the friend has heard nothing, a second friend enters and reports that Palamon has earned his pardon. They celebrate the fact when the wooer comes in and reports that he has seen the Jailer's Daughter acting mad over her love for Palamon. The Jailer's Brother as well as his daughter then enter, and they see for themselves the extent of her madness.

Act IV, Scene 2

Emilia walks in with pictures of Palamon and Arcite, trying to choose and end their strife. At first she prefers Arcite, but then switches to Palamon, realizing in the end that she does not know and cannot possibly choose. She laments that her chastity will be the object of violence and death. A Messenger comes in and reports that the fight is ready, six noble knights accompany Palamon and Arcite, three for each to help them in the fight. They agree to observe the fight with Emilia lamenting that whoever wins her must see his cousin die.

Act IV, Scene 3

A doctor examines the Jailer's Daughter and determines that the only way to cure her is to have the wooer present himself as if he were Palamon and express his love for her.

Act V, Scene 1

Theseus lets the challengers enter the tournament field and begin their prayers. Arcite leads a prayer to Mars, the god of war, and exits the stage. Palamon enters and leads a prayer to Venus, the goddess of love. Palamon exits. To the sound of recorders, Emilia enters dressed in white and wearing a wheaten wreath. Placing and lighting a silver hind full of incense on the altar, she leads a prayer to Diana, the chaste God of the hunt.

Act V, Scene 2

The doctor enters asking the Wooer if his plan has cured the Jailer's Daughter at all. The Wooer asserts that it has. The Jailer's Daughter enters to greet Palamon. Though the doctor must leave to be at the tournament, he says that within a few days the Jailer's Daughter will be cured. The Jailer's Daughter and the Wooer are told to stay together and they leave in love, the Wooer asserting he will not hurt her.

Act V, Scene 3

Theseus, Hippolyta, and Pirithous prepare to leave to watch the tournament while Emilia does not want to watch. Holding their two pictures in her hand, she thinks again on how she cannot make a choice between them. At first, she hears a cry for Palamon, believing him to be the winner and thinking it the most likely since "he looked all grace and success." Then she discovers that Arcite is the victor, thinking that she knew the whole time that Palamon "would miscarry," though she doesn't know why she thought this. Arcite enters to claim her, and Theseus praises him. Emilia, however, is unhappy with the necessary death of Palamon and thinks that heaven is forcing her to comfort the grieving fighter who will shortly see his cousin die.

Act V, Scene 4

Palamon laments his defeat with his knights who all are to die. The Jailer enters and informs Palamon that his daughter is doing well and will be married shortly, which comforts him. Palamon prepares to die and places his head on the block, but a Messenger rushes in, followed by Pirithous, to interrupt the execution. Pirithous explains that Arcite has been mortally wounded in an accident with his victory horse and, though living now, is near death. Theseus, Hippolyta, Emilia, and Arcite, in a chair carried by attendants, then enter. Palamon is sad to see him hurt. Arcite, then, tells him to take Emilia. He dies, and Theseus declares there will be a wedding after Arcite's funeral, offering some consolation over the ambivalence of these events.

Epilogue

A character called Epilogue enters and asks how the audience has liked the play. He observes that no one is smiling. Assuming they have not liked the play, he asks if any have found themselves in love with a beautiful girl. Sensing some hostility from the audience, he says that if they have enjoyed any aspect of this play, the players have succeeded, and if not, he's sure better plays will be coming that will make them love the acting company again. He ends the epilogue by wishing the audience a good night.

CHARACTER LIST

Prologue The character that begins the play, advertising its ambitious links to Geoffrey Chaucer and a hope that they are able to live up to his memory.

Theseus The powerful duke of Athens, husband to Hippolyta and brother-in-law to Emilia. He is also the intimate friend of Pirithous. When the Three Queens come from Thebes to lament the treatment of their husbands' bodies, Theseus conquers Thebes and brings back Palamon and Arcite.

Hippolyta Queen of the Amazons and, eventually, the wife of Theseus. She travels to Athens with her sister Emilia and, with Emilia, often urges Theseus to act mercifully in his governing of Athens.

Pirithous The intimate friend of Theseus. He secures the pardon of Arcite, allowing him to be exiled from Athens rather than imprisoned in it forever.

Palamon Cousin of Arcite, nephew of Creon, the first to see and fall in love with Emilia. Loses the fight with Arcite for her love but, because of Arcite's death in an accident with a horse, marries her in the end. Also, he is the love object for the Jailer's Daughter.

Arcite Cousin of Palamon, nephew of Creon, the second to see and fall in love with Emilia. Sentenced to banishment instead of life in prison by Theseus, he returns to Athens in disguise as a runner and wrestler. Defeats Palamon in the tournament for Emilia but then dies in an accident shortly after.

Hymen God of marriage, the first to enter the stage in Act I, Scene 1, part of the wedding procession of Theseus and Hippolyta.

A Boy Who sings.

Artesius An Athenian soldier, a character mentioned only once. Theseus turns to him to help plan his attack on Thebes.

Three Queens All widows of the kings who died attacking Thebes. Creon has not allowed their bodies to be properly buried, and so they come to Theseus seeking revenge and the right to have proper funerals for their husbands.

Valerius A Theban. He announces the war against the attacking Athenians to Palamon and Arcite.

A Herald Announces to Theseus that they have found Palamon and Arcite unconscious though alive on the battlefield, noting how well they fought before being struck down.

A Woman Attendant to Emilia, she is with Emilia when Emilia is observed by Palamon and Arcite outside their prison window.

An Athenian Gentleman Announces to Emilia that the knights who will support Palamon and Arcite in their tournament have arrived.

Messengers Announce all the various things happening during the preparations for the tournament between Palamon and Arcite off stage to Emilia, as well as the mortal wounds of Arcite to Palamon after the tournament.

A Servant Reports to Emilia the results of the tournament.

The Jailer Runs Theseus's prison.

The Jailer's Daughter Falls in love with Palamon and helps him escape. When she cannot find him in the woods where she left him, she goes mad, eventually ending up with the Wooer who pretends to be Palamon.

The Jailer's Brother Brings the Jailer's Daughter to her father after she has gone mad.

The Wooer Of the Jailer's Daughter; he wins her hand in marriage eventually by pretending to be Palamon.

Two Friends of the Jailer Announce that the Jailer has been cleared of punishment for his daughter's letting Palamon escape and that his daughter has gone mad.

A Doctor Helps cure the Jailer's Daughter.

Six Countrymen   Help put on the Morris Dance for Theseus.

Gerald   A schoolmaster, the leader of those putting on the Morris Dance.

Nell   A country wench.

Four other country wenches: Friz, Maudline, Luce, and Barbery.

Epilogue   Asks the audience if they have in the end enjoyed the play. Comments that the audience's faces seem to indicate they did not enjoy its sad ending.

CHARACTER STUDIES
Theseus

Theseus is an extremely important figure in Greek mythology and a character in quite a few plays of the European Renaissance (Shakespeare cast Theseus in his *A Midsummer Night's Dream* as well). He was perhaps the most famous of the legendary kings of Athens, slayer of the Minotaur, conquerer of the Amazons, best friend to Pirithous, and lover to Hippolyta and then Phaedra, unions that would have immense consequences for the mythical world they inhabit and that would inspire many plays and poems during Shakespeare's time and after.

In *The Two Noble Kinsmen*, however, we do not see a Theseus of mythic grandeur and accomplishment, but rather King Theseus, the effective, judicious, and right-dealing leader of Athens. While the other characters seem to be carried away by their emotions in the play, often acting in ways directly opposed to their own self-interest, Theseus is a calm and calculating figure in the play. Theseus's main strength comes from his ability to empathize with the supplications of female characters in the play. In fact, though he is the center of political power in the play, much of his decision making is guided by his reactions to female suffering and requests for mercy.

Early on in the play, Theseus, when confronted with the Three Queens' suffering, is not at first compelled to help until he begins to be swayed by the suffering of the dead kings expressed through the Queens' narrative. After a particularly poignant narrative by the first queen Act I, Scene 1, Theseus cannot contain how moved he is and begs the queen not to kneel:

> Pray you, kneel not;
> I was transported with your speech and suffered
> Your knees to wrong themselves. I have heard the fortunes
> Of your dead lords, which gives me such lamenting
> As wakes my vengeance and revenge for 'em.
> King Capaneus was your lord; the day
> That he should marry you, at such a season
> As now it is with me, I met your groom
> By Mars's altar; you were that time fair—
> Not Juno's mantle fairer than your tresses,
> Nor in more bounty spread her. Your wheaten wreath
> Was then nor threshed nor blasted; Fortune at you
> Dimpled her cheek with smiles. Hercules, our kinsman—
> Then weaker than your eyes—laid by his club;
> He tumbled down upon his Nemean hide
> And swore his sinews thawed. O grief and time,
> Fearful consumers, you will all devour!
>
> (1.1.55–70)

These first extended lines by Theseus couple his sympathy and care with a powerful intellect and philosophic nature. Yet it also signals to the audience how captivated Theseus is by the influence and image of women. Theseus is "transported [by] her speech" as well as the image of her beauty, which "grief and time" had taken. Throughout the play, the combination of powerful military and political rule and attention to the cries of mercy and aid from others is one of his major motivations.

As the above passage shows, Theseus, too, has a keen eye for veracity and quality. He senses the truth of feeling and depth of need in the Three Queens just as, when Palamon's and Arcite's badly battered but living bodies are brought to him, he senses the quality of their vigor. Being told by a herald that, though they are not "in a state of life" (1.4.24), Palamon and Arcite still "breathe and have the name of men" (1.4.26–27), Theseus is impressed with them, despite their being his enemies, saying:

> Then like men use 'em.
> The very lees of such, millions of rates,
> Exceed the wine of others. All our surgeons
> Convent in their behoof; our richest balms,
> Rather than niggard, waste; their lives
>   concern us
> Much more than Thebes is worth.
>
> (1.4.28–33)

An appreciation of quality, of truth, and of what is right in governing directs. Theseus through the play, but as the repeated mercies he offers to Palamon and Arcite show, based on the pleadings of Hippolyta and Emilia, his governing is swayed by an appreciation for suffering.

In a play so full of striking and irrational passions, of deep friendships that clash against romantic destinies, Theseus is a rare island in the play of stability, rationality, and dedication. His very close friendship with Pirithous does not drive him to the jealous passions of Palamon and Arcite, nor to the ambivalence over romantic relationships that Emilia possesses based in her close relationship with Flavina. He is a resolute dispenser of justice, who, at the end of the play, knows his place and duty even among the gods, as he says in some of the last lines of the play: "The gods my justice / take from my hand, and they themselves become / The executioners" (5.4.120–122).

Palamon and Arcite

The play's title *The Two Noble Kinsmen* underscores the nobility of the two protagonists Palamon and Arcite. In the first act of the play, their nobility is front and center, noted by Theseus and the rest of the Athenians even as they lay nearly lifeless on the battlefield after fighting with great acumen. Yet the play uses these two characters' nobility as a point of contrast for the shallow and immediate love for Emilia that tears apart what was one of the most intimate male friendships ever seen on stage.

Palamon and Arcite's intimate, obsessive, and contradictory relationship is at the heart of the play. They are cousins, both related to the cruel King Creon, and the audience first sees them in an intimate discourse in which they lament the dilapidated state of Thebes under their uncle's rule. The audience knows, however, from the first time we hear one of them speak, that their relationship is closer and stronger than simply what their family relation allows. Arcite first greets Palamon saying "Dear Palamon, dearer in love than blood / And our prime cousin, yet unhardened in/ the crimes of nature, let us leave the city / Thebes, and the temptings in't, / before we further / Sully our gloss of youth" (1.2.1–5). These lines underscore the two men's attempt to use their friendship as a barrier to the outside world—as a safe space in which they will remain devoted to each other and uncorrupted by the world.

This protective quality of their friendship is what they invoke when they find themselves in an Athenian jail cell facing a life sentence. Arcite argues in jail that the prison can be a "holy sanctuary / To keep us from corruption of worse men. / We are young and yet desire the ways of honour, / That liberty and common conversation, / The poison of pure spirits, might, like women, / Woo us to wander from. What worthy blessing / Can be but our imaginations / May make it ours?" (2.2.71–78). Their friendship, seemingly, though not ultimately, free from the rivalries of political and romantic relationships, offers comfort to the two men even in the most adverse circumstances.

The nature of Palamon and Arcite's friendship, however, is deeper than what might be conventionally thought of as simply friendship, and there is a deep love, charged with the language of sexual and romantic desire, that often is invoked when the men describe their relationship. When Arcite says "We are one another's wife" (2.2.80) or when Palamon asks rhetorically, "Is there record of any two that loved / Better than we do Arcite?" (2.2.113–114), the audience gets a window into an almost romantically intimate male friendship—one with the potential to stand in for, and even to exceed in the quality of experience, the traditional heterosexual relationships their prison term denies them.

Their bond, however, proves throughout the play to be as fragile as it is intense. When Palamon sees Emilia for the first time and points her out to Arcite, it takes only a few lines before the audience has seen their relationship, which had just been expressed in some of the most romantic and intimate language of the play, crumble into bitter and senseless jealousy. Palamon and Arcite's relationship, tender even in the throes of intense rivalry, works as an extended critique and exploration of intense and instant love. This is the love that Petrarch, an Italian poet of the 14th century who became the major model for poets like Shakespeare of how to write love poetry, celebrated in his collection of sonnets *The Canzoniere*. A Petrarchan lover needs only to see the object of desire once to completely fall in love with her. This act of instant love at first sight tears their friendship apart.

As the two men are separated by Theseus's pardon of Arcite, the two men remain as fascinated with each other as they are with Emilia. Arcite's first thoughts of exile include both Emilia and Palamon:

> Banished the kingdom? 'Tis a benefit,
> A mercy I must thank 'em for, but banished
> The free enjoying of that face I die for,
> O 'twas a studied punishment, a death
> Beyond imagination—such a vengeance
> That, were I old and wicked, all my sins
> Could never pluck upon me. Palamon,
> Thou hast the start now; thou shalt stay and see
> Her bright eyes break each morning 'gainst thy window.
>
> (2.3.1–9)

Their mutual obsession over Emilia transforms their relationship and yet it does not destroy it, they are as passionate about one another as they

had been previously, but in the wake of their rivalrous love for Emilia, their passion takes on bitter and angry qualities. Yet, being enraged with one another is not an easy task, as Arcite reveals before they are about to take the field and fight:

> I am in labour
> To push your name, your ancient love, our kindred,
> Out of my memory, and i'th' selfsame place
> To seat something I would confound. So hoist we
> The sails that must these vessels port even where
> The heavenly limiter pleases.
>
> (5.1.24–29)

Arcite must work hard to hate Palamon, to lie to himself by replacing thoughts and memories of Palamon with something he can hate more readily. Palamon responds warmly, embracing him one last time. The oscillation between hatred and love, compassion and militancy defines their relationship and drives the plot, as well as making these two characters some of the most compelling in early literature.

Shakespeare exploits this dichotomy between war and love in the prayers of the two men. While Arcite prays to Mars, the god of war, Palamon prays to Venus, the goddess of love. This division suggests that Palamon, the first to see Emilia and the one who ends up with her, has been more devoted to love the whole time, while Arcite, the second to see Emilia and the one to actually win her in war, though eventually a mortal victim of violence himself, has been the more militant of the two. Together, these characters showcase the workings of a relationship driven by love, obsession, and jealousy, combining their famed work of soldiers with their ability, for better or worse, to love deeply.

Emilia

Emilia is beautiful and compassionate, able to inspire compassion in Theseus and strong love in Palamon and Arcite. Though she will become the

Palamon and Arcite see Emilia in the garden from a 1465 manuscript of Boccaccio's *Il Teseide. (Art by the Master of the Hours of the duke of Burgundy)*

intense focus of Palamon and Arcite's love, even from her earliest words, Emilia seems to share a closer and more profound bond with women, as becomes clear in her first extended set of lines in the play:

> Pray you say nothing, pray you;
> Who cannot feel nor see the rain, being in't,
> Knows neither wet nor dry. If that you were
> The ground-piece of some painter, I would buy you
> T'instruct me 'gainst a capital grief, indeed
> Such heart-pierced demonstration; but alas,
> Being a natural sister of our sex,
> Your sorrow beats so ardently upon me
> That it shall make a counter-reflect 'gainst
> My brother's heart and warm it to some pity,
> Though it were made of stone. Pray have good comfort.
>
> (1.1.119–129)

The intimacy she feels with the third queen is uniquely feminine and a challenge to Theseus's "stone" heart. These early lines are an appropriate introduction to her character, fascinated by the power of a woman's bond to another woman.

As Theseus goes to conquer Thebes to allow the Three Queens to recover the bodies of their husbands, Hippolyta and Emilia stay behind, with Emilia meditating on the close relationship between Pirithous and Theseus and how it reminds her of her own intimate friendship:

> EMILIA. . . . . I was acquainted
> Once with a time when I enjoyed a playfellow;
> You were at wars when she the grave enriched,
> Who made too proud the bed; took leave o'th' moon—
> Which then looked pale at parting—when our count
> Was each eleven.
>
> HIPPOLYTA. 'Twas Flavina.
>
> EMILIA. Yes.
> You talk of Pirithous' and Theseus' love;
> Theirs has more ground, is more maturely seasoned,
> More buckled with strong judgement, and their needs
> The one of th'other may be said to water
> Their intertangled roots of love: but I
> And she I sigh and spoke of were things innocent
> Lov'd for we did, and like the elements
> That know not what nor why, yet do effect
> Rare issues by their operance, our souls
> Did so to one another; what she liked
> Was then of me approved, what not, condemned,
> no more arraignment . . .
>
> (1.3.49–66)

Emilia and Flavina's friendship was rooted in a deep bond that defies any explanation, they simply love because that is what they do. Emilia's devotion to Flavina, continuing in some ways even after her death, is based on feelings innate to the people involved, in some ways similar to the friendship between Pirithous and Theseus and between Palamon and Arcite.

The tender certainty of her words contrasts strikingly with her appraisal of Palamon and Arcite, the two men fighting over her. Where Flavina inspired a deep devotion in her effortlessly, Palamon and Arcite cannot, even through their increasingly drastic actions, get Emilia to care much for them at all. She asserts after her discussion of her friendship with Flavina that she intends never to marry, and even when she understands the depth of Palamon's and Arcite's obsession over her, she suggests a truce in which neither agrees to love her:

Swear 'em never more
To make me their contention, or to know me,
To tread upon thy dukedom, and to be,
Wherever they shall travel, ever strangers
To one another.

(3.6.253–257)

They, of course, refuse this truce, but it underscores how strongly Emilia would prefer to not be the object of their love. To this end, it is not surprising that, when Arcite dies and she is to be married, at last, to Palamon, she never expresses any gratitude or love toward Palamon. Her last words in the play are to Arcite, ushering him to death and mourning him: "I'll close thine eyes, prince. Blessèd souls be with thee! / Thou art a right good man, and while I live, / This day I give to tears" (5.4.95–97). In the end, the woman who never chose to love a man, and lost the woman whose love she most cherished, is ushered off the stage married to Palamon, a final, ambivalent, and slightly tragic act that underscores the lack of agency she possesses over her social and sexual destiny. Because she would not choose either Palamon or Arcite, she is denied any choice at all.

Jailer's Daughter

The Jailer's Daughter, who falls madly in love with Palamon, risking almost everything in the process, is a fascinating complement to the love Palamon himself feels for Emilia. Completely illogical, based on an instant look with little else to guide her, and completely unabashed by the object of her affec-

tion's indifference to herself, her love is based, and in the end results, in a sort of madness. Her character is able to expose the pathos of rushed and impulsive love, revealing it to be selfish, delusional, and ultimately dangerous.

Her first major act in the play is to help Palamon escape from prison, placing him—without supplies and still in his braces—in a remote part of the woods. In doing this, she neither is greatly praised by the Jailer nor, it seems, fazed by the fact that her actions will mean her father's condemnation to death. She loves Palamon in spite of her own knowledge, driven by feelings she does not fully understand, as in this soliloquy given right after she has allowed Palamon to escape:

Why should I love this gentleman? 'Tis odds
He never will affect me. I am base,
My father the mean keeper of his prison,
And he a prince. To marry him is hopeless,
To be his whore is witless. Out upon't
What pushes are we wenches driven to
When fifteen once has found us! First I saw him;
I, seeing, thought he was a goodly man;
He has as much to please a woman in him—
If he please to bestow it so—as ever
These eyes yet looked on. Next I pitied him,
And so would any young wench, o' my
    conscience,
That ever dreamed, or vowed her maidenhead
To a young handsome man. Then I loved him,
Extremely loved him, infinitely loved him,
And yet he had a cousin, fair as he too
But in my heart was Palamon . . .

(2.4.1–17)

The Jailer's Daughter, in these lines, reveals an analysis of love that other characters rarely present in the play. She is walking the audience through the process of developing her obsessive love of Palamon. The logic with which she lays out the history of her affections for him stands in stark contrast with the instant love of Palamon and Arcite for Emilia. Yet, as with the heterosexual desires of Palamon and Arcite, her love for Palamon is revealed to be shallow and interchangeable as, in the state of madness, she is able to believe that her Wooer is Palamon and marries him anyway, throwing the sincerity of her desire into question and arguing, as many Renaissance texts such as Ariosto's *Orlando Furioso* had before, that love is a kind of madness.

DIFFICULTIES OF THE PLAY

The Two Noble Kinsmen is difficult because it is rather different from the bulk of Shakespeare's earlier work. As a result of both the changing historical and cultural climate of the time, as well as the involvement of the collaborator John Fletcher, it features many themes and generic styles not found in much of the Renaissance drama that most students are used to encountering. One of these major themes is the presence of ritual and performance within the play. Though plays such as *Hamlet* and *A Midsummer Night's Dream* contain performances, they are closer to plays than the dances and masques from which the rituals and performances in *The Two Noble Kinsmen* are drawn. Masques were a popular dramatic form under King James I (r. 1603–1625), which depended on highly stylized staging and abstract personifications (characters could have names like "Pleasure" or "Virtue") and were mostly enjoyed by upper-class dramatic consumers. Some of the most famous masques in English were written by Shakespeare's friend and rival Ben Jonson (a masque also appears in another of Shakespeare's last plays, *The Tempest*). Scenes that draw heavily from the masque tradition in *The Two Noble Kinsmen* include the opening scene with the marriage procession of Theseus and Hippolyta (Act I, Scene 1) and Arcite, Palamon, and Emilia's three prayers in Act V, Scene 1 (see Difficult Passages for a guide on Emilia's prayer). Scenes that show ritual acts include the funeral scene in Act I, Scene 5 and the Morris Dance in Act III, Scene 5.

Perhaps the largest problem with understanding *The Two Noble Kinsmen* is that its major source is a work that many Renaissance readers and theatergoers would have known but few modern readers do. Geoffrey Chaucer's glorious "The Knight's Tale" is the first, longest, and grandest of his *Canterbury Tales*. "The Knight's Tale" was written in Middle English; its story is drawn from Boccaccio's *Teseida*, a work itself influenced by the Roman poet Statius's *Thebaid*, which contains the story of the "seven against Thebes," the war in which the Three Queens' husbands were killed. *The Two Noble Kinsmen*, perhaps more than earlier works by Shakespeare, depends on a more educated audience familiar with this background story. That the play's title page claims it to have been performed at Blackfriar's, an indoor theater, rather than an outdoor theater like the famed Globe, also suggests a more upper-class audience, as indoor theaters often charged higher admission prices than their outdoor counterparts. Though Shakespeare and Fletcher certainly wished, as the Prologue makes clear, for their work to be seen as following in the footsteps of Chaucer, it is not necessary to know the plot of "The Knight's Tale" to appreciate *The Two Noble Kinsmen*. The two playwrights follow the story of Palamon and Arcite (the Jailer's Daughter subplot is not from Chaucer and has no clear source) so closely that one need not have an extensive background in Chaucer to understand it. Yet, knowing the sources to which Shakespeare and Fletcher were so ambitiously linking their own work is essential to appreciate the boldness of the play. Drama had not been considered high literature like lyric poetry, romance, or epic. The bold assertion that drama could take on no less than Geoffrey Chaucer, in Renaissance readers' minds the greatest medieval poet writing in English, would have greatly informed an audience's experience with this play.

Though the language of *The Two Noble Kinsmen* is no more difficult than other plays by Shakespeare, the normally metaphor-rich and imagery-laden poetry of the actors' speeches are, in this play, allowed to go especially long. Drawing yet again from the early-17th-century masque tradition, the speeches often go on uninterrupted, developing extended arguments about the nature of friendship, the purity of one's love, the treacherousness of an enemy, and more. Such passages, like any extended passage in Shakespeare, require special attention and the aid of a good scholarly edition's notes.

KEY PASSAGES
Act I, Scene 3, 57–87

EMILIA. You talk of Pirithous' and Theseus'
  love;
Theirs has more ground, is more maturely
  seasoned,
More buckled with strong judgement, and
  their needs
The one of th'other may be said to water
Their intertangled roots of love: but I
And she I sigh and spoke of were things
  innocent,
Loved for we did, and like the elements
That know not what nor why, yet do effect
Rare issues by their operance, our souls did so
  to one another; what she liked
Was then of me approved, what not,
  condemned,
No more arraignment; the flower that I would
  pluck
And put between my breasts—O then but
  beginning
To swell about the blossom—she would long
Till she had such another, and commit it
To the like innocent cradle, where,
  phoenix-like,
They died in perfume; on my head no toy
But was her pattern; her affections—pretty,
Though happily her careless wear—I followed
For my most serious decking; had mine ear
Stol'n some new air, or at adventure hummed
  one
From musical coinage, why, it was a note
Whereon her spirits would soujourn—rather
  dwell on—
And sing it in her slumbers. This rehearsal—
Which seely innocence wots well, comes in
Like old importment's bastard—has this end,
That the true love 'tween maid and maid
  may be
More than in sex dividual.

HIPPOLYTA. You're out of breath,
And this high-speeded pace is but to say
That you shall never—like the maid Flavina—
Love any that's called man.

EMILIA. I am sure I shall not.

Emilia, in her comparison of her friendship with the late Flavina with the friendship between Pirithous and Theseus, contrasts innocent nature and developed experience early in this passage. She emphasizes the maturity and deep-rootedness of Pirithous and Theseus' friendship. They are so intertwined that they cannot help but answer each other's needs. Flavina and Emilia's relationship, however, does not reflect a mature growth into synergy but rather a natural affinity and disposition to love each other. Their friendship was innocent, natural to their beings, practically written into their very bodies—their friendship involves a combination of souls. The language here contrasts the earthy, material descriptions of the friendship between Theseus and Pirithous with the more abstract and transcendent quality of her friendship with the late Flavina.

Emelye (Emilia) in the garden from the 1896 Kelmscott edition of Chaucer's "The Knight's Tale" *(Illustration by Edward Burne-Jones)*

The imagery that Emilia uses is intensely intimate: Whenever Emilia would place a flower between her breasts, Flavina would long to do the same. There is an interesting relationship in this passage between the sensual imagery of a flower "but beginning / to swell about the blossom" and the innocence of their friendship that unites their bodies. In fact, as Emilia's description of their friendship develops, her examples move from the abstract and intellectual ("what she liked / Was then of me approved . . .") to increasingly more bodily and sensual ("had mine ear / Stol'n some new air, or at adventure hummed one / From musical coinage, why, it was a note / Whereon her spirits would sojourn—rather dwell on— / And sing it in her slumbers."). The two women shaped each other by their preferences, actions, and deep-rooted love. The language of this passage works in such a way as to emphasize the mutual nature of this process.

The climax of this passage comes in Emilia's assertion that ". . . the true love 'tween maid and maid may be / More than in sex dividual." That Emilia asserts her love for Flavina with the potential to be truer and simply "more" than the love between different sexes places her character in opposition to the love triangle plot that will center around her throughout the rest of the play. Hippolyta's response to Emilia, "You're out of breath, / And this high-speeded pace is but to say / That you shall never—like the maid Flavina—Love any that's called man," indicates that Emilia's speech has been a passionate one, leaving her excited and out of breath. Her memories of Flavina invoke passion in her that neither Palamon nor Arcite will ever be able to invoke. This passage, presented before Palamon and Arcite fall in love with Emilia, allows the audience to understand why their love for her is not only not mutual but misguided—her passion rests with the dead Flavina, whom she emulates, even as she is dead, in her chastity and devotion to the love between maids.

Act II, Scene 2, 71–110

ARCITE. Let's think this prison holy sanctuary,
To keep us from corruption of worse men.
We are young and yet desire the ways of honour,
That liberty and common conversation,
The poison of pure spirits, might, like women
Woo us to wander from. What worthy blessing
Can be but our imaginations
May make it ours? And here being thus together,
We are an endless mine to one another;
We are one another's wife, ever begetting
New births of love; we are father, friends, acquaintances;
We are in one another, families;
I am your heir, and you are mine; this place
Is our inheritance; no hard oppressor
Dare take this from us; here, with a little patience,
We shall live long, and loving. No surfeits seek us;
The hand of war hurts none here, nor the seas
Swallow their youth. Were we at liberty,
A wife might part us lawfully, or business;
Quarrels consume us; envy of ill men
Crave our acquaintance. I might sicken, cousin,
Where you should never know it, and so perish
Without your noble hand to close mine eyes,
Or prayers to the gods. A thousand chances,
Were we from hence, would sever us.

PALAMON. You have made me—
I thank you, cousin Arcite—almost wanton
With my captivity. What a misery
It is to live abroad, and everywhere!
'Tis like a beast, methinks. I find the court here—
I am sure, a more content; and all those pleasures
That woo the wills of men to vanity
I see through now, and am sufficient
To tell the world 'tis but a gaudy shadow
That old Time as he passes by, takes with him.
What had we been, old in the court of Creon,
Where sin is justice, lust and ignorance
The virtues of the great ones? Cousin Arcite,

Had not the loving gods found this place
 for us,
We had died as they do, ill old men, unwept,
And had their epitaphs, the people's curses.

Palamon and Arcite have found themselves facing a life sentence in an Athenian prison cell far from home. After initially realizing that they will never get to marry nor have children, Arcite offers this consolation: Their friendship itself can be a sort of protective entity in their lives, based on the intimacy of their friendship and the seclusion of their prison cell. The language of this passage is intimate, sacred, and transcendent. Arcite imagines that their new permanent home will be like a "holy sanctuary"—a metaphor that emphasizes the prison's ability to be a separate, safe, and spiritual place honoring their friendship by keeping it away "from corruption of worse men." As they realize that they want to be honorable, it becomes clear that the safety of their honor is only enhanced by the protection of the prison walls.

Arcite actually foreshadows their friendship's destruction in noting that "the poison of pure spirits, might, like women, / Woo us to wander from [the ways of honor]." He understands honor to be a spatial phenomenon, a route which one must keep but one that can be easily lost. This theme of honor as spatial allows the prison to take on spiritual meaning; it is a protective space for their friendship, keeping them safe together while keeping the corruption of the world out. The insularity of the prison cell, Arcite proposes, can only be enhanced by their imagination. In this speech, the prison cell becomes a kind of microcosm, a little world, which operates by its own, small versions of the life processes that go on outside. Though neither of them will ever have a wife, it is possible for them to be wives to each other, giving birth not to babies but to "new births of love." The prison seems to have the power to expand their relationship out of the realm of simple friendship into an all-encompassing love that includes "fathers, friends, acquaintances." Indeed, it seems that the prison is the safest place for their friendship and love to grow:

I am your heir, and you are mine; this place
Is our inheritance; no hard oppressor
Dare take this from us; here, with a little
 patience,
We shall live long and loving.

The prison then is a place where love and possessions are kept safe, by having nothing and going nowhere. Indeed, by being shut out from the outside world entirely, they are able to live in near complete safety.

The intimacy of the passage then turns specifically to one another, and Arcite's words take an almost romantic turn. The prison's great strength is that they shall never be separated, and when one dies, Arcite imagines it will be him first, the other will be there to close his eyes and pray to the gods. This passage will take on special resonance when Arcite does die in front of Palamon, but it is Emilia who will close his eyes.

Arcite is successful is converting Palamon to his way of thinking—with Palamon's response reflecting the same insular language as that of Arcite. Had they been free in Thebes, he believes, they would certainly have fallen into corruption—the love the two men have for each other is pure, held safely within the prison and preserved from outside influence.

Of course, as we know, this ends up being a fiction—Palamon and Arcite are torn apart inside their prison sanctuary because, even in prison, the outside world finds its way in and pollutes the purity and innocence of close friendship with the social consequences and personal jealousy of romantic love. Just as Flavina's death forced Emilia to face the world alone, without her same-sex soul mate, the unexpected interference of the outside world will rip Palamon and Arcite apart as well. However, given the ease with which the two men fall into jealousy, the audience is left to decide how genuine these sentiments, so passionately expressed by Palamon and Arcite, were.

Act III, Scene 2, 1–38

JAILER'S DAUGHTER. He has mistook the
 brake I meant, is gone

After his fancy. 'Tis now well-nigh morning.
No matter; would it were perpetual night,
And darkness lord o'th' world. Hark, 'tis a
  wolf!
In me hath grief slain fear, and but for one
  thing,
I care for nothing, and that's Palamon.
I reck not if the wolves would jaw me, so
He had this file. What if I hallowed for him?
I cannot hallow; if I whooped, what then?
If he not answered, I should call a wolf,
And do him but that service. I have heard
Strange howls this livelong night; why may't
  not be
They have made prey of him? He has no
  weapons;
He cannot run; the jingling of his gyves
Might call fell things to listen, who have in
  them
A sense to know a man unarmed, and can
Smell where resistance is. I'll set it down
He's torn to pieces; they howled many
  together,
And then they fed on him; so much for that.
Be bold to ring the bell. How stand I then?
All's chared when he is gone. No, no, I lie;
My father's to be hanged for his escape,
Myself to beg, if I prized life so much
As to deny my act, but that I would not,
Should I try death by dozens. I am moped;
Food took I none these two days,
Sipped some water. I have not closed mine eyes
Save when my lids scoured off their brine. Alas,
Dissolve, my life; let not my sense unsettle,
Lest I should drown, or stab, or hang myself.
O state of nature, fail together in me,
Since thy best props are warped! So which way
  now?
The best way is the next way to a grave;
Each errant step beside is torment. Lo,
The moon is down, the crickets chirp, the
  screech owl
Calls in the dawn. All offices are done
Save what I fail in; but the point is this—
An end, and that is all.

The Jailer's Daughter is an exemplar for the effects of maddening love on someone whose own social position has very little agency. In this passage, as she seeks Palamon in the place where she had left him after facilitating his escape, the Jailer's Daughter sinks into madness and despair. Like the passage between Palamon and Arcite above, the Jailer's Daughter's soliloquy centers around the theme of captivity and freedom, safe containment and liberated wandering. As Palamon had been safely in her care in the prison, under the Jailer's Daughter's watchful and authoritative presence, Palamon's freedom destroys her sense of closeness to him, and in this passage she deals with the various consequences of having set him loose out into the world.

As Palamon has entered the outside world, this passage makes clear that for the Jailer's Daughter the outside world is now about nothing except for Palamon:

> . . . 'Tis now well-nigh morning.
> No matter; would it were perpetual night,
> And darkness lord o'th'world. Hark, 'tis a
>   wolf!
> In me hath grief slain fear, and but for one
>   thing,
> I care for nothing, and that's Palamon.

The tone and pace of this passage is frantic and nervous, revealing the obsession and fear of its speaker. Her words reveal that the world for her, whether light or dark, safe or full of dangers such as a wolf nearby, is only Palamon, and without him, there is no reason to live. Her thoughts follow his safety exclusively, when she imagines he is torn to pieces by the wolves she hears, she declares that "all's chared when he is gone." The passage reads like a dialogue within one person as she decides what she must do to find him as well as mourn the consequences of her decision to free him. Her father is sentenced to death, she has denied herself food and only taken a little water. The passage reflects the panic and dread that her decisions have caused. Her last words in this scene are haunting in their resolution to give up on living: ". . . All offices are done / Save what I fail in; but the point is this— /An end, and that is all." She has succeeded in doing everything except giving Palamon the file, and yet that is enough to drive her to self-destruction and madness.

This passage provides a meditation, one act later than the dialogue between Palamon and Arcite in their prison cell, on the tensions between freedom and confinement. Her lines emphasize the expansiveness of her surroundings, the danger of nature, and the uncertainty of where she and Palamon are. Just as the window of the prison had opened up new dangers and frustrations for Palamon and Arcite, the prison door that the Jailer's Daughter opened offers no fewer challenges and crises, a fact that this passage offers to the reader through its panicked, uncertain, and rambling tone.

Act V, Scene 4, 86–96

PALAMON. O miserable end of our alliance!
The gods are mighty, Arcite. If thy heart,
Thy worthy, manly heart, be yet unbroken,
Give me thy last words. I am Palamon,
One that yet loves thee dying.

ARCITE. Take Emilia,
And with her all the world's joy. Reach thy
  hand—
Farewell; I have told my last hour. I was false,
Yet never treacherous; forgive me, cousin.
One kiss from fair Emilia— *(they kiss)* 'tis done;
Take her, I die
He dies

PALAMON. Thy brave soul seek Elysium!

Palamon and Arcite's long friendship and deep love, existent even in rivalry, comes to an end in these poignant, yet troubling lines. The dialogue between Palamon and Arcite is charged by the shocking reversal of fortune that had just occurred. Palamon who was to die after his loss to Arcite now watches Arcite die because of an accident on a horse, a complete and random reversal. This

shock reverberates through their dialogue, inaugurated with the dramatic exclamation by Palamon: "O miserable end of our alliance!" A deep sadness radiates from Palamon's words as he longs to be the recipient of Arcite's final words. There is a desperation behind these lines of wanting to return to the unity they once had before the tournament, a desire to restore their friendship and, in some ways, return to their former selves, as Palamon cries out "I am Palamon, / One that yet loves thee dying." This assertion reforms the once challenger Palamon back to the friend whose love for Arcite was so deep he doubted there was love like it in the world.

Arcite's response is defensive and not as loving. He hands over Emilia, but with a sense of great unhappiness: "Take Emilia, / And with her all the world's joy . . ." His tone, though warm, is somewhat defensive: ". . . I was false / Yet never treacherous; forgive me, cousin." This line seems more a method of clearing his own conscience than of showing love for Palamon. In fact, Arcite does not return Palamon's sentiment, dying without ever saying that he loves Palamon as well. He dies wanting only a kiss from Emilia, and it is Emilia, not Palamon as Arcite had earlier desired, who closes his eyes. Though Arcite's dying words are warm, they do invite a skeptical reading in which Arcite may have, in the end, not loved Palamon as he once did, not returned to the state of deep friendship that Palamon, seeing him dying, seems to have taken on.

DIFFICULT PASSAGES
Act V, Scene 1, 137–173

EMILIA. O sacred, shadowy, cold, and
  constant queen,
Abandoner of revels, mute contemplative,
Sweet, solitary, white as chaste, and pure
As wind-fanned snow, who to thy female
  knights
Allow'st no more blood than will make a
  blush,
Which is their order's robe, I here, thy priest,
Am humbled for thine altar. O, vouchsafe
With that thy rare green eye, which never yet
Beheld thing maculate, look on thy virgin;

And, sacred silver mistress, lend thine ear—
Which nev'r heard scurril term, into whose
   port
Ne'er entered wanton sound—to my petition,
Seasoned with holy fear. This is my last
Of vestal office; I am bride-habited,
But maiden-hearted. A husband I have
   'pointed,
But do not know him; out of two I should
Choose one, and pray for his success, but I
Am guiltless of election; of mine eyes
Were I to lose one—they are equal precious—
I could doom neither; that which perished
   should
Go to't unsentenced. Therefore, most modest
   queen,
He of the two pretenders that best loves me
And has the truest title in't, let him
Take off my wheaten garland, or else grant
The file and quality I hold I may
Continue in thy band
   Here the hind vanishes under the altar, and in
   the place ascends a rose tree, having one rose
   upon it
See what our general of ebbs and flows
Out from the bowels of her holy altar
With sacred act advances—but one rose!
If well inspired, this battle shall confound
Both these brave knights, and I, virgin flower,
Must grow alone, unplucked.
   Here is heard a sudden twang of instruments,
   and the rose falls from the tree
The flower is fall'n, the tree descends. O
   mistress
Thou here dischargest me; I shall be
   gathered—
I think so, but I know not thy own will.
Unclasp thy mystery. *(Aside)* I hope she's
   pleased;
Her signs were gracious

This prayer, a beautiful climax to a scene in which
all three members of the dangerous love triangle
offer prayers, is full of the style of the Jacobean
masque (see Difficulties of the Play for more on the

Arcite, Emilia, and Palamon pray to their respective
deities from a 1465 manuscript of Boccaccio's *Il Teseide.*
(Art by the Master of the Hours of the duke of Burgundy)

masque) with its symbolic, complicated staging and
prayerful tone directed to classical gods. Though
Palamon and Arcite direct their prayers to classical
gods as well, Emilia's is by far the greatest spectacle. Whereas Palamon and Arcite's prayers seek to
enhance their powers to conquer Emilia, Emilia's
prayer is for both of them to lose so that she may
remain, as she has hoped to remain throughout the
play, a virgin, never marrying a man.

Emilia's prayer, unlike the more boisterous
prayers to Venus and Mars, proceeds at a quiet,
meditative pace. Rather than rousing a group of
men to fight, the purpose of Palamon and Arcite's
prayers, this prayer is more private. She praises
Diana as being against "revels" and "a mute contemplative"—emphasizing her calm and protective presence in Emilia's life, a presence that seems
unique to women. Emilia, in the early lines, is
especially interested in Diana's powers to keep
women from feeling desire for men, she "allow'st
no more blood than will make a blush, / Which
is thy order's robe"—allows her women followers
no more desire than would allow them to blush.
The major theme of Emilia's praise for Diana in
this prayer will be that of her complete purity. Her
eye "never yet / beheld thing maculate," her ear

"nev'r heard scurril term." Anything flawed in any way has never been able to penetrate Diana's purity.

The prayer then moves to a near soliloquy, as Emilia begins to tell the audience her real feelings over the competition for her by Palamon and Arcite. She may be dressed like a bride ("bride-habited"), but her heart is still a maid, wishing not to be married. Though she must have a husband, and she must choose between the two, she has no desire to choose, nor can she. Emilia, then, turns the choice over to Diana, asking her to let the truest one marry her or let her remain a virgin.

The major difficulty in this passage is that Diana is never mentioned by name, only alluded to through the objects on stage associated with her (the hind) and to the adjectives that describe her ("sweet, solitary, white as chaste, and pure . . ."), so it is left to the audience to know these signs associated with Diana. Also, the staging of the rose tree, which, by the falling of its rose signals to Emilia that she will no longer be a maid and will be married to one of the men, depends on the audience recognizing the symbolism of the rose as representing virginity—a symbol in Western literature that goes back to the Middle Ages in works such as Guillaume de Lorris and Jean de Meun's *Le roman de la rose* (incidentally, a work that had a major influence on Geoffrey Chaucer, Shakespeare's main source for this play).

Epilogue, 1–18

EPILOGUE. I would now ask ye how ye like
  the play,
But, as it is with schoolboys, cannot say;
I am cruel fearful. Pray yet stay a while,
And let me look upon ye. No man smile?
Then it goes hard, I see. He that has
Loved a young handsome wench, then, show
  his face—
'Tis strange if none be here—and if he will,
Against his conscience, let him hiss, and kill
Our market. 'Tis in vain, I see, to stay ye.
Have at the worst can come, then! Now, what
  say ye?
And yet mistake me not—I am not bold—

We have no such cause. If the tale we have
  told—
For 'tis no other—any way content ye
(For to that honest purpose it was meant ye)
We have our end; and ye shall have ere long,
I dare say, many a better to prolong
Your old loves to us. We and all our might
Rest at your service. Gentlemen, good night.

This Epilogue is a very unusual way to end a play. Rather than assume that the audience has enjoyed it, thanking them for attending, or even immediately wishing them goodnight, the Epilogue comes onto the stage to rather self-consciously ask whether or not the audience enjoyed the play. This in itself is not a very unusual act, except that the Epilogue is "cruel fearful" about their response and seems to be unable to maintain the audience's attention, asking them "Pray yet stay awhile / And let me look upon ye." Seeing that no one is smiling, he assumes they do not like the play. But he knows that those in the audience who have loved a young woman, and there certainly must be some, can make sure this play will not be a success, as long as they are willing to do it "against [their] conscience." After realizing it is impossible to get the audience to stay, the Epilogue claims that they have only tried to please the audience with the play, and if they have succeeded in doing so, then they have met their goal. If the audience does not like this play, the Epilogue is sure they will have better ones soon to "prolong" their "old loves."

This Epilogue can be difficult for readers because it depends on a knowledge of the mores of Renaissance theater—mores that this play has broken. As a tragicomedy, a combination of tragedy and comedy modeled after Guarini's Italian play *The Faithful Shepherd (Il pastor fido),* this play was part of a new movement in the early 17th century to move away from the traditional divisions of tragedy, history, and comedy plays that had dominated the early years of English Renaissance theater. These plays, however, as was the case with an earlier Fletcher play *The Faithful Shepherdess* published in 1610 and staged some years before, were at times misinterpreted and disliked by audiences. When the reader knows this history of audience reception, he or she can come to see the importance of this Epilogue in anticipating the audience distaste for this story with its challenging and in some ways unsatisfying ending.

CRITICAL INTRODUCTION TO THE PLAY

The Two Noble Kinsmen is one of the least appreciated of Shakespeare's works, because of both content, which at times has been considered scandalous, and the debate over whether or not Shakespeare had anything to do with the writing of the play (for more on this debate, see the Classic Criticism section). Yet the play has striking merits, as a stunning tragicomedy and a piercing meditation into the passionate nature of human relationships. To appreciate and understand this play, one needs not only to appreciate the ways in which the play interrogates the character's relationships, passions, and actions but also the language of the play itself, which is often rich with metaphor, fanciful description, and playful rhythm.

Political and military power is an important theme throughout the play, but most strikingly in the early scenes of Act I. The audience, faced with this scene, would recall Shakespeare's earlier work *A Midsummer Night's Dream,* which also began with talk of a wedding celebration for Theseus and Hippolyta, with Theseus saying to Hippolyta:

> Hippolyta, I wooed thee with my sword,
> And won thy love doing injuries.
> But I will wed thee in another key—
> With pomp, with triumph and with revelling.
>
> (*AMND* Act I, Scene 1)

Theseus has conquered Hippolyta and her native land, yet this act of military conquest is meant to dissolve into the pleasures of marriage and ceremony. In *The Two Noble Kinsmen,* however, the pleasures and pomp of the wedding, the procession under way with a boy strewing flowers and Hymen carrying a torch will give way to military conquest.

As the queens interrupt, they are in essence pulling Theseus away from his domestic and romantic happiness with Hippolyta and forcing him to return to the role of the military conqueror. The stark contrast between the glory of Theseus's wedding procession and the meek supplication of the Three Queens whose husbands have been killed in a failed siege of Thebes is a poignant reminder of this contrast. Theseus, as a character, must always mediate between his powerful military prowess and his attention and sympathy to the needs and fears of the women around him. As his relationship to Hippolyta was forged with both love and violence, so, too, are his relationships with the Three Queens, whose supplications to him aim to activate his military side to intervene on their behalf.

Palamon and Arcite, as well, oscillate between military power and romantic, sympathetic feeling for both Emilia and one another. Their impressive ability as soldiers is well remarked almost immediately by a herald who brings them on stage after they have been defeated by Theseus's army, as Theseus describes them:

> By th'helm of Mars, I saw them in the war,
> Like to a pair of lions, smeared with prey,
> Make lanes in troops aghast. I fixed my note
> Constantly on them, for they were a mark
> Worth a god's view.
>
> (Act I, Scene 4)

Yet, Palamon's and Arcite's acumen on the battlefield is, in the early scenes of the play, combined with a sense of justice, purity, and emotional attachment for one another. Like Theseus, the two men, at least early on in the play, attempt to use their physical strength for the benefit of right governance, rather than blind ambition for power. Theseus and Palamon and Arcite, though they fight on different sides, are both united in their distrust and hatred for Creon, a fact Palamon makes clear:

> He,
> A most unbounded tyrant, whose successes
> Makes heaven unfeared, and villainy assured

Beyond its power there's nothing; almost puts
Faith in a fever, and deifies alone
Voluble chance; who only attributes
The faculties of other instruments
To his own nerves and act; commands men
  service,
And what they win in't, boot and glory; one
That fears not to do harm; good, dares not.
  Let
The blood of mine that's sib to him be sucked
From me with leeches; let them break and fall
Off me with that corruption.

(Act I, Scene 2)

The longing for purity, however, does not last for the two men, who become bitterly entangled in a love triangle with a woman who has no genuine love for either of them. The play, then, seems to be interested in how the sober-minded and devoted friends end up caught in a self-centered madness over Emilia. The contrast between stable control and passionate irrationality is one of the major driving factors of this play, exemplified not only by Palamon and Arcite but the Jailer's Daughter as well.

Romance, as a genre, often features displaced soldiers or travelers loving someone they observe in the strange land in which they find themselves. One of the most famous examples of this genre for Renaissance readers in England would have been Sir Philip Sidney's *Arcadia,* published in its authoritative edition in 1593, in which two men wash ashore after a shipwreck and pursue two ladies through a series of adventures in a new and strange kingdom. Shakespeare turned to romance in many of his later plays, including *The Winter's Tale* and *As You Like It,* both works based on popular prose romances of Shakespeare's time (Greene's *Pandosto* and Lyly's *Rosalind*). In *The Two Noble Kinsmen,* we have, similarly to *The Winter's Tale,* a story about friendship challenged by the jealousy that romantic love for women can create between male friends, but what makes this play unique among Shakespeare's canon is the intensity of same-sex friendship in this play. Friendship is not looked

upon simply with nostalgia for a simpler time, it is seen as a preferable way of living one's life, with the play often seeming to show that heterosexual love is a more destructive, random, and selfish force than same-sex friendship. To this end, to understand *The Two Noble Kinsmen,* one must understand the sort of friendships that exist in the play and what they are trying to say about the nature of human love, affection, and jealousy.

The friendship between Pirithous and Theseus emerges in the play as one of the only friendships that is stable, present, and fully integrated into the demands of social, political, and romantic living. Theseus will be married to Hippolyta, but this has no effect on his strong friendship with Pirithous, described by Emilia as "maturely seasoned, / More buckled with strong judgement," and so intense and mutual that "their needs / the one of th'other may be said to water / Their intertangled roots of love" (Act 1, Scene 3). Pirithous and Theseus are understood as being close allies, understanding deeply each other's needs and supporting each other throughout their lives. Emilia believes she had a similar, if less impressive, friendship with the late Flavina. She describes the friendship to Hippolyta

But I
And she I sigh and spoke of were things
  innocent,
Loved for we did, and like the elements
That know not what nor why, yet do effect
Rare issues by their operance, our souls
Did so to one another; what she liked
Was then of me approved, what not,
  condemned.

(Act I, Scene 3)

Emilia imagines that her friendship with Flavina was, though immature, deeply seated in their beings and based on natural and complete feelings between them.

Palamon and Arcite's friendship, though always strong, reaches its most exalted state right before its collapse. While in prison together, the two men begin to realize that their love is unrivaled in the world and that, though they can never marry or have children during their life sentences, they can be "one another's wife, ever begetting / New births of love" (Act II, Scene 2). Their friendship, unlike that of Pirithous and Theseus, is more of an escape from the reality of their situation than a support system for engagement with the realities of life. The escapist quality of their language in describing their friendship helps to underscore the problems that will come when they begin to feel jealous of each other and, more important, when their jail cell opens to the outside world of Athens.

Though friendship is explored, explained, and analyzed throughout the play, love is treated as a mysterious and destructive force throughout *The Two Noble Kinsmen*. Beginning with Theseus's love for Hippolyta enforced by conquest, love and violence are linked throughout the play. Palamon and Arcite, mere lines after proclaiming the depth of their love, turn violently toward each other when they realize they both love Emilia, a woman neither of the men has ever met:

> PALAMON. O that now, that now
> Thy false self and thy friend had but this
>   fortune
> To be one hour at liberty, and grasp
> Our good swords in our hands, I would
>   quickly teach thee
> What 'twere to filch affection from another.
> Thou art baser in it than a cutpurse.
> Put but thy head out of this window more,
> And, as I have a soul, I'll nail thy life to't.
>   (Act II, Scene 2)

The protective shell of their friendship and the prison cell has now been interrupted by the outside world and longs to spill out into it in order to settle their difference. Romantic love for Palamon and Arcite is a disruptive force urging the men to cross boundaries, break rules, and sneak around—quite a stark contrast to the peaceful seclusion of their friendship before their rival loves for Emilia.

The maddening potential of love is most clearly seen in the play through the Jailer's Daughter, who condemns her own father to death by allowing Palamon to escape as proof of her love for him. She loves him against her own reason, knowing that he does not seem to love her back nor is particularly grateful that she released him. Her madness at the fear of his death lasts for the whole play and only has the hope for being cured when she is eventually paired with the Wooer who pretends to be Palamon. Her desire, it seems, is arbitrary and interchangeable, hardly tied to a specific person and somewhat foolish in nature. That Palamon and Arcite fall in love, too, with a woman they do not know who does not love them back parallels the Jailor's Daughter's maddening love.

The play, in addition to its critique of love, contains a recurring theme of chastity, but a kind of productive chastity that is able to be regenerated. The Prologue compares the play to virginity, but a kind that can be renewed again and again. Arcite describes their love, certainly not able to bear children, as "ever begetting / new births of love" (Act II, Scene 2), echoing the renewable chastity of the Prologue, and Emilia, the object of affection who has no desire to be loved, clings to chastity even as it becomes clearer and clearer that she must give it up. The importance of chastity speaks to a kind of transcendence present in the play that is always at odds with the social competition going on in society. In Emilia's prayer before the tournament, she wishes to remain a virgin, but as the rose tree makes clear and as the tournament, the social ritual of determining who will win her love, progresses, society in the end beats out chastity, just as romantic love seems to win over friendship.

Yet, romantic love's victory in the play is deeply unsatisfying to the audience, a fact admitted by the Epilogue at the end of the play. In fact, the ending is the last and perhaps greatest obstacle to understanding the play. In the end, Arcite wins the tournament but dies in a random and deeply unfair accident. Palamon then wins Emilia's love, handed over to him by the dying Arcite, but we are given no sense that Emilia favors this in any way—her reaction to Palamon is a mystery. That the end of the play lacks a clear moral is odd for Shakespeare, who often gives his audiences a clear sense of resolution in his plays, and so this lack is all the more a striking moment to be considered and one that deeply questions romantic love, marriage, human passions, and the fairness of fate.

EXTRACTS OF CLASSIC CRITICISM
August Wilhelm von Schlegel (1767–1845)
[Excerpted from *Lectures on Dramatic Art and Literature* (1808). Schlegel translated the plays of Shakespeare into German and was an important influence on Samuel Coleridge and other romantics.]

The Two Noble Kinsmen is deserving of more particular mention, as it is the joint production of Shakespeare and Fletcher. I see no ground for calling this in question; the piece, it is true, did not make its appearance till after the death of both; but what could be the motive with the editor or printer for any deception, as Fletcher's name was at the time in as great, at least, if not greater celebrity than Shakespeare's? Were it the sole production of Fletcher, it would, undoubtedly, have to be ranked as the best of his serious and heroic pieces. However; it would be unfair to a writer of talent to take from him a work simply because it seems too good for him. Might not Fletcher, who in his thoughts and images not unfrequently shows an affinity to Shakespeare, have for once had the good fortune to approach closer to him than usual? It would still be more dangerous to rest on the similarity of separate passages to others in Shakespeare. This might rather arise from imitation. I rely therefore entirely on the historical statement, which, probably, originated in a tradition of the players. There are connoisseurs, who, in the pictures of Raphael, (which, as is well known, were not always wholly executed by himself,) take upon them to determine what parts were painted by

Francesco Penni, or Giulio Romano, or some other scholar. I wish them success with the nicety of their discrimination; they are at least secure from contradiction, as we have no certain information on the subject. I would only remind these connoisseurs, that Giulio Romano was himself deceived by a copy from Raphael of Andrea del Sarto's, and that, too, with regard to a figure which he had himself assisted in painting. The case in point is, however, a much more complicated problem in criticism. The design of Raphael's figure was at least his own, and the execution only was distributed in part among his scholars. But to find out how much of *The Two Noble Kinsmen* may belong to Shakespeare, we must not only be able to tell the difference of hands in the execution, but also to determine the influence of Shakespeare on the plan of the whole. When, however, he once joined another poet in the production of a work, he must also have accommodated himself, in a certain degree, to his views, and renounced the prerogative of unfolding his inmost peculiarity. Amidst so many grounds for doubting, if I might be allowed to hazard an opinion, I should say, that I think I can perceive the mind of Shakespeare in a certain ideal purity, which distinguishes this piece from all others of Fletcher's, and in the conscientious fidelity with which the story adheres to that of Chaucer's *Palamon and Arcite* ["The Knight's Tale" from Chaucer's *Canterbury Tales*]. In the style Shakespeare's hand is at first discoverable in a brevity and fulness of thought bordering on obscurity; in a colour of the expression, almost all the poets of that time bear a strong resemblance to each other. The first acts are most carefully laboured; afterwards the piece is drawn out to too great a length and in an epic manner; the dramatic law of quickening the action towards the conclusion, is not sufficiently observed. The part of the jailor's daughter, whose insanity is artlessly conducted in pure monologues, is certainly not Shakespeare's; for, in that case, we must suppose hm to have had an intention of arrogantly imitating his own Ophelia. Moreover, it was then a very general custom for two or even three poets to join together in the production of one play. Besides the constant example of Beaumont and Fletcher, we have many others. The consultations, respecting the plan, were generally held at merry meetings in taverns.

William Spalding (1809–1859) [Excerpted from *A Letter on Shakespeare's authorship of The Two Noble Kinsmen; a drama commonly ascribed to John Fletcher* (1833). Spalding was a professor at Edinburgh University.]

As I wish to make you a convert to the affirmative opinion [that Shakespeare is the author], it may be wise to acquaint you that you will not be alone in it, if you shall finally see reason to embrace it. Shakespeare, you know, suffered a long eclipse, which left him in obscurity till the beginning of the last century, when he reappeared surrounded by annotators, a class of men who have followed a narrow track, but yet are greater benefactors to us than we are ready to acknowledge. The commentators have given little attention to the question before us; but some of the best of them have declared incidentally for Shakespeare's claim, and though even the editors who have professed this belief have not yet inserted the work as his, this is only among many evil results of the slavish system to which they all adhere. . . .

The first difference which may be pointed out between Shakespeare and Fletcher, is that of their versification. You have learned from a study of the poets themselves in what the difference consists. Shakespeare's versification is broken and full of pauses, he is sparing of double terminations to his verses, and has a marked fondness for ending speeches or

scenes with hemi-stitches. Fletcher's rhythm is of a newer and smoother cast, often keeping the lines distinct and without breaks through whole speeches, abounding in double endings, and very seldom leaving a line incomplete at the end of a sentence or scene. And the opposite taste of the two poets in their choice and arrangement of words, gives an opposite character to the whole modulation of their verses. Fletcher's is sweet and flowing, and peculiarly fitted either for declamation or the softness of sorrow: Shakespeare's ear is tuned to the stateliest solemnity of thought, or the abruptness and vehemence of passion. The present drama exhibits in whole scenes the qualities of Shakespeare's versification; and there are other scenes which are marked by those of Fletcher's; the difference is one reason for separating the authorship.

Samuel Taylor Coleridge (1772–1834) [Excerpted from *Shakspeare, with Introductory Remarks on Poetry, the Drama, and the Stage* (1818). Coleridge, best known for poems such as "The Rime of the Ancient Mariner," was also an important critic.]

On comparing the prison scene of Palamon and Arcite, Act ii. sc. 2, with the dialogue between the same speakers, Act I. sc. 2, I can scarcely retain a doubt as to the first act's having been written by Shakespeare. Assuredly it was not written by B. and F. [Beaumont and Fletcher]. I hold Jonson more probable than either of these two.

The main presumption, however, for Shakespeare's share in this play rests on a point, to which the sturdy critics of this edition (and indeed all before them) were blind,—that is, the construction of the blank verse, which proves beyond all doubt any intentional imitation, if not the proper hand, of Shakespeare. Now, whatever improbability there is in the former, (which supposes

Fletcher conscious of the inferiority, the too poematic *minus* dramatic nature, of his versification, and of which there is neither proof, nor likelihood,) adds so much to the probability of the latter. On the other hand, the harshness of many of these very passages, a harshness unrelieved by any lyrical interbreathings, and still more the want of profundity in the thoughts, keep me from an absolute decision.

Algernon Charles Swinburne (1837–1909)

[From his Prologue to *The Two Noble Kinsmen*, excerpted from *The Poems of Algernon Charles Swinburne* (1905). Swinburne was a well-known poet, with a style often described as decadent. As a critic, he wrote extensively on Shakespeare.]

. . .

Sweet as the dewfall, splendid as the south,
Love touched with speech Boccaccio's golden
    mouth,
Joy thrilled and filled its utterance full with
    song,
And sorrow smiled on doom that wrought no
    wrong.
A starrier lustre of lordlier music rose
Beyond the sundering bar of seas and snows
When Chaucer's thought took life and light
    from his
And England's crown was one with Italy's.
Loftiest and last, by grace of Shakespeare's
    word,
Arose above their quiring spheres a third,
Arose, and flashed, and faltered: song's deep
    sky
Saw Shakespeare pass in light, in music die.
No light like his, no music, man might give
To bid the darkened sphere, left songless, live.
Soft though the sound of Fletcher's rose and
    rang
And lit the lunar darkness as it sang,
Below the singing stars the cloud-crossed
    moon

Gave back the sunken sun's a trembling tune.
As when at highest high tide the sovereign sea
Pauses, and patience doubts if passion be,
Till gradual ripples ebb, recede, recoil,
Shine, smile, and whisper, laughing as they
    toil,
Stark silence fell, at turn of fate's high tide,
Upon his broken song when Shakespeare died,
Till Fletcher's light sweet speech took heart to
    say
What evening, should it speak for morning,
    may.
And fourfold now the gradual glory shines
That shows once more in heaven two twinborn
    signs,
Two brethren stars whose light no cloud may
    fret,
No soul whereon their story dawns forget.

Henry Hallam (1777–1859)

[From *Introduction to the Literature of Europe in the Fifteenth, Sixteenth, and Seventeenth Centuries* (1839). Hallam was a distinguished historian. He was also the father of Arthur Henry Hallam, made famous by Tennyson's poem *In Memoriam.*]

The Two Noble Kinsmen is a play that has been honored by a tradition of Shakespeare's concern in it. The evidence as to this is the titlepage of the first edition; which, though it may seem much at first sight, is next to nothing in our old drama, full of misnomers of this kind. The editors of Beaumont and Fletcher have insisted upon what they take for marks of Shakespeare's style; and Schlegel, after "seeing no reason for doubting so probable an opinion," detects the spirit of Shakespeare in a certain ideal purity which distinguishes this from other plays of Fletcher, and in the conscientious fidelity with which it follows the Knight's Tale in Chaucer. *The Two Noble Kinsmen* has much of that elevated sense of honor, friendship, fidelity, and love, which belongs, I think, more characteristically to Fletcher, who had drunk at the fountain of Castilian romance, than to one in whose vast mind this conventional morality of particular classes was subordinated to the universal nature of man. In this sense, Fletcher is always, in his tragic compositions, a very ideal poet. The subject itself is fitter for him than for Shakespeare. In the language and conduct of this play, with great deference to better and more attentive critics, I see imitation of Shakespeare rather than such resemblances as denote his powerful stamp. The madness of the gaoler's daughter, where some have imagined they saw the masterhand, is doubtless suggested by that of Ophelia, but with an inferiority of taste and feeling which it seems impossible not to recognize. The painful and degrading symptom of female insanity, which Shakespeare has touched with his gentle hand, is dwelt upon by Fletcher with all his innate impurity. Can any one believe that the former would have written the last scene in which the gaoler's daughter appears on the stage? Shlegel has too fine taste to believe that this character came from Shakespeare, and it is given up by the latest assertor of his claim to a participation in the play.

MODERN CRITICISM AND CRITICAL CONTROVERSIES

Modern criticism of *The Two Noble Kinsmen* starting in the early decades of the 20th century began to move beyond the classic question of whether or not Shakespeare actually wrote the play (for excerpts of this, see the Classic Criticism section) to considering the nature of Shakespeare and Fletcher's collaboration—as well as exploring the themes of gender, desire, and literary precedent throughout the play. Theodore Spencer's 1939 article *"The Two Noble Kinsmen"* was an early example of a piece of scholarship moving beyond the authorship question. Spencer puts the question of whether Shakespeare has written any of the play or not by turning to Alfred Hart, whose 1934

article "Shakespeare and the vocabulary of *The Two Noble Kinsmen*" had used detailed analysis of passages from the play to show that Shakespeare was indeed behind many of the scenes. Spencer then goes on to compare in detail the passages written by Shakespeare versus those of Fletcher in order to suggest a difference in their styles. His main concern is to find out which passages are written by Shakespeare so he can subject them to detailed analysis. In the end, however, Spencer does not have a high opinion of the play, because he sees Fletcher's writing too much in it, he writes, "but most of [*The Two Noble Kinsmen*] is Fletcher's, and, for our present purposes, not worth careful analysis" (275).

As *The Two Noble Kinsmen* is one of the most stunning examples of Renaissance playwriting collaboration (a very common practice in the Renaissance), the relationship between Shakespeare and

An early-17th-century portrait of John Fletcher by an unknown artist.

Fletcher in regard to the text has been, for many scholars, a fascinating window into the collaborative practice of playmaking. Charles H. Frey, in his edited volume of essays, *Shakespeare, Fletcher, and The Two Noble Kinsmen,* published in 1989, gathers a collection of essays by various scholars that seek to understand the relationship between Shakespeare and Fletcher in this play. The essays in the collection consider the play from many different angles—with quite a few delving into the nature of collaboration and what this play means for our ideas about a canon of Shakespeare's work. One essay in the collection, Michael D. Bristol's "*The Two Noble Kinsmen:* Shakespeare and the Problem of Authority," takes up the question of what this play, "neither definitively included nor definitively excluded" from the list of Shakespeare's works, can tell the reader about Shakespeare's canonical work. He writes:

> The play offers a particularly useful point of departure for consideration of "Shakespeare's" authority. In the first place, the problem of attribution and authenticity invites consideration of the basis on which institutionalized scholarship acknowledges literary paternity and therefore the cultural force of particular documents. Second, the narrative material itself can be read as a demonstration or reenactment of the origin and foundation of civil authority in which Theseus's unification of the scattered communities of Attica into the Athenian polis is the exemplary illustration . . . I maintain that in both aspects of the problem *The Two Noble Kinsmen* should be regarded as an ominous text. (79)

By *ominous,* he means the way the play challenges our ideas of "the distinction between the canonical and the uncanonical." Indeed, the idea of Shakespeare as a solitary genius producing plays that must be held sacred as testaments to the great mind of their author is severely questioned by this play according to much of the modern criticism that surrounds it.

Modern criticism as well has reshaped the scholarly view of the Jailer's Daughter. Early critics saw this character as proof positive that the play, or at least the scenes containing her, were not written by Shakespeare. She was seen as a cheap parody and imitation of Ophelia in *Hamlet,* a depiction well beneath Shakespeare's genius. However, modern critics see in the Jailer's Daughter, however her character was created between the minds of Shakespeare and Fletcher, an interesting commentary on the gender politics of chivalry, reading her madness as a sort of resistance. A prime example of this strategy is Douglas Bruster's 1995 article "The Jailer's Daughter and the Politics of Madwomen's Language." Bruster argues that despite her complete lack of control in society, her madness is itself a powerful window into Jacobean society or, in Bruster's words "it is precisely in the mad language of this otherwise disempowered character that we get the richest picture of the arrangements of power in the play, of social relations in the early modern playhouse, and of transformations in the Jacobean culture that produced *The Two Noble Kinsmen*" (277).

Some historical readings of the play have also emerged in the recent scholarship. Peter Herman's essay "'Is This Winning?': Prince Henry's Death and the Problem of Chivalry in *The Two Noble Kinsmen*" argues that the death of King James's heir Prince Henry undermined some chivalric conventions of which the play itself is also skeptical. Queer readings of the play have also become more popular.

Nonetheless, historical inquiry into the nature of Shakespeare and Fletcher's collaboration forms the largest part of the recent criticism. As John Fletcher's reputation increased through the 1990s, critics began to see him not as a flawed and inferior imitator of Shakespeare but as an important dramatist in his own right. More nuanced and sympathetic readings of his work resulted, and interest in this play naturally increased.

THE PLAY TODAY

The Two Noble Kinsmen has the distinction of being the only play in the Shakespeare canon that has never been made into a movie. Despite this exclusion, the second half of the 20th century has seen a number of performances of the play, many of which are documented and described in Eugene M. Waith's critical edition of the play (see Waith, 34–42). The first 20th-century revival of the play known to scholars was in 1928 in London. There was a public reading of the play in 1936, thanks to the Nottingham Shakespeare Society, as well as a radio broadcast of the play in England in 1956. Waith notes a successful performance of the play in 1973 at the York Festival of the Arts in England. In 1979, there were all-male performances in Edinburgh and London. Also in 1979, the play was performed at the Globe Playhouse of Los Angeles. A performance by the Jean Cocteau Repertory Company in 1981 in New York City was not wholly praised, though the performance by Phyllis Deitschel as the Jailer's Daughter was considered a highlight. In 1985, the play was put on by the Berkeley Shakespeare Festival in California, a successful performance according to Waith. Quite strikingly, the Royal Shakespeare Company gave *The Two Noble Kinsmen* the honor, in 1986, of being the first play performed at their Swan Theater in Stratford-upon-Avon, Shakespeare's birthplace. The play was featured the same year at the New Jersey Shakespeare Festival. Beyond Waith's scope, a more recent production of the play opened in October 2003 at the Public Theater/Martinson Hall in New York City. The most recent New York City staging of the play was produced by the Guerrilla Shakespeare Company in early 2010.

While early critical discussion of the play centered nearly exclusively on the question of authorship and collaboration, the play now is far more represented in college classrooms and scholarly publications as a work deeply invested in issues of gender and identity. The homoerotically charged friendship of Palamon and Arcite, as well as the relationship of Hippolyta and Flavina, raises some critical questions about this play's relationship to issues of sexual identity. The play is also studied frequently as a critique of chivalry and patriarchy, focusing on the meaningless outcome of the tournament for Emilia's love. Students, as well, often find in the play a striking critique of what is commonly called "love at first sight." The love that dominates film, television, and popular literature—love without rationality, only passion—is strongly critiqued in this play.

Despite the fact that *The Two Noble Kinsmen* remains among the least read and least studied works of the Shakespearean canon, the play speaks to some of the most current issues in literary criticism, including gender identity, the politics of love, the role of women in society, the proper way to govern a political body, and the ethics of mercy and compassion. As scholars and students look for new hidden gems among the Shakespearean canon, *The Two Noble Kinsmen* is more and more frequently one of the places they look.

FIVE TOPICS FOR DISCUSSION AND WRITING

1. **Friendship:** What is *The Two Noble Kinsmen* trying to say about the nature of friendship? In the play, we are presented with friendships that are both strong and healthy (Pirithous and Theseus, for example, and the past friendship between Flavina and Emilia) as well as the passionately intimate yet vexed friendship between Palamon and Arcite. Are we meant to condemn Palamon and Arcite's behavior? To see it as an inevitability of such a passionate friendship? Also, why do you think Pirithous and Theseus are able to remain close over so many years while Palamon and Arcite run into jealousy and bitterness?

2. **Romantic love:** What is the play trying to say about romantic love? In the play we see Palamon and Arcite, as well as the Jailer's Daughter, all fall in love simply by seeing the other person. They often love in spite of their own safety, the relationships around them, and even the maintenance of their sanity. We often hear that love can drive people crazy, but this play takes this to its extreme. What do you think Shakespeare is trying to say about the way we fall in love? about the idea of love at first sight? about the complex relationship between romantic love and friendship?

3. **Ritual:** Ritual is very important in this play. The play begins with a marriage procession that is interrupted so that widows may lobby Theseus to help them perform the proper funeral rituals on their dead kings, Arcite and the Jailer's Daughter become caught up in a series of games and dances in the middle of pursuing their loves, and Palamon and Arcite must in the end settle their differences during a very public tournament. What role do these rituals play in the plot? What is the play trying to say about rituals and their importance in society and in individual lives?

4. **The Jailer's Daughter:** Many commentators have noted how closely Shakespeare and Fletcher model this play after Chaucer's "The Knight's Tale" from *The Canterbury Tales,* yet the Jailer's Daughter is not from Chaucer, and there is no clear source from which her story originated. Some people see the Jailer's Daughter as a kind of imitation of Ophelia in Shakespeare's *Hamlet.* Wherever her origins may lie, why do you think the Jailer's Daughter is in this play? What does she add that the story of Palamon and Arcite's love for Emilia does not offer? What symbolism may there be in the fact that she is the daughter of the Jailer?

5. **Tragedy and comedy:** This play is often called a tragicomedy, a combination of a tragedy and comedy. Comedies tend to end in marriage, while tragedies end in death. This play notably ends with both. Is the ending a happy one? Does the play leave the audience feeling that everything has been resolved as it should be? Why does the Epilogue seem to think the audience did not like the ending? What reasons would an audience have for disliking the play's ending? Do you feel as if all the characters at the end of the play are satisfied with the way all the various love stories have turned out?

Bibliography

Berggren, Paula S. "'For what we lack / We laugh': Incompletion and *The Two Noble Kinsmen.*" *Modern Language Studies* 14, no. 4 (1984): 3–17.

Bertram, Paul. *Shakespeare and the Two Noble Kinsmen.* New Brunswick, N.J.: Rutgers University Press, 1965.

Bradbrook, M. C. "Shakespeare and His Collaborators." In *Shakespeare,* edited by Clifford Leech and J. M. R. Margeson, 21–36. Toronto: University of Toronto Press, 1972.

Briggs, Julia. "'Chaucer . . . the Story Gives': *Troilus and Cressida* and *The Two Noble Kinsmen.*" In *Shakespeare and the Middle Ages: Essays on the Performance and Adaptation of the Plays with Medieval Sources or Settings,* edited by Martha W. Driver, Sid Ray, Michael Almereyda, and Dakin Matthews, 161–177. Jefferson, N.C.: McFarland, 2009.

———. "Tears at the Wedding: Shakespeare's Last Phase." In *Shakespeare's Late Plays: New Readings,* edited by Jennifer Richards and James Knowles, 210–227. Edinburgh: Edinburgh University Press, 1999.

Bruster, Douglas. "The Jailer's Daughter and the Politics of Madwomen's Language." *Shakespeare Quarterly* 46 (1995): 277–300.

Cobb, Christopher J. *The Staging of Romance in Late Shakespeare: Text and Theatrical Technique.* Newark: University of Delaware Press, 2007.

Donaldson, E. Talbot. *The Swan at the Well: Shakespeare Reading Chaucer.* New Haven, Conn.: Yale University Press, 1985.

Finkelpearl, Philip J. "Two Distincts, Division None: Shakespeare's and Fletcher's *The Two Noble Kinsmen* of 1613." In *Elizabethan Theater: Essays in Honor of S. Schoenbaum,* edited by R. B. Parker and S. P. Zitner, 184–199. Newark: University of Delaware Press, 1996.

Frey, Charles, ed. *Shakespeare, Fletcher, and "The Two Noble Kinsmen."* Columbia: University of Missouri Press, 1989.

Greenblatt, Stephen, Walter Cohen, Jean E. Howard, and Katharine Eisaman Maus, eds. *The Norton Shakespeare.* 2nd ed. New York: W. W. Norton, 2008.

Hart, Alfred. "Shakespeare and the Vocabulary of *The Two Noble Kinsmen.*" *RES* 10 (1934): 274–287.

Herman, Peter C. "'Is This Winning?': Prince Henry's Death and the Problem of Chivalry in *The Two Noble Kinsmen*." *South Atlantic Review* 62 (1997): 1–31.

Iyengar, Sujata. "Moorish Dancing in *The Two Noble Kinsmen*." *Medieval and Renaissance Drama in England: An Annual Gathering of Research, Criticism and Reviews* 20 (2007): 85–107.

Lynch, Kathryn L. "The Three Noble Kinsmen: Chaucer, Shakespeare, Fletcher." In *Images of Matter: Essays on British Literature of the Middle Ages and Renaissance,* edited by Yvonne Bruce, 72–91. Newark: University of Delaware Press, 2005.

Mesterházy, Lili. "The Taming of *The Two Noble Kinsmen*." In *Shakespeare and His Collaborators over the Centuries,* edited by Pavel Drábek, Klára Kolinská, Matthew Nicholls, and John Russell Brown, 77–84. Newcastle upon Tyne, England: Cambridge Scholars, 2008.

Potter, Lois, ed. *The Two Noble Kinsmen.* Surrey, England: Thomas Nelson, 1997.

Shannon, Laurie J. "Emilia's Argument: Friendship and 'Human Title' in *The Two Noble Kinsmen*." *English Literary Renaissance* 64 (1997): 657–682.

Sinfield, Alan. "Cultural Materialism and Intertextuality: The Limits of Queer Reading in *A Midsummer Night's Dream* and *The Two Noble Kinsmen*." *Shakespeare Survey: An Annual Survey of Shakespeare Studies and Production* 56 (2003): 67–78.

Spencer, Theodore. *"The Two Noble Kinsmen."* *Modern Philology* 36 (1939): 255–276.

Steiner, George. "Two Noble Kinsmen." *PN Review* 31, no. 2 (2004): 16–20.

Stewart, Alan. "'Near Akin': The Trials of Friendship in *The Two Noble Kinsmen*." In *Shakespeare's Late Plays: New Readings,* edited by Jennifer Richards and James Knowles, 57–71. Edinburgh: Edinburgh University Press, 1999.

Waith, Eugene M. *The Two Noble Kinsmen.* Oxford: Clarendon, 1989.

—Timothy J. Duffy

The Winter's Tale

꧁꧂

INTRODUCTION

The Winter's Tale is Shakespeare's great play of hope restored. The play's double plot shows love withstanding the pain of loss and the ravages of time. We see a man lose his mind and destroy much of what is dear to him, only to regain as much of it as time and circumstance will permit. *The Winter's Tale* is also a great adventure story, transpiring across seas and deserts, royal courts and humble shepherd's cottages. Replete with rich, often highly self-conscious language, *The Winter's Tale* shows a playwright fully in command of the artifices and devices of his craft, yet determined to use them to acknowledge and discover larger truths abut human passions and loyalties. The play encompasses scenes as horrible as Antigonus being torn limb from limb by a bear and as humorous as the ousted courtier Autolycus trying to eke out a living swindling country bumpkins.

The Winter's Tale, first performed in 1611, epitomizes the spirit of what critics term Shakespeare's "late romances"—plays of reconciliation after estrangement, celebration after loss. Other late romances include *Cymbeline* and *Pericles, Prince of Tyre*, both written before *The Winter's Tale*, and *The Tempest*, written just after it. These plays were intended for the Blackfriars theater, whose layout encouraged more ornate and detailed productions. Romances often involve unusual juxtapositions of genres and emotions. *The Winter's Tale* depicts the sudden and extreme jealousy of Leontes, king of Sicilia, whose false suspicion of his wife for adultery leads him to destroy all that is dear to him. The play also reflects thematic elements of Shakespeare's source for the play, a narrative prose work called *Pandosto* by his contemporary Robert Greene (who before his death had spoken of Shakespeare resentfully as "the upstart crow"). Greene's work was subtitled *The Triumph of Time*. Shakespeare jettisoned this subtitle but retained the theme denoted by it. He used it to suggest the way time not only heals all wounds, as the proverb goes, but restores losses, makes tragedies into comedies. Much of the play's appeal and part of its strangeness lies in its mixing of the tragic and comic. The sudden mood-shift in the middle of the play is disconcerting, yet it shows Shakespeare's consummate nimbleness in taking just what he needs from each genre to build a satisfying and intriguing story.

In the spirit of the ancient Greek romances from which it draws much of its narrative and emotional vocabulary, the play takes place across vast geographical reaches and over two decades. The story is fantastic in many ways, but it is bolstered by a fundamental emotional realism, with envy, remorse, love, bravery, trickery all coming to the fore at different points. If the play had ended after the courtier Antigonus was eaten by a bear while trying to provide safety for Leontes' rejected infant daughter, Perdita, it would have been a tragedy as thoroughly sad as any of Shakespeare's. One calamity follows another: The king's repudiation of his best friend, Polixenes; his sudden, vituperative hatred of his wife, Hermione, accused of adultery

Autolycus sells ribbons to the Clown and a ballad to Mopsa and Dorca in Act IV, Scene 4 of *The Winter's Tale,* in this print published by Virtue and Company in the 19th century. *(Painting by Charles Robert Leslie; engraving by Lumb Stocks)*

but in fact faithful; and the wasting away of his son and heir Mamillius, who dies apparently because he is so upset by the accusations against his mother. Only when the play's action is removed from court, to the countryside setting of the humble rustics who take the abandoned Perdita in, do we see the fostering of life, hope, harmony. Nature and art, whose complex relationship is at the philosophical heart of the latter half of the play, combine to produce a magical, even exuberant ending. Both the stunning surprise of Hermione's return to life and the brilliant, joyous nature of the earlier dialogue between Perdita and Polixenes' son Florizel during their bucolic courtship show Shakespeare's full command of the scale of human feeling. *The Winter's Tale* both examines and embodies the power of imagination to inform and transform reality.

BACKGROUND

The Winter's Tale was first classified as a comedy in the 1623 folio. Only later did Edward Dowden, a late-19th-century Anglo-Irish man of letters, identify *The Winter's Tale, The Tempest, Pericles,* and *Cymbeline* as "romances." All four of these plays involve divided families, have moments of

magic or miracle, and, after much travail, end in marriage and harmony. The form, in its artificiality and delight in stagecraft has been seen as influenced by the contemporary Jacobean masque. *Pericles* and *The Winter's Tale* are also, of the four Shakespearean romances, the two that most bear the imprint of the "Greek novel" or "Hellenistic romance," a form influential on European literature through the 16th century. The Greek novel portrays two young lovers, often of high rank, and their adventures, taking place in exotic climes centering around the Mediterranean, with most of the action taking place on sea voyages. Anybody who has read an example of this genre and then reads a plot summary of *The Winter's Tale* will be struck by the resemblances. But *The Winter's Tale* is not limited by the genre of the Greek novel; not only does its dramatic form make it more multidimensional, but Leontes' emotional depth, both in rage and in penance, is an aspect that could not have flourished within the tight generic leashing of the Greek novel form.

Shakespeare's textual source was Robert Greene's 1588 *Pandosto, or the Triumph of Time.* Greene, who died in his 30s, was a slightly older contemporary of Shakespeare and arguably the first to make mention of the man from Stratford in a document that has been preserved. Greene was associated with the Euphuistic movement of writers who employed a deliberately ornate ornamental prose. *Pandosto* is highly influenced by the Greek novel, but its artificiality is more jagged than refined, and it has jarring and downbeat elements at odds with the serene harmony of its parent genre. Pandosto is the character called Leontes in *The Winter's Tale:* the king who becomes jealous of his wife's closeness to his best friend and causes the death of his wife and son. But in Greene's work, Pandosto is the king of Bohemia, not of Sicilia, which is the domain of Pandosto's friend. Greene's scenario is darker. Not only does Pandosto's wife never come back to life, but when Pandosto meets his long-lost daughter, Fawnia, he feels desire for her and inveighs her to marry him. Fawnia is repulsed, but later loves him as a father once his true identity is revealed. Unlike Leontes in Shakespeare's play, the Pandosto figure commits suicide. However, the tone of the two plays is not as different as this might imply. Greene, in a highly self-conscious way, seems to have Pandosto commit suicide to add a tragical "stratagem" to a comical outcome, which means that Pandosto's demise does not detract from the positive outcome of the story; it merely makes it easier for the young lovers to stay on course for a happy life. The subtitle of Greene's work, *The Triumph of Time,* is highly pertinent to the tone of Shakespeare's play: In *The Winter's Tale,* truth and justice will out, and the workings of time will smooth out iniquity, remedy suffering, and bring consolation to the forlorn.

Shakespeare also modernizes Greene's story by switching the locales of Bohemia and Sicilia. In Greene's story, Sicilia is the pastoral place where the action moves once the baby is cast away, building on the classical associations of Sicily with pastoral poetry. In Shakespeare's time, Bohemia was known as by far the more rustic place, and he thus turned around the two. This gesture also shows a certain distancing of *The Winter's Tale* from the pastoral as a genre. Despite the presence of a great pastoral episode in Act IV, Scene 4, the play as a whole is, in terms of genre, much more a romance or tragicomedy than a pastoral. Despite similarities between *The Winter's Tale* and *As You Like It,* especially in the characters of Autolycus and Jaques and the cynical attitude toward the potential depravity of the court, *The Winter's Tale* is much less pastoral than the earlier play.

Date and Text of the Play

There is no quarto text of *The Winter's Tale;* in other words, it seems to have first appeared in print in the 1623 folio. It is believed that the First Folio version was derived from the manuscript written down by Ralph Crane at the time of the play's production, generally taken to be a reliable copy. There are few textual controversies regarding the play. It is known to have been first performed in 1611 and was performed again for the wedding of Princess Elizabeth, daughter of King James, to Frederick, king of Bohemia, in 1613. It is tempting to see the Bohemia referred to in the play as linked to the princess's marriage, but the marriage was not yet contracted when the play was written, probably in 1610 or early 1611, and "Bohemia" was in the original Greene story. Most scholars believe *The Winter's Tale* was written after *Cymbeline,* but some, including Gary Taylor and Stanley Wells, believe it came before.

SYNOPSIS
Brief Synopsis

Leontes, king of Sicilia, has been entertaining his childhood friend Polixenes, king of Bohemia, for nine months, and is reluctant to let him go home. Exhorting his wife, Hermione, to convince Polixenes to stay, Leontes suddenly suspects his wife of being *too* eager to retain Polixenes. Struck by a fit of jealousy, Leontes threatens to lash out at Polixenes, who is rescued by Leontes' courtier, Camillo, who both flee. Though realizing that his young son, Mamillius, is in fact his own, Leontes is convinced the child Hermione is now bearing is a bastard. Determined to prove Hermione guilty, he asks the advice of the oracle at Delphi, imprisoning his wife while he waits. Soon, messengers return from the oracle saying Leontes is totally wrong, that all he has accused are blameless. Leontes is determined to continue on with the trial when news is brought of Mamillius's death. Initially seeing this as an adverse judgment from Apollo, Leontes repents, but it is too late to save Mamillius, news of whose death is brought. To add to the tragedy, Paulina, Hermione's attendant, announces the death of the queen. Meanwhile, the baby has been taken for safekeeping by Paulina's husband, Antigonus. This mission ends in sadness as Antigonus's fleet is wrecked in a storm, and the courtier himself is killed and eaten by a bear. The baby, though, survives, along with instructions as to her true identity left by Antigonus. An Old Shepherd and his son, a Clown, watch all this and rescue the baby, who is named Perdita, raising her as a peasant girl in the Bohemian countryside. Perdita grows up, and is courted by Florizel, the son of Polixenes. While

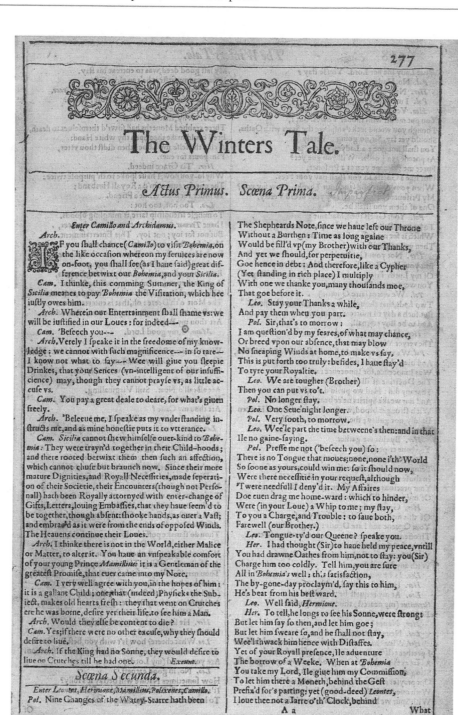

277

The VVinters Tale.

Actus Primus. Scœna Prima.

Enter Camillo and Archidamus.

Arch. IF you shall chance (*Camillo*) to visit *Bohemia*, on the like occasion whereon my seruices are now on-foot, you shall see (as I haue said) great difference betwixt our *Bohemia*, and your *Sicilia*.

Cam. I thinke, this comming Summer, the King of *Sicilia* meanes to pay *Bohemia* the Visitation, which hee iustly owes him.

Arch. Wherein our Entertainment shall shame vs: we will be iustified in our Loues: for indeed——

Cam. 'Beseech you——

Arch. Verely I speake it in the freedome of my knowledge: we cannot with such magnificence—— in so rare—— I know not what to say—— Wee will giue you sleepie Drinkes, that your Sences (vn-intelligent of our insufficience) may, though they cannot prayse vs, as little accuse vs.

Cam. You pay a great deale to deare, for what's giuen freely.

Arch. 'Beleeue me, I speake as my vnderstanding instructs me, and as mine honestie puts it to vtterance.

Cam. *Sicilia* cannot shew himselfe ouer-kind to *Bohemia*: They were trayn'd together in their Child-hoods; and there rooted betwixt them then such an affection, which cannot chuse but braunch now. Since their more mature Dignities, and Royall Necessities, made seperation of their Societie, their Encounters (though not Personall) hath been Royally attornyed with enter-change of Gifts, Letters, louing Embassies, that they haue seem'd to be together, though absent: shooke hands, as ouer a Vast; and embrac'd as it were from the ends of opposed Winds. The Heauens continue their Loues.

Arch. I thinke there is not in the World, either Malice or Matter, to alter it. You haue an vnspeakable comfort of your young Prince *Mamillius*: it is a Gentleman of the greatest Promise, that euer came into my Note.

Cam. I very well agree with you, in the hopes of him: it is a gallant Child; one that (indeed) Physicks the Subiect, makes old hearts fresh: they that went on Crutches ere he was borne, desire yet their life, to see him a Man.

Arch. Would they else be content to die?

Cam. Yes; if there were no other excuse, why they should desire to liue.

Arch. If the King had no Sonne, they would desire to liue on Crutches till he had one.   *Exeunt.*

Scœna Secunda.

Enter Leontes, Hermione, Mamillius, Polixenes, Camillo.

Pol. Nine Changes of the Watry-Starre hath been The Shepheards Note, since we haue left our Throne Without a Burthen: Time as long againe Would be fill'd vp (my Brother) with our Thanks, And yet we should, for perpetuitie, Goe hence in debt: And therefore, like a Cypher (Yet standing in rich place) I multiply With one we thanke you, many thousands moe, That goe before it.

Leo. Stay your Thanks a while, And pay them when you part.

Pol. Sir, that's to morrow: I am question'd by my feares, of what may chance, Or breed vpon our absence, that may blow No sneaping Winds at home, to make vs say, This is put forth too truly: besides, I haue stay'd To tyre your Royaltie.

Leo. We are tougher (Brother) Then you can put vs to't.

Pol. No longer stay.

Leo. One Seue'night longer.

Pol. Very sooth, to morrow.

Leo. Wee'le part the time betweene's then: and in that Ile no gaine-saying.

Pol. Presse me not ('beseech you) so: There is no Tongue that moues; none, none i'th' World So soone as yours, could win me: so it should now, Were there necessitie in your request, although 'Twere needfull I deny'd it. My Affaires Doe euen drag me home-ward: which to hinder, Were (in your Loue) a Whip to me; my stay, To you a Charge, and Trouble: to saue both, Farewell (our Brother.)

Leo. Tongue-ty'd our Queene? speake you.

Her. I had thought (Sir) to haue held my peace, vntill You had drawne Oathes from him, not to stay: you (Sir) Charge him too coldly. Tell him, you are sure All in *Bohemia's* well: this satisfaction, The by-gone-day proclaym'd, say this to him, He's beat from his best ward.

Leo. Well said, *Hermione*.

Her. To tell, he longs to see his Sonne, were strong: But let him say so then, and let him goe; But let him sweare so, and he shall not stay, Wee'l thwack him hence with Distaffes. Yet of your Royall presence, Ile aduenture The borrow of a Weeke. When at *Bohemia* You take my Lord, Ile giue him my Commission, To let him there a Moneth, behind the Gest Prefix'd for's parting: yet (good-deed) *Leontes*, I loue thee not a Iarre o'th' Clock, behind

A a   What

Title page of the First Folio edition of *The Winter's Tale*, published in 1623 they conduct their romance in a down-to-earth idyll epitomized by the itinerant peddler Autolycus, Perdita and Florizel are unwittingly spied upon by Polixenes, who, though enchanted by Perdita, nonetheless bans the match. Fleeing from his wrath, the young couple come to Sicilia, where Florizel introduces himself to the penitent Leontes, eventually, under pressure, disclosing the truth of why he is running away from his homeland. The Old Shepherd and the Clown, meanwhile, have proven Perdita's parentage to Polixenes by virtue of the material—"the fardel"—Antigonus left with her. Polixenes and Leontes reconcile and prepare for the marriage of their children, and Leontes joyfully reunites with his daughter. Paulina, who has presided over Leontes' repentance, has commissioned a lifelike statue of Hermione by a famous Italian sculptor. As the ensemble gazes at the statue, it suddenly breathes and moves—Hermione is alive. Overjoyed by the miraculous restoration of his mistreated wife, Leontes concludes the play with a declaration of harmony and serenity.

Act I, Scene 1

Camillo and Archidamus, two counselors, are talking. Camillo, a servant of the king of Sicilia (Sicily), where the scene takes place, says that his master plans to visit Bohemia, where Archidamus's master resides. Archidamus says that Bohemia is so much less luxurious than Sicilia that he will have to give the Sicilians tranquilizing alcohol to numb them to the disparity. Camillo reveals that the king of Sicilia and the king of Bohemia have been best friends since childhood and are as twins to one another. The Bohemian king is visiting the Sicilian king now; next summer, the Sicilian king will return the favor. They have found their friendship as close in adulthood as it once was in childhood. To add to the spirit of contentment and optimism, Mamillius, the king of Sicilia's son, is a fine young boy who excites hope for the future in all who see him.

Act I, Scene 2

Polixenes, king of Bohemia, has stayed at the Sicilian court of his friend Leontes for nine months, and now, with regret, says it is time to go. Hermione, Leontes' wife, joins her husband in pleading that Polixenes stay a week longer. Hermione does this at great length, showing herself at least as adamant as her husband in detaining Polixenes. Leontes is at first pleased by his queen's fervor in persuading his cherished friend to stay. But, in the glory of satisfaction and good cheer that the accomplishment of this goal conjures, Leontes' feelings begin to sour. Leontes suddenly becomes suspicious, concluding that Hermione and Polixenes are lovers, and then leaping to the fear that Mamillius, his beloved boy, may not in fact be his son. Examining Mamillius, he concludes their physical resemblance to be unmistakable, yet Polixenes and Hermione both realize that Leontes seems unsettled. Camillo observes to his master that it is Hermione's entreaties, not Leontes, which have made Polixenes stay. His statement unintentionally drives Leontes into rage. He accuses Camillo of being privy to the illicit relationship. Camillo denies this but agrees to poison Polixenes away from the court provided that Leontes not reveal his suspicion to Hermione and that he still treats Polixenes superficially as a friend. Camillo then has reservations about poisoning Polixenes, not only because he does not believe the Bohemian king to be guilty, but because he feels it is not his place as a servant to poison an anointed king. Polixenes comes by, having realized something is amiss at the court. After some inquiry, Camillo yields the truth to Polixenes, telling him Leontes suspects him and Hermione of adultery. Polixenes agrees to leave, bewildered at his friend's jealousy but understanding that, if Leontes in fact believed this to be happening, that, given his love for his queen and his previous trust for Polixenes, he would indeed be angry. Camillo prepares to spirit Polixenes out of Sicilia.

Act II, Scene 1

Hermione looks in on her son, Mamillius, and asks him, as a way of helping him get to sleep, to tell her a story. Saying that a sad tale is best for winter, Mamillius begins to tell a story of a man who dwelt by a churchyard when Leontes comes in, flush with the news of Polixenes' swift departure. Ordering Mamillius to leave, Leontes confronts Hermione to her face with the accusations of adultery. Hermione, seeing some insanity has afflicted Leontes, alternately protests her innocence and pleads with her husband to see reason. Antigonus firmly stands up to Leontes, insisting on Hermione's innocence. The queen is taken away to prison.

Act II, Scene 2

Paulina, Antigonus's wife, visits Hermione in prison. Emilia, a lady-in-waiting to the queen, says Hermione is doing well under the circumstances, as is confirmed by the Jailer. Paulina asks Emilia to relate to the queen her willingness to convey the baby Hermione is about to bear to Leontes, hoping the king will relent once he sees the baby and recognizes it as his own child.

Act II, Scene 3

Leontes cannot sleep, still fueled by jealousy and rage. He has alternating moments of reason, such as praising the nobility of Mamillius for becoming despondent in the wake of his mother's punishment, waiting until Cleomenes and Dion, two courtiers of his, return from the oracle at Delphi with an answer as to Hermione's guilt before executing her. But when Paulina presents the baby to him, he becomes livid, excoriating her as a witch. He orders Antigonus to silence his wife and fumes as Antigonus protests that husbands worldwide have shown themselves unable to perform this task. Leontes then orders Antigonus to take the baby—a girl—away and abandon her in the wilderness. Antigonus reluctantly accepts this task, rent with grief at the prospect. Suddenly, it is announced that Cleomenes and Dion have returned from the oracle.

Act III, Scene 1

Cleomenes and Dion, speaking favorably of the peace and serenity of Delphi, return to Sicilia, carrying the verdict of the oracle, which they have not opened.

Act III, Scene 2

The trial of Hermione is conducted. She protests her innocence, saying she was only as close to Polixenes as her husband dictated and her own sense of royal propriety—instilled in her by her Russian imperial background—mandated. Hermione says she has lost her husband's love, the company of her son, and even the fundamental motherly privilege of nursing her newborn. She submits herself to the judgment of the oracle, whose verdict is delivered by Cleomenes and Dion. The oracle says that Hermione is utterly innocent, that Leontes is deluded, and that Camillo acted wisely. Leontes refuses to believe the oracle and is about to proceed with the trial when news comes of Mamillius's death. Leontes instantly realizes that this is a sign that he is wrong, and he begins to step back from his rage. Hermione, though, is stricken and is taken out from the trial scene, though Leontes does not think she is seriously ill. Leontes repents and recants his accusations. But an agitated Paulina bursts in and, after a train of accusations against Leontes, announces the death of the queen. Paulina sees Leontes is touched and contrite and pardons him. Leontes vows to face a life of penitence and sorrow.

Act III, Scene 3

Antigonus and his mariners approach the seacoast of Bohemia. Antigonus reveals he dreamt the night before that Hermione, her spirit passed to the other world, has commanded him to name the baby Perdita and has also told Antigonus that, because of his participation in Leontes' cruel plan, he will never see Paulina again. Writing down a set of messages concerning Perdita's ancestry, including her name, and setting it on the ground near her, Antigonus leaves the baby and rushes off in the midst of a storm. As he flees, a bear catches sight of him, attacks him, and lengthily devours him. An Old Shepherd and his son, a Clown, watch the storm; the Clown recounts to the Old Shepherd his witnessing of Antigonus's death throes as he is eaten by a bear, as well as the shipwreck of the mariners the Sicilian courtier had brought with him. Finding the baby along with the boxes of messages and gold Antigonus had left they take Perdita to their humble home.

Act IV, Scene 1

The personification of Time recounts the passage of 16 years, Leontes' continuing contrition and purgation of his errors, as well as the maturation of Polixenes' son, Florizel, who courts Perdita, raised as the daughter of the Old Shepherd.

Act IV, Scene 2

Polixenes tells Camillo, who has remained in his service since he left Sicilia, that he knows Florizel is courting a woman beneath his station. They vow to spy on the young couple, disguising themselves in order to do so.

Act IV, Scene 3

Autolycus, a former courtier of Bohemia who was fired and has fallen on hard times, merrily sings a song of the coming of early spring. Autolycus takes out his boxes of fabrics and prepares to sell them for more than the just price to the rustic locals. Encountering the Clown, Autolycus pretends that he is someone who has been robbed by Autolycus, thus eliciting the Clown's sympathy. While telling the Clown his sad story, Autolycus picks the Clown's pocket.

Act IV, Scene 4

Conscious of the inequality of their relationship, Florizel and Perdita play a masquerade. Florizel pretends to be the shepherd Doricles, while Perdita assumes the dignity of a queen. Thus creating an ideal world where the apparent inequality between them is parodied if not wiped out, the two lovers court. The Old Shepherd comes in, accompanied by the Clown, as well as Polixenes and Camillo in disguise, and two young lasses of the precinct, Mopsa and Dorcas. Perdita presents the two old men with rosemary and rue, saying that other flowers at the ebb of the year, such as the gillyflower and the carnation, are too base to be presented to a gentleman. Polixenes protests, saying that

nature is too masterful not to already instill any art even in its most rude productions. Florizel and Perdita continue their pastoral masquerade while Polixenes looks on, admiring Perdita's beauty and sensing innate nobility in her. A servant comes in, announcing the arrival of Autolycus. Autolycus sells ribbons, which the Clown buys for Mopsa, with whom he is in love, and also for Dorcas. Autolycus sells the two young women a ballad of two women in love with the same man, which they then sing. Polixenes, feeling threatened by the evident love between his son and a low-born girl, by stages reveals himself to his son, after eliciting from him a declaration that he intends to persist in loving Perdita in spite of his father's opposition. Showing himself for who he really is, Polixenes excoriates the Old Shepherd for having tolerated this romance between people of two different social classes. Polixenes storms out, just too late to hear Perdita's retort that the sun shines on her as much as on the king. Camillo, remaining behind and recognizing Perdita's real identity, proposes to Florizel a scheme by which the young lovers can remain united and win back the favor of the king—to flee to Sicilia. Florizel reluctantly agrees. As they are bound for the coast, they encounter Autolycus, who overhears their purpose and agenda. Returning to the Old Shepherd's house, Autolycus interrupts a conversation between the Old Shepherd and the Clown where the younger man urges his father to reveal that Perdita is but his adopted daughter, thus indicating that he did not really aspire to infringe upon the rank of the royal family by a marriage with Florizel. Autolycus persuades them that his familiarity with the court will allow them to convince the king that they were not intriguing to marry into the royal family. They agree to pay him some of the gold that Antigonus had left with Perdita if Autolycus with conduct them to the king.

Act V, Scene 1

In the Sicilian court, Cleomenes assures Leontes he has done enough penitence and that now it is time to remarry, that the state needs an heir to reign

Mopsa in *The Winter's Tale.* This is a print from Charles Heath's 1848 edition of *The Heroines of Shakspeare: Comprising the Principal Female Characters in the Plays of the Great Poet. (Painting by A. Egg; engraving by B. Eyles)*

after him. Paulina, though, reminds the king of the oracle's pronouncement that he should not remarry until his lost child be found and, in addition, that even if he dies childless, he can leave his throne to the strongest as, she says, Alexander the Great is known to have done. Florizel's arrival is reported to the court. The young prince presents himself before Leontes as representing Polixenes and claims that Perdita, who is with him, is the daughter of Smalus, king of Libya, a potentate known to Leontes. A Bohemian lord enters, though, and informs Leontes that Florizel's tale is a falsehood and that Polixenes is arriving intent upon stopping his son's marriage. Furthermore, he has captured the Old Shepherd and the Clown. Florizel interjects that Camillo must have betrayed him. On

hearing the name of his former courtier, Leontes snaps to a different kind of attention, reminded of the trauma of the past. Eliciting from Florizel that his intended is not in fact a king's daughter, Leontes is sympathetic to their plight but warns them that he doubts Polixenes will see their side of the issue. Florizel says that if Leontes petitions Polixenes to accept Perdita as his bride, Polixenes would instantly capitulate, Paulina points out Perdita's resemblance to Hermione, while Leontes pledges to try to bring harmony between Florizel and Polixenes.

Act V, Scene 2

Autolycus elicits from two gentlemen that the Old Shepherd and the Clown have conveyed the fardel to the king and that a commotion had ensued. Another gentleman, Rogero (spelled Ruggiero in certain editions), quickly confirms that Perdita has been identified as the king's daughter and that bonfires blaze in celebration. The gentlemen recount the reconciliation between Polixenes and Leontes and Leontes' recognition of his found daughter as well as his confession to her of how her mother had died and his role in the calamity. The Old Shepherd and the Clown also informed the king of how Antigonus died and his fleet was wrecked, thus delivering the news to Paulina of the death of her husband. Paulina, though, is so moved by Leontes' confession that she tells Perdita that there is a lifelike statue of the late queen, recently carved by the acclaimed sculptor Giulio Romano, in a secluded house nearby. In recounting this story, the gentlemen relate that Paulina has often been seen surreptitiously visiting this house. The Old Shepherd and Clown reencounter Autolycus, who informs them that by benefit of the king's recognition of their role in succoring Perdita when she was a baby, they are now made gentlemen.

Act V, Scene 3

Paulina shows the collected ensemble, including Leontes, Polixenes, Perdita, Florizel, the Old Shepherd, the Clown, and Camillo, to her removed house. There she takes them on a gallery tour, which impresses Leontes, but he still presses Paulina to show him Hermione's statue. Paulina takes them to the room where the statue is lodged. They are awed by how lifelike it is—Leontes comments that the statue seems to have more wrinkles than he remembered Hermione having. Paulina says that attests to the sculptor's skill, in showing how Hermione would look if still alive. Paulina warns Leontes, before lifting the final curtain and totally revealing the statue, that it will look so lifelike that he might think it is alive. Leontes persists in his steady curiosity. Paulina lifts the veil, revealing the statue—which shows breath and color. Paulina orders the statue to descend—at which point the statue becomes animated. And walks down to embrace Leontes. Hermione is alive. Paulina informs her Perdita had been found. Leontes and Hermione happily reunite, while Paulina commends the happiness of all, except herself, her husband having been slain. Leontes promises that she shall have the hand of Camillo, whose affection for Paulina he has noticed. The happy throng leaves the stage in mutual celebration and joy.

CHARACTER LIST

Leontes King of Sicilia, husband of Hermione and father of Mamillius and Perdita. Best friends with Polixenes since childhood, he turns against his fellow king when he suspects him of having an affair with Hermione. After Mamillius dies and Paulina reports Hermione dead, Leontes repents of his fit of jealous rage and visits the graves of his wife and son daily. Leontes' courtiers put pressure on him to remarry so that there can be a new heir to the throne. When Florizel and Perdita flee from Polixenes' wrath, Leontes thinks of his two lost children and is overjoyed to find out their identities. After he is led by Paulina to the statue of Hermione, Leontes is stunned to see it step into life and resumes his marriage and his benevolent kingship.

Hermione Wife of Leontes, mother of Mamillius and Perdita, and daughter of the emperor of Russia. Hermione had lived happily with Leontes until the visit of Polixenes of Bohemia, who, at her husband's behest, she welcomes. Coming under suspicion by her husband for her excessive warmth toward Polixenes, Hermione is imprisoned even as she bears Leontes his second child. Reported dead by Paulina, after the child, deemed illegitimate, is ordered to be abandoned in the wild, Hermione is mourned by her repentant husband for 16 years. Allegedly depicted by the sculptor Giulio Romano in a very lifelike statue, Hermione steps back into life, regalness, and motherhood when Paulina brings the ensemble to see her.

Polixenes King of Bohemia, father of Florizel. Polixenes visits the court of his childhood friend Leontes, and after nine months avows his wish to go home. Urged by Leontes and Hermione to stay on one extra week, he yet suddenly flees when told of Leontes' new suspicion of his closeness to Hermione. After 16 years pass, Polixenes finds out his son, Florizel, is interested in a young shepherd girl. Ascertaining the truth of this rumor by himself assuming disguise as a shepherd, Polixenes forbids the marriage. Pursuing Florizel and Perdita to Sicilia, Polixenes finds out his son's beloved is truly a princess and is reunited in joy with his son and his old friend.

Mamillius Son of Leontes and Hermione. A young boy at the time of Polixenes' visit to Bohemia, Mamillius is seen as a figure of great promise and hope. Telling his father of a "winter's tale" of sadness and darkness, Mamillius begins to wilt when his mother is suspected of adultery, and he dies from sorrow.

Perdita Daughter of Hermione and Leontes. Born while her mother is in prison for suspected adultery, Perdita—whose name means "lost"—is ordered cast out into the wilderness. Taken by Antigonus to Bohemia, Perdita is rescued by the Old Shepherd and the Clown and is brought up in humble circumstances. Catching the eye of the young prince Florizel, she soon becomes his betrothed. After the romance is discovered by Polixenes, Perdita and Florizel flee to Sicilia, where she is acknowledged as the daughter of

Leontes and sees her mother come back to life in time for her marriage to Florizel.

Florizel Son of Polixenes (Polixenes' wife is unnamed in the play). The same age as Mamillius, he is grown to young manhood by the time he courts the presumed shepherd's daughter, Perdita. Found out by his father, he flees with Perdita to Leontes, at first telling to the king of Sicilia a false story about Perdita being the daughter of Smalus, king of Libya. Exposed by Camillo, Florizel defends his love for Perdita, which is vindicated once her ancestry is known. Florizel is reconciled with his father and marries Perdita.

Antigonus Nobleman of the Sicilian court, bidden to cast Perdita out into the wilderness. He takes her successfully to Bohemia but is captured and eaten by a bear there, leaving his wife, Paulina, a widow.

Paulina Noblewoman, wife of Antigonus, and loyal friend of Hermione. Defending the queen when she is accused of adultery, Paulina brings Leontes the sad news of his wife's passing. When Perdita returns to Sicilia, Paulina takes the Sicilian and Bohemian royal families to the statue of Hermione, which she has commissioned. The statue steps into life, and the lives of nearly everyone are redeemed, except Paulina, who has lost her husband, Antigonus. Leontes, though, knows that Camillo has feelings for Paulina and announces a marriage between the two.

Camillo Nobleman of the Sicilian court who is given orders by Leontes to poison Polixenes. Refusing these orders, he gives Polixenes surreptitious safe conduct out of Sicilia and stays with the Bohemian king as a valued servant for 16 years. Accompanying Polixenes as he spies on the romance of Florizel and Perdita, he is reunited with his old master, Leontes, when Polixenes arrives pursuing the fleeing young couple. As part of the general concord at play's end, he marries Paulina, who had been without a husband since the death of Antigonus,

The Old Shepherd Father of the Clown and foster-father of Perdita, he finds the little royal baby in the wild and brings her up as her daughter. Excoriated by Polixenes for sanctioning his lowly daughter to be courted by Prince Florizel, the Shepherd is nonetheless made a gentleman after Perdita's true ancestry is exposed.

The Clown (son of the Old Shepherd) Observer with his father of the mauling of Antigonus, he encounters Autolycus and is robbed by him. The Clown is in love with Mopsa and buys her ribbons from Autolycus. Along with his father, he is made a gentleman at the end of the play

Autolycus Formerly a member of Polixenes' court, he has been cashiered and begins to sell various items as a mode of swindling naive country people. A figure of both comedy and subversion, Autolycus nonetheless, in delivering the "fardel" containing proof of Perdita's true ancestry to Polixenes, helps bring about the reconciliatory denouement of the play.

Emilia Lady-in-waiting to Hermione who attends her in prison.

Cleomenes and Dion Two courtiers of Leontes who seek the pronouncement of the oracle at Delphi as to Hermione's innocence. Cleomenes and Dion are later present in Act V for the reuniting of Leontes and Perdita.

Mopsa and Dorcas Two young women of the country who live near the Old Shepherd. Mopsa is the beloved of the Clown.

CHARACTER STUDIES
Leontes

Given all of Leontes' crimes, why is he not simply a villain? How can the audience forgive him? We can begin to work this out by examining some of the traits that emerge after he has recovered from his fit of insanity. Leontes is not judgmental of Florizel even when he finds out the young prince has not been telling the truth. But neither does he seize the opportunity to exploit division between father and son, warning Florizel that Polixenes will be angry, and that this anger, though regrettable (Leontes has learned the lesson of anger management), is not unreasonable. Leontes is the sympathetic yet strong father-figure to Florizel he would have

Leontes orders Antigonus to abandon the baby Perdita in the wilderness in Act II, Scene 3 of *The Winter's Tale*. This is a print from the Boydell Shakespeare Gallery project, which was first conceived in 1786 and lasted until 1805. *(Painting by John Opie; engraving by Jean Pierre Simon)*

wished to have been to Mamillius had the young prince lived. Leontes may well have caused Mamillius's death, but in his counsel to Florizel he shows himself a wise and generous father-figure. Shakespeare, as compared to his source, Robert Greene, speeds up Leontes' jealousy, almost as if to get it over with so rapidly we will not hold lasting prejudice against the character, so he can be around at the end, unlike Greene's Pandosto.

Another reason we are not totally turned against Leontes is because Mamillius's death has mythic aspects—he is the child who is hoped for, then vanishes untimely, like Marcellus in Virgil's *Aeneid,* or potentially like the sacrifice of Isaac in the Bible. The tonalities here are too archetypal for Leontes to have caused the death all by himself; indeed, some have seen foreshadowing of the death even in the particular joy the young boy's presence is spoken of by Camillo and Archidamus at the beginning.

Leontes' penitence is also sincere, more than just lip service. The miracle at the end would not have been possible had the king not been genuinely sorry and purged himself through repeated formal acts of contrition for his misdeeds, which had caused the deaths of his son, Antigonus, and (he thinks) Hermione. The redemptive miracle of the statue come to life is dependent upon Leontes' moral cleansing of himself, in psychological terms as miraculous as Hermione's reanimation. Leontes has to learn to stop yearning for childhood as a place where time did not pass. Time has to be allowed into the circle in order to triumph. In a sense, we are close to the Christian doctrine of the "fortunate fall."

Leontes never goes totally mad, never totally forgets himself. He insists on having a full trial, a full legal procedure, to determine Hermione's guilt; he does not execute her at a whim. Anne Boleyn and Catherine Howard, the two wives of Henry VIII who were executed, did not receive such deliberate justice. The only moment where Leontes abandons procedural norms is when the verdict of the oracle is delivered. This flies in the face of what he believes, so that for a brief interval he casts aside precedent and normative procedure and disregards the oracle. The swift delivery of the news of Mamillius's death, however, makes him instantly realize he has transgressed the boundaries of his power, and his protracted, steadfast penitence begins.

Leontes has to pass a crucial test even after his penitence. The nature of this test is clearer if one examines Robert Greene's *Pandosto,* the novel that provided the source for Shakespeare's story. In *Pandosto,* as we have seen, the king conceives incestuous desires for the girl who turns out to be his daughter. There is the scantest hint of this in Shakespeare's play, quickly replaced by Leontes' unambiguous affirmation of support for Florizel in his suit for Perdita, even if it meant stretching the idea of what kind of royal marriage is permissible (and also threatening the potentiality of re-achieved concord with Polixenes). Leontes' reunion with Perdita is a testing ground for what happens next. Paulina is sure Leontes loves Perdita by the time she unveils the statue. In the 19th century, Perdita was often seen as a feminine avatar of miraculous nature. But she is more comprehensively part of the ensemble, with a particular capacity to bring out the best in people, her real and surrogate fathers especially. Leontes misses his wife and son. He has never known his daughter, so has no real idea of her. Part of the daughter's beauty is that morally and cognitively she leads us to the return of the mother. Her joyousness and laughter are also the window through which we contemplate the reanimation of her mother, Hermione.

Hermione

Hermione is a proud woman, and this pride comes out both in her sense that she—an emperor's daughter—should not be so basely treated when she is accused, and her gracious reticence about what had actually happened in the gap between her disappearance and her reconciliation with Leontes. She said nothing to either prove or disprove the supposition that she had ever been a statue. We would expect nothing less from a woman of Hermione's dignity and bearing. Leontes lost himself; Hermione was never in any danger of so doing. Though Hermione cannot be much older than in her late twenties when she is first accused, Shakespeare gives her the command and force of a considerably older woman. She is not just a consort or a domestic adornment but somebody worthy of respect, attention, and admiration. Shakespeare is tacitly saying, perhaps with the insight coming from his approaching 50, that sometimes women of middle age look just as attractive as younger maidens, even if they have a few wrinkles. Hermione vies with Gertrude in *Hamlet* in terms of being the oldest woman who still registers as physically attractive; and Hermione has a happier ending. At the end, Hermione is recognized by Leontes as the three-dimensional figure she had always been. He has ceased to objectify her and has acknowledged her dignity and personhood.

Instead of the mother she should have had, Perdita is brought up by two older men. The Old Shepherd and Clown fill the breach when Leontes is immobilized by guilt that succeeds rage, Antigonus is eaten, and Polixenes is far away and uninformed. They enable the development of reparation that characterizes the last two acts. They establish a sort of primitive civil society in which Perdita can grow to adulthood. The nobility of the young shepherdess is doubtless attributable to her high birth, but it has not been interfered with by the ambience provided by the Old Shepherd and the Clown. Most literally, they not only do not make her into a common young woman, but they do not interfere with her sexually. They are nurturers, caretakers, custodians, stewards, and they see Perdita as somebody to watch over and to protect. Mopsa is in the play so the Clown does not fall in love with Perdita—young enough to be his daughter, yet also his foster-sibling, but toward whom he shows nothing but disinterested affection. The Old Shepherd and Clown also serve as shepherds to the audience. They calm down the audience after the storms, literal and figurative, of Act III. They provide a clearing, a breathing space, a still yet productive interlude. After the selfishness of Leontes, they provide a counter example of people who put other people before themselves, an example that is succoring and heartening. The Old Shepherd and the Clown are vulgar, but not unscrupulous; they are not lowlifes. They are close to being "nature's gentlemen." When the Old Shepherd weeps over the joy of Perdita's reunion, it is remarked of the newly ennobled old man that these are not the last gentleman's tears he will shed. This witticism is an apt comment on the burdens of social status and the carefree joys of its absence. But, despite this remark, the Old Shepherd will most likely carry his natural dignity wisely into his new, unaccustomed station.

Paulina is also a character not motivated by selfish aims. Her dedication is to justice and to the good of the royal family. She is not just virtuous, though, but also uncanny and even intimidating. Paulina several times associates herself with witchcraft, refers to the possibility of herself being burnt, accuses the king of being a heretic when he threatens to so burn her, and warns that the revival of Hermione the statue will be taken for witchcraft. Paulina is the person with the most courage to point out Leontes' jealousy for what it is, to scold the powerful king to his face, and defend the queen's "gracious innocent soul" against the king's "tyrannous passion." Paulina does not protest against Leontes' arbitrary actions out of resent-

ment or spite. She implores Leontes to be reconverted to his old self and hopes the sight of his innocent daughter will restore him. Once Leontes repents, Paulina, though not yet totally forgiving, does not abandon him.

Camillo

At the beginning, Camillo is the person to whom Leontes confides and confesses, but Paulina becomes that over his 16-year purgative hiatus. This is almost reminiscent of the role of the Virgin Mary in Roman Catholicism, though of course in that context, only men would literally hear confession, and far from being a religiously sanctioned figure, Paulina is accused of being a witch. Yet, far from this, Paulina, over and above being a moral compass, is also a healer. She helps heal Hermione (if she has in fact been secretly visiting her all these years—in other words, if the statue is not really a statue) by succoring her in the hope of seeing Perdita again and has helped Leontes atone and find a new purpose in repentance. Paulina is a healer, very nearly a physician—for the most part as effective in the mode of the female physician as the only attested specimen of that variety in Shakespeare, Helena in *All's Well That Ends Well*, who seems less content in the professional role of healer. Through this all, Paulina has to endure the absence of Antigonus, then, at the end, the blow of the revelation of his violent death, making her the only unhappy person in a group of suddenly redeemed "precious winners." In giving her the hand of Camillo, Leontes includes her in the winning circle. This is partially a recognition that the only reason he is in a position to do this is because Paulina has been there for him and has cared for him and has not shunned him or rejected him out of contempt after Mamillius's real and Hermione's supposed deaths. (Interestingly, Paulina's three daughters by Antigonus, mentioned by Antigonus in Act I, are not exactly mentioned at the end.) Paulina and Leontes have a very intense relationship, striking in that it is between a man and a woman who are not connected by blood, marriage, or love. Paulina has taken Leontes' measure and has both judged and forgiven him. The woman whom Leontes termed an "audacious lady" plays an unusual large role for a secondary female character in Shakespeare.

Paulina's husband, Antigonus, is a figure of less depth, though more pathos. Antigonus goes to his death believing Polixenes is Hermione's baby's father, and that in laying Perdita down on a site in Bohemia, he is putting her in the land of her true father. He also uses Hermione's appearance in the dream to conclude that she is dead, while the end of the play gives us as much reason to think she was alive at the time. Even though Antigonus dies, his affirmation of the truth prepares the way for the wholesomeness of the upbringing of the baby so briefly in his charge. His being consumed by a bear, though, shows both the precarious social structure of Leontes' court, as well as opening up the entire theme of the power and bounty of nature that will dominate the next two acts. Like Mamillius, Antigonus's death is one of the play's most tragic moments; yet, again like Mamillius, Antigonus is not missed within the final economy of the play.

Polixenes

Polixenes is more an enigma to us than his boyhood friend Leontes. Although he has a son, we never see anything of his wife, who is never named, although she is spoken of in Act I. We presume that she is dead by the time Florizel is an adult. Polixenes is stunned and outraged by his friend's suspicion of him but does not hold a grudge. When Camillo speaks, in Act IV, of his wish to return to Sicilia, Polixenes forbids it, not because he resents Leontes, but because he values Camillo's companionship; he explicitly recognizes the penitence of Leontes, though an actor could if he so wishes supply a sarcastic intonation to that recognition. Polixenes seems the stern father in his evaluation of Perdita's suitability as a mate for his son. Yet, in intellectual terms, he undercuts his own rationale for objecting by commending the mingling of the baser and nobler stocks in the plant world in his dialogue with Perdita. That the rustic girl of such great natural beauty is in fact of high royal descent

is something the audience knows and Polixenes does not.

Polixenes, as a leader, is complacent, establishmentarian, and conventional—in other words, a normal authority figure. Shakespeare does not paint him as villainous or even especially obtuse. He is what one should expect in the situation, and he has possibility for growth when plausible circumstances allow it. He is not psychotic like Leontes after his jealousy, and society, as Shakespeare well realized, can get by being led by somebody who is merely conventional and establishmentarian.

The first time Polixenes speaks of a woman with any feeling is when he sees Perdita in Act IV, where the country lass seems to arouse some interest in him even as he scorns her as not good enough for his son—this and Leontes' brief gaze at her in Act V (quickly rebuked by Paulina) are the two slight residues of the Pandosto incest theme in Greene. But both older men quickly remove themselves to emeritus status in erotic terms; Polixenes, though at first not wanting her to marry his son for class reasons, is deeply respectful of her dignity and intrinsic merit.

Perdita presents Polixenes and Camillo with rosemary and rue in Act IV, Scene 4 of *The Winter's Tale*. This is a print from the Boydell Shakespeare Gallery project, which was first conceived in 1786 and lasted until 1805. (*Painting by Francis Wheatley; engraving by James Fittler*)

Interestingly, it is Polixenes who is the champion of mixture in nature, who wants the carnations and gillyvors in the garland, even though Perdita deems them not good enough. In a sense, the Bohemian king is anticipatorily (and unconsciously) rebutting his own insistence that Perdita is too vulgar to marry his son. He is recognizing that nature can produce art of its own, a point that stands in a philosophical sense, even after Perdita's royal birth is recognized and contributes to, or mirrors, the ease with which the Old Shepherd and Clown are ennobled. In the flower scene, this irony works in Polixenes' favor; we feel that his natural disposition recognizes that quality can come from humble origins, even if the official rhetoric of his role as king requires he says otherwise. Polixenes shares this quality with his son, Florizel. The overtly flowery and even slightly comic quality of the name describes somebody who is connected with nature, who, though young and inexperienced, is adventurous, open to life—the latter phrase in the sense both of being experimental and being tolerant. What is striking about all the characters we meet in Bohemia, in Act IV, is how, despite their different stations and demeanors—from king to knave, from prince to humble shepherd, from noble wooer to cunning cheat—they are all somewhat of a piece. They all delight in nature and would never find themselves ensnared in the insincerity that in many ways brings on the crisis at the court in Sicilia. It is against this background that we should understand Autolycus. Even though he is dishonest and unprincipled, he is not malicious. Autolycus might be unnerving in a less serene context; he is excused by his milieu. Autolycus verges on criminality, but in the end, he helps shape the action in an affirmative way; he is at once cutpurse, scamp, improviser, and artificer. One should watch one's wallet with him, but any roguery will not be on an epic or tragic level. Although, as many critics have remarked, Autolycus is not included in the final concord of the play, his anarchic energies have nonetheless contributed, paradoxically, to this harmonious finale.

The only character who is equally of both milieus is one who received scant attention from a good many commentators—Camillo. Formerly a member of Leontes' court, he flees with Polixenes after the Sicilian king's wrath becomes clear. He then serves his new lord faithfully, though yearning to return home both for home's sake and to honor the repentance of his former master. Camillo marries Paulina at the end not just because he is an extra, unattached character available for nuptial settlement but also because he has similarly learned from experience, been both weathered and mellowed, toughened and softened, by it. Camillo's compassion and insight are unobtrusive, but they stand among the principal ethical ballasts of the play's world.

DIFFICULTIES OF THE PLAY

The Winter's Tale, although a much beloved play, is arguably one of Shakespeare's most difficult. Three particular issues are particularly perplexing. These are the play's intended historical setting and treatment of time; the innovative combination of tragedy and comedy; and the challenge posed to what Coleridge termed our "suspension of disbelief" posed by the revival of Hermione the statue.

Time and History

The controversial role of Time at the beginning of Act IV—Time is actually personified and addresses the audience, briefing us on what has happened in the 16-year gap—is usually discussed with respect to the classical unities. But it also bears on the entire issue of how history and the past are represented in the play. There are references that are not only Christian but contemporary in the play—"Whitsun pastorals" refers not only to the Christian holiday of Pentecost but to the festive plays put on for that day in Shakespeare's and his original audience's own time. The play's setting in time is thus pre-Christian. But this does not mean that its morality is un-Christian. The themes of penitence and forgiveness and the reform of the self are consummately Christian ones, and the sense of miracle in Shakespeare's later plays, though never presented in an overtly religious manner is yet shadowed by Christianity. There are also several patterns in the play that mirror those in the Bible, particularly the idea of the younger generation atoning for the mistakes of the old, solving problems that their elders have bungled.

The historical setting of the play, indeed, is nebulous. A terminus a quo is set by Paulina's mention of Alexander the Great in Act V, Scene 1; the action cannot be earlier than 323 B.C.E. No explicit mention of Christianity is made in the play, nor are modern Western European states mentioned. Bohemia is a medieval Slavic kingdom, although technically the name, which was applied by the Romans to a Celtic tribe in the area, has a classical pedigree. So does Libya, where the father Florizel claims for Perdita resides. The one referent that definitely marks the play's setting as post-Christian is Russia, a word unattested before 900 C.E., from where Hermione's proud lineage traces its pedigree. Other references to Christianity, such as those to Puritans or Whitsun pastorals, denote practices contemporary with Shakespeare and explode any idea of fixing the play in a rigid historical setting. The New Testament parable of the Prodigal Son is also cited. Shakespeare does not deliberately purge the play of all Christian references, but the tendency toward avoidance of them points to the playwright's use of the generalized, fantastic setting of antiquity, with strange yet not totally unfamiliar names and landscapes, as a background for the play. In this, Shakespeare followed Greene's precedent, but his use of names is notable in its own right: Many of the play's names—Antigonus, Leontes, Camillo (i.e., Camillus), Paulina—are names borne by Greeks and Romans who lived between 550 B.C.E. and the birth of Christ. It is this setting, attitudinally and psychologically, that provides the canvas upon which the play's awesome events unfold, even though nothing in the play is remotely intended to be historically literal.

In Act IV, Scene 4, Polixenes says that, if Florizel continues to see Perdita, he will hold him "not further of our blood, no, not our kin, far than Deucalion off." As Jonathan Bate points out, the mention of Deucalion, the Noah-like figure in the Greek Flood myth related by the Roman poet Ovid, conjures the pattern of destruction and reparation reenacted in the play, as the world is destroyed, yet, through a remnant, is reborn. Yet why not just mention Noah? It seems a deliberate avoidance of biblical reference and confirms the non-Christian universe of the play, as Shakespeare pointedly does not use the Judeo-Christian parallel of Noah, which would be otherwise ready to hand. Another reason is that Polixenes' assertion would actually not be true with respect to Noah, as according to the Bible, Noah is the ancestor of all mankind. Though this is also assumed of Deucalion, it is not (in the *Metamorphoses* of Ovid, Shakespeare's source for this story) explicitly said.

If one were to literalize the setting—as Charles Kean did in his 1856 production—one would set the play in the classical world. Yet this would be, and was, too simple a solution. Shakespeare uses names such as Antigonus or Paulina for their Hellenistic associations; names like Antigonus (Antigonus Gonatas) and Paulina (feminine form of a Roman name, for instance, L. Aemilius Paulus, conqueror of Greece for Rome in the second century B.C.E.), gave Shakespeare the vague setting of majestic high drama and antiquity used by practitioners in the tradition of the Greek romance as well as much of European tragedy (including, for instance, the German *Trauerspiel,* or mourning play) up until the early 18th century, Shakespeare was very much in contact with this imaginary classical-medieval milieu through his cultural situation, and these names have to be understood as part of his participation in a tradition of representation that, for him, was still ongoing.

Tragedy and Comedy

Why is the play both a tragedy and a comedy? Why are there, in effect, two different plays? Even though in practice there was not always a strict division between tragedy and comedy in the ancient world—Euripides' plays often had happy endings but were classified as tragedies—the theory of drama in ancient literary criticism had rigorously partitioned the two. But, in the Renaissance, certain Italian critics, such as Giovanni Battista Guarini, postulated the form of "tragicomedy." Significantly, Guarini did not mean *tragicomedy* as simply a statistical balance between tragedy and comedy but having both elements present, in different admixtures, in the same compounds. Tragicomedy, for instance, permitted the tragic poet to modulate elements of tragedy and comedy, altering a dolorous outcome to furnish a moment of a recognition, a hazard of fortune, but not a calamitous end, according to Guarini. Another slightly earlier Italian critic, Lodovico Castelvetro, is suggestive with respect to the catalytic role recognition plays in *The Winter's Tale* when he stated that people can be kept from recognition by the changes brought about by time alone. This explains why, in a sense, Time is personified in the play, to represent the difficulties that lie between the plot as it stands and the possibilities for recognition that are ultimately seen in the coming-alive of Hermione, which, as a recognition scene, substitutes for what would, in Aristotelian terms, be a tragic catharsis. Much of Act V is a happy rewriting of potentially tragic phenomena. When Leontes and Perdita are reunited, Rogero reports the response is "Nothing but bonfires." The bonfire, as far back as Aeschylus, is a symbol of destruction and renewal; here, its use is one of unrestrained celebration: Perdita is found, against hope, in the teeth of years of futile lament.

Castelvetro also spoke of adultery as the concealment of identity. This is true in *The Winter's Tale,* although since there is no real adultery, "Sir Smile," the simulating neighbor-adulterer, is but an image in Leontes' deluded psyche. It is Leontes, the diagnostician of a false adultery, who loses his own identity. Shakespeare's sudden pivot from tragedy to comedy must be understood in light of the ideas of Castelvetro and especially Guarini. The tragicomedy was a genuinely new genre that added to the possibilities of the ancient dramatic forms. (As Louis L. Martz has pointed out in the context of *The Winter's Tale,* some ancient plays, such as Aeschylus's *Oresteia,* ended affirmatively after much bloodshed and despair, but tragicom-

edy in the Guarinian sense includes not only a happy outcome but laughter and celebration, both of which are abundant in Shakespeare's play.) What it retains from tragedy is the sense that the characters are higher than themselves, that in their lives and actions they confront the ultimate questions. Certainly this is true both of Leontes' jealousy and of the reparation and reconciliation scenes in the last two acts—the emotions conjured there are not those of ordinary life, they are elevated states that call us to attention and respect. Even the pastoral scene in Act IV, Scene 4 is, especially compared to other pastoral scenes in Shakespeare, a paradigm, not simply a fair reflection, of life. And the overall theme of the disruption and reunion of an immediate family is at its base profoundly tragic. As Castelvetro says, "It is not usual to lose knowledge of persons closely joined in blood," thus Leontes' recognition of Perdita, and, above all, Hermione has the magnitude of a tragic action.

Yet the play also has comedic elements. The reunion of estranged family members, the conclusion with a marriage—the hallmark of comedy since the ancient Greek dramatist Menander—and the humor provided by Autolycus all are comic indicators, the last perhaps not on its own, as many of Shakespeare's tragedies have deliberately humorous interludes. But Autolycus's charming knavery takes place in a context of rustic pastoral, and that makes all the difference. Though the sheep-shearing scene in Act IV, Scene 4 is not the complete idyll critics such as Dowden made it out to be—it is in many ways a space for healing after trauma, and conscious of the pain and loss it avoids—it does embed Autolycus's pranks within a context of festivity and delight. Like such musical pieces of the following century such as Johann Sebastian Bach's "Sheep May Safely Graze" or George Frideric Handel's opera *Acis and Galatea,* or paintings of that era such as the *fêtes galantes* of Jean Antoine Watteau, the sheep-shearing scene celebrates nature's bounty with more than an undertone of melancholy. Though this undertone may be there in some of Shakespeare's other pastoral scenes—great comedy is never totally either funny or happy—it

Hermione pleads her innocence before Leontes in Act II, Scene I of *The Winter's Tale*. This illustration was designed for a 1918 edition of Charles and Mary Lamb's *Tales from Shakespeare*. (Illustration by Louis Rhead)

is manifestly there in *The Winter's Tale* because so much of the play has to do with death, loss, and pain.

Notably, Leontes, the chief figure of the play—the figure who was its title character in Greene's novel—is himself a tragicomic figure. His bluster and certainty have a tragic effect, but their braggadocio and swagger, his sense of his "just censure" and "true opinion" is incipiently comic, not totally unlike the otherwise very different Malvolio in *Twelfth Night*. Leontes is not, at least in reality, an absolute monarch. His lords feel free to stand up to him, to contradict him, to point out to him

the limits of reality. In Act V, when deliberating remarriage, his relations to Dion, Paulina, and Cleomenes are consultative, and he appears genuinely open to their advice, even if the final decision remains his. There is very nearly a sense, for all the king's authority, that the other characters have what the Spanish Jesuit thinker Francisco Suárez would call the "right of resistance." It can be argued that it is in this play that we spend the most time, in all of Shakespeare's work, with a legitimate king whose title to the throne is undisputed and see how he governs. Given that kingship is such an impotent theme in Shakespeare's work and in the England in which he lived, the evidence provided by this play as to his opinion of the role and responsibility of the king is fascinating. This is especially true in that the later Shakespeare worked in a very court-centered context, and the pageantry and overt theatricality of the late romances are often seen as cognate with the staged masques that were the preferred dramatic form of the court of James I. In *The Winter's Tale*, kings have unlimited civic authority. But their moral authority can be incomplete. This seems more comedic than tragic.

Leontes also seems accessible because we know him so intimately. We see his domestic life, as we would in a comedy. The men with happier lives, by contrast, have domestic existences that are less visible. Polixenes is a more remote figure because we never see his home. Polixenes' wife is not named, and we know nothing of her life (though we presume her dead as she is absent) or of the nature of his relationship with her. The same, interestingly, is true of the Old Shepherd's wife, the Clown's mother, so their father-son relationship stands as an inverse, parodic mirror-image of Florizel's and Polixenes'. The Old Shepherd does refer to his wife when he uses her past example as domestic manager to exhort Perdita to prepare the domestic table. Perdita becomes a substitute for the dead mother, just as she is with respect to Florizel's mother and, until the awakening of the statue, to her own. Bohemian society has a sense of ongoingness: We are not just at the court. The cure for the tragedy of the first three acts only comes from the humble pastures of Bohemia. We never see the Bohemian court, never see Polixenes as king in situ. In Sicilia, we have a comedic context with a tragic plot; in Bohemia, we have joy, in many ways outside the more traditional comedic context. This is one of the reasons the Perdita-Florizel dialogue in Act IV, Scene 4 has such an elevated, dignified tone to it; it is well outside the generic realm of comic badinage.

It could be said that all the late romances mingle tragedy and comedy, yet the intermingling in *The Winter's Tale* is particularly worth exploring. It is one thing to say the play contains both tragic and comic elements, another thing to say how they converge or at least coalesce. What provides the unity? Perhaps it is the tragic elements in the comic, the comic in the tragic. The first three acts of the play, as horrific as are both the suspicions of adultery and the unreasoning jealousy that lies behind them, have a comedic aspect in that, like many of Shakespeare's comedies, they involve misunderstanding. In her trial scene (Act III, Scene 2) Hermione makes the following statement:

> For Polixenes, with whom I am accused,
> I do confess I loved him as in honour he
>   required,
> With such a kind of love as might become
> A lady like me, with a love even such,
> So and no other, as yourself commanded:
> Which not to have done I think had been
>   in me
> Both disobedience and ingratitude
> To you and toward your friend, whose love
>   had spoke,
> Even since it could speak, from an infant, freely
> That it was yours.

This passage is only not obscure if one reads it as Hermione saying that she found Polixenes hard to take, found his presence odious and intolerable, but put up with the Bohemian potentate's long visit because of her husband's friendship with him and her sense that a lady of her station could not be observed to be rude. Thus, the jarring note genuinely sensed by Leontes in Hermione's

pleading with Polixenes to stay on may not have been a secret liaison between the two but Hermione's actual discomfort with Polixenes, which she masked by protesting too much the other way, overdoing it. Hermione was overdoing it out of an excess of scruple, because in her inner heart she did not care much about Polixenes but was willing to go through the motions. Leontes misinterpreted.

The relationship between Leontes and Polixenes themselves is also subject to misunderstanding. It should be remembered that, as much as Leontes and Polixenes were friendly in youth, they had not seen each other as adults until Polixenes' current long visit. Though their reestablishment of intimacy seems unruffled, it is important to realize that this is the first time Leontes has encountered Polixenes as an adult and as a married man. Polixenes is a new factor in Leontes and Hermione's marriage. This raises the following questions: Does Leontes really like Polixenes, and vice versa, as adults as much as they did when they were children? Why had they not reconnected previously? (Both men have sons of 10 or so years, so they had been adults for some time.) Conversely, what if the childhood intimacy between the two men was renewed too seamlessly—in other words, if there were homosexual undercurrents in the relationship during the time when the two then-boys "frisked like twinned lambs I' the sun," this latency added an extra sense of tension. (Sir John Gielgud's 1951 performance of Leontes in Peter Brook's production influenced many later performances that made this suggestion.) Perhaps it is Hermione, not Leontes, who was originally jealous of Polixenes' place at the Sicilian court. Because of this sense of confusion, which verges on the grotesque and farcical, the sexual transgression here is as comic as it is tragic.

As masterfully as Shakespeare crossed the tragic-comic gap in this play, and as much of a prism as it constitutes for understanding all four romances, in a sense Shakespeare, in *The Winter's Tale*, has gone as far as he could go with such a mixture. Later readers such as the Russian novelist Leo Tolstoy, who criticized the artificiality of Shakespeare, could have grounds to point to *The Winter's Tale* as a prime instance, despite Shakespeare's manifest contention that artifice is ultimately natural. Though most would not agree with this, undeniably Shakespeare here explored the potential of this sort of fantastic setting as much as he could; in his next and final romance, *The Tempest,* the equally magical and miraculous action was shifted to a setting resembling the contemporary New World.

Because of the theme of suspected adultery in both, *The Winter's Tale* is often compared to the tragedy *Othello.* The difference, though, between *Othello* and *The Winter's Tale* is that, in the latter, Leontes was the architect of his own downfall, which can be blamed on his own unreasonable jealousy, resentment, and rage. Othello, on the other hand, was deluded by Iago. Unlike Othello, Leontes is a king, with authority to orchestrate downfalls, his own and others, whereas Othello is only a general and a vice-gerent. It is true that in *The Winter's Tale,* there are limits to absolute monarchy, Leontes defends himself from being a tyrant and makes at least a show of following due process. There is a sense, even though the king's will commands all, that the people will not support him if he is deemed to be arbitrary or capricious. But Leontes has such authority that no man other than himself can take him down. Othello, though, however powerful and strong, is yet vulnerable enough to be taken down by others.

Othello's downfall was authored by a malevolent schemer who somehow insinuated himself into the power structure of a major Mediterranean city. Leontes' society manages to repair itself—minus a prince (Mamillius is the only person permanently lost in *The Winter's Tale* and should not be forgotten). But the society can heal itself because its own serious flaw was internal, endemic to Leontes. Othello did not go mad. He was driven mad by the malignant Iago. And, after Othello is dead and buried, Venice has to ask itself how it could be that a malignant menace like Iago was permitted to insinuate himself into the power structure? What kind of Venice does Venice want to be? Sicilia does not, on the other hand, have to ask itself these fundamental questions. Even if Leontes had killed himself in *The Winter's Tale,* and it had thus been generally a tragedy, the society has in it the capacity to heal and to grow and to regraft itself, although this will take years of wan, forlorn mourning, and pining first. The society of *Othello* will not rest until the appalling calamity of letting the most prominent men fall into pendition is subject to a rigorous review process, an inquest, a sense of what precisely went wrong. How on earth did a trivial entity such as Iago deprive them of one of the best generals and of the daughter of one of its prominent citizens?

If, indeed, Othello was brought down by his own self-doubt and vulnerability, Venice also has to ask itself how it failed in either promoting Othello or in so stressing him out because of his racial background and outsider status that he was that vulnerable. Othello failed, Venice may well have set him up to fail. The society of *The Winter's Tale* has to ask itself none of these questions. The servants are either dead (Antigonus) or constructive (Paulina). The society has no challengers from the outside, only things gone wrong on the inside, which can be fixed. Even when Florizel seeks to renew his dynastic bloodline with new, vernacular energy, Perdita turns out to be his royal peer. Autolycus is a snapper-up of unconsidered trifles, not, like Iago, a whipper-up of unconsidered trifles into entities that bring down a marriage and a politico-military career and seriously wound a state. Hermione is thought to be a statue and then reenters life. Even after she is definitely dead, there will—because of her husband's disgrace, and despite her victimhood—be no statues of Desdemona.

Two questions arise in Act I, Scene 2: The one that arises to Leontes, why does Hermione not just do a pro forma echoing of her husband's injunctions for Polixenes to stay? Often when guests leave, their hosts politely observe that they are sorry they could not stay longer, but in reality they are only too happy for them to go. Leontes and Hermione both seem so insistent on Polixenes staying that suspicions arise that either, as Leontes suspects, Hermione and Polixenes are having an illicit affair or, perhaps, that Leontes wants Polixenes to stay in order to detain or waylay him. In the Bible, for instance, hosts often enjoin guests to stay when they do not have their best interests at heart, much like Laban with his nephew Jacob in Genesis. In a way, asking a guest to stay longer is the ultimate in hospitality. But in another way, enjoining a guest to stay when they want to leave, when, as Polixenes contends, his work—his business as king—requires he go home, is an act, unconscious or conscious, of hostility. At the moment when Polixenes and Leontes seem as close as two human beings can be outside of a romantic relationship, the good feelings somehow are so rich and festive, they surfeit and curdle into suspicion and jealousy. Even though the particular shape of these negative feelings is Leontes' suspicion of Hermione's adultery, the anxiety that Polixenes being asked to stay foments has to do with the delicate boundaries of hospitality, a very important notion in a still fairly traditional society such as the one in this play.

The Statue That Comes to Life

The biggest difficulty of the play, though, is the statue that comes to life. Certainly, the unbelievability of this event is part of the play's sense of miracle, of deliverance. Equally certainly, we are provided with enough internal evidence to conclude that this is all just a trick staged by Paulina, that the Giulio Romano story is just a diversion, that Hermione had been alive all those years, and Paulina was just waiting for the right moment. But even if we conclude empirically that this is what has happened in the play—not an unambiguous certainty—we are surely not meant to think it was just a stunt, a connivance. There is too much emotional weight, too much wonderment attached to it. Hermione's return may not be supernatural, but it is still nonetheless a miracle. (In some ways, of course, Shakespeare is thinking about his own stagecraft here, as he was with respect to Prospero's magic in *The Tempest*.) A line often appreciated more than examined in this respect is Leontes' acclamatory remark on Hermione's revival, "if

The statue of Hermione descends after Paulina lifts the veil in Act V, Scene 3 of *The Winter's Tale*. This is a print from the Boydell Shakespeare Gallery project, which was first conceived in 1786 and lasted until 1805. *(Painting by William Hamilton; engraving by Robert Thew)*

this be magic, let it be lawful as eating." This is usually taken as a kind of relaxation signal, as a suggestion that the mechanics of the revival process not be labored over too much, and that the wonderful fact simply lead to general merriment and celebration. But perhaps we should look at the phrase most literally. What is "lawful as eating"? Eating, for one thing, is itself contingent on being animate, on being biological and not mineral. Eating is something that Hermione the statue could not do, but Hermione the reanimated person can. Eating is also a physical process as necessary to human sustenance as sex, but far less controversial—Leontes has not, earlier in the play, lost his head over it. But eating is also an everyday practice, just the kind of activity that Florizel, in Act IV, had told Perdita that when she did it, it was so special that he wished it would last forever. Hermione has undergone this process in reverse, freed from being eternal and enabled once again to partake in everyday things. Without physically being in Bohemia, Leontes has learned the lesson from Act IV about art and nature arguably depending upon and partially comprising one another. Leontes' comment directs us away from the contradictions in the miracle of statues coming to life, only to make us newly aware of the miracle that life itself has a meaning, that we value other people and learn from experience in our relationships with them. With this in mind, both readings, both varieties of complexity—that Hermione was literally a statue, and that Paulina arranged the entire spectacle from the beginning—end up with the same moral, of a full affirmation, of life and the human spirit.

KEY PASSAGES
Act I, Scene 2, 108–118

LEONTES. Too hot, too hot! [*Aside.*]
To mingle friendship far is mingling bloods.
I have tremor cordis on me; my heart dances;
But not for joy, "not joy." This entertainment
May a free face put on; derive a liberty
From heartiness, from bounty, fertile bosom,
And well become the agent: 't may, I grant:
But to be paddling palms and pinching fingers,
As now they are; and making practis'd smiles
As in a looking-glass; and then to sigh, as
  'twere
The mort o'the deer: O, that is entertainment
My bosom likes not, nor my brows,
  "Mamillius,
Art thou my boy? . . ."

Leontes' utterance of "too hot" is the pivot for the play's first downward turn. The warmth, the joy, the pleasantry of his reaffirmation of his friendship with Polixenes have overflowed into something very different. (This sense of overflow is even foreshadowed in the opening Camillo and Archidamus scene, where their formal language has a turbid sexual undertone which, in retrospect, it can be seen as struggling to repress.) The king had wanted his wife to urge his friend to stay more but now wonders at her fervor. To like your husband's friends is one thing, but, he indicates, there is such a thing as liking them too much. He had earlier been alive with delight but now he is quivering with upset and jealousy. Leontes realizes that he may, as he later says, be making something out of nothing, but he cannot help but read the symptoms

exhibited by Polixenes and Hermione—the smiling, the overt affection they show to each other—as manifestations of a deeper, illicit understanding. There is throughout the passage a sense of a spoliation from surfeit, of a realization, a consummation of all that is good having gone awry through there simply being too much of it, so much that Leontes fantasizes that what are in all likelihood the ceremonial politenesses of the court are in fact heartfelt signs of a secret romance. When Leontes asks Mamillius if he is his boy, Mamillius thinks this is just a reassuring gesture of affection, as parents will do with children, but in fact it is the by-product of a network of suspicion that will eventually speed the poor little prince to his grave.

Act III, Scene 1, 1–17

CLEOMENES. The climate's delicate, the air most sweet,
Fertile the isle, the temple much surpassing
The common praise it bears.

DION. I shall report,
For most it caught me, the celestial habits,
Methinks I so should term them, and the reverence
Of the grave wearers. O, the sacrifice!
How ceremonious, solemn and unearthly
It was i'the offering!

CLEOMENES. But of all, the burst
And the ear-deafening voice o'the oracle,
Kin to Jove's thunder, so surprised my sense,
That I was nothing.

DION. If the event o'the journey
Prove as successful to the queen,—O be't so!—
As it hath been to us rare, pleasant, speedy,
The time is worth the use on't.

As the two courtiers return to give the oracle's verdict—which, being sealed, they do not know the content of—there is a sense of sacredness amid tumult, calm serenity. This pause, this counterpoint, is the first sense of placidity and peace in the play, and even though it cannot serve to immediately quell the wrath of Leontes, it still provides a precedent for the play's convincing change of mood in Act IV. Dion and Cleomenes are two people doing their job, and as such they represent a welcome change from the fervid, self-involved Leontes and the court, which must reverberate at his every whim. The pair are surprised that the oracle exceeds even their report of it, is dignified and awesome, and its seat a place of ceremoniousness and respect. Significantly, echoes of language used to different purposes elsewhere in the play enrich the meaning. When Cleomenes says that he felt like "nothing" in the wake of the thunder, he uses the same word employed by Leontes when he is wondering at the thin on-the-ground evidence for his own suspicions. The supernatural quality of the oracle anticipates the supernatural event of Hermione's returning to life. Dion's reference to the speediness of the journey also sets up the modulation of time in the play, the rapid speeding-up of the action with the 16 years' gap, yet the ability of time to operate slowly as well as quickly. The news of what turns out to be Hermione's innocence is delivered rapidly; the realization, all of it, and the enactment of the results of that judgment, take decades. The passage also established the play's sense of the sacred—pagan, not Christian, gods are evoked, but the sense of peace, power, and might has its echoes in Christian language, which, however, does not appear literally in the play. The scene is an interlude, a pause, perhaps in the immediate theatrical sense, a distraction. But it paves the way for the astonishing developments that make the play fortunate and inspirational.

Act III, Scene 3, 91–104

ANTIGONUS. O, the most piteous cry of the poor souls! sometimes to see 'em, and not to see 'em; now the ship boring the moon with her main-mast, and anon swallowed with yest and froth, as you'ld thrust a cork into a hogshead. And then for the land-service, to see how the bear tore out his shoulder-bone; how he cried to me for help and said his name was Antigonus, a nobleman. But to make an end of the ship, to see how the sea flap-dragoned it: but, first, how the poor souls roared, and the sea mocked them; and how the poor gentleman roared and the bear mocked him, both roaring louder than the sea or weather.

Antigonus screams out his status as a nobleman, because that is so bound up with his identity. He has lived all his life accustomed to the hierarchy at court and the degree of importance it confers on him. His being eaten by a bear shows that social status is no barrier to the appetite of a savage animal, that at this point of vulnerability all men are truly equal. That Antigonus's nobility does not avail him as his body is "borne" off by a bear (as Maurice Hunt has pointed out) demonstrates the universality of human circumstance. (This is indirectly intensified by the fact that the audience, having seen Antigonus mainly in the role of a much-put-upon servant to the king, is probably not even subconsciously aware of his nobility—his proclamation of it is in a sense the first news we have of it.) Antigonus's death also prepares the viewer to accept the Old Shepherd and the Clown as worthy guardians of Perdita and as constructive forces in her upbringing, an upbringing that will help repair the damages of the play's first half. In other words, the witness by the Clown of Antigonus's destruction contains the seeds of the eventual regeneration of the play's society. That the humble Clown is the one speaking this, and that he is doing so in prose, gives him not only an everyman's perspective but a distance that allows him to be both detached and pitying, to feel compassion for the victims but yet to soberly see things for what they are. The passage alternates between concrete description ("boring the moon with her main-mast," "swallowed with yest and froth," "flap-dragoned") and emotive response ("how the poor souls roared, and the sea mocked them"). The Clown feels sorry for the people he cannot help, and he will soon play a nurturing role for the young baby Antigonus had tried to bring to safety. But, from this point on, the play will belong to the Clown and to his father, in spirit and in station, as much as it will to "noblemen" such as Antigonus.

Act IV, Scene 4, 136–147

FLORIZEL. What you do
Still betters what is done. When you speak,
  sweet,
I'd have you do it ever; when you sing,
I'd have you buy and sell so; so give alms;
Pray so, and for the ordering of your affairs,
To sing them too: when you dance, I wish you
A wave of the sea, that might ever do
Nothing but that; move still, still so, and own
No other function; each your doing,
So singular in each particular,
Crowns what you are doing in the present
  deeds,
So all your acts are queens.

This is quite possibly the most beautiful and most complex expression of love in Shakespearean drama. Florizel is responding to Perdita's actions as a shepherdess. For Florizel, Perdita is so loved, so valued, that nothing she does can ever be just that, just a momentary activity. He wishes that she would prolong it, because a prolonged version of anything she would do would, no matter what it was, be consummate beauty. But this wish to extend the momentary is not made out of a desire to transcend Time but rather to give due recognition to whatever is happening in the moment, to delight in it to the point of full appreciation, not want to see it just lost in the shuffle. Despite the magnificence of the language, many of the activities Florizel mentions are ordinary ones, and some, such as buying and selling and ordering one's affairs, are in the acceptance of whatever Perdita may do as the obverse of the idealized vocabulary usually associated with love. Florizel's celebration of Perdita involves a radical appreciation of whatever she may do. Particularly salient is the plea that when Perdita dances, she might become "a wave of the sea and own no other function." Through not so much freezing time but repeating the same gesture indefinitely, the immediate action—whether dancing or doing business—is liberated from utility, becomes valuable in itself. It is the being, not the doing, of Perdita that is celebrated; yet her cumulative doings are what indicate for Florizel the pinnacle of her being that is so beloved by him. As Marjorie Garber has pointed out, at the heart of the passage is a pun on *still*—*still* as meaning continuity of action, as still doing something, and *still* as fixed, stationary. The two "stills" have very different resonances, one prolonging time, one freezing it, but Florizel's lines layer those senses on top of each other, conjuring a motile perpetuity of the frozen moment. This is how acts can be queens, how things done in the ordinary way can be endowed with consummate, cherished value. For an act—a pretense in the theatrical sense as well as a deed in the worldly sense—to become a queen is for it to be transformed, from something functional and done in the service of a broader meaning to something laureled for its own sake and that of criminal honor. Florizel sees love as the reconciliation of action and understanding, of a delight that does not just exult in passing sensation but seeks a deep coming-to-terms with what it delights in. Florizel's love is not rash or heedless. He has thought about his feeling. The passage is more than a love song, more than praise of Perdita's personal qualities. It is an understanding of how she matters with respect to the whole world; it lauds her within the widest and wisest context possible. Charles Forker describes Perdita as representing "nature in its least adulterated state" while also existing in a "sophisticated setting," and Florizel's praise of her shows how this pastoral paradox is conceptually possible.

DIFFICULT PASSAGES
Act I, Scene 2, 135–146

LEONTES. Come, sir page.
Look at me with your welkin eye. Sweet
  villain,
Most dearest, my collop! Can thy dam,
  may't be
Affection! Thy intention stabs the centre.
Thou dost make possible things not so held,

Communicat'st with dreams—how can
  this be?
With what's unreal thou coative art
And fellow'st nothing. Then 'tis very credent
Thou may'st co-join with something, and thou
  dost,
And that beyond commission, and I find it,
And that to the infection of my brains
And hardening of my brows.

This is renowned as the most difficult passage in *The Winter's Tale*. One feels when Polixenes asks "What mean'st Sicilia?" immediately afterwards he is not just befuddled by the sudden change of mood of his friend, as elsewhere in the scene, but genuinely does not comprehend what he is saying in the literal, denotative sense. A way to become oriented toward this perplexing speech is to realize that in the first instance he is speaking to Mamillius, his son. At this point, he still believes Mamillius is his son (he could certainly not be Polixenes', as Mamillius was born during the long period of the two friends' separation). In fact, the passages before the difficult portion are all about how physically alike Mamillius is to him. What Leontes, in a sense, is asking himself is can the woman who gave birth to a son so like me in fact be now committing adultery with my best friend? This possibility both baffles and enrages Leontes, to the point where after "Can thy dam, may't be" (where "thy dam" is Hermione, the boy's mother) Leontes suddenly breaks off and, in a rhetorical figure the Renaissance would have termed *anacoluthon*, there is an abrupt switch in meaning and structure within a sentence. Leontes stands back from himself, from his own musings, and asks himself if affection—both in the context of his love for Hermione and his incipient envy of his former friend Polixenes for his supposed affair with Hermione—can become so intense—"intention" here refers to *intensity*, not *intentionality* in the modern sense—that it can "stab the centre," undo all that is normal and healthy, all Leontes had previously relied on. *Affection* means both love and the curdling of that love in jealousy, and this acquired double intensity makes possible suspicions not seen by the senses, that are invisible, indiscernible, but nonetheless keenly felt by Leontes. As with the "I have drunk, and seen the spider" speech later on, Leontes is at his most passionate when he verges on having perspective on himself and his slide into lunacy. Clearly, in this speech, one can see his awareness of his own irrationality, his realization that it is not built on any sensory or empirical foundation—but ultimately, he does not thrash his way out of the madness. This wayward affection follows nothing, but is co-active—cooperative in production, one might say—in making meaning despite that. There are echoes here of a dark parody of the Christian doctrine of creation *ex nihilo,* where God makes something out of nothing. Wayward affection can do the same. But instead of creating something firm and enduring, it spawns the unsure web of fear and loathing in which Leontes is enmeshed. When this obscure power is admitted, then the effect of wayward affection becomes "credent"—plausible—and exceeds its original commission, begins to take illicit power within the brain. Leontes, again, seems on the verge of realizing how he has gone astray, but his reasoning processes are too muddled, too infested with the traces of his jealousy, to fully cohere. There is also a suspicion of the very language Leontes uses to formulate his accusations, an awareness that, as rhetoric, it may be built on shifting sands. Leontes, in other words, nascently, but incompletely, turns the suspicion he holds of Hermione toward himself and his own language but then shies away from it before it entails actually confronting his delusions and misapprehensions. Thus, the obscurity the audience finds is part of the psychological problem here. An added layer of complexity is that this capacity to conjure reality out of phantasms—to make something of out of an airy, vacant foundation—is just what happens in the latter half of the play, where love and beauty are regained through ignoring or transcending the boundaries between nature and art, reality and imagination. It is not this combination that is inherently wrong but the wretched turn it has taken within Leontes' mind.

Act IV, Scene 4, 79–95

PERDITA. Sir, the year growing ancient,
Not yet on summer's death, nor on the birth
Of trembling winter, the fairest flowers o'the
    season,
Are our carnations and streak'd gillyvors,
Which some call nature's bastards: of that kind
Our rustic garden's barren, and I care not
To get slips of them.

POLIXENES. Wherefore gentle maiden,
Do you neglect them?

PERDITA. For I have heard it said
There is an art, which, in their piedness, shares
With great creating nature.

POLIXENES. Say there be,
Yet nature is made better by no mean,
But nature makes that mean: so o'er that art
Which you say adds to nature, is an art
That nature makes. You see, sweet maid we
    marry
A gentler scion to the wildest stock,
And make conceive a bark of baser kind
By bud of noble race. This is an art
Which does mend nature—change it rather,
    but
That art itself is nature.

It is fairly easy to see here that Polixenes is saying that art and nature should not be distinguished as opposites but understood in the context of nature's mastery over everything, which makes even art natural, and is also in itself a type of art. The first major difficulty of the passage, though, lies in the narrative context. Polixenes is spying on Florizel because he is concerned about Florizel's romantic interest in Perdita and the possibility that he may want to marry the girl. Polixenes is trying to prevent, in human life, the combination of that which he deems greater and lesser; yet he is pleading with the maiden to include the carnations and gillyvors in the garland despite her rejection of their lowly origins. In other words,

Another depiction of Perdita presenting Polixenes and Camillo with rosemary and rue while Florizel and Mopsa look on in Act IV, Scene 4 of *The Winter's Tale*. This is a print from Malcolm C. Salaman's 1916 edition of *Shakespeare in Pictorial Art*. (Painting by C. R. Leslie)

his botanical attitudes are directly contradictory to his social ones. We can conclude that Polixenes realizes the truth of this point unconsciously; however, it may be that he is deliberately toying with Perdita to try to reveal her aspirations of making an advantageous marriage, or, more far-fetched, that he suspects Perdita's true parentage all the time and is just playing a game, as Perdita and Florizel, pretending to be shepherd and shepherdess, know that they are.

The second difficulty of the passage is in deciding just what is being said about the flowers. Perdita's description of the carnations and gillyvors clearly marks them as base and ignoble. But this baseness is not because they are so natural as to be unacceptable in a garland that, by its conception as an arrangement, is inherently artful—which would be the most obvious, most convenient reading. It is because the carnations and gillyvors are gaudy; they look like somebody had painted them. In other words, they look artificial, almost as if somehow some sort of rogue artist had gotten into nature's creativity and tampered with it. What Polixenes seeks to assure Perdita of is that, if nature is truly all-pervasive, then there is nothing foreign to it. Art cannot adulterate or pervert nature, as where else does art come from other than nature? There is potentially a larger context here, as Leontes had earlier suspected Hermione's language with respect to Polixenes of being artful and had seen the accused adulterers of covering up their deeds. Leontes has, as we have discussed, fallen into this trap because he fails to comprehend the artificiality and politeness of her language. Polixenes goes the other way; he understands the place of art precisely because he sees it is not unnatural. This means he does not ask for a pure or unvarnished nature. Divisions between the pure and impure cannot be maintained if the true abundance of nature is properly acknowledged.

The difficulty of this interchange is compounded by certain difficulties in the setting. When Autolycus first sings his song about the appearance of daffodils and the resurgence of red blood in the winter's pale, we think the scene will be set in early spring. But Perdita makes clear that we are at the end of the year, in late autumn, perhaps late in November or early in December. (This is another sense, aside from the one introduced by Mamillius, in which the play is "a winter's tale.") In this dawdling finale of the year, the weather is clement but the characteristic flowers of the season have waned, so that vestiges are all that is extant for Perdita to garland the two older men. The scene is set at a time whose fading belies the festivity of the scene and indicates that the spring of full reconciliation and acceptance has to round another bend before it can be realized. The shifting nature of the climatological milieu is further intensified when Perdita presents Polixenes and Camillo with midsummer flowers because they are middle-aged. This is a comment on the passage of time, on the sense that a new generation, represented by Florizel and Perdita, is coming to provide a new redemptive dimension. But the immediate thrust of the lines is to further confuse the situation, to highlight the permeability between what Barbara Everett terms "making and breaking" in the play. The audience immediately grasps the theme of the common terrain between art and nature, but the full impli-

cations of the passage demand further, rigorous scrutiny.

CRITICAL INTRODUCTION TO THE PLAY

What does *The Winter's Tale,* as a title, mean precisely? Why does Mamillius mention it? He is the most innocent character in the play. Even his mother, who is not guilty of the charges arrayed against her, understands their nature. But Mamillius does not, though by the time he dies he understands that his mother has been taken away from him. Not only, incongruously, is it the child, Mamillius, who tells the mother a bedtime story, but instead of a reassuring lullaby, it threatens to be a dark story. It starts with "A man dwelt by a churchyard," a phrase that might may raise images of piety, but Mamillius means *churchyard* in the sense of *graveyard*. He is telling an eldritch, uncanny story, both out of a childish love of the bizarre and creepy and a more adult foreboding of the doom that awaits him. Mamillius, who gets very little stage time in the play, is an odd character: At one point lauded by his father as a sportive little scamp, there is also an odd lack of masculinity about his personality. Even before he is taken ill, he seems wan and vulnerable, and his name has maternal and mammary associations. His comment about the shape of women's eyebrows shows either an affinity with the female or a precocious male interest in the female, or perhaps even a wish to be an infant again; it is not the sort of remark one conventionally expects a young child to make. In other words, the young boy is such an enigma that to have him be the one who pronounces the play's enigmatic title doubles the bewilderment. That Mamillius never gets to tell his story is a source of vexation to those who would attach a ready meaning to the play's title. Some have speculated that Mamillius is foreseeing Leontes' repentant visit to the young prince's own grave and the supposed grave of Hermione during his 16-year penitence, that in a sense he is anticipating his own death. Others have, daringly, speculated that the entire action of the play from this point on is part of

Mamillius's "Winter's Tale," that in a sense the whole remaining play is only his dark scenario of how things might play out. This is a far-fetched possibility, but it does strike at the incongruity of the play's title being sounded by its youngest, most tragic, and most ephemeral character. What "Winter's Tale" meant in the general parlance of Shakespeare's time is well known. It was a rousing, entertaining, but unlikely story, not necessarily making any claim to realism.

This lack of realism means that those who interpret the play on too literal a level often go awry. As Ben Jonson, Shakespeare's younger and more formally educated contemporary, first pointed out, there is no "seacoast of Bohemia." Bohemia—roughly the present Czech Republic—is totally landlocked as everybody well knew. It has been pointed out (by Isaac Asimov among others) that Bohemia had access to the sea at Trieste in the 13th century, and that technically there had at some point been a seacoast of Bohemia. This is a nice riposte to Jonson's over-meticulousness on the subject, but the larger point is that the play did not aim at geographical realism and mixes a heady brew of different and often clashing times, places, and names in the service of its fantastic and diverting story.

The romance genre's disregard of actual geography and history privileges a vague exoticism over denotative fact and detail. Shakespeare makes clear that one of the ways the play is a winter's tale is that it is a tall tale, a shaggy-dog story, something that should not be taken too seriously or too literally. This accords with the play's general blessing of art, whether it be in a sculpture becoming a person or in nature's art of grafting baser and greater stocks. Whatever literal certainty the play lacked was more than compensated for by its imaginative reach. But there is also a sense in which the play is skeptical of too much art. *The Winter's Tale* is replete with a critique of the artificiality of court. The anger that ruins the Sicilian court is also a kind of emotional release of unexamined tensions that were being repressed; this is pertinent even if Leontes' suspicions are as groundless as the overwhelm-

ing majority of commentators think they are. The play's characters transcend their juvenile and rivalrous feelings only after they have been fully ventilated and purged by the rough weather of life, and by Polixenes in literal, and Leontes in emotional terms, both "seeing a different part of the world." The fortunes of the play improve significantly once we get away from court, which seems to foster suspicion and jealousy rather than the easy acceptance and celebration of the country. In important ways, even though the marriage of Florizel and Perdita does not turn out to be a mixed marriage in class terms, the Old Shepherd's and the Clown's ennoblement constitutes a kind of a stepping into the middle class, a sign of increased mobility and opportunity. The society at the end is considerably more open than it was at the beginning.

But not every character benefits from this openness. In a sense, the plot of the play has to work out in such a way as to eliminate the two extras, Mamillius and Antigonus. With them out of the way, Camillo can marry Paulina, and Florizel and Perdita's marriage will unite two thrones, one of which would otherwise have been occupied by Mamillius. Of course, in the unfolding of the dramatic plot, these resolutions are astonishing gifts of unexpected joy, restorations of a hope deemed forever lost. But these restorations do fit squarely into a preconceived and rather conventional plot structure. (This sense of the transformation of social roles is anticipated by Florizel's pretending to be a servant, and for that matter, Perdita's "pretending" to be a lady, in Act IV.)

The play is full of kings, queens, and princes, but it is not a political play—in fact, all three of the other romances are more political. At no time, for instance, is Polixenes thought by Leontes to be a threat to his throne; Leontes' jealousy is private, not public (compare Oedipus's suspicions of Creon and Tiresias in Sophocles' *Oedipus Tyrannus;* when he does not like their criticism of him, Oedipus suspects them of intriguing for the throne). The only sense of Leontes as a public figure and of the importance of the disposition of the realm is in Act V, Scene 1. Polixenes is essentially play-acting with respect to his opposition to his son's marriage—compared to the enraged Leontes, the Bohemian monarch is a pussycat. His opposition has far more the air of a dramatic plot complication than a potentially tragic circumstance. Indeed, without Polixenes' opposition, Perdita's true parentage would not be revealed nor would all the miracles and reconciliations at the end would be brought about. So there is something providential, something harmonious. Neither king ever suffers a challenge of State; even after Leontes' grotesque behavior, he does not lose his throne nor is there an alternative wielder of power. Polixenes twice leaves his country and also is away from his capital for weeks on end, without any fear of usurpation. One feels the main characters are royalty not because of any associations with power but because only by being free of the constraints of ordinary men and women can they provide so thorough an example of loss and retrieved joy.

This sense of an authority valued, but not overly sanctified, extends to the play's own artistry. *The Winter's Tale* raises the specter of the need to believe in miracles without trusting too much in the mechanism of miracles, having miracles be too much of a gimmick. Again we have the precedent of Euripides (who, though Shakespeare did not read his works provides a crucial analogue for the entire genre of the Shakespearean romance). Euripides' technique of having a god descend refers to deus ex machina device to save the day at once salvaged tragic circumstances from total despair and also led to a perhaps gratuitous sense of an easy way out of life's problems.

This artificiality can sometimes seem to prevail over passion in the play. Samuel Taylor Coleridge greatly admired the play but saw Leontes' jealousy as "perfectly philosophical," not filled with a more atavistic, visceral rage. Coming from another direction, the German romantic critic Friedrich Schlegel chided Shakespeare for apparently not giving the reader the full picture of the antecedents to the jealousy, stating that Shakespeare "might have wished slightly to indicate" that there was some basis, however thin, for the king's suspicion.

Schlegel desires this not because he wants the king to be at all justified but because a minimal trace of evidence would make his reaction less intellectual. That two great critics found Leontes' anger not "real" enough points to the pervasive presence of artificiality as an animating conceit in the play. Most later readers, though, cherished this valuation of the artificial as precisely the ripe deposits of Shakespeare's late wisdom that made encountering the romance plays such a distinctive and worthwhile experience.

Themes

Despite the play's happy outcome, as much is decided by chance as by fate. Leontes' casting away of the daughter he deems a bastard into "strange fortune" where "chance may nurse or end it" is meant vindictively. But, totally by chance (in other words, by no design within the play, but by that of the playwright), the Old Shepherd and the Clown find Perdita, nurse and raise her and, by an inscrutable stroke of luck, contribute to the reuniting of Leontes' sundered family and the reparation of his cruel crime.

Jealousy is a major theme in the play's first part. Leontes may be as jealous of Hermione's freedom to flirt with Polixenes as he is of any supposed relationship. Is Leontes perversely expressing the sexual desire he himself feels for Polixenes? Does his rage emanate from a subconscious awareness of his own latent bisexuality? Even if one rejects this interpretation, it is undeniable that there is something already awry beneath Leontes' ostensible happiness at the beginning. When we first see him, Leontes exudes a sense of being so happy that the happiness brims over into discord and suspicion, a happiness that out of its own surplus percolates unsavory emotions.

These negative feelings come to a head in the trial of Hermione and the expulsion of Perdita. And much of the action of the latter half of the play, even when that action occurs far off in Bohemia, has to do with the rehabilitation, the moral rescue, of Leontes. The praise and appeal of Perdita in Act IV has to do with Act V, as one of the things that is happening in Act V is that Leontes is learning to love, and reaccepting the old Hermione, the Hermione who is at least 40, and understanding that, even though Perdita is the beauty in season at the moment, she is Florizel's to love, as Hermione is his, to love and to ask forgiveness of.

Leontes is the major character, the lead role. His persistence in living through what must be a dolorous regimen of penitence is admirable not just in its recognition of guilt, its new turning, but also in its sheer stamina. This stamina is assisted both by Paulina's perseverance in attending a man she must, after the catastrophe, have found distasteful and by the cyclic renewal of nature and life enacted by Perdita and Florizel, and finally brought home to Leontes in Act V.

Though the play is not explicitly Christian, there is a tacit understanding that Leontes has not only erred but sinned, that he needs to come to an internal reckoning of what he has done wrong, make atonement, and seek amendment for it. Despite his penitence, a full forgiveness remains latent in him, not fully manifest, until the astonishing events of Act V provide the agency for the forgiveness to be realized. But, even here, all does not happen at once. Leontes is repentant, and Hermione has accepted his repentance. But she has not yet forgiven him. Vladimir Jankélévitch underscores the difference between repentance and forgiveness when he says that repentance can be feigned, can be posed or gestural, but forgiveness is a thoroughgoing, inward conversion. Until he sees Perdita, Leontes has repented but not yet earned forgiveness. And only when Leontes is in a state to be fully forgiven can Hermione come back to life. Much about their relationship will have to be renegotiated after the curtain falls. But they have been reunited and become wife and husband to each other once again through their shared parentage of Perdita and, by adoption, Florizel. The major themes of the play can be said to be, in the first part, jealousy, and in the second, restitution.

Structure

In terms of place, the structure of the play can be divided into three parts: Sicilia, Bohemia, and back to Sicilia. The developments in Bohemia redeem the catastrophes of Sicilia, but the action has to leave Bohemia and come back to Sicilia to fully have and achieve its effect. In terms of tone, the play can be divided into two: the first half tragic, the second half comic. Within this structure, there are internal interruptions, as when the serenity of Cleomenes and Dion on returning to the oracle provides a leavening lacuna in the storm of hatred aroused by Leontes, or in Act IV when Polixenes' wrath over his son's courtship momentarily disrupts Bohemia's bucolic serenity. The play, by its very premise, is a violation of what were taken by Renaissance and early modern critics to be Aristotle's maxims as to "the classical unities"—the unities of place, time, and action. Shakespeare has often been castigated for violating these, and *The Winter's Tale* involves one of the most striking examples. The generation-long gap in the play's action, so wide that Time actually has to come on stage and not only apologize for but personify itself, stretches like an arch between the two halves of the action, unifying them but also foregrounding their separation. Part of the structure of the play is its pacing. After a slow beginning, the play careens through a series of horrifying developments, until equilibrium is reached with the festive but nonetheless slow-paced, even gravid Act IV. In Act V, the pace picks up once again, yet there is still something quite deliberate about it, as if the play is taking the first tentative steps of, to use the metaphor at hand, a statue come back to life.

The gulf between Polixenes and Leontes first seeing each other and their sojourn together in Sicilia is more or less the same as the gap between their quarrel and Hermione's restoration to life. Of the three stages to their relationship, they only are really close in their third encounter, when there is no longer any possible jealousy between them. Everything else was utopian overestimation. The play thus also has tacit structures that emerge when its experimentation with levels of time is fully understood.

There are also characters that are structurally paired. Florizel "replaces" Mamillius as the male heir; Camillo "replaces" Antigonus as Paulina's husband. At the end of the play, Leontes and Polixenes stand as firm friends, firmer in fact, than they were at the beginning. These pairs and complementarities add to the sense of structure in a play whose middle reaches have often been chaotic and sprawling. Part of the tension here is that Shakespeare is not only adopting a plot from a narrative source, as he often did, but also a plot from a longish romance that traced in generic origins to even longer romances. There are many occurrences and complications, to include which the structural frame of the five-act drama has to be stretched near its maximum.

Style and Imagery

The play is a highly self-conscious one, replete with formal and meditative thinking about art and its role in healing and renewal. This may be because, as Samuel Johnson winsomely argued, "It is impossible for any man to rid himself of his profession," or, as later critics have put it, Shakespeare was making a deliberate statement about the nature of his own artistic practice in the play. Yet this self-awareness does not make the play a mere repository of artifice. The play's style also is expressive enough to deal with the sharp swings of emotion and mood that occur within its weave. To this effect, repetition and/or foreshadowing are often used. For instance, in Act V, when Autolycus and the two gentlemen ask Rogero what has transpired in the meeting of the king and Perdita, Rogero's answer is "Nothing but bonfires." In other words, nothing but celebration and joy, symbolized by the lighting of the flames. An act earlier, Florizel had stated that he apprehended "nothing but jollity."

There are also certain keywords that have little manifestly to do with the play's theme or action but that crop up at certain strategic circumstances. When Antigonus pleads that Hermione is true, Leontes roughly asks him, "What, lack I credit?" When Leontes accuses his entire court of being liars, a lord implores him to "Give us better credit." The word *credit* does not enter the play again until Act V, when a lord reporting that Florizel and a shepherd's daughter have eloped to Sicilia notes the incredibility of the news by saying it would "bear no credit" were not the proof virtually in front of them. But the use of the word accelerates hereupon. When the second gentleman asks what has become of Antigonus, the tale of his being killed by a bear is given with the rider that it is a story so stunning it will, as it were, bear listening to even "if credit be asleep." *Credit* throughout is used in the sense of trust. Yet it also has a larger resonance, of dreams, phantasms that are unlikely or fantastic. Sometimes these are darkly so, as in Leontes' suspicion. Sometimes they are happily so, as in the miraculous reunion at the end. But the reiteration of the word heightens the sense of the suspension of disbelief, reaching even to the level of the paranormal, that pervades the play.

More direct foreshadowing is also employed. When the Leontes-Perdita reunion is reported, the third gentleman says, "Who was most marble there changed color." Color has been used throughout the play to talk about dress, beauty, and adornment. When Paulina presents the statue to Leontes, she says "The statue is but newly fix'd, the color's not dry." When Hermione comes to life, the potential of the marble/color imagery used earlier with respect to Perdita is fully reaped.

The Winter's Tale is famous for its commingling of art and nature, but some of its imagery presents nature in a far rougher guise. When Antigonus accepts the mission to carry baby Perdita away from the court, he addresses the baby and pleads that "kites and ravens may be its nurses" and also involves tales where "wolves and bears, casting their savageness aside, have done like offices of pity." This no doubt refers to the Latin legend of Romulus, Remus, and the founding of Rome, but it also captures, through animal imagery, the terror and violence that Leontes' fit has suddenly conjured in once-peaceful Sicilia.

In those few moments when Leontes is sufficiently detached from his own turmoil to be able to look at himself with any honesty, he comments:

There may be in the cup
A spider steep'd, and one may drink, depart,

And yet partake no venom, for his knowledge
Is not infected: but if one present
The abhorr'd ingredient to his eye, make
  known
How he hath drunk, he cracks his gorge, his
  sides,
With violent hefts. I have drunk,
and seen the spider.

The animal venom is used as a figure for the human suspicion, demonstrating its wildness in the way it operates outside norms of civilized conduct. But the spider metaphor also externalizes the situation so much that we think Leontes is about to have some perspective on himself, how he has fallen captive to rumors swelled within his heart.

Perdita in *The Winter's Tale*. This is a print from Charles Heath's 1848 edition of *The Heroines of Shakspeare: Comprising the Principal Female Characters in the Plays of the Great Poet. (Painting by J. Hayter; engraving by W. H. Mote)*

That he remains illusioned renders the spider metaphor all the more stinging in its effect.

Shakespeare also uses more delicate metaphorical registers in the poem. For instance, as Harold Bloom points out, Perdita recites the lovely catalog of flowers to Polixenes, starting with

daffodils,
That come before the swallow dares, and take
The winds of March with beauty; violets dim,
But sweeter than the lids of Juno's eyes
Or Cytherea's breath.

Hero, she is speaking of flowers that are not there, are out of season; imagining them, conjoining them. Many of the play's images operate in this transformative way, opening the drama up to the imagination and its ability to see beyond what is apparent.

The Poetry of the Play

Most of the play is written in blank verse, unrhymed iambic pentameter. There are moments when rhyme is used, most conspicuously in Time's declamation in the prologue to Act IV. Other passages, such as the verdict of the oracle, are not rhymed but are put in a deliberately concentrated, terse arrangement, much like the prophecy in *Cymbeline*, which in both cases lends the aphoristic pronouncements a sense of authority. Aside from those examples, much of the play is written in elevated speech that is arranged on the page as poetry. These passages often involve rhetorical declamation, where the language of the speeches is intensified not only to achieve the maximum emotional effect but also to carry the most heft in the immediate dramatic context. Paulina, for instance, asks Leontes in Act III, Scene 2, "What studied torments, tyrant, hast for me? / What wheels, racks, fires? / What flaying, boiling in leads or oils?" This is language that is amplified not just to achieve a certain sublimity of register but to resound to the immediate audience of Leontes' court and the theatrical audience beyond. In Act IV, poetry is used not just to embroider language but to constitute its emotional heart. Perdita and Florizel, in their pastoral courtship, not only are consciously "poetic" in their speech but have feelings for each other that are not merely dressed up by poetry but are epitomized by it. When Florizel says to Perdita, "These your unusual weeds to each part of you / Dost give a life /; no shepherdess / but Flora peering in April's front," he is saying in effect that she is her costume and that her costume is her, that there is no artificiality because she herself personifies the art of nature better than any imitation can. This is indicative of how elemental the force of poetry in the play becomes as it enters its later, more redemptive phases. The play's poetry also, in its assurance and stateliness, is charged with handling the drastic teetering between emotional extremes in the play. Poetic, metaphorical language can entertain several states of feeling at once more readily than prose—at least prose in the colloquial-dialogue mode in which Shakespeare tended to use it. This becomes evident in the passage where Perdita is composing her garland for Polixenes, where her evocation of the flowers that are gone and unavailable comes to seem almost like a mourning dirge, although nested in a context of ceremonious praise. When Perdita directly addresses Proserpina, the mythological maiden whose passage to the underworld and marriage to its ruler, Dis, symbolizes the absence of warm weather for half the year: "O Proserpina, / For the flowers that now, frighted of nature's continual productivity even in fallow time, The play offers poetry as a reassuring backbeat to its sweeping permutations, thou lett'st fall / From Dis's wagon," she is talking about death, the death of the year, death in nature. But the buoyancy of the poetry embeds this acknowledgment within the context and reversals.

But the play is aware that poetry is part of overall discourse and has a social function; that it can be conventional; that, as Autolycus does, ballads can be bought and sold for the bemusement of the gullible. When the wonderful offstage developments of Leontes' reconciliation with his regained daughter are brought by Rogero to the other observers, Rogero states that the joy is so great

"that ballad makers cannot be able to express it." That this statement is itself uttered in prose shows that a play that is characterized by such dazzling poetry nonetheless does not see poetry alone as sufficient to express the range of emotion at work in the play. The play concerns the ability of language, and by implication art, to overcome suffering by transforming experience. But it also recognized that this transformation of language is only dearly won as wisdom wrung from the unrelenting setbacks of the first three acts.

The Prose of the Play

It is in the turn of the play's fortunes that the fascinating nature of the relations between poetry and prose in *The Winter's Tale* can be seen. Before he is pursued by a bear, Antigonus speaks in fevered blank verse giving his final benediction to Perdita ("Blossom, speed thee well!") and coming to terms with his own complicity in abandoning the baby ("Weep I cannot. but my heart bleeds, and most accursed am I / to be by oath adjoin'd to do this.") After Antigonus is killed and the Old Shepherd enters the stage, Shakespeare uses prose to radically slow down the pace of the action, make it more meditative and ruminative, giving the audience a chance to catch its breath after the dramatic chase as well as for the new, more pastoral mood of the play to coalesce. The Old Shepherd muses about the one age nobody in the scene—he, his son, Antigonus, or Perdita—is, an adolescent, wishing that "youth would sleep out the rest" between "ten and three-and-twenty." Apparently complaining that a bunch of teenage roughs—"boiled brains between nineteen and two-and-twenty" have stolen two of his best sheep amid the storm, the Old Shepherd's grumbles cast him as, in the deepest sense of the word, a prosaic person, someone whose aspirations are best expressed in prose. He is long past that volatile age himself; his aspirations, whatever they are, have been ventilated or satisfied; he is content to observe life and get by as best he can. What he does not know is that his life is about to be changed by the infusion of a far more radical youth than the adolescent rapscallions, an infant innocence that will renew him and that he will renew through his tending and caring. When the Shepherd finds Perdita, he sounds the same general themes that Antigonus has—that sexual misdeeds have brought a young baby of clearly elevated background to this pass—but he does so in much earthier language; compare the Old Shepherd's "stair work, some trunk-work, some behind-door work" to Antigonus's "That, for thy mother's fault, art thou exposed to loss and what may follow!" In the very next scene, a similar prose-poetry contrast. In Act IV, Scene 1, the personified figure of Time speaks in elevated verse of the power of the theater to bridge chronological and for that matter geographical gaps, giving a panoramic view of what has happened in both the play's venues as the years have sped by. Not only does Time speak in verse, but he speaks in rhymed verse, each succeeding two lines a couplet, fortifying the sense of pattern and design in the content of his speech: Then, in Act IV, Scene 1, Polixenes and Camillo take the stage. Even though the conversation takes place at the Bohemian court, the two talk in prose, avoiding the ceremonious, official palaver of the first act with its, as it turns out, superficial concord. The offhanded acceptance of life's circumstances that characterizes the two men's prose conversation extends into the next scene. Autolycus sings in rhyme and lives by, among other things, packaging rhymed ballads and selling them to young women. But verse for Autolycus is advertising; prose is the medium in which he lives. When Autolycus, likening himself to the classical mythological figure of that name who was a son of Hermes, characterizes himself as "a snapper-up of unconsidered trifles," the line resonates—it has long been counted one of the most famous lines in the play—not just because it so epitomizes Autolycus's character but because it introduces the play's viewer to a new milieu of prose, a milieu where there will be more time for laughter and cajolery, where, unlike in the poetry-dominated world of Sicilia, life and fate cannot become horrifically unstable in an instant. When Perdita and Florizel reintroduce a high poetic register, it is at first a mode of play; for all she knows,

Perdita is a country lass affecting the mock majesty of a put-on pastoral. The young lovers have integrated the prose of their milieu into the poetry that the tenderness and the dignity of their love calls for. They have the spontaneity of Autolycus and his long prose meanderings, although in terms of character, worthy of the soaring flights of their poetic declamations.

EXTRACTS OF CLASSIC CRITICISM

John Dryden (1631–1700) [From *Defence of the Epilogue* (1672). Dryden was an English poet, dramatist, and literary critic who so dominated the literary scene of his day that it came to be known as the Age of Dryden. He produced some of the first substantive criticism of Shakespeare.]

The Winter's Tale, Love's Labours Lost, Measure for Measure, which were either grounded on impossibilities, or at least so meanly written, that the comedy neither caused your mirth, nor the serious part your concernment.

Samuel Johnson (1709–1784) [Excerpted from *The Plays of William Shakespeare* (1765). Samuel Johnson was one of the great critics in all of English literary history. He produced a landmark edition of Shakespeare's plays.]

This play is, for all its absurdities, as Dr. Warburton points out, very entertaining. The character of Autolycus is very naturally conceived, and strongly represented.

Edward Dowden (1843–1913) [Excerpted from *Shakspere: His Mind and Art* (1875). Dowden was an Irish critic, university lecturer, and poet.]

Serenity Shakespeare did attain. Once again before the end, the setting is bright and tender. While in some Warwickshire field, one breezy morning, when the daffodil began to peer, the poet did conceive his Autolycus, there might seem to be almost a return of the light-heartedness of youth. But the same play that contains Autolycus, contains the grave and noble figure of Hermione. From its elevation and calm Shakespeare's heart can pass into the simple merriment of rustic festivity; he can enjoy the open-mouthed happiness of country Clowns; he is delighted by the gay defiance of order and honesty which Autolycus, most charming of rogues, professes; he is touched and exquisitely thrilled by the pure and vivid joy of Perdita among her followers. Now that Shakespeare is most a householder he enters most into the pleasures of truantship. And in like manner it is when he is most grave that he can smile most brightly, most tenderly. But one kind of laughter Shakespeare at this time found detestable—the laughter of an Antonio or a Sebastian, barren and forced laughter of narrow heads and irreverent and loveless hearts. The sly knavery of Autolycus has nothing in it that is criminal; heaven is his accomplice. "If I had a mind to be honest, I see Fortune would not suffer me; she drops booties in my mouth." Whether Schiller's Franz Moor made many robbers may be doubtful. But certainly no person of spirit can read *A Winter's Tale* without feeling a dishonest and delightful itching of the fingers, an interest not wholly virtuous in his neighbor's bleaching-green, and an impatience to be off for once on an adventure of roving and rogueing with Autolycus.

Algernon Charles Swinburne (1837–1909)

[Excerpted from *A Study of Shakespeare* (1880). Swinburne, best known as a poet, was also an interesting critic.]

The wild wind of the "Winter's Tale" at its opening would seem to blow us back into a winterier world indeed. And to the very end I must confess that I have in so much of the spirit of Rachel weeping in Ramah as

not be comforted because Mamillius is not. It is well for those whose hearts are light enough to take perfect comfort even in the substitution of his sister Perdita; for in *The Winter's Tale* we have Clowns and rustics who become gentlemen, and very decent ones at that—the boy who died of "thoughts high for one so tender." Even the beautiful suggestion that Shakespeare as he wrote had in mind his own dead little son still fresh and living at his heart can hardly add more than a touch of additional tenderness to our perfect and piteous delight in him. And even in her daughter's embrace it seems hard if his mother should have utterly forgotten the little voice that had only time to tell her just eight words of that ghost story which neither she nor we were ever to hear ended.

Anna Jameson (1794–1860)

[Excerpted from *Shakespeare's Heroines: Characteristics of Women, Moral, Practical & Historical* (1833). An important early female critic of Shakespeare, Jameson saw Shakespeare as the "Poet of Womankind," whose female characters exemplify all characteristics and complexities of women's natures.]

The character of Hermione exhibits what is never found in the other sex, but rarely in our own—yet sometimes—dignity without pride, love without passion, and tenderness without weakness. To conceive a character in which there enters so much of the negative, required perhaps no rare and astonishing effort of genius, such as created a Juliet, a Miranda, or a Lady Macbeth; but to delineate such a character in the poetical form, to develop it through the medium of action and dialogue, without the aid of description to preserve its tranquil, mild and serious beauty, its unimpassioned dignity, and at the same time keep the strongest hold upon our sympathy and our imagination and out of this exterior calm, produce the most profound pathos, the most vivid impression of life and internal power: it is this which renders the character of Hermione one of Shakespeare's masterpieces.

Charlotte Lennox (1730—1804) [Charlotte Ramsay Lennox was a novelist, poet, playwright, magazine editor, and translator. Her novels include *The Life of Harriot Stuart, Euphemia,* and *The Female Quixote.* Her *Shakespear Illustrated, or the Novels and Histories on which the Plays of Shakespear Are Founded* examines the works from which Shakespeare derived his plots.]

For how can it be imagined that Hermione, a virtuous and affectionate wife, would conceal herself during sixteen years in a solitary house, though she was sensible that her repentant husband was all that time consuming away with grief and remorse for her death: and what reason could she have for choosing to live in such a miserable confinement when she might have been happy in her husband's affection and shared his throne? How ridiculous also in a great Queen, on so interesting an occasion, to submit to

Antigonus and Hermione (Viola Allen) kneel before Leontes in Act II, Scene I of *The Winter's Tale,* in this photograph published by the Byron Company in 1904.

such buffoonery as standing on a pedestal, motionless, her eyes fixed, and at least to be conjured down by a magical command of Paulina . . . the novel has nothing in it half so low and improbable as this contrivance of the statue; and indeed wherever Shakespeare has altered or invented, his Winter's Tale is greatly inferior to the old paltry story that furnished him with the subject of it.

MODERN CRITICISM AND CRITICAL CONTROVERSIES

Interestingly, amid a generally more skeptical critical climate, many Shakespeareans in modern times continue to believe that the romance genre affirms life and art in the way Edward Dowden suggested in the 19th century. Indeed, the late 20th century came to particularly value Shakespeare's later plays for their experimentation, disjunctiveness, reclamation of joy and beauty from the peril of their uttermost opposites.

In the 19th century, critics often emphasized the role of Perdita, particularly her freshness, pertinacity, and eloquence. Part of this had to do with the emergence of the actress as a major force in the theater; in Shakespeare's era, of course, female roles were performed by boys, and even through the 18th century, the actress was not seen as a figure of high repute. In the 19th century, a woman actor became a legitimate figure in society and partially in consequence the female roles in Shakespeare—particularly those in which young, attractive women were represented—were highlighted. In turn, the pastoral fourth act of the play was so exalted as to almost make the entire Leontes plot disposable. The 20th century tended to focus on Shakespeare's plays as unities and less on individual roles. With respect to *The Winter's Tale,* the emphasis shifted from Perdita's spiritual fertility to Leontes' penitence and the questions of artistry and craft raised by Hermione's return to life. It is only a slight exaggeration to say that the 19th century's emphasis on Perdita was replaced by the 20th century's emphasis on Hermione. G. Wilson Knight, one of the most influential Shakespeareans of the mid-20th century, saw Hermione's revival as effected by "rays from the heart of life" and saw its primary motif as "comic restoration." Whereas the 19th century (as in the Dowden quote excerpted above) concentrated on the seeming pastoral bliss in Act IV, the 20th century emphasized the sense of miraculous restoration after the collapse of all hope in Act V. Derek Traversi provided an important corrective to Dowden's posture by pointing out the important structural connections between the two final acts, no longer seeing Act IV as a joyous but anomalous irruption of nature and creativity. This was partially due to the 19th century regarding Shakespearean dramas as vehicles for star turns by lead actors, and Perdita, for obvious reasons, was more of a lead role than a woman who is a "statue" for most of the play. The 20th century, though, took a more ensemble-oriented view of theater, emphasizing the production and the director's skill over individual bravura renditions of parts, and in that context Hermione became more emphasized, especially as Paulina's "conjuring" her to life could itself be seen as a piece of stagecraft.

G. Wilson Knight was both exemplary and characteristic in seeing Hermione's revival as both an affirmation of life and a complex outcome wrought by premeditated art (whether Paulina's, Giulio Romano's, or Shakespeare's). Knight's discussion of Leontes "working out" his sin parallels the other sort of "working out" in the building of the statue as well as the art/nature layering in Polixenes' and Perdita's dialogue. H. W. Fawkner has refined the category of romance into that of the "miracle play" that operates outside of causality entirely, where radical shifts in states of being can manifest themselves. Critics such as Northrop Frye, Frank Kermode, and Denis Donoghue have all valued the play's capacity for renewal, seeing in it a dialogue between nature and civilization that ultimately ratifies art's ability to create new meanings of valuable ethical consequence. The sense that this at once mellow and intellectually worked-out stance has something to do with the place the plays occupy in the context of Shakespeare's career was influential on ideas of "late style" such as those popularized by the late Edward W. Said. Stanley Cavell, also writing in an ethical and, in his case, philosophical mode, has classified *The Winter's Tale* as a "comedy of remarriage." *Pericles* could also be classified as such, since the title character and Thaisa are reunited after a gap of time similar to that encompassed by Hermione's supposed death. Cavell's treatment of the play is valuable in that it shows how a dapper understanding overcomes the radical skepticism of reality evidenced by Leontes' delusion. In this way, Leontes is saved from Othello's grim fate. Harold Bloom, though, goes well beyond Cavell when he terms Leontes, in arguably the best single line of criticism the play has ever inspired, "an Othello who is his own Iago," stressing the solipsism and the potential schizophrenic bisexuality in the Sicilian king's disposition. Bloom's criticism manages to hold in one hand the delights of Perdita and the pastoral scene, the maleficent rage of Leontes, and the moral and artistic questions raised by Hermione's revival. Bloom sees the play as both "a pastoral lyric" and a "psychological novel," and this insight enables him to see the breadth of Shakespeare's achievement, evident also in his insight that Shakespeare is neither totally illusionistic nor spectacular; in other words, he neither absorbs spectacle entirely into the frame of the drama, nor does he foreground it too much as a "special effect." Bloom is also the critic to note most forcefully that much of the beauty of Perdita's litany comes from her evocation of absent flowers. This line of thought is seen in a more overtly deconstructive form in Howard Felperin's work, which lucidly sketches the operation of absence and difference in the play while still remaining well within the affirmation of the romance genre, life, and art that characterizes the vast majority of recent criticism of *The Winter's Tale*. Thomas G. Bishop, in his idea of "a theatre of wonder" similarly combines rigorous critique with a capacity for belief and a faith in regeneration.

A student of Bloom's, Kenneth Gross has given the most complex account of Hermione as statue. He points out that the properties of a statue are correlatives for how Leontes' rage has robbed her of her subjectivity and intentionality. Correspondingly, the lifelike nature of the statue when first encountered embodies our wish for the properties of life, perhaps as distinct from life itself. Gross qualifies the exaltation of the miracle by noting that the very idea of a statue objectifies and fossilizes Hermione's being, even when it is ostensibly fully restored. Similar insights manifest themselves in a more feminist direction in Lynn Enterline's assertion that Hermione's silence at the end is an indicator that she is still disempowered, still not authorized to speak, and that there are in fact rival practices of artifice in the play, Paulina's woman-centered stagecraft having to contend against the prerogatives of ceremony and composition exercised by the play's male suzerains. The philosopher Babette Babich's discussions of sculpture as the recognition of self and other—objectifying but not losing touch with the self—allow us to position the Hermione sculpture as a clearing space that parallels Leontes' long self-discipline and ascetic penitence.

Marjorie Garber makes much of the closeness of Paulina's name to that of the Apostle Paul, suggesting that she serves a "visibly Christian" role that calls the people of the play to redemption. Garber, though, qualifies this by noting the mythic, classical, and natural elements in the play, continuing the tendency to value its pluralism, synthesis, and conceptual expansiveness. Historicist and cultural materialist criticism has had an impact on the play, but perhaps not so much as with respect to Shakespeare's other works. *The Winter's Tale,* set in a fictive past, does not raise the political issues evoked by *The Tempest,* set in "the real world." In addition, the entire appreciation of the romances as a type of play is so recent that academia inclines to still want to value the triumphs over despair that the play offers. Whatever the source of this tendency, it cannot be seriously denied that work on *The Winter's Tale* has overwhelmingly affirmed a positive, constructive appreciation of the play's complex imaginative power. What Charlotte Lennox called "the paltry story" used by Shakespeare to create his late masterwork has continued to resonate 400 years after the play was first performed.

THE PLAY TODAY

As with most of the plays in the Shakespearean canon that fall between standard genres, *The Winter's Tale* has been staged more frequently and successfully in the past hundred years than ever before. The multiple genres in which the play can be seen as operating may well aid its adaptability to contemporary circumstances. The widely available 1981 BBC production directed by Jane Howell exhibits the typical way in which the play has been presented in recent times. Anna Calder-Marshall's Hermione epitomizes the deliberate strength of Hermione, bringing out an interesting but little-noticed aspect of the character: that Hermione is not the sort of woman one would expect to see as a victim of such a plight as she becomes ensnared in; that somebody of her confidence and serenity would be the last person we would expect to find herself in desperate straits. Jeremy Kemp's Leontes also is representative in playing Leontes in the first few acts as manic, fevered, driven over the edge by phantom speculation. Simon Russell Beale, in Sam Mendes' 2009 production at the Brooklyn Academy of Music, played Leontes as not so much reminiscent of Othello as of both Falstaff and Hamlet, his struggle with his domestic situation an image of a larger struggle with representation, identity, and selfhood.

The play's overt detailing of spectacle and theatricality has often led to very ornate productions, but there is also a countertradition perhaps originating from Trevor Nunn's 1969 production of bare-bones minimalist staging, which certainly makes the play's rapid shifts of scene and circumstance easier to accommodate. Other productions have been more radical. Inevitably, a certain familiarity sets in with respect to the background and theatrical assumptions of staging the play, so such gestures as Matthew Warchus's, in moving the setting of the play to the pre-desegregation American South, are often necessary provocations.

Casting can also operate as a principle of interpretation. Often, in the early 20th century, the same actress would play Hermione and Perdita, with a different actress playing the role of the revived statue at the end. This happened, for instance, in Viola Allen's 1905 rendition of the roles, although at 38 Allen was considerably older than both characters are in the play. As the focus on Perdita's spirited innocence was replaced, in the 20th century, by a stress on Hermione's suffering and regeneration, this practice faded, although it was memorably revived by Judi Dench in 1969.

One can often tell who the most important female character in the judgment of the director is by seeing whether the more famous actress was cast in the role of Hermione or Perdita. Casting of actors is a tacit interpretation of the play. Leontes, on the other hand, will inevitably be the leading male character, and the figure second to him in terms of being a star turn is arguably not Florizel but Autolycus, as is shown by Ethan Hawke's playing Autolycus in Sam Mendes' 2009 production. When Florizel is played by famous actors, it is often when they are very young and on the rise, as was the case with Jeremy Irons in the 1971 Old Vic production.

The recent productions have been able to, through stagecraft, frame questions about the play that have tended to be sidestepped in the critical archive. Playing Hermione visibly pregnant, as for instance was done in a summer 2005 performance staged at the University of California, Santa Cruz, supplies a greater correlative to Leontes' jealousy, both in the possibility that Polixenes may be the father and, more speculatively, that the very idea of childbirth upsets Leontes, although one might observe that this then would *not* have been the case when Mamillius was born. Casting is also used as a way to comment on doublings in the play. In the 1998 Royal Shakespeare Company production, Emily Bruni played both Mamillius and Perdita, commenting not only on the cross-gender impersonation that was a necessary facet of Elizabethan drama but in the complementarity of the two children; Perdita "replaces" Mamillius. The casting also raises questions of what would have been Mamillius's relationship to Florizel if the former had lived: Would they have been rivals or would they have experienced the notable level of affection that their fathers did? In the same production,

Alexandra Gilbreath plays a very different Hermione than Calder-Marshall's, rendering the queen tormented, anguished, as reminiscent of Euripides' Medea as any other role. Antony Sher's Leontes is similarly highly expressive, so that the couple together seem deeply abnormal, unusual, and this preternatural quality cannot be so totally remedied by the harmonious ending as most literary perspectives on the play would have it. In this way, the dramatic rendering of the play has made *The Winter's Tale* a riskier work than has been its recent fate in the academy.

As of 2011, a feature film of *The Winter's Tale* was said to be in the works, starring Dougray Scott as Leontes. This spotlighted the growing visibility of the play on popular culture, as seen in the film *The Sisterhood of the Traveling Pants 2,* based on Ann Brashers's fiction, in which the character played by America Ferrera is rehearsing for a staging of *The Winter's Tale.* General connections can be drawn between the movie's themes of distance, maturation, and reconnection and those at work in Shakespeare's drama.

Academic critics as well are turning more and more often to *The Winter's Tale* to explore themes that seem especially relevant in our time, and the play's reputation has never been higher. Frank Kermode, in one the last essays he wrote for the *London Review of Books* in 2010, referred to the play as "a work of enormous rhetorical and linguistic range." Harold Bloom, in the introduction to his 2010 volume on *The Winter's Tale* in his *Bloom's Shakespeare through the Ages* series, wrote, "Perhaps the high art of Shakespeare nowhere else is so married to human and natural vitality as in *The Winter's Tale.*" Finally, Jonathan Franzen's much-heralded 2010 novel *Freedom* included a key subtext emanating from *The Winter's Tale;* the epigraph to Franzen's novel is from Paulina's "precious winners" speech from Act V. The novel's concern with who is married to whom at the end, as well as its larger philosophical sense of broken and repaired marriages, and how children of the next generation construct themselves in relation to them, is clearly informed by Shakespeare.

FIVE TOPICS FOR DISCUSSION AND WRITING

1. **Jealousy:** Does Leontes have any ground, whatsoever, for his jealousy of Hermione? How do others react to his suspicions? How does Leontes recover from, and atone for, his jealousy. If you have read *Othello,* you might want to compare Leontes' jealousy to Othello's, both in terms of its nature and its circumstances.

2. **The statue:** What point is Shakespeare making by having the statue of Hermione come to life? Is it an allegorical point about art and nature? Is there ever really a statue, or is it a hoax staged by Paulina? What level of realism does Shakespeare want us to apply to the entire idea of the statue? How do we read the statue in light of the philosophical debates about art and nature in Act IV?

3. **Court versus country:** As long as the action is at the court of Leontes, the atmosphere is filled with rage and suspicion; as soon as the action gravitates the country, joy and the constructive unfolding of life take over. Is the atmosphere at court just a side effect of Leontes' distemper? Or is Shakespeare making a serious critique of the often cruel accusations and arbitrary punishment that characterized courts in his day? How much is *The Winter's Tale* a "pastoral" play, in other words one that praises the innocent life of the countryside?

4. **Comedy or tragedy:** If you had to choose—if there were no alternative—would you classify the play as a tragedy or a comedy? Does the presence of Autolycus bend the tone of the work toward comedy? Or does the loss of 20 years for Leontes and Hermione, not to mention the deaths of Antigonus and Mamillius, make it a tragedy despite the reconciliatory ending? Does it matter whether it is one or the other? Do you find something liberating about Shakespeare's evasion of the opposition between the genres, or is it disturbing?

5. **Chief female character:** Who is the most important female character, Hermione or Perdita? Who is the play's "heroine"? Or should this status belongs to Paulina, who, after all, makes the happy ending possible? How does considering this question address the status of male-female relationships in the play, especially in the light of the vulnerability of Hermione to the false accusations of her husband?

Bibliography

Bishop, Thomas G. *Shakespeare and the Theatre of Wonder.* Cambridge: Cambridge University Press, 1996.

Enterline, Lynn. "'You Speak a Language That I Understand Not': The Rhetoric of Animation in *The Winter's Tale.*" *Shakespeare Quarterly* 48, no. 1 (1997): 17–44.

Estrin, Barbara L. "'Bettering' the Generic Domain of The Winter's Tale." *Exemplaria: A Journal of Theory in Medieval and Renaissance Studies* 20, no. 3 (Fall 2008): 183–213.

Everett, Barbara. "Making and Breaking in Shakespeare's Romances." *London Review of Books* 29, no 6 (March 22, 2007): 21.

Felperin, Howard. *Shakespearean Romance.* Princeton, N.J.: Princeton University Press, 1972.

Forker, Charles R. "Negotiating the Paradoxes of Art and Nature in *The Winter's Tale.*" In *Approaches to Teaching Shakespeare's "The Tempest" and Other Late Romances,* edited by Maurice Hunt, 94–102. New York: Modern Language Association, 1992.

Garber, Marjorie. *Shakespeare After All.* New York: Random House, 2004.

Gross, Kenneth. *Dream of the Moving Statue.* Ithaca, N.Y.: Cornell University Press, 1992.

Knapp, James. "Visual and Ethical Truth in *The Winter's Tale.*" *Shakespeare Quarterly* 55, no. 3 (2004): 253–257.

Lim, Walter. "Knowledge and Belief in *The Winter's Tale.*" *SEL: Studies in English Literature 1500–1900* 41, no. 2 (Spring 2001): 317–334.

McDonald, Russ. *Shakespeare's Late Style.* Cambridge: Cambridge University Press, 2006.

Zender, Karl. *Shakespeare, Midlife, and Generativity.* Baton Rouge: Louisiana State University Press, 2009.

FILM AND VIDEO PRODUCTIONS

Dunlop, Frank, dir. *The Winter's Tale*. With Laurence Harvey, Jane Asher, and Diana Churchill. Cressida Productions, 1967.

Howell, Jane, dir. *The Winter's Tale*. With Robert Stephens, Jeremy Kemp, and Anna Calder-Marshall. BBC, 1981.

Marston, Theodore, and Barry O'Neill, dirs. *The Winter's Tale*. Silent. With Anna Rosemond, Martin Faust, and Frank Hall Crane. Thanhouser Film Corporation, 1910.

—Nicholas Birns

Contributors' Notes

Karley Adney teaches English at Butler University and Ivy Tech Community College. Her research involves examining adaptations of Shakespeare in various forms, ranging from retellings for children to film versions of the plays. She is the coauthor of Facts On File's *Critical Companion to J. K. Rowling.*

Mark G. Aune is associate professor in the English Department at California University of Pennsylvania. His research and teaching interests include Shakespeare and performance, Shakespeare and film, and media change. His articles and reviews have appeared in *Shakespeare Bulletin, Shakespeare, Early Modern Literary Studies,* and *Theatre Journal.*

William Baker is University Trustee Professor and Distinguished Research Professor, Department of English and University Libraries, at Northern Illinois University. He has authored or edited some 30 books devoted to literary studies, textual theory, and bibliography. He has been the recipient of numerous fellowships, grants, and honors. He is a Research Fellow with the National Endowment for the Humanities, and his work has been lauded by the *Times Literary Supplement.* He also earned *CHOICE* Book of the Year Awards for his edition of Wilkie Collins's correspondence (1999) and for *Harold Pinter: A Bibliographical History* (2006). He serves as coeditor (with Kenneth Womack) for the *Year's Work in English Studies,* published annually by Oxford University Press.

Lisa M. Barksdale-Shaw is a doctoral student in the Department of English at Michigan State University. She has a juris doctorate degree from the University of Michigan Law School. She has been the recipient of several fellowships, grants, and honors.

David Bevington is the Phyllis Fay Horton Distinguished Service Professor Emeritus in the Humanities at the University of Chicago. His books include *From "Mankind" to Marlowe* (1962), *Tudor Drama and Politics* (1968), *Action Is Eloquence* (1985), *Shakespeare: The Seven Ages of Human Experience* (2005), *This Wide and Universal Theater: Shakespeare in Performance (Then and Now)* (2007), *Shakespeare's Ideas* (2008), and *Shakespeare and Biography* (2010). He is the editor of *Medieval Drama* (1975), *The Bantam Shakespeare* series, and *The Complete Works of Shakespeare,* 6th edition (2008). He is a senior editor of the *Revels Student Editions, the Revels Plays, The Norton Anthology of Renaissance Drama,* and the forthcoming Cambridge edition of the works of Ben Jonson.

Melissa A. Birks worked for nearly 18 years as a reporter and editor at five newspapers around the country before earning her master's degree in English from Northern Illinois University. She now teaches composition at ITT Technical Institute in the Chicago suburbs.

Nicholas Birns is an associate teaching professor at Eugene Lang College, the New School, New York. His publications include *Theory after Theory: An Intellectual History of Literary Theory from 1950 to the Early 21st Century* (Broadview, 2010) and *A Companion to Australian Literature since 1900* (Camden House, 2007, coedited with Rebecca McNeer), which was named a *CHOICE* Outstanding Academic Book for 2008. He is the current secretary-treasurer of the Council of Editors of Learned Journals (CELJ).

John Boe is a lecturer at U.C. Davis and editor of the journal *Writing on the Edge.* He has published two books, as well as many articles, essays, reviews, stories, and poems. Every summer, he teaches Shakespeare in London to American college students.

Catherine Brown studied English literature at Gonville and Caius College under the poet J. H. Prynne and received a Ph.D. in Russian-English comparative literature at Cambridge. Her book *The Art of Comparison: How Novels and Critics Compare* is forthcoming in March 2011 from Legenda. She has taught at the Universities of Cambridge and of Greenwich and is currently at New College, Oxford, pursuing research interests in poetic justice and narrative morphology.

Chris Butler is completing his Ph.D. at Sheffield Hallam University, researching theological meanings in Elizabethan literature. He has written articles on *As You Like It*, primogeniture, and Ireland; Sir Edward Dyer's "Hee that his mirth hath loste . . ."; and the second Earl of Essex and the links between literature and politics in the long 1590s. He also reviews books for the Shakespeare "general" section of *The Year's Work in English Studies*.

Daniel J. Cadman is a research student at Sheffield Hallam University, where he is currently completing his doctoral thesis on early modern neo-Senecan drama. He has provided book reviews for a number of peer-reviewed journals and writes the section on Shakespeare's Problem Plays for *The Year's Work in English Studies*. He is also a contributor to the *Lost Plays Database*.

John Cameron is a doctoral candidate at Dalhousie University. His dissertation, entitled "Setting Machiavelli to School: Shakespeare and the Drama of Political and Military Strategy," deals with the relation between Shakespeare's plays and the writings of Niccolò Machiavelli. He has taught courses at Dalhousie University and Saint Mary's University.

Michael Carlson is completing his degree in English and Theology at Loyola University Chicago, graduating with departmental honors in both programs. His research is funded through Loyola University's Mulcahy Scholarship grant.

Sarah Carter is a lecturer in early modern literature and has taught at several universities in the United Kingdom, most recently at the University of Hull and the University of Sheffield. She researches the reception of Ovid and gender politics in the period and has published articles in this area as well as critical histories of Shakespeare's plays. She has just completed her first book, *Ovidian Myth and Sexual Deviance in Early Modern English Literature*, to be published in 2011 by Palgrave Macmillan.

Asha Choubey is an associate professor of English and head of the Department of Humanities at MJP Rohilkhand University, Bareilly, U.P. India. She has published more than 40 papers in refereed journals and anthologies and has written two books: *Women on Women* and *The Fictional Milieu of Nayantara Sahgal*.

Annaliese Connolly is senior lecturer in English at Sheffield Hallam University. Recent publications include "Guy of Warwick, Godfrey of Bouillon and Elizabethan Repertory" in *Early Theatre* and "Shakespeare and the Fairy King: Re-viewing the Cultural and Political Contexts of *A Midsummer Night's Dream*" in *A Midsummer Night's Dream*, edited by Regina Buccola.

Michael J. Cummings began his career as a public-school teacher in Muncy, Pennsylvania, in 1964 and taught English in Elmira, New York, from 1965 to 1968 at the Arthur W. Booth School and Elmira Free Academy. In 1968, he joined Grit Publishing Company in Williamsport, Pennsylvania, starting as a reporter and eventually becoming managing editor. In 1984, he became a freelance writer, specializing in feature writing and medical writing. In 1988, he became an English instructor at the Pennsylvania College of Technology in Williamsport.

Julia A. Daly is a doctoral student at Sheffield Hallam University.

James M. Decker is associate professor of English at Illinois Central College. He is the author of *Ideology* (2003) and *Henry Miller and Narrative Form: Constructing the Self, Rejecting Modernity* (2005). In addition to contributing numerous articles to such publications as *College Literature* and *Style,* he is the editor of *Nexus: The International Henry Miller Journal.*

Aaron Drucker is completing his Ph.D. at Claremont Graduate University. His research focuses on Milton, pedagogy, and the philosophy of reformation. He teaches literature and composition for the Los Angeles Community Colleges.

Timothy J. Duffy is a doctoral candidate in English at the University of Virginia.

Andrew Duxfield is a lecturer in Renaissance literature at Queen's University, Belfast, where he teaches on topics ranging from revenge tragedy to the Renaissance book. His principal area of interest is the work of Christopher Marlowe, on which he has published a number of articles and book chapters. He is currently finishing work on a book-length study of ideas of unification in Marlowe's plays.

Gabriel Egan coedits the journals *Theatre Notebook* for the Society for Theatre Research and *Shakespeare* for the British Shakespeare Association. He teaches Shakespeare, theater history, critical theory, and hand-printing. He is the author of *The Struggle for Shakespeare's Text* (2010), *Green Shakespeare* (2006), and *Shakespeare and Marx* (2004).

Elizabeth Ford is a postgraduate student at Cardiff University, researching the role of the stage clown in the composition and revision of Shakespeare's plays. Her thesis is due for completion next year. She has scholarly articles forthcoming in the journals *Early Theatre* and *Scintilla.*

Michelle Franklin received her M.A. in British Literature from San Diego State University. She has over a decade of experience writing, proofreading, teaching, and tutoring.

Stacy Furrer received her M.F.A. in Creative Writing and Writing for the Performing Arts in 2010 from University of California Riverside, in Palm Desert.

Louise C. Geddes is an assistant professor of English at Dominican College of Blauvelt, in New York. Her main interest is early modern drama in performance, and she has published work on the nature of sacrificial violence in Shakespeare's Roman plays. Her current project considers the stage history of the story of Pyramus and Thisbe, as a means of dissecting the Shakespearean text as an object of celebrity.

Johann Gregory is completing his doctoral research on Shakespeare's *Troilus and Cressida* at Cardiff University, where he also teaches courses on medieval and Renaissance literature. His latest publication is an article on paratexts and matters of taste in the journal *Shakespeare.*

Patricia Ann Griffin has produced the first modern edition of William Sampson's *The Vow Breaker, or The Fair Maid of Clifton* (1636), with textual notes and a substantial critical introduction.

Lisa Hopkins is professor of English at Sheffield Hallam University and coeditor of *Shakespeare,* the journal of the British Shakespeare Association. Her publications include *Shakespeare on the Edge: Border-crossing in the Tragedies and the* Henriad (Ashgate, 2005), *Beginning Shakespeare* (Manchester University Press, 2005), and *Shakespeare's The Tempest: The Relationship between Text and Film* (New Mermaids, 2008).

Colleen Kennedy is a Ph.D. student in the English department at Ohio State University. Her research interests include early modern embodiment and the sensory history of early modern drama and poetry.

Emily Kingery is a doctoral candidate at Northern Illinois University in the fields of linguistics and bibliographic and textual studies. Her academic interests include literary history, form, and genre and the teaching of literature and composition. She has been published in *Notes and Queries* and the *Journal of the Midwest Modern Language Association.*

Adam H. Kitzes is an associate professor of English at the University of North Dakota. He is the author of *The Politics of Melancholy from*

Spenser to Milton (Routledge, 2006), as well as articles on early modern writers, including Shakespeare, John Donne, Thomas Browne, Barnabe Riche, and others. His current research examines Elizabethan conspiracies, as found in pamphlets and plays.

Buff Lindau directs marketing and public relations for Saint Michael's College in Vermont, where she serves as a member of the president's cabinet. Her doctoral thesis was one of the earliest literature works in women's studies, *Feminism in the English Novel: George Eliot, Virginia Woolf and Doris Lessing* (University of South Carolina, 1979). She is the coeditor of the anthology *Women in Society.*

Julia MacDonald is a lecturer in early British literature at the University of North Texas. She has published on the lyric poetry of Ben Jonson, the temporality of the passions in Spenser's *Faerie Queene,* and *Macbeth.* Currently, she is completing a book entitled *The Sense of Time in Spenser and Shakespeare.*

Christopher Madson received his Ph.D. from the University at Buffalo. His research interests focus on Stuart-era city comedies and civil war poetry. He is currently writing about representations of prostitution and syphilis in the works of Dekker, Marston, and Shakespeare.

Anthony G. Medici received Ph.D. in English and American literature in 2003 from Northern Illinois University. His dissertation was on the American critic and memoirist Alfred Kazin. His research interests include the rare book trade, avant-garde music, and modern and counterculture literature and art.

Jolene C. Mendel is an instructor at the University of Memphis. She has presented numerous papers on 16th-century literature at major conferences. Her book *Women of the Crusades* was published in August 2010.

Deborah Montuori is an associate professor of English at Shippensburg University, where she specializes in Early Modern British Literature

with an emphasis on drama. A frequent reviewer for *The Shakespeare Bulletin,* she has also published and presented papers on Ben Jonson, Christopher Marlowe, Thomas Middleton, and, of course, William Shakespeare.

Nicholas Moschovakis has published essays in *Shakespeare Quarterly* (2002); in an award-winning Shakespearean special issue of *College Literature* (2005); in *Shakespeare and Historical Formalism* (Ashgate 2007); and in *Macbeth: New Critical Essays,* which he edited (Routledge 2008). He is now at work on a study of Shakespeare and allusiveness.

Jessica C. Murphy received her Ph.D. in English from the University of California Santa Barbara and is currently assistant professor of literary studies at the University of Texas at Dallas. Her research and teaching focus on the literature and culture of Shakespeare's England.

William Nelles is a professor of English at the University of Massachusetts Dartmouth. His publications include *Frameworks: Narrative Levels and Embedded Narrative* (1997), as well as numerous journal articles on literature and narrative theory, including an essay on Shakespeare's Sonnets in *ELR* 39.1 (2009).

John J. Norton is an associate professor of English at Concordia University Irvine. His research interests focus on 18th-century literature, world literature, and the intersection of literature and religion.

Michael Petersen is assistant professor of English at Wright College, Chicago. He specializes in early modern British literature and film.

Eleni Kyriakou Pilla is adjunct professor of English at Northern Arizona University where she teaches Shakespeare. Her most recent publications are on spatial sexualities in *Othello* and the translation of the Shakespearean Sonnets.

Kelly Quinn is associate professor of English at the University of Western Ontario. She is the author of a number of scholarly articles on early modern literature.

Robert H. Ray is a professor of English at Baylor University, where he regularly teaches courses in Shakespeare. He also has taught Shakespeare in England in the Baylor-in-London Program. Ray is the editor of *Approaches to Teaching Shakespeare's "King Lear"* (1986), published by the Modern Language Association. He also contributed an essay for the MLA volume on teaching *Hamlet* and has published many articles on Shakespeare and other writers, as well as books on Donne, Herbert, and Marvell.

James Reitter is assistant professor of English at the University of Wisconsin Sheboygan. He earned his Ph.D. in English from the University of Louisiana at Lafayette in 2006. He has published in a variety of academic and creative journals, including *Interdisciplinary Humanities* and *The South Carolina Review*.

Peter Roberts has recently completed his doctoral thesis, an edition of Gabriel Harvey's anti-Nashe tracts, at Cardiff University. He has published articles on the works of Shakespeare and his contemporaries Thomas Nashe, Robert Greene, and John Lyly. He is currently preparing an edition of *The True Tragedy of Richard III*.

Joseph Rosenblum is a retired English teacher, the compiler of *Shakespeare: A Bibliography,* and the general editor of *The Greenwood Companion to Shakespeare*.

David Rush completed his doctorate at the University of Sussex and has since published on critical theory, memory studies, and contemporary literature. In 2011, he will take a post as lecturer in English and head of General Studies at Baze University, Abuja, Nigeria.

Jeanette Roberts Shumaker is a professor of English at San Diego State University, Imperial Valley Campus. She teaches British literature and publishes on Irish and Victorian fiction. With William Baker, she coauthored *Leonard Merrick: A Forgotten Novelist's Novelist* (Fairleigh Dickinson University Press, 2009).

Peter Smith is reader in Renaissance Literature at Nottingham Trent University. He is the author of *Social Shakespeare* and coeditor of *Hamlet: Theory in Practice*. His study of literary scatology, *Between Two Stools,* is forthcoming, and he is currently working on a stage history of *Twelfth Night*. He has edited texts of *The Shoemaker's Holiday, The Jew of Malta,* and *Edward II*. His essays and reviews have appeared in *Critical Survey, Renaissance Quarterly, Review of English Studies, Shakespeare, Shakespeare Bulletin,* and *Shakespeare Survey*. He is a also regular contributor to *Times Higher Education* and the U.K. Correspondent for *Cahiers Elisabethains*.

Matthew Steggle is reader in English at Sheffield Hallam University. His publications include *Wars of the Theatres* (1998); *Richard Brome: Place and Politics on the Caroline Stage* (2004); and *Laughing and Weeping in Early Modern Theatres* (2007). Together with Eric Rasmussen, he has coedited *Cynthia's Revels* for the forthcoming *Cambridge Works of Ben Jonson*. His current project is a text of *Measure for Measure* for the third edition of Stephen Greenblatt's *Norton Shakespeare*.

Helen Vella-Bonavita is associate dean for International Faculty of Education and Arts and an associate professor of English at Edith Cowan University, Australia. She is editor of *Caelius Secundus Curio, His Historie of the Warr of Malta*.

James Wells is associate professor of English and director of the M.A. program in English at Belmont University. He teaches courses in Shakespeare, early modern English literature, British literature, drama, and composition. He has published articles on *Coriolanus* and *Macbeth* and is the editor of *The Second Part of Henry the Fourth* for the New Kittredge Shakespeare series (2009).

Kate Wilkinson is an associate lecturer at Sheffield Hallam University, with a particular interest in Shakespeare's history plays in performance. She is the author of several scholarly articles and numerous theater and book reviews.

Kenneth Womack is professor of English and Associate Dean for Academic Affairs at Penn State University's Altoona College. He serves as editor of *Interdisciplinary Literary Studies: A Journal of Criticism and Theory* and as coeditor (with William Baker) of Oxford University Press's *Year's Work in English Studies*. He is the author or editor of some 20 books, including *Postwar Academic Fiction: Satire, Ethics, Community* (2001), *Key Concepts in Literary Theory* (2002), *Long and Winding Roads: The Evolving Artistry of the Beatles* (2007), and the novel *John Doe No. 2 and the Dreamland Motel* (2010). Since 1992, Womack has served as a correspondent and member of the International Committee for the *World Shakespeare Bibliography*.

Richard Wood is an associate lecturer in English Studies at Sheffield Hallam University, where he is completing his doctorate on Sir Philip Sidney's *Arcadia*. He is the author of the entry on Shakespeare's poetry in *The Year's Work in English Studies* (Oxford) and journal articles on Sidney in *Early Modern Literary Studies* and the *Sidney Journal*.

Index